Lecture Notes in Computer Science 11678

More information about this series at http://www.springer.com/series/7412

Mario Vento · Gennaro Percannella (Eds.)

Computer Analysis of Images and Patterns

18th International Conference, CAIP 2019
Salerno, Italy, September 3–5, 2019
Proceedings, Part I

 Springer

Editors
Mario Vento 🆔
Department of Computer and Electrical
Engineering and Applied Mathematics
University of Salerno
Fisciano (SA), Italy

Gennaro Percannella 🆔
Department of Computer and Electrical
Engineering and Applied Mathematics
University of Salerno
Fisciano (SA), Italy

ISSN 0302-9743   ISSN 1611-3349   (electronic)
Lecture Notes in Computer Science
ISBN 978-3-030-29887-6   ISBN 978-3-030-29888-3   (eBook)
https://doi.org/10.1007/978-3-030-29888-3

LNCS Sublibrary: SL6 – Image Processing, Computer Vision, Pattern Recognition, and Graphics

This Springer imprint is published by the registered company Springer Nature Switzerland AG
The registered company address is: Gewerbestrasse 11, 6330 Cham, Switzerland

Preface

This book is one of two volumes for the proceedings of the 18th international Conference on Computer Analysis of Images and Patterns (CAIP 2019), which was held in Salerno, Italy, during September 3–5, 2019.

CAIP is a series of biennial international conferences devoted to all aspects of computer vision, image analysis and processing, pattern recognition, and related fields. Previous conferences were held in Ystad, Valletta, York, Seville, Münster, Vienna, Paris, Groningen, Warsaw, Ljubljana, Kiel, Prague, Budapest, Dresden, Leipzig, Wismar, and Berlin.

The conference included a main track held during September 3–5 at the Grand Hotel Salerno in the center of the city of Salerno. The conference hosted four keynote talks provided by world-renowned experts: James Ferryman (University of Reading, UK) gave a talk on "Biometrics and Surveillance on the Move: Vision for Border Security," Luc Brun (ENSICAEN, France) on "Graph Classification," Gian Luca Marcialis (University of Cagliari, Italy) on "Fingerprint Presentation Attacks Detection: from the "loss of innocence" to the "International Fingerprint Liveness Detection" competition," and Nicolai Petkov (University of Groningen, The Netherlands) on "Representation learning with trainable COSFIRE filters."

The scientific program of the conference was extended with satellite events held at the University of Salerno on the day before and after the main event. In particular, two tutorials on "Contemporary Deep Learning Models and their Applications," by Aditya Nigam and Arnav Bhavsar (Indian Institute of Technology Mandi) and on "Active Object Recognition: a survey of a (re-)emerging domain," by Francesco Setti (University of Verona, Italy) were given on September 2; while on September 6 we had a contest entitled "Which is Which? - Evaluation of local descriptors for image matching in real-world scenarios," organized by Fabio Bellavia and Carlo Colombo (University of Florence, Italy), together with two workshops, namely "Deep-learning based computer vision for UAV," by Hamideh Kerdegari and Manzoor Razaak (Kingston University, UK) and Matthew Broadbent (Lancaster University, UK), and "Visual Computing and Machine Learning for Biomedical Applications," by Sara Colantonio and Daniela Giorgi (ISTI-CNR, Italy) and Bogdan J. Matuszewski (UCLan, UK).

The program covered high-quality scientific contributions in deep learning, 3D vision, biomedical image and pattern analysis, biometrics, brain-inspired methods, document analysis, face and gestures, feature extraction, graph-based methods, high-dimensional topology methods, human pose estimation, image/video indexing and retrieval, image restoration, keypoint detection, machine learning for image and pattern analysis, mobile multimedia, model-based vision, motion and tracking, object recognition, segmentation, shape representation and analysis, and vision for robotics.

The contributions for CAIP 2019 were selected based on a minimum of two, but mostly three reviews. Among 183 submissions, 106 were accepted with an acceptance rate of 58%.

We are grateful to the Steering Committee of CAIP for giving us the honor of organizing this reputable conference in Italy. We thank the International Association for Pattern Recognition (IAPR) that endorsed the conference, Springer that offered the best paper award, and the Italian Association for Computer Vision, Pattern Recognition and Machine Learning (CVPL) that offered the CVPL prize assigned to a young researcher, author of the best paper presented the conference. We thank the University of Salerno for the sponsorship and, specifically, its Department of Computer and Electrical Engineering and Applied Mathematics, also SAST Gmbh, A.I. Tech srl, and AI4Health srl as gold sponsors, and Nexsoft spa, Gesan srl, and Hanwha Techwin Europe Ltd. as silver sponsors.

We thank the authors for submitting their valuable works to CAIP; this is of prime importance for the success of the event. However, the success of a conference also depends on a number of volunteers. We would like to thank the reviewers and the Program Committee members for their excellent work. We also thank the local Organizing Committee and all the other volunteers who helped us organize CAIP 2019.

We hope that all participants had a pleasant and fruitful stay in Salerno.

September 2019   Mario Vento
                                                         Gennaro Percannella

Organization

CAIP 2019 was organized by the Intelligent Machines for the recognition of Video, Images and Audio (MIVIA) Laboratory, Department of Computer and Electrical Engineering and Applied Mathematics, University of Salerno, Italy.

Executive Committees

Conference Chairs

Mario Vento	University of Salerno, Italy
Gennaro Percannella	University of Salerno, Italy

Program Chairs

Pasquale Foggia	University of Salerno, Italy
Luca Greco	University of Salerno, Italy
Pierluigi Ritrovato	University of Salerno, Italy
Nicola Strisciuglio	University of Groningen, The Netherlands

Local Organizing Committee

Vincenzo Carletti	University of Salerno, Italy
Antonio Greco	University of Salerno, Italy
Alessia Saggese	University of Salerno, Italy
Vincenzo Vigilante	University of Salerno, Italy

Web and Publicity Chair

Vincenzo Carletti	University of Salerno, Italy

Steering Committee

George Azzopardi	University of Groningen, The Netherlands
Michael Felsberg	Linköping University, Sweden
Edwin Hancock	University of York, UK
Xiaoyi Jiang	University of Münster, Germany
Reinhard Klette	Auckland University of Technology, New Zealand
Walter G. Kropatsch	Vienna University of Technology, Austria
Gennaro Percannella	University of Salerno, Italy
Nicolai Petkov	University of Groningen, The Netherlands
Pedro Real Jurado	University of Seville, Spain
Mario Vento	University of Salerno, Italy

Program Committee

Marco Aiello	University of Stuttgart, Germany
Enrique Alegre	University of Leon, Spain
Muhammad Raza Ali	InfoTech, Pakistan
Furqan Aziz	Institute of Management Sciences, Pakistan
George Azzopardi	University of Groningen, The Netherlands
Andrew Bagdanov	Computer Vision Center, Spain
Donald Bailey	Massey University, New Zealand
Antonio Bandera	University of Malaga, Spain
Ardhendu Behera	Edge Hill University, UK
Abdel Belaid	University of Lorraine, France
Fabio Bellavia	University of Florence, Italy
Michael Biehl	University of Groningen, The Netherlands
Gunilla Borgefors	Uppsala University, Sweden
Kerstin Bunte	University of Groningen, The Netherlands
Kenneth Camilleri	University of Malta, Malta
Vincenzo Carletti	University of Salerno, Italy
Modesto Castrillon Santana	University of Las Palmas de Gran Canaria, Spain
Kwok-Ping Chan	University of Hong Kong, SAR China
Rama Chellappa	University of Maryland, USA
Dmitry Chetverikov	Hungarian Academy of Sciences, Hungary
Danilo Coimbra	Federal University of Bahia, Brazil
Carlo Colombo	University of Florence, Italy
Donatello Conte	University of Tours, France
Carl James Debono	University of Malta, Malta
Santa Di Cataldo	Politecnico di Torino, Italy
Mariella Dimiccoli	Institut de Robòtica i Informàtica Industrial, Spain
Junyu Dong	University of China, China
Alexandre Falcao	University of Campinas (Unicamp), Brazil
Giovanni Maria Farinella	University of Catania, Italy
Reuben A. Farrugia	University of Malta, Malta
Gernot Fink	TU Dortmund University, Germany
Patrizio Frosini	University of Bologna, Italy
Eduardo Garea	Advanced Technologies Applications Center, Cuba
Benoit Gaüzère	Normandie Université, France
Daniela Giorgi	ISTI-CNR, Italy
Rocio Gonzalez-Diaz	University of Seville, Spain
Javier Gonzalez-Jimenez	University of Malaga, Spain
Antonio Greco	University of Salerno, Italy
Cosmin Grigorescu	European Patent Office, EU
Miguel A. Gutiérrez-Naranjo	University of Seville, Spain
Michal Haindl	Czech Academy of Sciences, Czech Republic
Vaclav Hlavac	Czech Technical University in Prague, Czech Republic
Yo-Ping Huang	National Taipei University of Technology, Taiwan

Atsushi Imiya	IMIT Chiba University, Japan
Xiaoyi Jiang	University of Münster, Germany
Maria Jose Jimenez	University of Seville, Spain
Martin Kampel	Vienna University of Technology, Austria
Hamideh Kerdegari	Kingston University of London, UK
Nahum Kiryati	Tel Aviv University, Israel
Reinhard Klette	Auckland University of Technology, New Zealand
Walter G. Kropatsch	Vienna University of Technology, Austria
Wenqi Li	King's College London, UK
Guo-Shiang Lin	China Medical University, Taiwan
Agnieszka Lisowska	University of Silesia, Poland
Josep Llados	Universitat Autònoma de Barcelona, Spain
Rebeca Marfil	University of Malaga, Spain
Manuel J. Marín-Jiménez	University of Cordoba, Spain
Heydi Mendez-Vazquez	Advanced Technologies Applications Center, Cuba
Eckart Michaelsen	Fraunhofer IOSB, Germany
Mariofanna Milanova	University of Arkansas at Little Rock, USA
Adrian Muscat	University of Malta, Malta
Paolo Napoletano	University of Milan Bicocca, Italy
Andreas Neocleous	University of Groningen, The Netherlands
Mark Nixon	University of Southampton, UK
Stavros Ntalampiras	University of Milan, Italy
Darian Onchis	University of Vienna, Austria
Arkadiusz Orłowski	Warsaw University of Life Sciences, Poland
Constantinos Pattichis	University of Cyprus, Cyprus
Marios Pattichis	University of New Mexico, USA
Gennaro Percannella	University of Salerno, Italy
Nicolai Petkov	University of Groningen, The Netherlands
Fiora Pirri	University of Rome Sapienza, Italy
Giovanni Poggi	University of Naples Federico II, Italy
Xianbiao Qi	Shenzhen Research Institute of Big Data, China
Manzoor Razaak	Kingston University, UK
Pedro Real Jurado	University of Seville, Spain
Emanuele Rodolà	University of Rome Sapienza, Italy
Robert Sablatnig	Vienna University of Technology, Austria
Alessia Saggese	University of Salerno, Italy
Hideo Saito	Keio University, Japan
Albert Ali Salah	Utrecht University, Turkey
Angel Sanchez	Rey Juan Carlos University, Spain
Lidia Sánchez-González	University of León, Spain
Antonio-José Sánchez-Salmerón	Universitat Politècnica de València, Spain
Gabriella Sanniti di Baja	ICAR-CNR, Italy
Carlo Sansone	University of Naples Federico II, Italy
Sudeep Sarkar	University of South Florida, USA
Christos Schizas	University of Cyprus, Cyprus

Klamer Schutte   TNO, The Netherlands
Francesc Serratosa   Universitat Rovira i Virgili, Spain
Fabrizio Smeraldi   Queen Mary University of London, UK
Akihiro Sugimoto   National Institute of Informatics, Japan
Bart Ter Haar Romeny   Eindhoven University of Technology, The Netherlands
Bernard Tiddeman   Aberystwyth University, UK
Klaus Toennies   Otto-von-Guericke University, Germany
Javier Toro   Desarrollo para la Ciencia y la Tecnología, Venezuela
Andrea Torsello   University of Venice Ca Foscari, Italy
Francesco Tortorella   University of Salerno, Italy
Carlos M.   University of Las Palmas de Gran Canaria, Spain
  Travieso-Gonzalez
Radim Tylecek   University of Edinburgh, UK
Herwig Unger   FernUniversität in Hagen, Germany
Ernest Valveny   Universitat Autònoma de Barcelona, Spain
Mario Vento   University of Salerno, Italy
Vincenzo Vigilante   University of Salerno, Italy
Arnold Wiliem   University of Queensland, Australia
Michael H. F. Wilkinson   University of Groningen, The Netherlands
Richard Wilson   University of York, UK
Wei Wi Yan   Auckland University of Technology, New Zealand
Zhao Zhang   Hefei University of Technology, China

Invited Speakers

James Ferryman   University of Reading, UK
Luc Brun   ENSICAEN, France
Gian Luca Marcialis   University of Cagliari, Italy
Nicolai Petkov   University of Groningen, The Netherlands

Tutorials

Aditya Nigam   Indian Institute of Technology Mandi, India
Arnav Bhavsar   Indian Institute of Technology Mandi, India
Francesco Setti   University of Verona, Italy

Workshops

Hamideh Kerdegari   Kingston University, UK
Manzoor Razaak   Kingston University, UK
Matthew Broadbent   Lancaster University, UK
Sara Colantonio   ISTI-CNR, Italy
Daniela Giorgi   ISTI-CNR, Italy
Bogdan J. Matuszewski   UCLan, UK

Contest

Fabio Bellavia   University of Florence, Italy
Carlo Colombo   University of Florence, Italy

Additional Reviewer

W. Al-Nabki   A. Griffin   M. Norouzifard
M. G. Al-Sarayreh   D. Helm   E. Paluzo-Hidalgo
D. Batavia   J. Hladůvka   C. Pramerdorfer
M. G. Bergomi   H. Ho   E. Rusakov
P. Bhowmick   C. Istin   J. R. R. Sarmiento
R. Biswas   A. Joshhi   J. Smith
P. Blanco   D. Kossmann   M. Soriano-Trigueros
M. Callieri   P. Marín-Reyes   E. Talavera
D. Chaves   F. A. Moreno   F. Wolf
D. Freire-Obregón   M. Mortara   D. Zuñiga-Noël
A. Gangwar   F. Moya

Endorsing Institution

International Association for Pattern Recognition (IAPR)

Sponsoring Institutions

Department of Computer and Electrical Engineering and Applied Mathematics, University of Salerno
Springer Lecture Notes in Computer Science
Italian Association for Computer Vision, Pattern Recognition and Machine Learning (CVPL)

Sponsoring Companies

A.I. Tech srl
SAST Gmbh
AI4Health srl
Gesan srl
Hanwha Techwin Europe Ltd
Nexsoft SpA

Contents – Part I

Poster Session

Contents – Part II

Intelligent Systems

HMDHBN: Hidden Markov Inducing a Dynamic Hierarchical Bayesian Network for Tumor Growth Prediction

Samya Amiri[1] and Mohamed Ali Mahjoub[2(✉)]

[1] Institut Supérieur d'Informatique et des Techniques de Communication de Hammam Sousse, LATIS - Laboratory of Advanced Technology and Intelligent Systems, University of Sousse, 4011 Sousse, Tunisia
amiri.sam6@gmail.com
[2] Ecole Nationale d'Ingénieurs de Sousse, LATIS - Laboratory of Advanced Technology and Intelligent Systems, University of Sousse, 4023 Sousse, Tunisia
Mohamedali.mahjoub@eniso.rnu.tn

Abstract. Radiomics transform medical images into a rich source of information and a main tool for the tumor growth survey, which is the result of multiple processes at different scales composing a complex system. To model the tumor evolution in both time and space we propose to exploit radiomic features within a multi-scale architecture that models the biological events at different levels. The proposed framework is based on the HMM architecture that encodes the relation between radiomic features as observed phenomena and the mechanical interactions within the tumor as a hidden process. On the other hand, it models the Tumor evolution through time thanks to its dynamic aspect. While, to represent the biological interactions, we use a Hierarchical Bayesian Network where we associate a level for each scale (Tissue, *cell-cluster*, cell scale). Thus, the HMM induces a Dynamic Hierarchical Bayesian Network that encodes the tumor growth aspects and factors.

Keywords: Tumor growth modeling · Bayesian network · HMM · Hierarchical BN · Dynamic BN · MRI

1 Introduction

Cancer has an epidemiological aspect. Although the overall death rates decrease, this is not the case for several cancer types [1,2]. New strategies for prevention, detection, and treatment are essential. Indeed, Cancer is a biological system with complex pathophysiology resulting from the interaction of several biological mechanisms, making detection, progress evaluation and treatment tasks very challenging and highly dependent on several factors. Thus, modeling is essential to better understand the governing mechanisms of these diseases [3].

In cancer research, modeling is applied for three different purposes: the diagnoses (tumor detection); the forecast (the prediction of the system evolution) and

© Springer Nature Switzerland AG 2019
M. Vento and G. Percannella (Eds.): CAIP 2019, LNCS 11678, pp. 3–14, 2019.
https://doi.org/10.1007/978-3-030-29888-3_1

the treatment (evaluation of the therapeutic strategies). In this paper, we are interested in predicting the tumor evolution in time and space which is clinically important for cancerologists [4].

The literature is rich with models that differ according to several aspects: the modeling scale, the used techniques and the precision of the information that they supply [4]. Microscopic scale models handle the elementary interactions and investigate on the cellular level. These models are suitable to study, to analyze and understand the mechanisms governing the tumor however, the simulation of these models on the tumor scale (107 cells at least) is not possible. The macroscopic models that represent on the tissue scale, are more suitable for the clinical application. At this level, tumor growth modeling has long been considered as a mathematical problem. Models are continuous and essentially based on differential equations. Their major limitation is parameters estimation. This task can be done by deterministic or statistical methods. In the first case, the parameters are difficult to estimate from the clinical data while in the second case, we lose the personalization of the model and its adaptation to the patient. In contrast, reaction-diffusion models derived from longitudinal imaging are purely patient specific and don't take into account the tumor growth pattern of the population trend [8].

To overcome mathematical modeling limitations, recent works address the tumor growth modeling from a machine learning perspective exploiting medical images that represent a rich source of knowledge; this has been encouraged by the improvement of automatic feature extraction and segmentation algorithms [19–22]. In [8], a statistical group learning approach to predict the tumor growth pattern is proposed it incorporates both the population trend and personalized data, in order to discover high-level features from multimodal imaging data. A deep convolutional neural network approach is developed to model the voxel-wise spatio-temporal tumor progression. Zhang et al. investigate the possibility of using deep convolutional neural networks (ConvNets) to directly represent and learn the cell invasion and mass-effect, and to predict the subsequent involvement regions of a tumor [9]. A different idea based on voxel motion is proposed in [10]. The authors propose to compute the optical flow of voxels over time, and estimate the future deformable field via an autoregressive model. This method is able to predict entire brain MR scan, however, the tumor growth pattern of population trend is still not involved. Moreover, this method might over-simplify the tumor growth process, since it infers the future growth in a linear manner (most tumor growth are nonlinear).

From another perspective, several works in literature attempt to include major biological events at tissue, cellular and *sub*-cellular scales in the tumor growth process [6,7]. Thus, they propose *multi*-scale models that incorporate multiple data: cancer cell proliferation, intrusion and micro- environment attributes... These models are motivated by: (i) Testing hypothesis and making predictions when there is insufficient information about the biological system under study. (ii) Trying to displace some of the in-*vivo* and in-*vitro* experiments [5].

Probabilistic Graphical Models (PGM) represent a potential solution to address the mentioned model's limitations. Indeed, they are powerful tools for modeling uncertainties and imprecise probabilistic systems. They play a crucial role in scientific data analysis, machine learning, robotics, cognitive science, and artificial intelligence [12]. Moreover; they have been widely applied for multiple problems such as forecasting [11], decision making [13], classification [14]... Especially, Bayesian network that has been adapted to different application domains, giving birth to multiple versions: Dynamic Bayesian Network (DBN) which introduces the time dimension, Hierarchical Bayesian Network (HBN) that allows distinguishing further levels of variability and HMM that may be considered as the simple example of DBN.

Considering the needs of tumor growth modeling in handling tumor variability, uncertainty and missed data, integrating complex tumor mechanisms (multi-level interactions, multiple factors...), and aggregating the population trend and the individualized characteristics of the patient, PGMs and more specifically BN are suitable for the tumor system modeling. In fact, BNs are increasingly applied in complex systems modeling and decision-making tools development thanks to the following strengths: inter-disciplinarily (integrating variables of different natures); graphical representation; the ability to extend models by introducing new data observations; good management of uncertainty, noise or incomplete data. In particular, they are characterized by adaptability to meet new needs. Thus, general BNs can be extended to handle new requirements: discovery of causality [16], cognitive modeling [11,16], evolution over time [16]...

In this paper, we propose a multi-scale BN based model for tumor growth modeling. The proposed framework is based on the HMM architecture: on the one hand, such graphical model encodes the relation between radiomics as observed phenomena and the mechanical interactions within the tumor as a hidden process. On the other hand, it models the Tumor evolution through time thanks to its dynamic aspect. To represent the biological interactions we use a hierarchical Bayesian Network where we associate a level for each scale (Tissue, *cell*-cluster, cell scale). Thus, the HMM induces a Dynamic Hierarchical Bayesian Network that encodes the tumor growth aspects and factors.

2   Hierarchical Bayesian Network

Hierarchical Bayesian Network (HBN) [23] is an altered version of BNs that deals with structured domains, through integrating knowledge about the structure of the data to improve both inference and learning. Thus, the network is a nesting of BNs or even HBNs that encodes the probabilistic dependencies between them, each node is an aggregation of simpler ones and represents a subset of the modeled system. In fact, the information we capture using medical images illustrates the macroscopic behavior of the tumor that results from other biological interactions in lower scales (cellular scale). Besides, if we consider that the multi-scale is a vertical decomposition of the tumor into a hierarchy, the sub-region of the tumor (edema (ED), non-enhancing solid core (NEN), necrotic/cystic core (C), enhancing core (EN)) can be considered as a horizontal decomposition. Hence, the tumor structure is very informative and have to be exploited to give an improved representation of this complex system.

To achieve the aforementioned goal, we propose a HBN that models these two dimensions (horizontal an vertical decomposition). First, considering the biological structure, three scales are identified: tissue scale, cell cluster scale and cellular scale. Each scale is represented with a simple BN see Fig. 1. Second, Considering the tumor structure, we identify different sub-regions in the top layer of the proposed HBN see Fig. 1.

Formally, the Hierarchical Bayesian Network is a triplet $\prec T, P, t \succ$ as defined in [23] where

- t is a type structure
- $T = \prec T, P, t \succ$ is an HBN-tree structure over t
- P is the HBN-Probabilistic Part related to T

We consider a type structure for each scale level, Fig. 1 shows the different tree structures. The HBN-tree structure is illustrated in Fig. 2.

2.1   Multi-scale Architecture

Tissue – Scale **Type Structure.** At the tissue scale, we consider three constituents representing (1) tumor cells, (2) normal cells, and (3) extracellular matrix (ECM). We further consider the different tumor sub-regions: edema (ED), non-enhancing solid core (NEN), necrotic/cystic core (C), enhancing core (EN). For the normal tissue we also differentiate sub-regions according to the Tissue type (example: white matter, gray matter and cerebro-spinal fluid for brain tissue). For each tumor sub-region we associate a $Tissue_s cale$ tree structure Fig. 2 composed of two nodes the first one represents the type of the tissue R_i (white circle) the second one represents the feature vector characterizing the region MR_i (black circle).

Cell-Cluster Type Structure. The representation of the tissue scale is based on the segmentation and annotation of the data. To refine it we perform an over-segmentation. Each supervoxel is an homogenous volume characterized with a unique feature vector and label. Biologically it represents a mass of cells having the same nature. The biological events evolving in each volume element are modeled using a *Cell – cluster* Type Structure which has the following attributes. First, we consider the nodes representing the super-voxels denoted by the symbol X_i i = 1, ..., N. Thus, each of those nodes may have the following states: proliferative, quiescent (predominantly hypoxic), nonviable (predominantly necrotic) and normal (Normal tissue cells). Second, M_i i = 1, ..., N, denote the measurements nodes representing the super voxel features.

A HBN variable is used to model the relation between adjacent cell clusters, it is an atomic type composed of binary nodes (state 0 or 1) that represent the superpixels S_i i = 1, ..., L, separating two adjacent super voxels. Each Superpixel node has the nodes representing the corresponding adjacent supervoxels as parent nodes. This node takes 1 if the supervoxels have the same parent node in the tissue scale else it takes 0.

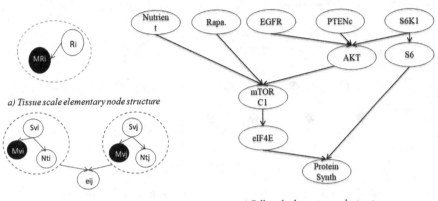

a) Tissue scale elementary node structure

b) Cell- clusters scale elementary node structure

c) Cell-scale elementary node structure

Fig. 1. The structure and parameters of the elementary Bayesian Network composing the HMDHBN architecture

Cellular Level. At the cellular scale we consider a cell signaling pathway consisting of key biological events such as induction, promotion or inhibition of *sub*-cellular [24]. Among them, the PI3K/AKT/mTOR pathway is an important regulator for the cell cycle and cell growth. In our work, we consider a simplified pathway components Fig. 1(c) [24].

In pathological conditions such as cancer, some components along pathway would either gain or loose functions, which means the protein level is either over- or under-expressed, respectively.

3 Hidden Markov Inducing a Dynamic Hierarchical Bayesian Network HMDHBN

Bayesian networks are extended to handle time in its dynamic version. To represent the tumor growth and the consequent space changes we propose to make dynamic the proposed hierarchical BN defined in the previous section. Hence, we intend to model not only the radiomic information given by one MRI, but the chronological alterations over time given a temporal sequence of MRIs. For that we consider a Hidden Markov Model to induce the Dynamic Hierarchical BN [24].

HMM is a graphical probabilistic model that represents the generation of the observed inputs from unobserved hidden states and their development over time. It captures the transitions among different states but not the conditional

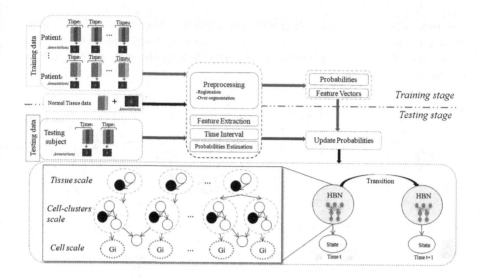

Fig. 2. The Proposed architecture for tumor growth Prediction

dependencies among variables. This problem is solved using the Hierarchical Bayesian network that will encode the inherent interactions within the tumor as a complex biological system. The aggregation of the two PGMs will produce a non-stationary DHBN, called Hidden Markov induced Hierarchical Dynamic Bayesian Network (HMDHBN).

The HMDHBN extends each hidden node of the traditional HMM into a hidden DHBN (called hidden graph), and develops the transition between nodes to describe the transition between the evolving networks. It models that multiple observed inputs T are generated by the unobserved hidden graphs. The conditional probability of data observation with respect to each DHBN and the conditional probability between DHBNs are used as the emission probability and the transition probability for HMDHBN, respectively.

In Fig. 2 we present the main steps of the proposed framework. During the training stage, we consider multi-model imaging data as the system input. First, the medical images of different modalities and different time points are registered along with the normal tissue images. Next, we perform the over segmentation to get homogeneous super-voxels; then features and time intervals are extracted. Probabilities are learned from each pairs of two time points (time t and time $t + 1$) for each patient (patient n and patient $n + 1$). This learning is a probabilistic representation of the population trend. Thus, to personalize the framework parameters, we consider two time points imaging of the testing subject. The same preprocessing and learning strategy is applied. Then a mixture is computed to get the personalized probabilities:

$$F_X(x) = \sum\nolimits_{i=1}^{k} \alpha_i p_X(i)(x).$$

During the testing stage, we construct the HMM as follows: The observed state nodes contain information depicted from the multi model images considered as our observed phenomena. For each voxel we associate a low-feature vector and its label. The Hidden nodes represent the Hierarchical BN that models the interactions within each scale (tissue scale, cell-cluster scale and cell scale), encodes the dependencies between different factors affecting this biological level and the relation between different scales. The prediction is then performed through the inference conducted upon the different BNs composing the framework and the HMM to get a new HBN describing the future state of the patient giving a new observed state for each voxel.

3.1 The Inference in the HMDHBN

Considering the composed structure of the proposed framework, a more sophisticated algorithm is needed to handle its specificity. For the hidden graphs which are HBNs the most economical technique for calculating beliefs is the message-passing algorithm [25]. Hence, each node within the network is associated to a belief state, that could be a vector. The belief state of each node are often directly retrieved given the belief states of its parent and children nodes. Whenever a modification in a node's belief state happens, either forced by some direct observation or indirectly, because of a modification of the state of a neighbor, the node calculates its new belief state and propagates the relevant data to its parent and children nodes. This process is then repeated till the network reaches convergence.

Belief calculation is performed naturally in 3 main steps: (i) Belief updating: alter a node's belief vector, according to the newest data coming from its neighbors. (ii) bottom-up propagation: Computing the messages that will be sent to parent nodes. (iii) Top-down propagation: Computing the messages that will be sent to children nodes. Formally, the belief at node i, is proportional to the product of the local evidence at that node $\Phi_i(x_i)$, and all the messages coming into node N:

$$M_i(x_i) \propto \Phi_i(x_i) \prod_{k \in N_i} m_{ki}(x_i)$$

where x_i is a random variable for the state of node i, and N_i denotes the neighbors of node i. The messages are determined by the message update rule:

$$m_{ki}(x_i) = \sum \Phi_k(x_k) \Phi_{ki}(x_i, x_k) \prod_{j \in N_k \setminus i} m_{jk}(x_k)$$

where $\Phi_{ki}(x_i, x_k)$ is the pairwise potential between nodes i and k. On the right-hand side, there is a product over all messages going into node k except for the one coming from node i. This product is marginalized in order to form the particular information that we want to send to the destination node.

Before inferring within the HBN, we perform inference on the HMM architecture using the forward backward algorithm. This will update the cell cluster probabilities according to the transition probabilities learned during the training stage. This update will generate an inner belief propagation to take into account the neighborhood dependencies and other parameters composing the tumor model.

As described, the Belief propagation within the HBN it self gives a personalized aspect to the framework while the transition probabilities of the HMM encodes the learned knowledge from the training data. Hence, through coupling these two nested PGMs we aggregate a general and personalized parametrization in the whole framework.

4   Tests and Experimental Results

4.1   Data and Measurements

To evaluate the performance of the proposed framework we consider *multi*-scans for two patients with brain tumor. The scans are taken at roughly 6 month intervals over three and a half (interval times between t1 and t2), with T1 protocols see Fig. 4. The pixel resolutions on these scans are 0.9375×0.9375 mm in-plane by 3.1 mm slice thickness. Manual tracing of the tumor was performed at both screening times (i.e. 4 manual segmentation per patient) to segment the different compartments. For each set of images, we first perform rigid registration between successive time points. Meanwhile, manual segmentation was performed for the non tumoral tissue, gray matter, white matter and cerebro-spinal fluid (CSF). The prediction performance is evaluated using measurements at the third time point by Dice score.

We evaluate the proposed method using a leave-one-out cross-validation, which not only facilitates comparison with the state-of-the-art model-based method (tumor status at time1 and time2 already known, predict next time point), but more importantly enables learning both population trend and patient-specific tumor growth patterns. The Fig. 4 shows the volume variation for the first patient plotted along with the ground truth volume.

We obtain the model's performance values by averaging results from the cross validation folds. Figure 5 shows qualitative predicting results at different time points. To further quantify the accuracy of the estimated posteriors, Dice coefficients of simulated tumors obtained using different sampling methods are compared in Table 1, where all sampling methods provided similar Dice coefficients for patient datasets. This confirms the accuracy of our method is satisfactory (Fig. 3).

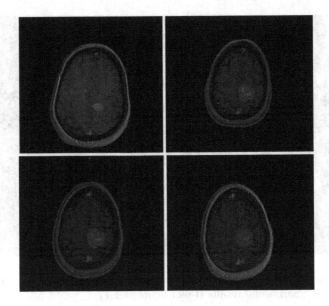

Fig. 3. Samples of the used dataset

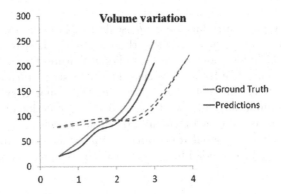

Fig. 4. The variation of the tumor mass volume for two patients.

Table 1. Prediction results evaluation

Method	HMM	DBN	HMDHBN
Mean Dice index	0.39 ± 0.40	0.53	0.76 ± 0.15

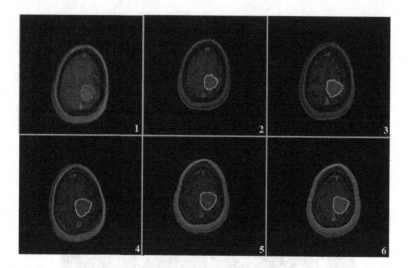

Fig. 5. Qualitative prediction results for several time points. Red color: ground truth; green color the experimental results (Color figure online)

5   Conclusion

In this paper we have introduced a *multi*-scale PGMs based model for tumor growth modeling. The proposed framework integrates a HBN within the HMM architecture as the hidden node while the radiomic features are considered as the observed phenomena. The HBN represents the tumor structure and encodes the dependencies between different factors governing the tumor growth. The HMM transitions allow updating the HBN to generate the prediction of the next time point state. Hence, it produce a Dynamic HBN that models the evolution of this complex system. The proposed framework alleviates the mathematical models limitation and may be extended to evaluate the treatment impact.

References

1. Jemal, A., et al.: Annual report to the nation on the status of cancer, 1975–2014, featuring survival. JNCI: J. Natl. Cancer Inst. **109**(9), djx030 (2017). Clerk Maxwell, J.: A Treatise on Electricity and Magnetism, 3rd edn, vol. 2, pp. 68–73. Clarendon, Oxford (1892)
2. Malvezzi, M., et al.: European cancer mortality predictions for the year 2018 with focus on colorectal cancer. Ann. Oncol. **29**(4), 1016–1022 (2018)
3. Hornberg, J.J., Bruggeman, F.J., Westerhoff, H.V., Lankelma, J.: Cancer: a systems biology disease. Biosystems **83**(2–3), 81–90 (2006). https://doi.org/10.1016/j.biosystems.2005.05.014
4. Masoudi-Nejad, A., Wang, E.: Cancer modeling and network biology: accelerating toward personalized medicine. In: Seminars in Cancer Biology, vol. 30, pp. 1–3. Academic Press, February 2015

5. Feng, Y., Boukhris, S.J., Ranjan, R., Valencia, R.A.: Biological systems: multiscale modeling based on mixture theory. In: De, S., Hwang, W., Kuhl, E. (eds.) Multiscale Modeling in Biomechanics and Mechanobiology, pp. 257–286. Springer, London (2015). https://doi.org/10.1007/978-1-4471-6599-6_11

6. Masoudi-Nejad, A., Bidkhori, G., Ashtiani, S.H., Najafi, A., Bozorgmehr, J.H., Wang, E.: Cancer systems biology and modeling: microscopic scale and multiscale approaches. In: Seminars in Cancer Biology, vol. 30, pp. 60–69. Academic Press, February 2015

7. Ghadiri, M., Heidari, M., Marashi, S.A., Mousavi, S.H.: A multiscale agent-based framework integrated with a constraint-based metabolic network model of cancer for simulating avascular tumor growth. Mol. BioSyst. **13**(9), 1888–1897 (2017)

8. Zhang, L., Lu, L., Summers, R.M., Kebebew, E., Yao, J.: Personalized pancreatic tumor growth prediction via group learning. In: Descoteaux, M., Maier-Hein, L., Franz, A., Jannin, P., Collins, D.L., Duchesne, S. (eds.) MICCAI 2017. LNCS, vol. 10434, pp. 424–432. Springer, Cham (2017). https://doi.org/10.1007/978-3-319-66185-8_48

9. Zhang, L., Lu, L., Summers, R.M., Kebebew, E., Yao, J.: Convolutional invasion and expansion networks for tumor growth prediction. IEEE Trans. Med. Imaging **37**(2), 638–648 (2018)

10. Weizman, L., et al.: Prediction of brain MR scans in longitudinal tumor follow-up studies. In: Ayache, N., Delingette, H., Golland, P., Mori, K. (eds.) MICCAI 2012. LNCS, vol. 7511, pp. 179–187. Springer, Heidelberg (2012). https://doi.org/10.1007/978-3-642-33418-4_23

11. Ibargüengoytia, P.H., Reyes, A., García, U.A., Romero, I., Pech, D.: Evaluating probabilistic graphical models for forecasting. In: 2015 18th International Conference on Intelligent System Application to Power Systems (ISAP), pp. 1–6. IEEE, September 2015

12. Ghahramani, Z.: Probabilistic machine learning and artificial intelligence. Nature **521**(7553), 452 (2015)

13. Lucas, P.: Bayesian networks in medicine: a model-based approach to medical decision making (2001)

14. Sucar, L.E., Bielza, C., Morales, E.F., Hernandez-Leal, P., Zaragoza, J.H., Larrañaga, P.: Multi-label classification with Bayesian network-based chain classifiers. Pattern Recogn. Lett. **41**, 14–22 (2014)

15. Tauber, S., Navarro, D.J., Perfors, A., Steyvers, M.: Bayesian models of cognition revisited: setting optimality aside and letting data drive psychological theory. Psychol. Rev. **124**(4), 410 (2017)

16. Pearl, J.: Bayesian networks (2011)

17. Forney, G.D.: The viterbi algorithm. Proc. IEEE **61**(3), 268–278 (1973)

18. Wu, M., Yang, X., Chan, C.: A dynamic analysis of IRS-PKR signaling in liver cells: a discrete modeling approach. PLoS One **4**(12), e8040 (2009)

19. Amiri, S., Rekik, I., Mahjoub, M.A.: Deep random forest-based learning transfer to SVM for brain tumor segmentation. In: 2016 2nd International Conference on Advanced Technologies for Signal and Image Processing (ATSIP), pp. 297–302. IEEE. March 2016

20. Amiri, S., Rekik, I., Mahjoub, M.A.: Bayesian network and structured random forest cooperative deep learning for automatic multi-label brain tumor segmentation. In: 2018 10th International Conference The International Conference on Agents and Artificial Intelligence (ICAART) (2018)

21. Amiri, S., Rekik, I., Mahjoub, M.A.: Dynamic multiscale tree learning using ensemble strong classifiers for multi-label segmentation of medical images with lesions. In: 2018 13th International Conference on Computer Vision Theory and Applications (VISAAP) (2018)
22. Amiri, S., Mahjoub, M.A., Rekik, I.: Dynamic multiscale tree learning using ensemble strong classifiers for multi-label segmentation of medical images with lesions. Neurocomputing (2018)
23. Gyftodimos, E., Flach, P.A.: Hierarchical bayesian networks: an approach to classification and learning for structured data. In: Vouros, G.A., Panayiotopoulos, T. (eds.) SETN 2004. LNCS (LNAI), vol. 3025, pp. 291–300. Springer, Heidelberg (2004). https://doi.org/10.1007/978-3-540-24674-9_31
24. Rahman, M.M., Feng, Y., Yankeelov, T.E., Oden, J.T.: A fully coupled space-time multiscale modeling framework for predicting tumor growth. Comput. Methods Appl. Mech. Eng. **320**, 261–286 (2017)
25. Zhu, S., Wang, Y.: Hidden Markov induced Dynamic Bayesian Network for recovering time evolving gene regulatory networks. Sci. Rep. **5**, 17841 (2015)
26. Pearl, J.: Probabilistic Reasoning in Intelligent Systems: Networks of Plausible Inference. Elsevier (2014)

MIVIABot: A Cognitive Robot for Smart Museum

Alessia Saggese, Mario Vento, and Vincenzo Vigilante[✉]

Università Degli Studi Di Salerno, 84084 Salerno, SA, Italy
{asaggese,mvento,vvigilante}@unisa.it

Abstract. Cognitive robots are robots provided with artificial intelligence capabilities, able to properly interact with people and with the objects in an a priori unknown environment, using advanced artificial intelligence algorithms. For instance, a humanoid robot can be perceived as a plausible tourist guide in a museum. Within this context, in this work we present how the latest findings in the field of machine learning and pattern recognition can be applied to equip a robot with sufficiently advanced perception capabilities in order to successfully guide visitors through the halls and the attraction in a museum.

The challenge of running all those algorithms on a mobile, embedded platform in real time is tackled on an architectural level, where all the artificial intelligence features are tuned to run with a low computational burden and a Neural Network accelerator is included in the hardware setup. Improved robustness and predictable latency is obtained avoiding the use of cloud services in the system.

Our robot, that we call MIVIABot, is able to decode and understand speech as well as extract soft biometrics from its interlocutor such as age, gender and emotional status. The robot can integrate all those elements in a dialog, using basic Natural Language Processing capabilities.

Keywords: Cognitive robotics · Machine learning · Cultural heritage

1 Introduction

In recent years, developments in fields of both Robotics and Artificial Intelligence allowed for building robots that are no more executors of a pre-programmed path, but are able to automatically adapt their behavior in function of the stimuli perceived from the environment which is typically not a-priori known.

That paradigm has its more meaningful application when robots have to confront an environment that is dynamic and its structure is non easy to model [14]. Such environments for instance are those which involve sharing the space with humans; the most basic application of such an idea is intelligent collision avoidance, where sensors are used to perceive the presence of obstacles at runtime [8,10]. In opposition, intelligent perception features are not required when a robot is bound to operate in a confined sterile area (robotic cell) where objects

© Springer Nature Switzerland AG 2019
M. Vento and G. Percannella (Eds.): CAIP 2019, LNCS 11678, pp. 15–25, 2019.
https://doi.org/10.1007/978-3-030-29888-3_2

to manipulate are in known positions and have a simple, predictable shape that can be thoroughly modeled.

The extreme expression of such a paradigm is when the only task of the robot is interaction with humans. That setting is called "social robotics" and applications such as automatic shop assistance or robotic museum guides are a clear example of that. The robotic part of the system is devoted to the imitation of a human gestures and allows for an automatic system to be socially accepted in a human context. Social acceptance of robot is a long-time studied subject [7]: it has been shown that social robots do not need to have to perfectly imitate human appearance but social acceptance works well when physical appearance is roughly similar but important features of the human behavior are recalled [18]. For example attention models are a crucial aspect of social robots [5]: the robot needs to direct its gaze towards its interlocutors, but also it needs to look away periodically otherwise it will provoke discomfort. Further features improve the *appearance of intelligence* that a robot may exhibit. For example a robot able to recognize gender and age of its interlocutor (as shown in [9]) is able to achieve a richer understanding of the surrounding environment and will be more effective in a simple conversation, gaining empathy and credibility.

Another important requirement in social robotics is related to the possibility to run all the software directly on board, without any needs of sending the sequence of image to be processed by using a wireless connection, for the processing over servers or on the cloud. Indeed, we need that the robot continues to be social even if the internet connection is not available; furthermore, the transmission of the sequence of images via wireless may introduce a latency that prevents the system to be really interactive with the persons.

As seen in the examples just described, perception of a dynamic, complex environment is configured as the basis of a cognitive robot system. In this work we propose an hw+sw robotic architecture that we call MIVIABot able tointegrate multiple advanced perception capabilities leveraging artificial intelligence techniques from the latest literature and particularizing them for the intended application, namely guiding tourists in a museum.

2   MIVIABot: The Proposed HW+SW Solution

2.1   The Architecture

The design of the hardware architecture is guided by the aims of the application and the constraints imposed. In particular, the application requires an anthropomorphic robot, that could be accepted as peer by its human interlocutor. It is not required a perfect understanding of speech and contexts but it is crucial that the robot is able to respond to simple inquiries identified by few keywords. Furthermore, to create a better relationship between the robot and its interlocutor, a personalized interaction is required, thus gender, age and emotional state of the interlocutor are recognized by the system. Of course all this needs to be recognized in real time: response time must be limited. Perfect recognition is not required, but a minimum performance is expected for the system to behave correctly. Furthermore, as previously stated, we want to avoid the use of cloud services to improve robustness against the absence of a stable internet connection.

For the task of guiding tourists in a museum, we use as base platform the Social Robot Pepper from Softbank Robotics, provided with an Intel Atom E3845. The choice is due to the anthropomorphous aspect that makes it ideal for social robotic applications. Furthermore it bundled with rich actuation capabilities. This paper focuses on perception and neglects actuation. Some built-in capabilities will be used in the working prototype, mainly related to speech synthesis and arm movement in a human-like fashion. Other built-in capabilities regarding intelligent perception are available: human detection, face tracking and soft biometrics, but performance of them is widely insufficient so we need to augment that capabilities with more powerful algorithms.

Best results in many perception-related fields are nowadays achieved by Deep Learning based methods, methods that use Deep artificial Neural Networks (DNNs) with many layers stacked on top of each other in order to extract more and more refined hierarchical features in an automated fashion. While the achieved performance and generalization capability is often significantly higher in DNN based solutions than in traditional ones, DNNs often require much more CPU time and memory. The light side is that computation required by DNNs is very scalable and easily parallelizable: vector processor yields a much higher efficiency than traditional general purpose ones and dedicated systems are more and more common on the market that leverage vector processing to drastically parallelize and speed up neural networks.

Starting from this assumption, in our architecture we augment computational capabilities of the Pepper robot using a NN-oriented embedded device where all DNNs run. An embedded device is needed that is both small and low power, in order for the mobile robot to be able to transport it and to be detached from electric source; the particular NN accelerator that we use in this prototype is the Nvidia Jetson TX2 [4]. Nvidia Jetson TX2 runs a GNU/Linux operating system. The hardware provides a 64 bit quad core ARM cpu with 8 gigabytes of main memory and a 256-core CUDA enabled GPU. CUDA technology enables GPU cores to be used for general purpose vector computation. Such an hardware configuration is enough to run the system in real time. Furthermore the Nvidia Jetson TX2 has a typical maximum energy consumption of only 7.5 W, that makes it suitable for mobile robot applications, where batteries are used as a power supply. With a common 3 cell 40 Wh lipo battery the system is able to run safely for 4 to 5 h. Finally its limited size allows seamless installation on the robot body.

The architecture is depicted in Fig. 1. The control software runs directly on the robot. The image is acquired from the camera and sent over to the network executor via an Ethernet point-to-point link using the HTTP protocol. We choose the HTTP Protocol because it is widely supported by many libraries and it is easy to understand and extend when it comes to APIs that follow a RESTful implementation. In the HTTP response, the data coming from the analysis of the image is returned to the control software and appropriate actions are performed.

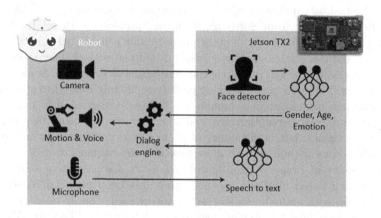

Fig. 1. The architecture of the proposed system.

2.2   Cognitive Capabilities

The main capabilities that we have added to the MIVIABot are the following:

- speech to text in our mother tongue (Italian);
- face detection for tracking, counting and face analysis;
- soft biometrics, namely gender, age and sentiment;

Speech to Text. We used the method *Wav2Letter* from [6] for automatic speech recognition (ASR). Differently from traditional systems where the system is composed of different independent modules, the system proposed in [6] is an end-to-end, Neural Network based system for ASR. Starting from the raw sound wave, the audio output from the microphone, it produces a textual representation that can be fed into a NLP module, such as a chatbot.

A traditional system would require training or tuning each single module on its own, i.e. the audio segmentation, silence detection, classification of the phonemes or letters and so on; one advantage of training the whole system end-to-end is that more complex patterns can be automatically discovered in the data and this improves generalization and overall performance. One great difficulty of training end-to-end Deep Learning based models for Speech Recognition is the absence of a public dataset of transcripted speech that is large enough and contains enough variability. Efforts are being made, for example in [2], but by now both quantity and quality of those data are lacking. This issue is less significant with English, but it becomes really severe when it comes to other languages, such as Italian. A way to address the lack of data in a specific language is *transfer learning* from one language to another [15]. For our application we start from the pre-trained model and fine-tune the network weights. A dropout value of 0.1 is furthermore used, since it is found to increase performance.

We train the system using data from the M-AILABS Speech Dataset [1] that contains audio-books and the text of them for a total of 128 books. The vox-forge dataset [3] contains transcriptions of dictated texts, for a total of 20 more hours of data and is used for training as well. To train the neural network from unaligned audio and text data we use the CTC algorithm [11]. While the neural network will give probability of each letter of the Italian alphabet from audio samples in a sliding window, the CTC algorithm will reconstruct the words from sequences of predictions, taking care of duplicate letters and word boundaries. CTC participates in backpropagation, where *prefix beam search* is used to efficiently match predicted test with actual text from the groundtruth, allowing the network to autonomously learn the alignment.

Finally we modify the CTC module to integrate a *Language Model* (LM) [12]. The LM module computes sentence-wise probabilities, that is the likelihood of a sequence of words and can be used to improve CTC predictions taking context into account. We used a simple *n-gram* LM and trained it with the text of the whole Italian version of Wikipedia.

In Sect. 3 we report the result data comparing results with and without the integration of the LM. Figure 2 shows the architecture of the ASR subsystem.

Fig. 2. The architecture of the speech recognition system. A spectrogram is extracted from each raw audio signal. For each time chunk the DNN will compute the probability $P_t(c)$ for each possible character c of the alphabet. On top of that information CTC loss is used for training. In the inference phase an appropriate decoder function will reconstruct the text from the character probabilities.

Face Detection. Many state of art methods are able to perform face detection with variable degrees of accuracy and efficiency, and with different constraints. For the purposes of this work it is important to choose an accurate face detector that is also efficient enough to not add much to the computational burden. In [16] a method called NPD is presented and has desired characteristics; it is a variant of the well known approach [19] but with strongly improved accuracy and even higher efficiency. The base approach is cascading, so that sequences of simple features are rapidly computed on a sliding window. If a feature in the sequence indicates the absence of a face, the rest of the sequence is not evaluated, making the approach fast. Main improvements are the use of a tree based sequence of features (that is, the result of a feature evaluation determines which feature will be evaluated next) and the use of a particular type of feature whose computation can be easily optimized.

Gender and Age. The authors of [21] present an architecture Convolutional Neural Networks specifically tailored for mobile devices, improving incrementally over their previous work. In that first work they showed that using *separable convolutions* accuracy can be retained while reducing the quantity of weights and the computation needed by an order of magnitude: those precious resource are typically scarce on mobile devices. In this work they also provide a guidance for tuning the accuracy-latency tradeoff with two hyperparameters, that affect the number of feature maps and the size of the input: the resource budget and the required accuracy can be traded by the user.

In [9] that architecture is leveraged to train an efficient classifier that is able to predict gender from face images using the huge collection of annotated images of the VGG-Face 2 Dataset, an extension of the dataset presented in [20].

In this work we use a similar approach to [9], but we add two improvements: The first improvement comes from the fact that we use a smaller variant of the original architecture: we choose to do that since we measure no significant harm to accuracy, while computation time is greatly reduced and also the memory footprint is much smaller. As seen in Fig. 3 he architecture chosen has a 96 × 96 input size, a width multiplier of 0.5 and a depth of 8 residual blocks.

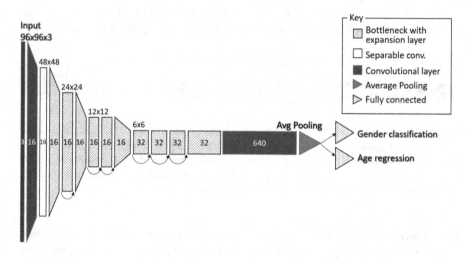

Fig. 3. The architecture of the multitask neural network for gender and age.

The second improvement comes from functionality expansion: we reuse most of the lower layers as feature extractors for both gender classification and age recognition, in a fashion that is called *multitask learning*. This procedure has been shown successful in previous work, with respect to different face analysis-related tasks [22]. Multitask learning is useful to reduce the computational load, since one pass of a single network provides the features needed to perform more prediction tasks; in many cases it is also shown to benefit generalization capability, since richer features, can be learned form a multi-attribute annotation.

When multitask learning the Neural Network is fed with face images and labels for different tasks; in our case we first train the network on gender recognition using 2 million images from the VGG-Face 2 Dataset alone, then we fine-tune the architecture feeding labels from both gender and age. For that second pass we use a different set of 10.000 faces taken from the *Labeled Faces in the Wild* (LFW) dataset [13], that contains both gender and age annotations. All the datasets the we use are acquired *in the wild*, which means that they are recorded in unconstrained conditions and so they are suitable to train a system bound to operate in similar uncontrolled settings, that is our goal.

Sentiment. Emotion recognition from faces in our project relies, as for gender recognition on the MobileNets neural network architecture that implements many modern concepts from the CNN literature and is designed to be lightweight and able to run in real time on system with limited computational capability. We trained the Network with a set of 400.000 face images that were downloaded from the internet and manually annotated in a dataset named AffectNet [17]. The Network is trained to distinguish between 7 classes of emotion: Neutral, Happy, Sad, Angry, Surprised, Scared and Disgusted. Since the dataset does not have a balance between classes (there are much more happy faces that disgusted ones, for example), we had to take into account the imbalance of the dataset in the training process. For that reason we used a weighted softmax loss function, where errors on less represented classes are weighted more: this prevents the network from leaning towards most represented classes.

Faces are tracked by considering overlap between successive frames: in this way robustness of the system is improved via majority voting: the robot will make its decision based on observation of a window of one second, compensating for randomly occurring classification errors.

3   Experimental Results

In this section we aim to demonstrate the performance of the different parts used in the proposed system.

3.1   Speech to Text

The performance of the speech to text subsystem is measured as Word Error Rate (WER), that is the fraction of correctly predicted words in the test set. The WER descends from the Letter Error Rate (LER), that is measured on the letter-level. LER is significant when prediction is performed on a letter-by-letter basis, i.e. without a Language Model, while, when a LM is used, WER is more significant because entire words are considered for making the prediction.

For fair performance measurement, the dataset is partitioned in two disjoint train and test subsets. Following the convention of previous work, 10 h are extracted for test purposes (7% of the dataset) while the rest of the dataset is used for training (128 h, 93%).

In Table 1 results on the test subset are reported. As expected the use of the LM allows many words to be corrected, achieving a final WER of 20.74%, even if the increment on LER is not as significant (7.01% with respect to 8.92% if the LM is not used).

Achieved performance is not extremely high when compared to commercial systems trained on private datasets, neither is in absolute terms, but it is empirically found to be sufficient for our application: the final system will use the ASR result only for word spotting, i.e. matching a word or a short phrase in a sentence. Such a performance would not be sufficient where an entire sentence is to be matched, since the high WER would severely jeopardize performance of matching.

Table 1. Results of the used ASR system on the test subset. Both Letter (LER) and Word (WER) error rates are reported, with or without the use of a Language Model (LM).

Version	LER	WER
IT simple	8.92%	34.9%
IT with LM	7.01%	20.74%

3.2   Gender Recognition and Age Estimation

The performance for gender and age recognition is reported on the LFW dataset. Gender accuracy is measured as correct recognition rate (how many images are correctly classified out of the total) while age regression accuracy is measured as Mean Absolute Error (MAE) that represents the average of the absolute difference $\delta_i = |p_i - g_i|$ between the predicted value p_i and the groundtruth value g_i.

The LFW dataset is divided in an identity-aware manner (also called "subject independent"), that is, the test set does not contain any subject that was present in the training set. 12,000 images are used for training and 2,500 for testing.

Table 2 reports achieved result on the test set for the original model, trained on the VGG-Face dataset for gender-only classification, and its multitask version, fine tuned on the LFW train partition for both gender classification and age regression.

From the result we observe a small increase of the gender recognition accuracy. The accuracy of the gender recognition ($\pm 7.7y$) allows for an estimation of the age range of the subject.

3.3   Emotion Recognition

Emotion recognition accuracy is measured as correct recognition rate over the 7 considered classes. On the test partition of AffectNet the achieved result is of

Table 2. Results of the used models for gender and age classification, compared with the result of the original model (gender only).

Model	Gender accuracy	Age MAE
Original gender	98.52%	N/A
Multitask	98.69%	7.7 years

66.1%. The result is to be considered high, since the human agreement measured on this dataset is low (60.7%). The distribution of error observed indicates that the accuracy is higher on most common classes such as Happy, Sad and Neutral, medium for Angry and Surprise, while it is significantly lower on classes such as Disgust and Fear, that are less represented in the dataset.

3.4 Computational Performance

In order to confirm the efficiency of the proposed architecture and the possibility to run everything simultaneously on board of the Jetson TX2, we also performed an analysis on the efficiency by evaluating the average time required by each step, namely face detection, age + gender and emotion recognition.

The processing is performed on VGA resolution images (640×480). In Table 3 we can find the average time needed by each processing step.

The achieved framerate is of about 4 fps: in a worst case scenario, where a face is present in the image, classification of age, gender and emotion are performed on the closest face detected. The average elaboration time is $131 + 98 + 48 = 277$ ms. When no face is detected the time is only 131 ms, allowing for even higher framerate, that means a lower latency and thus a more prompt response.

Table 3. Average latency measured on the target system (Jetson TX2).

Step	Latency (ms)
Face detection	131
Age+gender	98
Emotion recognition	48

It is important to highlight that a framerate between 3 and 4 fps can be considered sufficient to the task to assess the state and the characteristics of the interlocutor on a continuous basis. Anyway, we can also note that the highest time is consumed by the face detection step, that can not be avoided: in future implementation, a different approach to face detection can be considered, for instance by introducing a neural network based face detector that may result in fastest detection on the target platform due to its parallel nature.

4   Conclusion

In this work we aimed to build a social robot for guiding visitors inside a museum in Italy. The robot is equipped with state-of-the-art Deep Learning models for perception of the interlocutor state, namely speech to text, gender, age and emotion recognition. For speech to text a model known as Wav2Letter is fine tuned on Italian language, and a Language Model is added to improve performance on a word basis. Achieved word error rate is measured on a test partition and can be considered sufficient for recognizing short phrases, that is the aim of this application; performance would not be sufficient for recognizing entire sentences, and it would be object of improvement in successive works.

For what concerns gender and age classification, a sufficient performance is achieved for the three of them: a lightweight yet effective gender recognition architecture is chosen from previous work and it is improved adding age estimation capabilities, in a multitask fashion: the same convolutional feature extraction step will be shared among the two task yielding better computational efficiency. A separate, deeper variant of the same model is trained on a huge dataset of faces to recognize emotions, achieving again a sufficient result.

Said skills are integrated into an existing social robotic platform (namely, the Pepper Robot from Softbank Robotics) through the use of a Neural Network accelerator (NVIDIA Jetson TX2) interfaced with a Ethernet point to point link and standard Internet protocols. The use of such an accelerator is necessary to seamlessly run the Neural Networks since the robot CPU does not have sufficient capability to run the algorithms.

A robot equipped with such social skills is most likely to be accepted seamlessly as a guidance in a museum application by human interlocutors.

References

1. The M-AILABS Speech Dataset (2019). https://www.caito.de/2019/01/the-m-ailabs-speech-dataset/
2. Mozilla common voice, Italian dataset (2019). https://voice.mozilla.org/it/datasets
3. Voxforge, Italian dataset (2019). http://www.voxforge.org/it
4. Amert, T., Otterness, N., Yang, M., Anderson, J.H., Smith, F.D.: GPU scheduling on the NVIDIA TX2: hidden details revealed. In: 2017 IEEE Real-Time Systems Symposium (RTSS), pp. 104–115. IEEE (2017)
5. Bruce, A., Nourbakhsh, I., Simmons, R.: The role of expressiveness and attention in human-robot interaction. In: Proceedings 2002 IEEE International Conference on Robotics and Automation (Cat. No. 02CH37292), vol. 4, pp. 4138–4142. IEEE (2002)
6. Collobert, R., Puhrsch, C., Synnaeve, G.: Wav2Letter: an end-to-end convnet-based speech recognition system. arXiv preprint arXiv:1609.03193 (2016)
7. Duffy, B.R.: Anthropomorphism and the social robot. Robot. Auton. Syst. 42(3–4), 177–190 (2003)
8. Flacco, F., Kröger, T., De Luca, A., Khatib, O.: A depth space approach to human-robot collision avoidance. In: 2012 IEEE International Conference on Robotics and Automation, pp. 338–345. IEEE (2012)

9. Foggia, P., Greco, A., Percannella, G., Vento, M., Vigilante, V.: A system for gender recognition on mobile robots. In: Proceedings of the 2019 on Applications of Intelligent Systems (APPIS). ACM (2019)

10. Fulgenzi, C., Spalanzani, A., Laugier, C.: Dynamic obstacle avoidance in uncertain environment combining PVOs and occupancy grid. In: Proceedings 2007 IEEE International Conference on Robotics and Automation, pp. 1610–1616. IEEE (2007)

11. Graves, A., Fernández, S., Gomez, F., Schmidhuber, J.: Connectionist temporal classification: labelling unsegmented sequence data with recurrent neural networks. In: Proceedings of the 23rd International Conference on Machine Learning, pp. 369–376. ACM (2006)

12. Hannun, A.Y., Maas, A.L., Jurafsky, D., Ng, A.Y.: First-pass large vocabulary continuous speech recognition using bi-directional recurrent DNNs. arXiv preprint arXiv:1408.2873 (2014)

13. Huang, G.B., Mattar, M., Berg, T., Learned-Miller, E.: Labeled faces in the wild: a database for studying face recognition in unconstrained environments. In: Workshop on Faces in 'Real-Life' Images: Detection, Alignment, and Recognition (2008)

14. Kemp, C.C., Edsinger, A., Torres-Jara, E.: Challenges for robot manipulation in human environments [grand challenges of robotics]. IEEE Robot. Autom. Mag. **14**(1), 20–29 (2007)

15. Kunze, J., Kirsch, L., Kurenkov, I., Krug, A., Johannsmeier, J., Stober, S.: Transfer learning for speech recognition on a budget. arXiv preprint arXiv:1706.00290 (2017)

16. Liao, S., Jain, A.K., Li, S.Z.: A fast and accurate unconstrained face detector. IEEE Trans. Pattern Anal. Mach. Intell. **38**(2), 211–223 (2016)

17. Mollahosseini, A., Hasani, B., Mahoor, M.H.: AffectNet: a database for facial expression, valence, and arousal computing in the wild. IEEE Trans. Affect. Comput. **10**, 18–31 (2017)

18. Mori, M., MacDorman, K.F., Kageki, N.: The uncanny valley [from the field]. IEEE Robot. Autom. Mag. **19**(2), 98–100 (2012)

19. Viola, P., Jones, M.: Rapid object detection using a boosted cascade of simple features. In: IEEE Conference on Computer Vision and Pattern Recognition (CVPR). IEEE (2001)

20. Parkhi, O.M., Vedaldi, A., Zisserman, A., et al.: Deep face recognition. In: BMVC (2015)

21. Sandler, M., Howard, A., Zhu, M., Zhmoginov, A., Chen, L.C.: MobileNetV2: inverted residuals and linear bottlenecks. In: Proceedings of the IEEE Conference on Computer Vision and Pattern Recognition, pp. 4510–4520 (2018)

22. Savchenko, A.V.: Efficient facial representations for age, gender and identity recognition in organizing photo albums using multi-output CNN. arXiv preprint arXiv:1807.07718 (2018)

Two-Stage RGB-Based Action Detection Using Augmented 3D Poses

Konstantinos Papadopoulos[✉], Enjie Ghorbel[✉], Renato Baptista[✉],
Djamila Aouada[✉], and Björn Ottersten[✉]

Interdisciplinary Centre for Security, Reliability and Trust (SnT),
University of Luxembourg, Luxembourg, Luxembourg
{konstantinos.papadopoulos,enjie.ghorbel,renato.baptista,
djamila.aouada,bjorn.ottersten}@uni.lu

Abstract. In this paper, a novel approach for action detection from RGB sequences is proposed. This concept takes advantage of the recent development of CNNs to estimate 3D human poses from a monocular camera. To show the validity of our method, we propose a 3D skeleton-based two-stage action detection approach. For localizing actions in unsegmented sequences, Relative Joint Position (RJP) and Histogram Of Displacements (HOD) are used as inputs to a k-nearest neighbor binary classifier in order to define action segments. Afterwards, to recognize the localized action proposals, a compact Long Short-Term Memory (LSTM) network with a de-noising expansion unit is employed. Compared to previous RGB-based methods, our approach offers robustness to radial motion, view-invariance and low computational complexity. Results on the Online Action Detection dataset show that our method outperforms earlier RGB-based approaches.

Keywords: Action detection · LSTM · Pose estimation · Action proposals

1 Introduction

Action detection remains a very challenging topic in the field of computer vision and pattern recognition. The main goal of this research topic is to *localize* and *recognize* actions in untrimmed videos.

Numerous action detection approaches using a monocular camera have been proposed in the literature [6,10,19,25]. Nevertheless, due to the use of effective RGB-based human motion descriptors in a large spatio-temporal volume, these approaches are usually demanding in terms of computational time. As a result, they can be barely adapted to real-world applications such as security and video surveillance [1], healthcare [2,3], human-computer interaction [24], etc. Furthermore, they perform poorly in the presence of radial motion (defined as the perpendicular motion to the image plane), since this information is not encoded in 2D descriptors.

© Springer Nature Switzerland AG 2019
M. Vento and G. Percannella (Eds.): CAIP 2019, LNCS 11678, pp. 26–35, 2019.
https://doi.org/10.1007/978-3-030-29888-3_3

In order to face those challenges, many researchers have exploited the availability of 3D skeletons provided by RGB-D sensors [4,7,13,14]. This high-level representation has the advantage of being compact, largely discriminative and capturing both lateral and radial motion. However, RGB-D cameras present two major limitations in real-life scenarios: First, the acquisition of acceptable depth images and skeletons is only possible under specific lighting conditions. For instance, these devices are not suitable in outdoor settings. Second, acceptable estimation of depth maps is restricted within a very small range.

Inspired by the effectiveness of RGB-D based approaches, we propose to augment 2D data with a third dimension. This is achieved thanks to the tremendous advances in Convolutional Neural Network (CNN)-based approaches, which have made the estimation of relatively accurate 3D skeletons from a monocular video [17,20,28] possible. These estimated compact representations are used in both temporal localization of actions and action classification stages. As in [19], during the action localization phase, hand-crafted features are extracted at each instance using a temporal sliding window. The descriptors used in this stage are chosen to be both spatial with the specific use of *Relative Joint Positions* (RJP) [26], and spatio-temporal with the use of *Histogram of Oriented Displacements* (HOD) [9]. Each frame is classified by a k-Nearest Neighbor (kNN) classifier as *action* or *non-action* forming temporal segments of interest. During the second phase, action recognition is carried out using a Long Short-Term Memory (LSTM) network on the detected action segments. For the estimation of 3D poses, a state-of-the-art CNN-based 3D pose estimator [17] is chosen because of its real-time performance and the encoded temporal coherence. To validate the proposed concept, experiments are conducted on the challenging Online Action Detection dataset [13]. The obtained results show that our approach outperforms other RGB-based methods.

In summary, the contributions of this work are twofold. First, we introduce a novel framework for RGB-based action detection using 3D pose estimation which overcomes the issues of view-variation and radial motion. We argue that this concept can be combined with any 3D skeleton-based action detection approach. Second, a two-stage method for 3D skeleton-based action detection is proposed which uses hand-crafted features in the action localization stage and deep features in the action recognition stage. This two-stage approach is able to offer noise-free action proposals, by removing background frames in the detection stage. Therefore, the recognition part becomes more reliable, regardless of the method used.

The structure of this paper is organized as follows: In Sect. 2, the background and the motivation of our work are presented. Section 3 offers a detailed description of the proposed method. The experiments are given in Sect. 4. Finally, Sect. 5 concludes the paper and discusses future directions and extensions of this work.

2   Background

Given a long sequence of N frames $\mathbf{R} = \{\mathbf{R}_1, \ldots, \mathbf{R}_N\}$ of continuous activities, the goal of action detection is to find an action label l for each frame at an instance t, such that:

$$l(t) = G(\mathbf{R}_t), t \in [1, \ldots, N], \tag{1}$$

where l denotes one of the M actions of interest $\{a_1, \ldots, a_M\}$ or a background activity a_0 and G is the function which labels the frame $\mathbf{R}_t$.

In general, there are two categories of approaches for finding G; *single-stage* [4,13,14] and *multi-stage* [19,21]. Single-stage approaches are usually able to operate in an online manner, whereas multi-stage ones separate the detection from the recognition step in order to generate mostly noise-free action segments.

In this work, we follow a multi-stage strategy, since they have been shown to be more reliable [19,22]. This strategy, instead of directly estimating G, decomposes the problem into the estimation of two functions G_1 and G_2, such that $G = G_2 \circ G_1$. While G_1 allows the localization of actions via a binary classification, G_2 assigns a label to each frame containing an action. Papadopoulos et al. [19] proposed a two-stage RGB-based action detection concept in which, for finding G_1 during the first stage, 2D skeleton sequences are estimated by a state-of-the-art deep pose detector [18]. To achieve this, a function $f_{2D}(\cdot)$ is estimated to compute J joint positions $\mathbf{P^{2D}}(t) = \{\mathbf{P_1^{2D}}(t), \ldots, \mathbf{P_i^{2D}}(t), \ldots, \mathbf{P_J^{2D}}(t)\}$, with $\mathbf{P_i^{2D}}(t) = (x_i, y_i)$ at time instance t such that:

$$\mathbf{P^{2D}}(t) = f_{2D}(\mathbf{R}_t). \tag{2}$$

Instead of the RGB image $\mathbf{R}_t$, a 2D skeleton at an instance t is used as an input to G_1 to label each frame as action a_+ or non-action a_0, as defined below:

$$e(t) = G_1((\mathbf{P^{2D}}(t)), \quad e(t) \in \{a_0, a_+\}. \tag{3}$$

During the second stage, the final label l is computed using the estimated 'action' and 'non-action' labels from G_1 and by extracting motion features from RGB images using iDT [27]:

$$l(t) = G_2(G_1(\mathbf{P^{2D}}(t)), \mathbf{R}_T), \quad l \in [a_1, \ldots, a_M]. \tag{4}$$

Despite offering a compact spatio-temporal representation of actions and being relatively fast to compute, the pose estimation approach of (2) lacks 3D information and is dependent on features extracted from RGB images. This results in two issues: the first one is the sensitivity to view variation. Skeletons extracted by the pre-trained model in [18] are solely 2D, therefore any change in body orientation could potentially affect the classification performance. The second challenge is the limited capabilities of describing radial motion.

Taking these observations into consideration, we propose to further strengthen this concept by utilizing 3D skeleton information. For that purpose, we exploit the recent advances in deep learning which have enabled the development of a wide range of 3D pose estimators from monocular cameras [16,17,20]. These models find a function $f_{3D}(\cdot)$ which estimates, similarly to (2), the 3D pose $\mathbf{P^{3D}}(t)$ at each frame $\mathbf{R_t}$ as:

$$\mathbf{P^{3D}}(t) = f_{3D}(\mathbf{R_t}). \tag{5}$$

By incorporating the third dimension, a two-stage action detection method becomes dependent on the estimated 3D poses as follows:

$$l(t) = G_2(G_1(\mathbf{P^{3D}}(t)), \mathbf{P^{3D}}(t)); \tag{6}$$

thus, poses can be aligned using simple linear transformations, resulting in view-invariant representations. In addition, using 3D data, radial motion can be described more effectively.

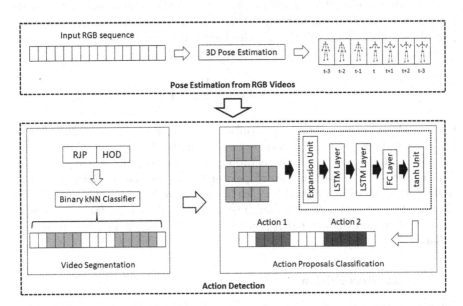

Fig. 1. The proposed model for 2D action detection. Initially, a 3D pose estimator extracts skeleton sequences from RGB frames which are then used for feature generation. In Video Segmentation stage, each frame is classified as action-of-interest or non-action, forming the video segments. These segments are labeled in Action Proposals Classification stage, using a LSTM-based network.

3   Proposed Approach

In this section, we propose to use the estimated 3D skeleton sequences P^{3D} as in (6) for carrying out action detection. To overcome view-point variability, a pre-processing of skeleton alignment is performed by estimating a linear transformation matrix between the absolute coordinate system and a local coordinate system defined using the spine and the hip joints of the skeleton as in [5,8]. To validate the use of 3D skeletons estimated from RGB images, a 3D skeleton-based approach for action detection is introduced. As shown in Fig. 1, we propose a two-stage approach: during the first stage, the video sequence is segmented into temporal regions of interest and during the second stage the generated video segments are recognized.

3.1   Action Localization

During the first stage, RJP [26] and HOD [9] descriptors are computed in a sliding temporal window around the current frame. The RJP descriptor computes the pairwise relative distances δ^{ij} between the J estimated joints, as shown below:

$$\delta^{ij} = \mathbf{P}_i^{3D} - \mathbf{P}_j^{3D}, \quad i,j \in [1,\ldots,J]. \tag{7}$$

In addition, we use HOD descriptor to describe the orientation of the joint motion in a temporal window around the current frame. To do that, for each pair of Cartesian planes xy, yz, xz, a displacement angle θ is computed between consecutive frames as shown below (for the pair xy):

$$\theta_j^{xy} = arctan\left(\frac{d(\mathbf{P}_{j_y}^{3D})}{d(\mathbf{P}_{j_x}^{3D})}\right), \tag{8}$$

where $d(\mathbf{P}_{j_x}^{3D})$ is the accumulated displacement of joint j in x coordinate in a temporal window around the current frame. The final feature vector is a concatenation of all histogram representations of $\theta_j^{xz}, \theta_j^{xy}, \theta_j^{yz}$ for $j \in [1,\ldots,J]$ in the quantitized 2D space for every pair of Cartesian planes. Both RJP and HOD features are concatenated for each frame, before being injected in the kNN classifier for the action localization. The classifier labels each frame as *action* or *non-action* and window-based patching is applied for filling any gaps in the *action* regions.

3.2   Action Recognition

After the generation of action proposals, the recognition stage takes place. Instead of relying on computationally expensive RGB-based descriptors which use a sizable spatio-temporal volume, such as iDT [27], we propose a compact yet efficient LSTM network using 3D skeletons as input. This end-to-end network allows to simultaneously learn features from sequences and classify actions. As shown in Fig. 1, it is composed of a data expansion unit, a compact LSTM unit with two layers, a fully connected layer and a tanh softmax unit. The expansion unit increases the dimensions of the sequences in order to decouple the noisy factors from the informative ones in the pose sequence. The expansion unit for an input pose $\mathbf{P}^{3D}$ is defined as follows:

$$\tilde{\mathbf{P}}^{3D} = tanh(W\mathbf{P}^{3D} + b). \tag{9}$$

By employing an LSTM unit of two hidden layers, we achieve a favorable balance between performance and compactness. LSTM networks are an advanced Recurrent Neural Network (RNN) architecture [12] which mitigates the problem of the vanishing gradient effect [11], and is capable of handling long-term dependencies. Such architectures have been proven to be effective in action classification [15,23]. Finally, a fully connected layer and a tanh softmax unit are utilized for the label prediction, as shown in Fig. 1.

4 Experiments

In this section, we present the details of our implementation, the experimental settings as well as the obtained results. To evaluate our method, we test it on the challenging Online Action Detection dataset [13].

4.1 Implementation Details

For the extraction of 3D skeletons from RGB sequences, we use the state-of-the-art VNect pose estimator [17]. VNect has two advantages over alternative 3D pose estimators: real-time performance and temporally-coherent skeletons. To achieve real-time performance, VNect is designed using Residual Networks (ResNet). The temporal coherence is ensured by the combination of 2D and 3D joint positions in a unified optimization framework. Temporal smoothing is also applied in order to establish stability and robustness. The available pre-trained model generates 3D poses of 21 joints.

For the localization of action proposals, we empirically choose a sliding window size of 11 and 21 frames for, respectively, computing the RJP and HOD descriptors. Furthermore, we choose to quantitize the 4D space using 8 bins for the computation of HOD features and we train our kNN classifier using 25 nearest neighbors.

In order to maintain a real-time performance without sacrificing the level of abstraction, we empirically use 2 LSTM layers and 256 hidden units per layer. The batch size is fixed to 2, because of the small size of the dataset. Moreover, we use a learning rate of 0.0002 and 200 epochs for the training part.

4.2 Dataset and Experimental Setup

We evaluate the proposed approach on the Online Action Detection Dataset [13] (Fig. 2). This dataset consists of 59 long sequences of 10 continuously performed actions captured by a Kinect v2 device. Thus, this dataset provides RGB and depth modalities along with 3D skeleton sequences. In each sequence, a subject is continuously performing the following activities: *no-activity*, *drinking*, *eating*, *writing*, *opening cupboard*, *opening oven*, *washing hands*, *sweeping*, *gargling*, *throwing trash* and *wiping*. For our experiments, we follow the cross-splitting protocol proposed in [13]. All the reported experiments were conducted on an Intel Xeon E5-1650v3 CPU, clocked at 3.5 GHz. For the evaluation of performance, *F1-score* is used as realized by [13]. F1-score conveys the balance between the precision and the recall and is widely used for the evaluation of action detection concepts.

4.3 Comparison with RGB-Based Approaches

Our approach denoted as *CNN-Skel-LSTM* is compared to two RGB-based action detection methods, namely *iDT-SW* [22] and *Skeleton-iDT* [19]. While

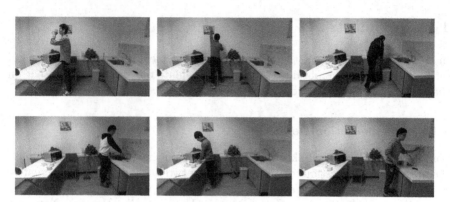

Fig. 2. Sample activities from the Online Action Detection dataset [13]

iDT-SW refers to a single-stage method using iDT, *Skeleton-iDT* indicates a double-stage approach using 2D CNN-based skeletons. In Table 1, the obtained per-class and average F1-scores are presented. Similar to Skeleton-iDT, our approach outperforms iDT-SW [22] since the two-stage concept is more effective in trimming action segments.

Our concept also performs better than Skeleton-iDT [19] approach in cases when there is intra-class variability of pose orientation. Recognition results are boosted in 'Drinking' and 'Eating' classes thanks to the use of 3D data, which offer significant view-invariance capabilities. In addition, our approach performs adequately when the subject is not facing the camera (e.g. 'Opening Oven'), by exploiting the radial motion description. However, in 'Opening Cupboard' class, the performance is low, due to the inaccurate estimation of 3D poses. Moreover, in 'Washing Hands' class, the motion is limited only in a small local area where the subject stays still and iDT approach is proven to be more effective in describing such motion.

4.4   CNN-Based Skeletons vs. Kinect-Based Skeletons

In order to determine the accuracy of the VNect-generated 3D poses for the task of action detection, we compare our approach against *RGBD-Skel-LSTM* case, in which the provided RGB-D skeleton sequences are utilized. The reported (see Table 1) average F1-score of this approach is marginally higher than the CNN-Skel-LSTM case. The RGBD-based skeleton sequences are more accurately estimated and more informative than the CNN-based ones (25 joints instead of 21). However, the reported results prove the potential of our approach, which goes in pair with the advances of the CNN-based 3D pose estimators.

4.5   Computational Time

One strong feature of the proposed approach is the fast execution time. Indeed, the first stage (segmentation) requires an average execution time of 0.125 s per

Table 1. F1-score performance of our proposed approach against literature.

	iDT-SW [22]	Skel-iDT [19]	CNN-Skel-LSTM	RGBD-Skel-LSTM
Drinking	0.350	0.218	0.580	0.330
Eating	0.353	0.404	0.601	0.627
Writing	0.582	0.619	0.685	0.646
Opening cupboard	0.453	0.499	0.347	0.536
Opening oven	0.294	0.581	0.624	0.650
Washing hands	0.591	0.759	0.652	0.577
Sweeping	0.467	0.430	0.513	0.673
Gargling	0.505	0.550	0.434	0.723
Throwing trash	0.425	0.573	0.594	0.446
Wiping	0.647	0.802	0.710	0.783
Average	**0.467**	**0.543**	**0.574**	**0.599**

frame (8 fps) to generate features, while the second stage requires an average of 0.061 s per frame (16.39 fps) to recognize the action. All these measurements were obtained on a single CPU-based implementation and can be further improved.

5 Conclusion

In this paper, we propose an action detection approach which utilizes estimated 3D poses from RGB data. Our concept solves effectively the challenges of radial motion, view dependency and computational complexity. For testing the proposed concept, a novel 3D-based action detection method is introduced. Our method uses estimated 3D skeletons for both determining the temporal regions of interest in a long video sequence and recognizing them, showing, at the same time, competitive detection performance (refer to Table 1). A future direction of our research is to investigate and develop CNN-based descriptors robust to noisy pose estimates, since, in our concept, noisy 3D poses degraded the recognition performance.

Acknowledgements. This work was funded by the European Union's Horizon 2020 research and innovation project STARR under grant agreement No.689947, and by the National Research Fund (FNR), Luxembourg, under the project C15/IS/10415355/3D-ACT/Björn Ottersten.

References

1. Baptista, R., Antunes, M., Aouada, D., Ottersten, B.: Anticipating suspicious actions using a small dataset of action templates. In: 13th International Joint Conference on Computer Vision, Imaging and Computer Graphics Theory and Applications (VISAPP) (2018)

2. Baptista, R., Antunes, M., Shabayek, A.E.R., Aouada, D., Ottersten, B.: Flexible feedback system for posture monitoring and correction. In: 2017 Fourth International Conference on Image Information Processing (ICIIP), pp. 1–6. IEEE (2017)
3. Baptista, R., Goncalves Almeida Antunes, M., Aouada, D., Ottersten, B.: Video-based feedback for assisting physical activity. In: 12th International Joint Conference on Computer Vision, Imaging and Computer Graphics Theory and Applications (VISAPP) (2017)
4. Boulahia, S.Y., Anquetil, E., Multon, F., Kulpa, R.: CuDi3D: curvilinear displacement based approach for online 3D action detection. Comput. Vis. Image Underst. **174**, 57–69 (2018)
5. Demisse, G.G., Papadopoulos, K., Aouada, D., Ottersten, B.: Pose encoding for robust skeleton-based action recognition. In: CVPRW: Visual Understanding of Humans in Crowd Scene, Salt Lake City, Utah, 18–22 June 2018 (2018)
6. Gaidon, A., Harchaoui, Z., Schmid, C.: Actom sequence models for efficient action detection. In: 2011 IEEE Conference on Computer Vision and Pattern Recognition (CVPR), pp. 3201–3208. IEEE (2011)
7. Garcia-Hernando, G., Kim, T.K.: Transition forests: learning discriminative temporal transitions for action recognition and detection. In: IEEE Conference on Computer Vision and Pattern Recognition (CVPR), pp. 432–440 (2017)
8. Ghorbel, E., Boonaert, J., Boutteau, R., Lecoeuche, S., Savatier, X.: An extension of kernel learning methods using a modified log-euclidean distance for fast and accurate skeleton-based human action recognition. Comput. Vis. Image Underst. **175**, 32–43 (2018)
9. Gowayyed, M.A., Torki, M., Hussein, M.E., El-Saban, M.: Histogram of oriented displacements (HOD): describing trajectories of human joints for action recognition. In: IJCAI, vol. 13, pp. 1351–1357 (2013)
10. Hoai, M., De la Torre, F.: Max-margin early event detectors. Int. J. Comput. Vis. **107**(2), 191–202 (2014)
11. Hochreiter, S., Schmidhuber, J.: Long short-term memory. Neural Comput. **9**(8), 1735–1780 (1997)
12. Kawakami, K.: Supervised sequence labelling with recurrent neural networks. Ph.D. thesis, Technical University of Munich (2008)
13. Li, Y., Lan, C., Xing, J., Zeng, W., Yuan, C., Liu, J.: Online human action detection using joint classification-regression recurrent neural networks. In: Leibe, B., Matas, J., Sebe, N., Welling, M. (eds.) ECCV 2016. LNCS, vol. 9911, pp. 203–220. Springer, Cham (2016). https://doi.org/10.1007/978-3-319-46478-7_13
14. Liu, C., Li, Y., Hu, Y., Liu, J.: Online action detection and forecast via multitask deep recurrent neural networks. In: 2017 IEEE International Conference on Acoustics, Speech and Signal Processing (ICASSP), pp. 1702–1706. IEEE (2017)
15. Liu, J., Wang, G., Hu, P., Duan, L.Y., Kot, A.C.: Global context-aware attention LSTM networks for 3D action recognition. In: The IEEE Conference on Computer Vision and Pattern Recognition (CVPR), vol. 7, p. 43 (2017)
16. Mehta, D., Rhodin, H., Casas, D., Sotnychenko, O., Xu, W., Theobalt, C.: Monocular 3D human pose estimation using transfer learning and improved CNN supervision. arxiv preprint. arXiv preprint arXiv:1611.09813, vol. 1, no. 3, p. 5 (2016)
17. Mehta, D., et al.: VNect: real-time 3D human pose estimation with a single RGB camera, vol. 36 (2017). http://gvv.mpi-inf.mpg.de/projects/VNect/
18. Newell, A., Yang, K., Deng, J.: Stacked hourglass networks for human pose estimation. In: Leibe, B., Matas, J., Sebe, N., Welling, M. (eds.) ECCV 2016. LNCS, vol. 9912, pp. 483–499. Springer, Cham (2016). https://doi.org/10.1007/978-3-319-46484-8_29

19. Papadopoulos, K., Antunes, M., Aouada, D., Ottersten, B.: A revisit of action detection using improved trajectories. In: IEEE International Conference on Acoustics, Speech and Signal Processing, Calgary, Alberta, Canada (2018)

20. Pavlakos, G., Zhou, X., Derpanis, K.G., Daniilidis, K.: Coarse-to-fine volumetric prediction for single-image 3D human pose. In: 2017 IEEE Conference on Computer Vision and Pattern Recognition (CVPR), pp. 1263–1272. IEEE (2017)

21. Shou, Z., Wang, D., Chang, S.F.: Temporal action localization in untrimmed videos via multi-stage CNNs. In: Proceedings of the IEEE Conference on Computer Vision and Pattern Recognition, pp. 1049–1058 (2016)

22. Shu, Z., Yun, K., Samaras, D.: Action detection with improved dense trajectories and sliding window. In: Agapito, L., Bronstein, M.M., Rother, C. (eds.) ECCV 2014. LNCS, vol. 8925, pp. 541–551. Springer, Cham (2015). https://doi.org/10.1007/978-3-319-16178-5_38

23. Song, S., Lan, C., Xing, J., Zeng, W., Liu, J.: Spatio-temporal attention-based lstm networks for 3D action recognition and detection. IEEE Trans. Image Process. **27**(7), 3459–3471 (2018)

24. Song, Y., Demirdjian, D., Davis, R.: Continuous body and hand gesture recognition for natural human-computer interaction. ACM Trans. Interact. Intell. Syst. (TiiS) **2**(1), 5 (2012)

25. Sun, C., Shetty, S., Sukthankar, R., Nevatia, R.: Temporal localization of fine-grained actions in videos by domain transfer from web images. In: Proceedings of the 23rd ACM International Conference on Multimedia, pp. 371–380. ACM (2015)

26. Vemulapalli, R., Arrate, F., Chellappa, R.: Human action recognition by representing 3D skeletons as points in a lie group. In: Proceedings of the IEEE Conference on Computer Vision and Pattern Recognition, pp. 588–595 (2014)

27. Wang, H., Schmid, C.: Action recognition with improved trajectories. In: Proceedings of the IEEE International Conference on Computer Vision (2013)

28. Yang, W., Ouyang, W., Wang, X., Ren, J., Li, H., Wang, X.: 3D human pose estimation in the wild by adversarial learning. In: Proceedings of the IEEE Conference on Computer Vision and Pattern Recognition, vol. 1 (2018)

Real-Time and GPU Processing

How Does Connected Components Labeling with Decision Trees Perform on GPUs?

Stefano Allegretti, Federico Bolelli[✉], Michele Cancilla, Federico Pollastri,
Laura Canalini, and Costantino Grana

Dipartimento di Ingegneria "Enzo Ferrari",
Università degli Studi di Modena e Reggio Emilia,
Via Vivarelli 10, 41125 Modena, MO, Italy
{stefano.allegretti,federico.bolelli,michele.cancilla,
federico.pollastri,laura.canalini,costantino.grana}@unimore.it

Abstract. In this paper the problem of Connected Components Labeling (CCL) in binary images using Graphic Processing Units (GPUs) is tackled by a different perspective. In the last decade, many novel algorithms have been released, specifically designed for GPUs. Because CCL literature concerning sequential algorithms is very rich, and includes many efficient solutions, designers of parallel algorithms were often inspired by techniques that had already proved successful in a sequential environment, such as the *Union-Find* paradigm for solving equivalences between provisional labels. However, the use of decision trees to minimize memory accesses, which is one of the main feature of the best performing sequential algorithms, was never taken into account when designing parallel CCL solutions. In fact, branches in the code tend to cause thread divergence, which usually leads to inefficiency. Anyway, this consideration does not necessarily apply to every possible scenario. Are we sure that the advantages of decision trees do not compensate for the cost of thread divergence? In order to answer this question, we chose three well-known sequential CCL algorithms, which employ decision trees as the cornerstone of their strategy, and we built a data-parallel version of each of them. Experimental tests on real case datasets show that, in most cases, these solutions outperform state-of-the-art algorithms, thus demonstrating the effectiveness of decision trees also in a parallel environment.

Keywords: Image processing · Connected components labeling · Parallel computing · GPU

1 Introduction

In the last decade, the great advance of Graphic Processing Units (GPUs) pushed the development of algorithms specifically designed for data parallel environ-

ⓒ Springer Nature Switzerland AG 2019
M. Vento and G. Percannella (Eds.): CAIP 2019, LNCS 11678, pp. 39–51, 2019.
https://doi.org/10.1007/978-3-030-29888-3_4

ments. On GPUs, threads are grouped into packets (warps) and run on *single-instruction, multiple-data* (SIMD) units. This structure, called SIMT (*single-instruction, multiple threads*) by NVIDIA, allows to execute the same instruction on multiple threads in parallel, thus offering a potential efficiency advantage [27]. It is commonly known that most sequential programs, when ported on GPU, break the parallel execution model. Indeed, only applications characterized by regular control flow and memory access patterns can benefit from this architecture [11].

During execution, each processing element performs the same procedure (kernel) on different data. All cores in a warp run like lock-step at same instruction, but next instruction can be fetched only when the previous one has been completed by all threads. If an instruction requires different amounts of time in different threads, such as when branches cause different execution flows, then all threads have to wait, decreasing the efficiency of the lock-step. This is the reason why intrinsically sequential algorithms must be redesigned to reduce/remove branches and fit GPU logic. But is this always necessary? Would this always improve performance? In this paper, focusing on the *Connected Component Labeling* (CCL) problem, we demonstrate that the best performing sequential algorithms can be easily implemented on GPU without changing their nature, and on real case scenarios they may perform significantly better than state-of-the-art algorithms specifically designed for GPUs. Given that CCL is a well-defined problem that provides an exact solution, the main difference among algorithms is the execution time. This is why the proposals of the last years focused on the performance optimization of both sequential and parallel algorithms.

The rest of this paper is organized as follows. In Sect. 2 the problem of labeling connected components on binary images is defined and the notation used throughout the paper is introduced. Section 3 resumes state-of-the-art algorithms for both CPUs and GPUs, describing strengths and weaknesses of each proposal. In Sect. 4 we describe how sequential algorithms have been implemented on GPU using CUDA. Then, to demonstrate the effectiveness of the proposed solution, an exhaustive set of experiments is reported in Sect. 5. Finally, Sect. 6 draws some conclusions.

2   Problem Definition

Given I, an image defined over a two dimensional rectangular lattice $\mathcal{L}$, and $I(p)$ the value of pixel $p \in \mathcal{L}$, with $p = (p_x, p_y)$, we define the *neighborhood* of a pixel as follows:

$$\mathcal{N}(p) = \{q \in \mathcal{L} \mid \max(|p_x - q_x|, |p_y - q_y|) \leq 1\} \tag{1}$$

Two pixels, p and q, are said to be *neighbors* if $q \in \mathcal{N}(p)$, that implies $p \in \mathcal{N}(q)$. From a visual perspective, p and q are *neighbors* if they share an edge *or* a vertex. The set defined in Eq. 1 is called 8-neighborhood of p.

In a binary image, meaningful regions are called *foreground* ($\mathcal{F}$), and the rest of the image is the *background* ($\mathcal{B}$). Following a common convention, we will assign value 1 to foreground pixels, and value 0 to background.

The aim of connected components labeling is to identify disjoint objects, composed of foreground pixels. So, given two foreground pixels $p, q \in \mathcal{F}$, the relation of *connectivity* $\diamond$ can be defined as:

$$p \diamond q \Leftrightarrow \exists \{s_i \in \mathcal{F} \mid s_1 = p, \, s_{n+1} = q, \, s_{i+1} \in \mathcal{N}(s_i), \, i = 1, \ldots, n\} \qquad (2)$$

We say that two pixels p, q are *connected* if the condition $p \diamond q$ is true. The above definition means that a path of connected foreground pixels exists, from p to q. Moreover, since pixel connectivity satisfies the properties of *reflexivity*, *symmetry* and *transitivity*, $\diamond$ is an equivalence relation. Equivalence classes based on $\diamond$ relationship are called *Connected Components* (CC).

Algorithm 1. *Union-Find* functions. P is the *Union-Find* array, a and b are provisional labels.

```
1: function FIND(P, a)
2:     while P[a] ≠ a do
3:         a ← P[a]
4:     return a

5: procedure UNION(P, a, b)
6:     a ← Find(P, a)
7:     b ← Find(P, b)
8:     if a < b then
9:         P[b] ← a
10:    else if b < a then
11:        P[a] ← b
```

The pixel connectivity associated to the neighborhood of Eq. 1 is usually called 8-connectivity, in contrast to the 4-connectivity, in which only pixels sharing an edge are considered neighbors and then connected. According to the *Gestalt Psychology*, CCL usually requires 8-connectivity, that is why we focus on it.

CCL algorithms assign a positive unique label (integer number) to all foreground pixels of a connected component of the image, marking background pixels with 0. Depending on the strategy used to perform the task, it can happen, at some point of the algorithm, that two connected pixels p, q are assigned different provisional labels. In that case, the two labels are said to be *equivalent*. Equivalent labels must be eventually modified, so that they result equal to a certain representative one, through a process of equivalence resolution.

Several strategies exist to solve equivalences, among which one of the most efficient exploits *Union-Find*, firstly applied to CCL by Dillencourt *et al.* [14]. The *Union-Find* data structure provides convenient procedures to keep track of a partition $\mathcal{P}$ of the set $\mathcal{S}$ of provisional labels. Two basic functions are defined on labels $a, b \in \mathcal{S}$:

- $Union(a, b)$: merges the subsets containing a and b.
- $Find(a)$: returns the representative label of the subset containing a.

The recording of an equivalence between labels is performed through a call to *Union*, while *Find* eases the resolution. The partition is represented as a forest of rooted trees, with a tree for every subset of $\mathcal{S}$. The forest can be represented as an array P, where $P[a]$ is the father node of a. A possible implementation of *Union-Find* functions is given in Algorithm 1.

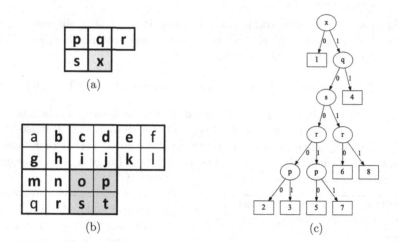

Fig. 1. (a) is the Rosenfeld mask used by SAUF to compute the label of pixel x during the first scan and (b) is the Grana mask used by BBDT and DRAG to compute the label of pixels o, p, s and t. Finally, (c) is one of the optimal decision trees associated to the Rosenfeld mask. Here ellipses (nodes) represent conditions to check and rectangles (leaves) are the actions to perform.

3   Connected Components Labeling Algorithms

Efficiency of connected components labeling is critical in many real-time applications [13,29,30], and this is the reason why many strategies have been proposed for efficiently addressing the problem [10].

Traditionally, on sequential machines a two scan algorithm is employed. It is composed of three steps:

- *First scan*: scans the input image using a mask of already visited pixels, such as the one in Fig. 1a, and assigns a temporary label to the current pixel/s, recording any equivalence between those found in the mask;
- *Flattening*: analyzes the registered equivalences and establishes the definitive labels to replace the provisional ones;
- *Second scan*: generates the output image replacing provisional with final labels.

When statistics about connected components are required (e.g. area, perimeter, circularity, centroid), the second scan can be avoided, reducing the total execution time.

Different solutions allowed performance improvements by avoiding redundant memory accesses [19,21,34]. One of the first improvements is the Scan Array-based Union-Find (SAUF) proposed by Wu *et al.* in [34]. This is a reference algorithm because of its very good performance and ease of understanding. The optimization introduced with SAUF reduces the number of neighbors visited during the first scan using a decision tree, such as the one shown in Fig. 1c. The idea is that if two already visited pixels are connected, their labels have already been marked as equivalent in the *Union-Find* data structure, so we do not even need to check their values.

Since 8-connectivity is usually employed to describe foreground objects, this algorithm was extended in [18,19] with the introduction of 2×2 blocks, in which all foreground pixels share the same label. In this case, the scanning mask is bigger (Fig. 1b), leading to a large number of combinations that produces a complex decision tree, whose construction is much harder. In [20] an optimal strategy to automatically build the decision tree by means of a dynamic programming approach has been proposed and demonstrated. This approach is commonly known as Block Based Decision Tree scanning (BBDT).

He *et al.* [21] were the first to realize that, thanks to the sequential approach taken, when the mask shifts horizontally through the image, it contains some pixels that were already inside the mask in the previous iteration. If those pixels were checked in the previous step, a repeated reading can be avoided. They addressed this problem condensing the information provided by the values of already seen pixels in a configuration state, and modeled the transition with a finite state machine. In [16] a general paradigm to leverage already seen pixels, which combines configuration transitions with decision trees, was proposed. This approach has again the advantage of saving memory accesses.

In [5,8], authors noticed the existence of identical and equivalent subtrees in the BBDT decision tree. *Identical* subtrees were merged together by the compiler optimizer, with the introduction of jumps in machine code, but *equivalent* ones were not. By also taking into account equivalent subtrees they converted the decision tree into a Directed Rooted Acyclic Graph, which they called DRAG. The code compression thus obtained, does not impact neither on the memory accesses, nor on the number of comparisons, but allows a significant reduction of the machine code footprint. This heavily reduces the memory requirements increasing the instruction cache hit rate and the run-time performance.

When moving to parallel architectures, CCL can be easily obtained by repeatedly propagating the minimum label to every pixel neighbor. Nevertheless, much better alternatives exist. Oliveira *et al.* [28] were the first to make use of the *Union-Find* approach in GPU. In their algorithm, the so called Union Find (UF), the output image is initialized with sequential values. Then, *Union-Find* primitives are used to join together trees of neighbor pixels. Finally, a flattening of trees updates the output image, completing the task. The algorithm is firstly performed on rectangular tiles, and then large connected components are merged in a subsequent step.

Optimized Label Equivalence (OLE) [23] is an iterative algorithm that records *Union-Find* trees in the output image itself. The algorithm consists of three kernels that are repeated in sequence until convergence. They aim at propagating the minimum label through each connected component, flattening equivalence trees at every step.

Zavalishin *et al.* [35] proposed Block Equivalence (BE), introducing the block-based strategy into a data-parallel algorithm. They make use of two additional data structures besides the output image: a block label map and a connectivity map, respectively to contain block labels and to record which blocks are connected together. The structure of the algorithm is the same as OLE, with the exception that it operates on blocks instead of single pixels. When convergence is met, a final kernel is responsible for copying block labels into pixels of the output image.

Komura Equivalence (KE) [24] was released as an improvement over Label Equivalence. Anyway, it has more in common with the Union Find algorithm. Indeed, their structures are almost equivalent. The main difference is the initialization step, which starts building *Union-Find* trees while assigning the initial values to the output image. The original version of the algorithm employs 4-connectivity. An 8-connectivity variation has been presented in [2].

Finally, Distanceless Label Propagation (DLP) [12] tries to put together positive aspects of both UF and LE. The general structure is similar to that of UF, with the difference that the *Union* operation is performed between each pixel and the minimum value found in a 2×2 square. Moreover, the *Union* procedure is implemented in an original and recursive manner.

4 Adapting Tree-Based Algorithms to GPUs

Algorithm 2. Summary of algorithms kernels. I and L are input and output images. The pixel (or block) on which a thread works is denoted as x.

```
1: kernel INITIALIZATION(L)
2:     L[id_x] ← id_x

3: kernel MERGE(I, L)
4:     DecisionTree(Mask(x))

5: kernel COMPRESSION(L)
6:     L[id_x] ← Find(L, id_x)

7: kernel FINALLABELING(L)
8:     label ← L[id_x]
9:     for all a ∈ Block(x) do
10:        if I(a) = 1 then
11:            L(a) ← label
12:        else
13:            L(a) ← 0
```

We adapt SAUF, BBDT and DRAG to a parallel environment, thus producing CUDA based CCL algorithms, that we call C-SAUF, C-BBDT and C-DRAG.

A GPU algorithm consists of a sequence of kernels, *i.e.*, procedures run by multiple threads of execution at the same time. In order to transform the aforementioned sequential algorithms into parallel ones, the three steps of which they are composed (*first scan*, *flattening*, and *second scan*) must be translated into appropriate kernels. In each of those steps, a certain operation is repeated over every element of a sequence. Thus, a naive parallel version consists in a concurrent execution of the same operation over the whole sequence. Unfortunately, the *first scan* cannot be translated in such a simple way, because of its inherently sequential nature: when thread t_x runs, working on pixel x, every foreground pixel in the neighborhood mask must already have a label. To address this issue, we assign an initial label to each foreground pixel, equal to its raster index (id_x). This choice has two important consequences. First, we can observe that there is

Table 1. Kernel composition of the proposed CUDA algorithms.

	C-SAUF	C-BBDT	C-DRAG	
Initialization	✓	✓	✓	Creates starting *Union-Find* trees
Merge	✓	✓	✓	Merges trees of equivalent labels
Compression	✓	✓	✓	Flattens trees
FinalLabeling		✓	✓	Copies block labels into pixels

no need to store provisional labels in the output image L, because calculating them is trivial. So, until *second scan*, L can be used as the *Union-Find* structure, thus removing the need to allocate additional memory for P. In fact, in our parallel algorithms, $L \equiv P$. The second consequence is that the *first scan* loses the aim of assigning provisional labels, and it is only required to record equivalences. Its job is performed by two different kernels: *Initialization* and *Merge*.

The first one initializes the *Union-Find* array L. Of course, at the beginning, every label is the root of a distinct tree. Thus, in this kernel, thread t_x performs $L[id_x] \leftarrow id_x$.

The second kernel, instead, deals with the recording of equivalences between labels. During execution, thread t_x traverses a decision tree in order to decide which action needs to be performed, while minimizing the average amount of memory accesses. When no neighbors of the scanning mask are foreground, nothing needs to be done. In all other cases, the current label needs to be merged with those of connected pixels, with the *Union* procedure. Moreover, the implementation of *Union* proposed in Algorithm 1 requires to introduce atomic operations to deal with the concurrent execution.

Then, it is easy to parallelize the *flattening* step: it translates into a kernel (*Compression*) in which thread t_x performs $L[id_x] \leftarrow Find(L, id_x)$ to link each provisional label to the representative of its *Union-Find* tree.

The last step of sequential algorithms is the *second scan*, which updates labels in the output image L. A large part of the job of *second scan* is not necessary in our parallel algorithms, because *Compression* kernel already solves label equivalences directly in the output image. In the case of C-SAUF, increasing foreground labels by one is the only remaining operation to perform, in order to ensure that connected components labels are positive numbers different from background. We avoid a specific kernel for this, shifting labels of foreground pixels by 1 since the beginning of the algorithm. This trick requires small changes to *Union-Find* functions. For C-BBDT and C-DRAG, a final processing of L is required to copy the label assigned to each block into its foreground pixels. This job is performed in *FinalLabeling* kernel. Table 1 sums up the structure of the proposed algorithms, while Algorithm 2 provides a possible implementation of the described kernels.

Table 2. Average run-time results in ms. The bold values represent the best performing CCL algorithm. Our proposals are identified with *.

	3DPeS	Fingerprints	Hamlet	Medical	MIRflickr	Tobacco800	XDOCS
C-SAUF*	0.560	0.487	2.867	1.699	0.571	3.846	14.870
C-BBDT*	0.535	0.472	2.444	1.249	0.529	3.374	12.305
C-DRAG*	**0.526**	**0.460**	**2.423**	**1.220**	**0.496**	**3.322**	**12.012**
OLE [23]	1.111	1.031	5.572	2.996	1.174	8.152	35.245
BE [35]	1.401	1.056	4.714	2.849	1.053	6.120	20.314
UF [28]	0.593	0.527	3.243	2.062	0.656	4.332	17.333
DLP [12]	0.657	0.484	3.323	1.719	0.597	5.031	18.182
KE [2]	0.565	0.478	2.893	1.644	0.523	4.007	15.445

5   Experimental Results

In order to produce a fair comparison, algorithms are tested and compared with state-of-the-art GPU implementations using the YACCLAB open-source benchmarking framework [9,17]. Since this tool has been originally developed for sequential algorithms, we have enriched its capabilities to run also GPU-based CCL algorithms.

Experiments are performed on a Windows 10 desktop computer with an Intel Core i7-4770 (4×32 KB L1 cache, 4×256 KB L2 cache, and 8 MB of L3 cache), 16 GB of RAM, and a Quadro K2200 NVIDIA GPU (640 CUDA cores and 4 GB of memory). Algorithms have been compiled for x64 architectures using Visual Studio 2017 (MSVC 19.13.26730) and CUDA 10 (NVCC V10.0.130) with optimizations enabled.

With the purpose of stressing algorithms behaviours, thus highlighting their strengths and weaknesses, we perform three different kind of tests on many real case and synthetically generated datasets provided by YACCLAB. Selected datasets cover most of the fields on which CCL is applied and are described in the following.

Medical [15] is a collection of 343 binary histological images with an average amount of 484 components to label. *Hamlet* is a scanned version of the Hamlet provided by the Gutenberg Project [32]. The dataset is composed of 104 images with an average amount of 1 447 components to label. *Fingerprints* [26] contains 960 images taken from fingerprint verification competitions (*FCV*2000, *FCV*2002 and *FCV*20040) and binarized using an adaptive threshold. *XDOCS*, is a set of 1 677 high-resolution historical document images retrieved from the large number of civil registries that are available since the constitution of the Italian state [4,6,7]. Images have an average amount of 15 282 components to analyze. *3DPeS* [3] contains surveillance images processed with background subtraction and Otsu thresholding. *MIRflickr* is a set of images containing the Otsu binarized version of the MIRFLICKR-25000 [22] dataset. It is composed of 25 000 standard resolution images taken from Flickr, with an average amount of 492

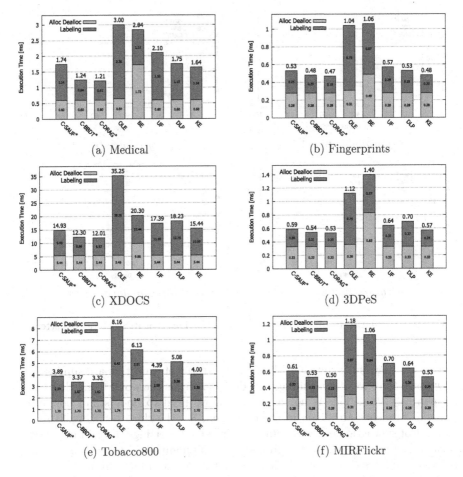

Fig. 2. Average run-time results with steps in ms. Lower is better.

connected components. *Tobacco800* [1, 25, 33] counts 1 290 document images collected and scanned using a wide variety of equipment over time. The images sizes vary from 1200 × 1600 up to 2500 × 3200.

As shown in Table 2, KE is confirmed to be the state-of-the-art GPU-specific algorithm, when taking into account the average run-time on all datasets. It is interesting to note that even a straightforward implementation of SAUF (C-SAUF) is able in many cases to outperform it. The two more complex tree-based algorithms (C-BBDT and C-DRAG) significantly reduce the computational requirements, with C-DRAG being always the best.

To better appreciate this results, it is useful to split the time required by memory allocation and the computation. Figure 2 shows that in some cases more than 50% of the time is dedicated to memory allocation, especially on small images. BE clearly suffers from the additional data structures. When moving to larger images (*e.g.* XDOCS), the reduced time allowed by C-BBDT and C-DRAG

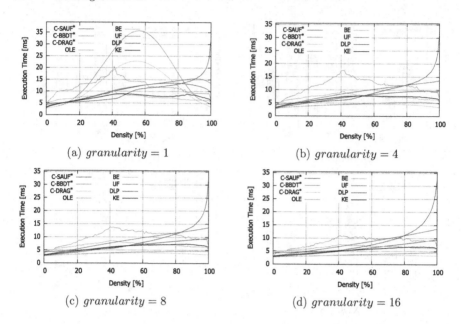

Fig. 3. Granularity results in ms on images at various densities. Lower is better.

is evident. How is this possible? Irregular patterns of execution are supposed to slow down the thread scheduling, so a decision tree is the worst thing that could happen to GPUs. This is not a myth, but we need to understand how often different branches are taken in the execution. So, the third test (Fig. 3) is run on a set of synthetic images generated by randomly setting a certain percentage (*density*) of pixel blocks to foreground. The minimum size of foreground blocks is called *granularity*. Resolution is 2048×2048, density ranges from 0% to 100% with a step of 1%, and granularity $g \in [1, 16]$ have been considered. Ten images have been generated for every couple of density-granularity values, for a total of 16 160 images, and charts report the average time per couple. When granularity is 1 (Fig. 3a), it is possible to observe that both C-BBDT and C-DRAG computational time explodes around density of 50%, in accordance with our expectation. The only cases in which those algorithms outperform GPU-specific ones is when density is below 10% or over 90%. Indeed, at low/high densities the decision is taken quickly by the first levels of the tree structures, saving a lot of memory accesses and without breaking the thread execution flow. Since images on which CCL is applied are usually in that range of densities, this explains the previously observed behavior. Moreover, when granularity grows (Fig. 3b–d), small portions of the image have irregular patterns requiring to explore deeper tree levels, while the vast majority tends to be all white or all black, again maximizing the tree performance.

6 Conclusions

In this paper we have addressed the problem of connected components labeling on GPU. We have focused our analysis on three 8-connectivity sequential algorithms relying on decision trees and we have adapted them to GPU programming paradigm, without altering their substance. Hence, we have compared these proposals against GPU state-of-the-art algorithms on real case datasets and the experimental results show their surprisingly good performance. An explanation of their effectiveness has been provided thanks to a set of additional tests on synthetic images. The C-DRAG algorithm always outperforms the other CUDA-designed proposals, highlighting the feasibility of decision trees on GPU. The source code of described algorithms is available in [31], allowing anyone to reproduce and verify our claims.

References

1. Agam, G., Argamon, S., Frieder, O., Grossman, D., Lewis, D.: The Complex Document Image Processing (CDIP) Test Collection Project. Illinois Institute of Technology (2006)
2. Allegretti, S., Bolelli, F., Cancilla, M., Grana, C.: Optimizing GPU-based connected components labeling algorithms. In: Third IEEE International Conference on Image Processing, Applications and Systems. IPAS (2018)
3. Baltieri, D., Vezzani, R., Cucchiara, R.: 3DPeS: 3D people dataset for surveillance and forensics. In: Proceedings of the 2011 Joint ACM Workshop on Human Gesture and Behavior Understanding, pp. 59–64. ACM (2011)
4. Bolelli, F.: Indexing of historical document images: ad hoc dewarping technique for handwritten text. In: Grana, C., Baraldi, L. (eds.) IRCDL 2017. CCIS, vol. 733, pp. 45–55. Springer, Cham (2017). https://doi.org/10.1007/978-3-319-68130-6_4
5. Bolelli, F., Baraldi, L., Cancilla, M., Grana, C.: Connected components labeling on DRAGs. In: International Conference on Pattern Recognition (2018)
6. Bolelli, F., Borghi, G., Grana, C.: Historical handwritten text images word spotting through sliding window HOG features. In: Battiato, S., Gallo, G., Schettini, R., Stanco, F. (eds.) ICIAP 2017. LNCS, vol. 10484, pp. 729–738. Springer, Cham (2017). https://doi.org/10.1007/978-3-319-68560-1_65
7. Bolelli, F., Borghi, G., Grana, C.: XDOCS: an application to index historical documents. In: Serra, G., Tasso, C. (eds.) IRCDL 2018. CCIS, vol. 806, pp. 151–162. Springer, Cham (2018). https://doi.org/10.1007/978-3-319-73165-0_15
8. Bolelli, F., Cancilla, M., Baraldi, L., Grana, C.: Connected components labeling on DRAGs: implementation and reproducibility notes. In: 24th International Conference on Pattern Recognition Workshops (2018)
9. Bolelli, F., Cancilla, M., Baraldi, L., Grana, C.: Toward reliable experiments on the performance of Connected Components Labeling algorithms. J. Real-Time Image Process. 1–16 (2018)
10. Bolelli, F., Cancilla, M., Grana, C.: Two more strategies to speed up connected components labeling algorithms. In: Battiato, S., Gallo, G., Schettini, R., Stanco, F. (eds.) ICIAP 2017. LNCS, vol. 10485, pp. 48–58. Springer, Cham (2017). https://doi.org/10.1007/978-3-319-68548-9_5

11. Brunie, N., Collange, S., Diamos, G.: Simultaneous branch and warp interweaving for sustained GPU performance. In: 39th Annual International Symposium on Computer Architecture (ISCA), pp. 49–60, June 2012
12. Cabaret, L., Lacassagne, L., Etiemble, D.: Distanceless label propagation: an efficient direct connected component labeling algorithm for GPUs. In: International Conference on Image Processing Theory, Tools and Applications. IPTA (2017)
13. Cucchiara, R., Grana, C., Prati, A., Vezzani, R.: Computer vision techniques for PDA accessibility of in-house video surveillance. In: First ACM SIGMM International Workshop on Video Surveillance, pp. 87–97 (2003)
14. Dillencourt, M.B., Samet, H., Tamminen, M.: A general approach to connected-component labeling for arbitrary image representations. J. ACM **39**(2), 253–280 (1992)
15. Dong, F., Irshad, H., Oh, E.Y., et al.: Computational pathology to discriminate benign from malignant intraductal proliferations of the breast. PloS One **9**(12), e114885 (2014)
16. Grana, C., Baraldi, L., Bolelli, F.: Optimized connected components labeling with pixel prediction. In: Blanc-Talon, J., Distante, C., Philips, W., Popescu, D., Scheunders, P. (eds.) ACIVS 2016. LNCS, vol. 10016, pp. 431–440. Springer, Cham (2016). https://doi.org/10.1007/978-3-319-48680-2_38
17. Grana, C., Bolelli, F., Baraldi, L., Vezzani, R.: YACCLAB - yet another connected components labeling benchmark. In: 23rd International Conference on Pattern Recognition. ICPR (2016)
18. Grana, C., Borghesani, D., Cucchiara, R.: Fast block based connected components labeling. In: 2009 16th IEEE International Conference on Image Processing (ICIP), pp. 4061–4064. IEEE (2009)
19. Grana, C., Borghesani, D., Cucchiara, R.: Optimized block-based connected components labeling with decision trees. IEEE Trans. Image Process. **19**(6), 1596–1609 (2010)
20. Grana, C., Montangero, M., Borghesani, D.: Optimal decision trees for local image processing algorithms. Pattern Recogn. Lett. **33**(16), 2302–2310 (2012)
21. He, L., Zhao, X., Chao, Y., Suzuki, K.: Configuration-transition-based connected-component labeling. IEEE Trans. Image Process. **23**(2), 943–951 (2014)
22. Huiskes, M.J., Lew, M.S.: The MIR flickr retrieval evaluation. In: Proceedings of the 2008 ACM International Conference on Multimedia Information Retrieval, MIR 2008. ACM, New York (2008)
23. Kalentev, O., Rai, A., Kemnitz, S., Schneider, R.: Connected component labeling on a 2D grid using CUDA. J. Parallel Distrib. Comput. **71**(4), 615–620 (2011)
24. Komura, Y.: GPU-based cluster-labeling algorithm without the use of conventional iteration: application to the Swendsen-Wang multi-cluster spin flip algorithm. Comput. Phys. Commun. **194**, 54–58 (2015)
25. Lewis, D., Agam, G., Argamon, S., Frieder, O., Grossman, D., Heard, J.: Building a test collection for complex document information processing. In: Proceedings of the 29th Annual International ACM SIGIR Conference on Research and Development in Information Retrieval, pp. 665–666. ACM (2006)
26. Maltoni, D., Maio, D., Jain, A., Prabhakar, S.: Handbook of Fingerprint Recognition. Springer, Heidelberg (2009). https://doi.org/10.1007/978-1-84882-254-2
27. Nickolls, J., Dally, W.J.: The GPU computing era. IEEE Micro **30**(2), 56–69 (2010)
28. Oliveira, V.M., Lotufo, R.A.: A study on connected components labeling algorithms using GPUs. In: SIBGRAPI, vol. 3, p. 4 (2010)

29. Pollastri, F., Bolelli, F., Paredes, R., Grana, C.: Improving skin lesion segmentation with generative adversarial networks. In: 2018 IEEE 31st International Symposium on Computer-Based Medical Systems (CBMS). IEEE (2018)
30. Pollastri, F., Bolelli, F., Paredes, R., Grana, C.: Augmenting data with GANs to segment melanoma skin lesions. Multimed. Tools Appl. J. (2019)
31. Source Code. https://github.com/prittt/YACCLAB. Accessed 30 Mar 2019
32. The Hamlet Dataset. http://www.gutenberg.org. Accessed 30 Mar 2019
33. The Legacy Tobacco Document Library (LTDL). University of California (2007)
34. Wu, K., Otoo, E., Suzuki, K.: Two strategies to speed up connected component labeling algorithms. Technical report LBNL-59102, Lawrence Berkeley National Laboratory (2005)
35. Zavalishin, S., Safonov, I., Bekhtin, Y., Kurilin, I.: Block equivalence algorithm for labeling 2D and 3D images on GPU. Electron. Imaging **2016**(2), 1–7 (2016)

A Compact Light Field Camera
for Real-Time Depth Estimation

Yuriy Anisimov$^{(\boxtimes)}$, Oliver Wasenmüller, and Didier Stricker

DFKI - German Research Center for Artificial Intelligence,
Trippstadter Street 122, 67663 Kaiserslautern, Germany
{yuriy.anisimov,oliver.wasenmueller,didier.stricker}@dfki.de

Abstract. Depth cameras are utilized in many applications. Recently light field approaches are increasingly being used for depth computation. While these approaches demonstrate the technical feasibility, they can not be brought into real-world application, since they have both a high computation time as well as a large design. Exactly these two drawbacks are overcome in this paper. For the first time, we present a depth camera based on the light field principle, which provides real-time depth information as well as a compact design.

Keywords: Light field · Depth estimation · Real-time

1 Introduction

In the recent years depth cameras got popular in different applications, such as automotive [15], industry [13], gaming [19], etc. The success factor of these cameras is in particular to record depth information, i.e. the distance of the scene to the camera in each pixel and in real time. The established technologies can basically be divided into two categories: active and passive depth cameras. Active cameras have high accuracy in poor lighting conditions and low texture in the scene as they emit active light; however, they are often larger in design, have a higher energy consumption and exhibit artifacts through the active lighting. For this reason, passive cameras are often used in commercial systems. Usually, these are stereo cameras, which are composed of two cameras determining the depths from the computed pixel disparities. For the quality of these cameras, the baseline, the distance between the individual cameras, is crucial. As a result, the baseline dictates the design and size of the camera.

As an alternative to stereo cameras, light field cameras have been explored recently. They either build using a micro-lens array or consist of several cameras, which are arranged in a matrix configuration (see Fig. 1b). From the redundant pixel information, correspondences and thus depth values can be calculated very efficiently and robustly. In the state-of-the-art such cameras were already described in detail. However, these systems suffer two major drawbacks: the depth estimation algorithms are not working in real-time but sometimes require

© Springer Nature Switzerland AG 2019
M. Vento and G. Percannella (Eds.): CAIP 2019, LNCS 11678, pp. 52–63, 2019.
https://doi.org/10.1007/978-3-030-29888-3_5

(a) Light Field Camera   (b) Depth Image

Fig. 1. In this paper, we propose a new compact light field camera, which is capable to compute depth information in real-time.

hours per image [3]; also, the camera systems are usually very large and thus prevent the practical use in filigree setups [9,14].

In this paper, we propose a novel system that handles these two disadvantages. We build a compact light field camera by placing an array of 4×4 single lenses in front of a full format CMOS sensor. Furthermore, we enable a real-time depth computation by developing the depth algorithm adequately with dedicated design decisions and suitable for embedded System-on-Chip (SoC).

2   Related Work

As mentioned previously, our proposed system is a passive depth camera, which means that no light is actively emitted to determine the depth (compared to Time-of-Flight cameras). Thus, we focus in this section on passive systems.

The most prominent category of passive depth cameras is stereo cameras. They are composed of two grayscale or color cameras, which are aligned in parallel with a given distance (baseline). Depth is estimated by computing the displacement (disparity) of all pixel from one camera to the other. The parallel alignment of the cameras ensures that corresponding pixels always lie in the same row in the other camera. Thus, the search for correspondence is considerably simplified. However, this correspondence search for just two pixels is prone to errors in many scenarios. In addition, a given baseline is required to ensure appropriate depth resolution. Thus, the baseline defines the size of the camera.

In this paper, we propose a compact light field camera which takes care of these challenges. Light field cameras have the advantage to estimate depth not out of just two corresponding pixels, but out of corresponding pixels of all cameras (in our case 16). This redundancy substantially increases the robustness. In the last years, several light field cameras were presented. However, some of them are quite large [9,14] preventing their usage in filigree machines. A famous commercial light field camera are the Lytro [5] and Raytrix [6] cameras. They use micro-lenses with different focus to create the light field. However, their

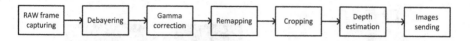

Fig. 2. Overview of the single processing steps in our proposed system. The depth estimation is detailed in Fig. 3.

fragility restricts a usage under industrial or automotive conditions. In addition, the emphasis of this system is to enable a refocus of images as post-processing. The systems also offer depth computation, but for single images only and not in real-time. In contrast, our system is robust for many environmental influences and at the same time provides the depth information as a video stream in real-time.

Focusing on the depth estimation algorithm itself, many approaches were recently presented. In 2013, Kim et al. in [3] proposed an accurate method for high-resolution light field depth estimation. It utilizes a concept of epipolar plane image, composed of the row or column slices of the light field images within an angular row or column respectively. In their work, the possible expansion of such light field processing for the 4-dimensional light field was shown. Work of Anisimov and Stricker [1] extends the previously mentioned paper. It proposes the generation of the initial disparity map, based on the limited number of light field images, together with the line fitting cost aggregation in the space of the whole light field with utilization of initial disparity map as the border for the computationally intensive search.

In the last years, the number of computer vision algorithms based on different types of neural networks is growing. An algorithm, proposed by Shin et al. in [11] is based on convolutional neural network, which uses not the whole light field, but the sets of images in different angular directions. The result of this algorithm can be considered as precise and the run time is relatively low (several seconds). A recently proposed method from [8] shows a way of CNN-driven depth estimation, which does not require ground truth for training. Nowadays with the recent GPU architectures the real-time performance of light field algorithms can be achieved. A work of Sabater et al. [9] shows the method for the rapid processing of real-world light field videos with wide baseline. It is based on normalized cross-correlation for correspondence matching and involves the pyramidal scheme for disparity estimation. An algorithm from [7] actively involves the distinct features of GPU architecture for the rapid processing of light field images using image shearing and tensor extraction. One of the accurate algorithms was published by [17], it utilizes the concept of spinning parallelogram operation extraction from the light field images and histogram-based processing on them.

3   Hardware

Since we want to design our light field camera as simple as possible, we customize an off-the-shelf full format sensor and equip it with a 4×4 lens array. In order to create a mobile system for real-time depth estimation, we utilize an embedded GPU-based computational platform.

3.1 Light Field Camera

The light field capturing device is built on the base of Ximea CB200CG-CM camera. It uses CMOSIS CMV20000 image sensor with 20 megapixel resolution together with 4 × 4 single lenses array, placed in the front of the sensor. In this configuration maximum effective resolution of a single light field image is equal to 704 × 704 pixels. Such a camera assembly approach is easier and more robust to manufacture compared to micro-lens approaches [5]. It is somewhat similar to the multi-camera light field capturing devices [9]; however, since all of the light field views are captured by a single image sensor, it can be considered as more resilient technology, because cameras synchronization and compensation of single sensors deviations do not need to be performed. The connection of the camera to the computational platform is provided via PCIe interface.

3.2 Computational Platform

The Jetson TX2 (see Fig. 4a) is used as computational platform for our system. It contains the Tegra X2 System-on-Chip, which consists of several ARM cores together with a CUDA-compatible graphics processing unit (GPU). This chip provides support for various peripheral interfaces, such as USB 3.0 or PCIe. Transmission of the processed images from the Jetson board to the recipient is provided by Ethernet interface using the socket-based client-server model.

4 Software

This section describes all software parts of our proposed system. The full pipeline is presented in Fig. 2. First, we need to pre-process the images in order to convert the raw information to usable RGB information. Second, calibration information is utilized to remap all images in order to ensure the epipolar constraint. As the last step, depth is estimated out of the 16 light field by a sophisticated depth algorithm with dedicated design decisions for real-time performance. In addition, the depth algorithm is efficiently implemented for the embedded GPU.

4.1 Pre-processing

The camera used in our system provides images in a RAW sensor format. Thus, some pre-processing steps need to be performed in order to convert images to the proper form for further processing.

The camera sensor captures the light intensity going through the color filter array. In our camera the color filter array utilizes the Bayer filter principle and consists of 2×2 three-colored patterns, which perceive green, blue and red colors.

In order to recover the color information from such an image, a so-called debay-ering needs to be applied. It uses the interpolation of same-colored neighborhood pixels in order to fully reconstruct the intensities values.

After this step, the luminance adjustment, the so-called gamma correction, is performed. A gamma value is selected automatically accordingly to the total scene illumination.

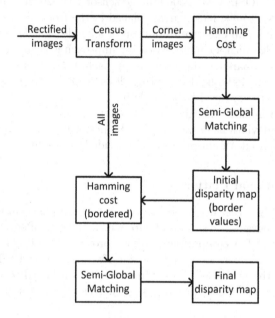

Fig. 3. Overview of the proposed real-time depth estimation algorithm.

4.2   Calibration

The camera calibration procedure provides the camera intrinsic values, such as camera focal length and camera center, which are required for the disparity-to-depth conversion, together with the extrinsic values, which represents the camera relative position. Both intrinsics and extrinsics are required for the images rectifi-cation, which simplifies the correspondence search problem and hence positively affects the accuracy of the further reconstruction.

The calibration procedure builds upon Zhang's pattern-based algorithm [18], which is extended here to multi-view case. First, the different positions of the calibration pattern are captured by all light field views. The detected coordinates of the pattern are used to estimate the initial single camera calibration values. These values are used for the stereo calibration between a reference view and other light field views. On the estimation of single and stereo calibration the Bundle Adjustment is performed. Based on two views at a maximum distance on the same axis, the reference stereo rectification is calculated. Out of that the global rotation matrix is estimated, and it is used afterwards to align all views to the common image plane. Two remapping tables for all views are generated using the previously computed values. Each of them describes rectified pixels position in X and Y directions respectively.

4.3 Efficient Depth Estimation

Accurate depth estimation in a short time is a challenging task. Most of the algorithms nowadays are concentrating more on the quality rather than on run time. In this work, we try to concentrate on both aspects. Good depth quality and objects' visual sharpness can be a product of the multi-view principle, while the short run time can be achieved by utilization of modern architectures with a high level of parallelism, such as GPU, together with dedicated design decisions. This depth estimation algorithm utilizes the well-tried computer vision techniques such as coarse-to-fine strategy and the semi-global matching (SGM) method [2]. The working flow of the depth estimation algorithm is presented in Fig. 3.

We consider a two-plane parametrization for the light field, described in [4], by which the light field $L(u, v, s, t)$ is presented by a plane (s, t) for the viewpoints and a plane (u, v) with the pixel information. This representation simplifies the further disparity-related structures estimation. For a given disparity hypothesis d and a reference image $(\hat{s}, \hat{t})$, the pixel position (u, v), corresponding to this disparity in the light-field view (s, t) is defined as

$$\hat{p}(u, v, s, t, d) = L(u + (\hat{s} - s)d, v + (\hat{t} - t)d, s, t). \tag{1}$$

The algorithm is based on the matching cost, generated from an image similarity measurement. In this work, the Census transform [16] is applied to the rectified views. With this operation the radiance value of a pixel in an original view is compared to pixels nearby within a set of pixels coordinates, lying in a window, resulting in a bit string. We use a 3×3 window as a neighborhood. Taking an image I, for every pixel (u, v) in this image, the pixel relation within a neighborhood coordinate set D is performed in a form

$$I_c(u, v) = \bigotimes_{[i,j] \in D} \xi(I(u, v), I(u + i, v + j)), \tag{2}$$

where $\otimes$ is the bit-wise concatenation. The pixel relation function $\xi()$ is defined as

$$\xi(p_1, p_2) = \begin{cases} 0, & p_1 \leqslant p_2 \\ 1, & p_1 > p_2 \end{cases}. \tag{3}$$

Having a pixel in a reference view, a matching cost function is defined through a Hamming distance between corresponding pixels in a form of two bit strings from Census-transformed images. For two Census-transformed light field images with coordinates $(\hat{s}, \hat{t})$ and (s, t)

$$C(u, v, d) = HD(L(u, v, \hat{s}, \hat{t}), \hat{p}(u, v, s, t, d)),\tag{4}$$

where HD is the Hamming distance function. For two vectors x_i and x_j ($|x_i| = |x_j| = n$, $|\ldots|$ stands for vector cardinality) it can be determined as a number of vectors elements with different values on corresponding positions ($\oplus$ denotes exclusive disjunction).

$$HD(x_i, x_j) = \sum_{k=1}^{n} x_{ik} \oplus x_{jk}.\tag{5}$$

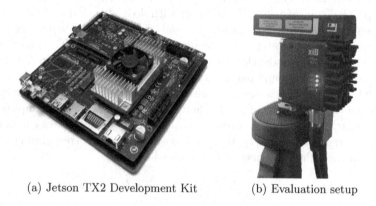

(a) Jetson TX2 Development Kit   (b) Evaluation setup

Fig. 4. Our real-time depth estimation is performed on an GPU-based SoC (a). For the evaluation of accuracy we added a reference laser scanner (b).

Matching cost generation is performed for every pixel in every light field view by

$$S(u, v, d) = \sum_{s=1}^{n} \sum_{t=1}^{m} HD(L(u, v, \hat{s}, \hat{t}), \hat{p}(u, v, s, t, d)).\tag{6}$$

Out of the matched costs, the final disparity map can be estimated as

$$D_s(p) = \arg\min_{d} C_s(p, d).\tag{7}$$

Performing of such operation can be considered as computationally expensive mainly because of the amount of data involved. One possible strategy could be to reduce the number of processed views; however, that would reduce the disparity map accuracy and object sharpness. Thus, we limit the area of the search for the right hypothesis by obtaining the initial coarse disparity map, based on four cross-lying images in the light field, with respect to reference image $(\hat{s}, \hat{t})$. The

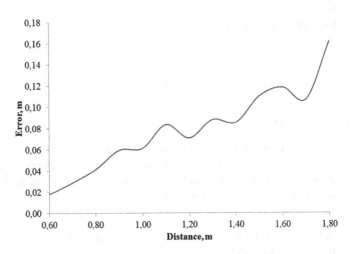

Fig. 5. Depth accuracy of our system.

results are used for creating the borders for the disparity search range. Having the data for initial disparity D_{min} and D_{max}, the range of disparity search in Eq. 6 is limited to $d = D_{min}(u,v) - \lambda, \ldots, D_{max}(u,v) + \lambda$, where λ stands for the bordering threshold, which can be adjusted for changing the degree of impact of the initial disparity map to the final one. With this design decision the execution time is drastically reduced, while the depth accuracy stays at the same high level. In order to improve quality of the disparity result, to make it smoother and to filter the discontinuities, the SGM method is used for the previously matched cost before applying Eq. 7 to it. The path-wise aggregation for each pixel $p = (u,v)$ and depth hypothesis d in a predefined range, after traversing in direction r, formulated as a 2-dimensional vector with the coordinate of a pixel traversing $r = \{\Delta u, \Delta v\}$, aggregated cost L_r is

$$
\begin{aligned}
L_r(p,d) = C(p,d) + \\
\min\,(L_r(p-r,d), \\
L_r(p-r,d-1) + P1, \\
L_r(p-r,d+1) + P1, \\
\min_t L_r(p-r,t) + P2),
\end{aligned}
\tag{8}
$$

where $P1$ and $P2$ are penalty parameters, $P2 \geqslant P1$. Traversed costs are then summarized through all traversing directions

$$
C_s(p,d) = \sum_r L_r(p,d).
\tag{9}
$$

Disparity-to-depth conversion is performed by a classical equation, based on the focal length f and the baseline b between two cameras on one axis at the maximum distance. The principles of light field parametrization allows to do it this way.

$$Z(p) = \frac{fb}{D_s(p)}. \tag{10}$$

4.4 Implementation

The main computations of our system are performed on GPU part of the Tegra TX2. The code is written in C/C++ and uses VisionWorks together with OpenCV libraries. Some of pre-processing steps, such as debayering and gamma correction, are performed by NVIDIA NPP library built-in functions.

Table 1. System run time for two different computation platforms. Please note that some parts are executed in parallel.

	Jetson TX2	GTX 1080 Ti
Capturing	30 ms	
Preprocessing	45 ms	16 ms
Depth (initial)	28 ms	2 ms
Depth (final)	100 ms	8 ms
Sending	17 ms	

5   Evaluation

In this section, we evaluate our novel depth camera system. We start with a quantitative evaluation and analyze the depth accuracy as well as the run-time of the proposed system. After that we demonstrate qualitative results of the system.

5.1   Quantitative Evaluation

Capturing ground truth data for real-world scenes is a challenging task. Using the depth information from other depth cameras can not be considered as a reliable metric, since their result might be flawed as well. Thus, we utilize data from an external laser measurement device (Bosch Zamo 3) as shown in Fig. 4b. This device has a depth accuracy of 3 mm, which is one order of magnitude higher than our system accuracy and can thus be considered as reliable. For the evaluation, we place our camera in front of a flat wall and align the image sensor parallel to it. In order to avoid any influence of the wall texture, we project twenty different patterns and average the results.

Figure 5 presents the depth accuracy with respect to the distance. The error increases quadratically for higher distances. For short distances the depth values have an error of below 2 cm, which is comparable to active devices. For higher distances the accuracy is still sufficient for many applications. An even further improved accuracy would be possible by choosing a bigger baseline for the camera matrix. However, we believe the chosen baseline is the best compromise between camera size and accuracy in the context of the described close range applications. An evaluation against other light field cameras is not possible, a.o. due to limited availability. The famous Lytro camera [5] is no longer on sale. In addition, they provide – like Raytrix [6] – offline processing of depth data only, which is not comparable with our novel real-time system (cp. Sect. 2).

Fig. 6. Qualitative results of the proposed system. The scenes are reconstructed with a high level of detail – even for homogeneous regions (wall), filigree objects (pillar) and crowded objects (plant hedge).

5.2 Running Time

As described in Sect. 3, our system utilizes a Nvidia Jetson TX2 for embedded processing. This platform is equipped with a Tegra X2 GPU. The run times are given in Table 1. With that setup we achieve a performance of up to 6 frames per second (FPS), which is sufficient for many applications.

In case higher frame rates are required, a more powerful hardware platform needs to be utilized. As an example, we evaluate our system running on an ordinary PC (CPU: Intel Xeon E5-1620 v3, GPU: Nvidia GTX 1080 Ti). With such a setup up to 32 FPS can be achieved.

5.3 Qualitative Evaluation

Figure 6 shows the qualitative results of our proposed system. The depth result is filtered in a way that it keeps distances in our target range of 0.5–2.0 m only. The objects are reconstructed with a high level of detail as visible e.g. for the plant hedge. In addition, smaller objects like the pillar are robustly detected, which is important for applications such as the automotive domain. For the flat wall with the homogeneous texture the depth is not very dense, but still depth is sufficiently robust.

6 Conclusion

In this paper, we proposed a novel passive depth camera. Compared to state-of-the-art approaches we provide real-time depth estimation as well as a compact design. The compact design is realized by using a full format sensor in combination with a lens array in a matrix configuration. We achieve real-time performance with a novel algorithm utilizing dedicated design decisions and an embedded optimization. In our evaluation we demonstrate the accuracy of the system in different scenarios.

As the next step, we will work on the density of the depth images. Some applications require dense depth in order to perform properly [15,19]. Thus, we will have a look at different filtering and interpolation approaches, which were successfully applied in other domains before [10].

Acknowledgements. This work was partially funded by the Federal Ministry of Education and Research (Germany) in the context of the project DAKARA (13N14318).

References

1. Anisimov, Y., Stricker, D.: Fast and efficient depth map estimation from light fields. In: International Conference on 3D Vision (3DV), pp. 337–346 (2017)
2. Hirschmuller, H.: Accurate and efficient stereo processing by semi-global matching and mutual information. In: IEEE Computer Vision and Pattern Recognition (CVPR), vol. 2, pp. 807–814 (2005)

3. Kim, C., et al.: Scene reconstruction from high spatio-angular resolution light fields. ACM Trans. Graph. **32**(4), 73 (2013)
4. Levoy, M., Hanrahan, P.: Light field rendering. In: Computer Graphics and Interactive Techniques. ACM (1996)
5. Lytro. http://www.lytro.com/
6. Raytrix. https://raytrix.de/
7. Qin, Y., et al.: GPU-based depth estimation for light field images. In: IEEE International Symposium on Intelligent Signal Processing and Communication Systems (ISPACS), pp. 640–645 (2017)
8. Peng, J., et al.: Unsupervised depth estimation from light field using a convolutional neural network. In: International Conference on 3D Vision (3DV), pp. 295–303 (2018)
9. Sabater, N., et al.: Dataset and pipeline for multi-view light-field video. In: IEEE Conference on Computer Vision and Pattern Recognition Workshops (CVPRW), pp. 1743–1753 (2017)
10. Schuster, R., et al.: FlowFields++: accurate optical flow correspondences meet robust interpolation. In: IEEE International Conference on Image Processing (ICIP) (2018)
11. Shin, C., et al.: EPINET: a fully-convolutional neural network using epipolar geometry for depth from light field images. In: IEEE Computer Vision and Pattern Recognition (CVPR), pp. 4748–4757 (2018)
12. Wanner, S., Goldluecke, B.: Globally consistent depth labeling of 4D light fields. In: IEEE Computer Vision and Pattern Recognition (CVPR), pp. 41–48 (2012)
13. Wasenmüller, O., et al.: Augmented reality 3D discrepancy check in industrial applications. In: IEEE International Symposium on Mixed and Augmented Reality (ISMAR), pp. 125–134 (2016)
14. Wilburn, B., et al.: High performance imaging using large camera arrays. ACM Trans. Graph. (TOG) **24**(3), 765–776 (2005)
15. Yoshida, T., et al.: Time-of-flight sensor depth enhancement for automotive exhaust gas. In: IEEE International Conference on Image Processing (ICIP), pp. 1955–1959 (2017)
16. Zabih, R., Woodfill, J.: Non-parametric local transforms for computing visual correspondence. In: Eklundh, J.-O. (ed.) ECCV 1994. LNCS, vol. 801, pp. 151–158. Springer, Heidelberg (1994). https://doi.org/10.1007/BFb0028345
17. Zhang, S., et al.: Robust depth estimation for light field via spinning parallelogram operator. Comput. Vis. Image Underst. **145**, 148–159 (2016)
18. Zhang, Z.: A flexible new technique for camera calibration. IEEE Trans. Pattern Anal. Mach. Intell. (PAMI) (2000)
19. Zhang, Z.: Microsoft kinect sensor and its effect. IEEE Multimed. **19**(2), 4–10 (2012)

A Real-Time Processing Stand-Alone Multiple Object Visual Tracking System

Mauro Fernández-Sanjurjo[✉], Manuel Mucientes, and Víctor M. Brea

Centro Singular de Investigación en Tecnoloxías Intelixentes (CiTIUS),
Universidade de Santiago de Compostela, Santiago de Compostela, Spain
{mauro.fernandez,manuel.mucientes,victor.brea}@usc.es

Abstract. Detection and tracking of multiple objects in real applications requires real-time performance, the management of tens of simultaneous objects, and handling frequent partial and total occlusions. Moreover, due to the software and hardware requirements of the different algorithms, this kind of systems require a distributed architecture to run in real-time. In this paper, we propose a vision based tracking system with three components: detection, tracking and data association. Tracking is based on a Discriminative Correlation Filter combined with a Kalman filter for occlusions handling. Also, our data association uses deep features to improve robustness. The complete system runs in real-time with tens of simultaneous objects, taking into account the runtimes of the Convolutional Neural Network detector, the tracking and the data association.

Keywords: Multiple object tracking · Convolutional Neural Network · Data association

1 Introduction

Real-life computer vision applications like traffic monitoring, autonomous vehicles, or surveillance in general usually require to detect and track tens of objects under the constraint of real-time processing in high resolution video like full HD and 4K formats without losing accuracy. All the above leads to the challenge of integrating seamlessly many heterogeneous solutions and hardware platforms into a stand-alone multiple object visual tracker. This does not mean a mere plug and play connection between trackers running on either CPU or GPU on the one hand, and top object detectors based on Convolutional Neural Networks

This research was partially funded by the Spanish Ministry of Economy and Competitiveness under grants TIN2017-84796-C2-1-R and RTI2018-097088-B-C32 (MICINN/FEDER), and the Galician Ministry of Education, Culture and Universities under grant ED431G/08. Mauro Fernández is supported by the Spanish Ministry of Economy and Competitiveness under grant BES-2015-071889. These grants are co-funded by the European Regional Development Fund (ERDF/FEDER program). We thank Dirección General de Tráfico (DGT) for their collaboration.

© Springer Nature Switzerland AG 2019
M. Vento and G. Percannella (Eds.): CAIP 2019, LNCS 11678, pp. 64–74, 2019.
https://doi.org/10.1007/978-3-030-29888-3_6

(ConvNets) running on high end desktop GPUs on the other hand, but their adaptation into a general architecture or framework combined with the insertion of decision-making processes along the data path to maximize performance metrics. Besides, motion prediction through, for instance, Bayesian filtering—Kalman filters, Particle filters, etc—, could also be included to deal with total occlusions.

In the last years, top trackers from the Visual Object Tracking (VOT) challenge [15] are based on two approaches: Discriminative Correlation Filters (DCF) based trackers, and deep-learning based trackers. On the one hand, DCF based trackers predict the target position training a correlation filter that can differentiate between the object of interest and the background [12–14]. On the other hand, deep-learning based trackers use ConvNets. SiamFC [10] is one of the first approaches of this kind. This tracker consists of two branches that apply an identical transformation—deep features extractor—to two inputs: the search image and the exemplar. Then, both representations are combined through cross-correlation, generating a score map that indicates the most probable position of the object. In [16] they propose SiamRPN, adding a Region Proposal Network (RPN) to a siamese network in order to generate bounding box proposals that go through a classification and a regression branch. DaSiamRPN [20] improves SiamRPN, focusing the training on semantic distractors, and adding a search region strategy for long-term tracking. All these trackers cannot cope with occlusions, nor by themselves provide a framework to deal with multiple objects.

In contrast to VOT, the Multiple Object Tracking (MOT) contest [5] focuses on data association, as they assume that detections are available in all time instants without computational cost and, therefore, perform tracking by detection. In [18] they solve the data associations by proposing extensions to the classical Multiple Hypothesis Tracking approach. In [11] they combine Kalman filtering with the Hungarian algorithm for data association, and in [19], they improve the proposal using deep features to make data association more robust to occlusions.

In summary, we find the following limitations in the proposed approaches for real-life situations: (i) high performance object detectors based on deep learning are too slow to perform tracking-by-detection, and so does with deep learning trackers when dealing with several objects in the scene; (ii) the number of simultaneous real-time tracked objects is low; and (iii) the time response constraint dictated by the application is severely compromised by the communication among processes on CPU and GPU platforms and/or different libraries or frameworks like Caffe2 [1], Pytorch [7] or OpenCV [6].

This paper aims at all the challenges outlined above. The main contributions of the paper are:

– A distributed architecture for a vision based tracking system which permits combining components of different technologies in a modular way for the correct exploitation of the available hardware resources, i.e. CPU and GPU.

– A complete system for visual tracking that can process tens of objects in real-time. It combines a Discriminative Correlation Filter (DCF) low-level tracker and a Kalman filter for the visual and motion information respectively. Difficult data association is performed using deep features correlation while simple associations are solved based on overlap. The system shows a significant improvement in MOTP and MOTA metrics compared to the baseline version despite performing detection only once every second.

2   Stand-Alone Multiple Object Visual Tracking Approach

Figure 1 shows the architecture of our system. It comprises three main components or visual tasks, namely, detection, tracking and data association. The proposed architecture serves two purposes. On the one hand, it allows the integration of the different parts of the system regardless of their underlying technologies. On the other hand, it is designed to provide a maximum use of the available hardware resources, that is, CPU and GPU. Each of the three modules of the architecture consists of a Docker [3] container with the specific dependencies necessary for their execution. In order to allow a modular integration of the different parts, Robot Operating System (ROS) [8] has been used as the framework for communication between processes for its flexibility, as well as for its support for computer vision tasks.

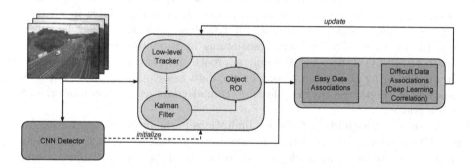

Fig. 1. Stand-alone multiple object visual tracking architecture. The blue box is the detection component. The orange block is the tracking. The green box is the data association module. (Color figure online)

Algorithm 1 presents an overview of the steps of our approach. At every time instant t, the system processes two inputs: the current video frame (Im_t) and the set of trackers in the last time frame Φ_{t-1}. First, the system calculates the new trackers position using two independent estimators: a discriminative correlation filter (DCF) tracker and a Kalman filter (Algorithm 1, lines 3–4). With the bounding boxes proposed by both methods, we estimate the region of

Fig. 2. Four images from the videos processed by our stand-alone multiple object visual tracking system. Videos are provided by the Spanish Traffic Authority (DGT) [2].

interest (ROI) in which the object might be located (Algorithm 1: 5). The larger the difference between the two trackers, the larger the ROI. Occlusions can be determined in cases where both predictors propose very different bounding boxes, since the bounding boxes provided by DCF will remain static, while those from the Kalman filter will follow the previous movement pattern of the object.

Our system is robust enough as not to need detections in every frame. If the time elapsed since the previous detection is greater than or equal to τ, detection is performed using a convolutional neural network (Algorithm 1: 6–7), which returns a set of detections Ψ_t. The aim of the detection component is twofold. First, it initializes every tracker or object of interest in the scene. Second, it refines the location and size of the bounding boxes of the trackers along their trajectories inside the data association component (see Fig. 1), improving tracking performance metrics. Thus, the frequency of detection calls sets a trade-off between tracking performance metrics and the number of objects that can be tracked at a given frame rate.

The data association block aims to assign each detection to its corresponding tracker and to identify objects that enter or leave the scene. In so doing, we build up the cost matrix IOU_t (see Algorithm 1: 8–10), where every entry is the Intersection Over Union (IOU) between a tracker $\overline{\varphi}_t^i$ and a detection ψ_t^j.

Algorithm 1. Our Stand-Alone Multi-Object Tracking System

Require:
  (a) Im_t: Video frame at current time t
  (b) $\Phi_{t-1} = \{\varphi_{t-1}^1, \varphi_{t-1}^2, \ldots, \varphi_{t-1}^n\}$

1 **Function** Track(Im_t, Φ_{t-1}):
2   **for** $i=1$ to n **do**
3      $dcf\_ROI_t^i$ =DCF_Track (φ_{t-1}^i)
4      $kalman\_ROI_t^i$ = Kalman_Predict (φ_{t-1}^i)
5      $\overline{\varphi}_t^i \leftarrow < ROI_t^i >$=Estimate_ROI $(dcf\_ROI_t^i, kalman\_ROI_t^i)$
6   **if** $time\_elapsed > \tau$ **then**
7      $\Psi_t \leftarrow \{\psi_t^1, \psi_t^2, \ldots, \psi_t^m\}$ =ConvNet_Detect()
8   **for** $i=1$ to n **do**
9   **for** $j=1$ to m **do**
10          $IOU_t^{i,j} = \dfrac{\overline{\varphi}_t^i \cap \psi_t^j}{\overline{\varphi}_t^i \cup \psi_t^j}$
11      $\{< \overline{\varphi}_t^\alpha, \psi_t^\beta >\}$ =Get_Easy_Associations (IOU_t)
12   **for** every α, β in $\{< \overline{\varphi}_t^\alpha, \psi_t^\beta >\}$ **do**
13   update_tracker $(\overline{\varphi}_t^\alpha, \psi_t^\beta)$
14   remove $(\overline{\varphi}_t^\alpha, \overline{\Phi}_t)$
15   remove (ψ_t^β, Ψ_t)
16   **for** $i=1$ to $size(\overline{\Phi}_t)$ **do**
17   **for** $j=1$ to $size(\Psi_t)$ **do**
18          $\rho_t^{i,j}, \overline{\varphi}_t^i$ =Deep_Learning_Correlation $(\varphi_{t-1}^i, \psi_t^j)$
19          $newIOU_t^{i,j} = \dfrac{\overline{\varphi}_t^i \cap \psi_t^j}{\overline{\varphi}_t^i \cup \psi_t^j}$
20          $\omega(i,j) = 1 - (\rho_t^{i,j} \cdot newIOU_t^{i,j})$
21      $\{< \overline{\varphi}_t^\alpha, \psi_t^\beta >\}$ =Hungarian (ω)
22   **for** every α, β in $\{< \overline{\varphi}_t^\alpha, \psi_t^\beta >\}$ **do**
23   update_tracker $(\overline{\varphi}_t^\alpha, \psi_t^\beta)$
24   remove $(\overline{\varphi}_t^\alpha, \overline{\Phi}_t)$
25   remove (ψ_t^β, Ψ_t)
26   **for** $i=1$ to $size(\overline{\Phi}_t)$ **do**
27   delete_tracker $(\overline{\varphi}_t^i)$
28   **for** $j=1$ to $size(\Psi_t)$ **do**
29   new_tracker (ψ_t^j)
30    $\Phi_t = \overline{\Phi}_t$
31   **return** Φ_t

Our approach makes assignments or data association in two steps. First, the system solves easy associations between trackers and detections (see Fig. 1). In so doing, the maximum IOU value is found ($maxIOU_t$). Then we iterate along the row and column of the cell with $maxIOU_t$ in order to find if there is any other $IOU_t^{i,j}$ complying with $IOU_t^{i,j} \geq \gamma \cdot maxIOU_t$. If not, we perform the assignment (Algorithm 1: 11). If so, this means that the IOU metric is not sufficiently discriminative, yielding a difficult association (see Fig. 1). Finally, easy associations between trackers and detections are updated through Algorithm 1: 12–15.

Second, difficult associations between trackers and detections are solved with a deep learning based tracker. This solution features high robustness, but with a much higher computational cost than that based on IOU. The deep learning tracker calculates the bounding boxes in the current frame and their score (correlation) from the last frame's trackers position (Algorithm 1: 16–18). With this information the cost of association for the tracker $\overline{\varphi}_t^i$ with the detection ψ_t^j is established as $\omega(i,j)$, using the IOU between $\overline{\varphi}_t^i$ and ψ_t^j, namely, $newIOU_t^{i,j}$, along with their correlation score $\rho_t^{i,j}$ (Algorithm 1: 19–20). Once the cost matrix is generated it is solved by the Hungarian method (Algorithm 1: 21). For every successful assignation ($<\varphi_t^\alpha, \psi_t^\beta>$), tracker φ_t^α is updated with detection ψ_t^β (Algorithm 1: 23). Finally, trackers not updated in the data association phase are candidates for being deleted, and detections not assigned are initialized as new trackers (Algorithm 1: 26–29).

3   Implementation Details

Our experimental configuration consists of a server with an Intel Xeon E52623v4 2.60 GHz CPU, 128 GB RAM and an NVidia GP102GL 24 GB (Tesla P40) as GPU. Nevertheless, our architecture allows for a complete distributed set up in which every module resides in a different machine.

In this current version of the architecture, we have included the ConvNet FPN with ResNeXt101 as backbone for object detection, as FPN is the basis for the three top entries in the last edition of the COCO detection challenge [17]. A Caffe2 implementation of FPN with ResNeXt101 takes 0.39 s in full HD video, so that tracking by detection through the overlap of successive detections throughout the video is discarded.

As DCF tracker we opt for KCF (Kernelized Correlation Filters) [14] as low-level tracker for its speed and for its implementation on a CPU, which can be parallelized to use all the available threads, thus increasing the number of tracked objects. As deep learning tracker for difficult associations between trackers and detections we build on DaSiamRPN, which offers very good results in long term tracking [15] with a speed of 200 fps [4]. However, its computation time does not scale well for several objects. Indeed, as far as we know, there is not any multiple object tracker in real-time with a deep learning solution. In order to cut processing time and cope with tens of objects at video frame rate, we have modified DaSiamRPN to initialize the network only the first time an object is identified. This is possible storing the feature vector and the states of all previously tracked objects. Still, we set an upper limit for the number of difficult data

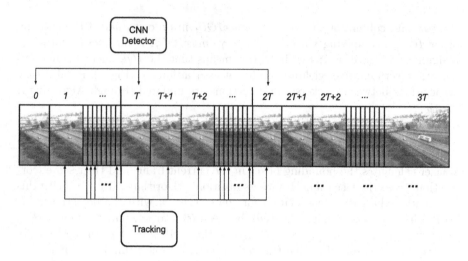

Fig. 3. Frame processing for our stand-alone multiple object visual tracker.

associations between trackers and detections solved with DaSiamRPN. If necessary, unsolved associations are handled during the next detection call. Finally, computation time is negligible for easy data associations.

Figure 3 illustrates how the different components of our architecture shown in Fig. 1 operate and interact with one another. Real-time processing of 30 fps in full HD video is met by cutting down the detector calls to only once per second, as our implementation of the FPN detector lasts 0.39 s in full HD video. Also, detections are being run or in parallel with the tracking. Detections during the first frame initialize the tracking module (see Fig. 1). The detection step produces a latency τ with respect to the original video as tracking in the first frame needs to wait for the detection to finish, unlike in the rest of frames with detection, in which no waiting will be required. Finally, it should be noted here that the tracking is run on CPU, while the detection and difficult associations between trackers and detections do it on GPU. Our stand-alone multiple object tracker succeeds in dealing with this situation.

Table 1 shows a time breakdown of our stand-alone approach for 30 fps full HD video. Detection times are not included since they are run in parallel while tracking the objects in the scene. Our system is able to track 60 objects simultaneously at 30 fps HD video. In so doing, 90% of the time frame of one second in a video has been reserved for tracking, while difficult data associations have been assigned the remaining 10%. The data association is only performed once the next detection arrives, in our case, once per second. The times of the rest of the parts of the system are disregarded as they are not sufficiently relevant for the calculations. The time it takes our system to track an object during a second of video (DCF + Kalman) is 0.21 s. If we leave 90% of the time for tracking we would have 0.9 s for the operation and with a single thread we could process 4 trackers at 30 fps full HD video. When having 15 threads for this task (as one is reserved for the detection module) on a single CPU, the number rises to 60. Once the next detection is reached, it is necessary to perform data association. As mentioned above, we set an upper limit of 10% for difficult associations, which is a realistic average. In this case, it would take 0.005 s per object, which amounts to 0.03 s for 6 objects, since, as previously mentioned, DaSiamRPN is not a scalable solution. This would be within the 0.1 s of available time.

We have also developed a fast version of our stand-alone tracking system that for each three consecutive frames, makes an execution of the tracking system in one frame and keeps the trackers unchanged in the next two. This fast tracking system has a good performance for real-life applications, and is able to track up to 180 simultaneous objects.

Table 1. Time breakdown of our stand-alone multiple object tracker at 30 fps full HD video.

Tracking times	
Max. number of objects tracked in real-time	60 objects
Time unit	30 frames in 1 s
Available time for tracking assuming 90%	$90\% = 0.9$ s
Available time for difficult data association assuming 10%	$10\% = 0.1$ s
Time to track 1 object during 1 s	0.21 s
Max. number of trackers in 0.9 s	$0.9/0.21 = 4$ trackers
Using 15 threads	$4 \times 15 = 60$ objects
Assuming 10% of complex data association	10% of $60 = 6$ objects
Time of DaSiamRPN	0.005 s per tracker
Average time in 6 objects	$0.005 \times 6 = 0.03$ s < 0.1 s

4   Results

We have tested our system for a traffic monitoring application. Figure 2 displays some images of the videos processed in this section. In order to assess the performance of our stand-alone multiple object visual tracker we construct our own dataset using three videos with more than 1,000 objects. As performance metrics we have used Multiple Object Tracking Precision (MOTP) and Multiple Object Tracking Accuracy (MOTA) [9]. Our system has been compared with two other approaches. The first one represents the ideal scenario in which the detector could be called in every frame of a video maintaining real-time performance, thus the low level tracking would not be necessary, simply a data association based on IOU would be enough to match the ground truth in consecutive frames (tracking-by-detection approach), named *Ideal_case*. It is worth mentioning here that in certain scenarios an assignment of ground truth bounding boxes by IOU in successive frames does not necessarily have to provide the perfect result (100%

Table 2. Approach, video, number of objects in the video (n_o) Multiple Object Tracking Precision (MOTP) and Multiple Object Tracking Accuracy (MOTA) for the three compared approaches.

Approach	Video	No	MOTP	MOTA
1. Ideal_case	video 1	589	100,00%	100,00%
2. Real_case			54,73%	56,22%
3. Ours			80,23%	97,87%
1. Ideal_case	video 2	218	100,00%	100,00%
2. Real_case			58,27%	84,74%
3. Ours			76,47%	92,48%
1. Ideal_case	video 3	244	100,00%	100,00%
2. Real_case			66,56%	67,38%
3. Ours			78,48%	92,31%

MOTP and 100% MOTA). However, it is always a good point to take as a reference to measure a tracking system. The second approach is the real case in which we could only run detection two times per second on average to guarantee real-time processing in the application, as an average call takes 0.39 s in a FPN with ImageNet and ResNeXt101. The assignment is made by IOU as in the previous case. This approach is named *Real_case*, and represents the baseline approach and it is the proposal that our system aims to significantly improve. To guarantee a fair comparison, in those cases in which a new object appears in the scene, this is added to the trackers list even though there is no detection in that particular frame. This affects our proposal and the *Real_case* approach since they do not use detection at all the frames, unlike the *Ideal_case*.

Table 3. Approach, video, misses (n_m), false positives (n_fp), mismatches (n_mm), percentage of increase in MOTP (%_p), percentage of increase in MOTA (%_a), percentage of decrease in misses (%_m), percentage of decrease in false positives (%_fp) and percentage of decrease in mismatches (%_mm) obtained with our system with respect to the real case in the videos of Table 2.

Approach	Video	n_m	n_fp	n_mm	%_p	%_a	%_m	%_fp	%_mm
1. Ideal_case	video 1	0	0	0					
2. Real_case		506	624	106					
3. Ours		38	21	1	46,59%	74,10%	92,49%	96,63%	99,06%
1. Ideal_case	video 2	0	0	0					
2. Real_case		994	1,579	139					
3. Ours		391	903	42	31,23%	9,14%	60,66%	42,81%	69,78%
1. Ideal_case	video 3	0	0	0					
2. Real_case		2,440	2,979	730					
3. Ours		390	1,018	42	17,91%	36,99%	84,02%	65,83%	94,25%

The results obtained in our dataset processing more than 1,000 objects are shown in Table 2. In view of the results we can see a clear improvement of our system with respect to the baseline, both in precision and accuracy, being in some cases close to the ideal case.

Table 3 shows a breakdown of the accuracy of the system in misses, false positives and mismatches. Misses are those ground truth objects that do not have an associated tracker, false positives are trackers that do not follow any real object and mismatches are identity switches. In view of the measures, we can observe an increase up to 46% in precision and 74% in accuracy, highlighting in the latter the maximum 99% of decrease in the number of mismatches thanks to data association.

5 Conclusions

We have presented a stand-alone multiple object visual tracking system that combines a DCF with a Kalman filter to handle occlusions, and solves the data association with deep features. The system runs in real-time—including the detector runtime—on a distributed architecture and, on a single CPU and GPU, is able to track tens of simultaneous objects in HD 1080 video. The proposal has been validated with several videos with more than 1,000 vehicles showing very good MOTP and MOTA metrics for up to 60 concurrent objects. Moreover, a fast version of the tracking system allows to track up to 180 simultaneous objects with a performance that is suitable for real-life applications.

References

1. Caffe2. https://caffe2.ai/. Accessed 15 Apr 2019
2. DGT: Dirección General de Tráfico. http://www.dgt.es/es/. Accessed 15 Apr 2019
3. Docker. https://www.docker.com/. Accessed 15 Apr 2019
4. Github: DaSiamRPN. https://github.com/foolwood/DaSiamRPN. Accessed 15 Apr 2019
5. MOTChallenge: The Multiple Object Tracking Benchmark. https://motchallenge.net/. Accessed 15 Apr 2019
6. OpenCV: Open Source Computer Vision Library. https://opencv.org/. Accessed 15 Apr 2019
7. Pytorch. https://pytorch.org/. Accessed 15 Apr 2019
8. ROS: The Robot Operating System. http://www.ros.org/. Accessed 13 Apr 2019
9. Bernardin, K., Stiefelhagen, R.: Evaluating multiple object tracking performance: the CLEAR MOT metrics. J. Image Video Process. 1 (2008)
10. Bertinetto, L., Valmadre, J., Henriques, J.F., Vedaldi, A., Torr, P.H.S.: Fully-convolutional siamese networks for object tracking. In: Hua, G., Jégou, H. (eds.) ECCV 2016. LNCS, vol. 9914, pp. 850–865. Springer, Cham (2016). https://doi.org/10.1007/978-3-319-48881-3_56
11. Bewley, A., Ge, Z., Ott, L., Ramos, F., Upcroft, B.: Simple online and realtime tracking. In: IEEE International Conference on Image Processing (ICIP) (2016)

12. Danelljan, M., Bhat, G., Khan, F.S., Felsberg, M.: ECO: efficient convolution oper-
    ators for tracking. In: IEEE Conference on Computer Vision and Pattern Recog-
    nition (CVPR) (2017)
13. Danelljan, M., Häger, G., Khan, F.S., Felsberg, M.: Discriminative scale space
    tracking. IEEE Trans. Pattern Anal. Mach. Intell. **39**(8), 1561–1575 (2017)
14. Henriques, J.F., Caseiro, R., Martins, P., Batista, J.: High-speed tracking with
    kernelized correlation filters. IEEE Trans. Pattern Anal. Mach. Intell. **37**(3), 583–
    596 (2015)
15. Kristan, M., et al.: The sixth visual object tracking VOT2018 challenge results,
    pp. 3–53, January 2019
16. Li, B., Yan, J., Wu, W., Zhu, Z., Hu, X.: High performance visual tracking with
    siamese region proposal network. In: The IEEE Conference on Computer Vision
    and Pattern Recognition (CVPR) (2018)
17. Lin, T.-Y., et al.: Microsoft COCO: common objects in context. In: Fleet, D.,
    Pajdla, T., Schiele, B., Tuytelaars, T. (eds.) ECCV 2014. LNCS, vol. 8693, pp.
    740–755. Springer, Cham (2014). https://doi.org/10.1007/978-3-319-10602-1_48
18. Reid, D., et al.: An algorithm for tracking multiple targets. IEEE Trans. Autom.
    Control **24**(6), 843–854 (1979)
19. Wojke, N., Bewley, A., Paulus, D.: Simple online and realtime tracking with a deep
    association metric. In: 2017 IEEE International Conference on Image Processing
    (ICIP), pp. 3645–3649. IEEE (2017)
20. Zhu, Z., Wang, Q., Bo, L., Wu, W., Yan, J., Hu, W.: Distractor-aware siamese
    networks for visual object tracking. In: European Conference on Computer Vision
    (2018)

Demo: Accelerating Depth-Map on Mobile Device Using CPU-GPU Co-processing

Peter Fasogbon[1]($\boxtimes$), Emre Aksu[1], and Lasse Heikkilä[2]

[1] Nokia Technologies, 33900 Tampere, Finland
{peter.fasogbon,emre.aksu}@nokia.com
[2] Vincit Oy, 33900 Tampere, Finland
lasse.heikkila@vincit.com

Abstract. With the growing use of smartphones, generating depth-map to accompany user acquisitions is becoming increasingly important for both manufacturers and consumers. Depth from Small Motion (DfSM) has been shown to be suitable approach since depth-maps can be generated with minimal effort such as handshaking motion, and without knowing camera calibration parameter. Direct porting of a desktop PC implementation of DfSM on mobile devices propose a major challenge due to its long execution time. The algorithm has been designed to run on desktop computers that have higher energy-efficient optimizations compared to mobile device with slower processors.

In this paper, we investigate ways to speed up the DfSM algorithm to run faster on mobile devices. After porting the algorithm to the mobile platform, we applied several optimization techniques using mobile CPU-GPU co-processing by exploiting OpenCL capabilities. We evaluate the impact of our optimizations on performance, memory allocation, and demonstrate about 3× speedup over mobile CPU implementation. We also show the portability of our optimizations by running on two different ANDROID devices.

Keywords: Depth-map · Bundle adjustment · OpenCL · DfSM · ANDROID

1 Introduction

Depth from small motion (DfSM) [6] is becoming popular among smartphone manufacturers especially due to its suitability for single lens depth estimation with minimal user effort such as natural hand-shake, and/or slight movement. Depth-map generation using these small motions can be offered to consumers to accompany their selfies, bothie and portraits camera shots. Other interesting applications include depth assisted segmentation and synthetic focusing of the cameras using depth information. The baseline between sequences of frames captured as a sudden motion is considered to be small if it is less than 8 mm,

© Springer Nature Switzerland AG 2019
M. Vento and G. Percannella (Eds.): CAIP 2019, LNCS 11678, pp. 75–86, 2019.
https://doi.org/10.1007/978-3-030-29888-3_7

Fig. 1. Depth-map demo. on an ANDROID device with proposed CPU-GPU co-processing using a selfie acquisition.

which restricts the viewing angle of a three-dimensional point to less than 0.2°
[6]. Therefore, the popular Structure from Motion (SfM) method [1,9] fails for
this scenario. As a result, several number of algorithms [6–8,10,11] have been
proposed for DfSM.

As this DfSM algorithm works effectively with acceptable execution time on
desktop PC (>10 min for full HD images [8]), deploying it on mobile device is
entirely a different problem. The direct porting of the representative PC algorithm [6] to mobile device does not necessarily bring the same improvement in
terms of execution time. Open Computing Language (OpenCL) [2,3] has been
largely used to accelerate computer vision algorithms using a General Purpose
Graphics Processing Unit (GPGPU) [2,12–15]. Most of the algorithm is written
in the ubiquitous C language and promotes a good programming portability. In
this paper, we carefully analyze the DfSM algorithm, and propose implementation that is influenced by the co-processing between the mobile CPU and GPU.

The following sections are organized as follows. First, we summarize representative DfSM algorithm [8] using mathematical representation and notations.
These notations make it easy to understand the acceleration with CPU-GPU
co-processing proposed in Sect. 3. Various experiments highlighting performance
achieved with the proposed acceleration as compared to optimized CPU implementations on the mobile device are provided in Sect. 4. Finally, we made conclusion and future direction in this work.

2   Background

Let us denote an image $M \times N$ where M, N correspond to the number of image
rows and columns respectively. Assuming optical lens distortion in Fig. 2(a), the
world point P_j is projected onto reference image coordinate C_0 and non-reference
one C_i as distorted $\tilde{p}_{0j}$ and $\tilde{p}_{ij}$ respectively. Both i and j signifies $j = 1 \dots m$
points and $i = 1 \dots n$ views. The i-th camera is transformed to the reference
plane using rotation matrix $\mathcal{R}_i$ followed by translation $\mathcal{T}_i$.

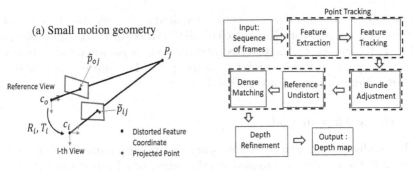

Fig. 2. Image showing (a) small motion geometry used in DfSM for uncalibrated camera, and (b) overview of the DfSM algorithm, where the blocks with dashed lines illustrates part of the algorithm we accelerate in this paper.

$$P_j = \frac{1}{\omega_j}[x_j, y_j, 1]^T \tag{1}$$

A backprojected 3D point P_j can be parametrized using the inverse depth w_j as shown in Eq. (1), where (x_j, y_j) is the undistorted normalized coordinate of $p_{0j}(u, v)$ derived from using the inverse of the intrinsic camera matrix $\mathcal{K}$ [8,19]. This intrinsic matrix embeds both the focal length and principal point.

In the following part of this section, we summarize the full DfSM algorithm illustrated in Fig. 2(b). This figure illustrates the general overview of the popular DfSM algorithm [8]. The enclosed blocks with dashed lines in the figure illustrate part of the algorithm we accelerate in this paper.

2.1 Point Tracking

Point tracking involves two steps: In the first step, (i) one extracts the feature pixels $\tilde{p}_{0j}$ on the reference plane using Harris corner detection [16]. In the second step, (ii) $\tilde{p}_{0j}$ is then track over all the non-reference images with the Kanade-Lukas-Tomashi (KLT) method [17]. At the end of these two earlier steps, only $\tilde{p}_{0j}$ that has consistent correspondence/pair with all the non-reference pixel $\tilde{p}_{ij}$ is retained.

2.2 Bundle Adjustment

Bundle adjustment [19–21] is used to find the optimal camera parameters ($\mathcal{K}$, $\mathcal{R}_i$, $\mathcal{T}_i$), radial distortion coefficients (k_1, k_2), and the inverse depth P_j values. A special non-linear optimization suitable for DfSM was proposed by Yu et al. [6]. The optimization involves the minimization of re-projection error using randomly initialized depth values.

2.3 Reference-Undistort

Before applying the dense matching, it is required to first remove the lens distortion from the images formed on the reference view coordinate. By using estimated radial coefficients k_1, k_2, all distorted reference points $\tilde{p}_{0j}$ are mapped to undistorted one p_{0j} using iterative inverse mapping [22]. This process takes about 10 to 12 iterations to have an acceptable distortion free p_{0j}.

2.4 Dense Matching [8]

A plane-induced homography $\mathcal{H}_{ik}$ is formulated using parameters $\mathcal{K}, R_j, T_j, P_j$, where k is the number of sampled depth planes, usually between 64 and 128 planes. This homography is then used to build an intensity profile through warping of all non-reference images onto a virtual image plane that is swept along the reference viewpoint. This approach for building intensity profile is known as plane sweep image matching [23].

The dense matching procedure requires two main operations (homography transformation and cubic interpolation) to create the intensity profile from RGB and edge detection of the non-reference images. Thereafter, a variance cost is derived from these intensity profiles. Finally, a Winner Takes All (WTA) strategy is applied on the cost volume to generate the depth-map.

3 Accelerated DfSM Using Mobile CPU-GPU

To better optimize the algorithm, we first measure the performance of the desktop C-function directly ported onto the mobile device. We use 10 "Full HD (1920 × 1080)" images from a "selfie" acquisition shown in Fig. 1. These tests

Table 1. Breakdown of full DfSM algorithm mobile CPU implementation using selfie example in Fig. 1.

Stages	C-Functions	Execution time (s)
I	*Read input frame sequence*	0.44
II	*Feature Extraction*	0.14
III	*Feature Tracking*	0.62
IV	*Bundle Adjustment*	0.24
V	*Reference-Undistort*	1.58
VI	*Dense Matching*	25.53
	Homography Transformation	
	Cubic Interpolation	
VII	*Depth Refinement*	1.52
		Total: 30.07

were made using a timing performance profiler we developed for Qualcomm Snapdragon chipset.

The algorithm is partitioned into seven core functions shown in Table 1. **Dense Matching** occupies most of the processing time at 25.53 s, followed by the **Reference-Undistort** at 1.58 s respectively. The optimization of these two functions is the key to improve performance on the mobile device. Therefore, we concentrate on accelerating these two most computationally expensive steps on GPU, while other parts of the algorithm were accelerated on CPU.

3.1   CPU Acceleration

The total number of features extracted and tracked has a major impact on the algorithms employed in **stages: II, III, IV**. As a result, we put effort into accelerating the point tracking part of the algorithm.

Grided Point Tracking. We proposed a grided point tracking idea, whereby we divide the full resolution image into grid of fixed size. We then extract only strongest Harris corners [16] in each enclosed grid by using Shi-Tomasi score [18] as the measure of best feature. With this approach, the total number of features that are tracked over all the non-reference images are reduced approximately four times ($\approx 4\times$).

In addition, rather than track features on the reference image sequentially over individual non-reference image, we parallelize this process using CPU multi-threading. As a result, all features on the non-reference images are tracked in a single pass, rather than many passes based on the total number of non-reference images, as done in the reference DfSM algorithm.

Bundle Adjustment. We use already optimized Ceres library with Huber loss function for the non-linear optimization [4,5]. The reduced number of features from the proposed Grided Point Tracking helps to reduce the whole execution time of the optimization procedure.

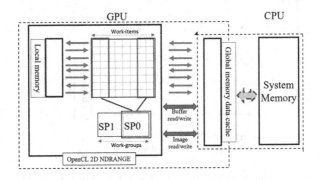

Fig. 3. A typical mobile device CPU-GPU architecture.

3.2 GPU Acceleration

Figure 3 shows a typical architecture of a mobile device. The GPU can be treated as an independent entity, and this is where the OpenCL operates. The data to be processed is transferred back and forth onto the GPU from the global cache. The Shader Processor (SP) is a GPU unit that executes the OpenCL kernels. Work-group is an OpenCL concept to arrange the SP, so that Work-items that belong to the same work-group are executed in parallel [2,15].

Reference-Undistort. To perform this operation with an OpenCL kernel function, we create $M \times N$ work-items using *clEnqueueNDRangeKernel*. Recall M and N are the number of image rows and columns respectively. We further partition these work-items into work-groups through empirical trial and test. These emprical tests ensure that we have the right work-group size in order to avoid register spilling that can worsen performance.

Inside the OpenCL kernel, we implement the iterative inverse mapping [22] using 12 iterations to remove the radial distortions. The distorted $\tilde{u}, \tilde{v}$-coordinate of $\tilde{p}_{i,j}$ are stacked as $M \times N \times 2$ input buffer using *clCreateBuffer*, where $\ldots \times 2$ specify the $\tilde{u}, \tilde{v}$-axes. Also, the camera parameters $\mathcal{K}$ and radial distortion k_1, k_2 are passed as input buffers. The $M \times N \times 2$ output buffer stores the outcome $p_{i,j}$ of the OpenCL kernel operation.

Dense Matching. The two main operations (homography transformation and cubic interpolation) were parallelized using a single OpenCL kernel. This helps to avoid unnecessary copy from/to the GPU in between the two operations, which naive approach will do. We take advantage of OpenCL capability to access local memory and temporarily store data inside the kernel.

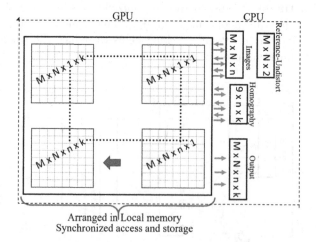

Fig. 4. Illustration of the dense matching OpenCL kernel operation. The homographic transformation and cubic interpolation process are performed together on the GPU.

The illustration of the kernel process is shown in Fig. 4. We create $n \times k$ work-items, where n, k are the number of images and depth-plane respectively. The input buffer to the GPU are (i) $M \times N \times n$ non-reference images, (ii) the undistorted $p_{i,j}$'s u, v-coordinate from Sect. 3.2, and (iii) $9 \times n \times k$ parameters of the homography transformation $\mathcal{H}_{ik}$.

The output buffer from the kernel operation is $M \times N \times n \times k$ in size. As the total number of specified work-item $n \times k$ does not have the same dimension as either the input buffer nor output buffer in Fig. 4, we are obliged to make some simple tricks and operations inside the OpenCL kernel to coordinate accessing of the data to and from the kernel.

The proposed acceleration is applied on non-reference RGB images and their corresponding edge detection images. The output buffer of the kernel operation is eventually used to generate the variance matching cost as in [8], followed by the Winner Takes All (WTA) strategy to extract the depth-map. These subsequent processes outside the OpenCL kernel (i.e variance cost and WTA) are performed using CPU multi-threading for speedup.

3.3   Other Acceleration

The reference-undistort operation is straightforward and easier than dense matching one. Although our dense matching approach provides faster kernel execution time than a naive implementation, it requires a big memory allocation for mobile devices. As a result, some device are expected to run out of memory when Full HD resolution with 10–15 images are used. This issue has motivated us to optimize our implementation further.

Memory Copying Prevention. Our implementation in Sect. 3.2 uses large copy to/from CPU operations, which leads to double allocation on CPU and GPU memory. Since CPU and GPU share the same memory for mobile devices, OpenCL can be used to eliminate this problem using the syntax below:

```
float* arr=static_cast<float*> (clEnqueueMapBuffer(queue,
... outputBuffer, CL_TRUE, CL_MAP_READ, 0,
... outputBufferSize, 0, nullptr, nullptr, &error));
```

As shown above, we allocate the data "*outputBuffer*" on the GPU using *clCreateBuffer*. This data can then be accessed from the CPU as float "*arr*" using mapping function *clEnqueueMapBuffer*. The resource allocation is eventually freed using *clEnqueueUnmapMemObject*.

Memory Optimization. Most mobile devices encounter "*out of memory*" issue as a result of large memory allocation in Sect. 3.2. In addition, a single maximum memory allocation for OpenCL on some devices can be significantly less than total available memory. For example, this problem was encountered on some mobile devices that have Adreno GPU.

We proposed to replace allocated 32-bit *float* in all our GPU implementation with an 8-bit integer *uint8*. This optimization does not necessarily bring extreme reduction in execution time since we must convert the output of the OpenCL kernel operation from *int* back to *float* for the remaining part of the algorithm on CPU. However, it makes it possible to free up memory space allocation on the mobile device, and thus avoid out of memory issue even with large image data ($\geq$15 images).

4   Experimental Results

To demonstrate the efficiency and practicality of the proposed implementation, we develop an interactive OpenCL demonstration for ANDROID mobile device. This application allows us to change various optimization parameters and thus ensure proper analysis of the proposed optimizations.

Figure 1 is a screen-shot of the implemented ANDROID application illustrating a reference image and its corresponding depth-map. The depth-map is generated using 10 non-reference frames from a portrait selfie. Two different mobile GPUs have been used for the experimental tests: (i) a Qualcomm Snapdragon chipset containing Adreno 540 GPU, and (ii) HiSilicon Kirin 970 chipset containing Mali-G72 MP12 GPU. Both devices have 4 GB RAM, 8 cores and support the OpenCL Embedded Profile for both CPU and GPU programming.

We execute the algorithm on the "selfie" acquisition using the two test ANDROID devices. The experimental outcome is summarized in Table 2. The execution times of the depth-map algorithm on mobile CPUs were about 30 s and 34 s, respectively. With the proposed CPU-GPU co-processing, we are able

Table 2. Speedup for CPU-GPU co-processing using the "selfie" image in Fig. 1.

Device	Stages	Processing time (s)	
		CPU-only	CPU-GPU w optimizations
Adreno 540	*I*- Read input frame sequence	0.44	0.41
	II- Feature Extraction	0.14	0.09
	III- Feature Tracking	0.62	0.05
	IV- Bundle Adjustment	0.24	0.17
	V- Reference-Undistort	**1.58**	**0.11**
	VI- Dense Matching	**25.53**	**6.38**
	VII- Depth Refinement	1.52	1.42
	Total:	*30.07*	*8.63*
Mali-G72 MP12	*I*- Read input frame sequence	0.51	0.47
	II- Feature Extraction	0.18	0.14
	III- Feature Tracking	1.22	0.09
	IV- Bundle Adjustment	0.45	0.32
	V- Reference-Undistort	**1.77**	**0.26**
	VI- Dense Matching	**27.74**	**9.99**
	VII- Depth Refinement	2.25	2.12
	Total:	*34.12*	*13.39*

to speed up both *Stage V: Refine-Undistort* and *Stage VI: Dense Matching* significantly by 14x and 3x respectively. The whole algorithm was improved 3x altogether on the final execution time.

4.1 Accuracy

We applied the exemplar DfSM algorithm [8] on sequence of "selfie" in Fig. 1 and "flower" acquisition in Fig. 5 respectively. Their output depth-maps are used as a baseline method to evaluate the deviation of our proposed bit optimizations in Sect. 3.3.

For evaluation purposes, we use the Root Mean Square Error (RMSE) that is evaluated on 10 depth-maps generated for each acquisition (selfie and Flower). Each depth-map is generated by randomly changing the reference frame in the video acquisition. The experimental outcome is shown in Table 3.

Table 3. Numerical comparison of the bit optimizations using 10 depth-maps. The generated depth-map of the exemplar DfSM algorithm [8] is used as the baseline method.

Acquisition	Method	RMSE
Selfie	*8-bit*	3.145
	32-bit	2.278
Flower	*8-bit*	4.145
	32-bit	6.091

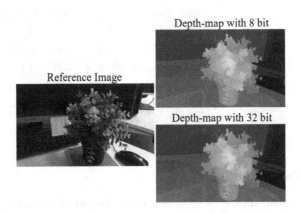

Fig. 5. Subjective visual comparison between depth-maps generated with 8-bit and 32-bit optimizations.

Using the RMSE error, the generated depth-map with 8-bit optimization is very close to the 32-bit ones and they are both not far from the ground-truth using exemplar DfSM [8]. In addition, we also show a visual comparison between the quality of the depth-map with the 8 and 32 bit optimizations in Fig. 5. There seems to be minimal difference in the visual quality.

Table 4. The total execution time for "flower" video acquisition, with OpenCL kernels running on Adreno 540 GPU. Scaling 1/4 signifies that the quarter of the full image resolution is used for the dense matching part of the whole algorithm.

Index	Nb. images	Scaling	CPU-only			CPU-GPU co-processing		
			w/o optimizations (s)			w optimizations (s)		
			Depth planes			Depth planes		
			16	32	64	16	32	64
1	2	1/4	2.671	3.085	3.946	0.887	1.000	1.218
2		1/2	4.355	6.023	9.239	1.803	2.376	3.365
3	10	1/4	5.627	7.515	11.721	2.392	2.446	3.157
4		1/2	**10.538**	**17.029**	**30.354**	**3.829**	**4.895**	**9.089**

Table 5. The total execution time for "flower" video acquisition, with OpenCL kernels running on Mali-G72 MP12 GPU. Scaling 1/4 signifies that the quarter of the full image resolution is used for the dense matching part of the whole algorithm.

Index	Nb. images	Scaling	CPU-only			CPU-GPU co-processing		
			w/o optimizations (s)			w optimizations (s)		
			Depth planes			Depth planes		
			16	32	64	16	32	64
1	2	1/4	3.027	3.566	4.48	1.954	1.995	2.538
2		1/2	4.815	6.353	10.265	2.538	4.109	5.267
3	10	1/4	6.526	8.295	12.297	4.058	3.639	6.483
4		1/2	**12.306**	**19.465**	**34.527**	**7.829**	**9.425**	**12.137**

4.2   Execution Time Validation

To further demonstrate the effectiveness of our proposed optimization schemes, the speedup gained from the proposed optimization strategies are summarized in Tables 4 and 5. These tests have been done on "flower" sequence shown in Fig. 5. We use various configuration options which can be seen on the table. The third column in the figure titled "Scaling" is only pertaining to *Dense Matching*. The scaling value 1/2 signifies that the full resolution image has been reduced with half factor under the dense matching. As soon as the dense matching algorithm is finalized, the generated depth-map image is upscale back to the original size.

In Tables 4 and 5, indexes 4 correspond to the execution time of the algorithm using 10 images, and 1/2 scaling. Our optimized implementation using CPU-GPU co-processing (9.089 s) provides about 3x acceleration over the CPU-only version (30.354 s). In addition, our implementation provides highest improvement on Qualcomm device when compared to HiSilicon one. There is a restriction on the total size that the OpenCL output buffer can handle using some Qualcomm device, and can affect effective working of the acceleration on some of their devices. Thanks to the memory optimization procedure in Sect. 3.3, one is able run the proposed acceleration on all mobile devices.

5 Conclusion

This paper presents a simple acceleration of the popular Depth from Small Motion algorithm for mobile devices using CPU-GPU co-processing. We have focused mostly on the GPU implementation part that brings significant improvement. However for the CPU part, we propose a grided feature extraction technique which extract fewer but significant feature points which ultimately speeds up the execution time. The experimental results on a real mobile platform powered by a Snapdragon Adreno and HiSilicon Mali show that by offloading the core computations to mobile GPU the processing time can be significantly reduced 3x, as compared to a well optimized multi-threaded CPU-only version.

As a future work, we plan to experiment with power consumption and make more test with other mobile platforms. There is further room for improvement on the GPU side especially in the depth refinement stage of the algorithm and it should be further explored.

References

1. Koenderink, J.J., Van Doorn, A.J.: Affine structure from motion. J. Opt. Soc. Am. A **8**(2), 377–385 (1991)
2. Munshi, A., Gaster, B., Mattson, T.G., Fung, J., Ginsburg, D.: OpenCL Programming Guide, 1st edn. Addison-Wesley Professional, Boston (2011)
3. Khronos Group: The OpenCL Specification v2.1 (2017). https://www.khronos.org/opencl
4. Huber, P.J.: Robust estimation of a location parameter. In: Kotz, S., Johnson, N.L. (eds.) Breakthroughs in Statistics: Methodology and Distribution. SSS, pp. 492–518. Springer, New York (1992). https://doi.org/10.1007/978-1-4612-4380-9_35
5. Agarwal, S., Mierle, K., et al.: Ceres Solver (2012). http://ceres-solver.org
6. Yu, F., Gallup, D.: 3D reconstruction from accidental motion. In: IEEE Conference on Computer Vision and Pattern Recognition, CVPR 2014, pp. 3986–3993 (2014)
7. Joshi, N., Zitnick, L.: Micro-baseline stereo. Microsoft Research Technical report, MSR-TR-2014-73, May 2014
8. Ha, H., Im, S., Park, J., Jeon, H.-G., Kweon, I.-S.: High-quality depth from uncalibrated small motion clip. In: IEEE Conference on Computer Vision and Pattern Recognition, CVPR 2016, pp. 5413–5421 (2016)

9. Schänberger, J.L., Frahm, J.: Structure-from-motion revisited. In: IEEE Conference on Computer Vision and Pattern Recognition (CVPR), pp. 4104–4113 (2016)
10. Corcoran, P., Javidnia, H.: Accurate depth map estimation from small motions. In: IEEE International Conference on Computer Vision Workshops (ICCVW), pp. 2453–2461 (2017)
11. Ham, C., Chang, M., Lucey, S., Singh, S.: Monocular depth from small motion video accelerated. In: International Conference on 3D Vision (3DV), pp. 575–583 (2017)
12. Lopez, M., Nykänen, H., Hannuksela, J., Silven, O., Vehvilainen, M.: Accelerating image recognition on mobile devices using GPGPU. In: Proceedings of the SPIE, pp. 7872–7882 (2011)
13. Rister, B., Wang, G., Wu, M., Cavallaro, J.R.: A fast and efficient sift detector using the mobile GPU. In: IEEE International Conference on Acoustics, Speech and Signal Processing, pp. 2674–2678 (2013)
14. Backes, L., Rico, A., Franke, B.: Experiences in speeding up computer vision applications on mobile computing platforms. In: International Conference on Embedded Computer Systems: Architectures, Modeling, and Simulation (SAMOS), pp. 1–8 (2015)
15. Wang, H., Yun, J., Bourd, A.: OpenCL optimization and best practices for Qualcomm adreno GPUs. In: Proceedings of the International Workshop on OpenCL, IWOCL 2018, pp. 16:1–16:8 (2018)
16. Harris, C., Stephens, M.: A combined corner and edge detector. In: Proceedings of the 4th Alvey Vision Conference, pp. 147–151 (1988)
17. Lucas, B.D., Kanade, T.: An iterative image registration technique with an application to stereo vision. In: Proceedings of the 7th International Joint Conference on Artificial Intelligence, IJCAI 1981, vol. 2, pp. 674–679 (1981)
18. Shi, J., Tomasi, C.: Good features to track. In: Proceedings of IEEE Conference on Computer Vision and Pattern Recognition, pp. 593–600 (1994)
19. Hartley, R., Zisserman, A.: Multiple View Geometry in Computer Vision, 2nd edn. Cambridge University Press, New York (2003)
20. Triggs, B., McLauchlan, P.F., Hartley, R.I., Fitzgibbon, A.W.: Bundle adjustment—a modern synthesis. In: Triggs, B., Zisserman, A., Szeliski, R. (eds.) IWVA 1999. LNCS, vol. 1883, pp. 298–372. Springer, Heidelberg (2000). https://doi.org/10.1007/3-540-44480-7_21
21. Zhang, Z.: A flexible new technique for camera calibration. IEEE Trans. Pattern Anal. Mach. Intell. **22**(11), 1330–1334 (2000)
22. Heikkila, J., Silven, O.: A four-step camera calibration procedure with implicit image correction. In: Proceedings of the 1997 Conference on Computer Vision and Pattern Recognition (CVPR 1997), pp. 1106–1112 (1997)
23. Collins, R.T.: A space-sweep approach to true multi-image matching. In: Proceedings of IEEE Computer Society Conference on Computer Vision and Pattern Recognition, pp. 358–363 (1996)

Image Segmentation

Skin Lesion Segmentation Ensemble
with Diverse Training Strategies

Laura Canalini, Federico Pollastri, Federico Bolelli[(✉)], Michele Cancilla,
Stefano Allegretti, and Costantino Grana

Dipartimento di Ingegneria "Enzo Ferrari",
Università degli Studi di Modena e Reggio Emilia,
Via Vivarelli 10, 41125 Modena, MO, Italy
{laura.canalini,federico.pollastri,federico.bolelli,michele.cancilla,
stefano.allegretti,costantino.grana}@unimore.it

Abstract. This paper presents a novel strategy to perform skin lesion
segmentation from dermoscopic images. We design an effective segmentation pipeline, and explore several pre-training methods to initialize
the features extractor, highlighting how different procedures lead the
Convolutional Neural Network (CNN) to focus on different features. An
encoder-decoder segmentation CNN is employed to take advantage of
each pre-trained features extractor. Experimental results reveal how multiple initialization strategies can be exploited, by means of an ensemble
method, to obtain state-of-the-art skin lesion segmentation accuracy.

Keywords: Deep learning · Convolutional Neural Networks ·
Transfer learning · Skin lesion segmentation

1 Introduction

Since 2016, the International Skin Imaging Collaboration (ISIC) has been gathering public datasets (Fig. 1) and hosting multiple challenges and workshops, stressing the relevance of skin lesion analysis [9]. Many efforts have been given in order
to aid professional dermatologists in the detection of malignant melanoma which,
being the most dangerous type of skin cancer, holds a substantial death rate.

Skin lesion segmentation is a fundamental step in the automated melanoma
detection process, defined as the recognition of the set of pixels that constitute
the skin lesion within the image. This task can be especially troublesome due to
the vast variety of skin characteristics among different people, and the subjec-
tivity of the definition of skin lesion borders. State-of-the-art approaches on this
field have proved once again the effectiveness of deep learning algorithms, as a
matter of fact, Convolutional Neural Networks (CNNs) are currently the cornerstone of medical images analysis. Segmentation CNNs are able to extract features
through a contracting path and exploit them to generate a segmentation mask
across the expanding path; the size of feature maps decreases progressively in the
former, whereas in the latter it increases back to the input resolution thanks to

© Springer Nature Switzerland AG 2019
M. Vento and G. Percannella (Eds.): CAIP 2019, LNCS 11678, pp. 89–101, 2019.
https://doi.org/10.1007/978-3-030-29888-3_8

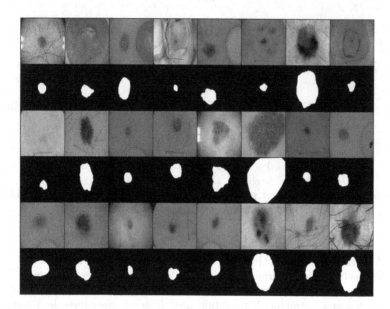

Fig. 1. Samples from the ISIC dataset: dermoscopic skin images coupled with their ground truth segmentation masks.

up-sampling operators and fractionally-strided convolutions, thus producing an encoder-decoder architecture. U-Net [29] is a noteworthy example of such kind of neural networks, it is characterized by an equal number of layers in the two distinct paths and by skip connections, which have the purpose of concatenating features between the two distinct sections.

Unfortunately, in order to be trained, deep learning algorithms require huge amounts of data, which are often hard to obtain and particularly expensive to annotate, especially in medical fields. The need for a large annotated medical imaging dataset can be mitigated by pre-training neural networks with an already existing collection of natural images, like ImageNet [10]. Indeed, the first convolutional layers of every CNN learn to recognize simple elements like lines and colors, making them useful across different tasks and datasets [23]. Learning features from wider datasets and re-using them in different tasks can be seen as a form of transfer learning. The choice of the dataset employed to learn low-level features can introduce biases towards certain features and characteristics, and this should be taken into account especially when dealing with medical imaging. For example, CNNs trained using ImageNet are strongly biased in recognizing textures rather than shapes [13].

In this work, we address the problem of skin lesion image segmentation taking into account the trade-off between training a model from scratch and employing images of a very different nature through transfer learning. In particular, we design a CNN-based ensemble model that, exploiting different pre-training strategies, obtains the state-of-the-art performance on skin lesion segmentation when trained on the ISIC skin lesions dataset and on synthetically generated samples.

The rest of the paper is organized as follows. In Sect. 2 relevant proposals on image segmentation are summed up. Section 3 describes the pre-training strategies adopted to push the effectiveness of the proposed ensemble strategy, which is then described in Sect. 4. In Sect. 5 the performance of our proposal are compared with state-of-the-art model, highlighting its validity. Finally, Sect. 6 draws some conclusions.

2 Related Work

In the last decades, a lot of effort has been devoted to solving the problem of automated skin lesion segmentation, promoting the development of different approaches: histogram thresholding [26,39], edge-based [8,30], region-merging [12,31], and supervised learning [11]. Nevertheless, CNNs are now one of the most powerful tools in machine learning and computer vision. They are able to learn features directly from input image data, with no need of hand-crafted features. In a typical classification task a convolutional network produces a single label as output. However, in other visual tasks such as segmentation [17,36], a pixel-wise output information is required, having a critical point in the mapping of low resolution features into input resolution.

In 2015, Ronneberger *et al.* proposed the so called U-Net [29], which consists of a contracting encoder network that extracts high resolution features from the input image and followed by an expanding decoder model to produce a full-resolution segmentation. This model employs skip connections between the downsampling and upsampling path, applying a concatenation operator in order to provide coarse contextual information when upsampling.

In DeepLabv1 [6], atrous convolutions were introduced. Instead of repeatedly reducing the dimension of feature maps, each convolutional filter of the network is upsampled in size and filled with zeroes in between filter values. This allows to avoid the use of pooling operations, which are responsible for the spatial resolution reduction, and thus cause a lower output segmentation quality. DeepLabv3+ [7] is a state-of-the-art segmentation CNN. It employs atrous convolutions, residual blocks [16], and a decoder module to refine the segmentation results.

In 2017, Mask R-CNN [15] was able to surpass other instance segmentation methods. This approach combines object detection, which aims to classify and localize individual objects using a bounding box, and semantic segmentation, which has the goal of classifying each pixel given a fixed set of classes. This strategy extends Faster R-CNN [14], adding a Fully Convolutional Network (FCN) to predict segmentation masks for each Region of Interest (RoI) in a pixel-to-pixel fashion.

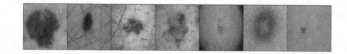

Fig. 2. One sample of each class from the third ISIC challenge task. From left to right: Melanoma, Melanocytic nevus, Basal cell carcinoma, Actinic keratosis, Benign keratosis, Dermatofibroma, and Vascular lesion.

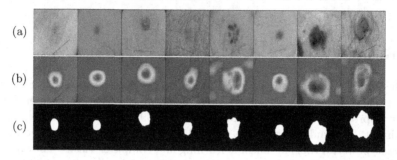

Fig. 3. Samples from the 2017 ISIC validation set (a), with corresponding Grad-Cam heatmaps (b) and segmentation masks (c).

3 Learning to Extract Features

In order to design an ensemble of CNNs that can effectively segment skin lesion images, we select DeepLabv3+ [7] with a ResNet-101 [16] backbone as the baseline architecture, and explore several pre-training strategies. This Section discloses three different pre-training methods employed to obtain three different initializations of ResNet-101, the features extractor for our segmentation neural network.

3.1 ISIC Task 3

The International Skin Imaging Collaboration, in 2018, hosted a challenge split in three tasks: lesion segmentation, lesion attribute detection and disease classification. A public dataset of 10 015 dermoscopic images was divided by experts into 7 different classes, illustrated in Fig. 2. In the interests of obtaining a features extractor effective on dermoscopic images, we train ResNet-101 to correctly classify skin lesion images in the 7 original classes, taking advantage of the 10 015 annotated samples from the ISIC dataset [34]. The network is trained for 15 epochs, using a weighted Cross-Entropy Loss, an initial learning rate of 0.0001, and the Adam optimizer [20]. Figure 3 provides a useful visualization of which sections of the input image mostly affect the hidden representation that the network obtains after the last convolutional layer, right before employing the fully-connected layers designed for classification. The heatmaps obtained by applying the Grad-Cam technique [32], suggest that our features extractor implicitly learns to coarsely detect the skin lesion.

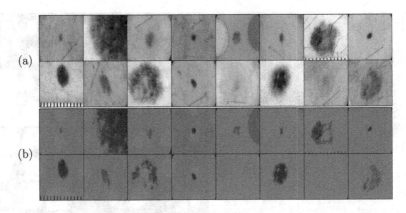

Fig. 4. Samples from the 2017 ISIC validation set (a) and the corresponding autoencoder output (b).

3.2 Autoencoder

Data annotation for the image segmentation task is extremely expensive, it requires an expert dermatologist to perform an extremely time consuming and uninspiring job. Therefore, we try to exploit many dermoscopic images that were never given manual annotation through a form of unsupervised learning. Taking advantage of the encoder-decoder architecture of DeepLabv3+, an autoencoder is built in order to obtain a version of ResNet able to map skin lesion images to a meaningful hidden representation. The model of our autoencoder is identical to DeepLabv3+ [7], with 3 output classes (RGB channels). It is trained using, again, the 10 015 images from the ISIC classification task for 10 epochs, employing the mean squared error loss. The learning rate is initially set to 0.0001 and then influenced by the Adam optimizer [20]. Figure 4 shows that the autoencoder struggles to recreate the original background skin color and texture, but promptly generates a coherent lesion in the correct position, which is the most important element for our final goal.

3.3 GAN

Generative Adversarial Networks (GANs) are often used to create unlabeled examples, which cannot be directly employed for the training of a supervised algorithm [38]. Following the approach introduced in [27, 28], we improve the role of GANs in the training process by designing an architecture able to generate both the skin lesion image and its segmentation mask, making it extremely easy to exploit new synthetic images as additional training data. We modify the GAN proposed by Karras *et al.* [19] in order to feed it 4-channels images: the first three channels are the R, G and B components and the fourth one is the binary segmentation mask. Instead of generating a fixed number of samples, the generator is required to provide new couples image-mask for each training batch. An example of the generated images is shown in Fig. 5.

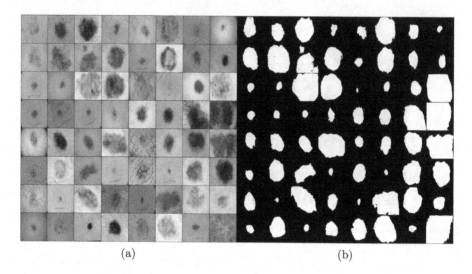

(a)   (b)

Fig. 5. GAN-generated skin lesion samples (a) and their segmentation masks (b).

The GAN is trained to generate 256×256 images and segmentation masks. Most images present realistic details, like a well delivered presence of hair, black corners representing real camera characteristics, and pen marks. Moreover, the generative model produces segmentation masks that look very coherent with the respective generated images.

4   Learning to Segment Skin Lesions

To take advantage of the pre-trained backbones, DeepLabv3+ is fine-tuned following the training protocol outlined in [7]. Input images are resized to 513×513 pixels, the learning rate is initially set to 0.007 and then multiplied by $(1 - \frac{iter}{max\_iter})^{0.9}$, following the poly policy [25]. The output stride is fixed to 16, the network is trained for 60 epochs, and the early stopping strategy is employed. During the whole fine-tuning process, the learning rate is multiplied by a factor of 10 for layers outside of ResNet-101, in order to take full advantage of the pre-training process applied to the features extractor. Data augmentation is performed by randomly rotating, flipping, shifting, shearing and scaling input images, and by changing the color contrasts.

To enhance the fine-tuning process, the official 2017 training set of 2 000 images is enlarged using several dermoscopic images gathered from the public ISIC archive. In order to remove potentially disadvantageous samples, every supplementary image is first fed to a state-of-the art segmentation CNN. Images segmented with an Intersection over Union lower than 0.60 are considered incorrect and thus removed from further analysis. To build the final training set, we select the 1 500 dermoscopic images that offer a ground truth segmentation mask

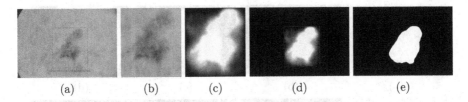

(a)   (b)   (c)   (d)   (e)

Fig. 6. Detection-Segmentation Pipeline: sample image from the 2017 ISIC test set with its predicted bounding box overlapped (a), the cropped and resized sample (b), the output of the ensemble method (c) that is rescaled to the original size (d) and the final segmentation mask (e).

where the skin lesion fills at least the 10% of the image. We thus obtain a 3 500 images training set.

4.1 Detection-Segmentation Pipeline

In order to encourage the network to focus on the correct section of input images, we remove redundant background from the input samples. During training, every ground truth segmentation mask is exploited to obtain the bounding box containing the skin lesion, and every dermoscopic image is cropped accordingly (Fig. 6a and b). Dur-

Table 1. Detection-segmentation pipelines comparison.

Pipeline strategy	Validation IoU
None	0.800
Crop	0.845
4-channels	0.848

ing inference, input samples are cropped in accordance with bounding boxes obtained through Mask R-CNN [15], pre-trained on the COCO dataset [24] and then fine-tuned on the 2017 ISIC original training set. Mask R-CNN produces bounding boxes with an Intersection over Union of 0.886 on the 2017 public test set. This pipeline, illustrated in Fig. 6, improves the Intersection over Union accuracy of the segmentation framework by 0.045. However, cropping images by means of an object detection network can erase meaningful portions of the segmentation CNN input, propagating the error from the first network to the next one. To tackle this drawback, bounding boxes can be directly supplied to the segmentation CNN, without forcing it to discard the sections of the input image classified as background by the detection tool. We thus feed the segmentation network with a 4-channels input: R, G, B, and the skin lesion bounding box in the form of a binary mask, where white pixels represent the foreground and black pixels represent the background. Improvements delivered by adding an object detection network to the process are shown in Table 1.

4.2 The Ensemble Method

As observed by Krogh et al. [21] and Chandra et al. [5], a key point on ensemble learning is that the hypotheses should be as accurate and as diverse as possible.

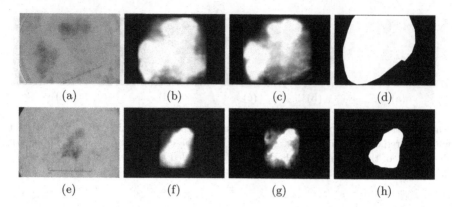

(a) (b) (c) (d)

(e) (f) (g) (h)

Fig. 7. Examples of model outputs when using different pre-trained feature extractors. (a) and (e) are the original images, (b) and (f) are the outputs when using a features extractor pre-trained with ImageNet, (c) and (g) are the outputs of the CNNs that exploit the features extractor described in Sect. 3.2. Finally, (d) and (h) represent the ground truth.

In our work, such properties were prompted by applying different strategies. Even though the performance of the various CNNs are comparable, different networks focus on different features, greatly increasing the effectiveness of the ensemble. Figure 7 displays how the features extractor pre-trained to build the autoencoder described in Sect. 3.2, seems to give much importance to darker shades of colours, whereas the CNN that employs the features extractor formerly used to classify natural images from ImageNet, produces segmentation masks less attentive to this particular feature, focusing on higher level structures instead.

For each pixel, its probability of being part of the skin lesion is obtained as the mean value across the selected CNNs. The output is then binarized with a dual-threshold method. A high threshold (0.80) is followed by blob analysis [3,4] and the biggest object center is assumed to be the tumor center. Afterwards, a lower threshold (0.40) is applied and the final segmentation mask is given by the region which contains the tumor center. Whenever the first high threshold does not yield any object, we only apply the second one and keep its result as segmentation mask.

5 Experimental Results

Experimental results of the proposed networks are summed up in Table 2. The first column shows the detection-segmentation pipeline of each CNN. It is important to notice that, when using the 4-channels strategy described in Sect. 4.1, the first layer of the features extractor is required to deal with four channels instead of three, and thus to be re-trained from scratch. Since every network described in Sect. 3 was pre-trained using dermoscopic images, we fine-tune them using the cropping strategy to avoid a random re-initialization of the first layer of filters.

Table 2. Analysis of the Neural Networks trained for the task. IoU is the Intersection over Union, TIoU is the Threshold Intersection over Union.

Pipeline strategy	Loss	Pre-training	Validation IoU	Validation TIoU	Test IoU	Test TIoU
Crop	Cross-Entropy	Classes	0.851	0.819	0.841	0.809
	Cross-Entropy	AE	0.856	0.837	0.838	0.810
	Cross-Entropy	GAN	0.854	0.834	0.838	0.814
	Tanimoto	Classes	0.855	0.832	**0.845**	0.818
	Tanimoto	AE	0.857	0.838	0.844	0.816
	Tanimoto	GAN	0.850	0.831	0.841	0.817
4-channels	Cross-Entropy	None	0.847	0.816	0.834	0.805
	Cross-Entropy	ImageNet	0.848	0.823	0.837	0.808
	Tanimoto	None	0.846	0.819	0.831	0.802
	Tanimoto	ImageNet	**0.859**	**0.840**	**0.845**	**0.819**

In order to further increase the diversity between predicted masks, and hence the effectiveness of the ensemble architecture, we employ two different loss functions during training (second column of Table 2): the cross-entropy loss[1] in its binary form and the Tanimoto distance defined as

$$L = 1 - \frac{\sum\limits_{i,j} t_{ij} p_{ij}}{\sum\limits_{i,j} t_{ij}^2 + \sum\limits_{i,j} p_{ij}^2 - \sum\limits_{i,j} t_{ij} p_{ij}} \qquad (1)$$

where t_{ij} is the target value of the pixel at coordinates (i, j), and p_{ij} is the real output. Note that t_{ij} is either 0 or 1, while p_{ij} is a real number in range $[0, 1]$.

The third column of Table 2 presents the pre-training procedure applied to each network. Values *Classes*, *AE*, and *GAN* refer to Sects. 3.1, 3.2, and 3.3 respectively. The value *None* represents a network trained from scratch, included for comparison. The last four columns of the Table present the accuracy of each network, on both the validation set and the test set from the ISIC 2017 challenge. IoU stands for Intersection over Union, which is the official evaluation metric of the 2017 ISIC challenge. TIoU means Threshold Intersection over Union, an adaptation of Intersection over Union that reflects the number of images in which automated segmentation fails, by giving a score of 0 to images segmented with an Intersection over Union lower than 0.65. Both of the metrics show similar results when testing different initialization methods, but stress the importance of employing a pre-trained feature extractor: CNNs trained from scratch (value *None* in the third column) show the worst results. Table 3 displays the results obtained by merging the output of resulting CNNs through the ensemble strategy described in Sect. 4.2. The proposed pipeline clearly outperforms state-of-the-art segmentation algorithms when applied on skin lesions.

---

[1] Cross-Entropy is the standard loss function employed when training DeepLab [6].

Table 3. Performance of the proposed method compared to the state-of-the-art. All the models have been trained and tested on the 2017 ISIC dataset. Reimplemented/retrained models are identified by *. IoU is the Intersection over Union, TIoU is the Threshold Intersection over Union.

Method	Test IoU	Test TIoU
Ours (ensemble)	**0.850**	0.827
SegAN [35]	0.785	—
GAN Augmented [27]	0.781	—
DCL-PSI [2]	0.777	—
DeepLabv3+* [7]	0.769	—
(RE)-DS-U-ResnetFCN34 [22]	0.772	—
SegNet* [1]	0.767	—
Challenge winners [37]	0.765	—
Tiramisu* [18]	0.765	—
U-Net* [29]	0.740	—

6 Conclusion

With this paper, we tackled the problem of skin lesion segmentation by a different perspective, introducing a novel ensemble strategy to improve state-of-the-art results. We presented multiple ways to initialize a features extractor without the need to employ biases-inducing datasets. The designed segmentation pipeline takes advantage of the multiple pre-training methods, improving the overall performance. Experimental results on the ISIC 2017 dataset show the effectiveness of our approach on skin lesion segmentation. The source code of the proposed model is available in [33].

Acknowledgments. This project has received funding from the European Union's Horizon 2020 research and innovation programme under grant agreement No. 825111, DeepHealth Project.

References

1. Badrinarayanan, V., Kendall, A., Cipolla, R.: SegNet: a deep convolutional encoder-decoder architecture for image segmentation. IEEE Trans. Pattern Anal. Mach. Intell. **39**(12), 2481–2495 (2017)
2. Bi, L., Kim, J., Ahn, E., Kumar, A., Feng, D., Fulham, M.: Step-wise integration of deep class-specific learning for dermoscopic image segmentation. Pattern Recogn. **85**, 78–89 (2019)
3. Bolelli, F., Baraldi, L., Cancilla, M., Grana, C.: Connected components labeling on DRAGs. In: International Conference on Pattern Recognition (2018)

4. Bolelli, F., Cancilla, M., Grana, C.: Two more strategies to speed up connected components labeling algorithms. In: Battiato, S., Gallo, G., Schettini, R., Stanco, F. (eds.) ICIAP 2017. LNCS, vol. 10485, pp. 48–58. Springer, Cham (2017). https:// doi.org/10.1007/978-3-319-68548-9_5

5. Chandra, A., Yao, X.: Evolving hybrid ensembles of learning machines for better generalisation. Neurocomputing **69**(7–9), 686–700 (2006)

6. Chen, L.C., Papandreou, G., Kokkinos, I., Murphy, K., Yuille, A.L.: Semantic image segmentation with deep convolutional nets and fully connected CRFs. arXiv preprint arXiv:1412.7062 (2014)

7. Chen, L.-C., Zhu, Y., Papandreou, G., Schroff, F., Adam, H.: Encoder-decoder with atrous separable convolution for semantic image segmentation. In: Ferrari, V., Hebert, M., Sminchisescu, C., Weiss, Y. (eds.) ECCV 2018. LNCS, vol. 11211, pp. 833–851. Springer, Cham (2018). https://doi.org/10.1007/978-3-030-01234-2_49

8. Chung, D.H., Sapiro, G.: Segmenting skin lesions with partial-differential-equations-based image processing algorithms. IEEE Trans. Med. Imaging **19**(7), 763–767 (2000)

9. Codella, N., Gutman, D., Celebi, M., et al.: Skin lesion analysis toward melanoma detection: a challenge at the 2017 international symposium on biomedical imaging (ISBI), hosted by the international skin imaging collaboration (ISIC). In: 2018 IEEE 15th International Symposium on Biomedical Imaging (ISBI 2018), pp. 168–172 (2018)

10. Deng, J., Dong, W., Socher, R., Li, L.J., Li, K., Fei-Fei, L.: ImageNet: a large-scale hierarchical image database. In: 2009 IEEE Conference on Computer Vision and Pattern Recognition, pp. 248–255. IEEE (2009)

11. Ganster, H., Pinz, P., Rohrer, R., et al.: Automated melanoma recognition. IEEE Trans. Med. Imaging **20**(3), 233–239 (2001)

12. Gao, J., Zhang, J., Fleming, M.G.: A novel multiresolution color image segmentation technique and its application to dermatoscopic image segmentation. In: Proceedings 2000 International Conference on Image Processing, vol. 3, pp. 408–411. IEEE (2000)

13. Geirhos, R., Rubisch, P., Michaelis, C., Bethge, M., Wichmann, F.A., Brendel, W.: ImageNet-trained CNNs are biased towards texture; increasing shape bias improves accuracy and robustness. arXiv preprint arXiv:1811.12231 (2018)

14. Girshick, R.: Fast R-CNN. In: Proceedings of the IEEE International Conference on Computer Vision, pp. 1440–1448 (2015)

15. He, K., Gkioxari, G., Dollár, P., Girshick, R.: Mask R-CNN. In: Proceedings of the IEEE International Conference on Computer Vision, pp. 2961–2969 (2017)

16. He, K., Zhang, X., Ren, S., Sun, J.: Deep residual learning for image recognition. In: Proceedings of the IEEE Conference on Computer Vision and Pattern Recognition, pp. 770–778 (2016)

17. Jafari, M.H., Nasr-Esfahani, E., Karimi, N., Soroushmehr, S.M.R., Samavi, S., Najarian, K.: Extraction of skin lesions from non-dermoscopic images for surgical excision of melanoma. Int. J. Comput. Assist. Radiol. Surg. **12**(6), 1021–1030 (2017)

18. Jégou, S., Drozdzal, M., Vazquez, D., Romero, A., Bengio, Y.: The one hundred layers tiramisu: fully convolutional DenseNets for semantic segmentation. In: Proceedings of the IEEE Conference on Computer Vision and Pattern Recognition Workshops, pp. 11–19 (2017)

19. Karras, T., Aila, T., Laine, S., Lehtinen, J.: Progressive growing of GANs for improved quality, stability, and variation. In: International Conference on Learning Representations (2018)

20. Kingma, D.P., Ba, J.: Adam: a method for stochastic optimization. arXiv preprint arXiv:1412.6980 (2014)
21. Krogh, A., Vedelsby, J.: Neural network ensembles, cross validation, and active learning. In: Advances in Neural Information Processing Systems, pp. 231–238 (1995)
22. Li, X., Yu, L., Fu, C.-W., Heng, P.-A.: Deeply supervised rotation equivariant network for lesion segmentation in dermoscopy images. In: Stoyanov, D., et al. (eds.) CARE/CLIP/OR 2.0/ISIC -2018. LNCS, vol. 11041, pp. 235–243. Springer, Cham (2018). https://doi.org/10.1007/978-3-030-01201-4_25
23. Li, Y., Yosinski, J., Clune, J., Lipson, H., Hopcroft, J.E.: convergent learning: do different neural networks learn the same representations? In: FE@ NIPS, pp. 196–212 (2015)
24. Lin, T.-Y., et al.: Microsoft COCO: common objects in context. In: Fleet, D., Pajdla, T., Schiele, B., Tuytelaars, T. (eds.) ECCV 2014. LNCS, vol. 8693, pp. 740–755. Springer, Cham (2014). https://doi.org/10.1007/978-3-319-10602-1_48
25. Liu, W., Rabinovich, A., Berg, A.C.: ParseNet: looking wider to see better. arXiv preprint arXiv:1506.04579 (2015)
26. Pellacani, G., Grana, C., Seidenari, S.: Algorithmic reproduction of asymmetry and border cut-off parameters according to the abcd rule for dermoscopy. J. Eur. Acad. Dermatol. Venereol. **20**(10), 1214–1219 (2006)
27. Pollastri, F., Bolelli, F., Grana, C.: Improving Skin lesion segmentation with generative adversarial networks. In: 31st International Symposium on Computer-Based Medical Systems (2018)
28. Pollastri, F., Bolelli, F., Paredes, R., Grana, C.: Augmenting data with GANs to segment melanoma skin lesions. In: Multimed. Tools Appl. J. MTAP, 1–8 (2019)
29. Ronneberger, O., Fischer, P., Brox, T.: U-Net: convolutional networks for biomedical image segmentation. In: Navab, N., Hornegger, J., Wells, W.M., Frangi, A.F. (eds.) MICCAI 2015. LNCS, vol. 9351, pp. 234–241. Springer, Cham (2015). https://doi.org/10.1007/978-3-319-24574-4_28
30. Rubegni, P., Ferrari, A., Cevenini, G., et al.: Differentiation between pigmented Spitz naevus and melanoma by digital dermoscopy and stepwise logistic discriminant analysis. Melanoma Res. **11**(1), 37–44 (2001)
31. Schmid, P.: Lesion detection in dermatoscopic images using anisotropic diffusion and morphological flooding. In: Proceedings 1999 International Conference on Image Processing, vol. 3, pp. 449–453. IEEE (1999)
32. Selvaraju, R.R., Cogswell, M., Das, A., et al.: Grad-CAM: visual explanations from deep networks via gradient-based localization. In: Proceedings of the IEEE International Conference on Computer Vision, pp. 618–626 (2017)
33. Source Code of the Proposed Model. https://github.com/PollastriFederico/skin_lesion_segmentation_ensemble. Accessed 21 July 2019
34. Tschandl, P., Rosendahl, C., Kittler, H.: The HAM10000 dataset, a large collection of multi-source dermatoscopic images of common pigmented skin lesions. Sci. Data **5**, 180161 (2018). https://doi.org/10.1038/sdata.2018.161
35. Xue, Y., Xu, T., Huang, X.: Adversarial learning with multi-scale loss for skin lesion segmentation. In: 2018 IEEE 15th International Symposium on Biomedical Imaging (ISBI 2018), pp. 859–863. IEEE (2018)
36. Yu, L., Chen, H., Dou, Q., Qin, J., Heng, P.A.: Automated melanoma recognition in dermoscopy images via very deep residual networks. IEEE Trans. Med. Imaging **36**(4), 994–1004 (2017)
37. Yuan, Y., Chao, M., Lo, Y.C.: Automatic skin lesion segmentation with fully convolutional-deconvolutional networks. arXiv preprint arXiv:1703.05165 (2017)

38. Zheng, Z., Zheng, L., Yang, Y.: Unlabeled samples generated by GAN improve the person re-identification baseline in vitro. arXiv preprint arXiv:1701.07717 (2017)
39. Zortea, M., Flores, E., Scharcanski, J.: A simple weighted thresholding method for the segmentation of pigmented skin lesions in macroscopic images. Pattern Recogn. **64**, 92–104 (2017)

Hough Based Evolutions for Enhancing Structures in 3D Electron Microscopy

Kireeti Bodduna[1,2,3(✉)], Joachim Weickert[1], and Achilleas S. Frangakis[2]

[1] Mathematical Image Analysis Group,
Faculty of Mathematics and Computer Science, Saarland University,
66041 Saarbrücken, Germany
{bodduna,weickert}@mia.uni-saarland.de

[2] Electron Microscopy Group, Institute of Biophysics,
Johann Wolfgang Goethe University Frankfurt, 60438 Frankfurt am Main, Germany
{bodduna,achilleas.frangakis}@biophysik.org

[3] Saarbrücken Graduate School of Computer Science, Saarland University,
66041 Saarbrücken, Germany

Abstract. Connecting interrupted line-like structures is a frequent problem in image processing. Here we focus on the specific needs that occur in 3D biophysical data analysis in electron microscopy (EM). We introduce a powerful framework for connecting line-like structures in 3D data sets by combining a specific semilocal Hough transform with a directional evolution equation. The Hough transform allows to find the principal orientations of the local structures in a robust way, and the evolution equation is designed as a partial differential equation that smoothes along these principal orientations. We evaluate the performance of our method for enhancing structures in both synthetic and real-world EM data. In contrast to traditional structure tensor based methods such as coherence-enhancing diffusion, our method can handle the missing wedge problem in EM, also known as limited angle tomography problem. A modified version of our approach is also able to tackle the discontinuities created due to the contrast transfer function correction of EM images.

Keywords: Structure enhancement · Electron microscopy ·
Hough transform · Partial differential equations ·
Missing wedge problem

1 Introduction

Enhancing oriented structures is a classical problem in image processing. Grading the quality of fabrics and wood, fingerprint analysis, and processing cellular structures from electron microscopes are specific areas where enhancing oriented structures is required. On a broader scale, this application is encountered in fluid dynamics, meteorology, forensic studies, computer vision, biomedical and biophysical image analysis.

© Springer Nature Switzerland AG 2019
M. Vento and G. Percannella (Eds.): CAIP 2019, LNCS 11678, pp. 102–112, 2019.
https://doi.org/10.1007/978-3-030-29888-3_9

In 2D, analysing and processing oriented structures has a long tradition, and the structure tensor [6] and its equivalent concepts plays a prominent role in this context. While early work by Kass and Witkin [12] and Rao and Schunck [16] apply it as a pure analysis tool, Weickert et al. [20,21] use it to steer a so-called coherence-enhancing anisotropic diffusion (CED) process. This has triggered several follow up works that employ diffusion based ideas to enhance oriented structures [9,17,19]. Mühlich et al. [14] have studied the presence of multiple orientations in a local neighbourhood. Stochastic models [22] have also been used for analysis of contour shapes in images. More recently, template matching based on orientation scores [3] has been proposed for detecting combined orientation and blob patterns.

In 3D, the first technique for coherence enhancement was proposed by Weickert et al. [21]. Related works to this anisotropic diffusion technique in 3D include papers by Krissian et al. [13] and by Payot et al. [15] for medical imaging applications. Also in our days, methods based on partial differential equations continue to be important for enhancing 3D data sets that are difficult and expensive to acquire, such that deep learning approaches are less suited. However, in order to achieve optimal quality, these methods should be well adapted to the imaging process.

Our Goals. In our work, the main goal is to design a filter that extends the application of oriented structure enhancement in 3D to the specific needs in Electron Microscopy (EM). One challenge in designing filters for EM data is the limited angle tomography problem, also known as missing wedge problem [7,8]. It arises from the geometric design of data acquisition using the electron microscope. One cannot acquire data from all orientations of the sample, which leads to presence of the missing wedge in the Fourier space. When one reconstructs the 3D data in the Cartesian space from individual projections, the data is blurred/smeared in the directions where the missing wedge exists. Figure 1 shows the directions in which the data is blurred at every pixel in the Cartesian space. Here we depict a particular xz plane. The two triangles represent the directions where the data is smeared at every pixel. This region extends throughout the y direction. Due to the smearing effect of the data, classical formulas based on gradient calculations cannot be considered for processing this reconstructed data in order to enhance the image structures. Another challenge in EM is created by discontinuities in the image structures due to the contrast transfer function (CTF) correction of EM data. We will see that the direct and modified approaches of the Hough based evolution (HE) method introduced by us in this work is effective in dealing with both problems.

Paper Structure. The organisation of our paper is as follows: In Sect. 2 we introduce the HE method. We also mention the specific changes that have to be made to the classical ideas used for structure enhancement, in order to adapt them to electron microscopy data. In Sect. 3, we compare the performance of the HE method with the popular CED approach on synthetic and EM data. We also discuss how the ideas used in the modelling of the HE algorithm lead to the

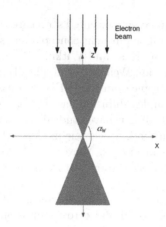

Fig. 1. Directions where the data is smeared at every pixel in Cartesian space due the presence of the missing wedge.

desired enhancement of oriented structures in the images. In Sect. 4, we conclude with a summary and give an outlook to future work.

2   Hough Based Evolution

2.1   A General Directional Data Evolution

Let $\Omega \subset \mathbb{R}^3$ denote a cuboid and consider some 3D data set $f : \Omega \to \mathbb{R}$. We can obtain a family $\{u(.,t) \,|\, t \geq 0\}$ of smoothed versions of f by regarding f as initial value of a 3D directional image evolution that satisfies the following partial differential equation:

$$\partial_t u = \partial_{\eta\eta} u = \boldsymbol{\eta}^\top \text{Hess}(u)\, \boldsymbol{\eta} \tag{1}$$

with reflecting boundary conditions. Here Hess(u) denotes the spatial Hessian of u. The smoothing direction $\boldsymbol{\eta}$ is space-variant and is characterised by its angles $\theta(\boldsymbol{x})$ and $\phi(\boldsymbol{x})$ in the spherical coordinate system:

$$\boldsymbol{\eta} = \boldsymbol{\eta}(\boldsymbol{x}) = \begin{pmatrix} \sin(\theta(\boldsymbol{x}))\cos(\phi(\boldsymbol{x})) \\ \sin(\theta(\boldsymbol{x}))\sin(\phi(\boldsymbol{x})) \\ \cos(\theta(\boldsymbol{x})) \end{pmatrix}. \tag{2}$$

Equations of type (1) have a long tradition, in particular in the 2D setting. For instance, for 2D mean curvature motion [1], one chooses $\boldsymbol{\eta}(\boldsymbol{x},t) \perp \boldsymbol{\nabla} u(\boldsymbol{x},t)$. Obviously such a choice – which smoothes along isophotes – cannot close interrupted structures. To this end, one needs more advanced local structure descriptors than the gradient, e.g. the Gabor transform based methods that are used in the evolution equation of Carmona and Zhong [4]. The Carmona–Zhong approach, however, is designed for processing 2D images and has not been adapted to tackle 3D EM data. We prefer another local structure descriptor that is etter suited for our specific needs. It is based on a semilocal Hough transform and shall be discussed next.

2.2   Choosing the Smoothing Direction with a Hough Transform

The novelty of our work is that we choose the smoothing direction $\eta(x)$ mentioned above using a semilocal Hough transform [2,5,11] on the original data f. To be more precise, we compute the Hough transform to find the direction $\eta(x)$ corresponding to the line segment in a local neighbourhood, which represents the orientation along which the image structure to be enhanced is present. It has to be mentioned that the Hough transform is very robust in detecting the local dominant direction because a small relative majority in the voting process suffices for obtaining the dominant direction. In this sense, for noise of isotropic nature, the Hough based image evolution is more robust when compared to structure tensor based methods such as CED. Moreover, as we will see in the upcoming section, our modified Hough based selection of dominant directions is able to tackle the missing wedge in EM. The following pseudo-code explains the complete algorithm and its parameters in detail.

Input: Original discrete data set f and the following parameters:
ρ_1 - radius of the sphere shaped neighbourhood,
ρ_2 - half of the length of the line segments,
T - threshold for the Hough transform,
τ - time step size of the explicit scheme,
$k_{\max}$ - total number of iterations.

Modified Hough Algorithm for Computing $\eta(x)$:

1. Select a ball B of radius ρ_1 around each pixel of f.
2. Line segments of half length ρ_2 centered at every pixel within B are considered by discretising the angles θ and ϕ.
3. The θ and ϕ values of the line segment which has the largest percentage of pixels with grey values $> T$ represent the local dominant direction η.
   To tackle the missing wedge, only line segments within the angle α_W from Figure 1 are considered in the voting process.

Main Algorithm:

1. Initialisation: $u^0 = f$
2. For $k = 0, 1, 2, ..., k_{\max} - 1$:
   $$u^{k+1} = u^k + \tau \cdot \eta^\top \mathrm{Hess}(u^k)\, \eta,$$
   where $\mathrm{Hess}(u^k)$ is approximated with central finite differences.

Output: Image with enhanced structures $u^{k_{\max}}$.

Note that we compute the Hough transform only for the initial data set f, not for its evolution $u(.,t)$. This saves computational time and leads to a linear method. We have not noticed qualitative differences compared to a nonlinear variant where we adapt the dominant direction to the evolving image $u(., t)$.

2.3 Modification of Classical Ideas for Adapting to EM Data

Let us now discuss the exact modifications we have made to classical concepts in order to adapt them better to the scenario of limited angle tomography.

Restricting the Search Space of Dominant Directions. It was already explained in Sect. 1 that the missing wedge problems arises due to the design of the data acquistion process: The specimen whose images are acquired cannot be tilted above a certain angle (generally 60°). Thus, we do not have projections from all the angles. This leads to missing information while reconstructing the 3D data from the available projections, which creates a smearing effect of the reconstructed data in the directions where the data cannot be collected. In order to tackle this, the modified Hough algorithm mentioned above just considers the line segments which are outside the wedge represented in Fig. 1, in the voting process. In other words, since our aim is to enhance the structures in the directions where we do not encounter the smearing effect, the search space of Hough directions is restricted by choosing $\alpha_W = 30°$ (Fig. 1). This value is chosen such that the search space is smaller than the entire space representing the directions where the data is not smeared.

Avoiding the Usage of Gradients. Due to the smearing effect of the EM data, classical formulas for gradient calculation can no longer be used for processing. Generally, gradients calculated on a Gaussian-smoothed image (with standard deviation σ) are used for making the decision in the voting process of the Hough transform. We instead use the grey values for making this decision as mentioned in the modified Hough algorithm. If dark structures are to be enhanced, we choose as Hough direction in 3D the one that contains the largest percentage of pixels with greyscale value below a certain threshold. For enhancing bright structures, we consider pixels above the threshold. Most of the previously designed filters mentioned in Sect. 1 are based on the structure tensor [6]. The structure tensor averages directional information over a local neighbourhood using gradient formulation. Thus, as we will see in the upcoming section, both gradient based Hough algorithm and CED (which is built upon the structure tensor) are not successful in enhancing the structures. On the other hand, we will also see that the usage of the grey value based Hough algorithm in the directional image evolution produces the desired results.

2.4 Numerical Algorithm

For discretising the 3D evolution Eq. (1), we use a straighforward explicit scheme as mentioned in the main algorithm of the pseudo-code. We use central derivative approximations to calculate the spatial derivatives in the Hessian. For a spatial grid size of 1, we observe experimentally L^2-stability if the time step size τ satisfies $\tau < \frac{1}{6}$. This stability bound is identical to the one for an explicit scheme

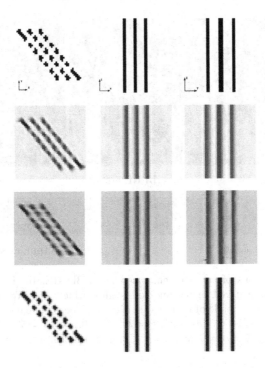

Fig. 2. Performance of the different approaches for a synthetic data set of size $49 \times 49 \times 49$. Left to Right: xy, xz, and yz slices. (a) First Row: Original data. (b) Second Row: Grey value based HE ($\rho_1 = 3$, $\rho_2 = 21$, $T = 10$, $\tau = 0.1$, $k_{max} = 10$). (c) Third Row: Gradient based HE ($\rho_1 = 3$, $\rho_2 = 21$, $T = 5$, $\sigma = 0.5$, $\tau = 0.1$, $k_{max} = 10$). (d) Fourth Row: CED ($\lambda = 1.0$, $\sigma = 0.5$, $\rho = 5.0$, $\alpha = 0.001$, $\tau = 0.1$, $k_{max} = 1000$).

for 3D homogeneous diffusion filtering. A more detailed theoretical study of the Hough based image evolution behaviour will be a topic for future research.

3   Results and Discussion

3.1   Synthetic Data

The Shepp–Logan phantom data set [10,18] is a popular synthetic data set used for testing 3D reconstruction algorithms. However, it is not suited for testing the capability of enhancing line-like structures in the presence of a missing wedge. A synthetic image for testing this particular capability of methods is simply missing in the image processing community. Thus, we have created a 3D image which mimics the effect of the missing wedge and also has discontinuous structures that need to be connected while enhancing them. Figure 2(a) shows different slices of the 3D data set we have created. We can clearly see the disconnected structures in the xy slice and the elongated/smeared structures in the other slices. This mimics the effect of the missing wedge. Figure 2(b) depicts the results of our

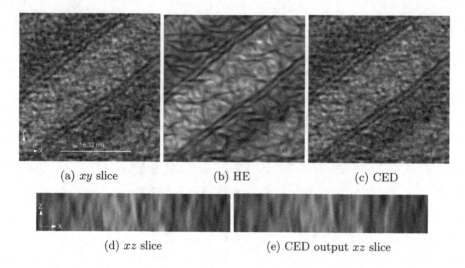

(a) xy slice   (b) HE   (c) CED

(d) xz slice   (e) CED output xz slice

Fig. 3. Cellular regions of rat liver enhanced using 3D HE. In (b) we can see the enhanced double walled cell membranes of neighbouring cells. We can also see the desmosomes (structures made of proteins) in directions perpendicular to the cell membrane. HE parameters: $\rho_1 = 3$, $\rho_2 = 21$, $T = 200$, $\tau = 0.1$, $k_{max} = 50$. CED parameters: $\lambda = 1.0$, $\sigma = 0.5$, $\rho = 5.0$, $\alpha = 0.001$, $\tau = 0.1$, $k_{max} = 100$. Data set size: $256 \times 256 \times 50$.

grey value based HE method. It is able to connect the disconnected structures. We observe that this approach outperforms both the gradient based HE method and CED whose results are presented in Figs. 2(c) and (d), respectively.

3.2 Real World Data

Figure 3(a), (d) shows a reconstructed 3D cellular region acquired from an electron microscope. One can see that the data in the z direction is smeared and resembles the above mentioned synthetic data set. Figure 3(b) displays the resulting enhanced cell structures using the HE algorithm. This image allows better visualisations than the original image in Fig. 3(a). The enhanced image (Fig. 3(b)) contains two double walled cell membranes of neighbouring cells. The structures arising in directions perpendicular to the cell membrane are the desmosome networks which are made of proteins. These networks bind neighbouring cells together. The structures are more evident in the enhanced image than the original image (Fig. 3(a)). Also, since the original image has more signal in the intra-cellular region than the extra-cellular region, the enhanced image also has clear desmosome networks in the intra-cellular region. Figure 3(c) depicts the result using CED with a straightforward explicit scheme. This structure tensor based enhancement method fails to enhance the structures in the presence of the missing wedge, as was explained in Sect. 2.3. Figure 3(e) shows the xz slice after applying CED. In the presence of a missing wedge, this method would always smooth in the z-direction as is visible in the image. This is because CED always

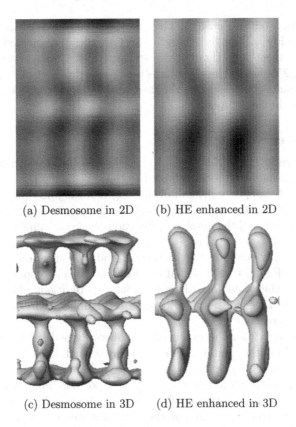

(a) Desmosome in 2D   (b) HE enhanced in 2D

(c) Desmosome in 3D   (d) HE enhanced in 3D

Fig. 4. Connecting disconnected desmosome structures. Visualisation threshold for both structures is 140. The length of each vertical desmosome is around 28 nm. Full data set size: $128 \times 128 \times 128$. Parmeters used: $\tau = 0.025$, $k_{\max} = 300$.

detects the coherent structures in the z-direction. Consequently, we do not get the desired structure enhancement in the xy slices; see Fig. 3(c). In the grey value based HE method, on the other hand, this is avoided by restricting the search space of angles and using grey value based detection of dominant orientations.

Another application of the HE is presented in Fig. 4. The vertical structures in white in Fig. 4(a) are discontinuous desmosomes. We infer that the presence of discontinuities in the horizontal direction is due the CTF correction of the data after acquisition. We see the desmosome structures in the extra-cellular regions clearly when compared to the images in the previous experiment. This is because several similar structures were averaged to get this final image. Due to this averaging, the missing wedge effect is minimised. Also, we just want to enhance the structures only in the direction perpendicular to the discontinuities. Hence, we need not perform the Hough transform. Smoothing in this required direction is governed by setting $\theta = 0°$. The result after removing the discontinuities using HE is displayed in Fig. 4(b). The graphical renderings of these structures are depicted in Fig. 4. The vertical structures are nicely connected.

It has to be mentioned that the cell structure data sets underwent an affine rescaling to $[0, 255]$ before the algorithms were applied. This facilitates the reproducibility of results while selecting the threshold parameter. It does not have any other effect on the model itself.

3.3   Parameter Selection

There are five parameters which need to be selected, out of which mainly two of them are critical and need to be adapted to the specific data set.

The radius of the sphere ρ_1, half of the length of the line segment ρ_2 and the threshold T for voting process in the Hough transform are the model parameters. The time step size τ and the number of iterations k_{max} are numerical parameters to reach a desired stopping time.

As already mentioned, τ has to obey a stability criterion caused by the explicit scheme. Fixing τ implies that the stopping time is proportional to k_{max}. We obtain smoother data for a larger number of iterations. Also, if the gaps to be closed are large, we need to increase the number of iterations until the structures get connected.

We suggest $\rho_1 = 3$ for the radius of the sphere shaped neighbourhood. This allows for searching the dominant orientation in a small neighbourhood instead of just around a specific pixel.

The selection of the parameters ρ_2 and T is important. They must be adapted to the data set. The parameter ρ_2, which specifies the length of the line segment, must be greater than the length of the discontinuites in order to detect and remove them. The threshold parameter T for the Hough transform voting process must be selected according to the greyscale range at which the structures are present in the image.

The spherical polar coordinate angles θ and ϕ are sampled 18 times each in their respective ranges.

Performing Gaussian smoothing and specifying the Gaussian standard deviation σ is only necessary for a gradient based Hough transform, due to the ill-posedness of differentiation. It is not required for our grey value based variant.

3.4   Computational Time

All the experiments in this work have been performed with ANSI C and CUDA on an Nvidia Quadro P5000 device. The computational time for the synthetic data experiment with grey value based HE method is 3.45 s. The time consumed for the real world data experiments is 84.6 s and 10 s, respectively.

4   Conclusions and Outlook

We have introduced a method that combines a semilocal Hough transform with a directional image evolution. This approach is designed to enhance oriented structures in 3D data sets from electron microscopy. Our variant of the Hough transform is robust with respect to the unwanted effects produced by the missing wedge effect in EM data. This helps to enhance structures in the data that are present in the directions where no smearing due to the missing projections occurs. Other methods which are based on derivative information, such as CED and gradient based HE, fail to overcome this problem. Additionally, our approach is also able to deal with the discontinuities that can occur in EM data due to the CTF correction.

In our future work we plan to also study applications beyond electron microscopy where the data acquisition is performed in a similar manner.

Acknowledgements. J.W. has received funding from the European Research Council (ERC) under the European Union's Horizon 2020 research and innovation programme (grant agreement no. 741215, ERC Advanced Grant INCOVID).

References

1. Alvarez, L., Lions, P.L., Morel, J.M.: Image selective smoothing and edge detection by nonlinear diffusion. II. SIAM J. Numer. Anal. **29**(3), 845–866 (1991)
2. Ballard, D.H.: Generalizing the Hough transform to detect arbitrary shapes. Pattern Recognit. **13**(2), 111–122 (1981)
3. Bekkers, E.J., Loog, M., ter Haar Romeny, B.M., Duits, R.: Template matching via densities on the roto-translation group. IEEE Trans. Pattern Anal. Mach. Intell. **40**(2), 452–466 (2018)
4. Carmona, R., Zhong, S.: Adaptive smoothing respecting feature directions. IEEE Trans. Image Process. **7**(3), 353–358 (1998)
5. Duda, R., Hart, P.E.: Use of the Hough transformation to detect lines and curves in pictures. Commun. ACM **15**(1), 11–15 (1972)
6. Förstner, W., Gülch, E.: A fast operator for detection and precise location of distinct points, corners and centres of circular features. In: Proceedings of the ISPRS Intercommission Conference on Fast Processing of Photogrammetric Data, Interlaken, Switzerland, pp. 281–305, June 1987
7. Frank, J.: Three-Dimensional Electron Microscopy of Macromolecular Assemblies: Visualization of Biological Molecules in their Native State. Oxford University Press, Oxford (2006)
8. Frank, J.: Electron Tomography: Three-dimensional Imaging with the Transmission Electron Microscope. Springer, New York (2013)
9. Franken, E., Duits, R., ter Haar Romeny, B.: Nonlinear diffusion on the 2D Euclidean motion group. In: Sgallari, F., Murli, F., Paragios, N. (eds.) SSVM 2007. LNCS, vol. 4485, pp. 461–472. Springer, Berlin (2007). https://doi.org/10.1007/978-3-540-72823-8_40
10. Gach, H.M., Tanase, C., Boada, F.: 2D & 3D Shepp-Logan phantom standards for MRI. In: Proceedings of the 2008 IEEE International Conference on Systems Engineering, Las Vegas, NV, USA, pp. 521–526, August 2008
11. Hough, P.: Methods and means for recognizing complex patterns. U.S. Patent No. 3,069,654, December 1962
12. Kass, M., Witkin, A.: Analyzing oriented patterns. Comput. Vis. Graph. Image Process. **37**, 362–385 (1987)

13. Krissian, K., Malandain, G., Ayache, N.: Directional anisotropic diffusion applied to segmentation of vessels in 3D images. In: ter Haar Romeny, B., Florack, L., Koenderink, J., Viergever, M. (eds.) Scale-Space 1997. LNCS, vol. 1252, pp. 345–348. Springer, Berlin (1997). https://doi.org/10.1007/3-540-63167-4_68
14. Mühlich, M., Aach, T.: Analysis of multiple orientations. IEEE Trans. Image Process. **18**(7), 1424–1437 (2009)
15. Payot, E., Guillemaud, R., Trousset, Y., Preteux, F.: An adaptive and constrained model for 3D X-ray vascular reconstruction. In: Grangeat, P., Amans, J.L. (eds.) Three-Dimensional Image Reconstruction in Radiation and Nuclear Medicine, Computational Imaging and Vision. CIVI, vol. 4, pp. 47–57. Springer, Dordrecht (1996). https://doi.org/10.1007/978-94-015-8749-5_4
16. Rao, A.R., Schunck, B.G.: Computing oriented texture fields. CVGIP: Graph. Models Image Process. **53**(2), 157–185 (1991)
17. Scharr, H.: Diffusion-like reconstruction schemes from linear data models. In: Franke, K., Müller, K.R., Nickolay, B., Schäfer, R. (eds.) DAGM 2006. LNCS, vol. 4174, pp. 51–60. Springer, Berlin (2006). https://doi.org/10.1007/11861898_6
18. Shepp, L.A., Logan, B.F.: The Fourier reconstruction of a head section. IEEE Trans. Nucl. Sci. **21**(3), 21–43 (1974)
19. Steidl, G., Teuber, T.: Anisotropic smoothing using double orientations. In: Tai, X.C., Mörken, K., Lysaker, M., Lie, K.A. (eds.) SSVM 2009. LNCS, vol. 5567, pp. 477–489. Springer, Berlin (2009). https://doi.org/10.1007/978-3-642-02256-2_40
20. Weickert, J.: Coherence-enhancing diffusion filtering. Int. J. Comput. Vis. **31**(2/3), 111–127 (1999)
21. Weickert, J., ter Haar Romeny, B.M., Lopez, A., van Enk, W.J.: Orientation analysis by coherence-enhancing diffusion. In: Proceedings of the 1997 Real World Computing Symposium, Tokyo, Japan, pp. 96–103, January 1997
22. Williams, L.R., Jacobs, D.W.: Stochastic completion fields: a neural model of illusory contour shape and salience. Neural Comput. **9**(4), 837–858 (1997)

Automated Segmentation of Nanoparticles in BF TEM Images by U-Net Binarization and Branch and Bound

Sahar Zafari[1]([✉]), Tuomas Eerola[1], Paulo Ferreira[3,4,5], Heikki Kälviäinen[1], and Alan Bovik[2]

[1] Computer Vision and Pattern Recognition Laboratory (CVPR),
Department of Computational and Process Engineering, School of Engineering
Science, Lappeenranta-Lahti University of Technology LUT, Lappeenranta, Finland
sahar.zafari@lut.fi
[2] Laboratory for Image and Video Engineering (LIVE),
Department of Electrical and Computer Engineering,
The University of Texas at Austin, Austin, TX 78712, USA
[3] Materials Science and Engineering Program,
The University of Texas at Austin, Austin, TX 78712, USA
[4] INL-International Iberian Nanotechnology Laboratory,
Av. Mestre José Veiga s/n, 4715-330 Braga, Portugal
[5] Mechanical Engineering Department and IDMEC, Instituto Superior Técnico,
University of Lisbon, Av. Rovisco Pais, 1049-001 Lisbon, Portugal

Abstract. Transmission electron microscopy (TEM) provides information about Inorganic nanoparticles that no other method is able to deliver. Yet, a major task when studying Inorganic nanoparticles using TEM is the automated analysis of the images, i.e. segmentation of individual nanoparticles. The current state-of-the-art methods generally rely on binarization routines that require parameterization, and on methods to segment the overlapping nanoparticles (NPs) using highly idealized nanoparticle shape models. It is unclear, however, that there is any way to determine the best set of parameters providing an optimal segmentation, given the great diversity of NPs characteristics, such as shape and size, that may be encountered. Towards remedying these barriers, this paper introduces a method for segmentation of NPs in Bright Field (BF) TEM images. The proposed method involves three main steps: binarization, contour evidence extraction, and contour estimation. For the binarization, a model based on the U-Net architecture is trained to convert an input image into its binarized version. The contour evidence extraction starts by recovering contour segments from a binarized image using concave contour points detection. The contour segments which belong to the same nanoparticle are grouped in the segment grouping step. The grouping is formulated as a combinatorial optimization problem and solved using the well-known branch and bound algorithm. Finally, the full contours of the NPs are estimated by an ellipse. The experiments on a real-world dataset consisting of 150 BF TEM images containing

© Springer Nature Switzerland AG 2019
M. Vento and G. Percannella (Eds.): CAIP 2019, LNCS 11678, pp. 113–125, 2019.
https://doi.org/10.1007/978-3-030-29888-3_10

approximately 2,700 NPs show that the proposed method outperforms five current state-of-art approaches in the overlapping NPs segmentation.

Keywords: Segmentation · Image processing · Concave points · Branch and bound · Overlapping · Nanoparticles · TEM images

1 Introduction

Inorganic nanoparticles (NPs) exhibit numerous properties that make them of interest to the research and industrial community [4, 9–11]. Numerous techniques for characterizing Inorganic NPs exist, and Transmission electron microscopy (TEM) represents one of the most appealing options because it can provide information about a broad range of their features, such as size, shape, texture, crystal structure, and composition. No other technique can provide as much information as TEM, primarily due to ability of the modern instruments to achieve both high contrast, high resolution, and diffraction composition [16]. However, studies of Inorganic NPs using TEM have suffered from poor statistical quality due to the difficulty of their segmentation in the image processing step. Although, the recent studies have made significant progress towards remedying the problem of inaccurate segmentation and the resultant poor statistical information [6, 20, 24], segmenting Inorganic NPs in TEM micrographs still rely on either global thresholding or local thresholding [2, 5]. Global thresholding [7, 13] has performed successfully in the past in some limited cases where the NPs are clearly distinguishable form background [20]. However, nonuniform backgrounds generally prevent this binarization technique from succeeding. The end result for global thresholding is numerous false negatives and some false positives resulting from a poor binarization. Local thresholding [1, 12, 18] supposedly has led to improved segmentation results in the presence of nonuniform backgrounds. However, this binarization technique also reproducibly fails to distinguish between the background and the NPs. A recent study [6] has proposed the use of variance hybridized mean local thresholding as a binarization routine, and this method shows promising results. When compared to the baseline of global thresholding, this novel binarization routine effectively eliminates false negatives while greatly reducing false positives, usually providing excellent segmentation. However, variance hybridized mean local thresholding contains a weakness in that it requires an optimized set of parameters to achieve a good binarization. Thus, one must specify values these parameters for each image in dataset in order to use the approach.

In this study, we advance the state-of-the-art by utilizing a binarization technique that does not require parameterization, as well as providing a superior technique for the segmentation of individual NPs from regions of nanoparticle overlap. We propose to use a binarization method based on the convolutional neural networks. The binarization is formulated as a semantic segmentation task in which each pixel in the image is assigned to an object class, the foreground and the background, and is implemented based on the well-known U-Net architecture [17]. We integrate the U-Net based binarization to our segmentation framework for overlapping NPs [24,25] that utilize concave points in the contours of nanoparticle bundles. We demonstrate that the U-Net based binarization produces accurate separation of NPs and background without causing fluctuations to the nanoparticle contours. This makes it possible to detect the concave points robustly and further allows accurate segmentation of individual NPs. We show that the proposed method outperforms five existing methods [6,14,20,22,26] with higher NP detection rate and segmentation accuracy.

2 Proposed Method

The proposed method is summarized in Fig. 1. Given an input grayscale image, the segmentation follows three sequential stages: binarization, contour evidence extraction, and contour estimation. First, the binarization of the image is performed using the well-known encoder-decoder deep framework called U-Net [17]. Second, the contour evidence extraction aims to find and inference the visible contour of each nanoparticle. This involves two separate tasks: contour segmentation and segment grouping. In the contour segmentation the contour segments are recovered from the binarized image using concave point detection and segment grouping, whereby contour segments belonging to the same nanoparticle are grouped by utilizing the branch and bound algorithm [24]. Finally, the contour evidences are utilized by ellipse fitting to estimate the full contours of the NPs.

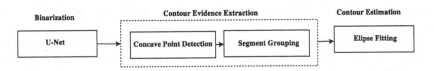

Fig. 1. Proposed segmentation method.

2.1 Binarization

The proposed method is organized in a sequential manner where the performance of each module directly impacts the performance of the next step. Binarization is a key step in computation flow that can directly affects the performance of contour evidence extraction. Due to uneven illumination, contrast variation, non-uniform background, and the likely presence of noise in NP images, the binarization is a challenging task. To this end, the binarization routine is formulated as a pixel classification problem that is performed by a convolutional encoding-decoding framework [21]. In particular, it is implemented by the U-Net architecture proposed by Ronneberger *et al.* [17]. The U-Net contains several layers of convolutional encoders and decoders, followed by the final pixelwise classification layer. Each encoder layer is composed of duplicated 3×3 convolution operations followed by a rectified linear unit (ReLU). Following that, the encoder layers downsample the feature maps using a 2×2 max pooling operation with stride 2. To avoid spatial information lost during downsampling, the encoder feature maps are up-sampled and summed to the corresponding decoder feature maps and passed to the next layer after rectification in the decoder layers. The final layer is 1×1 convolution to map each feature vector to the desired classes. To classify each pixel and to ensure that all predicted pixels are in the range $[0, 1]$ the sigmoid activation function is applied at the output layer.

The loss function for training the network was defined based on the Dice coefficient [27]. Given the prediction O_p and the ground truth O_g the dice coefficient (DSC) measures the similarity as follows:

$$DSC = \frac{2|O_p \cap Og|}{|O_p| + |Og|}. \tag{1}$$

The higher the DSC value, the greater the similarity. Since the training aims to minimize the loss function we instead used the negative dice coefficient (-DSC).

2.2 Concave Point Detection

Concave point detection has a pivotal role in contour segmentation and provides an important cue for further object segmentation (contour estimation). The main goal of the concave point detection is to find concave locations on the object boundaries and to utilize them to segment the contours of overlapping objects in such a way that each contour segment contains edge points from one object only [23].

Polygonal approximation is a well-known method to represent the objects contours by a sequence of dominant points. It can be used to reduce complexity, to smooth object contours, and to avoid detection of false concave points. Given the sequence of extracted contour points $C = \{c_1, c_2, ...\}$, the dominant points are determined by co-linear suppression. To be specific, every contour point c_i is examined for co-linearity, while it is compared to the previous and the next successive contour points. The point c_i is considered as a dominant point if it is not located on the line connecting $c_{i-1} = (x_{i-1}, y_{i-1})$ and $c_{i+1} = (x_{i+1}, y_{i+1})$ and the distance d_i from c_i to the line connecting c_{i-1} to c_{i+1} is larger than a pre-set threshold $d_i > d_{th}$.

Here, the d_{th} value was selected automatically using the method of Prasad *et al.* [15]. In this method, the threshold value d_{th} is selected automatically based on the angular distance between the slope of the actual line and the digitized line. After polygonal approximation and dominant point detection, the dominant point $c_{d,i} \in C_{dom}$ is considered to be a concave point if [26]

$$C_{con} = \{c_{d,i} \in C_{dom} \ : \ \overrightarrow{c_{d,i-1}c_{d,i}} \times \overrightarrow{c_{d,i}c_{d,i+1}} > 0\}. \tag{2}$$

2.3   Segment Grouping

Due to overlaps between objects and irregularities of the object shapes, a single object may produce multiple contour segments. Segment grouping is needed to merge all of the contour segments belonging to the same object. Let $S = \{S_1, S_2, \ldots, S_N\}$ be an ordered set of N contour segments in a connected component of an image. The aim is to group the contour segments into M subsets such that the contour segments that belong to individual objects are grouped together, and so that $M \leq N$.

Let ω_i be the group membership indicator giving the group index to which each contour segment S_i belongs to. Denote Ω as the ordered set of all membership indicators: $\{\omega_1, \omega_2, \ldots, \omega_N\}$. The grouping criterion is given by a scalar function $J(\cdot)$ of Ω which maps a possible grouping of the given contour segments onto the set of real numbers $\mathbb{R}$. J is the cost of grouping that ideally measures how the grouping Ω resembles the true contour segments of the objects. The grouping problem for the given set of S is to find the optimal membership set Ω^* such that the grouping criterion (cost of grouping) is minimized as

$$\Omega^* = \underset{\Omega}{\operatorname{argmin}} \; J(\Omega; S). \tag{3}$$

The grouping task is formulated as a combinatorial optimization problem which is solved using the branch and bound (BB) algorithm [24]. The BB algorithm can be applied with any grouping criterion J. However, the selection of the grouping criterion has a significant effect on the overall performance. The proposed grouping criterion is a hybrid cost function consisting of two parts [24]: (1) the *generic part* ($J_{\text{concavity}}$) that encapsulates the general convexity properties of the objects and (2) the *specific part* that encapsulates the properties of objects that are exclusive to a certain application, e.g., symmetry (J_{symmetry}), and ellipticity ($J_{\text{ellipticity}}$) as follows:

$$J = \underbrace{J_{\text{concavity}}}_{\text{Generic}} + \underbrace{\beta J_{\text{ellipticity}} + \gamma J_{\text{symmetry}}}_{\text{Specific}} \tag{4}$$

where β, γ are the weights for each term respectively.

The generic part encourages the convexity assumption of the objects to penalize the grouping of the contour segments belonging to different objects. This is achieved by incorporating a quantitative concavity measure. Given two contour segments s_i and s_j, the generic part of the cost function is defined as

$$J_{\text{concavity}} = \left(\frac{A_{s_i \cup s_j} - A_{\text{ch}, s_i \cup s_j}}{A_{S_i \cup S_j}} \right) \tag{5}$$

where $A_{s_i \cup s_j}$ is the area of a region bounded by s_i, s_j, and $A_{\text{ch}, s_i \cup s_j}$ is the upper bound on the area of any convex hull with contour points s_i and s_j.

The specific part is adapted to consider the application criteria and certain object properties. Considering the object under examination, several functions can be utilized. The ellipticity term measures the discrepancy between the fitted ellipse and the contour segments [26]. Given the contour segment S_i consisting of n points, $s_i = \{(x_k, y_k)\}_{k=1}^n$, and the corresponding fitted ellipse points, $s_{f,i} = \{(x_{f,k}, y_{f,k})\}_{k=1}^n$, the *ellipticity* term is defined as follows:

$$J_{\text{ellipticity}} = \frac{1}{n} \sum_{k=1}^n \sqrt{(x_k - x_{f,k})^2 + (y_k - y_{f,k})^2}. \tag{6}$$

The *symmetry* term penalizes the resulting objects that are non-symmetric. Let o_i and o_j be the centers of symmetry of the contour segments s_i and s_j obtained by aggregating the normal vector of the contour segments. The procedure applied is similar to the fast radial symmetry transform [8], but the gradient vectors are replaced by the normal vectors of the contour segments. This transform is referred to as the *normal symmetry transform* (NST).

In NST, every contour segment point gives a vote for the plausible radial symmetry at some specific distance from that point. Given the distance value n of the predefined range $[R_{min}\ R_{max}]$, for every contour segment point (x, y), NST determines the negatively affected pixels P_{-e} by

$$P_{-ve}(x, y) = (x, y) - round\left(\frac{n(x, y)}{\|n(x, y)\|} n\right), \tag{7}$$

and increments the corresponding point in the orientation projection image O_n by 1. The symmetry contribution S_n for the radius $n \in [R_{min}, R_{max}]$ is formulated as

$$S_n(x, y) = \left(\frac{|\tilde{O}_n(x, y)|}{k_n}\right) \tag{8}$$

where k_n is the scaling factor that normalizes O_n across different radii. $\tilde{O}_n$ is defined as

$$\tilde{O}_n(x, y) = \begin{cases} O_n(x, y), & \text{if } O_n(x, y) < k_r. \\ k_n, & \text{otherwise.} \end{cases} \tag{9}$$

The full NST transform S, by which the interest symmetric regions are defined, is given by the average of the symmetry contributions over all the radii $n \in [R_{min}, R_{max}]$ considered as

$$S = \frac{1}{|N|} \sum_{n \in [R_{min}, R_{max}]} S_n. \tag{10}$$

The centers of symmetry o_i and o_j of the contour segments are estimated as the average locations of the detected symmetric regions in S. The symmetry term J_{symmetry} is defined as the Euclidean distance between $o_i(x, y)$ and $o_j(x, y)$ as

$$J_{\text{symmetry}} = |o_i - o_j|. \tag{11}$$

This distance is normalized to $[0, 1]$ by diving it by the maximum diameter of the object.

2.4   Contour Estimation

Once the contour evidences have been obtained, contour estimation is carried out to infer the missing parts of the overlapping NPs. A widely known approach is Least Square Ellipse Fitting (LSEF) [3]. The purpose of LSEF is to compute the ellipse parameters by minimizing the sum of squared algebraic distances from the known contour evidences points to the ellipse.

3   Experiments

3.1   Data

The experiments were carried out using a dataset from an interesting real-world application [6]. The dataset consists of BF TEM images of nanocatalyst NPs, present in cathode of a proton exchange fuel cell captured in a JEOL 2010F operated 200 kV. This dataset contains 150 images, each of 1024×1024 pixels, containing a total of 2700 NPs. It should be noted that, in the original publication [6], the total number of NPs was reported as 2000. This is due to the fact that the paper considered only non-overlapping NPs.

As the quantity and diversity of the training samples are important factors in attempting to achieve high accuracy and only a small amount annotated images of NPs are available, we employ data augmentation to create a larger training dataset for image binarization. The augmented data were generated using affine transformations (rotation, shifts, and shearing). An expert annotated 20 binary masks consists of around 700 particles from the dataset. For training purposes in the U-Net framework around 1000 images were generated by data augmentation. The rest of Images in the dataset, 130, containing 2000 NPs was used as a final test set for binarization. The training images were zero-centered and normalized to unit variance. The network was trained for 20 epochs using the Adam optimization algorithm with a fixed initial rate of $1e-4$ and a mini-batch size of 8 patches in Keras. To asses the performance of U-Net, the training was performed using 10-Fold Cross Validation and the best performing model was recorded on each epoch. The model achieved the average accuracy of 98% ± 0.001, precision of 97% ± 0.002 and recall of 97% ± 0.003.

3.2   Performance Measure

To evaluate and to compare performances of the methods, the four different metrics were used. The detection performance was measured using the following three metrics: the true positive rate (TPR), the positive predictive value (PPV), and the accuracy (ACC), defined as follows:

$$TPR = \frac{TP}{TP + FN}, \tag{12}$$

$$PPV = \frac{TP}{TP + FP}, \tag{13}$$

$$ACC = \frac{TP}{TP + FP + FN}, \tag{14}$$

where true positive (TP) is the number of correctly detected NPs, false positive (FP) is the number of incorrect segmentation results, and false negative (FN) is the number of missed NPs.

To compute the number of correct or incorrect detection results, the Jaccard similarity coefficient (JSC) [19] was used. JSC was chosen since it interprets the similarity by the ratio of overlap between the ground truth NP and the segmented NP. JSC considers the amount of the common area between two NPs. Since we are often interested in area measurements this is an appropriate metric. Given the binary feature model of the segmented object I_p and the ground truth particle I_g, JSC is computed as

$$JSC = \frac{|I_p \cap I_g|}{|I_p \cup I_g|}. \tag{15}$$

The threshold value for the ratio of overlap (JSC threshold) was set to 0.6. In this way, if the area of overlap between segmented object I_p and the ground truth particle I_g was more than 60% then the segmented object considered as TP. The average JSC (AJSC) and DSC (ADSC) value were used as another measure of the segmentation and binarization performance.

3.3   Parameter Selection

The proposed method requires the following major parameters:

Weighting parameters β, γ define to what extent the ellipticity and symmetry features must be weighted in the computation of the grouping cost J. A lower value emphasizes non-ellipticity and non-symmetry features where higher values ensure that objects have perfect elliptical symmetry shapes. This parameter is useful when the objects are not perfectly elliptical or symmetry. In this work, NPs have perfect elliptical symmetry shapes; thus the symmetry and ellipticity terms were weighted equally to 0.5.

Radial range $[R_{min}, R_{max}]$ determines the range of radii at which the NST transform S is computed. The radial range should be defined as such that it covers the variety of all objects sizes available in the image. Considering the smallest and largest object axes, the radial ranges was set $R_{min} = 18$ and $R_{max} = 22$ for our NPs dataset.

3.4   Results

Binarization. The U-Net binarization methods were compared to six competing methods: hybridized variance (HV) [6], Otsu [13] Kittler [7], Niblack [12],

Table 1. Comparison of performances of binarization methods on the fuel cell NPs dataset. The best method based on each criterion is shown bolded.

	U-Net [17]	HV [6]	Otsu [13]	Kittler [7]	Niblack [12]	Sauvola [18]	Bresen [1]
AJSC	**93**	88	62	67	28	66	26
ADSC	**96**	93	72	78	42	78	41

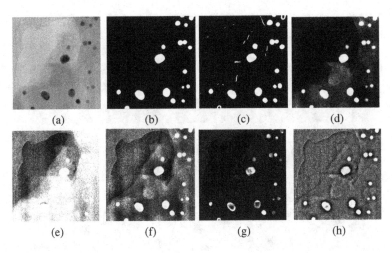

Fig. 2. An example of image binarization methods: (a) Original image; (b) U-Net [17]; (c) HV [6]; (d) Otsu [13]; (e) Kittler [7] (f) Niblack [12]; (g) Sauvola [18]; (h) Bernsen [1].

Sauvola [18], and Bresen [1]. The results of the image binarization methods applied to the Inorganic fuel cell datasets is presented in Table 1, From the result it can be seen that the proposed U-Net achieves the highest ADSC and AJSC scores compare to the competing methods. Figure 2 shows an example of image binarization methods applied to a BF TEM image containing NPs. As it can be seen in Fig. 2, the U-Net performs better as compared to the competing methods. This shows the superiority of U-Net which can handle various type of image degradation such as noise, non uniform background and uneven-illumination.

Segmentation. The proposed NPs segmentation methods were compared to five existing methods for overlapping NPs segmentation: hybridized variance (HV) [6], seed point-based contour evidence extraction (SCC) [20], concave point-based contour evidence extraction (CC) [22], nanoparticle segmentation (NPA) [14], and concave points extraction and contour segmentation (CECS) [26]. These methods were chosen since they have been previously successfully applied to the segmentation of NPs images. It should be noted that, due to the fact that the generic image binarization was not considered in [14,20,22,26], the proposed U-Net binarization method was applied also for SCC,CC,NPA and CECS methods.

Example results of these segmentation methods applied to an image of the fuel cell NPs dataset are shown in Fig. 3. As it can be seen, HV, CC, and NPA suffered from under-segmentation, while SCC and CECS experienced over-segmentation. The CC and CECS methods failed to achieve acceptable results on NPs whose shapes deviated substantially from an ellipse. The NPA and SCC methods failed to work when the sizes of the NPs varied widely. Our proposed method achieved satisfactory segmentation results and outperformed the other methods in this regard. Table 2 presents the corresponding performance statis-

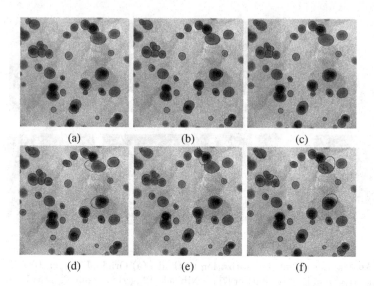

Fig. 3. Example results of the segmentation methods applied to an image of fuel cell NPs: (a) Proposed; (b) HV; (c) CC; (d) SCC; (e) NPA; (f) CECS.

tics of the competing segmentation methods when applied to the Inorganic fuel cell NPs dataset. The segmentation results show that the proposed method outperforms the other methods, achieving higher scores of TPR, PPV, and ACC. Figure 4 represents the effect of the Jaccard similarity threshold on the TPR, PPV, and ACC scores of the proposed segmentation and competing methods. The performance of all segmentation methods degraded when the JSC threshold was increased, while our proposed segmentation method was better than the other methods, achieving higher JSC threshold values.

Table 2. Comparison of performances of segmentation methods on the fuel cell NPs dataset. The best method based on each criterion is shown bolded.

Methods	TPR [%]	PPV [%]	ACC [%]	AJSC [%]
Proposed	**90**	**92**	**85**	**87**
HV [6]	89	91	83	85
CC [22]	81	87	74	82
SCC [20]	83	87	74	86
NPA [14]	80	87	73	87
CECS [26]	88	73	68	86

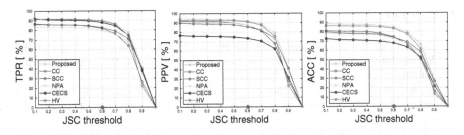

Fig. 4. Effect of different JSC threshold values on segmentation performance on the fuel cell NPs dataset: (a) TPR; (b) PPV; (c) ACC.

4   Conclusions

This paper presents a novel method for automated segmentation of NPs in BF TEM images. The proposed method consists of the following three main steps: the image binarization to divide the image into foreground (nanoparticles) and background, the contour evidence extraction to detect the visible part of each nanoparticle, and the contour estimation to estimate the nanoparticle contours. The binarization is performed using the well known U-Net deep encoder-decoder framework. The contour evidence extraction is performed by detecting concave points and finding contour segment groupings using the branch and bound algorithm. Finally, the contour estimation is performed using ellipse fitting. The experiments showed that the proposed method reduces the false negatives and false positives relative to all of the compared methods, while increasing the number of individual NPs segmented from regions of overlap. The proposed method achieves high detection and segmentation accuracies, and outperforms five competing methods on the real dataset of NPs images.

Acknowledgments. The research was carried out in the Computational Photonics Imaging (COMPHI) and the Automatic segmentation of overlapping objects for cell image analysis (CellVision) projects. The authors would like to thank Academy of Finland for funding the CellVision project (Decision No. 313598). The authors would like to acknowledge Prof. Heikki Haario and Dr. Jouni Sampo from the LUT University and Dr. Daniel Groom from University of Texas for their collaboration. Moreover, the authors would like to thank support of the fuel cell technologies office of the US Department of Energy (DoE), office of energy efficiency and renewable energy. Dr. Nancy Garland was the DoE technology development manager for this work. The work was subcontracted by Argonne National Laboratory, a DoE, office of science laboratory operated under contact no. DE-AC02-06CH1135 by U.Chicago, Argonne, LLC, DE-AC02-07CH11358.

References

1. Bernsen, J.: Dynamic thresholding of grey-level images. In: Proceedings of the Eighth International Conference on Pattern Recognition (ICPR), pp. 1251–1255 (2009)
2. Fisker, R., Carstensen, J., Hansen, M., Bødker, F., Mørup, S.: Estimation of nanoparticle size distributions by image analysis. J. Nanopart. Res. **2**(3), 267–277 (2000)
3. Fitzgibbon, A., Pilu, M., Fisher, R.B.: Direct least square fitting of ellipses. IEEE Trans. Pattern Anal. Mach. Intell. **21**(5), 476–480 (1999)
4. Gilbert, J.A., et al.: Pt catalyst degradation in aqueous and fuel cell environments studied via in-operando anomalous small-angle X-ray scattering. Electrochim. Acta **173**, 223–234 (2015)
5. Gontard, L.C., Ozkaya, D., Dunin-Borkowski, R.E.: A simple algorithm for measuring particle size distributions on an uneven background from TEM images. Ultramicroscopy **111**(2), 101–106 (2011)
6. Groom, D., Yu, K., Rasouli, S., Polarinakis, J., Bovik, A., Ferreira, P.: Automatic segmentation of inorganic nanoparticles in BF TEM micrographs. Ultramicroscopy **194**, 25–34 (2018)
7. Kittler, J., Illingworth, J.: Minimum error thresholding. Pattern Recognit. **19**(1), 41–47 (1986)
8. Loy, G., Zelinsky, A.: Fast radial symmetry for detecting points of interest. IEEE Trans. Pattern Anal. Mach. Intell. **25**(8), 959–973 (2003)
9. Melander, M., Latsa, V., Laasonen, K.: CO dissociation on iron nanoparticles: size and geometry effects. J. Chem. Phys. **139**(16), 164320 (2013)
10. Miller, J., et al.: The effect of gold particle size on AuAu bond length and reactivity toward oxygen in supported catalysts. J. Catal. **240**(2), 222–234 (2006)
11. Murray, C.B., Kagan, C.R., Bawendi, M.G.: Synthesis and characterization of monodisperse nanocrystals and close-packed nanocrystal assemblies. Ann. Rev. Mater. Sci. **30**(1), 545–610 (2000)
12. Niblack, W.: An Introduction to Digital Image Processing. Strandberg Publishing Company, Birkeroed (1985)
13. Otsu, N.: A threshold selection method from gray-level histograms. Automatica **11**(285–296), 23–27 (1975)
14. Park, C., Huang, J.Z., Ji, J.X., Ding, Y.: Segmentation, inference and classification of partially overlapping nanoparticles. IEEE Trans. Pattern Anal. Mach. Intell. **35**(3), 669–681 (2013)
15. Prasad, D.K., Leung, M.K.: Polygonal representation of digital curves. INTECH Open Access Publisher (2012)
16. Pyrz, W.D., Buttrey, D.J.: Particle size determination using TEM: a discussion of image acquisition and analysis for the novice microscopist. Langmuir **24**(20), 11350–11360 (2008)
17. Ronneberger, O., Fischer, P., Brox, T.: U-Net: convolutional networks for biomedical image segmentation. In: Navab, N., Hornegger, J., Wells, W.M., Frangi, A.F. (eds.) MICCAI 2015. LNCS, vol. 9351, pp. 234–241. Springer, Cham (2015). https://doi.org/10.1007/978-3-319-24574-4_28
18. Sauvola, J., Pietikäinen, M.: Adaptive document image binarization. Pattern Recognit. **33**(2), 225–236 (2000)
19. Taha, A.A., Hanbury, A.: Metrics for evaluating 3D medical image segmentation: analysis, selection, and tool. BMC Med. Imaging **15**(1), 29 (2015)

20. Zafari, S., Eerola, T., Sampo, J., Kälviäinen, H., Haario, H.: Segmentation of overlapping elliptical objects in silhouette images. IEEE Trans. Image Process. **24**(12), 5942–5952 (2015)
21. Zafari, S.: Segmentation of partially overlapping convex objects in silhouette images. Ph.D. thesis, Lappeenranta University of Technology (2018)
22. Zafari, S., Eerola, T., Sampo, J., Kälviäinen, H., Haario, H.: Segmentation of partially overlapping nanoparticles using concave points. In: Bebis, G., et al. (eds.) ISVC 2015. LNCS, vol. 9474, pp. 187–197. Springer, Cham (2015). https://doi.org/10.1007/978-3-319-27857-5_17
23. Zafari, S., Eerola, T., Sampo, J., Kälviäinen, H., Haario, H.: Comparison of concave point detection methods for overlapping convex objects segmentation. In: Sharma, P., Bianchi, F.M. (eds.) SCIA 2017. LNCS, vol. 10270, pp. 245–256. Springer, Cham (2017). https://doi.org/10.1007/978-3-319-59129-2_21
24. Zafari, S., Eerola, T., Sampo, J., Kälviäinen, H., Haario, H.: Segmentation of partially overlapping convex objects using branch and bound algorithm. In: Chen, C.-S., Lu, J., Ma, K.-K. (eds.) ACCV 2016. LNCS, vol. 10118, pp. 76–90. Springer, Cham (2017). https://doi.org/10.1007/978-3-319-54526-4_6
25. Zafari, S., Murashkina, M., Eerola, T., Sampo, J., Kälviäinen, H., Haario, H.: Resolving overlapping convex objects in silhouette images by concavity analysis and Gaussian process. arXiv preprint arXiv:1906.01049 (2019)
26. Zhang, W.H., Jiang, X., Liu, Y.M.: A method for recognizing overlapping elliptical bubbles in bubble image. Pattern Recognit. Lett. **33**(12), 1543–1548 (2012)
27. Zhang, W., et al.: Deep convolutional neural networks for multi-modality isointense infant brain image segmentation. NeuroImage **108**, 214–224 (2015)

Image and Texture Analysis

A Fractal-Based Approach to Network Characterization Applied to Texture Analysis

Lucas C. Ribas[1](✉), Antoine Manzanera[3], and Odemir M. Bruno[2]

[1] Institute of Mathematics and Computer Science, University of São Paulo - USP,
Avenida Trabalhador são-carlense, 400, São Carlos, SP 13566-590, Brazil
lucasribas@usp.br
[2] São Carlos Institute of Physics, University of São Paulo - USP,
PO Box 369, São Carlos, SP 13560-970, Brazil
bruno@ifsc.usp.br
[3] U2IS, ENSTA Paris, Institut Polytechnique de Paris,
828 Boulevard des Maréchaux, 91120 Palaiseau, France
antoine.manzanera@ensta-paristech.fr

Abstract. This work proposes a new method for texture analysis that combines fractal descriptors and complex network modeling. At first, the texture image is modeled as a network. Then, the network is converted into a surface where the Cartesian coordinates and the vertex degree is mapped into a 3D point in the surface. Then, we calculate a description vector of this surface using a method inspired by the Bouligand-Minkowski technique for estimating the fractal dimension of a surface. Specifically, the descriptor corresponds to the evolution of the volume occupied by the dilated surface, when the radius of the spherical structuring element increases. The feature vector is given by the concatenation of the volumes of the dilated surface for different radius values. Our proposal is an enhancement of the classic complex networks descriptors, where only the statistical information was considered. Our method was validated on four texture datasets and the results reveal that our method leads to highly discriminative textural features.

Keywords: Complex networks · Fractal dimension · Texture analysis

1 Introduction

Texture is a visual pattern related to the surface of a material or an object and it is considered as a key feature to image interpretation. Texture classification is used in many fields such as material science [43], industrial inspection [29], geology [42], etc. There are many classical texture characterization methods in the literature that can be divided into four different categories: statistical-based (e.g., gray-level co-occurrence matrices (GLCM) [22] and local binary patterns (LBP)

© Springer Nature Switzerland AG 2019
M. Vento and G. Percannella (Eds.): CAIP 2019, LNCS 11678, pp. 129–140, 2019.
https://doi.org/10.1007/978-3-030-29888-3_11

[32]), spectral methods (e.g. Gabor filters [24] and wavelet transform [41]), structural methods (e.g. morphological decomposition [27]) and model-based methods (e.g. Fractal models [5,6,37], complex networks [36] and stochastic models [34]).

Currently, methods based on complex networks theory have attracted significant attention of the computer vision community, due to the promising results and their capacity to represent the relationships among structural properties of texture [1,15,38]. The complex network techniques represent the texture image as a network and extract measures capable of characterizing precisely the structural patterns of texture modeled. In this sense, the network modeling is an important step whose aim is to represent different aspects like spatial and pixel intensity distribution, texture irregularities, auto-similarity scales, etc. [15]. Now a challenging problem is to find a relevant set of measures to extract from the network to characterize it. Previous works [7,10] use simple metrics based on degree distribution, however, it is noticeable that more complex measures are needed for a finer characterization [12,15].

To this end, we propose in this paper a new approach for texture analysis that uses fractal descriptors as measures for complex network characterization. The proposal is to use the fractal measures to characterize the network topology instead of using network statistical measures. To achieve this, firstly, the texture image is modeled as a network and this network is converted to a surface. Then, we calculate a feature vector using a method inspired by the Bouligand-Minkowski technique to estimate the fractal dimension of the surface that maps a network. The proposed signature is composed of the influence volume computed of this surface for different radius values. We verify the performance of the proposed approach in the classification of four texture image datasets and the results are compared to other literature methods.

The paper is organized as follows. In Sect. 2, we describe the proposed approach in detail. Section 3 reports the experimental setup. The results and discussion are presented in Sect. 3, followed by the conclusion in Sect. 4.

2   Proposed Method

2.1   Modeling Texture as Network

According to Backes et al. [7] a texture image I can be modeled as a network $G = (V, E)$ considering each pixel as a vertex. Each pixel $i \in V$ is characterized by its Cartesian coordinates x_i and y_i, and an integer value $I(i) \in [0, 255]$ which represents its gray-level. Two vertices (pixels) i and j are connected by a non-directed edge $e_{ij} \in E$ if the Euclidean distance between them is smaller or equal than a given value d, according to:

$$e_{ij} \in E \iff \sqrt{(x_i - x_j)^2 + (y_i - y_j)^2} \leq d \tag{1}$$

For each edge a weight $w(e_{ij})$ is defined by a normalized combination of the Euclidean distance and the difference of intensities between two pixels:

$$w(e_{ij}) = \frac{(x_i - x_j)^2 + (y_i - y_j)^2 + d^2 \frac{|I(i) - I(j)|}{255}}{2d^2} \qquad (2)$$

This weight function includes information about the pixel surroundings and the normalization of the difference of pixel intensity in the interval $[0, d^2]$ aims to balance the relative importance between geometric and color information in the texture representation [7]. Each network vertex i has a degree k_i, which is the number of edges connected to i. Note that until now the network vertices all have the same degree. Thus, it is necessary to apply a transformation in order to highlight texture properties. This can be done by applying a threshold t over the network, removing all edges whose weight is higher than a given value t and obtaining a new set of edges E_t. In this way, a set of thresholds $T, t \in T$ can be applied over the network in order to study the behavior of its properties along the successive transformations.

2.2 Fractal Dimension of Network Degrees

A way to describe how irregular is an object is to use the Fractal dimension, which can be estimated in various ways [17]. In this paper, we compute the fractal descriptors of the complex network using a method inspired by the Bouligand-Minkowski method, which is one of the most accurate approach to estimate the fractal dimension [4,9]. This method estimates the fractal dimension based on the size of the influence area $|S(r)|$ generated by the dilation of surface $S \subset \mathbb{R}^3$ using a radius r [17]. The Bouligand-Minkowski fractal dimension D of a surface S varying the radius r is defined as:

$$D(S) = 3 - \lim_{r \to 0} \frac{\log V_S(r)}{\log r}, \qquad (3)$$

where $V_S(r)$ is the influence volume achieved with the dilation process of all points s of the surface S using a sphere of radius r [4,17]. $V_S(r)$ can be calculated by the Euclidean Distance Transform (EDT) in order to achieve a fast algorithm [4,13]. The distance transform DT is the function defined as:

$$DT(x, y, k) = \min_{(x', y', k') \in S} d\left((x, y, k), (x', y', k')\right), \qquad (4)$$

for all points (x, y, k) from the cubic grid $\mathbb{N}^3$ [4,39]. This way, the set of possible radii (distances) R is

$$R = \{r : r = \sqrt{x^2 + y^2 + k^2}; (x, y, k) \in \mathbb{N}^3\}, \qquad (5)$$

with the values r sorted increasingly to create the set of possible radii $R = \{0, 1, \sqrt{2}, \sqrt{3}, 2\sqrt{2}, ..., r_{max}\}$ [39]. In this approach, the influence volume is computed by $V_S(r) = \#\{(x, y, k) : DT(x, y, k) = r\}$ [39].

In the proposed method, we apply the fractal dimension theory to characterize the topology of a network that models a texture image. To achieve this, a network modeling texture can be easily mapped onto a 3D surface $S \subset \mathbb{R}^3$, by converting the Cartesian coordinates (x_i, y_i) and the degree k_i of each vertex i into a 3D point $s_i = (x_i, y_i, k_i)$. In this way, we can characterize the network topology relating the degree and the vertex/pixel position in the image. Figure 1(a) illustrates a network modeling a texture image and (b) the degree of the vertices.

Figures 1(b) and (c) illustrate the mapping of the network onto a surface. Note that the Z axis is the degree of the vertices. The dilation process of this surface is shown in Figs. 1(d) and (e). Figure 2(a) shows the degree of vertices of a network modeling a texture image represented by an image. Figures 2(a)–(c) show the dilatation process of the surface that represents this network with each point of the 3D surface dilated by a sphere of radius r. Notice that more collisions happen among the dilated points as we increase the value of radius r. These collisions are directly related to the geometry of the surface S and determine the way the total influence volume $V_S(r)$ increases, according to the changes in the network topology. Thus, the pattern produced by the influence volume $V_S(r)$ for different radii can be used to describe the network topology and, consequently, the texture patterns.

2.3   Feature Vector

In this paper, we propose to use the influence volume $V_S(r)$ of the surface (that maps a network) as a feature vector. The influence volume provides a rich shape descriptor and it was used with success to discriminate texture in previous works [4,17]. Thus, the feature vector is composed of the concatenation of the influence volume $V_S(r)$ computed for different values of radius r:

$$\Psi_t^d = [V_S(1), V_S(\sqrt{2}), V_S(\sqrt{3}), ..., V_S(r_{max})], \tag{6}$$

where t is the value of threshold applied in the network, d is the distance used in network modeling and r_{max} is the maximum radius.

Note that the feature vector Ψ_t^d is built using all possible radius values from $r = 1$ to r_{max}. In order to analyze the behavior of the network topology from the successive transformation, we combine the feature vector Ψ_t^d for different values of threshold t, starting from t_0 to t_f, to finally get the complete texture signature as follows:

$$\Upsilon^d = [\Psi_{t_0}^d, \Psi_{t_1}^d, ..., \Psi_{t_f}^d]. \tag{7}$$

3   Results and Discussion

3.1   Experimental Setup

The proposed signature is computed for each image. After that, the supervised classification is carried out by applying a Canonical Analysis [11] followed by a Linear Discriminant Analysis (LDA) [16]. This is a simple classifier that emphasizes the features extracted by the methods. We apply the Canonical Analysis

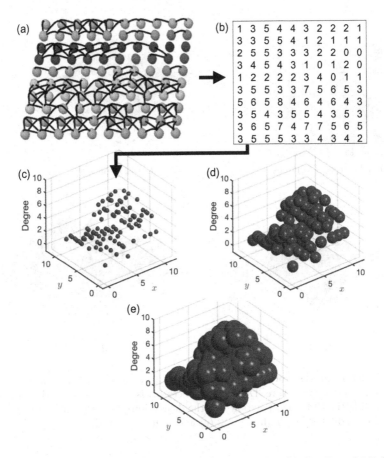

Fig. 1. Illustration of the proposed approach inspired by the Bouligand-Minkowski method for estimating the fractal dimension of a network. (a) Network modeling pixels. (b) Degree of the vertices. (c) 3D surface mapping the network in (a), converting each vertex into a 3D point. (d)–(e) Dilation process of the surface.

here due to the presence of high correlation of the volume features [39]. Basically, the canonical analysis is a geometric transformation of the feature space to generate new uncorrelated features. Thus, p–canonical variables can be obtained from the original features and the LDA supervised classification is accomplished by using the most significant p–variables [39]. To separate the training and testing sets we adopted the leave-one-out cross-validation scheme. Thus, one sample is used for testing and the remainder for training. This process is repeated for each sample of the dataset. The average accuracy of all tests is used as a performance measure.

To evaluate the methods the databases used as benchmark were:

– Brodatz [8]: just as in [7], this dataset is composed of 1776 texture images of 128×128 pixel size divided into 111 classes, 16 images per class.

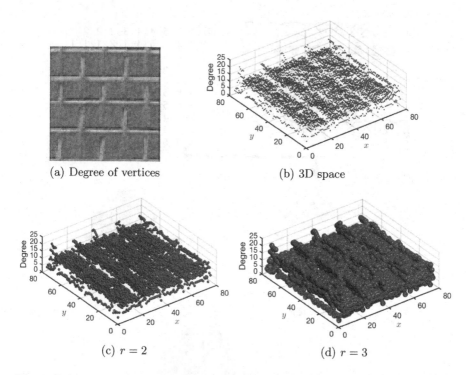

(a) Degree of vertices   (b) 3D space

(c) $r = 2$ (d) $r = 3$

Fig. 2. Dilation process for estimating the fractal dimension of the space × degree surface representing a texture. Degree of vertices (a) is mapped onto a 3D surface (b) by converting the Cartesian position and the degree into a point in the surface. Then, this surface is dilated, e.g. radius $r = 2$ (c) and radius $r = 3$ (d).

- Outex [31]: the dataset used in this work is composed of 68 texture classes from TC_Outex_00013 with 20 samples each of 128 × 128 pixel size without overlapping. The dataset has a total of 1 360 textures.
- USPTex [6]: this dataset is composed of 2 292 samples divided into 191 classes, 12 images per class, and each image has 128 × 128 pixels size.
- Vistex [35]: the database *Vision Texture* has 54 images 512 × 512 which were split into 16 sub-images 128 × 128 pixel size without overlapping, totalizing 864 images.

We compare the accuracy of our proposed method to other descriptors proposed in the literature. For fair comparison purposes, all methods are compared using the LDA classifier and leave-one-out cross-validation scheme. The compared methods are: Grey-Level Co-occurrence Matrix (GLCM) [21], Gray Level Difference Matrix (GLDM) [26], Windowed Fourier transforms [3], Gabor Filters [30], Fractal [5], Fractal Fourier [14], Local Binary Patterns (LBP) [32], Local Binary Patterns Variance (LBPV) [20], Complete Local Binary Pattern (CLBP) [19], Local Phase Quantization (LPQ) [33], Local Configuration Pattern

(LCP) [18], Local Frequency Descriptor (LFD) [28], Binarized Statistical Image Features (BSIF) [25] and Complex Network Texture Descriptors (CNTD) [7].

3.2 Parameter Evaluation

In this paper, the set of thresholds T and distance for connection d used are identical as the ones used in [7]. It was defined by an initial threshold $t_0 = 0.005$, an increment of $\Delta t = 0.015$ and a final threshold $t_f = 0.530$. The maximal distance d for connection of the vertices was set up as $d = 3$. Figure 3(a) shows the accuracy variation with respect to the number of the p-canonical variables used in the LDA classifier for different datasets and with a fixed value of maximal radius $r = 3$. Note that, for all datasets, the accuracy increases at a first moment, achieves an optimal accuracy and then stabilizes. Such behavior is expected and is a good indicator for adjusting the dimension of the descriptor, since the high number of features damages the efficiency of the classifier [39]. From the behavior observed in Fig. 3(a), we accomplish the remainder of the experiments using a total of 130 p–canonical variables.

Figure 3(b) presents the accuracy variation for all datasets when the maximal value of radius r_{max} is ranged. The original feature vector before the canonical analysis has the size of 36, 144, 288, 504, 792, 1 116, 1 512, 1 944, 2 484, 3 060, 3 672, 4 356, 5 112, 5 940, 6 804 for the 15 respective integer values of r_{max} between 1 and 15. We observe that, as we increase the maximal radius value the accuracy also increases. However, it begins to stabilize or decrease from the radius $r_{max} = 5$ and $r_{max} = 6$. Based on this behavior, we define the value of radius $r_{max} = 6$ as the maximum dilation radius. Therefore, we define the following feature vector $\Psi_t^d = [V_S(1), V_S(\sqrt{2}), V_S(\sqrt{3}), \ldots, V_S(\sqrt{36})]$.

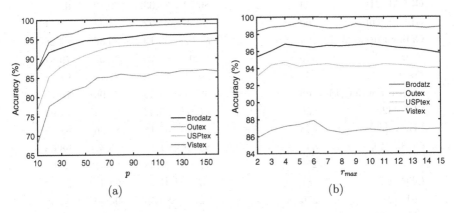

Fig. 3. Accuracy of our approach for different datasets. (a) Accuracy versus number of p–canonical variables. (b) Accuracy versus the maximal values of the radius.

3.3   Comparison with Other Methods

In this section, we performed comparisons with literature methods in order to evaluate the performance obtained by the proposed approach. In all experiments were used the LDA classifier with leave-one-out, except for CLBP descriptor (1-Nearest Neighborhood (1-NN) classifier with distance Chi-square), which followed the original paper. For our approach, it was adopted the parameter setup discussed in Sect. 3.2.

The results obtained by all the texture methods in the four datasets are presented in Table 1. We can note that the proposed approach achieved the best results when compared to the other literature methods in the four datasets. In the Brodatz and Vistex datasets, the CLBP and CNDT methods obtained the second best results. On the other hand, the second best accuracy in the Outex and USPTex datasets was obtained by the GLDM and CNDT methods.

We can also verify in Table 1 that our method reached higher accuracy than the CNDT method. The CNDT method is also based on complex networks, and we use in our approach the same network modeling as them. The difference between the CNDT method and our approach is the measure (statistical measures based on the degree histogram) used to characterize the network. Therefore, this suggests that our approach obtained superior performance due to the fractal measure extracted from the network. Our interpretation is that our volumetric fractal descriptors can characterize more richly the network topology,

Table 1. Comparison of accuracies of different texture analysis methods in four texture databases.

Methods	Number of features	Outex	USPTex	Brodatz	Vistex
GLCM [21]	24	80.73	83.63	90.43	92.24
GLDM [26]	60	86.76	91.92	94.43	97.11
Gabor Filters [30]	64	81.91	83.19	89.86	93.28
Fourier [3]	63	81.91	67.70	75.90	79.51
Fractal [5]	69	80.51	78.22	87.16	91.67
Fractal Fourier [14]	68	68.38	59.45	71.96	79.75
LBP [32]	256	81.10	85.42	93.64	97.92
LBPV [20]	555	75.66	55.13	86.26	88.65
CLBP [19]	648	85.80	91.13	95.32	98.03
BSIF [25]	256	77.43	77.48	91.44	88.66
LCP [18]	81	86.25	91.31	93.47	94.44
LFD [28]	276	82.57	83.59	90.99	94.68
LPQ [33]	256	79.41	85.29	92.51	92.48
CNTD [7]	108	86.76	91.71	95.27	98.03
Proposed approach	130	87.86	94.41	96.45	98.96

considering the degree and spatial arrangement of the vertices, in contrast with the CNDT method that only used the degree frequency.

On the other hand, the proposed method also outperformed the Fractal method [5] which also uses the volumetric fractal descriptors to describe the image. However, this approach uses the Cartesian coordinates and the gray intensities to represent the surface. This shows that the proposed approach that combines fractal measures and complex networks improves the ability of discrimination when compared to both approaches isolated.

We can also compare our results with learned descriptors (e.g. using convolutional neural network (CNN)). For comparison purposes, we considered the Outex and USPTex datasets, which are the most challenging. The results using the HardNet++ [2], InceptionV3 [40] and ResNet101 [23] methods for feature extraction were considered. On the USPTex dataset, our approach obtained the highest accuracies when compared to the InceptionV3 (92.71%) and HardNet++ (94.20%). On the other hand, the ResNet101 obtained an accuracy of 96.50%. For the Outex dataset, the accuracies were 86.98%, 88.97% and 89.34% for the InceptionV3, ResNet101 and HardNet++, respectively. Our approach overcomes the CNN methods in some cases and in others it obtain close results. Thus, our method is still competitive due to its simplicity.

4   Conclusion

In this paper, we have proposed a new method based on fractal descriptors and complex network for texture analysis. The method extracts fractal measures from a network that models a texture image. For this, we have proposed to map the network into a 3D surface by converting the Cartesian coordinates and the vertex degree as a point in the surface.

We have demonstrated how the texture description can be improved by combining the fractal descriptors and complex networks, instead of using only the fractal descriptor or complex network approaches separated. Experiments on four datasets indicate that our method significantly improved the classification rate with regard to the original complex networks method and fractal descriptors method. The results also showed that our approach overcomes the other compared literature methods. As future work, we believe that different techniques to estimate the fractal dimension of the network can be investigated. In addition, new ways to obtain the feature vector can be studied, such as using different sets of radius values. Another future idea is to extend the proposed approach to boundary shapes analysis. The proposed idea also opens a promising research field for network characterization using fractal measures.

Acknowledgments. Lucas Ribas gratefully acknowledges the financial support grant #2016/23763-8 and #2019/03277-0, São Paulo Research Foundation (FAPESP). Odemir Bruno thanks the financial support of CNPq (Grant #307797/2014-7) and FAPESP (Grant #s 14/08026-1 and 16/18809-9).

References

1. Ribas, L.C., Gonçalves, W.N., Bruno, O.M.: Dynamic texture analysis with diffusion in networks. Digit. Signal Proc. **92**, 109–126 (2019)
2. Mishchuk, A., Mishkin, D., Radenovic, F., Matas, J.: Working hard to know your neighbor's margins: local descriptor learning loss, December 2017
3. Azencott, R., Wang, J.P., Younes, L.: Texture classification using windowed Fourier filters. IEEE Trans. Pattern Anal. Mach. Intell. **19**(2), 148–153 (1997)
4. Backes, A.R., Bruno, O.M.: Plant leaf identification using color and multi-scale fractal dimension. In: Elmoataz, A., Lezoray, O., Nouboud, F., Mammass, D., Meunier, J. (eds.) ICISP 2010. LNCS, vol. 6134, pp. 463–470. Springer, Heidelberg (2010). https://doi.org/10.1007/978-3-642-13681-8_54
5. Backes, A.R., Casanova, D., Bruno, O.M.: Plant leaf identification based on volumetric fractal dimension. Int. J. Pattern Recognit Artif Intell. **23**(06), 1145–1160 (2009)
6. Backes, A.R., Casanova, D., Bruno, O.M.: Color texture analysis based on fractal descriptors. Pattern Recognit. **45**(5), 1984–1992 (2012)
7. Backes, A.R., Casanova, D., Bruno, O.M.: Texture analysis and classification: a complex network-based approach. Inf. Sci. **219**, 168–180 (2013)
8. Brodatz, P.: Textures: A Photographic Album for Artists and Designers. Dover Publications, New York (1966)
9. Bruno, O.M., de Oliveira Plotze, R., Falvo, M., de Castro, M.: Fractal dimension applied to plant identification. Inf. Sci. **178**(12), 2722–2733 (2008)
10. Chalumeau, T., da F. Costa, L., Laligant, O., Meriaudeau, F.: Texture discrimination using hierarchical complex networks. In: Damiani, E., Yétongnon, K., Schelkens, P., Dipanda, A., Legrand, L., Chbeir, R. (eds.) Signal Processing for Image Enhancement and Multimedia Processing. MMSA, vol. 31, pp. 95–102. Springer, Boston (2008). https://doi.org/10.1007/978-0-387-72500-0_9
11. Correa, D.C., Saito, J.H., da F. Costa, L.: Musical genres: beating to the rhythms of different drums. New J. Phys. **12**(5), 053030 (2010)
12. da F. Costa, L., Rodrigues, F.A., Travieso, G., Villas Boas, P.R.: Characterization of complex networks: a survey of measurements. Adv. Phys. **56**(1), 167–242 (2007)
13. Fabbri, R., da F. Costa, L., Torelli, J.C., Bruno, O.M.: 2D Euclidean distance transform algorithms: a comparative survey. ACM Comput. Surv. (CSUR) **40**(1), 2 (2008)
14. Florindo, J.B., Bruno, O.M.: Fractal descriptors based on Fourier spectrum applied to texture analysis. Phys. A **391**(20), 4909–4922 (2012)
15. Florindo, J.B., Casanova, D., Bruno, O.M.: Fractal measures of complex networks applied to texture analysis. J. Phys: Conf. Ser. **410**, 012091 (2013)
16. Fukunaga, K.: Introduction to Statistical Pattern Recognition, 2nd edn. Academic Press, New York (1990)
17. Gonçalves, W.N., Machado, B.B., Bruno, O.M.: Texture descriptor combining fractal dimension and artificial crawlers. Physica A Stat. Mech. Appl. **395**, 358–370 (2014)
18. Guo, Y., Zhao, G., Pietikäinen, M.: Texture classification using a linear configuration model based descriptor. In: BMVC, pp. 1–10. Citeseer (2011)
19. Guo, Z., Zhang, L., Zhang, D.: A completed modeling of local binary pattern operator for texture classification. IEEE Trans. Image Process. **19**(6), 1657–1663 (2010)

20. Guo, Z., Zhang, L., Zhang, D.: Rotation invariant texture classification using LBP variance (LBPV) with global matching. Pattern Recognit. **43**(3), 706–719 (2010)
21. Haralick, R.M.: Statistical and structural approaches to texture. Proc. IEEE **67**(5), 786–804 (1979)
22. Haralick, R.M., Shanmugam, K., Dinstein, I.H.: Textural features for image classification. IEEE Trans. Syst. Man Cybern. **6**, 610–621 (1973)
23. He, K., Zhang, X., Ren, S., Sun, J.: Deep residual learning for image recognition. In: Proceedings of the IEEE Conference on Computer Vision and Pattern Recognition, pp. 770–778 (2016)
24. Jain, A.K., Farrokhnia, F.: Unsupervised texture segmentation using Gabor filters. In: 1990 IEEE International Conference on Systems, Man and Cybernetics. Conference Proceedings, pp. 14–19. IEEE (1990)
25. Kannala, J., Rahtu, E.: BSIF: binarized statistical image features. In: 2012 21st International Conference on Pattern Recognition (ICPR), pp. 1363–1366. IEEE (2012)
26. Kim, J.K., Park, H.W.: Statistical textural features for detection of microcalcifications in digitized mammograms. IEEE Trans. Med. Imaging **18**(3), 231–238 (1999)
27. Lam, W.K., Li, C.K.: Rotated texture classification by improved iterative morphological decomposition. IEE Proc.-Vis. Image Signal Process. **144**(3), 171–179 (1997)
28. Maani, R., Kalra, S., Yang, Y.H.: Noise robust rotation invariant features for texture classification. Pattern Recognit. **46**(8), 2103–2116 (2013)
29. Malamas, E.N., Petrakis, E.G., Zervakis, M., Petit, L., Legat, J.D.: A survey on industrial vision systems, applications and tools. Image Vis. Comput. **21**(2), 171–188 (2003)
30. Manjunath, B.S., Ma, W.Y.: Texture features for browsing and retrieval of image data. IEEE Trans. Pattern Anal. Mach. Intell. **18**(8), 837–842 (1996)
31. Ojala, T., Mäenpää, T., Pietikäinen, M., Viertola, J., Kyllönen, J., Huovinen, S.: Outex: new framework for empirical evaluation of texture analysis algorithms (2002)
32. Ojala, T., Pietikainen, M., Maenpaa, T.: Multiresolution gray-scale and rotation invariant texture classification with local binary patterns. IEEE Trans. Pattern Anal. Mach. Intell. **24**(7), 971–987 (2002)
33. Ojansivu, V., Heikkilä, J.: Blur insensitive texture classification using local phase quantization. In: Elmoataz, A., Lezoray, O., Nouboud, F., Mammass, D. (eds.) ICISP 2008. LNCS, vol. 5099, pp. 236–243. Springer, Heidelberg (2008). https://doi.org/10.1007/978-3-540-69905-7_27
34. Panjwani, D.K., Healey, G.: Markov random field models for unsupervised segmentation of textured color images. IEEE Trans. Pattern Anal. Mach. Intell. **17**(10), 939–954 (1995)
35. Picard, R., Graczyk, C., Mann, S., Wachman, J., Picard, L., Campbell, L.: Vision Texture Database. Media Laboratory, MIT, Cambridge (1995)
36. Ribas, L.C., Junior, J.J., Scabini, L.F., Bruno, O.M.: Fusion of complex networks and randomized neural networks for texture analysis. arXiv preprint arXiv:1806.09170 (2018)
37. Ribas, L.C., Gonçalves, D.N., Oruê, J.P.M., Gonçalves, W.N.: Fractal dimension of maximum response filters applied to texture analysis. Pattern Recognit. Lett. **65**, 116–123 (2015)
38. Ribas, L.C., Neiva, M.B., Bruno, O.M.: Distance transform network for shape analysis. Inf. Sci. **470**, 28–42 (2019)

39. da S. Oliveira, M.W., Casanova, D., Florindo, J.B., Bruno, O.M.: Enhancing fractal descriptors on images by combining boundary and interior of Minkowski dilation. Phys. A: Stat. Mech. Appl. **416**, 41–48 (2014)
40. Szegedy, C., Vanhoucke, V., Ioffe, S., Shlens, J., Wojna, Z.: Rethinking the inception architecture for computer vision. In: Proceedings of the IEEE Conference on Computer Vision and Pattern Recognition, pp. 2818–2826 (2016)
41. de Ves, E., Acevedo, D., Ruedin, A., Benavent, X.: A statistical model for magnitudes and angles of wavelet frame coefficients and its application to texture retrieval. Pattern Recognit. **47**(9), 2925–2939 (2014)
42. Wenk, H.R.: Preferred Orientation in Deformed Metal and Rocks: An Introduction to Modern Texture Analysis. Elsevier, Amsterdam (2013)
43. Zimer, A.M., et al.: Investigation of AISI 1040 steel corrosion in H2S solution containing chloride ions by digital image processing coupled with electrochemical techniques. Corros. Sci. **53**(10), 3193–3201 (2011)

Binary Tomography Using Variants of Local Binary Patterns as Texture Priors

Judit Szűcs[(⊠)] and Péter Balázs

Department of Image Processing and Computer Graphics, University of Szeged,
Árpád tér 2., Szeged 6720, Hungary
{jszucs,pbalazs}@inf.u-szeged.hu

Abstract. In this paper, we propose a novel approach for binary image reconstruction from few projections. The binary reconstruction problem can be highly underdetermined and one way to reduce the search space of feasible solutions is to exploit some prior knowledge of the image to be reconstructed. We use texture information extracted from sample image patches as prior knowledge. Experimental results show that this approach can retain the structure of the image even if just a very few number of projections are used for the reconstruction.

Keywords: Binary Tomography · Image reconstruction ·
Texture descriptors · Local Binary Patterns · Simulated annealing

1 Introduction

The aim of Computerized Tomography is to reconstruct digital images from their projections, i.e., a collection of line integrals of the image taken along predefined straight lines. Filtered Backprojection is by far the most widely applied method to solve the reconstruction problem which works well when hundreds of projections are available, gathered with equal spacing on the whole angular range. When these conditions are not met, iterative reconstruction methods, such as variants of the Algebraic Reconstruction Technique (ART) can serve as alternatives [4,8]. However, when only a handful of projections are accessible and/or when the missing angle is large, these latter methods may also not ensure good image quality. On the other hand, in certain applications of tomography (crystallography, materials science, industrial non-destructive testing, etc.), one can assume that the object to reconstruct consist of just a few known materials, i.e., only a few different grayscale intensity values can appear in the image representing the object. Discrete Tomography (DT) [5,6] deals with such problems, trying to exploit the abovementioned prior information.

One of the DT reconstruction approaches is to formulate the problem as a system of linear equations and search for its solution, often just approximately. Due to the limited number of projections, this equation system may be highly underdetermined. On the other hand, noisy projections can cause the system to

© Springer Nature Switzerland AG 2019
M. Vento and G. Percannella (Eds.): CAIP 2019, LNCS 11678, pp. 141–154, 2019.
https://doi.org/10.1007/978-3-030-29888-3_12

become inconsistent. All these drawbacks can be compensated by the knowledge that the range of the discrete images to produce is a small discrete set, known beforehand (representing known materials the object of investigation consists of). Additional prior knowledge about the shape, topology and geometry of the object may also be exploited in order to facilitate the reconstruction. There are, among others, works focusing on perimeter preserving regularization [14], shape orientation [13], convexity [3], etc.

In this paper we study texture as shape prior in DT which was first investigated in [20]. Here, we extend the former work by studying several variants of the Local Binary Patterns (LBP) to describe the texture, and by conducting a comparative experiment on both synthetic and real images. The structure of the paper is the following. In Sect. 2 we give the basics of Binary Tomography. In Sect. 3 we describe different variants of Local Binary Patterns. In Sects. 4 and 5, respectively, we present the experimental setup and the results achieved. Finally, we summarize our work in Sect. 6.

2   Binary Tomography

A special case of DT is Binary Tomography (BT) where the object to reconstruct consists of a single material yielding that the corresponding image contains only 0s and 1s (representing the absence and presence of the material, respectively). Thus, the binary reconstruction problem can be traced back to solving equation

$$\mathbf{Ax} = \mathbf{b}, \tag{1}$$

where the matrix $\mathbf{A} \in \mathbb{R}^{k \times mn}$ describes the relationship between the k different beams and the pixels (a_{ij} gives the length of the line segment of the i-th projection ray in the j-th pixel), vector $\mathbf{b} \in \mathbb{R}^k$ contains the measured projection values, and $\mathbf{x} \in \{0,1\}^{mn}$ represents the unknown image of size $m \times n$, in a row-by-row vector form.

To overcome the difficulties arising from the underdeterminedness and inconsistency of (1), the binary reconstruction problem is commonly reformulated as a minimization problem

$$C(\mathbf{x}) = ||\mathbf{Ax} - \mathbf{b}||_2 + \gamma \cdot \Phi(\mathbf{x}) \;\rightarrow\; \min, \tag{2}$$

where $||\mathbf{Ax} - \mathbf{b}||_2$ is the data fitting term, $\Phi : \{0,1\}^{mn} \rightarrow \mathbb{R}$ is a function expressing how the image $\mathbf{x}$ fits to the prior information (smaller value means better result), and $\gamma \geq 0$ is a scaling constant.

3   Local Binary Patterns as Texture Descriptors

LBP is a visual descriptor mostly used for classification in computer vision, that is suitable to find image patterns or repetitions. It describes the relationship between the pixels and their 8-neighbors with an eight-digit binary code. Thus, there are 256 such binary codes, and as a result of an LBP process we gain a 256-dimensional feature vector ('LBP histogram' or 'LBP vector') describing the normalized distribution of the binary codes in the image. The original LBP algorithm was published in 1996, in [17]. Since then, many variants of the basic LBP version have been developed. In most of the implementations (also in the ones we use) the sample points are evenly distributed on a radius around a center pixel. If a point does not coincide with a pixel center, bilinear interpolation is used. For the sake of simplicity, we present here the versions using simply the 8-neighbors of the center pixel. Although LBP descriptors have been studied in many recent surveys for image classification [12,16,18], etc., as far as we know, they have never been used for image reconstruction, except in our preliminary work [20].

In order to explain different variants of LBP, consider an example grayscale matrix I defined in (3), where the center pixel is denoted by p_c and its 8-neighbors by $p_0, p_1, \cdots, p_7$, in a clockwise manner from the top-left pixel.

$$I = \begin{bmatrix} p_0 & p_1 & p_2 \\ p_7 & p_c & p_3 \\ p_6 & p_5 & p_4 \end{bmatrix} = \begin{bmatrix} 200 & 0 & 255 \\ 83 & 132 & 156 \\ 132 & 10 & 130 \end{bmatrix} \tag{3}$$

3.1 LBP (Local Binary Patterns)

The basic LBP algorithm [17] examines the relation between the center pixel p_c and its 8-neighbors $p_0, p_1, \cdots, p_7$ in a 3×3 window for each pixel, thereafter describes it as a sequence of zeros and ones. This results a binary code which is converted to decimal. The resulted codes for all image pixels are aggregated in a 256-dimensional histogram representing the frequency of each possible pattern. The LBP value in the center pixel p_c is defined as

$$LBP(p_c) = \sum_{i=0}^{N-1} d_i \cdot 2^i, \tag{4}$$

where N is the number of the sampling points (in our example, $N = 8$, since a 3×3 neighborhood is taken into account). The threshold function is

$$d_i = \begin{cases} 1 & p_i \geq p_c \\ 0 & p_i < p_c \end{cases}. \tag{5}$$

Example 1. The LBP value of the center pixel p_c of the matrix I defined in (3) is $LBP(p_c) = 1 \cdot 2^0 + 0 \cdot 2^1 + 1 \cdot 2^2 + 1 \cdot 2^3 + 0 \cdot 2^4 + 0 \cdot 2^5 + 1 \cdot 2^6 + 0 \cdot 2^7 = 77$.

3.2 FLBP (Fuzzy Local Binary Patterns)

A soft extension of LBP is Soft LBP [1] or Fuzzy LBP (FLBP) [7] which integrates fuzzy logic into the basic LBP process. FLBP is robust and continuous w.r.t. the output, i.e., small changes in the input image result in only small changes in the output. To improve the robustness of the basic LBP operator, the original threshold function is expanded by two fuzzy membership functions. Fuzzification allows FLBP to assign several (or even all) bins of the histogram to each pixel to some degree, not just a single one. While LBP is based on thresholding that makes it sensitive to noise, FLBP enables a more robust representation of image texture, by fuzzifying the calculated LBP codes using fuzzy rules and membership functions. The fuzzy rules are

- **R_0** : The smaller p_i is, with respect to p_c, the greater the certainty that d_i is 0.
- **R_1** : The bigger p_i is, with respect to p_c, the greater the certainty that d_i is 1.

Based on these rules, the membership functions $f_{0,T}(i)$ and $f_{1,T}(i)$ $(i = 1, \ldots, N)$ are defined as

$$f_{0,T}(i) = \begin{cases} 0 & p_i \geq p_c + T \\ \frac{T - p_i + p_c}{2 \cdot T} & p_c - T < p_i < p_c + T, \ T \neq 0 \\ 1 & p_i \leq p_c - T, \ T \neq 0 \\ 1 & p_i \leq p_c, \ T = 0 \end{cases} \tag{6}$$

$$f_{1,T}(i) = 1 - f_{0,T}(i), \tag{7}$$

where $T \in [0, 255]$ represents a parameter that controls the degree of fuzziness. The contribution $C_T(LBP)$ of each LBP code in a single bin of the FLBP histogram is defined as

$$C_T(LBP) = \prod_{i=0}^{N-1} f_{d_i,T}(i). \tag{8}$$

Thus, the crisp thresholding of (4) is replaced with the softer membership functions (6) and (7) yielding each 3×3 neighborhood may contribute to more than one bin of the FLBP histogram. It is important to note that the total contribution of each neighborhood to the bins equals 1.

Example 2. Consider again the center pixel p_c of matrix I defined in (3) and let $T = 10$. With this setting, some of the 8-neighbors yields a fix value in the LBP code: $p_0 = 1, p_1 = 0, p_2 = 1, p_3 = 1, p_5 = 0, p_7 = 0$. However, the membership functions of p_4 and p_6 are not crisp any more. These are $f_{0,T}(4) = \frac{10 - 130 + 132}{2 \cdot 10} = 0.6$, $f_{1,T}(4) = 0.4$, $f_{0,T}(6) = \frac{10 - 132 + 132}{2 \cdot 10} = 0.5$, and $f_{1,T}(6) = 0.5$. Thus we have the following contributions

- for the LBP code 00001101: $C_T(13) = f_{0,T}(4) \cdot f_{0,T}(6) = 0.6 \cdot 0.5 = 0.3$,
- for the LBP code 00011101: $C_T(29) = f_{1,T}(4) \cdot f_{0,T}(6) = 0.4 \cdot 0.5 = 0.2$,
- for the LBP code 01001101: $C_T(77) = f_{0,T}(4) \cdot f_{1,T}(6) = 0.6 \cdot 0.5 = 0.3$,
- for the LBP code 01011101: $C_T(93) = f_{1,T}(4) \cdot f_{1,T}(6) = 0.4 \cdot 0.5 = 0.2$.

Therefore, the $13^{th}, 29^{th}, 77^{th}, 93^{th}$ bins get the nonzero values calculated above. Finally, $C_T(13) + C_T(29) + C_T(77) + C_T(93) = 0.3 + 0.2 + 0.3 + 0.2 = 1$.

3.3   SLBP (Shift Local Binary Patterns)

The Shift Local Binary Patterns (SLBP) was introduced in [12] as a fast approximation of the computationally heavy FLBP. There, the authors described SLBP as generating a fixed number of local binary codes for each pixel position. An intensity limit l is added to specify the shift interval k:

$$k \in [-l, l] \cap \mathbb{Z} \Rightarrow |k| = 2 \cdot l + 1. \tag{9}$$

When k is changed, a new binary code is calculated and added to the histogram. The SLBP value of the center pixel with shift value k is defined as

$$SLBP(p_c, k) = \sum_{i=0}^{N-1} d_i \cdot 2^i, \tag{10}$$

where

$$d_i = \begin{cases} 1 & p_i \geq p_c + k \\ 0 & p_i < p_c + k \end{cases}. \tag{11}$$

Taking advantage of the fuzziness of the method, supposing high differences on the local 3×3 window, all the $|k|$ bins can have the same value, while in case of low contrast, the bins may represent greater deviation. Finally, the histogram is divided by $|k|$.

Example 3. For $l = 3$, $k \in [-3, 3]$ and $|k| = 7$, therefore 7 bins are taken into account. The SLBP value of the center pixel in the matrix I defined in (3) is

- for $k \in \{-3, -2\}$: $1 \cdot 2^0 + 0 \cdot 2^1 + 1 \cdot 2^2 + 1 \cdot 2^3 + 1 \cdot 2^4 + 0 \cdot 2^5 + 1 \cdot 2^6 + 0 \cdot 2^7 = 93$,
- for $k \in \{-1, 0\}$: $1 \cdot 2^0 + 0 \cdot 2^1 + 1 \cdot 2^2 + 1 \cdot 2^3 + 0 \cdot 2^4 + 0 \cdot 2^5 + 1 \cdot 2^6 + 0 \cdot 2^7 = 77$,
- for $k \in \{1, 2, 3\}$: $1 \cdot 2^0 + 0 \cdot 2^1 + 1 \cdot 2^2 + 1 \cdot 2^3 + 0 \cdot 2^4 + 0 \cdot 2^5 + 0 \cdot 2^6 + 0 \cdot 2^7 = 13$.

Thus, the 13th bin gets $3/7$ value, the 77th and the 93th bins get $2/7$ value, and the contribution to all other bins are zero.

3.4   DRLBP (Dominant Rotated Local Binary Patterns)

Caused by the fixed arrangement of weights, the basic LBP is not invariant to rotations and viewpoint changes. Thus, in [15] an extended LBP variant was proposed to ensure rotation-invariance. Its main idea is that the weights are aligned in a circular manner, so the effect of image rotations can be followed by rotating the weights by the same (unknown) angle. The dominant direction is defined as the index of the neighboring pixel whose difference from the central pixel is maximum:

$$D = \operatorname*{argmax}_{i \in \{0, \cdots, N-1\}} |p_i - p_c|, \tag{12}$$

which quantizes the dominant directions into N discrete values. Thus, (4) becomes

$$DRLBP(p_c) = \sum_{i=0}^{N-1} d_i \cdot 2^{\bmod(i-D,N)}, \tag{13}$$

where the mod operator circularly shifts the weights with respect to the dominant direction, while the sequence of weights remains the same. The shift results in a rotation invariance, as the weights exclusively depend on the neighborhood.

Example 4. The dominant direction in the position p_c of matrix I defined in (3) is $D = 1$ corresponding to the neighbor p_1 with the maximal difference $|0 - 132|$. Thus, $DRLBP(p_c) = 0 \cdot 2^0 + 1 \cdot 2^1 + 1 \cdot 2^2 + 0 \cdot 2^3 + 0 \cdot 2^4 + 1 \cdot 2^5 + 0 \cdot 2^6 + 1 \cdot 2^7 = 166$.

4   Experimental Setup

4.1   SA (Simulated Annealing)

To optimize the cost function in (2) we use simulated annealing (SA) [9]. In the cost function, $\Phi(\mathbf{x})$ measures the Euclidean distance between the LBP vector of the current image and all representative LBP vectors of the image patches observed in advance, and finally it takes the minimum. Formally,

$$\Phi(\mathbf{x}) = \min_t \{\|LBP(\mathbf{x}) - LBP(\mathbf{x_t})\|_2\} \tag{14}$$

where $\mathbf{x_1}, \mathbf{x_2}, \ldots, \mathbf{x_t}$ are the t sample images from the same class as of $\mathbf{x}$, known a priori. In our setting we observe 150 random patches of size 64×64 as prior dataset, thus $t = 150$. In (14) one could use any variant of the LBP descriptor. We choose here SLBP (with $k = 3$). The reason of this will be given later, in this paper. The pseudocode of the optimization is given in Algorithm 1.

All the parameters of the SA algorithm are set manually on an empirical way. The method starts each time from a random binary image. The stopping criteria of the algorithm is to reach 800 000 iterations or to perform 25 000 iterations without improving the optimal result. The initial temperature is set to $T_1 = 5\ 800$ while the cooling schedule is controlled by $\alpha = 0.99$. The SA algorithm may stay in identical temperature for some iterations. In our case this is fine-tuned by $\beta = 0.035$. Choosing a neighbor means randomly choosing and inverting some of the image pixels. We found that inverting only a single pixel per iteration cannot significantly decrease the cost value at the beginning. The number l of pixels to be inverted in each iteration depends on the previous cost value $f(s)$, more precisely, $l = \eta \cdot f(s)$ with $\eta = \beta/2 = 0.0176$. Based on empirical experiments we found that the value of the γ scaling parameter in the cost function had to be determined individually, for each image class. SA as well as the LBP algorithms were implemented in MATLAB. For LBP, FLBP, and SLBP we used implementations of [11,22].

Algorithm 1. Simulated Annealing

1: $s \leftarrow$ initial state
2: $T_1 \leftarrow$ initial temperature
3: $k \leftarrow 1$
4: $\alpha \in (0.5, 1)$
5: $\beta \in (0, 1)$
6: **while** ($stoppingCriteria == FALSE$) **do**
7:     $tempStay := 0$
8:     **while** ($tempStay < \beta \cdot f(s)$) **do**
9:        $actual := neighbor(s)$
10:       **if** ($f(actual) < f(s)$) **then**
11:          $s := actual$
12:       **else if** ($e^{\frac{f(s)-f(actual)}{T_k}} > rand(0,1)$) **then**
13:          $s := actual$
14:       **end if**
15:       $tempStay := tempStay + 1$
16:    **end while**
17:    $T_{k+1} := T_k \cdot \alpha$
18:    $k := k + 1$
19: **end while**

4.2 DART (Discrete Algebraic Reconstruction Technique)

DART is an algebraic reconstruction technique, which takes advantage of the properties of the discrete images: the range of image function is finite and contains just a small number of elements [2]. Its idea is that thresholding the result of an arbitrary continuous reconstruction method gives usually an approximately good result even for the discrete problem, except some inaccuracies at the boundary of the object in the image. Therefore, after performing a continuous reconstruction and thresholding it, DART iteratively refines the boundary. It is one of the most effective algorithms in the field of Binary Tomography. We will use this method here for a comparative study.

5 Results

5.1 Comparison of the LBP Variants

In [20] we applied only the basic LBP feature as prior information. In the reconstruction we took two priors into account: the image must be smooth and – in the same time – it must have a texture similar to the previously observed ones. Note that the texture information prior itself implicitly forces some degree of homogeneity (in case of homogeneous textures), too, thus smoothness prior could be omitted if the texture descriptor was sufficiently expressive. Performing experimental analysis on software phantom images (arising from several classes with different textures) we found that the concept of [20] is promising, especially in case of few projections. However, we also deduced that the expressive power of the standard LBP descriptor was not satisfactory enough, in some cases. Fortunately, an advantage of our approach is that it can be evolved by using other versions of LBP. Thus, we conduct here experiments with the aforementioned LBP versions.

It is clear that the same LBP vector can belong to many different (binary) matrices which may lead to an incorrect reconstruction [21]. To investigate this issue, we generated all the 512 binary matrices of size 3 × 3, and examined their LBP vectors. We found that if the center pixel is 0, in case of LBP and DRLBP the calculated vector is always the same, only the 255th bin had nonzero (one) value. On the other hand, both SLBP and FLBP provided 511 different vectors, and only the full zeros and full ones matrices had the same vectors. Thus, we can deduce, that the distinguishing power of SLBP and FLBP is greater than that of LBP or DRLBP. However, FLBP is extremely slow to compute compared to the other methods. The expected running times of the different variants of LBP are as follows, on the same binary image of size 64 × 64 (see also [12] for a thorough comparison), $LBP = 0.004$ s, $DRLBP = 0.0016$ s, $SLBP = 0.0028$ s, $FLBP = 1.6834$ s. Based on these observations we decided to use SLBP.

5.2   Measuring the Quality of Reconstructions

To determine the quality of reconstruction a commonly calculated measure is the Relative Mean Error [10] given by

$$RME = \frac{\sum_i |x_i^o - x_i^r|}{\sum_i x_i^o} \cdot 100\%, \tag{15}$$

where x_i^o and x_i^r stand for the i-th pixel of the original and reconstructed image, respectively. RME value gives the ratio of the pixel difference between the original and the result image, and the number of object pixels of the original image. Usually, the lower is the RME value, the better is the result. However, in case of textures this measure on its own is not always informative enough. There can be reconstructions that are visually acceptable, though they have high RME value. The chessboard image in Fig. 1c is a great example for this. Inverting it yields 200% RME, although the image has exactly the same texture and (horizontal and vertical) projections as the original one has. Thus, in the experiments we also calculated the projection difference $E_{proj} = ||\mathbf{Ax} - \mathbf{b}||_2$ and the SLBP difference $E_{SLBP} = \min_t\{||SLBP(\mathbf{x}) - SLBP(\mathbf{x_t})||_2\}$, i.e., the two terms of the cost function, separately.

5.3 Synthetic Images

Now that we have chosen the proper LBP variant, we can investigate reconstruction accuracy. In the first step, we generated software phantom images with simple textures (Fig. 1) of size 1024 × 1024. Then, we selected a random patch of size 64 × 64 from each phantom and we tried to reconstruct them from the horizontal and vertical projections. As prior information we used each time 150 randomly selected patches of size 64 × 64 from the same images. Due to the stochastic nature of SA, mean results of 20 runs of each image class are shown in the Table 1.

Table 1. Results on synthetic data.

Type	Time (s)	E_{proj}	E_{SLBP}	RME
Line image	598.61	1.41	0.91	0.00%
Grid image	421.23	1.41	0.74	0.00%
Chessboard image	4568.42	2.88	85.31	99.18%
Diagonal image	8144.78	3.76	232.35	99.74%

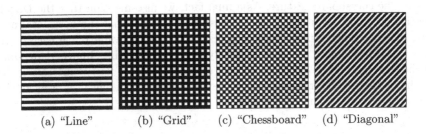

    (a) "Line"   (b) "Grid"   (c) "Chessboard"   (d) "Diagonal"

Fig. 1. Software phantom images.

As it clearly seen, in case of the "Line" and "Grid" images, the execution time is lower, RME is 0%, and both E_{proj} and E_{SLBP} are small. This is in accordance with the fact that these images are uniquely determined by their horizontal and vertical projections [19]. In case of the "Chessboard" and "Diagonal" images only E_{proj} is satisfactory. However, by increasing the γ weight of the SLBP term, the reconstructions can be forced to be more similar in texture to the observed patches. Nevertheless, fine-tuning this parameter is challenging.

To investigate the effect of increasing γ in case of the "Chessboard" image, consider the matrix

$$M = \begin{bmatrix} 1 & 0 \\ 0 & 1 \end{bmatrix}. \tag{16}$$

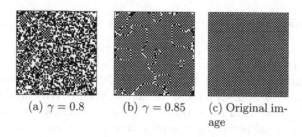

(a) $\gamma = 0.8$ (b) $\gamma = 0.85$ (c) Original image

Fig. 2. Reconstruction of the "Chessboard" image with increasing texture weights from the horizontal and vertical projections and the original image, respectively.

If we count the frequency of M being present as a submatrix in the reconstruction, we can get impression on how similar the reconstructed image is compared to the "Chessboard". Based on experiments we can say that increasing the SLBP weight from 0 to 0.8, there is no significant change in the frequency of M. Then, somewhere around 0.85 there is a big jump in frequency, and above 0.85 there is, again, no significant improvement. While the original image contains 1985 times M as submatrix, with SLBP weight 0.8 and 0.85 this frequency in the reconstructed image is 370 and 1729, respectively. The corresponding images are shown in Fig. 2a and b. We can observe that the image of Fig. 2a belonging to $\gamma = 0.8$ has no clear texture, while that of Fig. 2b with $\gamma = 0.85$ clearly reveals the chessboard texture. As a final fact, we also mention that the DART algorithm cannot reconstruct the "Chessboard" image from the horizontal and vertical projections. If first creates a grayscale image with value 0.5 at each pixel, and then thresholds it, resulting in a fully black or fully white image, depending on the threshold level. Similarly, in case of the "Diagonal" image increasing the weight of texture information can reduce the SLBP difference, as well as the projection error and the RME value.

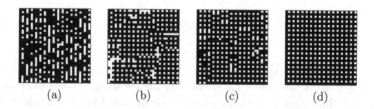

(a)   (b)   (c)   (d)

Fig. 3. Reconstruction of the "Grid" image using only its projection term, only the SLBP term, both terms, and the original image, respectively.

In our next experiment we optimized the objective function first taking into account only its projection term (omitting the SLBP term), then only the SLBP term, and finally both of them. The aim was to emphasize the importance of both terms. Table 2 together with the corresponding images of Fig. 3 show an evidence of this: the combination of both terms can ensure a reconstruction of Fig. 3d, that has low projection as well as low SLBP error. In the same time RME is also smaller, than those achieved using only one term of the objective function.

Table 2. Reconstruction attempts with one of the terms of the objective function, and with both of them.

	Figure 3a	Figure 3b	Figure 3c
Terms	Proj.	SLBP	Proj. + SLBP
RME (%)	98.44	187.11	79.30
E_{proj}	1.41	43.56	1.73
E_{SLBP}	53.42	20.91	19.27

5.4 Real Images

Owing to the auspicious results on the phantom images, we went on to test the algorithm on binary images (Fig. 4) coming from 3 different grayscale image classes. We reconstructed 10 image patches of size 64×64 from each class, using also only the horizontal and vertical projections. Figure 5 and Table 3 give one sample reconstruction of each class with their numerical data. We found that in most of the cases E_{proj} was less than 5 and E_{SLBP} was less than 30. The images reconstructed by our method are appealing and are similar in texture to the original images. DART, by its nature, prefers to create homogeneous areas, thus it fails to resemble the original texture. RMEs are high for both algorithms. However, we already discussed that it is not informative enough on its own. Taking a look at the E_{SLBP} values we are convinced that the SA-based method performs better in solving the reconstruction. We must add that our method needs 4–5 min for reconstructing an image whereas DART provides the reconstruction in a few seconds. This is the price we pay for better image quality.

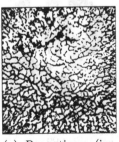 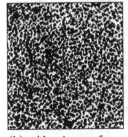 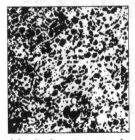

(a) Bone tissue (image class 1)   (b) Aluminum foam (image class 2)   (c) Carbonate sample (image class 3)

Fig. 4. Real images.

Of course, we cannot expect perfect reconstructions from only two projections. Still, the improvement in quality of our method is unquestionable. When the goal is for example to measure the density of the reconstructed image, the results of SA are promising.

Table 3. Sample reconstruction results on real images.

Image	Figure 5b	Figure 5c	Figure 5e	Figure 5f	Figure 5h	Figure 5i
E_{SLBP}	19.62	133.18	13.57	205.75	21.11	182.63
RME (%)	76.87	82.97	124.66	117.23	90.14	91.94

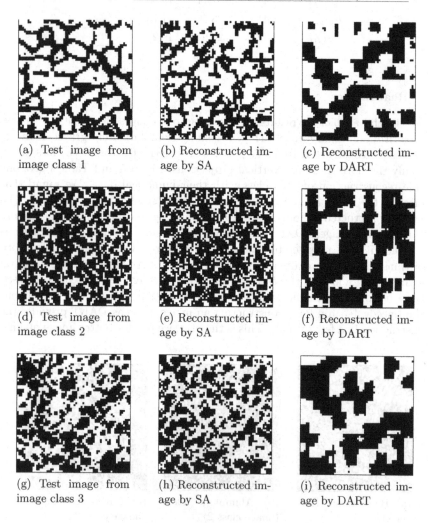

(a) Test image from image class 1

(b) Reconstructed image by SA

(c) Reconstructed image by DART

(d) Test image from image class 2

(e) Reconstructed image by SA

(f) Reconstructed image by DART

(g) Test image from image class 3

(h) Reconstructed image by SA

(i) Reconstructed image by DART

Fig. 5. Results.

6   Conclusion

In this paper we studied how texture information can improve the quality of binary tomographic reconstruction using few projections. We presented different versions of Local Binary Patterns and found that in our case the SLBP is the best choice. Integrating it into the reconstruction process we solved the corresponding optimization problem by SA. We observed that the widely used RME is not suitable in our case, to describe reconstruction quality, thus we investigated projection error and SLBP error of the reconstructions. We found that SLBP as texture prior information can significantly improve reconstruction quality, especially when only very few projections are available.

Acknowledgements. Judit Szűcs was supported by the UNKP-18-3 New National Excellence Program of the Ministry of Human Capacities. This research was supported by the project "Integrated program for training new generation of scientists in the fields of computer science", no. EFOP-3.6.3-VEKOP-16-2017-00002. The project has been supported by the European Union and co-funded by the European Social Fund. The authors thank Péter Bodnár for helping in implementation issues.

References

1. Ahonen, T., Pietikäinen, M.: Soft histograms for local binary patterns. In: Proceedings of the Finnish Signal Processing Symposium, FINSIG, vol. 5, p. 1 (2007)
2. Batenburg, K.J., Sijbers, J.: DART: a practical reconstruction algorithm for discrete tomography. IEEE Trans. Image Process. **20**(9), 2542–2553 (2011)
3. Brunetti, S., Del Lungo, A., Del Ristoro, F., Kuba, A., Nivat, M.: Reconstruction of 4-and 8-connected convex discrete sets from row and column projections. Linear Algebra Appl. **339**(1–3), 37–57 (2001)
4. Herman, G.T.: Fundamentals of Computerized Tomography: Image Reconstruction from Projections. Springer, London (2009). https://doi.org/10.1007/978-1-84628-723-7
5. Herman, G.T., Kuba, A.: Discrete Tomography: Foundations, Algorithms, and Applications. Springer, New York (1999). https://doi.org/10.1007/978-1-4612-1568-4
6. Herman, G.T., Kuba, A.: Advances in Discrete Tomography and its Applications. Springer, New York (2008). https://doi.org/10.1007/978-0-8176-4543-4
7. Iakovidis, D.K., Keramidas, E.G., Maroulis, D.: Fuzzy local binary patterns for ultrasound texture characterization. In: Campilho, A., Kamel, M. (eds.) ICIAR 2008. LNCS, vol. 5112, pp. 750–759. Springer, Heidelberg (2008). https://doi.org/10.1007/978-3-540-69812-8_74
8. Kak, A.C., Slaney, M.: Principles of Computerized Tomographic Imaging. IEEE Press, New York (1988)
9. Kirkpatrick, S., Gelatt, C.D., Vecchi, M.P., et al.: Optimization by simulated annealing. Science **220**(4598), 671–680 (1983)
10. Kuba, A., Herman, G.T., Matej, S., Todd-Pokropek, A.: Medical applications of discrete tomography. DIMACS Ser. Discret. Math. Theor. Comput. Sci. **55**, 195–208 (2000)

11. Kylberg, G.: FLBP and SLBP implementations for Matlab. http://www.cb.uu.se/~gustaf/textureDescriptors/

12. Kylberg, G., Sintorn, I.M.: Evaluation of noise robustness for local binary pattern descriptors in texture classification. EURASIP J. Image Video Process. **2013**(1), 17 (2013)

13. Lukić, T., Balázs, P.: Binary tomography reconstruction based on shape orientation. Pattern Recognit. Lett. **79**, 18–24 (2016)

14. Lukić, T., Lukity, A., Gogolák, L.: Binary tomography reconstruction method with perimeter preserving regularization. In: Proceedings of the 8th Conference of the Hungarian Association for Image Processing and Pattern Recognition, pp. 83–91 (2011)

15. Mehta, R., Egiazarian, K.: Dominant rotated local binary patterns (DRLBP) for texture classification. Pattern Recognit. Lett. **71**, 16–22 (2016)

16. Nanni, L., Lumini, A., Brahnam, S.: Survey on LBP based texture descriptors for image classification. Expert Syst. Appl. **39**(3), 3634–3641 (2012)

17. Ojala, T., Pietikäinen, M., Harwood, D.: A comparative study of texture measures with classification based on featured distributions. Pattern Recognit. **29**(1), 51–59 (1996)

18. Ojala, T., Pietikainen, M., Maenpaa, T.: Multiresolution gray-scale and rotation invariant texture classification with local binary patterns. IEEE Trans. Pattern Anal. Mach. Intell. **24**(7), 971–987 (2002)

19. Ryser, H.: Combinatorial properties of matrices of zeros and ones. Canad. J. Math. **9**, 371–377 (1957)

20. Szűcs, J., Balázs, P.: Binary image reconstruction using local binary pattern priors. Int. J. Circuits Syst. Signal Process. **11**, 296–299 (2017)

21. Waller, B., Nixon, M., Carter, J.: Image reconstruction from local binary patterns. In: International Conference on Signal-Image Technology and Internet-Based Systems, pp. 118–123 (2013)

22. Zhao, G.: LBP implementation for MATLAB. http://www.cse.oulu.fi/CMV/Downloads/LBPMatlab

Volumes of Blurred-Invariant Gaussians for Dynamic Texture Classification

Thanh Tuan Nguyen[1,2(✉)], Thanh Phuong Nguyen[1], Frédéric Bouchara[1], and Ngoc-Son Vu[3]

[1] Université de Toulon, Aix Marseille Université, CNRS, LIS, Marseille, France
[2] Faculty of IT, HCMC University of Technology and Education,
Ho Chi Minh City, Vietnam
tuannt@hcmute.edu.vn
[3] ETIS UMR 8051, Université de Paris Seine, UCP, ENSEA, CNRS, Cergy, France

Abstract. An effective model, which jointly captures shape and motion cues, for dynamic texture (DT) description is introduced by taking into account advantages of volumes of blurred-invariant features in three main following stages. First, a 3-dimensional Gaussian kernel is used to form smoothed sequences that allow to deal with well-known limitations of local encoding such as near uniform regions and sensitivity to noise. Second, a receptive volume of the Difference of Gaussians (DoG) is figured out to mitigate the negative impacts of environmental and illumination changes which are major challenges in DT understanding. Finally, a local encoding operator is addressed to construct a discriminative descriptor of enhancing patterns extracted from the filtered volumes. Evaluations on benchmark datasets (i.e., UCLA, DynTex, and DynTex++) for issue of DT classification have positively validated our crucial contributions.

Keywords: Dynamic texture · DoG · Gaussian filter · LBP · CLBP

1 Introduction

Dynamic textures (DTs) are textural characteristics repeated in temporal ranges, such as waves, trees, fire, clouds, fountain, blowing flag, etc. Analyzing to clarify them is an important task for different applications in computer vision. Various methods have been introduced with diverse procedures for describing DTs. In general, those can be roughly categorized into the following groups. *Optical-flow-based approaches* [18,20] efficiently represent the turbulent motion properties of DT videos in natural modes for issues of classifying DTs. In the meanwhile, filtering techniques are taken into account in *filtering-based approaches* to reduce the negative impacts of noise and illumination on encoding DT sequences. It should be noted that this technique is also effective for analyzing 2D texture images [14,35]. The group of *model-based approaches* [30,36] has mainly inherited the computational types of Linear Dynamical System [30] (LDS) and its

© Springer Nature Switzerland AG 2019
M. Vento and G. Percannella (Eds.): CAIP 2019, LNCS 11678, pp. 155–167, 2019.
https://doi.org/10.1007/978-3-030-29888-3_13

variants to model motions of DTs in spatio-temporal aspects, while *geometry-based approaches* [25,37,38] geometrically capture dynamic features for DT representation based on fractal analyses, such as dynamic fractal spectrum (DFS) [38], Multi-fractal spectrum (MFS) [37], and wavelet-based MFS [11]. Recently, *learning-based approaches* have been considerable due to their promising effect in DT recognition, which can be divided into two principle trends: deep learning methods (e.g., Convolutional Neural Networks (CNNs)) [1,2,22] utilize deep algorithms for learning features, and the other is dictionary-learning-based techniques [23,24] which are based on kernel sparse coding to produce learned dictionaries for DT description. Finally, *local-feature-based approaches* [15,16,31–34] are involved with Local Binary Pattern (LBP) operator which is fortunately applied for encoding still images thanks to its computational efficiency. For video representation, they mostly rely on two main LBP-based variants to enhance the capacity of discriminative power as follows: Volume LBP (VLBP) [39] formed on contiguous frames, and LBP-TOP [39] computed on three orthogonal planes.

Although achieving the positive performance on classifying DTs, some limitations have been enduring, such as in the filtering-based approaches: issues of noise and illumination [3]; in the local-feature-based methods: near uniform patterns, sensitivity to noise [15,32], and large dimensional problems [28,31,39]. In this paper, we propose an effectively computational framework to diminish these restrictions in the following steps. Firstly, a 3D Gaussian kernel is taken into account for analyzing videos as a pre-processing to point out blurred sequences with less sensitive to noise and near uniform regions. A receptive volume of DoG is then computed from these sequences to deal with the influences of environmental and illumination changes. Finally, a robust descriptor is structured by exploiting a local encoding operator (e.g., LBP, CLBP, etc) to jointly capture shape and motion cues of blurred-invariant features from three orthogonal planes of the filtered volumes. Experiments on various benchmarks have shown that our proposal promisingly performs compared to the state-of-the-art methods.

2 Proposed Method

Exploiting local features for video representation with an effective computation, the local-feature-based approaches have acquired promising results on DT recognition. In spite of that, their performance is still in restriction due to the problems of illumination, near uniform regions, and sensitivity to noise. In this section, we firstly recall LBP and its variants as well as Gaussian-based filtering kernels. We then introduce an efficient framework for DT representation based on above materials to address typical limitations of local encoding operators.

2.1 A Brief Review of LBP and Its Completed Model

A typical LBP code is defined as a chain of bits for describing local relationships between a center pixel and others in neighborhoods of a still image [19]. Accordingly, let $\mathcal{I}$ signify a 2D gray-scale image. A binary string for each pixel

$\mathbf{q} \in \mathcal{I}$ is formed by estimating the difference of gray-scale values of $\mathbf{q}$ and local neighbors $\{\mathbf{p}_i\}$ sampled its surrounding regions as

$$\text{LBP}_{P,R}(\mathbf{q}) = \left\{ sign\big(\mathcal{I}(\mathbf{p}_i) - \mathcal{I}(\mathbf{q})\big) \right\} \Big|_{i=0}^{P-1} \tag{1}$$

where P denotes a number of neighbors interpolated on a circle of radius R, $\mathcal{I}(.)$ comes out the gray-level of a pixel, and function $sign(.)$ is defined as

$$sign(x) = \begin{cases} 1, x \geq 0 \\ 0, \text{otherwise.} \end{cases} \tag{2}$$

In calculation of probability distributions for image texture representation, the LBP codes form a histogram with a large dimension of 2^P distinct values. In practice, two popular mappings are utilized to treat this shortcoming: $u2$ with $P(P-1)+3$ bins for uniform features and $riu2$ with $P+2$ bins for rotation invariant uniform features. In addition, other considerable mappings are also expected to improve the structuring operation, such as LBC [41] - an alternative of uniform patterns, $TAP^{\mathcal{A}}$ mapping [13] for addressing topological information.

Guo et al. [9] proposed a completed model of LBP (CLBP) in which three complemented components are incorporated in different ways for enhancing the performance: CLBP_S that is identical to the typical LBP, CLBP_M for capturing magnitude information, and CLBP_C for obtaining the difference between the gray-level of a center pixel and that of the mean on the whole image. Experiments in [9] also validated that the joint of three components (i.e., $\text{CLBP}_{S/M/C}$), which is used in our proposal, outperforms other configurations.

2.2   Blurred-Invariant Gaussian Volumes

A Gaussian filtering is a process of convolving a Gaussian kernel on a spatial domain. It should be in accordance with the regulation of a Gaussian distribution. In general, the n-dimensional Gaussian kernel is defined as follows.

$$\text{G}_\sigma^n(x_1, x_2, \ldots, x_n) = \frac{1}{(\sigma\sqrt{2\pi})^n} \exp\left(-\frac{x_1^2 + x_2^2 + \ldots + x_n^2}{2\sigma^2} \right) \tag{3}$$

in which σ means a pre-defined standard derivation, n denotes a number of spatial axes $\{x_i\}_{i=1}^n$ taken into account the convolutions.

For analysis of DT videos, the 3D Gaussian kernel should be applied as

$$\text{G}_\sigma^{3D}(x, y, t) = \frac{1}{(\sigma\sqrt{2\pi})^3} \exp\left(-\frac{x^2 + y^2 + t^2}{2\sigma^2} \right) \tag{4}$$

where x, y denote the spatial coordinates, t indicates the temporal coordinate. As a result of that, the difference of 3D Gaussian filters is computed as

$$\text{DoG}_{\sigma_1, \sigma_2}^{3D}(x, y, t) = \text{G}_{\sigma_1}^{3D}(x, y, t) - \text{G}_{\sigma_2}^{3D}(x, y, t) \tag{5}$$

Two above kernels $G_{\sigma_1}^{3D}$ and $DoG_{\sigma_1,\sigma_2}^{3D}$ are used to filter a DT video resulting in filtered volumes of blurred $(\mathcal{V}_G)$ and invariant $(\mathcal{V}_{DoG})$ features as follows.

$$\begin{cases} \mathcal{V}_{G_{\sigma_1}} = G_{\sigma_1}^{3D}(x,y,t) * \mathcal{V} \\ \mathcal{V}_{DoG_{\sigma_1,\sigma_2}} = |DoG_{\sigma_1,\sigma_2}^{3D}(x,y,t)| * \mathcal{V} \end{cases} \tag{6}$$

where $\mathcal{V}$ means a volume of DTs, $\sigma_1 < \sigma_2$, "$*$" is the convolutional operator. This volume filtering is illustrated in the second image line of Fig. 1.

Fig. 1. A sample of Gaussian filterings. (a) is an input gray-scale frame in a DT video. (b_1), (c_1) are 2D smoothed images of (a) using $\sigma_1 = 0.5$, $\sigma_2 = 4$ respectively, and (d_1) denotes the 2D DoG of them [17]. In the meanwhile, (b_2), (c_2) are 3D blurred frames of (a) with the above standard derivations, and (d_2) is the 3D DoG of (b_2) and (c_2).

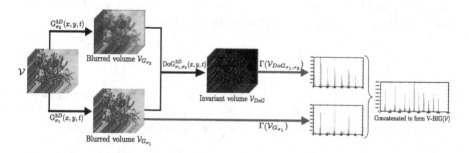

Fig. 2. (Best viewed in color) Our proposed framework for structuring volumes of blurred-invariant features. Therein, the black arrow denotes a pre-processing of Gaussian filters while the blue implies a process of encoding the filtered volumes. (Color figure online)

2.3   Proposed DT Descriptor

In this section, we propose a simple framework to efficiently capture appearance information and motion cues for DT representation. For a given video $\mathcal{V}$, the proposed framework consists of three major steps to encode DT characteristics (see Fig. 2 for graphical illustration). Firstly, the 3D Gaussian-based filters $G_{\sigma_1}^{3D}$ and $DoG_{\sigma_1,\sigma_2}^{3D}$ are taken into account for analyzing $\mathcal{V}$ as a pre-processing stage to figure out its corresponding filtered volumes, i.e., $\mathcal{V}_{G_{\sigma_1}}$ and $\mathcal{V}_{DoG_{\sigma_1,\sigma_2}}$, against the issues of noise and illumination. Secondly, each of these volumes is broken into the separative frames of image textures according to its three orthogonal planes $\{XY, XT, YT\}$. A local encoding operator Ψ is then utilized for these planes to extract spatial information and motion properties of DTs as follows.

$$\Gamma(\mathcal{V}_{G_{\sigma_1}/DoG_{\sigma_1,\sigma_2}}) = \left[\Psi(f_i \in XY), \Psi(f_j \in XT), \Psi(f_k \in YT)\right] \qquad (7)$$

where frames f_i, f_j, and f_k belong to the corresponding planes of a filtered volume, $\Psi(.)$ denotes a function of local encoding structures (e.g., LBP, CLBP, etc.) for capturing smoothing characteristics of spatio-temporal cues from $\mathcal{V}_{G_{\sigma_1}}$ and invariant features of those from $\mathcal{V}_{DoG_{\sigma_1,\sigma_2}}$. An instance for encoding $\mathcal{V}_{G_{\sigma_1}}$ is graphically illustrated in Fig. 3. Finally, the achieved histograms are normalized and concatenated to produce a robust descriptor based on the volumes of blurred-invariant Gaussians V-BIG($\mathcal{V}_{\sigma_1,\sigma_2}$) to enhance the performance.

$$\text{V-BIG}(\mathcal{V}_{\sigma_1,\sigma_2}) = \left[\Gamma(\mathcal{V}_{G_{\sigma_1}}), \Gamma(\mathcal{V}_{DoG_{\sigma_1,\sigma_2}})\right] \qquad (8)$$

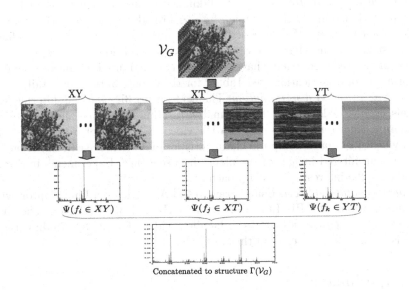

Fig. 3. Encoding model for a filtered volume $\mathcal{V}_G$.

2.4 Beneficial Properties of the Proposed Descriptor

Similar to FoSIG [17], our descriptor takes advantage of the following beneficial properties to enhance the discriminant power. In addition, V-BIG are involved with an important feature of informative voxel discrimination that leads to its outstanding performance compared to FoSIG in most of circumstances. Figure 1 shows a specific comparison of using 2D and 3D Gaussian filtering kernels, in which the outputs of the 3D filter seem more "stable" than that of 2D.

- *Robustness to changes of illumination and environment:* Filtered volumes $\mathcal{V}_G$ and $\mathcal{V}_{DoG}$ are robust against changes of illumination thanks to 3D Gaussian filtering kernels. Furthermore, the receptive DoG volume against scale changes, computed by two Gaussians of different scales, allows to capture features with more robustness to the major remaining problems of DT description: illumination, scale, and changes of environment.
- *Robustness to noise:* Instead of encoding on a raw video $\mathcal{V}$, its filtered volumes, i.e., $\mathcal{V}_G$ and $\mathcal{V}_{DoG}$, are addressed to exploit local features with more intensities to noise. It should be noted that the 2D Gaussian filtering kernel has been taken into account for analyzing neighborhoods at various regional scales of a pixel for textural image description [12], and capturing spatio-temporal information based on filtered images of the planes in a video [17]. Different from those, the 3D Gaussian filtering kernels is used to enrich discriminative information of voxels in consideration of the whole sequence. On the other hand, our proposal also integrates DoG filters to make descriptor more robust against environmental and illumination changes.
- *Forceful discriminative factors:* Well-known as an approximation of Laplacian of Gaussian (LoG), volume of $\mathcal{V}_{DoG}$ provides useful receptive properties for encoding DT features. In the meanwhile, volume of $\mathcal{V}_G$ produces robust smoothing characteristics for DT representation. As a result, these complemented components have significantly contributed to improve the performance of classification (see Table 2 for their contributions in detail).
- *Informative voxel discrimination:* Thanks to using 3D Gaussian filtering kernels, each voxel is enriched by informative discrimination that allows to *jointly capture shape and motion cues* of a DT video. It is different from FoSIG [17], in which just spatio-temporal characteristics of a voxel are calculated on 2D Gaussian filtered images of the planes in a sequence. Experiments in Sect. 3 validate the interest of this approach compared to [17].
- *Low computational cost:* Using a raw MATLAB code on a Linux laptop with configurations of CPU Intel Core i7 1.9 GHz and 4G RAM, our encoding algorithm just takes less 0.84 s to handle a video of $48 \times 48 \times 75$ dimension. It is about 0.08 s faster than that of FoSIG [17] (0.92 s).

3 Experiments

To evaluate the performance of our proposition, we address descriptor V-BIG for task of DT recognition on different benchmark DT datasets, i.e., UCLA

[30], DynTex [21], and DynTex++ [8]. For classifying, we utilize a linear multi-class SVM algorithm with the default parameters which is implemented in the LIBLINEAR[1] library [7]. The obtained rates are then evaluated in comparison with the state-of-the-art results.

3.1 Experimental Settings

To structure filtered volumes, we investigate $\sigma_1 = 0.5$, $\sigma_2 = \{1, 2, 3, 4, 5, 6\}$, and $x, y, t \in [-3\sigma, 3\sigma]$. For calculating the proposed descriptor, CLBP operator is exploited to capture local features of these volumes, i.e., $\Psi = \text{CLBP}_{\{(P,R)\}}^{riu2}$ with joint parameters of $riu2$ mapping, $\{(P, R)\} = \{(8, 1)\}$ for single-scale, and $\{(8, 1), (8, 2)\}$ for multi-scale to acquire more local relationships in further regions. As a result of those, the obtained descriptors have dimensions of 1200 and 2400 bins respectively. For comparison with the state of the art, the setting of $(\sigma_1, \sigma_2) = (0.5, 6)$ for the multi-scale encoding is appointed thanks to its outperformance on most of DT datasets. Empirically, it should be addressed $\sigma_2 \in [1, 6]$ due to a reduction of spatial information in case of $\sigma_2 > 6$.

3.2 Datasets and Protocols

The properties of benchmark datasets as well as experimental protocols, which are used for verifying our proposal, are exposed in this section. The summary in brief of those is shown in Table 1 for a convenient search.

UCLA Dataset: Saisan et al. [30] composed 50 categories of 200 DT sequences in $110 \times 160 \times 75$ dimension with four videos for each of groups. In experiments of DT recognition, a split version of $48 \times 48 \times 75$ is often used and divided into the challenging subsets as follows.

- *50-class:* DT classification using the original 50 categories with two protocols: *leave-one-out* (LOO) [3,33] and *4-fold cross validation* [15,32].
- *9-class* and *8-class:* 50 categories are readjusted in a different way to construct a sub-dataset of 9 groups named as "boiling water" (8), "plants" (108), "sea" (12), "fire" (8), "flowers" (12), "fountains" (20), "smoke" (4), "water" (12), and "waterfall" (16), in which the numbers in parentheses mean their quantities. As the dominance of "plants" class, it is discarded to form an 8-class scheme with more challenges [38]. Similarly, the protocol is set as in [8,15], that a half of samples in each group is randomly taken out for training and the remain for testing. The average rates of 20 runtimes on these schemes are reported as the final results.

DynTex Dataset: Péteri et al. [21] recorded more than 650 high-quality DT videos in differences of environmental conditions. Identical to [2,3,6], LOO is used to evaluate DT classification rates for all of the following sub-datsets.

---

[1] https://www.csie.ntu.edu.tw/~cjlin/liblinear.

- *DynTex35:* It is constructed as a challenging sub-dataset from clipping 35 videos as follows: randomly splitting each video at different cutting points but not in the half of X, Y, and T axes to acquire 8 non-overlapping sub-videos; further splitting along its T axis to obtain 2 more. As a result of that, *DynTex35* is ranged into 10 categories [3,32,39].
- *Alpha:* It consists of three categories of 20 sequences.
- *Beta:* It includes 162 videos grouped into 10 classes with different quantities.
- *Gamma:* It contains 10 classes of 264 DT videos with varied cardinalities.

DynTex++ Dataset: 345 raw videos of DynTex are pre-processed so that just the main turbulent motions are taken out and fixed in dimension of $50 \times 50 \times 50$ [8]. They are then grouped into 36 categories with 100 sub-videos for each, i.e., 3600 DTs in total. Similar to [3,8], a half of items of each group is randomly chosen for training and the remain for testing. The mean of 10 runtimes is reported as the final recognition rate.

Table 1. A summary of main properties of DT datasets.

Dataset	Sub-dataset	#Videos	Resolution	#Classes	Protocol
UCLA	50-class	200	$48 \times 48 \times 75$	50	LOO and 4fold
	9-class	200	$48 \times 48 \times 75$	9	50%/50%
	8-class	92	$48 \times 48 \times 75$	8	50%/50%
DynTex	DynTex35	350	Different dimensions	10	LOO
	Alpha	60	$352 \times 288 \times 250$	3	LOO
	Beta	162	$352 \times 288 \times 250$	10	LOO
	Gamma	264	$352 \times 288 \times 250$	10	LOO
DynTex++		3600	$50 \times 50 \times 50$	36	50%/50%

Note: LOO and 4fold are leave-one-out and four cross-fold validation respectively. 50%/50% denotes a protocol of taking randomly 50% samples for training and the remain (50%) for testing.

3.3   Experimental Results

Evaluations of our proposed descriptor V-BIG on the benchmark DT datasets are presented in Table 3, in which the highest rates are in bold. In the meanwhile, Table 2 shows the important contributions of each kind of filtered features in performing DT recognition. It can be verified from these tables that exploiting the filtered volumes of smooth-invariant patterns in video representation figures out a robust descriptor with outstanding operation. The experimental results are compared to those of the existing methods in Table 4. In general, our proposal is more efficient than the others, except deep-learning-based approaches utilizing a giant computational cost for DT description. It should be noted that

Table 2. Comparison rates (%) on DynTex++ between FoSIG [17] on filtered images and V-BIG on filtered volumes using settings of $riu2$ mapping and $\{(P, R)\} = \{(8, 1)\}$.

Descriptor	FoSIG$_{8,1}^{riu2}$ of [17]			Our V-BIG$_{8,1}^{riu2}$		
(σ_1, σ_2)	$G_{\sigma_1}^{2D}$	$DoG_{\sigma_1,\sigma_2}^{2D}$	$G_{\sigma_1}^{2D} + DoG_{\sigma_1,\sigma_2}^{2D}$	$G_{\sigma_1}^{3D}$	$DoG_{\sigma_1,\sigma_2}^{3D}$	$G_{\sigma_1}^{3D} + DoG_{\sigma_1,\sigma_2}^{3D}$
$(0.5, 3)$	95.73	93.19	96.38	96.01	94.61	96.45
$(0.5, 4)$	95.73	93.33	96.39	96.01	94.55	96.33
$(0.5, 5)$	95.73	93.52	96.12	96.01	94.26	96.14
$(0.5, 6)$	95.73	93.78	95.99	96.01	94.43	96.59

Table 3. Classification rates (%) on DT benchmark datasets.

Dataset	UCLA				DynTex				Dyn++
$\{(P, R)\}, (\sigma_1, \sigma_2)$	50-LOO	50-4fold	9-class	8-class	Dyn35	Alpha	Beta	Gamma	
$\{(8, 1)\}, (0.5, 1)$	98.50	99.00	96.90	96.74	98.57	100	93.83	94.32	96.53
$\{(8, 1)\}, (0.5, 2)$	**99.50**	**99.50**	97.70	96.96	97.43	100	93.83	93.56	96.51
$\{(8, 1)\}, (0.5, 3)$	99.00	**99.50**	97.75	96.74	98.57	100	93.21	92.42	96.45
$\{(8, 1)\}, (0.5, 4)$	98.50	99.00	**98.00**	96.41	98.57	100	93.21	92.80	96.33
$\{(8, 1)\}, (0.5, 5)$	98.50	99.00	97.65	97.72	98.57	100	93.21	92.80	96.14
$\{(8, 1)\}, (0.5, 6)$	99.00	**99.50**	97.80	**98.04**	98.86	100	93.83	92.80	96.59
$\{(8, 1), (8, 2)\}, (0.5, 1)$	99.00	99.00	97.55	96.30	**99.43**	100	94.44	93.94	96.59
$\{(8, 1), (8, 2)\}, (0.5, 2)$	99.00	99.00	97.15	96.96	98.57	100	94.44	**94.70**	96.52
$\{(8, 1), (8, 2)\}, (0.5, 3)$	98.50	99.00	97.00	96.63	99.14	100	94.44	**94.70**	96.57
$\{(8, 1), (8, 2)\}, (0.5, 4)$	99.00	99.00	97.65	96.30	98.57	100	**95.06**	94.32	96.42
$\{(8, 1), (8, 2)\}, (0.5, 5)$	99.00	99.00	97.45	96.20	99.14	100	**95.06**	94.32	96.61
$\{(8, 1), (8, 2)\}, (0.5, 6)$	**99.50**	**99.50**	97.95	97.50	**99.43**	100	**95.06**	94.32	**96.65**

Note: 50-LOO and 50-4fold denote results on 50-class breakdown using leave-one-out and four cross-fold validation. Dyn35 and Dyn++ are shortened for DynTex35 and DynTex++ sub-datasets respectively.

V-BIG also outperforms significantly FoSIG [17] with the same single-scale settings of CLBP$_{\{(8,1)\}}^{riu2}$ and $(\sigma_1, \sigma_2) = (0.5, 6)$ (see Tables 3 and 4). Hereafter, the proficiency of V-BIG on the specific datasets are assessed in detail.

UCLA Dataset: In this scenario, V-BIG outperforms on schemes of *50-LOO* and *50-4fold* with the settings for comparison (see Table 3). With rate of 99.5% for both of them, the proposed method deals with the same as performances of all existing approaches, including deep-learning-based techniques, i.e., DT-CNN [1] and PCANet-TOP [2] (see Table 4). In aspects of DT classification on *9-class* and *8-class*, our proposal achieves comparative results compared to the local-feature-based methods. More specifically, it can be seen in Table 4 that V-BIG's performance obtains recognition rates of 97.95%, 97.5% respectively, about 1.3% lower than those of the recent local-feature-based approaches, such as FoSIG's [17] (98.95%, 98.59%), CVLBC's [40] (99.20%, 99.02%), and MEWLSP's [34] (98.55%, 98.04%). It should be noted that their abilities are either not verified

Table 4. Comparison of recognition rates (%) on benchmark DT datasets

Group	Dataset Encoding method	UCLA 50-LOO	50-4fold	9-class	8-class	DynTex Dyn35	Alpha	Beta	Gamma	Dyn++
A	FDT [18]	98.50	99.00	97.70	99.35	98.86	98.33	93.21	91.67	95.31
	FD-MAP [18]	99.50	99.00	99.35	**99.57**	98.86	98.33	92.59	91.67	95.69
B	AR-LDS [30]	89.90^{N}	-	-	-	-	-	-	-	-
	KDT-MD [4]	-	97.50	-	-	-	-	-	-	-
	NLDR [26]	-	-	-	80.00	-	-	-	-	-
	Chaotic vector [36]	-	-	85.10^{N}	85.00^{N}	-	-	-	-	-
C	3D-OTF [37]	-	87.10	97.23	99.50	96.70	83.61	73.22	72.53	89.17
	WMFS [11]	-	-	97.11	96.96	-	-	-	-	-
	NLSSA [5]	-	-	-	-	-	-	-	-	92.40
	KSSA [5]	-	-	-	-	-	-	-	-	92.20
	DKSSA [5]	-	-	-	-	-	-	-	-	91.10
	DFS [38]	-	100	97.50	99.20	97.16	85.24	76.93	74.82	91.70
	2D+T [6]	-	-	-	-	-	85.00	67.00	63.00	-
	STLS [25]	-	99.50	97.40	99.50	98.20	89.40	80.80	79.80	94.50
D	MBSIF-TOP [3]	99.50^{N}	-	-	-	98.61^{N}	90.00^{N}	90.70^{N}	91.30^{N}	97.12^{N}
	DNGP [29]	-	-	**99.60**	99.40	-	-	-	-	93.80
E	VLBP [39]	-	89.50^{N}	96.30^{N}	91.96^{N}	81.14^{N}	-	-	-	94.98^{N}
	LBP-TOP [39]	-	94.50^{N}	96.00^{N}	93.67^{N}	92.45^{N}	98.33	88.89	84.85^{N}	94.05^{N}
	DDLBP with MJMI [28]	-	-	-	-	-	-	-	-	95.80
	CVLBP [31]	-	93.00^{N}	96.90^{N}	95.65^{N}	85.14^{N}	-	-	-	-
	HLBP [32]	95.00^{N}	95.00^{N}	98.35^{N}	97.50^{N}	98.57^{N}	-	-	-	96.28^{N}
	CLSP-TOP [15]	99.00^{N}	99.00^{N}	98.60^{N}	97.72^{N}	98.29^{N}	95.00^{N}	91.98^{N}	91.29^{N}	95.50^{N}
	MEWLSP [34]	96.50^{N}	96.50^{N}	98.55^{N}	98.04^{N}	99.71^{N}	-	-	-	98.48^{N}
	WLBPC [33]	-	96.50^{N}	97.17^{N}	97.61^{N}	-	-	-	-	95.01^{N}
	CVLBC [40]	98.50^{N}	99.00^{N}	99.20^{N}	99.02^{N}	98.86^{N}	-	-	-	91.31^{N}
	CSAP-TOP [16]	**99.50**	99.50	96.80	95.98	100	96.67	92.59	90.53	-
	FoSIG [17]	**99.50**	100	98.95	98.59	99.14	96.67	92.59	92.42	95.99
	Our V-BIG	**99.50**	99.50	97.95	97.50	99.43	100	95.06	94.32	96.65
F	DL-PEGASOS [8]	-	97.50	95.60	-	-	-	-	-	63.70
	PI-LBP+super hist [27]	-	100^{N}	98.20^{N}	-	-	-	-	-	-
	PD-LBP+super hist [27]	-	100^{N}	98.10^{N}	-	-	-	-	-	-
	PCA-cLBP [27]	-	-	-	-	-	-	-	-	92.40
	Orthogonal Tensor DL [24]	-	99.80	98.20	99.50	-	87.80	76.70	74.80	94.70
	Equiangular Kernel DL [23]	-	-	-	-	-	88.80	77.40	75.60	93.40
	st-TCoF [22]	-	-	-	-	100*	100*	98.11*	-	-
	PCANet-TOP [2]	99.50*	-	-	-	96.67*	90.74*	89.39*	-	-
	D3 [10]	-	-	-	-	100*	100*	98.11*	-	-
	DT-CNN-AlexNet [1]	-	99.50*	98.05*	98.48*	100*	99.38*	**99.62***	-	98.18*
	DT-CNN-GoogleNet [1]	-	99.50*	98.35*	99.02*	100*	100*	**99.62***	-	**98.58***

Note: "-" means "not available". Superscript "*" indicates results using deep learning algorithms. "N" indicates rates with 1-NN classifier. 50-LOO and 50-4fold denote results on 50-class breakdown using leave-one-out and four cross-fold validation respectively. Dyn35 and Dyn++ are abbreviated for DynTex35 and DynTex++ datasets respectively. Evaluations of VLBP and LBP-TOP operators are referred to the evaluations of implementations in [22,32]. Group A denotes *optical-flow-based* approaches, B: *model-based*, C: *geometry-based*, D: *filter-based*, E: *local-feature-based*, F: *learning-based*.

on the other challenging datasets (MEWLSP, CVLBC) or not better than ours on DynTex and DynTex++ (FoSIG).

DynTex Dataset: It can be observed from Table 4, our method obtains rate of 99.43% on *DynTex35*, the best result compared to all approaches, except

MEWLSP [34] (99.71%) and CSAP-TOP [16] (100%). However, MEWLSP has not been verified on the challenging DT datasets (i.e., *Alpha, Beta, Gamma*) as well as not perform better than ours in schemes of *50-LOO* and *50-4fold*. In the meanwhile, CSAP-TOP is only little higher than ours on this scheme, but not on the others (see Table 4). In terms of DT classification on the other variants of DynTex datasets, V-BIG achieves the best performance on *Alpha* with rate of 100% among the state of the art, over 3% better than FoSIG's [17] (96.67%) and the same as that of the deep-learning-based methods, i.e., DT-CNN [1], st-TCoF [22], and D3 [10]. It is also verified that our method outperforms prominently on *Beta* and *Gamma* sub-datasets, obtaining the best results compared to all non-deep-learning methods. Specifically, with rates of 95.06% and 94.32% on *Beta* and *Gamma* respectively, V-BIG is about 2% higher than FDT's [18] with 93.21% and FoSIG's [17] with 92.42% (see Table 4).

DynTex++ Dataset: On this scheme, our method gains the highest rate of 96.65% using the settings chosen for comparison (see Table 3). This performance is the best compared to the state-of-the-art results, excluding MEWLSP [34] with 98.48%, MBSIF-TOP [3] 97.12%, and DT-CNN [1] 98.18%, 98.58% for AlexNet and GoogleNet frameworks respectively (see Table 4). However, MEWLSP and MBSIF-TOP have either not been evaluated on the variants of DynTex (i.e., *Alpha, Beta, Gamma*) or not better than ours in recognition on most of datasets. Meanwhile, DT-CNN takes huge computation to learning DT features with complex algorithms. In comparison with FoSIG's [17], ours is also higher, 96.59% versus 95.99%, with the same settings of $\{(P, R)\} = \{(8, 1)\}$ and $(\sigma_1, \sigma_2) = (0.5, 6)$ (see Tables 2 and 3).

4   Conclusions

In this work, an efficient framework for DT representation has been proposed by exploiting the benefits of smooth-invariant features which are extracted from 3D Gaussian filtered volumes in order to construct a robust descriptor against the problems of illumination and noise. Evaluations for DT classification on the different benchmark datasets have verified that our method outperforms significantly compared to the state of the art. Furthermore, the experiments have also validated that encoding DT features based on the 3D filtered volumes allows to enrich more information of shape and motion cues than capturing spatio-temporal patterns based on the 2D Gaussian filtered images in the planes of a DT video [17]. In the further contexts, the advantages of these properties can be taken into account to form a descriptor with more discrimination.

References

1. Andrearczyk, V., Whelan, P.F.: Convolutional neural network on three orthogonal planes for dynamic texture classification. Pattern Recogn. **76**, 36–49 (2018)
2. Arashloo, S.R., Amirani, M.C., Noroozi, A.: Dynamic texture representation using a deep multi-scale convolutional network. JVCIR **43**, 89–97 (2017)

3. Arashloo, S.R., Kittler, J.: Dynamic texture recognition using multiscale binarized statistical image features. IEEE Trans. Multimed. 16(8), 2099–2109 (2014)
4. Chan, A.B., Vasconcelos, N.: Classifying video with kernel dynamic textures. In: CVPR, pp. 1–6 (2007)
5. Baktashmotlagh, M., Harandi, M., Lovell, B.C., Salzmann, M.: Discriminative nonlinear stationary subspace analysis for video classification. IEEE Trans. PAMI 36(12), 2353–2366 (2014)
6. Dubois, S., Péteri, R., Ménard, M.: Characterization and recognition of dynamic textures based on the 2D+T curvelet transform. Sig. Image Video Process. 9(4), 819–830 (2015)
7. Fan, R., Chang, K., Hsieh, C., Wang, X., Lin, C.: LIBLINEAR: a library for large linear classification. JMLR 9, 1871–1874 (2008)
8. Ghanem, B., Ahuja, N.: Maximum margin distance learning for dynamic texture recognition. In: Daniilidis, K., Maragos, P., Paragios, N. (eds.) ECCV 2010. LNCS, vol. 6312, pp. 223–236. Springer, Heidelberg (2010). https://doi.org/10.1007/978-3-642-15552-9_17
9. Guo, Z., Zhang, L., Zhang, D.: A completed modeling of local binary pattern operator for texture classification. IEEE Trans. IP 19(6), 1657–1663 (2010)
10. Hong, S., Ryu, J., Im, W., Yang, H.S.: D3: recognizing dynamic scenes with deep dual descriptor based on key frames and key segments. Neurocomputing 273, 611–621 (2018)
11. Ji, H., Yang, X., Ling, H., Xu, Y.: Wavelet domain multifractal analysis for static and dynamic texture classification. IEEE Trans. IP 22(1), 286–299 (2013)
12. Mäenpää, T., Pietikäinen, M.: Multi-scale binary patterns for texture analysis. In: Bigun, J., Gustavsson, T. (eds.) SCIA 2003. LNCS, vol. 2749, pp. 885–892. Springer, Heidelberg (2003). https://doi.org/10.1007/3-540-45103-X_117
13. Nguyen, T.P., Manzanera, A., Kropatsch, W.G., N'Guyen, X.S.: Topological attribute patterns for texture recognition. Pattern Recogn. Lett. 80, 91–97 (2016)
14. Nguyen, T.P., Vu, N., Manzanera, A.: Statistical binary patterns for rotational invariant texture classification. Neurocomputing 173, 1565–1577 (2016)
15. Nguyen, T.T., Nguyen, T.P., Bouchara, F.: Completed local structure patterns on three orthogonal planes for dynamic texture recognition. In: IPTA, pp. 1–6 (2017)
16. Nguyen, T.T., Nguyen, T.P., Bouchara, F.: Completed statistical adaptive patterns on three orthogonal planes for recognition of dynamic textures and scenes. J. Electron. Imaging 27(05), 053044 (2018)
17. Nguyen, T.T., Nguyen, T.P., Bouchara, F.: Smooth-invariant Gaussian features for dynamic texture recognition. In: ICIP (2019)
18. Nguyen, T.T., Nguyen, T.P., Bouchara, F., Nguyen, X.S.: Directional beams of dense trajectories for dynamic texture recognition. In: Blanc-Talon, J., Helbert, D., Philips, W., Popescu, D., Scheunders, P. (eds.) ACIVS 2018. LNCS, vol. 11182, pp. 74–86. Springer, Cham (2018). https://doi.org/10.1007/978-3-030-01449-0_7
19. Ojala, T., Pietikäinen, M., Mäenpää, T.: Multiresolution gray-scale and rotation invariant texture classification with local binary patterns. IEEE Trans. PAMI 24(7), 971–987 (2002)
20. Peh, C., Cheong, L.F.: Synergizing spatial and temporal texture. IEEE Trans. IP 11(10), 1179–1191 (2002)
21. Péteri, R., Fazekas, S., Huiskes, M.J.: Dyntex: a comprehensive database of dynamic textures. Pattern Recogn. Lett. 31(12), 1627–1632 (2010)
22. Qi, X., Li, C.G., Zhao, G., Hong, X., Pietikainen, M.: Dynamic texture and scene classification by transferring deep image features. Neurocomputing 171, 1230–1241 (2016)

23. Quan, Y., Bao, C., Ji, H.: Equiangular kernel dictionary learning with applications to dynamic texture analysis. In: CVPR, pp. 308–316 (2016)
24. Quan, Y., Huang, Y., Ji, H.: Dynamic texture recognition via orthogonal tensor dictionary learning. In: ICCV, pp. 73–81 (2015)
25. Quan, Y., Sun, Y., Xu, Y.: Spatiotemporal lacunarity spectrum for dynamic texture classification. CVIU **165**, 85–96 (2017)
26. Ravichandran, A., Chaudhry, R., Vidal, R.: View-invariant dynamic texture recognition using a bag of dynamical systems. In: CVPR, pp. 1651–1657 (2009)
27. Ren, J., Jiang, X., Yuan, J.: Dynamic texture recognition using enhanced LBP features. In: ICASSP, pp. 2400–2404 (2013)
28. Ren, J., Jiang, X., Yuan, J., Wang, G.: Optimizing LBP structure for visual recognition using binary quadratic programming. SPL **21**(11), 1346–1350 (2014)
29. Rivera, A.R., Chae, O.: Spatiotemporal directional number transitional graph for dynamic texture recognition. IEEE Trans. PAMI **37**(10), 2146–2152 (2015)
30. Saisan, P., Doretto, G., Wu, Y.N., Soatto, S.: Dynamic texture recognition. In: CVPR, pp. 58–63 (2001)
31. Tiwari, D., Tyagi, V.: Dynamic texture recognition based on completed volume local binary pattern. MSSP **27**(2), 563–575 (2016)
32. Tiwari, D., Tyagi, V.: A novel scheme based on local binary pattern for dynamic texture recognition. CVIU **150**, 58–65 (2016)
33. Tiwari, D., Tyagi, V.: Improved weber's law based local binary pattern for dynamic texture recognition. Multimed. Tools Appl. **76**(5), 6623–6640 (2017)
34. Tiwari, D., Tyagi, V.: Dynamic texture recognition using multiresolution edge-weighted local structure pattern. Comput. Electr. Eng. **62**, 485–498 (2017)
35. Vu, N., Nguyen, T.P., Garcia, C.: Improving texture categorization with biologically-inspired filtering. Image Vis. Comput. **32**(6–7), 424–436 (2014)
36. Wang, Y., Hu, S.: Chaotic features for dynamic textures recognition. Soft. Comput. **20**(5), 1977–1989 (2016)
37. Xu, Y., Huang, S.B., Ji, H., Fermüller, C.: Scale-space texture description on sift-like textons. CVIU **116**(9), 999–1013 (2012)
38. Xu, Y., Quan, Y., Zhang, Z., Ling, H., Ji, H.: Classifying dynamic textures via spatiotemporal fractal analysis. Pattern Recogn. **48**(10), 3239–3248 (2015)
39. Zhao, G., Pietikäinen, M.: Dynamic texture recognition using local binary patterns with an application to facial expressions. IEEE Trans. PAMI **29**(6), 915–928 (2007)
40. Zhao, X., Lin, Y., Heikkilä, J.: Dynamic texture recognition using volume local binary count patterns with an application to 2D face spoofing detection. IEEE Trans. Multimed. **20**(3), 552–566 (2018)
41. Zhao, Y., Huang, D.S., Jia, W.: Completed local binary count for rotation invariant texture classification. IEEE Trans. IP **21**(10), 4492–4497 (2012)

Machine Learning for Image and Pattern Analysis

Learning Visual Dictionaries from Class-Specific Superpixel Segmentation

César Castelo-Fernández[✉] and Alexandre X. Falcão

Laboratory of Image Data Science, Institute of Computing, University of Campinas, Campinas, SP, Brazil
{cesar.fernandez,afalcao}@ic.unicamp.br

Abstract. Visual dictionaries (Bag of Visual Words - BoVW) can be a very powerful technique for image description whenever exists a reduced number of training images, being an attractive alternative to deep learning techniques. Nevertheless, models for BoVW learning are usually unsupervised and rely on the same set of visual words for all images in the training set. We present a method that works with small supervised training sets. It first generates superpixels from multiple images of a same class, for interest point detection, and then builds one visual dictionary per class. We show that the detected interest points can be more relevant than the traditional ones (e.g., grid sampling) in the context of a given application—the classification of intestinal parasite images. The study uses three image datasets, with a total of 15 different species of parasites, and a diverse class, namely impurity, which makes the problem difficult with examples similar to all the remaining classes of parasites.

Keywords: Bag of Visual Words · Superpixels · Supervised learning · Intestinal parasites · Image classification

1 Introduction

Deep learning techniques have caught a lot of attention due to their excellent results in several problems [7,16]. As limitation, these techniques often require large training sets, either supervised or unsupervised ones. In some applications, the training sets can be small and, in the worst case, image annotation of large training sets may require the knowledge of specialists in the application domain. Although there are data augmentation techniques suitable for deep learning [13], we are interested in simpler and yet effective alternatives to learn features from a low number of supervised samples. In this paper, we revisit Visual Dictionaries (Bag of Visual Words - BoVW, or codebooks) [17] for that purpose and present a new BoVW approach that learns image features from class-specific superpixels.

The simplest way to construct a visual dictionary (unsupervised training) can be described as follows. The methods first detect interest points in the training

© Springer Nature Switzerland AG 2019
M. Vento and G. Percannella (Eds.): CAIP 2019, LNCS 11678, pp. 171–182, 2019.
https://doi.org/10.1007/978-3-030-29888-3_14

images and then extract a local image descriptor from each point. A visual dictionary can be constructed by finding groups of those local image descriptors and using the representative one from each group as *visual word* for the dictionary. After training, for a given image, its interest points lead to local image descriptors and the number of occurrences of the visual words closest to those local descriptors form a *histogram of the visual words* that characterizes the image. This process does not take into account the classes of the images and, at the end, a single dictionary is used to represent the entire dataset. We believe, however, that the use of pre-annotated images can help and this seems to have been under exploited in the literature.

In this paper, we propose to learn one dictionary for each category, which is based on the most relevant interest points for that category according to a class-specific superpixel segmentation method. For this purpose, we present a method that creates superpixels from multiple images by using a recently introduced framework, named *Iterative Spanning Forest* (ISF) [22]. This framework computes superpixels as optimum-path trees derived from an image graph with pixel properties. We essentially define the graph based on pixel properties from multiple images of a same class, after image alignment, and the result is a superpixel coordinate space that is common to all images from that class—i.e., a reference space more suitable to detect interest points, since the superpixels divide the image into regions, with similar color and texture, which adhere to the boundaries of the image objects.

The proposed approach is evaluated in the context of image classification of intestinal parasites, which is one from many examples of applications in the Sciences and Engineering that produce large unsupervised image datasets. Image annotation in such datasets requires knowledge from specialists. In this study, we are interested in classifying optical microscopy images from the 15 most common species of human intestinal parasites in Brazil. In this problem, a single exam can easily generate 2000 images of 4 million pixels with hundreds of thousands of objects for image classification. Among the 15 species of parasites, most objects are fecal impurities—a diverse class with examples similar to all classes of parasites (e.g., Fig. 1). These objects can be automatically separated into three groups: *Protozoan cysts* with similar impurities, *Helminth eggs* with similar impurities, and *Helminth larvae* with similar impurities [20]. However, it is still challenging the effective classification of the species of parasites in each group due to the presence of impurities and similarities between some classes.

Fig. 1. Examples of *Helminth eggs* (top) and similar fecal impurities (bottom).

The rest of this paper is organized as follows. Section 2 presents the basic concepts related to the construction of a BoVW model. Section 3 reviews related works and Sect. 4 presents the proposed approach for supervised visual dictionary learning. The experimental results are presented in Sect. 5 and, finally, the conclusions are stated in Sect. 6.

2   The Bag of Visual Words Model

Bag of Visual Words (BoVW) is a model that extracts local information from each image in a training set as a collection of local image descriptors and then organizes the local descriptors into groups to represent each image globally. The idea is to detect interest points in each image of a training set and then extract visual features from those points (local image descriptors) using some characterization algorithm. This task is performed for all images in the training set and, afterwards, the local image descriptors (feature vectors) are clustered to find groups with similar characteristics. Then, the representatives of the clusters are used as visual words for the dictionary.

A global descriptor for a given image can then be the histogram of visual words—i.e., the number of occurrences of each visual word to the closest local descriptor of that image. This coding scheme is usually referred to as *hard assignment*. One can also assign the distance between each local descriptor and the k nearest visual words to form a global image descriptor—a process usually more effective and referred to as *soft assignment*.

Finally, a supervised classifier can be trained based on those global image descriptors extracted from images of all classes and tested on new images.

The entire process can be divided into five steps:

1. Localization of interest points: Class-specific superpixel segmentation.
2. Learning of the most promising local image descriptors: BIC descriptor [19].
3. Construction of a visual dictionary: Class-specific clustering by OPF [14].
4. Coding of global image descriptors using the dictionary: Soft assignment.
5. Learning of a classifier using global image descriptors: Linear SVM [1].

3   Related Works

Most of the approaches found in the literature [4,9,17] use the Scale-Invariant Feature Transform (SIFT) or the Speeded-Up Robust Features (SURF) detectors to localize the interest points of the image and to characterize them. Nevertheless, works in the literature [3,12] showed that performing random sampling gives comparable results to SIFT and SURF.

Tian and Wang [21] and Haas *et al.* [6] have shown that the use of superpixels to extract the interest points improves the quality of the extracted descriptors. However, those works rely on the extraction of superpixels for each image, different from our work which uses class-specific superpixel segmentation.

On the other hand, recent works [15,18] have shown that it is possible to obtain good results using simpler descriptors, such as the Border/Interior Pixel Classification (BIC) descriptor [19]. BIC is a color descriptor capable of generating good-quality image description in much less time than SIFT/SURF.

Considering the task of building a visual dictionary, the visual words are mostly selected using the k-means clustering algorithm [17] or some variant of it [10]. The main problem of using k-means is that it needs to know *a-priori* the number of clusters, which is difficult to estimate for BoVW. Thus, it becomes important the use of clustering techniques that do not require this information.

De Souza et al. [18] have successfully used clustering by Optimum-Path Forest (OPF) [14] to build visual dictionaries, in a similar way as we use here. However, their methodology considers the construction of a single dictionary for the dataset, in contrast with ours which builds one specific dictionary for each class.

Liu and Caselles [9] proposed a supervised BoVW approach that uses a k-means algorithm with a new cost function which considers the label information as part of the feature vectors. The drawback of this approach, however, is that they still need to indicate the number of clusters *a-priori*.

As a matter of fact, most approaches in the literature, the traditional [17] and the recent ones [2,4,6,11,15,18,21], use a single visual dictionary for the entire dataset, without exploiting class information.

Finally, we would like to mention some recent improvements in BoVW modeling. Minaee *et al.* [11] use an adversarial autoencoder network to characterize the patches extracted from each image, outperforming some traditional methods. Gong *et al.* [4] mix CNN features with BoVW features and show that the proposed approach slightly outperforms some deep learning architectures. Recently, Li *et al.* [8] proposed a Fisher embedding dictionary algorithm that outperformed other dictionary methods.

4 Proposed Approach

We propose a method for superpixel segmentation from multiple images of a same class for the detection of more relevant points for local image description and the construction of class-specific visual dictionaries by OPF clustering [14]. This will allow for more effective global image description, given that the number of visual words in each dictionary is naturally found from the distribution of the local descriptors in the feature space rather than fixed *a-priori* by the user.

4.1 Interest Point Detection Using Superpixels

The generation of a superpixel segmentation from training images of a same class creates a coordinate space for the detection of common interest points related to that class and, in particular, related to object borders from the images. We then propose a method based on the Interactive Spanning Forest (ISF) framework [22], which allows to control boundary adherence and shape regularity in the generation of superpixels.

Interactive Spanning Forest Framework. In the ISF framework, one image is represented as a graph in which the pixels are the nodes, each represented by a feature vector (e.g., the color of the pixel), and the arcs between pixels are weighted by a function that takes into account distances in the feature space and in the image domain. For a given connectivity function (path-cost function), seed estimation algorithm, and seed recomputation procedure, the ISF algorithm computes a spanning forest rooted at the estimated seeds and, subsequently, repeats the process for recomputed seeds by a given number of iterations. The result is a superpixel segmentation in which each superpixel is a spanning tree rooted at one seed pixel. We essentially map the training images from a same class into a same image domain and apply the ISF algorithm by considering as features of each pixel all its color components from each training image.

Let $\mathcal{G}_{isf} = (\mathcal{I}, \mathcal{A})$ be a graph that represents an image $\mathcal{I}$ with its corresponding adjacency relation $\mathcal{A}$ (e.g. 4-neighbors). A path $\pi_{s \rightsquigarrow t} = \langle s = t_1, t_2, \cdots, t_n = t \rangle$ is a sequence of adjacent pixels with origin in s and terminus in t, being that a given path π_s can be extended by an arc (s, t) to form a new path π_t. A *predecessor map* is a function that either assigns to each pixel $s \in \mathcal{I}$ its predecessor $t \in \mathcal{I}$ or marks it as a *seed* in the graph. In this sense, a *spanning forest* is defined as a predecessor map with no cycles, i.e., for any pixel it is possible to obtain its root from the map. Next, an *optimum-path* is computed for any pixel $t \in \mathcal{I}$ by using a *cost function* $f(\cdot)$ which computes the value $f(\pi_t)$ of a path π_t with terminus in t. A path π_t is said to be optimum if $f(\pi_t) \leq f(\tau_t)$ for any other path $\tau_t \in \Pi_\mathcal{G}$ (the set of paths in $\mathcal{G}$). Using this function, we can define an optimal mapping C which contains the optimum path π_t^* for every $t \in \mathcal{I}$, as:

$$C(t) = \min_{\forall \pi_t \in \Pi_\mathcal{G}} \{f(\pi_t)\} \tag{1}$$

The final result of this optimization process is an optimum-path forest P, i.e., a forest whose all paths are optimum.

According to the authors, the function f can be defined as:

$$f_1(\pi_{s_j \rightsquigarrow s} \cdot \langle s, t \rangle) = f_1(\pi_s) + (\||\vec{v}(t) - \vec{\mu}(s_j)\||\alpha)^\beta + \||s, t\|| \tag{2}$$

where $\alpha \geq 0$ controls shape regularity, $\beta \geq 1$ controls boundary adherence, $\vec{v}(t)$ is the color vector of pixel t and $\vec{\mu}(s_j)$ is the mean color vector of the superpixel of the previous iteration whose seed if s_j.

Class-Specific Superpixels for Each Class. As we mentioned earlier, we would like to exploit the label information that we possess in the learning images together with the segmentation masks that we can extract from the parasite images using the methodology in [20].

Let $\lambda = \{\lambda_1, \cdots, \lambda_n\}$ be the labels (with values from 1 to c, i.e., the number of classes) and $\Phi = \{\phi_1, \cdots, \phi_n\}$ be the segmentation masks from the images $\mathcal{I} = \{\mathcal{I}_1, \cdots, \mathcal{I}_n\}$. A class-specific segmentation mask φ_i can be defined for class i as $\varphi_i = \bigcup_{\forall j, \lambda_j = i} [\phi_j]$. Next, we perform grid sampling inside each mask φ_i, obtaining the set of seeds $\mathcal{S}_i$ for class i.

Then, a class-specific multiband image $\mathcal{I}_i'$ is created for class i, such that $\mathcal{I}_i'(p) = \bigcup_{\forall j, \lambda_j = i}[\mathcal{I}_j(p)]$ is the color vector for each $p \in \mathcal{I}_i'$. This operation needs the images to be in the same reference space, which could be achieved using simple rotation/translation image registration (as is the case for this work) or more generally deformable image registration.

Next, the ISF algorithm is executed with the image $\mathcal{I}_i'$ and the set of seeds $\mathcal{S}_i$, obtaining the set of superpixels Ω_i for class i.

Finally, using the set Ω_i, we define the superpixels' boundaries mask Ω_i^m and perform a grid sampling on Ω_i^m, i.e., a set of uniformly-spaced points $\Psi_i = \{p_1, \cdots, p_k\}$ chosen from the superpixels' boundaries (interest points for class i).

Since we do not have the label information for the testing images, we then define the final set Ψ of interest points as $\Psi = \{\Psi_1, \cdots, \Psi_c\}$.

Figure 2 shows the results of the proposed approach.

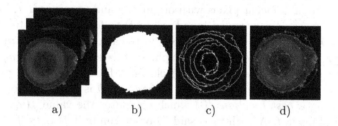

a)   b)   c)   d)

Fig. 2. Example of the superpixel-based interest point detection approach: (a) Multiband image $\mathcal{I}_i'$ for the class *H.diminuta* (*H.Eggs* dataset), (b) Class-specific segmentation mask φ_i, (c) Superpixels' boundaries Ω_i^m and (d) Set of chosen interest points Ψ_i.

4.2 Dictionary Estimation Using OPF Clustering

Clustering by Optimum-Path Forest. The Optimum-Path Forest (OPF) clustering algorithm [14] represents the training set as a k-nn graph $\mathcal{G}_{opf} = (\mathcal{N}, \mathcal{A})$ (samples and an adjacency relation), i.e., every sample is connected in $\mathcal{A}$ to its k nearest neighbors. Every vertex s in the graph is represented by the sample's feature vector $\vec{v}(s)$ and it is weighted by its Probability Density Function (PDF), which is estimated using the k-nn graph. The PDF is an estimation of how densely are the samples distributed. The PDF is computed as follows:

$$\rho(s) = \frac{1}{\sqrt{2\pi\sigma^2}|\mathcal{A}(s)|} \sum_{t \in \mathcal{A}(s)} \exp\left(\frac{-d^2(s,t)}{2\sigma^2}\right), \text{ where } \sigma = \max_{\forall(s,t) \in \mathcal{A}}\left\{\frac{d(s,t)}{3}\right\} \quad (3)$$

where $d(s,t)$ is the Euclidean distance between $\vec{v}(s)$ and $\vec{v}(t)$.

In a similar way to the ISF method, the OPF classifier performs an optimization process to find an optimum partition of the graph $\mathcal{G}_{opf}$ according to a cost function $f(\cdot)$, being that the optimum trees that are obtained represent the clusters in the data. The optimization process can be represented as:

$$V(t) = \max_{\forall \pi_t \in \mathcal{G}_{opf}} \{f(\pi_t)\} \quad (4)$$

which sets to $V(t)$ the cost of the optimum path $\pi_t^* \in \Pi_t$ with terminus in t among all the possible paths $\Pi_t \in \mathcal{G}_{opf}$ that lead to t.

According to the authors, the function f is defined as:

$$f_{min}(\langle t \rangle) = \begin{cases} \rho(t) \text{ if } t \in \mathcal{R} \\ h(t) \text{ otherwise} \end{cases} \quad f_{min}(\pi_s \cdot \langle s, t \rangle) = \min\{f_{min}(\pi_s), \rho(t)\} \quad (5)$$

where $\mathcal{R}$ is the set of initial roots in $\mathcal{G}_{opf}$, which are defined as the maxima of the PDF distribution of the vertices in $\mathcal{G}_{opf}$, and $h(t)$ is a *handicap* value that is used to avoid local minima in the PDF.

Note that the number k in the graph $\mathcal{G}_{opf}$ is not difficult to estimate, and the authors proposed the use of the graph-cut measure for multiple clusters [14].

Finally, once the optimization process from Eq. 4 is terminated, the visual words (visual dictionary) can be extracted from the resultant optimum trees. Let $\{\mathcal{T}_1, \cdots, \mathcal{T}_g\} \subset \mathcal{G}_{opf}$ be the set of optimum trees that represent the g resultant clusters, the visual dictionary $\mathcal{D} = \{\mathcal{W}_1, \cdots, \mathcal{W}_g\}$ can be defined as:

1. The centroids $\{c_1, \cdots, c_g\}$ of $\{\mathcal{T}_1, \cdots, \mathcal{T}_g\}$, where $c_i = \frac{1}{|\mathcal{T}_i|} \sum_{\forall s \in \mathcal{T}_i} \vec{v}(s)$
2. The medoids $\{m_1, \cdots, m_g\}$ of $\{\mathcal{T}_1, \cdots, \mathcal{T}_g\}$, where $m_i = \operatorname{argmin}_{\forall s \in \mathcal{T}_i}[d(s, c_i)]$
3. The roots $\{r_1, \cdots, r_g\}$ of $\{\mathcal{T}_1, \cdots, \mathcal{T}_g\}$

According to De Souza *et al.* [18], using the roots of the optimum trees gives better results in comparison to the other options.

Visual Dictionaries Specialized by Image Class. As we mentioned before, we propose to build independent visual dictionaries for each class with the aim of detecting the visual words that better represent each class.

Therefore, the set of visual dictionaries will be defined as $\mathcal{VD} = \{\mathcal{D}_1, \cdots, \mathcal{D}_c\}$, where c is the number of classes and $\mathcal{D}_i$ represents the visual words extracted for class i using the graph $\mathcal{G}_{opf}^i = (\mathcal{N}_i, \mathcal{A})$, where $\mathcal{N}_i$ is the set of local features extracted from the interest points Ψ_i that represent the class-specific superpixels Ω_i for class i.

5   Experiments

All the experiments were performed using an Intel® Core i7-7700 processor with 64 GB of RAM and running Ubuntu 16.04.

The intestinal parasite datasets used in this work were created at the University of Campinas' Laboratory of Image Data Science (LIDS) as part of the work developed in [20]. The images belong to the 15 most common species of parasites in Brazil organized in 3 datasets, which are detailed in Table 1.

It is important to note that the number of impurities present in each dataset is high compared to the other classes. Each dataset is splitted using stratified sampling into 3 subsets: (1) dictionary learning (10%); (2) classifier learning (45%) and; (3) classifier testing (45%).

Table 1. Datasets containing the 15 most common species of intestinal parasites in Brazil, organized as: (1) *Protozoan cysts*; (2) *Helminth eggs* and; (3) *Helminth larvae.*

Dataset	Samples	Classes	Samples per class (last class: impurities)
P.Cysts - protozoan cysts	9568	7	[719, 78, 724, 641, 1501, 189, 5716]
H.Eggs - helminth eggs	5112	9	[348, 80, 148, 122, 337, 375, 122, 236, 3344]
H.Larvae - helminth larvae	3544	2	[446, 3068]

5.1   Baseline and Performance Metrics for Comparisons

Three baseline techniques were used in the present work to evaluate our method:

1. BoVW-Grid-BIC-UnsupOPF-Soft: BoVW approach using grid sampling, BIC descriptor, unsupervised OPF clustering [18] and soft assignment.
2. BoVW-Grid-BIC-UnsupKmeans-Soft: BoVW approach using grid sampling, BIC descriptor, unsupervised k-means clustering and soft assignment.
3. BoVW-Grid-BIC-SupKmeans-Soft: BoVW approach using grid sampling, BIC descriptor, k-means clustering per class and soft assignment.

All the tests use the soft assignment strategy to build the histogram of visual words that represent each image (final feature vector) and a Linear SVM classifier (training and testing phases).

Note that our study was developed considering two performance metrics:

1. Accuracy (percentage of true positives), the most used measure in literature.
2. Cohen's Kappa, which considers the size of each class, giving a more realistic performance measure. It represents the level of agreement between two raters, in this case the classifier and the ground-truth of the datasets [5].

5.2   Evaluating the Impact of Dictionary Estimation and Interest Point Detection

We will evaluate in this section some aspects of the proposed methodology using the *P.Cysts* dataset (without considering the class of impurities) and we will use only the kappa measure for the sake of simplicity.

The dictionary estimation phase of BoVW is essential since it is responsible for defining the visual words that will represent the images. However, it is essential to note that in order to have good visual words, we need to have good strategies to define the interest points and to represent them.

Table 2 shows the kappa results using unsupervised OPF clustering for dictionary estimation (Unsup-OPF) compared to defining dictionaries per class (OPF-per-class). As we can see, the advantage of OPF-per-class over Unsup-OPF is small (1% more in the kappa measure), which reinforces the necessity of better techniques to define the interest points and characterize them. We are using a large patch size because BIC requires this to extract good visual features.

Regarding the interest point strategies, Table 3 shows the kappa results using grid sampling (Grid-samp) compared to the use of superpixels per class with ISF

Table 2. Tests regarding the dictionary estimation strategies: (1) Unsupervised OPF clustering and (2) OPF clustering per class. Both use grid sampling (patch size: 31 and stride: 8) to define the interest points and BIC to extract the local features.

DictEstim: Unsup-OPF		DictEstim: OPF-per-class	
kappa	# words	kappa	# words
80.53 ± 0.23	576 ± 8	$\mathbf{81.68 \pm 1.04}$	804 ± 9

(Spix-per-class-ISF). As it can be seen, the kappa measure of the Spix-per-class-ISF technique is 3% higher than Grid-samp's, which confirms that the proposed superpixel strategy actually improves the image characterization.

Table 3. Tests regarding the interest point detection strategies: (1) Grid sampling and (2) Superpixels per class with ISF (in the Lab color space). Both use patch size: 31 and stride: 8, BIC to extract the local features and OPF clustering per class to estimate the visual dictionary.

IntPointDet: Grid-samp		IntPointDet: Spix-per-class-ISF	
kappa	# words	kappa	# words
81.68 ± 1.04	804 ± 9	$\mathbf{84.09 \pm 0.72}$	1266 ± 35

5.3   Final Results

In this section we will present the results comparing our proposal with the baseline methods using all the datasets. We used the datasets with and without the class of impurities to show how this impacts in the final kappa and accuracy. As it can be seen in the Table 4, our methodology obtains better results regarding both measures kappa and accuracy, achieving considerable advantages in some cases. Also, it is important to note that the method based on k-means obtained in some cases a very low kappa value and a much higher accuracy; the reason for this is that they obtained an accuracy of 0% for several classes and the kappa score penalizes that behavior.

On the other hand, it is important to mention the difference in the dictionary size among the 4 methods. It is desirable to have a smaller dictionary (for faster classifier training/testing processes) as is the case of the $BoVW_{UnsupOPF}$ method. Nevertheless, the bigger dictionaries of our method are justified by the advantage in the kappa score.

Table 4. Final accuracy results of our proposal and the two baseline methods using all the datasets. Kappa and accuracy measures are shown as well as the number of visual words. $k = 1000$ for $BoVW_{UnsupKmeans}$ and $k = 200$ (for each class) for $BoVW_{SupKmeans}$. Best values for each dataset and each measure are in bold.

Method	Measure	Dataset				
		P.Cysts No imp	P.Cysts	H.Eggs No imp	H.Eggs	H.Larvae
Our method	kappa	**83.37 ± 1.20**	**57.09 ± 0.50**	**95.47 ± 0.44**	**72.65 ± 1.18**	**71.12 ± 2.62**
	acc	**87.41 ± 0.89**	**82.91 ± 0.33**	**96.26 ± 0.36**	**89.41 ± 0.53**	92.41 ± 0.96
	# words	1230 ± 34	1621 ± 8	633 ± 16	1099 ± 20	653 ± 29
$BoVW_{UnsupOPF}$	kappa	81.05 ± 0.43	50.94 ± 0.98	93.37 ± 0.75	63.70 ± 2.09	**71.52 ± 2.99**
	acc	85.65 ± 0.32	79.54 ± 0.34	94.54 ± 0.61	84.93 ± 1.15	**92.64 ± 0.93**
	# words	**587 ± 18**	653 ± 11	153 ± 8	224 ± 5	493 ± 25
$BoVW_{UnsupKmeans}$	kappa	44.03 ± 2.65	0.00 ± 0.00	51.22 ± 1.89	1.99 ± 2.52	0.00 ± 0.00
	acc	59.79 ± 1.81	76.44 ± 0.00	60.44 ± 1.48	69.26 ± 6.11	84.58 ± 0.00
	# words	1000 ± 0	1000 ± 0	1000 ± 0	1000 ± 0	1000 ± 0
$BoVW_{SupKmeans}$	kappa	56.06 ± 2.53	2.05 ± 2.90	71.47 ± 6.08	32.12 ± 13.14	0.00 ± 0.00
	acc	68.04 ± 1.72	76.58 ± 0.20	76.57 ± 4.91	79.46 ± 0.43	84.58 ± 0.00
	# words	1200 ± 0	1400 ± 0	1600 ± 0	1800 ± 0	**400 ± 0**

Finally, Table 5 shows the times to learn the visual dictionary and to extract the final feature vectors. The time needed to compute the visual dictionary is higher for our method because the Spix-per-class-ISF method defines a higher number of interest points and hence the time needed to compute the dictionary is higher. On the other hand, the feature vector extraction times are directly related to the size of the visual dictionary (soft assignment procedure).

Table 5. Final time results (in seconds) of our proposal and the two baseline methods using all the datasets. Dictionary learning and feature vector extraction times are shown. Lower values are in bold.

Method	Time	Dataset				
		P.Cysts No imp	P.Cysts	H.Eggs No imp	H.Eggs	H.Larvae
Our method	dict-learn	274 ± 26	1369 ± 167	205 ± 70	1692 ± 145	220 ± 16
	feat-vect-extr	427 ± 129	446 ± 303	785 ± 188	850 ± 459	148 ± 10
$BoVW_{UnsupOPF}$	dict-learn	192 ± 32	231 ± 53	**13 ± 4**	**77 ± 32**	94 ± 7
	feat-vect-extr	**243 ± 13**	**244 ± 51**	**55 ± 20**	306 ± 90	137 ± 16
$BoVW_{UnsupKmeans}$	dict-learn	891 ± 247	969 ± 322	955 ± 97	1258 ± 637	491 ± 220
	feat-vect-extr	340 ± 53	294 ± 96	433 ± 182	**284 ± 184**	135 ± 56
$BoVW_{SupKmeans}$	dict-learn	**42 ± 13**	**157 ± 84**	108 ± 69	197 ± 138	**41 ± 1**
	feat-vect-extr	373 ± 15	451 ± 118	516 ± 151	742 ± 380	122 ± 18

6 Conclusions

We have presented a novel approach to learn supervised visual dictionaries for image classification. We proposed to use superpixel techniques (ISF) to detect more relevant interest points and we are also using the images' label information for this process. Moreover, we successfully used the OPF classifier to build dictionaries that are specialized for each class in the dataset. The experiments showed that our approach is able to outperform the three baselines that were used for comparisons (based on k-means and unsupervised OPF clustering) in virtually all the cases. One drawback of our method is that it produces larger dictionaries than their counterparts, but this is justified by the performance obtained. Nevertheless, we would like to study alternatives to either produce smaller dictionaries or to reduce the dictionaries that are built by our method.

Acknowledgments. The authors thank FAPESP (grants 2014/12236-1 and 2017/03940-5) and CNPq (grant 303808/2018-7) for the financial support.

References

1. Cortes, C., Vapnik, V.: Support-vector networks. Mach. Learn. **20**(3), 273–297 (1995). https://doi.org/10.1007/BF00994018
2. Cortés, X., Conte, D., Cardot, H.: A new bag of visual words encoding method for human action recognition. In: 2018 24th International Conference on Pattern Recognition (ICPR), pp. 2480–2485, August 2018. https://doi.org/10.1109/ICPR. 2018.8545886
3. Fei-Fei, L., Perona, P.: A Bayesian hierarchical model for learning natural scene categories. In: 2005 IEEE Computer Society Conference on Computer Vision and Pattern Recognition (CVPR 2005), vol. 2, pp. 524–531, June 2005. https://doi. org/10.1109/CVPR.2005.16
4. Gong, X., Yuanyuan, L., Xie, Z.: An improved bag-of-visual-word based classification method for high-resolution remote sensing scene. In: 2018 26th International Conference on Geoinformatics, pp. 1–5, June 2018. https://doi.org/10.1109/ GEOINFORMATICS.2018.8557124
5. Gwet, K.L.: Handbook of Inter-Rater Reliability: The Definitive Guide to Measuring the Extent of Agreement Among Raters, 4th edn. Advanced Analytics, LLC, Gaithersburg (2014)
6. Haas, S., Donner, R., Burner, A., Holzer, M., Langs, G.: Superpixel-based interest points for effective bags of visual words medical image retrieval. In: Müller, H., Greenspan, H., Syeda-Mahmood, T. (eds.) MCBR-CDS 2011. LNCS, vol. 7075, pp. 58–68. Springer, Heidelberg (2012). https://doi.org/10.1007/978-3-642-28460-1_6
7. Krizhevsky, A., Sutskever, I., Hinton, G.E.: ImageNet classification with deep convolutional neural networks. In: Pereira, F., Burges, C.J.C., Bottou, L., Weinberger, K.Q. (eds.) Advances in Neural Information Processing Systems, vol. 25, pp. 1097–1105. Curran Associates, Inc. (2012)
8. Li, Z., Zhang, Z., Qin, J., Zhang, Z., Shao, L.: Discriminative fisher embedding dictionary learning algorithm for object recognition. IEEE Trans. Neural Netw. Learn. Syst. 1–15 (2019). https://doi.org/10.1109/TNNLS.2019.2910146
9. Liu, Y., Caselles, V.: Supervised visual vocabulary with category information. In: Blanc-Talon, J., Kleihorst, R., Philips, W., Popescu, D., Scheunders, P. (eds.) ACIVS 2011. LNCS, vol. 6915, pp. 13–21. Springer, Heidelberg (2011). https:// doi.org/10.1007/978-3-642-23687-7_2
10. Mikulik, A., Perdoch, M., Chum, O., Matas, J.: Learning vocabularies over a fine quantization. Int. J. Comput. Vis. **103**(1), 163–175 (2013). https://doi.org/10. 1007/s11263-012-0600-1

11. Minaee, S., et al.: MTBI identification from diffusion MR images using bag of adversarial visual features. IEEE Trans. Med. Imaging (2019, to appear). https://doi.org/10.1109/TMI.2019.2905917

12. Nowak, E., Jurie, F., Triggs, B.: Sampling strategies for bag-of-features image classification. In: Leonardis, A., Bischof, H., Pinz, A. (eds.) ECCV 2006. LNCS, vol. 3954, pp. 490–503. Springer, Heidelberg (2006). https://doi.org/10.1007/11744085_38

13. Peixinho, A.Z., Benato, B.C., Nonato, L.G., Falcão, A.X.: Delaunay triangulation data augmentation guided by visual analytics for deep learning. In: 2018 31st SIBGRAPI Conference on Graphics, Patterns and Images (SIBGRAPI), pp. 384–391, October 2018. https://doi.org/10.1109/SIBGRAPI.2018.00056

14. Rocha, L.M., Cappabianco, F.A.M., Falcão, A.X.: Data clustering as an optimum-path forest problem with applications in image analysis. Int. J. Imaging Syst. Technol. 19(2), 50–68 (2009). https://doi.org/10.1002/ima.v19:2

15. Silva, F.B., de O. Werneck, R., Goldenstein, S., Tabbone, S., da S. Torres, R.: Graph-based bag-of-words for classification. Pattern Recogn. 74, 266–285 (2018). https://doi.org/10.1016/j.patcog.2017.09.018

16. Simonyan, K., Zisserman, A.: Very deep convolutional networks for large-scale image recognition. arXiv abs/1409.1556 (2014)

17. Sivic, J., Zisserman, A.: Video Google: a text retrieval approach to object matching in videos. In: Proceedings of the Ninth IEEE International Conference on Computer Vision, ICCV 2003, vol. 2, pp. 1470–1477. IEEE Computer Society, Washington, DC (2003). https://doi.org/10.1109/ICCV.2003.1238663

18. de Souza, L.A., et al.: Learning visual representations with optimum-path forest and its applications to Barrett's esophagus and adenocarcinoma diagnosis. Neural Comput. Appl. (2019) https://doi.org/10.1007/s00521-018-03982-0

19. Stehling, R.O., Nascimento, M.A., Falcão, A.X.: A compact and efficient image retrieval approach based on border/interior pixel classification. In: Proceedings of the Eleventh International Conference on Information and Knowledge Management, CIKM 2002, pp. 102–109. ACM, New York (2002). https://doi.org/10.1145/584792.584812

20. Suzuki, C.T.N., Gomes, J.F., Falcão, A.X., Papa, J.P., Hoshino-Shimizu, S.: Automatic segmentation and classification of human intestinal parasites from microscopy images. IEEE Trans. Biomed. Eng. 60(3), 803–812 (2013). https://doi.org/10.1109/TBME.2012.2187204

21. Tian, L., Wang, S.: Improved bag-of-words model for person re-identification. Tsinghua Sci. Technol. 23(2), 145–156 (2018). https://doi.org/10.26599/TST.2018.9010060

22. Vargas-Muñoz, J., Chowdhury, A., Alexandre, E., Galvão, F., Miranda, P., Falcão, A.: An iterative spanning forest framework for superpixel segmentation. IEEE Trans. Image Process. (2019, to appear). https://doi.org/10.1109/TIP.2019.2897941

Towards Real-Time Image Enhancement GANs

Leonardo Galteri, Lorenzo Seidenari$^{(\boxtimes)}$, Marco Bertini,
and Alberto Del Bimbo

Università di Firenze - MICC, Florence, Italy
{leonardo.galteri,lorenzo.seidenari,
marco.bertini,alberto.delbimbo}@unifi.it
http://www.micc.unifi.it/

Abstract. Video stream compression, using lossy algorithms, is performed to reduce the bandwidth required for transmission. To improve the video quality, either for human view or for automatic video analysis, videos are post-processed to eliminate the introduced compression artifacts. Generative Adversarial Network have been shown to obtain extremely high quality results in image enhancement tasks; however, to obtain top quality results high capacity large generators are usually employed, resulting in high computational costs and processing time. In this paper we present an architecture that can be used to reduce the cost of generators, paving a way towards real-time frame enhancement with GANs.

With the proposed approach, enhanced images appear natural and pleasant to the eye. Locally high frequency patterns often differ from the raw uncompressed images. A possible application is to improve video conferencing, or live streaming. In these cases there is no original uncompressed video stream available. Therefore, we report results using popular no-reference metrics showing high naturalness and quality even for efficient networks.

1 Introduction

Every day a huge number of videos are produced, streamed and shared on the web, and many more are produced and used within private systems and networks, such as mobile phones, cameras and surveillance systems. To practically store and transmit these video streams it is necessary to compress them, to reduce bandwidth and storage requirements. Typically video is compressed using lossy algorithms, given the need to deal with large quantities of data, especially when dealing with HD and 4K resolutions that are becoming more and more common. The effect of these algorithms results in a more or less strong loss of content fidelity with respect to the original visual data, to achieve a better compression ratio. However, since one of the factors that accounts for user experience is image quality, compression algorithms are designed to reduce perceptual quality loss, according to some model of the human visual system.

© Springer Nature Switzerland AG 2019
M. Vento and G. Percannella (Eds.): CAIP 2019, LNCS 11678, pp. 183–195, 2019.
https://doi.org/10.1007/978-3-030-29888-3_15

A typical use case in which a high compression is desirable is that of video conferencing, in which video streams must be kept small to reduce communication latency and thus improve user experience. Another case is that of wireless cameras, in particular mobile and wearable ones, that may need to limit power consumption reducing the energy cost of image transmission applying strong compression. Also in the case of entertainment video streaming, like Netflix or Amazon Prime Video, there is need to reduce as much as possible the required bandwidth, to reduce network congestion and operational costs.

When compressing videos several artifacts appear as shown in Fig. 1. These artifacts are due to the different types of lossy compressions used. Considering MPEG-based algorithms such as H.264 and H.265/AVC or AV1, the most common and recent algorithm used nowadays, these artifacts are due to the chroma sub-sampling (i.e. dropping some color information of the original image) and the quantization of the DCT (or DST) coefficients; other artifacts are due to blocking processing of frames, due to how the original uncompressed frame is partitioned for compression, but is also due to erroneous motion compensated prediction [20]. These two causes are common also in image compression algorithms such as JPEG. Finally, another source of artifacts is associated with motion compensation and coding, such as flickering, caused by differences in frame reconstruction between intra-frames and inter-frames (i.e. key frames encoded as images and frames reconstructed using motion compensation) [31].

An approach to improve the perceived image quality while maintaining a high compression rate is to perform filtering on the reconstructed frames, to reduce the effect of the various artifacts. The most recent codecs, such as H.265 and AV1 envisage standardised deblocking filtering.

In this work we propose a solution to artifact removal based on convolutional neural networks trained on large sets of frame patches compressed with different quality factors. Our approach is independent with respect to the compression algorithm used to process a video; it can be used as a post-processing step on decompressed frames and therefore it can be applied on many lossy compression algorithms such as WebM, AV1, H.264/AVC and H.265/HEVC.

One of the main advantages of improving video quality working on artifact removal is that our method can be applied just on the receiving end of a coding pipeline, thus avoiding any modification to the existing compression pipelines, that are often optimized e.g. using dedicated hardware such as graphic cards, GPUs or SoCs. Another important aspect is that often streaming services use a dynamic adaptive streaming approach, that compose video streams using different versions encoded at different bit rates (and thus at different qualities) to cope with bandwidth availability; an example of this is the Dynamic Adaptive Streaming over HTTP (DASH) [27]. This means that we could not rely on an approach based on super-resolution, that would require image sub-sampling also on the coding end.

Fig. 1. Examples of video compression artifacts: (*top*) blocking artifacts on the bottom part of the green pole, color interpolation due to chroma sub-sampling on left and right of the umbrella; (*bottom*) ringing around the white on blue text in the street name sign; little vertical flickering (1–2 lines) of numbers and letters (in particular N and 7) between two following frames. (Color figure online)

2 Related Work

Improving image quality is a topic that has been vastly studied in the past, especially in the case of compression artifact removal. Many approaches are based on image processing techniques [5,8,14,18,19,30,32,34,35]. Recently, several learning based methods have been proposed [6,9,10,16,21,28,29].

Best results have been obtained using Deep Convolutional Neural Networks (DCNN), trained to restore image quality using couples of undistorted and distorted images. A major strength of this type of approach is that once the degrading process is known, e.g. video compression, generating data is extremely easy and does not requires hand labeling, but just to generate degraded images from high quality input. Degraded images will be fed as input to restoration networks while high quality sources will be regarded as ground truth or target images. Dong et al. [6] extended their previous work on super-resolution SRCNN with artifact removal CNN (AR-CNN) sharing a common architecture with SRCNN, following sparse coding pipelines. Svoboda et al. [28] follow a similar approach, obtaining improved results in image restoration by learning a feed-forward CNN. The main difference with respect to [6] is that the CNN is a standard multi-layered network in which the layers have no specific functions, using residual learning and skip connections. Recent works [3,9,33] tend to use deeper architectures, often employing residual blocks. Cavigelli et al. [3] trained 12-layers CNN to remove JPEG artifacts. Their CNN uses skip connection in a hierarchical fashion. Local frequency classifier are trained and exploited by Yoo et al. to condition and encoder-decoder architecture in reconstructing JPEG compressed images [33]. Galteri et al. are the first to propose a method that uses a GAN ensemble and a quality predictor that allows them to restore images of unknown quality [9]. Their method shows superior results in term of perceived quality.

To the best of our knowledge the only method restoring compressed video frames is proposed by He et al. [13]. Their method, tightly bound to HEVC coding, exploits coding unit to learn a two-stream CNN receiving a decoded frame and combines it with a feature map computed from the partition data.

2.1   Contribution

Unfortunately all best performing artifact removal methods do not perform in real-time, even on high-end GPUs. All the envisioned applications for such technology in video quality improvement have a less or more strict real-time constraint. In this paper we propose a GAN in which the generator is designed with efficiency in mind. Instead, the discriminator can be made large at will, since it only affects training efficiency. We show that on no-reference video and image quality assessment our approach produces frames that have scores higher than compressed frames.

3   Methodology

Our approach consists in regarding a frame from a compressed video as an image which has been distorted by some known process. Considering a raw frame I_t from a sequence we consider $I_t^C = C(I_t, I_{t-1}, I_{t-2}, \ldots, \theta)$ as its compressed version, where $C(\cdot)$ is some compression algorithm for video sequences such as H.264/AVC configured according to a parameters set θ.

Representing images as real valued tensors in $\mathbb{R}^{H \times W \times Ch}$, where W and H are width and height of the frame, and Ch is the number of channels, we would like to learn some function $G(\cdot)$ able to invert the compression process:

$$G\left(I_t^C\right) = I_t^R \approx I_t \tag{1}$$

where I_t^R denotes the restored version of I_t^C. In all models we use $Ch = 3$, since we are training over and restoring RGB video frames. We define the function $G(\cdot)$ as a fully convolutional neural network, whose weights are learned using a Generative Adversarial Framework. Using fully convolutional networks has the great benefit of not having to stick to a precise input resolution for frames and most importantly allows us to train the network over smaller frame crops and larger batches, speeding up the training. Considering the fact that the noise process induced by compression is local, our strategy does not compromise performance.

We apply adversarial training [12] which has recently shown remarkable performances in image processing and image generation tasks [4,9,17]. GAN training consist of the optimization of two networks named *generator* (G) and *discriminator* (D) where the generator is fed some noisy input and has the goal to create "fake" images able to induce the discriminator in mistakes. On the other hand the discriminator optimizes a classification loss rewarding solutions that correctly distinguish *fake* from real images. In our case we are not aiming at generating novel unseen images sampled from a distribution but our task regards the enhancement of a corrupted image. Interestingly such task can be tackled with GANs by conditioning the training. Our end goal is to obtain a $G(\cdot)$ function able to process compressed frames and remove artifacts. In our conditional GAN we provide to the discriminator positive examples $I_t | I_t^C$ and negative examples $I_t^R | I_t^C$, where $\cdot|\cdot$ indicates channel-wise concatenation. This means that, in case of samples of size $N \times N \times Ch$, the discriminator receives a sample with dimensions $N \times N \times 2 \cdot Ch$.

3.1 Generative Network

The architecture of our generator is based on MobileNetV2 [25], which is a very efficient network designed for mobile devices to perform classification tasks. Differently from [9], we replace standard residual blocks with bottleneck depthseparable convolutions blocks, as shown in Table 1, to reduce the overall amount of parameters. We set the expansion factor t to 6 for all the experiments.

Table 1. Bottleneck residual block used in our generator network.

Layer	Output
Conv2d 1×1, ReLU6	$m \times n \times t * c$
Dw Conv2d 3×3, ReLU6	$m \times n \times t * c$
Conv2d 1×1	$m \times n \times c$

After a first standard convolutional layer, feature maps are halved twice with strided convolutions and then we apply a chain of B bottleneck residual blocks. The number of convolution filters doubles each time the feature map dimensions are halved. We use two combinations of nearest-neighbour up-sampling and standard convolution layer to restore the original dimensions of feature maps. Finally, we generate the RGB image with a 1×1 convolution followed by a *tanh* activation, to keep the output values between the $[-1, 1]$ range. In all our trained models we employed Batch Normalization to stabilize the training process. Table 2 reports the number of filters, blocks and weights of the GAN used in a previous work [9], and two variations of the proposed network, called "Fast" and "Very Fast" since they are designed to attain real-time performance. It can be observed that the new GAN architectures have much smaller number of parameters, resulting in reduced computational costs, that allow to reach the required real-time performance.

Table 2. Parameters of the different GANs used. Compared to the previous work [9], our new "Fast" and "Very Fast" networks have much smaller number of parameters, resulting in improved computation time.

Model	# Filters	# Blocks	# Params
Galteri *et al.* [9]	64	16	5.1M
Our Fast	32	12	1.8M
Our Very Fast	8	16	145k

3.2 Discriminative Network

The structure of the discriminator network comprises mostly convolutional layers followed by LeakyReLU activation, with a final dense layer and a sigmoid activation. Since the complexity of this network does not affect the execution time during test phase, we have chosen for all our trainings a discriminator with a very large number of parameters, thus increasing its ability to discriminate fake patches from real ones. As in [9,10], sub-patches are fed to this network rather than whole images, because image compression operates at sub-patch level and those artifacts we aim to remove are generated inside them. The set of weights ψ of the D network are learned by minimizing:

$$l_d = -\log\left(D_\psi\left(I|I^C\right)\right)$$
$$-\log\left(1 - D_\psi\left(I^R|I^C\right)\right) \tag{2}$$

where $D(x)$ is taken from of the sigmoid activation of the discriminator network, with x indicating the concatenation on channels axis between the distorted input I^C and the correspondent real image I or the synthetic one I^R.

3.3 Content Losses

Here we describe the content losses used in combination with the adversarial loss for the generator. Content losses have the goal to limit the set of distributions to be modeled via the adversarial learning process inducing the generator to produce consistent image enhancement behavior.

Pixel-Wise MSE Loss. Mean Squared Error loss (MSE) is defined as:

$$l_{MSE} = \frac{1}{WH} \sum_{x=1}^{W} \sum_{y=1}^{H} \left(I_{x,y} - I_{x,y}^{R} \right)^2. \tag{3}$$

This loss is commonly used in image reconstruction and restoration tasks [6, 21,28]. l_{MSE} recovers low frequency details from a compressed image, but the drawback is that high frequency details are suppressed.

Perceptual Loss. Many contributions on image enhancement, restoration and super-resolution have employed the perceptual loss to optimize the network in a feature space rather than the pixel space [2,7,11,15]. We used such loss in our adversarial training to encourage reconstructed images and target ones to have similar feature representations. The similarity measure between two images is obtained by projecting I and I^R on a feature space of a pre-trained network, hence extracting some meaningful feature maps. The perceptual loss is the Euclidean distance between the extracted feature representations:

$$l_P = \frac{1}{W_f H_f} \sum_{x=1}^{W_f} \sum_{y=1}^{H_f} \left(\phi_j\left(I\right)_{x,y} - \phi_j\left(I^R\right)_{x,y} \right)^2 \tag{4}$$

where $\phi_j(I)$ indicates the activations of some j-th layer of the pre-trained network for an input image I, and W_f and H_f are respectively the width and the height of the feature maps. In this work we have chosen the VGG-19 model [26] as feature extractor, using the outputs of the pool4 layer of this network.

Adversarial Loss. The total loss of our generator is a weighted combination of the aforementioned losses:

$$l_{AR} = l_{MSE} + \lambda_1 l_P + \lambda_2 l_{adv}. \tag{5}$$

where l_{adv} is the standard adversarial loss:

$$l_{adv} = -\log\left(D_\psi\left(I^R|I^C\right)\right) \tag{6}$$

that rewards solutions that are able to "fool" the discriminator.

4   Experimental Results

We test our novel architectures with three popular no reference metrics. No reference (NR) image quality assessment (IQA) is the task of providing a score for an image, which has been possibly distorted by an unknown process, without having access to the original image. These metrics are designed to identify and quantify the presence of different types of artifacts that may be present in the image being analyzed, like blurriness, blocking, lack of contrast or saturation, etc.

All models are trained on DIV2K dataset [1]. DIV2K training set comprises 800 high resolution uncompressed images, which we compress using H.264 to generate degraded frames. As an augmentation strategy, considering the small size of DIV2K, we resize images at 256, 384 and 512 on their shorter side and then we randomly crop a patch of 224 × 224 pixels with random mirror flipping. This procedures allows to increase dataset size and increase diversity of pattern scales.

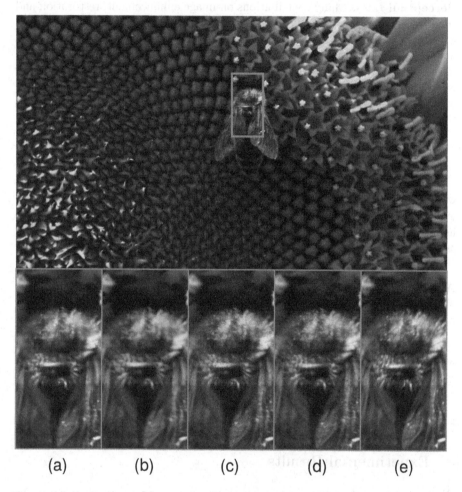

(a)   (b)   (c)   (d)   (e)

Fig. 2. Qualitative comparison of (leftmost) compressed frame with H.264 (CRF 28), (b–d) our Very Fast, Fast and Galteri *et al.* [9] networks with (e) uncompressed frame. Large frame obtained by our Fast network. Note the fine details of the wings and hairs of the bee obtained by the GAN based approaches, compared to the standard compressed version.

(a)   (b)   (c)   (d)   (e)

Fig. 3. Qualitative comparison of (a) compressed frame with H.264 (CRF 28), (b–d) our Very Fast, Fast and Galteri *et al.* [9] networks with (e) uncompressed frame. Large frame obtained by our Fast network. Note the fine details of the texture of the water and feathers of the duck obtained by the GAN based approaches, compared to the standard compressed version. Also ringing and blocking artifact in the body of the duck, that are present in the standard compressed version are eliminated.

Looking at qualitative examples in Figs. 2 and 3, it can be seen that the quality of imagery is largely improved by our networks in comparison with the source compressed frame; in particular finer details of the wings and hair of the bee and texture of water and feathers, as well as reduced ringing and blocking in the body of the duck. As also shown in [9,10,33], GAN image enhancement can lead to low performance in full reference metrics due to the fact that the overall pictures is improved by semantically consistent textures which, pixel-wise, may differ from the original uncompressed image.

As a test dataset we pick the following videos: *Mobile Calendar, Park Run, Shields, River Bed, Sunflower, Rush Hour, Tractor Pedestrian Area, Blue Sky* and *Station* from the Derf collection[1], since it consists of high resolution uncompressed videos allowing us to test the effect of compression on frames that have not undergone any corruption due to the compression process. We compress video aggressively, setting the constant rate factor (CRF) to 28; in comparison to a more high quality CRF setting (e.g. 10) this results in a ~10×–20× reduction of video size.

We use two image based no reference metrics (BRISQUE [22] and NIQE [24]) and a video specific no reference metric (VIIDEO [23]). We use different metrics since typically NR IQA methods are defined to handle specific types of artifacts. We report results in Table 3, for all metrics a lower score corresponds to a better image quality. For all the image quality enhancement approaches we report their time performance in terms of FPS, computed on videos at 720p resolution.

Interestingly our networks, even our "Very Fast", consistently improve image quality metrics. We run all experiments using a NVIDIA Titan Xp GPU card and our TensorFlow implementation. No further optimizations have been made such as using quantized networks or employing faster inference engines such as Caffe or TensorRT. We use as baseline the GAN presented in [9], which runs at 4 FPS. Interestingly our "Fast" network, running at 20 FPS, obtains comparable results. Our "Very Fast" network, running at 42 FPS is able to improve the compressed frames according to all metrics but does not reach the quality of original frames. When processing HD frames (i.e.1080p resolution) the GAN used in [9] reaches 2 FPS, while our "Very Fast" still obtains real-time performance at 20 FPS.

It can be noted that for NIQE and BRISQUE measures the score measured on enhanced frames for Galteri *et al.* [9] and the Fast network exceeds the one of raw frames. We believe that this must be read with obvious caution, and is likely to be motivated by the fact that these two metrics are assessing frames independently. Looking at the VIIDEO measure all of the proposed networks obtains improve consistently with respect to the compressed frames, but are not better quality than the raw frames.

Table 3. No reference quality assessment of our compression artifact removal networks. VIIDEO is specifically designed for sequences, while NIQE and BRISQUE are geared towards images. For all metrics lower figure is better.

	VIIDEO [23]	NIQE [24]	BRISQUE [22]	FPS@720p
H.264	0.520	4.890	41.93	-
Our Very Fast	0.388	4.574	25.12	42
Our Fast	**0.350**	3.714	**16.95**	20
Galteri *et al.* [9]	0.387	**3.594**	17.58	4
Uncompressed	0.276	4.329	23.73	-

---

[1] https://media.xiph.org/video/derf/.

5   Conclusion

Many applications based on video streaming impose a strict real-time constraint. Unfortunately existing image quality methods, that improve the quality of reconstruction of compressed frames, are not able to satisfy it. In this paper we move the first steps towards Real-Time GANs for image enhancement. Our Fast network is able to run at 20 FPS with no deterioration on the final results according to three popular image quality measures. Qualitative inspection of our frames confirm quantitative results, showing pleasant highly detailed frames.

Further speed-up can be obtained by exploiting specialized inference engines such as TensorRT and quantizing the models on 8bit. Our current solution do not employ any temporal coherence schema, we expect that adding a loss imposing frame-by-frame coherence may enhance further video quality.

Acknowledgments. We gratefully acknowledge the support of NVIDIA Corporation with the donation of the Titan X Pascal GPUs used for this research.

References

1. Agustsson, E., Timofte, R.: NTIRE 2017 challenge on single image super-resolution: dataset and study. In: Proceedings of IEEE CVPR Workshops (2017)
2. Bruna, J., Sprechmann, P., LeCun, Y.: Super-resolution with deep convolutional sufficient statistics. CoRR abs/1511.05666 (2015)
3. Cavigelli, L., Hager, P., Benini, L.: CAS-CNN: a deep convolutional neural network for image compression artifact suppression. In: Proceedings of IJCNN (2017)
4. Chu, M., Xie, Y., Leal-Taixé, L., Thuerey, N.: Temporally coherent GANs for video super-resolution (TecoGAN). arXiv preprint arXiv:1811.09393 (2018)
5. Dar, Y., Bruckstein, A.M., Elad, M., Giryes, R.: Postprocessing of compressed images via sequential denoising. IEEE Trans. Image Process. 25(7), 3044–3058 (2016)
6. Dong, C., Deng, Y., Change Loy, C., Tang, X.: Compression artifacts reduction by a deep convolutional network. In: Proceedings of ICCV (2015)
7. Dosovitskiy, A., Brox, T.: Generating images with perceptual similarity metrics based on deep networks. In: Proceedings of NIPS (2016)
8. Foi, A., Katkovnik, V., Egiazarian, K.: Pointwise shape-adaptive DCT for high-quality denoising and deblocking of grayscale and color images. IEEE Trans. Image Process. 16(5), 1395–1411 (2007)
9. Galteri, L., Seidenari, L., Bertini, M., Del Bimbo, A.: Deep universal generative adversarial compression artifact removal. IEEE Trans. Multimed. 21(8), 2131–2145 (2019)
10. Galteri, L., Seidenari, L., Bertini, M., Del Bimbo, A.: Deep generative adversarial compression artifact removal. In: Proceedings of ICCV (2017)
11. Gatys, L.A., Ecker, A.S., Bethge, M.: Texture synthesis and the controlled generation of natural stimuli using convolutional neural networks. CoRR abs/1505.07376 (2015)
12. Goodfellow, I., et al.: Generative adversarial nets. In: Proceedings of NIPS (2014)
13. He, X., Hu, Q., Zhang, X., Zhang, C., Lin, W., Han, X.: Enhancing HEVC compressed videos with a partition-masked convolutional neural network. In: Proceedings of ICIP (2018)

14. Jakhetiya, V., Lin, W., Jaiswal, S.P., Guntuku, S.C., Au, O.C.: Maximum a posterior and perceptually motivated reconstruction algorithm: a generic framework. IEEE Trans. Multimed. 19(1), 93–106 (2017)
15. Johnson, J., Alahi, A., Fei-Fei, L.: Perceptual losses for real-time style transfer and super-resolution. In: Leibe, B., Matas, J., Sebe, N., Welling, M. (eds.) ECCV 2016. LNCS, vol. 9906, pp. 694–711. Springer, Cham (2016). https://doi.org/10. 1007/978-3-319-46475-6_43
16. Kang, L.W., Hsu, C.C., Zhuang, B., Lin, C.W., Yeh, C.H.: Learning-based joint super-resolution and deblocking for a highly compressed image. IEEE Trans. Multimed. 17(7), 921–934 (2015)
17. Karras, T., Laine, S., Aila, T.: A style-based generator architecture for generative adversarial networks. arXiv preprint arXiv:1812.04948 (2018)
18. Li, T., He, X., Qing, L., Teng, Q., Chen, H.: An iterative framework of cascaded deblocking and super-resolution for compressed images. IEEE Trans. Multimed. 20(6), 1305–1320 (2017)
19. Li, Y., Guo, F., Tan, R.T., Brown, M.S.: A contrast enhancement framework with JPEG artifacts suppression. In: Fleet, D., Pajdla, T., Schiele, B., Tuytelaars, T. (eds.) ECCV 2014. LNCS, vol. 8690, pp. 174–188. Springer, Cham (2014). https:// doi.org/10.1007/978-3-319-10605-2_12
20. List, P., Joch, A., Lainema, J., Bjontegaard, G., Karczewicz, M.: Adaptive deblocking filter. IEEE Trans. Circ. Syst. Video Technol. 13(7), 614–619 (2003)
21. Mao, X., Shen, C., Yang, Y.B.: Image restoration using very deep convolutional encoder-decoder networks with symmetric skip connections. In: Proceedings of NIPS (2016)
22. Mittal, A., Moorthy, A.K., Bovik, A.C.: No-reference image quality assessment in the spatial domain. IEEE Trans. Image Process. 21(12), 4695–4708 (2012)
23. Mittal, A., Saad, M.A., Bovik, A.C.: A completely blind video integrity oracle. IEEE Trans. Image Process. 25(1), 289–300 (2016)
24. Mittal, A., Soundararajan, R., Bovik, A.C.: Making a "completely blind" image quality analyzer. IEEE Sig. Process. Lett. 20(3), 209–212 (2013)
25. Sandler, M., Howard, A., Zhu, M., Zhmoginov, A., Chen, L.C.: MobileNetV2: inverted residuals and linear bottlenecks. In: Proceedings of CVPR, June 2018
26. Simonyan, K., Zisserman, A.: Very deep convolutional networks for large-scale image recognition. In: Proceedings of ICLR (2015)
27. Stockhammer, T.: Dynamic adaptive streaming over HTTP-: standards and design principles. In: Proceedings of ACM MMSys, pp. 133–144. ACM (2011)
28. Svoboda, P., Hradis, M., Barina, D., Zemcik, P.: Compression artifacts removal using convolutional neural networks. arXiv preprint arXiv:1605.00366 (2016)
29. Wang, Z., Liu, D., Chang, S., Ling, Q., Yang, Y., Huang, T.S.: D3: deep dual-domain based fast restoration of JPEG-compressed images. In: Proceedings of CVPR (2016)
30. Wong, T.S., Bouman, C.A., Pollak, I., Fan, Z.: A document image model and estimation algorithm for optimized JPEG decompression. IEEE Trans. Image Process. 18(11), 2518–2535 (2009)
31. Yang, J.X., Wu, H.R.: Robust filtering technique for reduction of temporal fluctuation in H.264 video sequences. IEEE Trans. Circ. Syst. Video Technol. 20(3), 458–462 (2010)
32. Yang, S., Kittitornkun, S., Hu, Y.H., Nguyen, T.Q., Tull, D.L.: Blocking artifact free inverse discrete cosine transform. In: Proceedings of ICIP (2000)
33. Yoo, J., Lee, S.h., Kwak, N.: Image restoration by estimating frequency distribution of local patches. In: Proceedings of CVPR (2018)

34. Zhang, J., Xiong, R., Zhao, C., Zhang, Y., Ma, S., Gao, W.: CONCOLOR: constrained non-convex low-rank model for image deblocking. IEEE Trans. Image Process. **25**(3), 1246–1259 (2016)
35. Zhang, X., Xiong, R., Fan, X., Ma, S., Gao, W.: Compression artifact reduction by overlapped-block transform coefficient estimation with block similarity. IEEE Trans. Image Process. **22**(12), 4613–4626 (2013)

Multi-stream Convolutional Networks for Indoor Scene Recognition

Rao Muhammad Anwer[1,2]([envelope]), Fahad Shahbaz Khan[2,3]([envelope]),
Jorma Laaksonen[1]([envelope]), and Nazar Zaki[4]([envelope])

[1] Department of Computer Science, Aalto University School of Science,
Espoo, Finland
{rao.anwer,jorma.laaksonen}@aalto.fi
[2] Inception Institute of Artificial Intelligence, Abu Dhabi, UAE
[3] Computer Vision Laboratory, Linköping University, Linköping, Sweden
fahad.khan@liu.se
[4] Computer Science and Software Engineering Department,
College of Information Technology, United Arab Emirates University, Al Ain, UAE
Nzaki@uaeu.ac.ae

Abstract. Convolutional neural networks (CNNs) have recently achieved outstanding results for various vision tasks, including indoor scene understanding. The de facto practice employed by state-of-the-art indoor scene recognition approaches is to use RGB pixel values as input to CNN models that are trained on large amounts of labeled data (ImageNet or Places). Here, we investigate CNN architectures by augmenting RGB images with estimated depth and texture information, as multiple streams, for monocular indoor scene recognition. First, we exploit the recent advancements in the field of depth estimation from monocular images and use the estimated depth information to train a CNN model for learning deep depth features. Second, we train a CNN model to exploit the successful Local Binary Patterns (LBP) by using mapped coded images with explicit LBP encoding to capture texture information available in indoor scenes. We further investigate different fusion strategies to combine the learned deep depth and texture streams with the traditional RGB stream. Comprehensive experiments are performed on three indoor scene classification benchmarks: MIT-67, OCIS and SUN-397. The proposed multi-stream network significantly outperforms the standard RGB network by achieving an absolute gain of 9.3%, 4.7%, 7.3% on the MIT-67, OCIS and SUN-397 datasets respectively.

Keywords: Scene recognition · Depth features · Texture features

1 Introduction

Scene recognition is a fundamental problem in computer vision with numerous real-world applications. The problem can be divided into recognizing indoor

© Springer Nature Switzerland AG 2019
M. Vento and G. Percannella (Eds.): CAIP 2019, LNCS 11678, pp. 196–208, 2019.
https://doi.org/10.1007/978-3-030-29888-3_16

versus outdoor scene types. Initially, most approaches target the problem of outdoor scene classification with methods demonstrating impressive performance on standard benchmarks, such as fifteen scene categories [17]. Later, the problem of recognizing indoor scene categories have received much attention with the introduction of specialized indoor scene datasets, including MIT-67 [23]. Different to outdoor scene categorization, where global spatial layout is distinctive and one of the most discriminative cues, indoor scenes are better characterized either based on global spatial properties or local appearance information depending on the objects they contain. In this work, we investigate the challenging problem of automatically recognizing indoor scene categories.

In recent years, deep convolutional neural networks (CNNs) have revolutionized the field of computer vision setting new state-of-the-art results in many applications, including scene recognition [32]. In the typical scenario, deep networks or CNNs take raw pixel values as an input. They are trained using a large amount of labeled data and perform a series of convolution, local normalization and pooling operations (called layers). Generally, the final layers of a deep network are fully connected (FC) and employed for the classification purpose. Initially, deep learning based scene recognition approaches employed CNNs pre-trained on the ImageNet [26] for object recognition task. These pre-trained deep networks were then transferred for the scene recognition problem. However, recent approaches have shown superior results when training deep networks on a specialized large-scale scene recognition dataset [32]. In all cases, the de facto practice is to use RGB patches as input when training these networks.

As mentioned above, the standard procedure is to employ RGB pixel values as input for training deep networks. Besides color, texture features also provide a strong cue for scene identification at both the superordinate and basic category levels [24]. Significant research efforts have been dedicated in the past in designing discriminative texture features. One of the most successful hand-crafted texture descriptors is that of Local Binary Patterns (LBP) and its variants [12,21,22]. LBP is based on the signs of differences of neighboring pixels in an image and is invariant to monotonic gray scale variations. Recent studies [1,4] have investigated employing deep learning to design deep texture representations.

Other than color and texture, previous works [7,11,27,28] have shown the effectiveness of depth information and that depth images can be used simultaneously with RGB images to obtain improved recognition performance. However, most of these approaches require depth data acquired from depth sensors together with camera parameters to associate point clouds to image pixels. Despite increased availability of RGB-D sensors, standard large-scale object and scene recognition benchmarks (ImageNet and Places) still contain RGB images captured using different image sensors with no camera parameters to generate accurate point clouds. In a separate research line, recent works [5,20] have investigated estimating depth information from single monocular images. These methods employ RGB-D acquired through depth sensors during the training stage to infer the depth of each pixel in a single RGB image. Here, we aim to exploit these advancements in depth estimation from monocular images *and* hand-crafted discriminative texture features to integrate explicit depth and texture information for indoor scene recognition in the deep learning architecture.

In this work, we propose a multi-stream deep architecture where the estimated depth and texture streams are fused with the standard RGB image stream for monocular indoor scene recognition. The three streams can be integrated at different stages in the deep learning architecture to make use of the complementary information available in these different modalities. In the first strategy, the three streams are integrated at an early stage by aggregating the RGB, texture and estimated depth image channels as the input to train a joint multi-stream deep CNN model. In the second strategy, the three streams are trained separately and combined at a later stage of the deep network. To the best of our knowledge, we are the first to propose a multi-stream deep architecture and investigate fusion strategies to combine RGB, estimated depth and texture information for monocular indoor scene recognition. Figure 1 shows example indoor scene categories from the MIT-67 dataset and their respective classification accuracies (in %) when using different streams and their combination in the proposed multi-stream architecture.

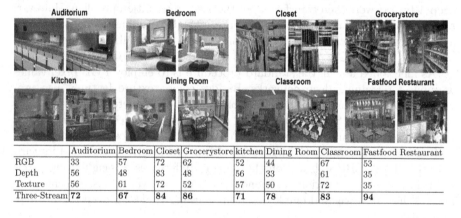

	Auditorium	Bedroom	Closet	Grocerystore	kitchen	Dining Room	Classroom	Fastfood Restaurant
RGB	33	57	72	62	52	44	67	53
Depth	56	48	83	48	56	33	61	35
Texture	56	61	72	52	57	50	72	35
Three-Stream	72	67	84	86	71	78	83	94

Fig. 1. Example categories from MIT-67 indoor scene dataset and their respective classification accuracies (in %) when using different streams: baseline standard RGB, estimated depth and texture. We also show the classification accuracies when combining these streams in our late fusion based three-stream architecture. The classification results are consistently improved with our three-stream architecture, highlighting the complementary information possessed by the three streams.

2   Related Work

Indoor Scene Recognition: Recently, indoor scene recognition has gained a lot of attention [6,8,14–16]. Koskela [16] propose an approach where CNNs, trained on object recognition data, using different architectures are employed as feature extractors in a standard linear-SVM-based multi-feature scene recognition framework. A discriminative image representation based on discriminative mid-level convolutional activations is proposed by [14] to counter variability in indoor scenes. Guo et al. [6] propose an approach by integrating local convolutional supervision layer that is constructed upon the convolutional layers of deep network. The work of [15] proposes an approach based on spectral transformation of CNN activations integrated as a unitary transformation within a deep network. All these aforementioned deep learning based approaches are trained using RGB pixel values of an image.

Depth Estimation: Recent approaches [5,19,20] employ deep learning to learn depth estimation in monocular images. The work of [5] proposes a multi-scale convolutional architecture for depth prediction, surface normals and semantic labeling. Li et al. [19] introduce an approach by regressing CNN features together with a post-processing refinement step employing conditional random fields (CRF) for depth estimation. The work of [20] proposes a deep convolutional neural field model that jointly learns the unary term and pairwise term of continuous CRF in a unified CNN framework. Different to [5], where the depth map is directly regressed via convolutions from an input image, the approach of [20] explicitly models the relations of neighbouring superpixels by employing CRF. Both unary and binary potentials are learned in a unified deep network framework. Here, we employ deep convolutional neural field model of [20] as a depth estimation strategy for our monocular deep depth network stream. In our multi-stream architecture, the monocular depth stream is trained from scratch, on the large-scale ImageNet and Places datasets, for indoor scene recognition.

Texture Representation: Robust texture description is one of the fundamental problems in computer vision and is extensively studied in literature. Among existing methods, the Local Binary Patterns (LBP) descriptor [22] is one of the most popular hand-crafted texture description methods and several of its variants have been proposed in literature [21]. Recent approaches [1,4] have investigated deep learning for the problem of texture description. Cimpoi et al. [4] propose to encode convolutional layers of the deep network using the Fisher Vector scheme. Rao et al. [1] investigate the problem of learning texture representation and integrate LBP within deep learning architecture. In that approach, LBP codes are mapped to points in a 3D metric space using the approach of [18]. Here, we employ the strategy proposed in [1] to learn the texture stream and combine it with RGB and estimated depth streams in a multi-stream deep architecture for indoor scene recognition.

3 Our Multi-stream Deep Architecture

Here, we present our multi-stream deep architecture for indoor scene recognition. We also investigate fusion schemes to integrate different modalities in the deep learning architecture. We base our approach on the VGG architecture [3] that takes as input an image of 224×224 pixels and consists of five convolutional (conv) and three fully-connected (FC) layers.

3.1 Deep Depth Stream

The first step in designing of the depth stream is to compute the estimated depth image given its RGB counterpart. We employ the method of [20] for depth estimation of each pixel in a monocular image. The depth estimation approach employs continuous CRF to explicitly model the relations of neighbouring superpixels. Both unary and binary terms of continuous CRF are learned in an unified deep network framework. In the depth estimation model, each image is comprised of small regions, termed as superpixels, with nodes of a graphical model defined on them. Each superpixel in an image is described by the depth value of its centroid. Let I be an image and $y = [\text{sp}_1, \ldots, sp_m]^\top \in \mathbb{R}^m$ be a vector of all m superpixels in image I. The conditional probability distribution of the data is then modelled by employing the following density function:

$$P(y \mid I) = \frac{1}{Z(I)} \exp(-EN(y, I)), \tag{1}$$

where EN is the energy function and the partition function represented by Z is defined as:

$$Z(I) = \int_y \exp\left\{-EN(y, I)\right\} dy. \tag{2}$$

Due to the continuous nature of the depth values y, no approximation method is required to be applied. The subsequent MAP inference problem is then solved in order to obtain the depth value of a new image. The energy function is written as a combination of unary potentials UN and pairwise potentials PV over the superpixels $\mathcal{M}$ and edges $\mathcal{S}$ of the image I:

$$EN(y, I) = \sum_{p \in \mathcal{M}} UN(y_p, I) + \sum_{(p,q) \in \mathcal{S}} PV(y_p, y_q, I), \tag{3}$$

Here, the unary potential UN regresses the depth value for a single superpixel whereas the pairwise potential PV invigorates the superpixel neighborhoods with similar appearances to hold similar depth values. In the work of [20], both the unary potentials UN and the pairwise potentials PV are learned jointly in a unified deep network framework. The deep network comprises the following components: a continuous CRF loss layer consisting of a unary part and a pairwise part. Given an input image, image patches centred around each superpixel centroid are considered. Each image patch is used as an input to the unary part which is fed into the deep network. The network returns a single value representing the regressed depth value of the superpixel. The unary part of the deep network consists of five convolutional and four fully-connected layers. The unary potential is formulated by the output of the deep network by considering the following least square loss:

$$UN(y_p, I; \theta) = (y_p - z_p(\theta))^2, \forall p = 1, \ldots, m, \tag{4}$$

Here, z_p is the regressed depth of the homogeneous region (superpixel) p, parameterized by the deep network parameters θ. In case of the pairwise part of the network, the input is the similarity vectors of all neighboring superpixel pairs, fed to the FC layer with shared parameters among different superpixel pairs. The pairwise term enables neighboring superpixels with similar appearances to have similar depth values. Three types of pairwise similarities are considered: color histogram difference, color difference and texture disparity based on LBP. The output is then a 1-dimensional similarity vector for each of the neighboring superpixel pairs. Consequently, outputs from the unary and the pairwise terms are taken by the continuous CRF loss layer in order to minimize the negative log-likelihood. Standard RGB-D datasets, including NYUD2 have the same viewing angles for both the camera and the depth sensor. This implies that objects in a depth image possess the same 2D shapes as in RGB image with the only difference is that the RGB values are replaced by depth values. The estimated depth images alleviate the problem of intra-object variations, which is desired for scene understanding. During the construction of the depth stream, we first estimate depth values of the input RGB image using the approach described above resulting in a single-channel depth map. The estimated depth values are log-normalized to the range of $[0, 255]$ and duplicated into three channels which are then input to the deep learning framework. Figure 2 shows example RGB images and their corresponding estimated depth maps.

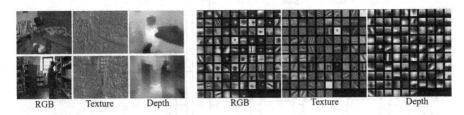

RGB   Texture   Depth   RGB   Texture   Depth

Fig. 2. On the left: example RGB images and the corresponding texture coded mapped images (visualized here in color) together with estimated depth images. On the right: visualization of filter weights from the RGB, texture and estimated depth CNN models.

3.2   Deep Texture Stream

In addition to the standard RGB and estimated depth streams, we propose to integrate an explicit texture stream for indoor scene recognition since texture features have shown to be crucial for scene understanding. Here, we base our texture stream on the popular LBP descriptor [22] where the neighborhood of a pixel is described by its binary derivatives used to form a short code for the neighborhood description of the pixel. These short codes are binary numbers (lower than threshold (0) or higher than the threshold (1)), where each LBP code can be regarded as a micro-texton. Each pixel in the image is allocated a code of the texture primitive with its best local neighborhood match.

When integrating the LBP operator in the deep learning architecture, a straightforward way is to directly employ LBP codes as an input to the deep network. However, the direct incorporation of LBP codes as input is infeasible since the convolution operations, equivalent to a weighted average of the input values, employed within CNNs are unsuitable for the unordered nature of the values of the LBP code. To counter this issue, the work of [18] proposes to map the LBP code values to points in a 3D metric space. In this metric space, the Euclidean distance approximates the distance between the LBP code values. Such a transformation enables averaging of LBP code values during convolution operations within CNN models. First, a distance $\delta_{j,k}$ is defined between the LBP codes $LBPT_j$ and $LBPT_k$. In the work of [18], Earth Mover's Distance (EMD) [25] is employed since it takes into account both the different bit values and their locations. Afterwards, a mapping is derived of the LBP codes into a DM-dimensional space which approximately preserves the distance between them. The mapping is derived by applying Multi Dimensional Scaling (MDS) [2]. The mapping enables the transfer of LBP code values into a representation that is suitable to be used as input to the deep network. As in [1,18], the dimensionality DM is set to three and the resulting texture representation is used to train a texture stream for indoor scene recognition. Figure 2 shows example RGB images and their corresponding texture coded mapped images.

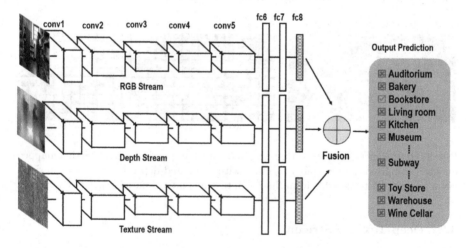

Fig. 3. Our late fusion based multi-stream deep architecture. In this architecture, RGB, estimated depth and texture streams are kept separate and the point of fusion, which combines the three network towers, is at the end of the network.

3.3   Multi-stream Fusion Strategies

We consider two fusion strategies to integrate the RGB, estimated depth and texture streams in a multi-stream architecture. In the first strategy, termed as early fusion, the three network streams are combined at an early stage as inputs to the deep network. As a result, the input to CNN is of $224 \times 224 \times N$ dimensions, where N is the number of image channels. When combining the three streams in an early fusion strategy, the number of image channels is $N = 7$ (3 RGB, 1 depth and 3 texture). A joint deep model is trained due to the aggregation of the image channels. In the second fusion strategy, termed as late fusion, the three networks are trained separately. The standard RGB stream network takes raw RGB values as input. The texture stream network takes texture coded mapped image as an input to the CNN model. This texture coded mapped image is obtained by first computing the LBP encoding that transforms intensity values in an image to one of the 256 LBP codes. The code values are then mapped into a 3D metric space, as described above, resulting in a 3-channel texture coded mapped image. The depth image is obtained by converting an RGB image to an estimated depth map, based on the procedure described earlier, to be used as an input to the depth stream. Consequently, the three streams are fused at the final stages of the deep network either by using FC layer activations with linear SVMs or combining the score predictions from individual streams. Figure 3 shows our late fusion based three stream architecture. The three streams are separately trained, from scratch, on both ImageNet [26] and Places [32] datasets. Figure 2 shows the VGG architecture based visualization of filter weights from the RGB, texture and estimated depth models trained on the ImageNet.

4 Experimental Results

Experimental Setup: We train our multi-stream network, described in Sect. 3, from scratch on the ImageNet 2012 [26] and Places 365 [32] training sets, respectively. In all cases, the learning rate is set to 0.001. The weight decay which contributes reducing the training error of the deep network is set to 0.0005. The momentum rate which is associated with the gradient descent method employed to minimize the objective function is set to 0.9. In case of fine-tuning the pretrained deep models, we employ training samples with a batch size of 80, a momentum value of 0.9 and an initial learning rate of 0.005. Furthermore, in all experiments the recognition results are reported as the mean classification accuracy over all scene categories in a scene recognition dataset. From the network prediction, the scene category label providing the highest confidence is assigned to the test image. The overall results are obtained by calculating the mean recognition score over all scene classes in each scene recognition dataset.

Datasets: MIT-67 [23] consists of 15,620 images of 67 indoor scene categories. We follow the standard protocol provided by the authors [23] by using 80 images per scene category for training and another 20 images for testing. **OCIS** [14] is the recently introduced large-scale object categories in indoor scenes dataset. It comprises of 15,324 images spanning more than 1300 commonly encountered indoor object categories. We follow the standard protocol provided by the authors [14] by defining a train-test split of (67% vs 33%) for each category. **SUN-397** [30] dataset consists of 108,754 images of 397 scene categories.

Here, the scene categories are both from indoor and outdoor environments. Each category in this dataset has at least 100 images. We follow the standard protocol provided by the authors [30] by dividing the dataset into 50 training and 50 test images per scene category. Since our aim is to investigate indoor scene recognition, we focus on the 177 indoor scene categories for the baseline comparison. Later, we show the results on the full SUN-397 dataset for state-of-the-art comparison.

Baseline Comparison: We compare our three-stream approach with the baseline standard RGB stream. Further, both early and late fusion strategies are evaluated for fusing the RGB, estimated depth and texture streams. For a fair comparison, we employ the same network architecture together with the same set of parameters for both the standard RGB and our multi-stream networks. Table 1 shows the baseline comparison with deep models trained on both ImageNet and Places datasets. We first discuss the results based on deep models pre-trained on the ImageNet. The baseline standard RGB deep network achieves average classification scores of 63.0%, 39.1%, and 46.0% on the MIT-67, OCIS, and SUN-397 datasets, respectively. The estimated depth based deep stream obtains mean recognition rates of 41.0%, 25.2%, and 26.0% on the MIT-67, OCIS and SUN-397 datasets, respectively. The texture coded deep image stream yields average classification accuracies of 59.1%, 33.6%, and 38.9% on the three scene datasets. In the case of the two fusion strategies, superior results are obtained with late fusion. The late fusion based two-stream network with RGB and depth streams obtains average classification scores of 67.1%, 40.9%, and 48.4% on the MIT-67, OCIS and SUN-397 datasets, respectively. Further, the late fusion based two-stream network with RGB and texture streams achieves average recognition rates of 69.3%, 42.5%, and 51.1% on the MIT-67, OCIS and SUN-397 datasets, respectively. The proposed late fusion based three-stream deep network significantly outperforms the baseline standard RGB deep stream on all datasets. Significant absolute gains of 9.3%, 4.7%, and 7.3% is achieved on the MIT-67, OCIS and SUN-397 datasets, respectively.

Other than the OCIS dataset, results are improved overall when employing deep models pre-trained on the Places scene dataset. The inferior recognition results in the case of the OCIS dataset are likely due to the fact that this dataset is based on indoor objects as categories instead of scenes. When comparing models trained on the Places dataset, our late fusion based three-stream deep architecture provides a substantial gains of 7.6%, 5.7%, and 4.9% on the MIT-67, OCIS and SUN-397 datasets respectively, compared to the baseline RGB stream.

We further analyze the impact of integrating depth and texture information within the deep learning architecture by looking into different indoor scene hierarchies available in the SUN-397 dataset. The indoor categories in the SUN-397 dataset are further annotated with the following scene hierarchies: shopping/dining with 40 indoor scene classes, workplace (office building, factory, lab, etc.) with 40 indoor scene classes, home/hotel with 35 indoor scene classes, transportation (vehicle interiors, stations, etc.) with 21 indoor scene classes, sports/leisure with 22 indoor scene classes, and cultural (art, education, religion,

Table 1. Comparison (overall accuracy in %) of our proposed three-stream deep architecture with the baseline standard RGB stream on the three scene datasets. We show multi-stream results with both early and late fusion schemes using deep networks either pre-trained on ImageNet or Places. Our proposed late-fusion based three-stream architecture significantly outperforms the baseline standard RGB stream on *all* datasets.

Architecture	Pre-training: imagenet			Pre-training: places		
	MIT-67	OCIS	SUN-397	MIT-67	OCIS	SUN-397
RGB deep stream (baseline)	63.0	39.1	46.0	73.6	32.5	58.6
Depth deep stream	41.0	25.2	26.0	51.5	21.4	34.6
Texture deep stream	59.1	33.6	38.9	68.7	27.2	49.3
Two-stream {RGB, depth} (early fusion)	65.2	39.5	46.7	74.3	32.8	59.3
Two-stream {RGB, depth} (late fusion)	67.1	40.9	48.4	76.5	34.1	60.5
Two-stream {RGB, texture} (early fusion)	65.7	39.9	47.9	75.3	33.3	59.7
Two-stream {RGB, texture} (late fusion)	69.3	42.5	51.1	78.8	36.5	61.8
Three-stream {RGB, depth, texture} (early fusion)	67.8	40.7	48.8	76.5	34.9	60.6
Three-stream {RGB, depth, texture} (late fusion)	**72.3**	**43.8**	**53.3**	**81.2**	**38.2**	**63.5**

Table 2. Comparison (overall accuracy in %) of our three-stream deep architecture with the baseline standard RGB stream on different indoor scene hierarchies available in SUN-397 dataset. The proposed three-stream deep architecture (late fusion) consistently improves the baseline standard RGB stream on all indoor scene hierarchies.

Architecture	Shopping/dining	Workplace	Home/hotel	Transportation	Sports/leisure	Cultural
RGB deep stream (baseline)	38.4	46.5	44.3	56.1	63.8	43.6
Ours {RGB, depth, texture} (late fusion)	**45.5**	**52.5**	**54.3**	**64.7**	**67.6**	**51.3**

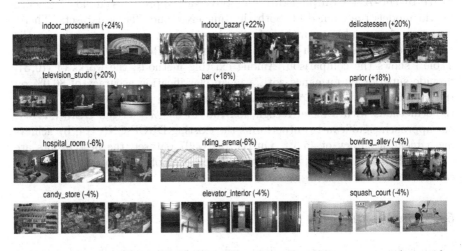

indoor_proscenium (+24%)   indoor_bazar (+22%)   delicatessen (+20%)

television_studio (+20%)   bar (+18%)   parlor (+18%)

hospital_room (-6%)   riding_arena(-6%)   bowling_alley (-4%)

candy_store (-4%)   elevator_interior (-4%)   squash_court (-4%)

Fig. 4. Example images from SUN-397 indoor categories where our approach provides the biggest increase (top) and the biggest decrease (bottom), compared to the baseline.

Table 3. Comparison (overall accuracy in %) with the state-of-the-art approaches.

Method	Publication	MIT-67	OCIS	SUN-397
Multi-scale hybrid CNNs [10]	CVPR 2016	86.0	-	70.2
DRCF-CNN [14]	TIP 2016	71.8	32.0	-
SLSIF-CNN [8]	TIP 2016	74.4	-	-
PatchNets [29]	TIP 2017	84.9	-	**71.7**
LSHybrid-CNNs [6]	TIP 2017	83.8	-	67.6
Hybrid CNN models [31]	TCSVT 2017	86.0	-	70.7
Spectral-CNNs [15]	ICCV 2017	84.3	-	67.6
SCF-CNNs [13]	MVA 2018	83.1	-	-
This paper	-	**86.4**	**45.3**	69.2

military, law, politics, etc.) with 36 indoor scene classes. Note that some indoor scene categories are shared across different scene hierarchies. Table 2 shows the results obtained using the standard RGB and our three-stream network on the six scene hierarchies. Our approach provides significant gains of 7.1%, 6.0%, 10.0%, 3.8%, 7.5% and 7.3% on the six scene hierarchies (shopping/dining, Workplace, home/hotel, transportation, sports/leisure, and cultural), respectively. Figure 4 shows example images from different indoor scene categories from the SUN-397 dataset on which our three-stream architecture provides the biggest improvement (top) and the biggest drop (bottom), compared to the standard RGB network.

State-of-the-Art Comparison: State-of-the-art approaches employ very deep hybrid models pre-trained on both the ImageNet and Places datasets. Therefore, we also combine our late fusion based three-stream network, at the score/prediction level, with the very deep networks: ResNet-50 architecture [9]. Table 3 shows the comparison. Among existing methods, the works of [10,31] provide superior performance with a mean classification accuracy of 86.0% on the MIT-67 dataset. Our approach achieves improved results compared to both these methods with a mean recognition rate of 86.4%. On the OCIS dataset, our approach significantly outperforms the existing DRCF-CNN [14] by achieving a mean accuracy of 45.3%. On the SUN-397 dataset, the best results are obtained by PatchNets [29] approach. Our approach obtains an average classification accuracy of 69.2%.

5   Conclusions

We introduced a three-stream deep architecture for monocular indoor scene recognition. In addition to the standard RGB, we proposed to integrate explicit estimated depth and texture streams in the deep learning architecture. We further investigated different fusion strategies to integrate the three sources of information. To the best of our knowledge, we are the first to investigate fusion strategies to integrate RGB, estimated depth and texture information for monocular indoor scene recognition.

Acknowledgement. This work has been supported by the Academy of Finland project number 313988 *Deep neural networks in scene graph generation for perception of visual multimedia semantics* and the European Union's Horizon 2020 research and innovation programme under grant agreement No 780069 *Methods for Managing Audiovisual Data: Combining Automatic Efficiency with Human Accuracy.* Computational resources have been provided by the Aalto Science-IT project and NVIDIA Corporation.

References

1. Anwer, R.M., Khan, F.S., van de Weijer, J., Molinier, M., Laaksonen, J.: Binary patterns encoded convolutional neural networks for texture recognition and remote sensing scene classification. ISPRS J. Photogramm. Remote Sens. **138**, 74–85 (2018)
2. Borg, I., Groenen, F.: Modern Multidimensional Scaling: Theory and Applications. Springer, New York (2005). https://doi.org/10.1007/0-387-28981-X
3. Chatfield, K., Simonyan, K., Vedaldi, A., Zisserman, A.: Return of the devil in the details: delving deep into convolutional nets. In: BMVC (2014)
4. Cimpoi, M., Maji, S., Vedaldi, A.: Deep filter banks for texture recognition and segmentation. In: CVPR, pp. 3828–3836 (2015)
5. Eigen, D., Fergus, R.: Predicting depth, surface normals and semantic labels with a common multi-scale convolutional architecture. In: ICCV (2015)
6. Guo, S., Huang, W., Wang, L., Qiao, Y.: Locally supervised deep hybrid model for scene recognition. TIP **26**(2), 808–820 (2017)
7. Gupta, S., Arbelaez, P., Girshick, R., Malik, J.: Local binary features for texture classification: taxonomy and experimental study. IJCV **112**(2), 133–149 (2015)
8. Hayat, M., Khan, S., Bennamoun, M., An, S.: A spatial layout and scale invariant feature representation for indoor scene classification. TIP **25**(10), 4829–4841 (2016)
9. He, K., Zhang, X., Ren, S., Sun, J.: Deep residual learning for image recognition. In: CVPR (2016)
10. Herranz, L., Jiang, S., Li, X.: Scene recognition with CNNs: objects, scales and dataset bias. In: CVPR (2016)
11. Hoffman, J., Gupta, S., Darrell, T.: Learning with side information through modality hallucination. In: CVPR (2016)
12. Khan, F.S., Anwer, R.M., van de Weijer, J., Felsberg, M., Laaksonen, J.: Compact color-texture description for texture classification. PRL **51**, 16–22 (2015)
13. Khan, F.S., van de Weijer, J., Anwer, R.M., Bagdanov, A., Felsberg, M., Laaksonen, J.: Scale coding bag of deep features for human attribute and action recognition. MVA **29**(1), 25–71 (2018)
14. Khan, S., Hayat, M., Bennamoun, M., Togneri, R., Sohel, F.: A discriminative representation of convolutional features for indoor scene recognition. TIP **25**(7), 3372–3383 (2016)
15. Khan, S., Hayat, M., Porikli, F.: Scene categorization with spectral features. In: ICCV (2017)
16. Koskela, M., Laaksonen, J.: Convolutional network features for scene recognition. In: ACM MM (2014)

17. Lazebnik, S., Schmid, C., Ponce, J.: Beyond bags of features: spatial pyramid matching for recognizing natural scene categories. In: CVPR, pp. 2169–2178 (2006)
18. Levi, G., Hassner, T.: Emotion recognition in the wild via convolutional neural networks and mapped binary patterns. In: ICMI (2015)
19. Li, B., Shen, C., Dai, Y., van den Hengel, A., He, M.: Depth and surface normal estimation from monocular images using regression on deep features and hierarchical CRFs. In: CVPR (2015)
20. Liu, F., Shen, C., Lin, G., Reid, I.: Learning depth from single monocular images using deep convolutional neural fields. PAMI 38(10), 2024–2039 (2016)
21. Liu, L., Fieguth, P., Guo, Y., Wang, X., Pietikainen, M.: Local binary features for texture classification: taxonomy and experimental study. PR 62, 135–160 (2017)
22. Ojala, T., Pietikainen, M., Maenpaa, T.: Multiresolution gray-scale and rotation invariant texture classification with local binary patterns. PAMI 24(7), 971–987 (2002)
23. Quattoni, A., Torralba, A.: Recognizing indoor scenes. In: CVPR (2009)
24. Renninger, L.W., Malik, J.: When is scene identification just texture recognition? Vis. Res. 44(19), 2301–2311 (2004)
25. Rubner, Y., Tomasi, C., Guibas, L.: The earth mover's distance as a metric for image retrieval. IJCV 40(2), 99–121 (2000)
26. Russakovsky, O., et al.: ImageNet large scale visual recognition challenge. arXiv preprint arXiv:1409.0575 (2014)
27. Song, X., Herranz, L., Jiang, S.: Depth CNNs for RGB-D scene recognition: learning from scratch better than transferring from RGB-CNNs. In: AAAI (2017)
28. Wang, A., Cai, J., Lu, J., Cham, T.J.: Modality and component aware feature fusion for RGB-D scene classification. In: CVPR (2016)
29. Wang, Z., Wang, L., Wang, Y., Zhang, B., Qiao, Y.: Weakly supervised patchnets: describing and aggregating local patches for scene recognition. TIP 26(4), 2028–2041 (2017)
30. Xiao, J., Hays, J., Ehinger, K., Oliva, A., Torralba, A.: Sun database: large-scale scene recognition from abbey to zoo. In: CVPR (2010)
31. Xie, G.S., Zhang, X.Y., Yan, S., Liu, C.L.: Hybrid CNN and dictionary-based models for scene recognition and domain adaptation. TCSVT 27(6), 1263–1274 (2016)
32. Zhou, B., Lapedriza, A., Xiao, J., Torralba, A., Oliva, A.: Learning deep features for scene recognition using places database. In: NIPS, pp. 487–495 (2014)

Learning Controllable Face Generator from Disjoint Datasets

Jing Li$^{(\boxtimes)}$, Yongkang Wong , and Terence Sim

School of Computing, National University of Singapore, Singapore, Singapore
{lijing,wongyk,tsim}@comp.nus.edu.sg

Abstract. Recently, GANs have become popular for synthesizing photorealistic facial images with desired facial attributes. However, crucial to the success of such networks is the availability of large-scale datasets that are fully-attributed, *i.e.*, datasets in which the Cartesian product of all attribute values is present, as otherwise the learning becomes skewed. Such fully-attributed datasets are impractically expensive to collect. Many existing datasets are only partially-attributed, and do not have any subjects in common. It thus becomes important to be able to jointly learn from such datasets. In this paper, we propose a GAN-based facial image generator that can be trained on partially-attributed disjoint datasets. The key idea is to use a smaller, fully-attributed dataset to bridge the learning. Our generator (i) provides independent control of multiple attributes, and (ii) renders photorealistic facial images with target attributes.

Keywords: Face generator · Disentanglement · Disjoint-learning

1 Introduction

Research in facial image synthesis has spanned at least two decades in both computer graphics and computer vision. Much research employs machine learning approaches, and thus central to their success has been the collection and sharing of diverse facial image datasets that exhibit attribute variations, *i.e.*, images of subjects captured under different illumination conditions, head pose, facial expressions, *etc.*

However, many datasets (*e.g.*, CelebA [12], Multi-PIE [5]) exhibits a trade-off between subject diversity and image variations. Datasets acquired under laboratory settings typically contain a limited number (∼hundreds) of subjects, each captured under many different controlled imaging conditions; while datasets collected "in-the-wild" tend to consist of many (∼tens of thousands) subjects, each captured under only a few unknown and uncontrolled imaging conditions. For machine learning purposes, the ideal training dataset should contain a large number of subjects, each imaged under many different conditions. Moreover, all these

This research is supported by the National Research Foundation, Prime Minister's Office, Singapore under its Strategic Capability Research Centres Funding Initiative.

© Springer Nature Switzerland AG 2019
M. Vento and G. Percannella (Eds.): CAIP 2019, LNCS 11678, pp. 209–223, 2019.
https://doi.org/10.1007/978-3-030-29888-3_17

attributes should be present in all possible combinations, as otherwise the learning would be skewed. Alas, collecting such fully-attributed dataset, where the full Cartesian product of all attribute values is present, is impractically expensive. Thus, it becomes important to learn from partially-attributed disjoint datasets, where each dataset exhibits variations in only one or a few attributes.

In fact, this joint-learning ability becomes *crucial* for face synthesis methods that employ deep networks, because such networks require large datasets for effective training. Recently, Generative Adversarial Network (GAN) [4] has been adopted to manipulate multiple attribute for facial images [2,18]. Unfortunately, these generators are hampered by their inability to learn from partially-attributed disjoint datasets.

In this paper, we propose a GAN-based facial image generator that can be learned from multiple partially-attributed disjoint datasets. The key idea is to use a smaller yet fully-attributed dataset to bridge the learning. Our proposed generator manipulates attributes for a facial image by extracting a disentangled attribute feature vector and by performing transformations on it. We demonstrate our method by learning to disentangle illumination, pose, and subject identity, and by rendering novel faces not seen in training under all variations of the said attributes. Our contributions are: (1) A novel GAN-based facial image generator with explicit control over attributes, thereby permitting the synthesis of arbitrary combinations of said attributes; (2) A learning method that learns from multiple partially-attributed disjoint datasets, thereby greatly increasing the learning capability of GAN-based generators. As a side benefit, our network also permits accurate analyses of facial image attributes.

2 Related Work

Face synthesis is widely studied in the literature. Compared with conventional methods [1,6,17] using handcraft feature models to capture attributes, deep learning methods [9,18,20] have been favored for image generation by taking advantage of vast real-life face images. For instance, Yang *et al.* [20] proposed a recurrent convolutional autoencoder network to rotate faces in images. Kulkarni *et al.* [9] presented a deep convolutional inverse graphics network, which learns disentangled pose, illumination, and identity features and allows for manipulation of multiple attributes.

Among deep learning methods, GAN-based models [4] has been favored for generating photorealistic images by training a generator against a discriminator. There are several works addressing multi-attribute manipulation for facial images. Li *et al.* [11] proposed a two-stage method for transfering attributes while preserving identity for a facial image. The method generates photorealistic face images but requires a set of reference facial images with target attribute for each input image. TD-GAN [18] learned to disentangle face attributes by integrating face generator with a tag mapping network to explore the consistency between images and their tags. Although this method is able to directly generate images from tags of target attributes, it requires for a set of training images with almost Cartesian product of all attribute variations. Recently StarGAN [2] allows simultaneous training of multiple datasets with different domains within a single network. It takes both image and domain information and learns to flexibly translate the image into corresponding domain. StarGAN is shown to perform well on synthesizing facial expressions of images from CelebA [12] dataset using features learned from RaFD [10] dataset. Although expression label of CelebA dataset are not explicitly used during training, there exist various facial expressions. Thus CelebA and RaFD are not completely disjoint with respect to facial expression. Furthermore, manipulation of facial attributes such as expressions and hair color, involves only local changes of images. It is unclear how effective it is to the manipulation of global facial attributes (*e.g.,* pose).

All the above methods suffer from a serious drawback: they require a training dataset that is fully-attributed. This makes them impractical since such datasets are expensive to collect. It would be more practical to be able to learn from partially-attributed disjoint datasets, and still retain the ability to control rendering attributes, while generating realistic images. This paper proposes such a method: the key idea is to use a small bridging dataset that mediates between the disjoint datasets.

3   Proposed Face Generator Framework

We propose a face generator network (Fig. 1) that learns disentangled and discriminative embedding for different attributes, including illumination, pose, ID and latent information useful for image rendering. Within this embedding, an attribute manipulation network, shown on the right panel of Fig. 1, is devised to modify illumination and pose feature by learning a transform matrix from two one-hot vectors (*i.e.,* c^l and c^p) that indicates target illumination and pose.

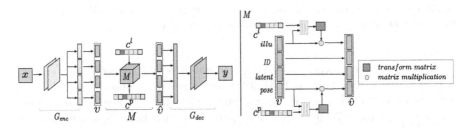

Fig. 1. Structure of proposed controllable multi-attribute face generator network. The face generator is composed of an encoder G_{enc}, an attribute manipulator network M, and a decoder G_{dec}. G_{enc} encodes a facial image into illumination, pose, ID and latent subspaces.

We train the proposed network for two disjoint facial image datasets: $\mathcal{A}$ with frontal pose but variable illuminations and $\mathcal{C}$ in reverse. To address the attribute disentanglement and rendering of images with attributes absent in both $\mathcal{A}$ and

$\mathcal{C}$ (*e.g.*, facial images with 45° illumination and 45° pose), we employ a small fully-attributed bridging dataset $\mathcal{B}$, which can be easily collected in practice as it requires only a few subjects. The training method (shown in Fig. 2) works by applying two-stream attribute manipulations on an input facial image: one is to manipulate illumination to target c^l and the other is to manipulate pose to target c^p. We train the proposed model with following objectives.

Attribute Disentanglement and Discriminability. These are two desirable properties for attribute subspace, because disentanglement allows for changing an attribute for a facial image without tempering others, and discriminative attribute subspace makes it easy for attribute manipulation operation and attribute interpolation.

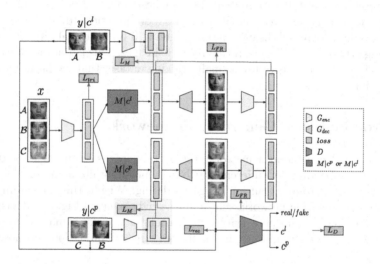

Fig. 2. Overview of proposed method. For each image x, the model changes it separately to illumination c^l and pose c^p, resulting in two images.

To achieve this objective, we adopt triplet loss [14] (denoted as L_{tri}) in each of illumination, pose and ID subspaces learned by encoder G_{enc}[1]. The intrinsic idea of triplet loss is to minimize intra-class distance and maximize inter-class distance. While triplet loss is designed for training discriminative feature subspace, it also achieves attribute disentanglement. Take illumination as an example, pose and identity variations are untangled from illumination attribute subspace, because facial images with same illumination but different poses and identities are enforced to be close in the subspace by triplet loss objective. Similarly, illumination and identity are untangled in pose subspace, and illumination and pose are untangled in ID subspace.

---

[1] For convenience, we normalized each feature vector in embedding subspaces in network.

Attribute Manipulation. This is performed by transforming a normalized attribute feature vector from one class to target class. We conduct two separate manipulations on illumination and pose, denoted as M^{illu} and M^{pose} for training images. We pair each image x with a target image y conditioned on M^{illu}/M^{pose}, and enforce the transformed attribute feature vector of x to be same with that of y. Nevertheless, there is no target image for M^{pose} of $\mathcal{A}$ images and M^{illu} of $\mathcal{C}$ images. We hence select a pseudo target image from the other dataset. We denote image pairs as *homogeneous pair* and *heterogeneous pair* as Fig. 3. Homogeneous pairs come from a same dataset and differs in only one particular attribute. We propose a loss function for homogeneous pairs as:

$$L_{h1}(\mathcal{S}, attr) = \mathbb{E}_{x,y \sim \mathcal{S}} \left[\|v_x^{\overline{attr}} - v_y^{\overline{attr}}\|_2^2 + \|v_x^{ID} - v_y^{ID}\|_2^2 + \|M^{attr}(v_x^{attr}, c^{attr}) - v_y^{attr}\|_2^2 \right] \quad (1)$$

where $\mathcal{S} \in \{\mathcal{A}, \mathcal{B}, \mathcal{C}\}$, $attr \in \{illu, pose\}$ and $\overline{attr} = \{illu, pose\} - attr$. We sum up the homogeneous loss as: $L_{ho} = L_{h1}(\mathcal{A}, illu) + L_{h1}(\mathcal{C}, pose) + L_{h1}(\mathcal{B}, illu) + L_{h1}(\mathcal{B}, pose)$. In homogeneous pairs, images come from two partially-attributed datasets with different attributes. Therefore, only the distance between the transformed attribute feature vector and its pseudo target attribute feature is considered in heterogeneous loss:

$$L_{he} = \mathbb{E} \left[\|M^{pose}(v_{x_{\mathcal{A}}}^{pose}, c^p) - v_{y_{\mathcal{C}}}^{pose}\|_2^2 + \|M^{illu}(v_{x_{\mathcal{C}}}^{illu}, c^l) - v_{y_{\mathcal{A}}}^{illu}\|_2^2 \right] \quad (2)$$

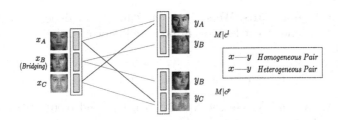

Fig. 3. Attribute transform pairs. Homogeneous images are from same dataset with same identity, and heterogeneous images are from two disjoint datasets with different identity. Each pair demonstrates variation in either illumination or pose.

Photorealistic Image Generation. This is achieved by regression loss and GAN loss. Firstly, since the face generator follows autoencoder architecture, we use L2 loss as L_{rec} for homogeneous pairs. In addition, we train face generator against a discriminator D, and employ GAN loss for realistic facial image generation by:

$$L_{GAN} = \mathbb{E}_{x \sim r} \log D(x) + \mathbb{E}_{x \sim g} \log(1 - D(x)) \quad (3)$$

In order to encourage face generator generate images with correct target illumination and pose, we apply two 1-of-2N classifiers [15], C, on top of feature layers of discriminator to predict illumination and pose of the generated images. 1-of-2N classifier is designed with the purpose of classifying a real image x_r

to first N labels and a generated image x_g to the last N labels, where N is the number of attribute classes. By considering a same attribute class of real and generated images as different label, adversarial training pushes real and generated domains as close to each other as possible, thus preserving attributes of generated images. Cross-entropy loss is used to train C:

$$L_{C_{attr}} = \sum_j -\{[c_r^{attr} \ \mathbf{0}]\}_j \log(\{C_{attr}(x_r)\}_j) + \sum_j -\{[\mathbf{0} \ c_g^{attr}]\}_j \log(\{C_{attr}(x_g)\}_j) \quad (4)$$

where $\mathbf{0}$ is a N-dim zero vector, $j \in [1, 2N]$ is the j-th index of attribute class.

Identity Preservation. In proposed method, discriminator D is employed to enforce the distribution of generated images to be similar to that of real images. However, due to that $\mathcal{A}$ and $\mathcal{C}$ are partially-attributed, the real images with non-frontal illumination and non-frontal pose for D only comes from $\mathcal{B}$. This would result in that the generated images $M^{pose}(x_A)$ and $M^{illu}(x_C)$ appear to be like faces of $\mathcal{B}$ with same attribute conditions. To address this problem, we propose a feature reconstruction loss to preserve the facial identity of generated images. Specifically, we extract the semantic feature of each generated image by the encoder G_{enc}, and enforce the semantic feature to be same as the one that is used for generating the current image. See Fig. 2 for illustration. The feature reconstruction loss is presented as:

$$L_{FR} = \mathbb{E}_{v \sim G_{enc}(x)} \|v - G_{enc}(G_{dec}(v))\|_2^2 \quad (5)$$

Implementation Details. We set (64, 64, 256, 64) for dimensions of illumination, pose, ID and latent features in proposed networks. We trained our face generator by:

$$L = L_{rec} + \lambda_1(L_{tri}^{illu} + L_{tri}^{pose} + L_{tri}^{ID}) + \lambda_2(L_{ho} + L_{he}) + \lambda_3 L_{FR} + \lambda_4(L_{GAN} + L_{C_{illu}} + L_{C_{pose}}) \quad (6)$$

where λ_1, λ_2, λ_3 and λ_4 are set to 0.01, 0.5, 0.5, and 0.001. We set triplet margins for illumination, pose and identity features to be 1.8, 1.8, and 0.7. Adam optimizer is used to train the G and M with learning rate at 0.001 and decay rate at 0.01, and D with learning rate at 0.001 and decay rate at 0.01.

4   Experiments

Dataset and Preprocessing. We evaluated the proposed generator on CMU-PIE [16], Multi-PIE [5] and CAS-PEAL [3] datasets (see Table 1). All images were aligned using chin and forehead position detected by Dlibrary [8] and cropped to 128×128 pixels.

Table 1. Details of experimental datasets. Note that we label 67° illumination of CMU-PIE to be same with 90° illumination of Multi-PIE and CAS-PEAL, as they are visually similar in images.

Dataset	Subjects	Images	Illumination	Pose	Light
CMU-PIE [16]	68	2380	0°, ±30°, ±67°	0°, ±15°, ±30°, ±45°	Off
Multi-PIE [5]	336	11760	0°, ±45°, ±90°	0°, ±15°, ±30°, ±45°	On
CAS-PEAL [3]	233	920	0°, ±45°, ±90°	0°	Off

Table 2. Experimental configurations. • denotes single attribute face dataset and ∗ denotes the small scale bridging face dataset. Note that subjects of each subset in the table is non-overlapped.

Scenario	Training data	Data source
I (Ideal)	Fully-attribute dataset with 200 subjects	Multi-PIE
II (w/o bridge)	• Pose attribute subset with 100 subjects	Multi-PIE
	• Illumination attribute subset with 100 subjects	Multi-PIE
III (w/ bridge)	• Pose attribute subset with 100 subjects	Multi-PIE
	• Illumination attribute subset with 100 subjects	Multi-PIE
	∗ Bridging dataset with 20 subjects	Multi-PIE
IV (cross dataset)	• Pose attribute subset with 200 subjects	Multi-PIE
	• Illumination attribute subset with 200 subjects	CAS-PEAL
	∗ Bridging dataset with 20 subjects	CMU-PIE

Experimental Configuration. We considered four scenarios to investigate how face generator performs with different training dataset configurations (Table 2). Scenario I is the ideal training configuration where each subject has multiple images captured under all factors (*i.e.*, controlled poses and illumination conditions). It benchmarks the best performance that can be achieved by a face generator. In Scenario II, the training was conducted using two face datasets with single attribute variation. This scenario stresses testing the proposed model under extreme learning condition. In Scenario III, we added on top of Scenario II a bridging dataset with small number of subjects. The newly added bridging dataset provided *guidance information* during model training stage. In Scenario IV, we designed a configuration that mimics realistic scenario, where partially-attributed datasets come from different data sources.

Evaluation. We evaluated the learned face generator with two aspects, namely feature subpaces and image quality. The feature subpaces were evaluated by performing a series of classification tasks on attribute feature vectors, and the image quality was evaluated by Fréchet Inception Distance (FID) [7], a measure of similarity between the generated images and real images.

4.1   Experiments on Multi-PIE

We firstly investigated the importance of a fully-attribute training dataset to the learning of a multi-attribute face generator by comparing our method in Scenario I, II and III.

Feature Subspaces. We evaluated the discriminability and disentanglement of semantic attribute subspaces by performing classification tasks on the testing images of 116 subjects in Multi-PIE. For illumination and pose classification, we used images of 50 subjects as galleries and images of the remaining 66 subjects as probes. For face verification, we randomly selected 17 images for each of 116 subjects as galleries and used the remaining 18 images as probes. We employed KNN method using Euclidean Distance metric for each task.

Table 3. Classification accuracy on feature subspaces for Multi-PIE experiments.

		Illumination	Pose	ID
Scenario I (ideal)	Illu subspace	**100.00%**	14.68%	0.20%
	Pose subspace	20.39%	**100.00%**	0.0%
	ID subspace	29.09%	20.56%	**100.00%**
Scenario II (w/o bridge)	Illu subspace	66.36%	35.76%	0.86%
	Pose subspace	43.03%	80.04%	0.51%
	ID subspace	64.03%	50.87%	83.92%
Scenario III (w/bridge)	Illu subspace	99.61%	15.24%	0.51%
	Pose subspace	24.11%	93.72%	0.15%
	ID subspace	27.84%	19.22%	99.79%

We showed the classification results in Table 3. As can be seen, the baseline Scenario I achieved the best performance, 100% accuracy, for all three classification tasks. However, the performance quickly drops in Scenario II, where much lower accuracy rates (66.36%, 80.04%, 83.92%) were attained for illumination, pose classifications and face verification in corresponding subspace. Moreover, it can be noted that substantial results were achieved in unassociated subspaces for illumination and pose classification tasks. This is because that the training data sets were partially-attributed, hence the learned model cannot disentangle facial images with non-frontal illumination and non-frontal pose. With a small fully-attributed bridging dataset in Scenario III, we attained classification performance that approaches ideal Scenario I.

Table 4. Image quality evaluation for Multi-PIE experiments.

	FID	Illumination	Pose	ID
Scenario I (ideal)	19.59	99.15%	95.59%	91.50%
Scenario II (w/o bridge)	139.81	36.69%	70.69%	65.65%
Scenario III (w/bridge)	37.79	98.15%	95.04%	86.07%

Image Quality. We evaluated quality of generated images by computing FID scores between synthesized images and real images of testing Multi-PIE subjects. We also evaluated attribute preservation of generated images by performing illumination and pose classifications as well as face verification on generated images of testing subjects. We used the testing images as galleries and the generated images as probes. We conducted the experiments by using a pretrained face network [19] as feature extractor, PCA for reducing feature dimension and then SVM classification method. The results are shown in Table 4, in which Scenario I achieves the best performance for all evaluation on generated images with smallest FID score and largest classification accuracy rates. In scenario II, the quality of generated images drops to 139.81. This is mainly because the model learned was unable to generate photorealistic images with unseen illumination and pose. By using a small bridging dataset, our method was able to synthesize images with target attributes and preserved facial identity, where FID score was reduced to 37.79, and classification performance was improved by 61.46%, 24.35%, 20.42% for illumination, pose and identity, respectively.

We illustrated some example images in Fig. 4. As can be seen, model II failed to generate convincing results, especially images with illumination changed. This is consistent with the low illumination classification accuracy using feature vectors (66.36%) and synthesized images (36.69%). It also fell short of changing poses for facial images with non-frontal illumination absent during training (face 2, 4). On the other hand, model I and III succeeded to generate photorealistic facial images, even if testing images were at random pose and illumination. Generally, model I achieved better holistic image quality, while model III preserved better local details, such as eye regions in face 1 and 2. One possible reason is that model I learned more variations for each attribute condition and failed preserve local details while trying to capture global structure.

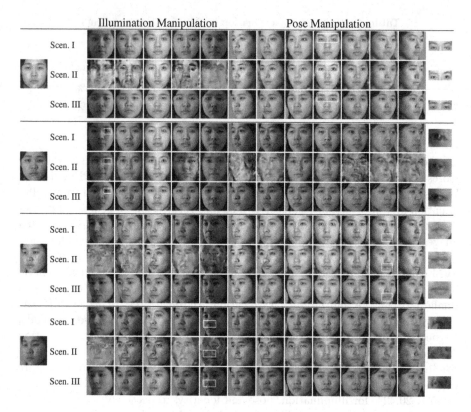

Fig. 4. Comparison of generated images for models in Scenario I, Scenario II and Scenario III. Each face was changed in illumination and pose, respectively. It is clear that the use of the bridging dataset (Scenario III) improves image quality.

4.2   Cross Dataset Experiments

We compared our method with existing methods, namely TD-GAN [18] and StarGAN [2], in Scenario IV, where each subset of training data came from different datasets.

Feature Subspaces. Both our method and TD-GAN learn disentangled attribute feature subspaces for input images. In the same line, we compared their feature subspaces by performing a series of classification tasks. We used images of 116 subjects from Multi-PIE, 33 subjects from CAS-PEAL, and 48 subjects from CMU-PIE as testing data. For illumination and pose classification, we use CMU-PIE images as galleries and Multi-PIE as well as CAS-PEAL images as probes. For face verification, we split images of each subject into two equal subsets, one for training and the other for testing.

The results were presented in Table 5. As can be seen, our method attained higher accuracy rates in all tasks than TD-GAN. This is because our method concerns both inter-class and intra-class distance for attribute feature vectors,

Table 5. Classification accuracy on feature spaces for cross dataset experiments.

	Illumination	Pose	ID
TD-GAN [18]	96.88%	31.34%	7.05%
Our method	**99.72%**	**100.00%**	**99.78%**

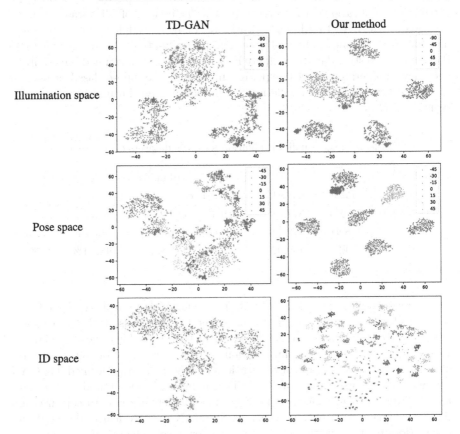

Fig. 5. (Best viewed in color) Visualization of feature subspaces of TD-GAN (LEFT) and our method (RIGHT). Illumination and pose class center learned by tag network as ⋆ in the figures. We denote • for CMU-PIE images, + for CAS-PEAL images and use the lighter color for Multi-PIE images. Our method achieves better separation of illumination, pose and identity attributes, leading to more accurate classification of said attributes. (Color figure online)

whereas TD-GAN only considers inter-class distance by enforcing feature vectors of same class to be close.

We plotted the feature subspaces in Fig. 5 using t-SNE [13]. It can be seen that TD-GAN network failed to disentangle face attributes, while our method performed well in attribute disentanglement. The main reason for TD-GAN's poor performance is that it employed L2 loss to enforce an attribute feature of an image to be close to that learned from its label. However, without considering inter-class distance, L2 loss leads to the trivial feature vectors where their norm $\|v\|_2^2$ equals to 0.

Image Quality. We evaluated quality of generated images by FID scores and attribute classifications performance on testing images of all datasets. Being reminded that CAS-PEAL and Multi-PIE images used here were partially-attributed, so we only compared generated partially-attributed images for these datasets with testing data to compute FID score. Also, we examined the attribute accuracy of generated images by performing illumination, pose classification and face identification tasks on galleries and probes as used during feature analysis mentioned above.

Table 6. Image quality evaluation for cross datasets experiments.

Method	FID			Illumination	Pose	ID
	Multi-PIE	CAS-PEAL	CMU-PIE			
TD-GAN [18]	310.49	377.58	329.49	94.25%	59.34%	54.86%
StarGAN [2]	118.41	172.31	142.60	**95.09%**	97.55%	**80.72%**
Ours	34.33	139.02	55.35	94.83%	**98.51%**	69.97%

We presented the results in Table 6. It was shown that our method generated more photorealistic facial images than other two methods, with the smallest FID scores for all datasets. In addition, our method was able to generate images with target attributes, with illumination and pose classification accuracy rates at 94.83% and 98.51%. In face verification, our method outperformed TD-GAN yet performed worse than StarGAN. This is because our method learns high-level attribute features in bottleneck layer, and therefore fails to capture high frequency image information. Whereas StarGAN directly learns the attribute translation in the network and can preserve low-level image feature.

The generated images are shown in Fig. 6. As shown, TD-GAN failed to generate photorealistic facial images. StarGAN was able to preserve the identity of synthesized images as it directly learns the attribute translation method without learning semantic feature space. Yet StarGAN performed poorly in pose manipulation that involves spatial change in images (see the ghosting effects in pose manipulation results). In general, our method can generates images with reasonable image quality and preserves identity.

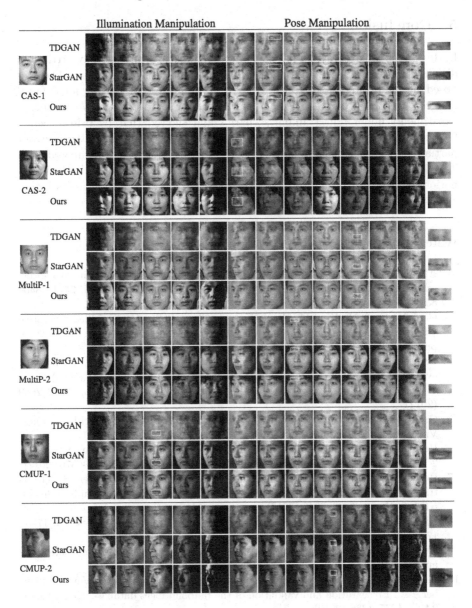

Fig. 6. Comparison of generated images for our method and TD-GAN, StarGAN. Each face was changed in illumination and pose, respectively. Our method renders images with better visual quality.

5 Conclusion

In this paper, we presented a face generator that learns from partially-attributed disjoint datasets, along with a smaller fully-attributed briding dataset. The proposed method allows for explicit control over multiple attributes for a facial image by learning a disentangled and discriminative feature space. We conducted experiments under four training scenarios and showed that by using a small bridging dataset, the disentanglement and rendering of multiple attributes for partially-attributed disjoint datasets can be easily addressed. Compared with TD-GAN and StarGAN, our method renders superior images in both illumination and pose variations. As a side benefit, our network also achieves higher classification accuracy of the said attributes.

References

1. Almaddah, A., Vural, S., Mae, Y., Ohara, K., Arai, T.: Face relighting using discriminative 2D spherical spaces for face recognition. Mach. Vis. Appl. **25**(4), 845–857 (2014)
2. Choi, Y., Choi, M., Kim, M., Ha, J., Kim, S., Choo, J.: StarGAN: unified generative adversarial networks for multi-domain image-to-image translation. In: CVPR 2018, pp. 8789–8797 (2018)
3. Gao, W., et al.: The CAS-PEAL large-scale chinese face database and baseline evaluations. IEEE Trans. Syst. Man Cybern. Part A **38**(1), 149–161 (2008)
4. Goodfellow, I.J., et al.: Generative adversarial nets. In: NIPS 2014, pp. 2672–2680 (2014)
5. Gross, R., Matthews, I.A., Cohn, J.F., Kanade, T., Baker, S.: Multi-PIE. Image Vis. Comput. **28**(5), 807–813 (2010)
6. Heo, J., Savvides, M.: 3-D generic elastic models for fast and texture preserving 2-D novel pose synthesis. IEEE Trans. Inf. Forensics Secur. **7**(2), 563–576 (2012)
7. Heusel, M., Ramsauer, H., Unterthiner, T., Nessler, B., Hochreiter, S.: GANs trained by a two time-scale update rule converge to a local nash equilibrium. In: NIPS 2017, pp. 6629–6640 (2017)
8. King, D.E.: Dlib-ml: a machine learning toolkit. J. Mach. Learn. Res. **10**, 1755–1758 (2009)
9. Kulkarni, T.D., Whitney, W.F., Kohli, P., Tenenbaum, J.B.: Deep convolutional inverse graphics network. In: NIPS 2015, pp. 2539–2547 (2015)
10. Langner, O., Dotsch, R., Bijlstra, G., Wigboldus, D.H., Hawk, S.T., Van Knippenberg, A.: Presentation and validation of the radboud faces database. Cogn. Emot. **24**(8), 1377–1388 (2010)
11. Li, M., Zuo, W., Zhang, D.: Convolutional network for attribute-driven and identity-preserving human face generation. CoRR abs/1608.06434 (2016)
12. Liu, Z., Luo, P., Wang, X., Tang, X.: Deep learning face attributes in the wild. In: ICCV 2015, pp. 3730–3738 (2015)
13. van der Maaten, L., Hinton, G.: Visualizing data using t-SNE. J. Mach. Learn. Res. **9**(Nov), 2579–2605 (2008)
14. Schroff, F., Kalenichenko, D., Philbin, J.: FaceNet: a unified embedding for face recognition and clustering. In: CVPR 2015, pp. 815–823 (2015)

15. Shen, Y., Luo, P., Yan, J., Wang, X., Tang, X.: FaceID-GAN: learning a symmetry three-player GAN for identity-preserving face synthesis. In: CVPR 2018, pp. 821–830 (2018)
16. Sim, T., Baker, S., Bsat, M.: The CMU pose, illumination, and expression (PIE) database. In: AFGR 2002, pp. 53–58 (2002)
17. Thies, J., Zollhöfer, M., Nießner, M., Valgaerts, L., Stamminger, M., Theobalt, C.: Real-time expression transfer for facial reenactment. ACM Trans. Graph. **34**(6), 183:1–183:14 (2015)
18. Wang, C., Wang, C., Xu, C., Tao, D.: Tag disentangled generative adversarial networks for object image re-rendering. In: IJCAI (2017)
19. Wu, X., He, R., Sun, Z., Tan, T.: A light CNN for deep face representation with noisy labels. IEEE Trans. Inf. Forensics Secur. **13**(11), 2884–2896 (2018)
20. Yang, J., Reed, S.E., Yang, M., Lee, H.: Weakly-supervised disentangling with recurrent transformations for 3D view synthesis. In: NIPS 2015, pp. 1099–1107 (2015)

Learning Discriminatory Deep Clustering Models

A. Alqahtani[1,2], X. Xie[1]([✉]), J. Deng[1], and M. W. Jones[1]

[1] Department of Computer Science, Swansea University, Swansea, UK
x.xie@swansea.ac.uk
http://csvision.swan.ac.uk
[2] Department of Computer Science, King Khalid University, Abha, Saudi Arabia

Abstract. Deep convolutional auto-encoder (DCAE) allows to obtain useful features via its internal layer and provide an abstracted latent representation, which has been exploited for clustering analysis. DCAE allows a deep clustering method to extract similar patterns in lower-dimensional representation and find idealistic representative centers for distributed data. In this paper, we present a deep clustering model carried out in presence of varying degrees of supervision. We propose a new version of DCAE to include a supervision component. It introduces a mechanism to inject various levels of supervision into the learning process. This mechanism helps to effectively reconcile extracted latent representations and provided supervising knowledge in order to produce the best discriminative attributes. The key idea of our approach is distinguishing the discriminatory power of numerous structures, through varying degrees of supervision, when searching for a compact structure to form robust clusters. We evaluate our model on MNIST, USPS, MNIST fashion, SVHN datasets and show clustering accuracy on different supervisory levels.

Keywords: Deep convolutional auto-encoder · Embedded clustering · Supervision

1 Introduction

In recent years, deep learning methods have shown their robust ability in representation learning and achieved considerable success in many tasks. It transforms raw data into a more abstract representation. A Deep convolutional auto-encoder (DCAE) is a deep unsupervised model for representation learning. It maps inputs into a new latent space, allowing to obtain useful features via its encoding layer. This high-level representation provides beneficial properties that can support traditional clustering algorithms in demonstrating satisfying performance. DCAE has been exploited for clustering analysis, allowing such clustering algorithms to deal with an abstract latent representation in a low-dimensional space. Different approaches to unsupervised deep clustering have

M. Vento and G. Percannella (Eds.): CAIP 2019, LNCS 11678, pp. 224–233, 2019.
https://doi.org/10.1007/978-3-030-29888-3_18

been developed utilizing deep neural networks. A detailed survey can be found in [10]. For instance, DCAE with embedded clustering [2] is an unsupervised clustering method that simultaneously captures representative features and the relationships among images. In this procedure, the discriminative patterns are only discovered through certain parts or objects in an image in an unsupervised manner. The goal of this method is to learn feature representations and cluster assignments simultaneously, utilizing the strength of DCAE to learn high-level features. Two objective functions were utilized: one is embedded into a DCAE model to minimize the distance between features and their corresponding cluster centers, while the other one minimizes the reconstruction error of the DCAE. During optimization, all data representations are assigned to their new identical cluster centers and then cluster centers are updated iteratively allowing the model to achieve a stable clustering performance. The defined clustering objective, as well as the reconstruction objective, are simultaneously utilized to update parameters of transforming network.

Providing partial supervision to the clustering process, semi-supervised clustering aims to cluster a large amount of unlabeled data in the presence of a minimal supervision. Basu et al. [3] studied the effect of using a small amount of labeled data to generate initial seeds for K-means. Pedrycz et al. [11] also proposed a fuzzy clustering algorithm with partial supervision. Other works utilize pairwise constrained clustering method as semi-supervised process, which has been applied to partitioning clustering [14], hierarchical clustering [4], and density-based clustering [13]. Similarly, supervised clustering includes a supervisory scheme into the clustering process aiming to improve unsupervised clustering algorithms through exploiting supervised information [15]. Pedrycz et al. [12] presented fuzzy clustering algorithm with supervision that carried out in the presence of label information. Eick et al. [6,7] introduced supervised clustering methods, which suppose that all obtained clusters hold ground truth labels aiming to identify class-uniform clusters. Al-Harbi et al. [1] also proposed a supervised clustering method by modifying the K-means algorithm to be used as a classifier.

Even though conventional semi-supervised and supervised clustering approaches have received a lot of attention, with the revolution of deep learning, limited attention has been paid to semi-supervised and supervised deep clustering models compared with unsupervised deep clustering. Therefore, providing a way to inject varying degrees of supervision into the body of the deep learning process and exploring the influence of adding supervision knowledge into a deep clustering model are worthwhile to understand discriminatory power obtained by patterns or provided by supervision components.

In this paper, we focus on a deep clustering model, where varying degrees of supervision can be injected into the body of the learning process. We propose a new version of DCAE to involve a supervision component. Injecting supervision allows us to experience different discriminatory powers, which can be provided by supervisory knowledge or obtained by data-driven discriminative attributes and examine the clustering performance through different levels of supervision.

The proposed method is aimed at forming a kind of a structure that reconciles structure discovered by the clustering process and structure provided by labeling patterns. This mechanism makes the features derived from the encoding layer are the best discriminative attributes. An available side of background knowledge along with representative patterns in latent space can be leveraged to find the best partitioning of data and maximize the purity of clusters. Experimental results illustrate the influence of adding supervision into the body of the learning process. In this study, we consider three different learning levels: supervised, semi-supervised and unsupervised. We evaluate our experimental models on MNIST, USPS, MNIST fashion, SVHN datasets and show clustering accuracy of our model through supervised, semi-supervised and unsupervised learning levels.

2   Method

The proposed approach is a DCAE with embedded clustering that is carried out in presence of varying degrees of supervision. It introduces a mechanism to inject various levels of supervision into the body of the learning process. This allows us to explore the leverage of supervised information into the performance of a deep clustering method. In this paper, we consider three different learning levels: supervised, semi-supervised and unsupervised. Each experimental model consists of combination objective functions. All objectives are simultaneously optimized.

2.1   DCAE with Embedded Clustering

DCAE is learned to capture representative features through its encoding layer by minimizing the reconstruction error using the Euclidean (L2) loss function.

$$E_1 = \frac{1}{2N} \sum_{i=1}^{n} \parallel x^i - y_i \parallel^2 \qquad (1)$$

where y is a reconstructed image, and x is an original image.

Although DCAE learns an effective representation via its encoding layer, it does not explicitly force representation forming compact clustering. In [2], we proposed a DCAE with embedded clustering that learns feature representations and clusters assignments simultaneously. It embeds K-means clustering into a DCAE framework and minimizes the distance between data points and their assigned centers in the latent space as follows:

$$E_2 = \frac{1}{2N} \sum_{n=1}^{N} \parallel h^t(x_n) - c_n^* \parallel^2 \qquad (2)$$

where N is the number of data examples, $h^t(*)$ denotes the encoded representation obtained at the tth iteration, (x_n) is the nth example in the dataset x. And c_n^* is the assigned centroids to the nth example. For further detail of DCAE with embedded clustering, readers can refer to [2].

2.2   Architecture and Extended Output Layer

Using the extended version of the DCAE with embedded clustering method allows us to inject supervision and utilize its strength to obtain discriminative and robust features from the encoding layer and allows the deep clustering method to extract discriminative features and cluster assignments, simultaneously.

DCAE architecture consists of three convolutional layers. This is followed by two fully-connected layers, of which the second layer has 10 neurons. These are considered as hidden representations learned through the training process. A single fully-connected layer is followed by three deconvolutional layers as the decoding part. ReLU is utilized as the activation function. Table 1 has shown a detailed configuration of DCAE network architecture. Our extensions to this architecture are as follows. Firstly, instead of a reconstruction layer at the end of the DCAE, extra layers are added at the end of the network just after the reconstruction layer. This allows the passing of supervision knowledge across the learning process and also the examination of clustering performance with different discriminatory power that is provided by supervision or obtained from data-driven discriminative attributes. Secondly, the learned features given by the encoding layer are optimized to form compact and discriminative clusters using K-means, which minimizes the distance between a feature representation and their respective centroid. Thirdly, instead of only minimizing the reconstruction loss and cross-entropy loss, we iteratively optimize the mapping function of the encoding part and cluster centers to obtain more effective clustering.

Table 1. Detailed configuration of the DCAE network architecture used in the experiments.

Layer	MNIST	USPS	MNIST fashion	SVHN
Convolutional	$5 \times 5 \times 32$	$4 \times 4 \times 32$	$5 \times 5 \times 32$	$5 \times 5 \times 32$
Convolutional	$5 \times 5 \times 64$	$4 \times 4 \times 64$	$5 \times 5 \times 64$	$5 \times 5 \times 64$
Convolutional	$3 \times 3 \times 128$	$2 \times 2 \times 128$	$3 \times 3 \times 128$	$2 \times 2 \times 128$
Fully connected	1152	512	1152	2048
Fully connected	10	10	10	10
Fully connected	1152	512	1152	2048
Deconvolutional	$3 \times 3 \times 128$	$2 \times 2 \times 128$	$3 \times 3 \times 128$	$2 \times 2 \times 128$
Deconvolutional	$5 \times 5 \times 64$	$3 \times 3 \times 64$	$5 \times 5 \times 64$	$5 \times 5 \times 64$
Deconvolutional	$5 \times 5 \times 32$	$3 \times 3 \times 32$	$5 \times 5 \times 32$	$5 \times 5 \times 32$

In supervised and semi-supervised models, we have used same architectures, showing on Table 1. Instead of a reconstruction layer at the end of the DCAE, we flatten the output of the reconstruction layer and feed them into a certain number of nodes in the last layer. The number of nodes depends on the task at hand, i.e. the number of provided classes (e.g. ten nodes for the supervised case and two nodes for the semi-supervised case). A softmax function is used for the final prediction. The final architecture of our extended model for a DCAE with embedded clustering is presented in Fig. 1.

Two forms of labels are used: **true labels** and **parent-class labels** to reflect two different levels of supervision. True labels are provided in supervised training process. Parent-class labels are used in semi-supervised deep clustering, that is true class labels are combined to form parent-class labels. For example, in clustering digit images using the proposed DCAE, the parent-class labels are defined as:

$$ParentLabel = \begin{cases} 0 & Labels < 5 \\ 1 & otherwise \end{cases} \tag{3}$$

The categorical cross-entropy function between network predictions and provided labels is defined as:

$$E_3 = -\sum_j t_{i,j} log(p_{i,j}) \tag{4}$$

where p is prediction, t is the provided label, i denotes the number of samples, and j denotes the class.

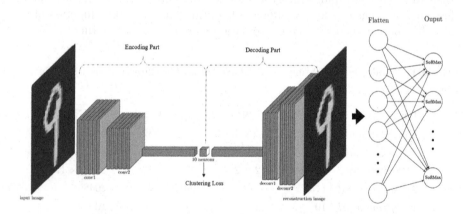

Fig. 1. The architecture of our proposed model.

In the DCAE hidden layer, encoded features are used to compute clustering loss function that minimizes the distance between data points and their corresponding cluster centers, Eq. (2). The overall cost function is thus a combination of reconstructions loss $E1$, clustering residual in latent space $E2$, and categorical cross-entropy loss $E3$ that minimizes the classification error with either supervised or semi-supervised scheme:

$$\min_{W,b} E_1 + E_2 + E_3 \tag{5}$$

3   Experiments and Discussion

The proposed method was implemented using Keras and Theano in Python and evaluated on four different datasets including MNIST, USPS, MNIST fashion, and SVHN, which are the most commonly used datasets in the area of deep clustering. Specifications of these datasets are presented in Table 2. The model was trained end-to-end without involving any pre-training and fine-tuning procedures. All weights and cluster centers were initialized randomly. *Adam* optimizer was used where each batch contains 100 random shuffled images.

Table 2. Details of datasets used in our experiments.

Dataset	Examples	Classes	Image size	Channels
MNIST	70000	10	28×28	1
USPS	11000	10	16×16	1
MNIST fashion	70000	10	28×28	1
SVHN	99289	10	32×32	3

For MNIST dataset, the experiments were performed using four different numbers of trained examples, i.e. 2000, 4000, 6000, 8000. We trained our supervised model using these settings with the same number of iteration. The comparative results are shown in Table 3, which supports our hypothesis that a small amount of labeled data can add enough discriminative ability to unsupervised deep clustering. Note that the results are the accuracy of clustering not classification use reconstructed image.

Table 3. Number of trained samples and clustering accuracy.

Trained examples	Clustering accuracy
2000	94.24%
4000	96.48%
6000	97.52%
8000	98.06%

In order to visualize the impact of supervision in deep clustering, the t-SNE visualization method [9] was applied as a visual assessment to show adding supervision is able to guide the clustering task to obtain more appropriate data partitioning. Figure 2 shows the latent representation of our proposed methods in 2D space using different levels of supervisions, where color coding of the ground truth label are used to visualize the clustering results. This shows that adding a supervision component into DCAE with embedded clustering produces significantly more compact clusters. The learned features involves a supervised process have tighter structures and larger inter-cluster distances compared with semi-supervised and unsupervised models. Injecting supervision into the learning process effectively reconciles data-driven-obtained representations and the provided supervisory knowledge to form the best partitioning of data and to maximize the purity of clusters. With the semi-supervised approach (Fig. 2b), the clustering result show typical compact clusters, producing much better clustering results compared with unsupervised models (Fig. 2c), which shows the learned features are sparse and not compacted. Figure 2d shows that the data distribution on latent space using normal DCAE which was trained only to optimize reconstruction error. Compared to Fig. 2c which enforces compact representation on hidden layer, the clusters forming by normal DCAE have higher intra-cluster variance and lower inter-cluster difference. By adopting semi-supervised (see Fig. 2b) and supervised (see Fig. 2a), intra-cluster variances are reduced significantly while the inter-cluster distances are enlarged. Especially, less cluster outliers are observed in Fig. 2a.

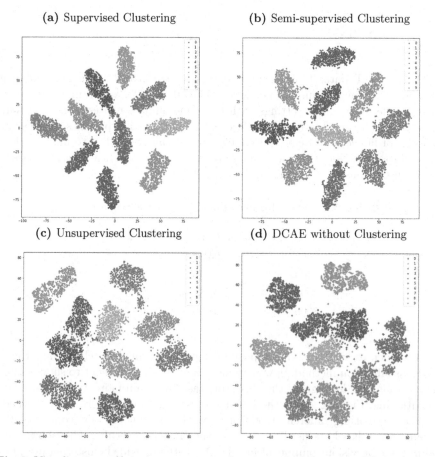

(a) Supervised Clustering   **(b)** Semi-supervised Clustering

(c) Unsupervised Clustering   **(d)** DCAE without Clustering

Fig. 2. Visualizations of latent representation for our method through a different supervisions levels on MNIST testing set.

In addition, we analyze the invariance properties of learned representation given different levels of supervision. We have trained five different models with varying degrees of supervision: supervised, semi-supervised with three different percentages of supervision (20%, 30%, 50%), and unsupervised. We apply a range of rotation-based transformations (rotate by 90°, 180°, 270°, flip horizontally, flip horizontally and rotate by 90°, 180°, 270°) to each image. We follow [5,8] to measure the variance properties by calculating Mean Squared Error (MSE) between the features of the original images and the transformed ones. The result is shown in Fig. 3. The figure compares the invariance properties of learned representation in five different models. Overall, the experiment empirically confirms that the features are more invariant when no supervision is provided. In other words, the features learned by the unsupervised model are more invariant compared to features learned with supervision.

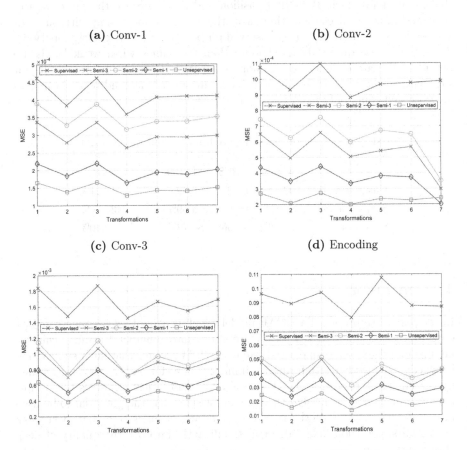

(a) Conv-1   **(b)** Conv-2

(c) Conv-3   **(d)** Encoding

Fig. 3. Invariance properties of the learned representation in different layers from five different models.

We empirically evaluated the performance of representation learning of DCAE with different supervisory schemes by calculating the clustering accuracy against the true label. These experiments show a discriminative representation can form a kind of structure that reconciles structure discovered by clustering process and structure formed by labeling patterns. An available side of label information along with data-driven patterns were efficiently brought together to support the clustering process. Injecting true labels or partial supervision into the DCAE with an embedded clustering method allows the clustering algorithm to perform much better compared with the models that utilize an unsupervised learning process. Label consistency can add a discriminative power that clearly guides the clustering algorithm to obtain the best, most accurate compacted groups compared with data-driven discriminative attributes. Table 4 summarizes the results on four different datasets including MNIST, USPS, and more challenging ones, such as MNIST fashion and SVHN. Since the performances were evaluated on a classification task, the accuracy increasing with supervision knowledge enforced can be observed on both cases. Particularly for SVHN dataset, the accuracy is boosted more than two times when weak labels are provided. We argue that the common structures are not well formed without supervision where there are large variances in appearance and noisy in images are observed commonly in SVHN dataset.

Table 4. Comparison of clustering accuracy on four different datasets.

	MNIST	USPS	MNIST fashion	SVHN
Unsupervised [2]	92.14%	89.23%	60.42%	17.41%
Semi-supervised	97.77%	91.92%	63.59%	34.96%
Supervised	98.82%	95.06%	88.73%	92.40%

4   Conclusion

In the paper, we proposed a DCAE model which is capable of learning compact data representation that can be incorporated into different learning schemes, i.e. unsupervised, semi-supervised, supervised. We found that such supervision knowledge greatly helps to form discriminative transformations that are learned by the encoding part of a DCAE model and significantly improves the performance of clustering. It implies that the latent space has the potential to be used for image generation/ synthesis. The results also demonstrate that even weak or partial supervision knowledge can significantly improve the quality of deep clustering.

Acknowledgment. This work is supported by EPSRC EP/N028139/1.

References

1. Al-Harbi, S.H., Rayward-Smith, V.J.: Adapting k-means for supervised clustering. Appl. Intell. **24**(3), 219–226 (2006)
2. Alqahtani, A., Xie, X., Deng, J., Jones, M.: A deep convolutional auto-encoder with embedded clustering. In: IEEE ICIP, pp. 4058–4062 (2018)
3. Basu, S., Banerjee, A., Mooney, R.: Semi-supervised clustering by seeding. In: ICML (2002)
4. Davidson, I., Ravi, S.S.: Agglomerative hierarchical clustering with constraints: theoretical and empirical results. In: Jorge, A.M., Torgo, L., Brazdil, P., Camacho, R., Gama, J. (eds.) PKDD 2005. LNCS (LNAI), vol. 3721, pp. 59–70. Springer, Heidelberg (2005). https://doi.org/10.1007/11564126_11
5. Dosovitskiy, A., Fischer, P., Springenberg, J.T., Riedmiller, M., Brox, T.: Discriminative unsupervised feature learning with exemplar convolutional neural networks. IEEE T-PAMI **38**(9), 1734–1747 (2016)
6. Eick, C.F., Vaezian, B., Jiang, D., Wang, J.: Discovery of interesting regions in spatial data sets using supervised clustering. In: Fürnkranz, J., Scheffer, T., Spiliopoulou, M. (eds.) PKDD 2006. LNCS (LNAI), vol. 4213, pp. 127–138. Springer, Heidelberg (2006). https://doi.org/10.1007/11871637_16
7. Eick, C.F., Zeidat, N., Zhao, Z.: Supervised clustering-algorithms and benefits. In: IEEE ICTAI, pp. 774–776 (2004)
8. Kavukcuoglu, K., Fergus, R., LeCun, Y., et al.: Learning invariant features through topographic filter maps. In: 2009 IEEE CVPR, pp. 1605–1612 (2009)
9. van der Maaten, L., Hinton, G.: Visualizing data using t-SNE. J. Mach. Learn. Res. **9**(Nov), 2579–2605 (2008)
10. Min, E., Guo, X., Liu, Q., Zhang, G., Cui, J., Long, J.: A survey of clustering with deep learning: from the perspective of network architecture. IEEE Access **6**, 39501–39514 (2018)
11. Pedrycz, W., Waletzky, J.: Fuzzy clustering with partial supervision. IEEE T-SMC-B **27**(5), 787–795 (1997)
12. Pedrycz, W., Vukovich, G.: Fuzzy clustering with supervision. Pattern Recogn. **37**(7), 1339–1349 (2004)
13. Ruiz, C., Spiliopoulou, M., Menasalvas, E.: Density-based semi-supervised clustering. Data Min. Knowl. Discov. **21**(3), 345–370 (2010)
14. Wagstaff, K., Cardie, C., Rogers, S., Schrödl, S., et al.: Constrained k-means clustering with background knowledge. In: ICML, vol. 1, pp. 577–584 (2001)
15. Zaghian, A., Noorbehbahani, F.: A novel supervised cluster adjustment method using a fast exact nearest neighbor search algorithm. Pattern Anal. Appl. **20**(3), 701–715 (2017)

Multi-stream Convolutional Autoencoder and 2D Generative Adversarial Network for Glioma Classification

Muhaddisa Barat Ali[1]($\boxtimes$), Irene Yu-Hua Gu[1]($\boxtimes$), and Asgeir Store Jakola[2]($\boxtimes$)

[1] Department of Electrical Engineering, Chalmers University of Technology,
41296 Gothenburg, Sweden
{barat,irenegu}@chalmers.se
[2] Department of Clinical Neuroscience, Sahlgrenska University Hospital,
41345 Gothenburg, Sweden
asgeir.jakola@vgregion.se

Abstract. Diagnosis and timely treatment play an important role in preventing brain tumor growth. Deep learning methods have gained much attention lately. Obtaining a large amount of annotated medical data remains a challenging issue. Furthermore, high dimensional features of brain images could lead to over-fitting. In this paper, we address the above issues. Firstly, we propose an architecture for Generative Adversarial Networks to generate good quality synthetic 2D MRIs from multi-modality MRIs (T1 contrast-enhanced, T2, FLAIR). Secondly, we propose a deep learning scheme based on 3-streams of Convolutional Autoencoders (CAEs) followed by sensor information fusion. The rational behind using CAEs is that it may improve glioma classification performance (as comparing with conventional CNNs), since CAEs offer noise robustness and also efficient feature reduction hence possibly reduce the over-fitting. A two-round training strategy is also applied by pre-training on GAN augmented synthetic MRIs followed by refined-training on original MRIs. Experiments on BraTS 2017 dataset have demonstrated the effectiveness of the proposed scheme (test accuracy 92.04%). Comparison with several exiting schemes has provided further support to the proposed scheme.

Keywords: Brain tumor classification · Glioma grading ·
Deep learning · Image synthesis · Generative Adversarial Networks ·
Multi-stream Convolutional Autoencoders · Information fusion

1 Introduction

According to statistics reported in 2016 [1], gliomas are considered as one of the main reasons of brain cancer in both adults and children. Magnetic Resonance Imaging (MRI) is a key diagnostic tool for brain tumor analysis, monitoring and surgery planning. In clinical practice, doctors often look for multiple modalities

© Springer Nature Switzerland AG 2019
M. Vento and G. Percannella (Eds.): CAIP 2019, LNCS 11678, pp. 234–245, 2019.
https://doi.org/10.1007/978-3-030-29888-3_19

of MRI such as T1 (native), T1ce (T1 contrast enhanced), T2 (T2-weighted) and FLAIR (fluid attenuated inversion recovery) for the diagnosis of gliomas. According to World Health Organization (WHO) gliomas have been divided into low-grade (LGG, WHO grade II) and high-grade (HGG, WHO grade III and IV) subtypes [2]. Since non-invasive prediction of glioma type is very important for physicians to plan the treatment precisely. In previous studies, some machine learning techniques have been used. For instance, SVM was used in [5] to predict patient survival and molecular subtype. Yu et al. [6] proposed a noninvasive way to reveal IDH mutation by SVM. Pan et al. [7] used CNN for HGG/LGG classification. Akkus et al. [8] and Ge et al. [13] introduced multi-sensor CNN strategy for the classification of glioma and prediction of 1p19q codeletion in LGG.

In recent years, deep learning has gained popularity in many computer vision tasks. For classification, a Convolutional Neural Network (CNN) learns different levels of features which are further optimized for decision making. Some of these features might be more general and useful other than this specific task. Hence, before optimizing the network for the decision making, one can focus on the intermediate level for learning good data representation. One of the widely used feature learning algorithm is Stacked AutoEncoder (SAE) that consists of an encoder part and a decoder part with fully connected layers [3]. Later, to deal with the image data Convolutional Auto-Encoder (CAE) was introduced [4]. The basic principle of a CAE aims to learn internal representation (encoding) from an image dataset such that the reconstruction error is minimized. Its non-linear abstraction adapts to the underlying manifold structure of the data that makes high level features in the latent space.

In medical imaging, one of the main challenges is to deal with the limited amount of data and its corresponding annotations. Although grand challenges have been met using the publicly available medical datasets, the small dataset size limits its usage to solve specific medical problems. Recently, a new data augmentation technique and its variations have gained popularity, known as Generative Adversarial Networks [9]. Among many generative models, it is capable of producing sharp realistic images. The GAN frameworks have been used in various medical imaging applications [10,11]. Most studies have proposed image-to-image translation such as label-to-segmentation [10], segmentation-to-image [12] or cross-modality translation [11].

Although Convolutional Autoencoders (CAEs) have been used in some medical applications e.g., segmentation and Alzheimer's disease detection, to the best of our knowledge it has not been applied to brain tumor (e.g. glioma) characterization and grading. The rational behind employing CAEs is that it may improve glioma classification performance (comparing with CNNs), since CAEs offer noise robustness and also efficient feature reduction, it may reduce the over-fitting when feature dimension is high. A further issue of concern is the insufficient amount of training data in deep learning, since our glioma dataset only contains 285 subjects due to practical medical limitation. Simple data augmentation such as flipping, scaling and rotation of tumor images does not generate sufficient good tumor statistics. Motivated by the above issues, this paper proposes a novel scheme that uses multi-stream CAEs and GAN augmented images on multi-modality MRIs for glioma characterization and grading. The main contributions of this paper include:

- Propose an architecture of GAN, using original and GAN augmented multi-modality MRIs for enlarging the training dataset.
- Extract high-level glioma features through applying 3-streams of CAEs and multi-modality MRIs (T1ce, T2, FLAIR)-information fusion.
- Apply a 2-round training strategy by pre-training on GAN augmented MRIs followed by refined-training on original MRIs.
- Compare our results with several existing methods.

2   Overview of the Proposed Scheme

The basic idea is to improve glioma classification by a scheme based on multi-stream CAE and GAN image augmentation. The block diagram of the proposed scheme is given in Fig. 1. Input 2D images from multi-modality MRIs (T1-contrast enhanced (T1ce), T2, FLAIR) are fed into DCGAN (Deep Convolutional GAN) to generate synthetic 2D images in each modality. The training phase consists of two steps. First, synthetic images are fed into a multi-stream Convolutional Autoencoder (CAE) for extraction of features by each stream of CAE (T1ce-MRI, T2-MRI, FLAIR-MRI) during the pre-training phase. Second, original 2D MRIs are then used for the refined-training phase where a fusion layer is added followed by fully connected layers for classification. Further details are described in the following subsections.

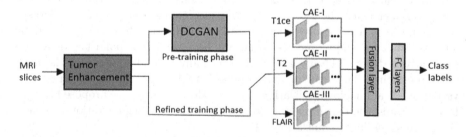

Fig. 1. The block diagram of our proposed scheme for glioma classification. DCGAN (Deep Convolutional GAN), CAE: Convolutional Autoencoder

2.1   Multi-stream Convolutional Autoencoder (CAE)

Our data source consists of 3 types of MRI-modality: T1ce (T1 contrast enhanced), T2 and FLAIR. Each 2D slice from a 3D MRI scan is resized. For the 3 modalities of MRIs, we train 3 Convolutional Autoencoders denoted as CAE-I, CAE-II and CAE-III respectively. In each CAE, the encoder part consists of 6 convolutional layers for extracting high dimensional feature maps followed by

Table 1. The proposed architecture of CAE for a single stream

Layer	Filters	Output size
Encoder layer:		
Conv-1+BN+ReLU	3 * 3 * 64	64 * 64 * 64
Conv-2+Maxpool+BN+ReLU	3 * 3 * 128	64 * 64 * 128
Conv-3+Maxpool+BN+ReLU	3 * 3 * 128	32 * 32 * 128
Conv-4+BN+ReLU	3 * 3 * 256	16 * 16 * 256
Conv-5+Maxpool+BN+ReLU	3 * 3 * 256	8 * 8 * 512
Conv-6+BN+ReLU	3 * 3 * 512	8 * 8 * 512
Decoder layer:		
Upsample+Conv-7+BN+ReLU	3 * 3 * 256	16 * 16 * 256
Conv-8+BN+ReLU	3 * 3 * 256	16 * 16 * 256
Upsample+Conv-9+BN+ReLU	3 * 3 * 128	32 * 32 * 128
Upsample+Conv-10+BN+ReLU	3 * 3 * 128	64 * 64 * 128
Conv-11+BN+ReLU	3 * 3 * 1	64 * 64 * 1

the decoder with 5 convolutional layers for reconstruction. Since, this overcomplete representation gives the CAE possibility to learn the identity function. To prevent over representation, max-pooling as suggested in [11] is used to enforce the learning of plausible features. The proposed architecture of a single stream in a multi-stream CAE is given in Table 1. The latent features in multi-stream CAE are then fused in fusion layer before classification. As can be seen in Fig. 1, input MRI slices from different modalities are fed in parallel to the corresponding streams of the framework. The kernel size for all the layers is set as 3 * 3 in order to learn more complex features. These high-level features are fused in fusion layer that consists of an aggregation layer followed by a bilinear layer [13,19]. The feature maps are aggregated by element-wise multiplication of features and the bilinear feature layer captures the interaction of features with each other at spatial locations. Finally, fully connected layers (FCs) are applied as the last layers with random initialization and dropout regularization followed by a softmax layer that determines the class labels. The last layers are trained during refined training with MR slice images from the original dataset.

2.2 Generating Synthetic Multi-modality MRIs

For the problem of insufficient training dataset, it is partially resolved by slicing the 3D volume images to the maximum possible number of 2D slices with tumor regions. These 2D slices are extracted from all directions of 3D volume images (e.g. axial, coronal and sagittal). This strategy increases the diversity to some extent in the training set and prevents the model from over-fitting to specific directional views.

To further enlarge the training datatset, we generate augmented images using a Generative Adversarial Network (GAN) [9]. GANs are specific networks of generative model that consists of two sub-networks, G a generator and D, a discriminator. G learns a mapping from an input image z (typically from a uniform distribution p_z) and maps to an image y in the target domain p_g. While D learns to discriminate between the fake samples $G(y)$ and the real samples y. During the training, both D and G learn simultaneously with G aiming at generating images with high probability to look real and achieve the goal $p_g = p_{data}$. Conversely, D aims to distinguish the fake and the real images. This is done by optimizing the following adversarial loss function:

$$\mathcal{L}_{GAN}(G, D) = E_{y \sim p_{data}} log D(y) + E_{z \sim p_z} log(1 - D(G(z))) \tag{1}$$

where G learns to minimize the loss function $\mathcal{L}_{GAN}$ for images with $y \not\sim p_{data}$ and D learns to maximize $\mathcal{L}_{GAN}$ for images with $y \sim p_{data}$ simultaneously. The aim is that G is capable of producing more realistic images that D may not distinguish between the real and the synthesized ones.

GAN Architecture: We have used DCGAN (Deep Convolutional GAN) for our experiments where both D and G networks are deep CNNs as described in Table 2 [16]. For each MRI-modality, DCGAN is trained separately to generate the corresponding synthesized images. A small image size 64 * 64 is selected to avoid GAN from mode collapse when it generates a limited diverse range of images. The generator network takes a vector of 100 random samples drawn from a uniform distribution as the input and generates the corresponding type of MRIs. While the discriminator takes the original and generated images and outputs one decision: real or fake?

Table 2. DCGAN (Deep Convolutional GAN) architecture

Layer	Filters	Output size
Discriminator D:		
Conv-1+stride 2+BN+LeakyReLU(0.2)	5 * 5 * 128	32 * 32 * 128
Conv-2+stride 2+BN+LeakyReLU(0.2)	5 * 5 * 256	16 * 16 * 256
Conv-3+stride 2+BN+LeakyReLU(0.2)	5 * 5 * 512	8 * 8 * 512
Conv-4+stride 2+BN+LeakyReLU(0.2)	5 * 5 * 1024	4 * 4 * 1024
Dense+sigmoid	-	1
Generator G:		
Dense+ReLU+reshape	16384	4 * 4 * 1024
ConvTranspose-1+stride 2+BN+ReLU	4 * 4 * 512	8 * 8 * 512
ConvTranspose-2+stride 2+BN+ReLU	4 * 4 * 256	16 * 16 * 256
ConvTranspose-3+stride 2+BN+ReLU	4 * 4 * 128	32 * 32 * 128
ConvTranspose-4+stride 2+BN+ReLU	4 * 4 * 64	64 * 64 * 64
Conv-5+Tanh	4 * 4 * 3	64 * 64 * 3

3   Experimental Results

Setup: We implemented our network using KERAS library [15] with Tensor Flow backend on a workstation with Intel-i7 3.40 GHz CPU, 48G RAM and an NVIDIA Titan Xp 12 GB GPU. For the DCGAN model, *Adam* optimizer with a mini batch size of 64, learning rate of $\alpha = 0.002$ and a binary crossentropy loss function were used for training both D and G networks. The training of DCGAN was continued until the output probability of discriminator approaches to 0.5 called the *Nash Equilibrium* point.

For training each stream of the network, *Adam* optimizer with mean square error loss function, learning rate of $\alpha = 0.002$ and mini batch size of 16 were used for 200 epochs. Here, the performance was evaluated by the loss vs epochs curve. We used $L2$-norm regularization with the parameter value of $1e^{-4}$ for convolutional layers of each CAE. For refined training of the Multi-stream CAE, early stopping strategy was used when the best validation performance was achieved. We also used the spatial dropout with a rate of 0.5 for the 2 FC-layers. Finally, the categorical cross-entropy was applied as loss function for evaluating the performance of the proposed scheme.

3.1   Data Pre-processing

Pre-processing has a big impact on the performance. The dataset used in this work consists of 3D volume MRIs including low grade gliomas (LGG) and high grade gliomas (HGG), publicly accessible from the MICCAI BraTS'2017 competition [14]. It contains data from four modalities along with corresponding mask annotations, where only three types (T1ce, T2 and FLAIR) were used in our experiments. Detail information of the dataset is described in Table 3.

Table 3. Description of BraTS 2017 dataset

Class	#3D data in T1ce/T2/FLAIR	# slices in each direction	# slices in T1ce/T2/FLAIR
HGG	210	5 + 5 + 5	15 * 210 = 3150
LGG	75	15 + 15 + 15	45 * 75 = 3375

The dataset was divided into 3 subsets: training (60%), validation (20%) and test (20%). All possible 2D slice regions containing tumors from 3 different directions (axial, sagittal, coronal) were extracted. Tumor mask annotations were used to enhance the tumor regions by using a saliency-aware approach. First we masked the volume data with the corresponding tumor mask. Then, non-tumor regions were suppressed by reducing the pixel intensity values to 1/3 of the original values. In this way, the location of tumor and information on surrounding tissues were preserved that enabled the network to focus more on tumor regions. After slicing the volume in three directional axis, the slices without tumor were discarded. So, we obtain the masked slices for all 3 subsets named as D_{train}, D_{val}

and D_{test} respectively. Further, to save the computation, slices were cropped to get rid of the surrounding black regions, rescaled and then normalized. Figure 2 shows an example of the pre-processed slice images.

For training the GAN, all possible slices with tumor region from D_{train} were used. Since our data size is still small to train the GAN network, we incorporated horizontal flipping to double the size of D_{train}. For refined training, only original slice images were used. To keep the balance between the two classes, LGG slices were extracted triple times than the HGG class. The total number of slices used for each class is summarized in Table 3.

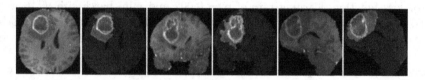

Fig. 2. Example of saliency aware approach on a HGG subject for all 3 directions (axial, coronal, sagittal) of its T1ce-modality. Each original image is followed by its corresponding enhanced tumor masked slice.

3.2 Results of DCGAN Data Augmentation

The architecture in Sect. 2.2 was employed to generate the DCGAN augmented slice images. The slice images from the dataset were partitioned into D_{train}, D_{val} and D_{test} so that no image from the same subject fell into other subsets. GAN was trained on D_{train}. The same D_{train} was used for refined training in each run. The discriminator's performance of training DCGAN was evaluated by the loss as a function of epochs which is shown in Fig. 3.

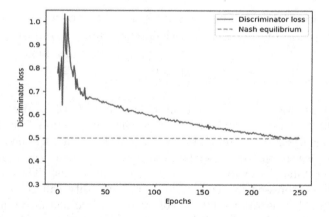

Fig. 3. Discriminator loss of DCGAN training for generating T1ce-MRIs for HGG class.

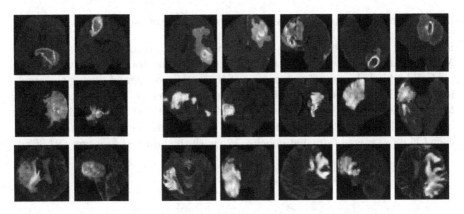

Fig. 4. Examples for DCGAN synthesized MRIs vs original MRIs. Left 2 Columns: Original MR image slices. Right 5 columns: DCGAN synthesized MRIs; Rows 1–3: T1ce-MRIs, FLAIR, T2-MRIs.

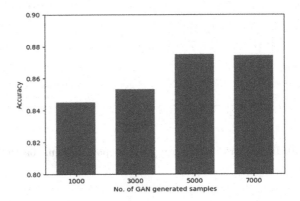

Fig. 5. Classification accuracy on T1ce-MRIs by using different number of DCGAN synthesized T1ce-MRIs.

Observing Fig. 3 it shows that the loss curve reduces to approximately 50% at 250 epochs which means that both the generator and discriminator struggled for reaching to an equilibrium state. We generated the augmented image slices at this point. The experiment was repeated for each MRI-modality separately. Few examples of DCGAN augmented data are shown in Fig. 4. To evaluate the quality of generated images, we trained a single CAE with same modality (T1ce-MRIs) of 4 number of different sized synthetic data groups. Figure 5 shows the test accuracy of classification with each of the synthesized image group.

Increasing the number of synthesized images above 5000 did not seem to show noticeable changes in performance. This indicates the limit of the diversity that our GAN had generated. For the next parts of experiment, we continued with this size of the synthetic data.

3.3   Results on Multi-stream CAE and Comparison

Employing the architecture of CAE described in Sect. 2.1 for all GAN augmented MRI-modalities (T1ce, T2 and FLAIR) has led to the training of Multi-stream CAE. The final classification accuracy of the proposed method during the training and validation is shown in Fig. 6. Observing the results in Fig. 6, one can see that the training curve was converged at 99.83% after 150 epochs and continues with a small gap from the validation curve. For this run, the best validation accuracy (95.63%) was obtained at epoch $= 125$ with the best test accuracy (93.36%).

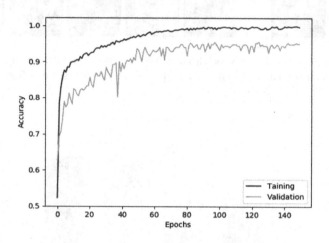

Fig. 6. Refined training performance using the proposed scheme on HGG/LGG classification.

Table 4(a) shows the overall accuracy on the test set, while Table 4(b) shows the corresponding confusion matrix. Observing the results from Table 4, one can see that reasonable good performance has been obtained. To further analyze the robustness of the proposed scheme, we repeated the experiments 5 times where dataset was randomly partitioned in D_{train}, D_{valid} and D_{test} each time

Table 4. Performance for HGG/LGG classification at epoch $= 125$. (a) Test accuracy; (b) The corresponding confusion matrix.

	Training(%)	Validation(%)	Test (%)
Accuracy	99.83	95.63	**93.36**

(a)

Actual/Predicted	HGG(%)	LGG(%)
HGG	**94.23**	5.66
LGG	7.45	**92.54**

(b)

in each run. Observe Table 5 for a summary of experiments. First, the proposed scheme was employed on single stream CAE using individual MRI-modality and the performance is reported accordingly in 2nd, 3rd and 4th column of Table 5. Then, the features from multi-streams CAE were fused for information fusion to obtain the overall performance of the proposed framework which is added in the last column of Table 5. Among the individual MRI-modality, T1ce gave the best test accuracy with 87.51% compared to FLAIR (84.21%) and T2 (74.79%). This complies with the doctor's visual examination. The results also show that feature information fusion has boosted up the test accuracy by a noticeable amount (92.04%) as compared to that of individual modalities of MRIs.

Table 5. Test performance of the proposed scheme on individual MRI-modality and multi-modality inputs.

Run	T1ce (%)	FLAIR (%)	T2 (%)	3-Modality fusion (%)
1	**87.51**	80.54	70.49	92.64
2	86.21	**84.21**	74.71	**93.36**
3	87.51	79.69	72.26	92.49
4	86.13	83.52	74.02	90.52
5	87.14	80.77	**74.79**	91.19
Average	**86.90**	**81.75**	**73.25**	**92.04**

Comparison with State-of-the-Art: Although there exists some reported works on different medical datasets and different sub-categories of gliomas, we selected the few ones that have used MICCAI BraTS dataset with HGG/LGG classes for fair comparison. Table 6 shows comparison to 3 existing methods. Observing the last row of Table 6 where we have put our results for giving indications on the relative improved performance of our scheme among other methods.

Table 6. Comparison with existing methods for HGG/LGG classification using BraTS dataset.

Method	# of subjects	Test accuracy %
Ye [17]	274	82.1
Ge [18]	285	88.07
Ge [13]	285	90.87
Proposed scheme	**285**	**92.04**

4   Conclusion

In this study, we focused on the intermediate goal of learning big synthetic data by the proposed Multi-stream CAE framework. The primary aim of deploying CAEs (compared to CNN) was to offer the noise robustness and to mitigate the over-fitting when using a small dataset for glioma classification. Our test results have shown that the features learned by the proposed approach using the original plus GAN generated images are effective in 2 stage training process for glioma classification. Comparing the results from the proposed scheme and the results of [13] (reproduced by us), it shows that our CAE-based scheme using the original and GAN-augmented data has led to enhanced glioma classification (92.04%, improved by 1.17%). Future work will be on extending our tests on more datasets, also extending the experiments to classify gliomas with/without IDH mutations, and 1p19q codeletion.

References

1. Siegel, R.L., Miller, K.D., Jemal, A.: Cancer statistics, 2017. Cancer J. Clin. **67**(1), 7–30 (2017)
2. Cha, S.: Update on brain tumor imaging: from anatomy to physiology. Am. J. Neuroradiol. **27**(3), 475–487 (2006)
3. Vincent, P., Larochelle, H., Lajoie, I., Bengio, Y., Manzagol, P.-A.: Stacked denoising autoencoders: learning useful representations in a deep network with a local denoising criterion. J. Mach. Learn. Res. **11**, 3371–3408 (2010)
4. Masci, J., Meier, U., Cireşan, D., Schmidhuber, J.: Stacked convolutional auto-encoders for hierarchical feature extraction. In: Honkela, T., Duch, W., Girolami, M., Kaski, S. (eds.) ICANN 2011. LNCS, vol. 6791, pp. 52–59. Springer, Heidelberg (2011). https://doi.org/10.1007/978-3-642-21735-7_7
5. Macyszyn, L., Akbari, H., et al.: Imaging patterns predict patient survival and molecular subtype in glioblastoma via machine learning techniques. Neuro-Oncology **18**(3), 417–425 (2015)
6. Yu, J., Shi, Z., et al.: Noninvasive IDH1 mutation estimation based on a quantitative radiomics approach for grade II glioma. Eur. Radiol. **27**(8), 3509–3522 (2017)
7. Pan, Y., et al.: Brain tumor grading based on neural networks and convolutional neural networks. In: 2015 37th Annual International Conference of the IEEE Engineering in Medicine and Biology Society (EMBC), Milan, pp. 699–702 (2015)
8. Akkus, Z., Ali, I., et al.: Predicting 1p19q Chromosomal Deletion of Low-Grade Gliomas from MR Images using Deep Learning. arXiv preprint arXiv: 1611.06939 (2016)
9. Goodfellow, I., et al.: Generative adversarial nets. In: Advances in Neural Information Processing Systems, pp. 2672–2680 (2014)
10. Costa, P., et al.: Towards Adversarial Retinal Image Synthesis. arXiv preprint arXiv:1701.08974 (2017)
11. Ben-Cohen, A., Klang, E., Raskin, S.P., Amitai, M.M., Greenspan, H.: Virtual PET images from CT data using deep convolutional networks; Initial results. arXiv preprint arXiv:1707.09585 (2017)

12. Xue, Y., Xu, T., Zhang, H., Long, R., Huang, X.: SegAN: adversarial network with multi-scale L1 loss for medical image segmentation. arXiv preprint arXiv:1706.01805 (2017)
13. Ge, C., Gu, I.Y., Jakola, A.S., Yang, J.: Deep learning and multi-sensor fusion for glioma classification using multistream 2D convolutional networks. In: 2018 40th Annual International Conference of the IEEE Engineering in Medicine and Biology Society (EMBC), Honolulu, HI, pp. 5894–5897 (2018)
14. Menze, B.H., et al.: The multimodal Brain Tumor Image Segmentation Benchmark (BRATS). IEEE Trans. Med. Imaging **34**(10), 1993–2024 (2015)
15. Chollet, F., et al.: Keras (2015). https://github.com/fchollet/keras
16. Radford, A., Metz, L., Chintala, S.: Unsupervised representation learning with deep convolutional generative adversarial networks. arXiv preprint arXiv: 1511.06434 (2015)
17. Ye, F., Pu, J., Wang, J., Li, Y., Zha, H.: Glioma grading based on 3D multimodal convolutional neural network and privileged learning. In: 2017 IEEE International Conference on Bioinformatics and Biomedicine (BIBM), Kansas City, MO, pp. 759–763 (2017)
18. Ge, C., Qu, Q., Gu, I.Y., Jakola, A.S.: 3D multi-scale convolutional networks for glioma grading using MR images. In: 2018 25th IEEE International Conference on Image Processing (ICIP), Athens, pp. 141–145 (2018)
19. Diba, A., et al.: Deep temporal linear encoding networks. In: 2017 IEEE Conference on Computer Vision and Pattern Recognition (CVPR), pp. 1541–1550 (2017)

Object Contour and Edge Detection
with RefineContourNet

André Peter Kelm[1]([✉])(iD), Vijesh Soorya Rao[2](iD), and Udo Zölzer[1]

[1] Department of Signal Processing and Communications,
Helmut Schmidt University, Holstenhofweg 85, 22043 Hamburg, Germany
{andre.kelm,udo.zoelzer}@hsu-hamburg.de
[2] Department of Mechatronics,
Hamburg University of Technology,
Am Schwarzenberg-Campus 1, 21073 Hamburg, Germany
vijesh.rao@tuhh.de

Abstract. A ResNet-based multi-path refinement CNN is used for object contour detection. For this task, we prioritise the effective utilization of the high-level abstraction capability of a ResNet, which leads to state-of-the-art results for edge detection. Keeping our focus in mind, we fuse high, mid and low-level features in that specific order, which differs from many other approaches. The tensor with the highest-levelled features is set as the starting point to combine it layer-by-layer with features of a lower abstraction level until it reaches the lowest level. We train this network on a modified PASCAL VOC 2012 dataset for object contour detection and evaluate on a refined PASCAL-val dataset reaching an excellent performance and an Optimal Dataset Scale (ODS) of 0.752. Furthermore, by fine-training on the BSDS500 dataset, we reach state-of-the-art results for edge-detection with an ODS of 0.824.

Keywords: Object contour detection · Edge detection ·
Multi-path refinement CNN

1 Introduction

Object contour detection extracts information about the object shape in images. Reliable detectors distinguish between desired object contours and edges from the background. Resulting object contour maps are very useful for supporting and/or improving various computer vision applications, like semantic segmentation [5,31,35], object proposal [24] and object flow estimation [25,31].

Holistically-Nested Edge Detection (HED) [32] has shown that it is beneficial to use features of a pre-trained classification network to capture desired image boundaries and suppressing undesired edges. Khoreva et al. [13] have specifically trained the HED on object contour detection and proven the potential of HED for this task. Yang et al. have used a Fully Convolutional Encoder-Decoder Network (CEDN) to produce contour maps, in which the object contours of certain

© Springer Nature Switzerland AG 2019
M. Vento and G. Percannella (Eds.): CAIP 2019, LNCS 11678, pp. 246–258, 2019.
https://doi.org/10.1007/978-3-030-29888-3_20

object classes are highlighted and other edges are suppressed more effectively than before [34]. Convolutional Oriented Boundaries (COB) [21] outperforms these results by using multi-scale oriented contours derived from a HED-like network architecture together with an efficient hierarchical image segmentation algorithm. A common feature in all this work is that a Very Deep Convolutional Network for Large-Scale Image Recognition (VGG) [28] and its classifying ability is used as a backbone network. Obviously, this backbone and its effective use are the major keys to the results achieved, but the new methods outlined before do not use the latest classification networks, like Deep Residual Learning for Image Recognition (ResNet) [12], which show a higher classification ability than VGG. We use a ResNet as backbone and propose a strategy to prioritise the effective utilization of the high-level abstraction capability for object contour detection. Accordingly, we choose a fitting architecture and a customized training procedure. We outperform the methods mentioned previously and achieve a very robust detector with an excellent performance on the validation data of a refined PASCAL VOC [10]. High-level edge detection is closely related to object contour detection, because object contours are often an important subset of the desired detection. Continuing, we will introduce the edge detection task and show that, unlike object contour detection, there is unexploited potential for using the high abstraction capability of classification networks.

Edge detection has a rich history and – as one of the classic vision problems – plays a role in almost any vision pipeline with applications like optical flow estimation [17], image segmentation [7] or generative image inpainting [22,33]. Classical low-level detectors, such as Canny [6] and Sobel [29], or the recently applied edge-detection with the Phase Stretch Transform [2], filter the entire image and do not distinguish between semantic edges and the rest. Edge detection is no longer limited only to low-level computer vision problems. Even the evaluation method established to date – the Berkeley Segmentation Dataset and the Benchmark 500 (BSDS500) [1] – requires high-level image processing algorithms for good results. Before Convolutional Neural Networks (CNNs) became popular, algorithms like the gPb [1], which uses contour detection together with hierarchical image segmentation, reached impressive results. In recent years, edge detectors, such as DeepNet [14] and N^4-Fields [11] have begun to use operations from CNNs to reach a higher-level detection. DeepEdge [3] and DeepContour [27] are CNN applications that use more high-level features to extract contours, and show that this capability improves the detection of certain edges. HED uses higher abstraction abilities than previous methods by combining multi-scale features and multi-level features extracted of a pre-learned CNN, and improves edge detection. Latest edge detectors such as the Crisp Edge Detector (CED) [31], Richer Convolutional Features (RCF) [20], COB and a High-for-Low features algorithm (HFL) [4] make use of their backbone classification nets for edge detection in different ways. But some of these networks are based on older backbone CNNs like the VGG and/or use simple HED-like skip-layer architectures. Similarly for object contour detection, we assume recent work has unexploited potential in the utilization of pre-trained classification abilities, in terms of architecture, backbone network, training procedure and datasets. We contribute a simple but decisive strategy, a network architecture choice following our strategy and unconventional training methods to reach state-of-the-art.

Section 2 will briefly summarize the closest related work, Sect. 3 contains main contributions, like concept, realization and special training procedures for the proposed detector, Sect. 4 compares the method with other relevant methods and Sect. 5 concludes the paper.

2   Related Work

AlexNet [16] was a breakthrough for image classification and was extended to solve other computer vision tasks, such as image segmentation, object contour, and edge detection. The step from image classification to image segmentation with the Fully Convolutional Network (FCN) [26] has favored new edge detection algorithms such as HED, as it allows a pixel-wise classification of an image. HED has successfully used the logistic loss function for the edge or non-edge binary classification. Our approach uses the same loss function, but differs in term of another weighting factor, network architecture, and backbone network. Another image segmentation network, Learning Deconvolution Network for Semantic Segmentation [23], has favored the development of the CEDN, demonstrating the strong relationship between image segmentation, object contour detection and edge detection. The good results of the CEDN inspired us to consider recent image segmentation networks for our task. Yang et al. created a new contour dataset using a Conditional-Random-Fields (CRF) [15] refining method. CEDN and edge detector networks such as COB and HFL have an older backbone net and are outperformed by RCF, which is based on a ResNet and improved the edge detection. RCF has the same backbone network, but differs from our approach in using a different network architecture because it uses a skip-layer structure for feature concatenation like HED. We state that this simple concatenation is not effective enough for edge detection, and we propose to use a more advanced network structure. We have the hypothesis that an effective network architecture for edge detection should prioritise the high abstraction capability itself. As the deepest feature maps are the next ones to the classification layer, we propose to use them as the starting point to refine them layer-by-layer with features of a lower level until it reaches the level of classical edge detection algorithms. Our required properties are combined in RefineNet [18] and that is why we have used the publicly available code from Guosheng Lin et al. as the basis of our approach. Parallelly to the implementation of our method, the CED from the work Learning to Predict Crisp Boundaries from Deng et al. [8] has used a similar bottom-up architecture and surpasses RCF and achieves state-of-the-art. The work from Wang et al. Deep Crisp Boundaries [31] further develops this method and improved state-of-the-art results. Our approach mainly differs from theirs in its conceptualization. They also focus on producing "crisp" (thinned) boundaries, as they have shown that this benefits their results. We assume in contrast, that by focusing on the effective utilization of the high abstraction capability of a backbone network, we could achieve better results.

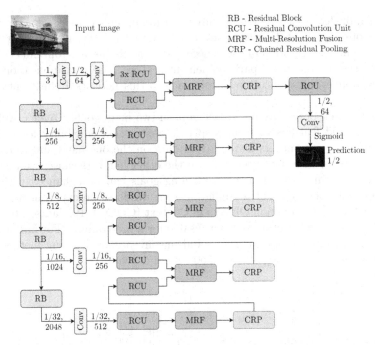

Fig. 1. RefineContourNet - modified RefineNet [18], where last layers are changed, such that there is one feature map at the end and a sigmoid activation function that predicts the probability of presence of contour

3   RefineContourNet

3.1   Concept

Detecting edges with classical low-level methods can visualize the high amount of edges in many images. To distinguish between meaningful edges and undesired edges, a semantic context is required. Our selected contexts are the object contours of the 20 classes of the PASCAL VOC dataset. If context is clear and some low-level vision functions are available, the most important ability for an object contour detector is the high-level abstraction capability, so that edges can be distinguished in the sense of context. For this reason, our concept focuses on the effective use of the high-level abstraction ability of a modern classification network for object contour detection. With this strategy, we choose the architecture, backbone network, training procedure and datasets.

We hypothesize that an effective edge detection network architecture should prioritize the above mentioned capability. For this we propose to give preference to the deepest feature maps of the backbone network and to use them as the starting point in a refinement architecture. To connect the high-level classification ability with the pixel-wise detection stage, we assume, that a step-by-step refinement, where deep features are fused with features of the next shallower level until the shallowest level is reached, should be more effective than skip-layers with a simple feature concatenation architecture. In most classification networks, features of different abstraction levels have different resolutions. To merge these features, a multi-resolution fusion is necessary. The RefineNet from Lin et al. [18] provides the desired multi-path refinement and we base our application upon that and name our application in reference to this network RefineContourNet (RCN).

The training procedure has to accomplish two main goals: To effectively use the pre-trained features to form a specific abstraction capability for identifying desired object contours learned from data on the one hand and to connect this to the pixel-wise detection stage on the other hand. Because training data of object contours is limited, both training goals can be enhanced with data augmentation methods. For a similar reason, we do some experiments with a modified Microsoft Common Objects in Context (COCO) [19] dataset, to create an additional object contour dataset, usable for a pre-training. For fine-training on edge-detection, we offer a simple and unconventional training method that considers the individuality of BSDS500's hand-drawn labels.

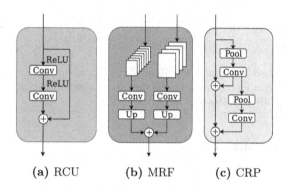

(a) RCU   (b) MRF   (c) CRP

Fig. 2. Block diagrams of refinement path operations

3.2   Image Segmentation Network for Contour Detection

The main difference between an image segmentation network and a contour detection network lies in the definition of the objective function. Instead of defining a multi-label segmentation, an object contour can be defined binary. We use the logistic regression loss function

$$
\begin{aligned}
\mathrm{L}(h_\Theta(x), y) = &-y \cdot \beta \log(h_\Theta(x)) \\
&- (1 - y) \cdot \log(1 - h_\Theta(x)),
\end{aligned}
\tag{1}
$$

with $h_\Theta(x) \in [0,1]$, $y \in \{0,1\}$ and $\beta = 10$, where $h_\Theta(x)$ is the prediction for a pixel x with the corresponding binary label y. Θ symbolizes the learned parameters and β is a weighting factor for enhancing the contour detection due to the large imbalance between the contour and the non-contour pixels. Changing the loss function results in a change of the last layer of the RefineNet according to the binary loss function. The 21 feature map layers previously used to segment 20 PASCAL-VOC classes, including background class, will be replaced by a single feature map sufficient for binary classification of contours.

3.3 Network Architecture

Figure 1 shows the RefineContourNet. For clarity, the connections between the blocks specifies the resolution of the feature maps and the size of the feature channel dimension. The Residual Blocks (RB) are part of the ResNet-101. RefineNet has introduced three different refinement path blocks: The Residual Convolution Unit (RCU), the Multi-Resolution Fusion (MRF) and the Chained Residual Pooling (CRP). They are arranged in a row to use the higher-level features as input to combine them with the lower-level features of the RB at the same level. The RCU in Fig. 2(a) has residual convolutional layers and enriches the network with more parameters. It can adjust and modify the input for MRF. The MRF block adapts the input first by performing a convolution operation, in order to adjust the channel dimension of the feature space corresponding to the higher-level ones with the lower level. Then, the smaller resolution feature maps get upsampled by bicubic interpolation to have same tensor dimensions as the larger ones, after which they are added, as shown in Fig. 2(b). The goal of the CRP is to gather more context from the feature maps than a normal max pooling layer. Several pooling blocks are concatenated and each block consists of a max-pooling with higher stride length and a convolutional operation. Illustration of CRP with two max-pooling operations is shown in Fig. 2(c). In the final refinement step, the original image gets downsampled by a strided convolution and feeded in an extra path with 3 RCUs, which improves our results.

4 Evaluation

We have done various experiments with different combinations of refinement blocks per multipath, and we have always observed the best results by placing the three blocks sequentially in a row, as shown in Fig. 1.

4.1 Training

The final network architecture has 148 convolutional layers resulting in approximately 81.4 million parameters. For each epoch, 1000 random images are selected from the training set, and the data is augmented by random cropping, vertical flipping, and scaling between 0.7 and 1.3. To find an optimal training method, we have examined the following training variants:

- **RCN-VOC** is trained only on the CRF-refined object contour dataset proposed by Yang et al. [34].

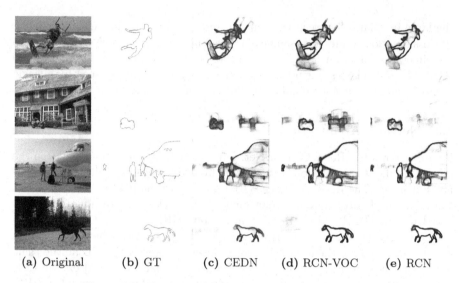

(a) Original   (b) GT   (c) CEDN   (d) RCN-VOC   (e) RCN

Fig. 3. Visualization of object contour detection methods

- **RCN-COCO** is pre-trained on a modified COCO dataset, where we have considered only the 20 PASCAL VOC classes and have produced contours. COCO segmentation masks and from those generated contours are not accurate, so we enrich them with additional contours. For this we use our own object contour detector RCN-VOC and set a high threshold to add only confident contour detections.
- **RCN** is pre-trained on the modified COCO and trained on the refined PASCAL VOC.

Training the network for edge detection involves fine-training on the validation and train sets of the BSDS500 dataset. The BSDS contains individual, hand-drawn contours for the same images created by different people. We take the subjective decisions into account of which edge is a desired edge and which is not, by simply using all individual labels, and let the CNN form a compromise. To give an indication of how such training affects the results, we fine-train one of the networks only on the drawings of one single person, called **RCN-VOC-1**. All trainings and modifications are done in MatConvNet [30].

4.2   Object Contour Detection Evaluation

For evaluation, we use Piotr's Computer Vision Matlab Toolbox [9], the included Non-Maximum-Suppression (NMS) algorithm for thinning the soft object contour maps and a subset of 1103 images of a CRF-refined PASCAL val2012. We calculate the Precision and Recall (PR) curve for the RCN models, CEDN, HED

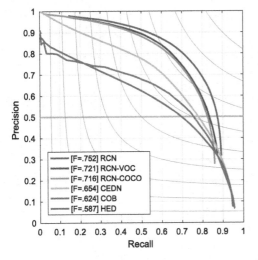

Table 1. Comparison on refined PASCAL val2012

Net	ODS	OIS	AP
RCN	**.752**	**.773**	.641
RCN-VOC	.721	.746	.613
RCN-COCO	.716	.741	**.719**
CEDN	.654	.657	.679
COB	.624	.657	.593
HED	.587	.598	.568

Fig. 4. PR-curves on refined PASCAL val2012

and COB in Fig. 4. In Table 1 the Optimal Dataset Scale (ODS), Optimal Image Scale (OIS) and the Average Precision (AP) for the methods are noted. The quantitative analysis reveals that the RCN models significantly perform better in comparison to the other methods on all three metrics. This is also reflected in the visual results, cf. Fig. 3. The RCN-VOC and RCN have upper hand in suppressing the undesired edges, such as inner contours of the objects. At the same time, they also can recognize object contours more clearly. A disadvantage is that the contour predictions are thicker than in CEDN, which is due to the halved resolution owed by the network architecture. Nevertheless, the detection is very robust and the NMS can effectively calculate 1-pixel thinned object contours.

4.3   Edge Detection Evaluation

The results of a quantitative evaluation of the RCN on unseen test images of BSDS500 are represented in the PR-curves in Fig. 6. ODS, OIS and AP from methods such as RCN, CED, RCF, COB and HED are listed in Table 2. The proposed RCN achieves the state-of-the-art with a higher ODS than recent methods, closely followed by CED. In Fig. 5 results of CED and RCN are visualized for some test images. Careful analysis of the results reveals that RCN detects some relevant edges, cf. inner contours of the snowshoes (1st row), face of the young man (2nd row), snout of the llama (4th row), which CED no longer recognizes. As for the object contour detection task, the disadvantage of the thicker edge predictions persists for the RCN. However, the NMS works more precisely for edge prediction maps from RCN, as the bit depth per pixel is increased from 8 to

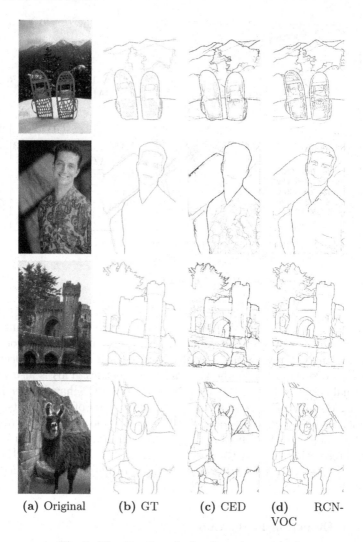

(a) Original   (b) GT   (c) CED   (d)   RCN-
                                                VOC

Fig. 5. Visualization of edge detection methods

16 bits. The difference is evident in the results for background edges in the image of the young man (2nd row), since an absolute maximum of the CED prediction could not be clearly distinguished, RCN edges are thinned more effectively.

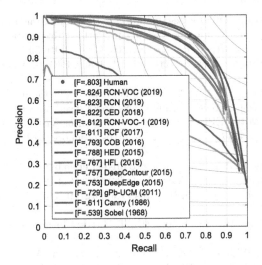

Table 2. Comparison on BSDS500

Net	ODS	OIS	AP
RCN-VOC	**.824**	.839	.837
RCN	.823	.838	.853
CED	.822	**.840**	**.895**
RCN-VOC-1	.812	.827	.822
RCF	.811	.830	.846
Human	.803	.803	-
COB	.793	.819	.849
HED	.788	.808	.840

Fig. 6. PR-curves on BSDS500

5 Conclusion

The strategy, of using the high abstraction capability for object contour and edge detection more effectively than previous methods, results in outstanding object contour detection and state-of-the-art for edge detection. Our concept that the bottom-up multipath refinement architecture of RefineNet [18] is beneficial for edge detection gets supported by these results. With the unconventional training methods, such as the pre-training with a modified COCO dataset or by simply using all individual labels for fine-training on BSDS500, we have been able to improve the detections further.

References

1. Arbelaez, P., Maire, M., Fowlkes, C., Malik, J.: Contour detection and hierarchical image segmentation. IEEE Trans. Pattern Anal. Mach. Intell. **33**(5), 898–916 (2011). https://doi.org/10.1109/TPAMI.2010.161
2. Asghari, M.H., Jalali, B.: Physics-inspired image edge detection. In: 2014 IEEE Global Conference on Signal and Information Processing (GlobalSIP), pp. 293–296, December 2014. https://doi.org/10.1109/GlobalSIP.2014.7032125
3. Bertasius, G., Shi, J., Torresani, L.: DeepEdge: a multi-scale bifurcated deep network for top-down contour detection. In: 2015 IEEE Conference on Computer Vision and Pattern Recognition (CVPR), pp. 4380–4389, June 2015. https://doi.org/10.1109/CVPR.2015.7299067
4. Bertasius, G., Shi, J., Torresani, L.: High-for-low and low-for-high: efficient boundary detection from deep object features and its applications to high-level vision. In: 2015 IEEE International Conference on Computer Vision (ICCV), pp. 504–512, December 2015. https://doi.org/10.1109/ICCV.2015.65

5. Bertasius, G., Shi, J., Torresani, L.: Semantic segmentation with boundary neural fields. In: 2016 IEEE Conference on Computer Vision and Pattern Recognition (CVPR), pp. 3602–3610, June 2016. https://doi.org/10.1109/CVPR.2016.392

6. Canny, J.: A computational approach to edge detection. IEEE Trans. Pattern Anal. Mach. Intell. **6**, 679–698 (1986)

7. Chen, L., Barron, J.T., Papandreou, G., Murphy, K., Yuille, A.L.: Semantic image segmentation with task-specific edge detection using CNNs and a discriminatively trained domain transform. In: 2016 IEEE Conference on Computer Vision and Pattern Recognition (CVPR), pp. 4545–4554, June 2016. https://doi.org/10.1109/CVPR.2016.492

8. Deng, R., Shen, C., Liu, S., Wang, H., Liu, X.: Learning to predict crisp boundaries. In: Ferrari, V., Hebert, M., Sminchisescu, C., Weiss, Y. (eds.) ECCV 2018. LNCS, vol. 11210, pp. 570–586. Springer, Cham (2018). https://doi.org/10.1007/978-3-030-01231-1_35

9. Dollár, P.: Piotr's Computer Vision Matlab Toolbox (PMT). https://github.com/pdollar/toolbox

10. Everingham, M., Van Gool, L., Williams, C.K.I., Winn, J., Zisserman, A.: The PASCAL Visual Object Classes Challenge 2012 (VOC2012) Results. http://www.pascal-network.org/challenges/VOC/voc2012/workshop/index.html

11. Ganin, Y., Lempitsky, V.: N^4-fields: neural network nearest neighbor fields for image transforms. In: Cremers, D., Reid, I., Saito, H., Yang, M.-H. (eds.) ACCV 2014. LNCS, vol. 9004, pp. 536–551. Springer, Cham (2015). https://doi.org/10.1007/978-3-319-16808-1_36

12. He, K., Zhang, X., Ren, S., Sun, J.: Deep residual learning for image recognition. In: 2016 IEEE Conference on Computer Vision and Pattern Recognition (CVPR), pp. 770–778, June 2016. https://doi.org/10.1109/CVPR.2016.90

13. Khoreva, A., Benenson, R., Omran, M., Hein, M., Schiele, B.: Weakly supervised object boundaries. In: 2016 IEEE Conference on Computer Vision and Pattern Recognition (CVPR), pp. 183–192, June 2016. https://doi.org/10.1109/CVPR.2016.27

14. Kivinen, J., Williams, C., Heess, N.: Visual boundary prediction: a deep neural prediction network and quality dissection. In: Kaski, S., Corander, J. (eds.) Proceedings of the Seventeenth International Conference on Artificial Intelligence and Statistics. Proceedings of Machine Learning Research, PMLR, Reykjavik, Iceland, 22–25 April 2014, vol. 33, pp. 512–521 (2014). http://proceedings.mlr.press/v33/kivinen14.html

15. Krähenbühl, P., Koltun, V.: Efficient inference in fully connected CRFs with Gaussian edge potentials. In: Shawe-Taylor, J., Zemel, R.S., Bartlett, P.L., Pereira, F., Weinberger, K.Q. (eds.) Advances in Neural Information Processing Systems 24, pp. 109–117. Curran Associates, Inc. (2011). http://papers.nips.cc/paper/4296-efficient-inference-in-fully-connected-crfs-with-gaussian-edge-potentials.pdf

16. Krizhevsky, A., Sutskever, I., Hinton, G.E.: ImageNet classification with deep convolutional neural networks. In: Pereira, F., Burges, C.J.C., Bottou, L., Weinberger, K.Q. (eds.) Advances in Neural Information Processing Systems 25, pp. 1097–1105. Curran Associates, Inc. (2012). http://papers.nips.cc/paper/4824-imagenet-classification-with-deep-convolutional-neural-networks.pdf

17. Lei, P., Li, F., Todorovic, S.: Boundary flow: a Siamese network that predicts boundary motion without training on motion. In: 2018 IEEE/CVF Conference on Computer Vision and Pattern Recognition, pp. 3282–3290, June 2018. https://doi.org/10.1109/CVPR.2018.00346

18. Lin, G., Milan, A., Shen, C., Reid, I.: RefineNet: multi-path refinement networks for high-resolution semantic segmentation. In: 2017 IEEE Conference on Computer Vision and Pattern Recognition (CVPR), pp. 5168–5177, July 2017. https://doi.org/10.1109/CVPR.2017.549

19. Lin, T.-Y., et al.: Microsoft COCO: common objects in context. In: Fleet, D., Pajdla, T., Schiele, B., Tuytelaars, T. (eds.) ECCV 2014. LNCS, vol. 8693, pp. 740–755. Springer, Cham (2014). https://doi.org/10.1007/978-3-319-10602-1_48

20. Liu, Y., et al.: Richer convolutional features for edge detection. IEEE Trans. Pattern Anal. Mach. Intell. 1 (2018). https://doi.org/10.1109/TPAMI.2018.2878849

21. Maninis, K., Pont-Tuset, J., Arbeláez, P., Gool, L.V.: Convolutional oriented boundaries: from image segmentation to high-level tasks. IEEE Trans. Pattern Anal. Mach. Intell. (TPAMI) 40(4), 819–833 (2017)

22. Nazeri, K., Ng, E., Joseph, T., Qureshi, F.Z., Ebrahimi, M.: EdgeConnect: generative image inpainting with adversarial edge learning. CoRR abs/1901.00212 (2019). http://arxiv.org/abs/1901.00212

23. Noh, H., Hong, S., Han, B.: Learning deconvolution network for semantic segmentation. In: 2015 IEEE International Conference on Computer Vision (ICCV), pp. 1520–1528, December 2015. https://doi.org/10.1109/ICCV.2015.178

24. Pont-Tuset, J., Arbeláez, P., Barron, J., Marques, F., Malik, J.: Multiscale combinatorial grouping for image segmentation and object proposal generation. arXiv:1503.00848, March 2015

25. Revaud, J., Weinzaepfel, P., Harchaoui, Z., Schmid, C.: EpicFlow: Edge-preserving interpolation of correspondences for optical flow. In: 2015 IEEE Conference on Computer Vision and Pattern Recognition (CVPR), pp. 1164–1172, June 2015. https://doi.org/10.1109/CVPR.2015.7298720

26. Shelhamer, E., Long, J., Darrell, T.: Fully convolutional networks for semantic segmentation. IEEE Trans. Pattern Anal. Mach. Intell. 39(4), 640–651 (2017). https://doi.org/10.1109/TPAMI.2016.2572683

27. Shen, W., Wang, X., Wang, Y., Bai, X., Zhang, Z.: DeepContour: a deep convolutional feature learned by positive-sharing loss for contour detection. In: 2015 IEEE Conference on Computer Vision and Pattern Recognition (CVPR), pp. 3982–3991, June 2015. https://doi.org/10.1109/CVPR.2015.7299024

28. Simonyan, K., Zisserman, A.: Very deep convolutional networks for large-scale image recognition. CoRR abs/1409.1556 (2014)

29. Sobel, I.: Camera models and machine perception. Camera models and machine perception. Technical report, Stanford University, California, Department of Computer Science (1970)

30. Vedaldi, A., Lenc, K.: Matconvnet - convolutional neural networks for MATLAB. In: Proceedings of the 23rd ACM International Conference on Multimedia (2015)

31. Wang, Y., Zhao, X., Li, Y., Huang, K.: Deep crisp boundaries: from boundaries to higher-level tasks. IEEE Trans. Image Process. 28(3), 1285–1298 (2019). https://doi.org/10.1109/TIP.2018.2874279

32. Xie, S., Tu, Z.: Holistically-nested edge detection. In: 2015 IEEE International Conference on Computer Vision (ICCV), pp. 1395–1403, December 2015. https://doi.org/10.1109/ICCV.2015.164

33. Xu, S., Liu, D., Xiong, Z.: Edge-guided generative adversarial network for image inpainting. In: 2017 IEEE Visual Communications and Image Processing (VCIP), pp. 1–4, December 2017. https://doi.org/10.1109/VCIP.2017.8305138

34. Yang, J., Price, B., Cohen, S., Lee, H., Yang, M.: Object contour detection with a fully convolutional encoder-decoder network. In: 2016 IEEE Conference on Computer Vision and Pattern Recognition (CVPR), pp. 193–202, June 2016. https://doi.org/10.1109/CVPR.2016.28

35. Zhang, H., Jiang, K., Zhang, Y., Li, Q., Xia, C., Chen, X.: Discriminative feature learning for video semantic segmentation. In: 2014 International Conference on Virtual Reality and Visualization, pp. 321–326, August 2014. https://doi.org/10.1109/ICVRV.2014.65

LYTNet: A Convolutional Neural Network for Real-Time Pedestrian Traffic Lights and Zebra Crossing Recognition for the Visually Impaired

Samuel Yu, Heon Lee[(⊠)], and John Kim

Shanghai American School, Puxi West, Shanghai 201103, China
{samuel01px2020,heon01px2020,john01px2020}@saschina.org

Abstract. Currently, the visually impaired rely on either a sighted human, guide dog, or white cane to safely navigate. However, the training of guide dogs is extremely expensive, and canes cannot provide essential information regarding the color of traffic lights and direction of crosswalks. In this paper, we propose a deep learning based solution that provides information regarding the traffic light mode and the position of the zebra crossing. Previous solutions that utilize machine learning only provide one piece of information and are mostly binary: only detecting red or green lights. The proposed convolutional neural network, LYTNet, is designed for comprehensiveness, accuracy, and computational efficiency. LYTNet delivers both of the two most important pieces of information for the visually impaired to cross the road. We provide five classes of pedestrian traffic lights rather than the commonly seen three or four, and a direction vector representing the midline of the zebra crossing that is converted from the 2D image plane to real-world positions. We created our own dataset of pedestrian traffic lights containing over 5000 photos taken at hundreds of intersections in Shanghai. The experiments carried out achieve a classification accuracy of 94%, average angle error of 6.35°, with a frame rate of 20 frames per second when testing the network on an iPhone 7 with additional post-processing steps.

Keywords: Visually impaired · LYTNet ·
Convolutional neural network · Classification · Machine learning ·
Regression · Pedestrian traffic lights

1 Introduction

The primary issue that the visually impaired face is not with obstacles, which can be detected by their cane, but with information that requires the ability to see. When we interviewed numerous visually impaired people, there was a shared concern regarding safely crossing the road when traveling alone. The reason for this concern is that the visually impaired cannot be informed of the

© Springer Nature Switzerland AG 2019
M. Vento and G. Percannella (Eds.): CAIP 2019, LNCS 11678, pp. 259–270, 2019.
https://doi.org/10.1007/978-3-030-29888-3_21

color of pedestrian traffic lights and the direction in which they should cross the road to stay on the pedestrian zebra crossing. When interviewed, they reached a consensus that the information stated above is the most essential for crossing roads.

To solve this problem, some hardware products have been developed [5]. However, they are too financially burdening due to both the cost of the product itself and possible reliance on external servers to run the algorithm. The financial concern is especially important for the visually impaired community in developing countries, such as the people we interviewed who live in China. Accordingly, our paper addresses this issue by discussing LYTNet that can later be deployed on a mobile phone, both ios and android, and run locally. This method would be a cheap, comprehensive, and easily accessible alternative that supplements white-canes for the visually impaired community.

We propose LYTNet, an image classifier, to classify whether or not there is a traffic light in the image, and if so, what color/mode it is in. We also implement a zebra crossing detector in LYTNet that outputs coordinates for the midline of the zebra crossing.

The main contributions of our work are as follows:

- To the best of our knowledge, we are the first to create a convolutional neural network (LYTNet) that outputs both the mode of the pedestrian traffic light and midline of the zebra crossing
- We create and publish the largest pedestrian traffic light dataset, consisting of 5059 photos with labels of both the mode of traffic lights and the direction vector of the zebra crossing [16]
- We design a lightweight deep learning model (LYTNet) that can be deployed efficiently on a mobile phone application and is able to run at 20 frames per second (FPS)
- We train a unique deep learning model (LYTNet) that uses one-step image classification instead of multiple steps, and matches previous attempts that only focus on traffic light detection

The rest of the paper is organized in the following manner: Sect. 2 discusses previous work and contributions made to the development and advancements in the detection of pedestrian traffic light detectors and zebra crossings; Sect. 3 describes the proposed method of pedestrian traffic light and zebra crossing classifier; Sect. 4 provides experiment results and comparisons against a published method; Sect. 5 concludes the paper and explores possible future work.

2   Related Works

Some industrialized countries have developed acoustic pedestrian traffic lights that produce sound when the light is green, and is used as a signal for the visually impaired to know when to cross the street [3,7,13]. However, for less economically developed countries, crossing streets is still a problem for the blind, and acoustic pedestrian traffic lights are not ubiquitous even in developed nations [13].

The task of detecting traffic light for autonomous driving has been explored by many and has developed over the years [1,9,14,19]. Behrendt et al. [4] created a model that is able to detect traffic lights as small as 3 × 10 pixels and with relatively high accuracy. Though most models for traffic lights have a high precision and recall rate of nearly 100% and show practical usage, the same cannot be said for pedestrian traffic lights. Pedestrian traffic lights differ because they are complex shaped and usually differ based on the region in which the pedestrian traffic light is placed. Traffic lights, on the other hand, are simple circles in nearly all countries.

Shioyama et al. [18] were one of the first to develop an algorithm to detect pedestrian traffic lights and the length of the zebra-crossing. Others such as Mascetti et al. and Charette et al. [6,13] both developed an analytic image processing algorithm, which undergoes candidate extraction, candidate recognition, and candidate classification. Cheng et al. [7] proposed a more robust real-time pedestrian traffic lights detection algorithm, which gets rid of the analytic image processing method and uses candidate extraction and a concise machine learning scheme.

A limitation that many attempts faced was the speed of hardware. Thus, Ivanchenko et al. [11] created an algorithm specifically for mobile devices with an accelerator to detect pedestrian traffic lights in real time. Angin et al. [2] incorporated external servers to remove the limitation of hardware and provide more accurate information. Though the external servers are able to run deeper models than phones, it requires fast and stable internet connection at all times. Moreover, the advancement of efficient neural networks such as MobileNet v2 enable a deep-learning approach to be implemented on a mobile device [17].

Direction is another factor to consider when helping the visually impaired cross the street. Though the visually impaired can have a good sense of the general direction to cross the road in familiar environments, relying on one's memory has its limitations [10]. Therefore, solutions to provide specific direction have also been devised. Other than detecting the color of pedestrian traffic lights, Ivanchenko et al. [10] also created an algorithm for detecting zebra crossings. The system obtains information of how much of the zebra-crossing is visible to help the visually impaired know whether or not they are generally facing in the correct direction, but it does not provide the specific location of the zebra crossing. Poggi et al., Lausser et al., and Banich [8,12,15] also use deep learning neural network within computer vision to detect zebra crossings to help the visually impaired cross streets. However, no deep learning method is able to output both traffic light and zebra crossing information simultaneously.

3   Proposed Method

Our method is performed on our labeled test-set. The training, test, and validation sets do not overlap.

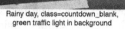

Rainy day, class=countdown_blank,   Snowy day, class=green   Dusk, class=red
green traffic light in background

Fig. 1. Sample images taken in different weather and lighting conditions. Other pedestrian traffic lights or vehicle/bicycle traffic lights can be seen in the images. The two endpoints of the zebra crossing are labelled as seen on the images. (Color figure online)

3.1 Dataset Collection and Pre-processing

Our data consists of images of street intersection scenes in Shanghai, China in varying weather and lighting conditions. Images were captured with two different cameras, an iPhone 7 and iPhone 6s at a resolution of 4032×3024 [16]. The camera was positioned at varying heights and angles around the vertical and transverse axes, but the angle around the longitudinal axis was kept relatively constant under the assumption that the visually impaired are able to keep the phone in a horizontal orientation. At an intersection, images were captured at varying positions relative to the center of the crosswalk, and at different positions on the crosswalk. Images may contain multiple pedestrian traffic lights, or other traffic lights such as vehicle and bicycle traffic lights.

The final dataset consists of 5059 images [16]. Each image was labelled with a ground truth class for traffic lights: red, green, countdown_green, countdown_blank, and none. Sample images are shown in Fig. 1. Images were also labelled with 2 image coordinates (x, y) representing the endpoints of the zebra crossing as pictured on the image. The image coordinates define the midline of the zebra crossing. In a significant number of the images, the mid-line of the zebra crossing was obstructed by pedestrians, cars, bicycles, or motorcycles. Statistics regarding the labelled images are shown in Table 1.

Prior to training, each image was re-sized to a resolution of 876×657. During each epoch, a random crop of size 768×576 and a random horizontal flip was applied to each image to prevent over-fitting. The training dataset was partitioned into 5 equal groups and 5-fold cross validation was performed. Images used in the validation dataset were directly re-sized from 4032×3024 to 768×576 without any transformations applied.

3.2 Classification and Regression Algorithm

Our neural network, LYTNet, follows the framework of MobileNet v2, a lightweight neural network designed to operate on mobile phones. MobileNet v2 primarily uses depthwise separable convolutions. In a depthwise separable convolution, a "depthwise" convolution is first performed: the channels of the

Table 1. Composition of dataset

	Red	Green	CD green	CD blank	None	Total
Number of images	1477	1303	963	904	412	5059
Percentage of dataset	29.2%	25.8%	19.0%	17.9%	8.1%	100.0%

input image are separated and different filters are used for every convolution over each channel. Then, a pointwise convolution (regular convolution of kernel size 1×1) is used to collapse the channels to a depth of 1. For an input of dimensions $h_i \cdot w_i \cdot d_i$ convolved with stride 1 with a kernel of size $k \cdot k$ and d_j output channels, the cost of a standard convolution is $h_i \cdot w_i \cdot k^2 \cdot d_i \cdot d_j$ while the cost of a depthwise separable convolution is $h_i \cdot w_i \cdot d_i \cdot (k^2 + d_j)$ [17]. Thus, the total cost of a depthwise separable convolution is $\frac{k^2 \cdot d_j}{k^2 + d_j}$ times less than a standard convolution while having similar performance [17]. Each "bottleneck" block consists of a 1×1 convolution to expand the number of channels by a factor of t, and a depthwise separable convolution of stride s and output channels c. Multiple fully connected layers were used to achieve the two desired outputs of the network: the classification and the endpoints of the zebra crossing. Compared to MobileNet v2, LYTNet was adapted for a larger input of $768 \times 576 \times 3$ in order for the pedestrian traffic lights to retain a certain degree of clarity. We used a 2×2 max-pool layer after the first convolution to decrease the size of the output and thus increase the speed of the network. LYTNet also features significantly fewer bottleneck layers (10 vs 17) compared to MobileNet v2 [17]. Table 2 shows the detailed structure of our network.

Fig. 2. The image on the left is the base image that was taken perpendicular to the zebra crossing and positioned in the center of the crossing, at a camera height of 1.4 m. Using our matrix, each point in the base image is mapped to a new point, creating the birds-eye image on the right. We can see that the zebra crossing is bounded by a rectangle with a midline centered and perpendicular to the x-axis.

During training, we used the Adam optimizer with momentum 0.9 and initial learning rate of 0.001. The learning rate was decreased by a factor of 10 at 150,

Table 2. Structure of our network

Input	Operator	t	c	n	s
768 × 576 × 3	conv2d 3 × 3	-	32	1	2
384 × 288 × 32	maxpool 2 × 2	-	-	1	-
192 × 144 × 32	Bottleneck	1	16	1	1
192 × 144 × 16	Bottleneck	6	24	1	2
96 × 72 × 24	Bottleneck	6	24	2	1
96 × 72 × 24	Bottleneck	6	32	1	2
48 × 36 × 32	Bottleneck	6	64	1	2
24 × 18 × 64	Bottleneck	6	64	2	1
24 × 18 × 64	Bottleneck	6	96	1	1
12 × 9 × 160	Bottleneck	6	160	2	1
12 × 9 × 160	Bottleneck	6	320	1	1
12 × 9 × 320	conv2d 1 × 1	-	1280	1	1
12 × 9 × 1280	avgpool 12 × 9	-	1280	1	-
1280	FC	-	160	1	-
160	FC	-	5	1	-
1280	FC	-	80	1	-
80	FC	-	4	1	-

400, and 650 epochs, with the network converging at around 800 epochs. We used a combination of cross-entropy loss (for image classification to calculate the loss for classification) and mean-squared-error loss (for regression to calculate the loss for direction) function is defined as:

$$L = \omega \cdot MSE + (1 - \omega) \cdot CE + \lambda \cdot R(W) \tag{1}$$

in which $R(W)$ is L-2 regularization. We used the value $\omega = 0.5$ during training.

3.3 Conversion of 2D Image Coordinates to 3D World Coordinates

The predicted endpoints output from the network are assumed to be accurate in regards to the 2D image. However, the appearance of objects and the zebra crossing in the image plane is an incorrect representation of the position of objects in the 3D world. Since the desired object, the zebra crossing, is on the ground, it has a fixed z-value of $z = 1$, enabling the conversion of a 2D image to a 2D birds-eye perspective image to achieve the desired 3D real-world information of the zebra crossing.

On our base image in Fig. 2, we define four points: (1671,1440), (2361,1440), (4032,2171), (0,2171) and four corresponding points in the real world: (1671,212), (2361,212), (2361,2812), (1671,2812), with the points defined on the xy-plane such that $0 \le x < 4032$ and $0 \le y < 3024$. The matrix

$$\begin{bmatrix} -1.17079727 \cdot 10^{-1} & -1.56391162 \cdot 10^0 & 2.25203273 \cdot 10^3 \\ 0 & -2.59783431 \cdot 10^0 & 3.71606050 \cdot 10^3 \\ 0 & -7.75749810 \cdot 10^{-4} & 1.00000000 \cdot 10^0 \end{bmatrix}$$

maps each point on the image $(x, y, 1)$ to its corresponding point in the real-world. Assuming a fixed height, and a fixed angle around the transverse and longitudinal axes, the matrix will perfectly map each point on the image to the correct birds-eye-view point. Though this is not the case due to varying heights and angles around the transverse axis, the matrix provides the rough position of zebra crossing in the real world, which is sufficient for the purposes of guiding the visually impaired to a correct orientation.

3.4   Mobile Application

As a proof of concept, an application was created using Swift. LYTNet is deployed in the application. Additional post-processing steps are implemented in the application to increase safety and convert zebra crossing data into information for the visually impaired. Accordingly, the softmax probabilities of each class is stored in phone memory, and the probabilities are averaged over five consecutive frames. Since countdown_blank and countdown_green represent the same mode of traffic light - a green light that has numbers counting down - the probabilities of either class are added together. A probability threshold of 0.8 is set for the application to output a decision. This is used to prevent a decision from being made before or after the pedestrian traffic light changes color. If one frame of the five frame average is different, the probability threshold would not be reached. Users will be alerted by a choice of beeps or vibrations whenever the five-frame average changes to a different traffic light mode. The average of the endpoint coordinates is also taken over five consecutive frames to provide more stable instructions for the user. The direction is retrieved from the angle of the direction vector in the birds-eye perspective.

A threshold of $10°$ was set for $\Delta\theta$ before instructions are output to the user. If $\Delta\theta < -10°$ then an instruction for the user to rotate left is output, and if $\Delta\theta > 10°$ an instruction for the user to rotate right is output. The x-intercept of the line through the start and end-points is calculated with:

$$x_{int} = \frac{x_1 y_2 - x_2 y_1}{y_2 - y_1}. \tag{2}$$

For an image with width w and midline at $(w-1)/2$, if $x_{int} > (w-1)/2 + w \cdot 0.085$, instructions are given to move left, and if $x_{int} < (w-1)/2 - w \cdot 0.085$, instructions are given to move right. In our defined area of the zebra crossing in transformed base image, the edges of the zebra crossing are within 8.5% of the midline. With a constant width for the zebra crossing, if x_{int} is outside of the 8.5% range, the user will be outside of the zebra crossing. Refer to Fig. 3 for a flow chart of the demo application and Fig. 4 for a screenshot of our demo application.

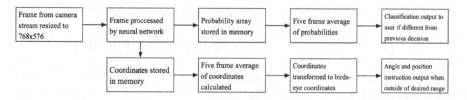

Fig. 3. Our application continuously iterates through this flow chart at 20 fps.

Fig. 4. Sample screenshots from our demo application. In order from top to bottom is the: position instruction, orientation instruction, 5-frame average class, delay, frame rate, and current detected class. The blue line is the direction vector for the specific frame, and the red line is the five-frame average direction vector. (Color figure online)

Table 3. Comparison of different network widths

Width	Accuracy (%)	Angle error (degrees)	Start-point error	Frame rate (fps)
1.4	93.50	6.80	0.0805	15.69
1.25	92.96	6.73	0.0810	17.19
1.0	94.18	6.27	0.0763	20.32
0.9375	93.50	6.44	0.0768	21.69
0.875	93.23	7.08	0.0854	23.41
0.75	92.96	7.16	0.0825	24.33
0.5	89.99	7.19	0.0853	28.30

4   Experiments

We trained our network using 3456 images from our dataset and 864 images for validation [16]. Our testing dataset consists of 739 images. The width multiplier changes the number of output channels at each layer. A smaller width multiplier decreases the number of channels and makes the network less computationally expensive, but sacrifices accuracy. As seen in Table 3, networks using a higher width multiplier also have a lower accuracy due to overfitting. We performed further testing using the network with width multiplier 1.0, as it achieves the highest accuracy while maintaining near real-time speed when tested on an iPhone 7. The precisions and recalls of countdown_blank and none are the lowest out of all classes, which may be due to the limited number of training samples for those two classes (Table 4). However, the precision and recall of red traffic lights, the most important class, is greater than 96%.

Table 4. Precision and recalls by class

	Red	Green	Countdown green	Countdown blank	None
Precision	0.97	0.94	0.99	0.86	0.92
Recall	0.96	0.94	0.96	0.92	0.87
F1 score	0.96	0.94	0.97	0.89	0.89

When the zebra crossing is clear/unblocked, the angle error, startpoint, and endpoint errors are significantly better than when it is obstructed (Table 5). For an obstructed zebra crossing, insufficient information is provided in the image for the network to output precise endpoints.

Figure 5 shows various outputs of our network. In (A), the network correctly predicts no traffic light despite two green car traffic lights taking a prominent place in the background, and is able to somewhat accurately predict the coordinates despite the zebra crossing appearing faint. In (B), the model correctly predicted the class despite the symbol being underexposed by the camera. (C) and (D) show examples of the model correctly predicting the traffic light despite rainy and snowy weather. (B), (C), and (D) all show the network predicting coordinates close to the ground truth.

To prove the effectiveness of LYTNet, we retrained it using only red, green, and none class pictures from our own dataset and tested it on the PTLR dataset [7]. Due to the small size of the PTLR training dataset, we were unable to perform further training or fine-tuning using the dataset without significant overfitting. Using the China portion of the PTLR dataset, we compared our algorithm with Cheng et al.'s algorithm, which is the most recent attempt for pedestrian traffic light detection to our knowledge.

LYTNet was able to outperform their algorithm in regards to the F1 score, despite the disadvantage of insufficient training data from the PTLR dataset to train our network (Table 6). Furthermore, LYTNet provides additional information about the direction of the zebra crossing, giving the visually impaired a more comprehensive set of information for crossing the street, and outputs information regarding 4 different modes of traffic lights rather than only 2. We also achieve a similar frame rate to Cheng et al.'s algorithm, which achieved a frame rate of 21, albeit on a different mobile device.

Table 5. Comparison of network performance on clear and obstructed zebra crossings

	Number of images	Angle error	Startpoint error	Endpoint error
Clear	594	5.86	0.0725	0.476
Obstructed	154	7.97	0.0918	0.0649
All	739	6.27	0.0763	0.0510

Fig. 5. Example correct outputs from our neural network. The class is labelled on top of each image. Blue dots are ground truth coordinates and red dots are predicted coordinates. (Color figure online)

Table 6. Precision and recall of our network and Cheng et al.'s algorithm

		Our network	Cheng et al.'s algorithm
Red	Recall	**92.23**	86.43
	Precision	96.24	**96.67**
	F1 Score	**94.19**	91.26
Green	Recall	**92.15**	91.30
	Precision	**98.83**	98.03
	F1 Score	**95.37**	94.55

5   Conclusion

In this paper, we proposed LYTNet, a convolutional neural network that uses image classification to detect the color of pedestrian traffic lights and to provide the direction and position of the zebra crossing to assist the visually impaired in crossing the street. LYTNet uses techniques taken from MobileNet v2, and was trained on our dataset, which is one of the largest pedestrian traffic light datasets in the world [16]. Images were captured at hundreds of traffic intersections within Shanghai at a variety of different heights, angles, and positions relative to the zebra crossing.

Unlike previous methods that use multiple steps like detecting candidate areas, LYTNet uses image classification, a one-step approach. Since the network can learn features from an entire image rather than only detecting the pedestrian traffic light symbol, it has the advantage of being more robust in cases such as images with multiple pedestrian traffic lights. With sufficient training data, the network can draw clues from the context of an image along with the traffic light color to reach the correct prediction.

Additionally, LYTNet provides the advantage of being more comprehensive than previous methods as it classifies the traffic light between five total classes compared to 3 or 4 in previous attempts. Furthermore, our network is also capable of outputting zebra crossing information, which other methods do not provide. Thus, LYTNet elegantly combines the two most needed pieces of information without requiring two separate algorithms. Furthermore, our network is able to match the performance of the algorithm proposed by Cheng et al.

In the future, we will improve the robustness of our deep learning model through the expansion of our dataset, for further generalization. For the two classes with the least data, none and countdown_blank, additional data can greatly improve the precisions and recalls. Data from other areas around the world can also be collected to separately train the network to perform optimally in another region with pedestrian traffic lights with differently shaped symbols. Our demonstration mobile application will be further developed into a working application that converts the output into auditory and sensory information for the visually impaired.

Acknowledgements. We would like to express our sincerest gratitude to Professor Chunhua Shen, Dr. Facheng Li, and Dr. Rongyi Lan for their insight and expertise when helping us in our research.

References

1. Almeida, T., Macedo, H., Matos, L.: A traffic light recognition device. In: Latifi, S. (ed.) Information Technology - New Generations. AISC, vol. 738, pp. 369–375. Springer, Cham (2018). https://doi.org/10.1007/978-3-319-77028-4_49
2. Angin, P., Bhargava, B., Helal, S.: A mobile-cloud collaborative traffic lights detector for blind navigation, pp. 396–401, January 2010. https://doi.org/10.1109/MDM.2010.71
3. Barlow, J., Bentzen, B., Tabor, L.: Accessible Pedestrian Signals. National Cooperative Highway Research Program, Washington, D.C (2003)
4. Behrendt, K., Novak, L., Botros, R.: A deep learning approach to traffic lights: detection, tracking, and classification, pp. 1370–1377, May 2017. https://doi.org/10.1109/ICRA.2017.7989163
5. Blaauw, F., Krieke, L., Emerencia, A., Aiello, M., Jonge, P.: Personalized advice for enhancing well-being using automated impulse response analysis – AIRA, June 2017
6. de Charette, R., Nashashibi, F.: Traffic light recognition using image processing compared to learning processes, pp. 333–338, November 2009. https://doi.org/10.1109/IROS.2009.5353941
7. Cheng, R., Wang, K., Yang, K., Long, N., Bai, J., Liu, D.: Real-time pedestrian crossing lights detection algorithm for the visually impaired. Multimed. Tools Appl. **77**, 20651–20671 (2017). https://doi.org/10.1007/s11042-017-5472-5
8. Banich, J.D.: Zebra crosswalk detection assisted by neural networks, June 2016

9. Gong, J., Jiang, Y., Xiong, G., Guan, C., Tao, G., Chen, H.: The recognition and tracking of traffic lights based on color segmentation and CAMSHIFT for intelligent vehicles, pp. 431–435, July 2010. https://doi.org/10.1109/IVS.2010.5548083

10. Ivanchenko, V., Coughlan, J., Shen, H.: Crosswatch: a camera phone system for orienting visually impaired pedestrians at traffic intersections. In: Miesenberger, K., Klaus, J., Zagler, W., Karshmer, A. (eds.) ICCHP 2008. LNCS, vol. 5105, pp. 1122–1128. Springer, Heidelberg (2008). https://doi.org/10.1007/978-3-540-70540-6_168

11. Ivanchenko, V., Coughlan, J., Shen, H.: Real-time walk light detection with a mobile phone. In: Miesenberger, K., Klaus, J., Zagler, W., Karshmer, A. (eds.) ICCHP 2010. LNCS, vol. 6180, pp. 229–234. Springer, Heidelberg (2010). https://doi.org/10.1007/978-3-642-14100-3_34

12. Lausser, L., Schwenker, F., Palm, G.: Detecting zebra crossings utilizing AdaBoost, pp. 535–540, January 2008

13. Mascetti, S., Ahmetovic, D., Gerino, A., Bernareggi, C., Busso, M., Rizzi, A.: Robust traffic lights detection on mobile devices for pedestrians with visual impairment. Comput. Vis. Image Understand. **148** (2015). https://doi.org/10.1016/j.cviu.2015.11.017

14. Omachi, M., Omachi, S.: Traffic light detection with color and edge information, pp. 284–287, January 2009. https://doi.org/10.1109/ICCSIT.2009.5234518

15. Poggi, M., Nanni, L., Mattoccia, S.: Crosswalk recognition through point-cloud processing and deep-learning suited to a wearable mobility aid for the visually impaired. In: Murino, V., Puppo, E., Sona, D., Cristani, M., Sansone, C. (eds.) ICIAP 2015. LNCS, vol. 9281, pp. 282–289. Springer, Cham (2015). https://doi.org/10.1007/978-3-319-23222-5_35

16. Samuel, Y., Heon, L., John, K.: PTL-dataset, April 2019. https://github.com/samuelyu2002/PTL-Dataset

17. Sandler, M., Howard, A., Zhu, M., Zhmoginov, A., Chen, L.C.: MobileNetV2: inverted residuals and linear bottlenecks, pp. 4510–4520, June 2018. https://doi.org/10.1109/CVPR.2018.00474

18. Shioyama, T., Wu, H., Nakamura, N., Kitawaki, S.: Measurement of the length of pedestrian crossings and detection of traffic lights from image data. Meas. Sci. Technol **13**, 1450–1457 (2002). https://doi.org/10.1088/0957-0233/13/9/311

19. Varan, S., Singh, S., Kunte, R.S., Sudhaker, S., Philip, B.: A road traffic signal recognition system based on template matching employing tree classifier, pp. 360–365, January 2008. https://doi.org/10.1109/ICCIMA.2007.190

A Sequential CNN Approach for Foreign Object Detection in Hyperspectral Images

Mahmoud Al-Sarayreh[1(✉)], Marlon M. Reis[2], Wei Qi Yan[1],
and Reinhard Klette[1(✉)]

[1] School of Engineering, Computer and Mathematical Sciences,
Auckland University of Technology, Auckland, New Zealand
{malsaray,wyan,rklette}@aut.ac.nz
[2] AgResearch, Palmerston North, New Zealand
marlon.m.reis@agresearch.co.nz

Abstract. This paper reports about potentials of hyperspectral imaging for object detection, especially on an application of foreign object detection (FOD) in meat products. A sequential deep-learning framework is proposed by using region-proposal networks (RPNs) and 3D convolutional networks (CNNs). Two independent datasets of images, contaminated with many types of foreign materials, were used for training and testing the proposed model. Results show that the proposed RPN model outperforms a selected search method in terms of accuracy, efficiency, and run-time. An FOD model based on RPN and 3D-CNN, or selected search with a 3D-CNN solve FOD with an average precision of 81.0% or 50.6%, respectively. This study demonstrates opportunities when using hyperspectral imaging systems for real-time object detection by using both spectral and spatial features combined.

1 Introduction

Food inspection and monitoring are essential processes in the modern food industry. The main task in these processes is to ensure that the products are safe, wholesome, and comply with international standards and legislations [1,2]. In the meat industry, there are two fundamental types of inspections, product-based or carcass-based inspections. Meat-product inspection processes include the correction of labelling and packaging, and a prevention of recall incidents due to physical or microbial contamination. Foreign matters (i.e., foreign objects or foreign bodies) are defined as a kind of physical contamination in meat products, which can accidentally fall in meat products during processing and packaging. These objects could be glass, metal, paper, or plastic objects [1–3].

Existing technologies for automated *foreign object detection* (FOD) in the food industry [1,2] include metal detectors, magnetic separators, optical sorting systems, microwave imaging, *nuclear magnetic resonance imaging* (NMRI), ultrasound systems, and X-ray imaging. Each technology has its assumptions for a specific type of food, specific types of foreign objects, advantages, and

© Springer Nature Switzerland AG 2019
M. Vento and G. Percannella (Eds.): CAIP 2019, LNCS 11678, pp. 271–283, 2019.
https://doi.org/10.1007/978-3-030-29888-3_22

drawbacks [1,2]. For example, X-ray imaging systems perform accurately for detecting metal and plastic objects. However, they have limitations regarding work-environment safety, large-scale foreign materials, high costs, and radiation emissions [1,2,4–6]. *Hyperspectral imaging* (HSI) systems are robust, rapid, and non-destructive tools for presenting both the chemical composition and spatial distributions of materials; these distributions are presented as a 3D image volume [7]. Thus, HSI images are commonly used in the food industry, for example for predicting safety or quality attributes [7–9], biological contaminant detection [10], or a detection of physical contamination [9].

Meat processing, regarding quality and safety of products, is gaining more attention in the meat industry and related research. The industry aims at preventing recall occurrences throughout the whole meat processing chain, and at keeping products free of physical contaminants causing that recalls occur during the process [3]. In general, meat is considered as being one of the food types that have a high probability of recall occurrences [3]. Costs for preventing these incidents are high in the meat industry; inspections to avoid foreign matters in meat products are typically performed manually and thus subjected to human errors, cause labour costs, and are time-consuming. As an emerging technology, *snapshot* HSI systems [11,12] can be used for automating the detection process of foreign objects in meat products, which positively reflects on accuracy, costs, and speed of the whole inspection process.

This paper aims at investigating the robustness of snapshot HSI systems for real-time detection and localisation of foreign objects that may contaminate food products. Moreover, we investigate the efficiency of supervised learning approaches for FOD in food products. The main contribution of this paper is to propose and evaluate a novel sequential deep-learning framework for FOD in meat products, including the development and evaluation of a novel region-proposal model for object detection tasks and a 3D *convolutional neural network* (3D-CNN) model for classifying normal and abnormal regions in HSI images.

The rest of the paper is organised as follows. Section 2 reviews state-of-the-art techniques which are related to this research. Section 3 describes the used dataset and HSI imaging system. Section 4 describes the proposed methods and models for FOD. Experimental results and analysis of the proposed framework are given in Sect. 5. Section 6 concludes.

2   Related Work

FOD systems based on imaging follow one of two main approaches for implementing FOD detection models. In a supervised learning approach, prior knowledge about the expected foreign objects and their physical properties is needed for training the models [13–15]. An unsupervised learning approach (anomaly detection) requires an understanding of normal materials while training the models on the desired materials [16].

Supervised learning approaches demonstrate robustness and efficiency for many FOD tasks such as FOD in airfield pavements [13]. The accuracy of such approaches depends on used features for FOD and representations of foreign materials which are taken into consideration [13,15]. Handcrafted image features, such as *scale invariant feature transform* (SIFT)[17], *histograms of oriented gradients* (HOG) [18] or *local binary patterns* (LBP) [19], are considered to be insufficient for dealing with complex images (i.e complex normal and abnormal regions) for FOD tasks [13].

Recently, CNN-based models gain much attention and show an efficiency for dealing with several tasks in computer vision research, such as image recognition [20] or object detection [21–23,25,27,28]. Object detection applies, for example, *region-proposal networks* (RPNs) or target-regression approaches. The RPN was proposed in faster R-CNN [23] and mask R-CNN [24] algorithms. In these algorithms, both region-proposal and classification were designed in a single model by sharing features of the RPN model [23,24]. RPN-based algorithms show efficiency, both in terms of run-time and accuracy, in comparison with algorithms following "traditional" (i.e., non-neural networks) methods for generating region proposals [21,22], such as selective search [26] or sliding windows.

Target regression was used for localisation tasks in the *single shot MultiBox detector* (SSD) [28] and in *You-only-look-once* (YOLO) [27] algorithms. Both SSD and YOLO algorithms showed better performance regarding run-time, but lower accuracy compared to RPN-based algorithms. Moreover, SSD and YOLO show limitations in the detection of small objects due to their design [13].

In [13], a multi-stage deep-learning algorithm was proposed for FOD, including three steps, an RPN model for generating a set of candidates of objects, a spatial transformer network (STN) for rectifying the resulting candidates, and a CNN network for classifying candidates into object categories or background. A comparison in [13] shows that sequential approaches (i.e., multi-stage algorithms) for FOD are better than FOD detection in a single algorithm such as faster R-CNN or SSD, where the comparison reports that the multi-stage algorithm [13] is faster and more accurate than faster R-CNN and SSD algorithms for this kind of object detection problems (i.e., FOD on airfield pavements).

3   Dataset and HSI System

A collection of fresh red-meat samples were procured from two local supermarkets. The total number of samples is 184, including lamb (67), beef (73), and pork (44). All of the samples were chosen from loin and leg chops. The samples were chosen from eight different commercial products which are commonly found in New Zealand shops. The meat samples were randomly separated into 102, 40, 40 meat samples for training, validation, and testing purposes.

An HSI imaging system was implemented, for imaging the collected meat samples, by using an NIR snapshot camera [11,12], a set of illumination units, a controlled movable conveyor belt, and a computer running an image acquisition software. Figure 1 demonstrates the main components of the used HSI system; we refer the reader to [11] for all technical and experimental details of the used HSI system.

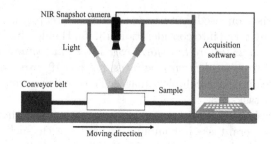

Fig. 1. Demonstration of the main components of the used snapshot HSI system.

For simulating the FOD problem in meat products, several sets of materials were collected and then "contaminated" with meat samples. These materials are categorised as glass, soft and hard plastic, transparent plastic, papers, and metals. In all material categories, a wide range of colours was taken into account. Moreover, these materials were grouped into two sets: One set was considered in training and validation processes, and the other set was totally left for only testing and evaluating the proposed methods. Figure 2, left, shows examples of these materials that were used for validation and testing phases.

The HSI system was used for collecting a set of 2,988 snapshot HSI images, including 1,000 images of normal (i.e., without adding any foreign materials) training meat samples, 937 images of contaminated training meat samples (i.e., contaminated by adding a random set of foreign materials), 250 images of normal validation samples, 220 images of contaminated validation samples, and 581 images of contaminated testing meat samples. Figure 2, right, shows a selected set of images (from validation and testing sets) of meat products contaminated with foreign objects. After collecting the images, all images were calibrated and post-processed, including illumination correction and normalisation steps, by using an approach as presented in [11].

4   The Proposed Framework

A snapshot HSI camera is a robust tool for collecting spectral data at video rate; it is portable similar to RGB cameras with the advantage of having more spectral information of materials in scenes. This fact inspired us to investigate this tool for solving object detection for FOD in meat products. We believe this study is the first case of object detection by HSI imaging, which is an important step towards the real-time use of HSI imaging systems.

The proposed framework was inspired by methods and models presented in [13,20,21,23]. The proposed framework is a combination of several modules in a sequential order. The framework consists of three modules: An RPN module for generating a set of candidates with a probability for being foreign materials or normal materials, a filtering module for reducing the number of these candidates by certain rules for having regions with high probability for being foreign

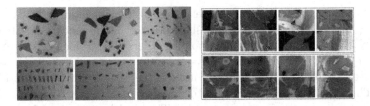

Fig. 2. *Left, top*: Examples of used foreign materials in training and validation images. *Left, bottom*: Set of materials used in testing images. *Right, top*: Selected HSI images from the validation set. *Right, bottom*: Selected HSI images from the testing set. Images on the right are false-colour images extracted from HSI images. (Color figure online)

materials, and a 3D-CNN module for a final classification of the resulting top regions. Figure 3 illustrates the proposed framework and its sequential flow. The next sections describe these modules in detail.

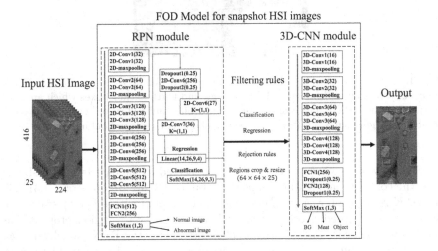

Fig. 3. Proposed FOD model for meat products by using snapshot HSI images.

4.1 RPN Module

Deep learning requires a large set of labelled images. Transfer learning is commonly used for handling the issue of a small dataset by initialising models with an already existing and well-trained model. Unfortunately, this approach is not applicable on HSI images due to their dimensions (i.e., the 3D hypercube) and because there is not yet any pre-trained model for these kind of images. Thus, we decided for a two-step learning approach for implementing and training the proposed RPN model.

First, a customised VGG16 model [20] was implemented and adapted for handling an HSI image as input. As shown in Fig. 3, the model consists of five 2D-CNN blocks, including five max-pooling layers with a pooling size of 2 and striding of $(2,2)$, followed by two fully-connected layers and an output layer for two classes. In all 2D-CNN layers, we use a kernel size of (3×3) and striding of $(1,1)$. The main task of this model is to recognise an HSI image as being normal or abnormal (i.e., with foreign materials). The model was trained by using the normal and abnormal images of our training dataset. During the training, we used real-time data augmentation processes, such as randomly rotation, shift, and zoom. Empirically, after observing convergence on training and validation datasets, the modelling stopped and only the 2D-CNN layers, excluding the final max-pooling layer, are saved and then used as *base-layers* for the RPN model.

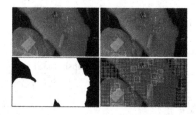

Fig. 4. *Top*: Input snapshot HSI and its annotated bounding boxes. *Bottom*: Mask image of the input HSI image and labels of ground truth anchor boxes which are used in training the RPN model; colours red, green, blue and yellow present ground truth of objects, background, meat, and objects anchors. (Color figure online)

Second, a small CNN network is fully connected to the base-layers for sliding over the convolutional feature maps (here we use sliding windows of 3×3) [23]. Then, K reference boxes (*anchors*) [23] are computed with different scales and aspect ratios to predict region proposals of objects. Each region proposal has a classification score and location coefficients. Thus, the RPN model takes an HSI image as input and generates a series of rectangular object candidates with corresponding classification scores of being ether a *background region*, a *meat region*, or a *foreign object*.

In [13,23] the RPN network was designed for generating a set of object candidates with objectiveness scores, while the proposed RPN network is implemented individually for solving a complete classification task for each predicted candidate region. For training the proposed RPN model, we use *intersection over union* (IoU) between anchor boxes and annotated bounding boxes for selecting the set of anchors with a high probability of being an object (ground-truth anchors for objects with $IoU > 0.5$), and also anchors with a high probability of being meat or background regions (ground-truth anchors for meat and background regions with $IoU < 0.2$). For distinguishing between meat regions and background regions, manually generated mask images are used for selecting a set of anchors with a high probability of being a background region. Figure 4 shows an example of the selected anchors, for each class, for training the proposed RPN model.

In training processes, an adaptive mini-patch approach was used for defining the number of ground truth anchor boxes of each class. In a mini-patch, the number of best anchors of foreign objects was selected and, randomly, the same number of anchors of meat and background regions was selected; this approach makes the mini-patch balanced and representative. In back propagation processes, we used a loss function as in [23]. The loss function is a combination between a categorical cross-entropy loss for the classification task and smooth L_1 for the regression task. For the regression task, the selected anchors were masked. Thus, the only anchors of foreign objects were encoded as in [23] and contributed in the loss function. For optimising the network weights, we use *stochastic gradient descent* (SGD) algorithms for adjusting the model weights and a best model selection.

4.2   Filtering Module

In fact, RPN networks produce much fewer candidate regions compared to a standard sliding-window paradigm; the number of candidates depends on the size of the feature map, not on the size of the image. These candidates are still very large for the final classification and consist of many false-alarm regions. Thus, we sought for applying a set of steps and rules, as an intermediate phase before the final classification, for filtering these candidates into candidates with high probabilities for being foreign objects. These steps are defined, as shown in Fig. 3, as follows:

Classification: The proposed RPN network was designed for predicting a set for bounding boxes and each box has its own probability p of being ether an object, background, or meat region in the HSI image. Thus, the rejection rule of i-th predicted box as follow:

$$\begin{cases} \text{Rejected,} & \text{if } p^i_{background} > t_1 \text{ or } p^i_{meat} > t_2 \text{ or } p^i_{object} < t_3 \\ \text{Accepted,} & \text{otherwise} \end{cases}$$

where t_1, t_2, and t_3 are hard thresholds and set to be 0.7, 0.7, and 0.8 in our experiments, respectively. By using this rule, boxes with high probabilities for being background and meat regions are discarded, which reduces the number of boxes by around 60% compared to the total number, and only boxes with high probabilities for being foreign objects remain for the next step.

Regression: Coordinates of remaining boxes are computed by using the predicted regression coefficient of the RPN network. Then, all boxes that have any negative coordinate (i.e., outside the image borders) or have a size less than 64 pixel are labelled as non-valid boxes (to be discarded).

Intersection: Figure 5 shows the remaining boxes as groups of boxes around each object in the image. Empirically, we observe that there are many small boxes located inside the best-predicted box. Thus, we use the intersection measure as a tool for eliminating these small boxes. First, all boxes are sorted and listed based on the probability of being objects. Second, intersections between the i-th box B_i (i.e., box with the highest probability) and the others are computed. Then, all boxes that have an intersection of 1.0 with B_i are discarded and the same process is repeated until all boxes in the list are processed.

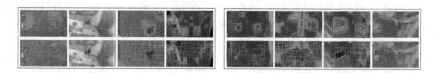

Fig. 5. Visual comparison between resulting candidate boxes of the RPN network (*top row*), and selective search (*bottom row*).

Non-maximum suppression (NMS): As in [13,23,25], NMS is used to remove the boxes that have high degrees of overlapping; IoU is used for quantifying the overlapping between predicted boxes. Empirically, we used an IoU of 0.8 as a threshold in our NMS step, with a top rule of 150 for defining the maximum number of the remaining boxes; top 150 is the maximum, while, empirically, the remaining boxes are much less.

After applying these steps and rules, the resulting bounding boxes are ready for final classification. The resulting boxes are cropped from the input image and then resized into a fixed size of $64 \times 64 \times 25$. These cropped boxes are used as independent HSI images and as input for the next module (i.e., the 3D-CNN model).

4.3   3D-CNN Classification Module

Although the bounding boxes resulting from the RPN and filtering modules are very good candidates for FOD, still some boxes are related to background or meat regions in the image. For an accurate FOD, we add a classification module for classifying the resulting bounding boxes into background, meat, or foreign objects by using 3D-CNNs; those are an efficient tool for using both spectral and spatial information of HSI images [11].

The proposed 3D-CNN model, as shown in Fig. 3, consists of a hierarchical structure of ten 3D-CNNs with a kernel size of $3 \times 3 \times 3$, four 3D max-pooling layers with a pooling size of 2, two dropout layers with a ratio of 0.25, and two fully-connected layers of size 256 and 128. For classification, a softmax layer (with 3 nodes) was added as an output layer, where 3 defines the predefined classes (i.e., background, meat, and foreign object). In all CNNs and fully-connected layers, we use *rectified linear units* (ReLUs) for activating the output of these layers. Figure 3 sketches the flow and the details of layers of the proposed 3D-CNN classification model.

For training the 3D-CNN model, a random HSI image is selected from the training dataset; then, the reference anchors of the image are computed based on the defined scales and aspect ratios. Next, the anchors are labelled as described in Sect. 4.1 by using IoU and the masked images. Adaptively, a set of anchors is selected from each class and cropped into a size of $64 \times 64 \times 25$; the patch size is adaptive and depends on the number of best anchors that have high overlapping with the annotated ground truth. The selected patch is now fed into the model and a categorical cross-entropy loss function is used for computing the error between actual and predicted outputs, while an SGD algorithm is used for optimising the model weights.

In the testing phase, the resulting candidate boxes by the region proposal module are fed to the classification module for having the probabilities, of being either a foreign object, meat, or background regions, of these candidates. Then, a hard threshold (t_4) is used for keeping only boxes with high probabilities of being foreign objects and eliminating the other candidates; empirically, t_4 was set to be 0.8 based on our experiments and datasets.

5   Experimental Results and Analysis

In the RPN model we use the scales [24, 48, 64] and aspect ratios [1:1, 1:2, 2:1] for training and implementation of the model. In both RPN and 3D-CNN models, we used an SGD algorithm with a momentum of 0.9, a weight decay of 0.0001, and an initial learning rate of 0.001. The models were trained for 5 K epochs; after each 1 K epochs, the learning rate decayed by 0.1%.

For comparison, an FOD model was implemented by using a common selective search method [12,13,22,23,26] and the proposed 3D-CNN classification model. In the selective search method, first three PCA images of an HSI image are used as input due to the high dimensionality of the HSI images. The localisation accuracy of the candidate regions is very important for having an accurate object detection algorithm [13,23]. Thus, we first evaluate the performance of the proposed RPN network for both the validation and testing dataset.

Table 1 shows the performance of the RPN network in comparison with the selective search method. The RPN network achieves a higher recall rate for different IoU thresholds, including 0.5, 0.4, and 0.3, compared to the selective search method. On average for the IoU thresholds, the RPN network provides a recall rate of 73.6% and 0.97.1% for validation and testing dataset, respectively, while the selective search method achieves recalls of 58.8% and 91%. The RPN network shows accurate localisation (i.e., a high recall with an IoU of 0.5) and detection (i.e., a high recall on average of three IoUs), with fewer candidates in comparison to the selective search method.

Figure 5 shows a qualitative comparison between resulting candidates of RPN network and selective search. Candidate regions of the RPN network look accurate and distributed only around the foreign objects in the image, while normal regions in the image look "clean from detection".

For FOD evaluation, we use *average precision* (AP), following [13,23,24,27, 28], as a measure based on three IoU thresholds. Table 2 shows the evaluation of FOD by RPN and 3D-CNN networks, and FOD by selective search and 3D-CNN. The resulting AP shows that FOD with RPN outperforms FOD with the

Table 1. Performance evaluation on HSI images for the proposed RPN network, in comparison with a standard selective search method. "Avg No." shows the number of generated regions, on average for the whole dataset, by each method.

Method	IoU >	Validation set			Testing set		
		Recall No.	Recall rate	Avg No.	Recall No.	Recall rate	Avg No.
Selective search	0.5	658	47.3	183	1793	83.3	212
	0.4	834	59.9		1993	92.5	
	0.3	960	69.1		2090	97.1	
	Avg		58.8			91.0	
RPN	0.5	835	60.0	Top50	1934	89.8	Top50
	0.4	883	63.5		1968	91.4	
	0.3	909	65.3		1980	92.0	
	Avg		63.0			91.1	
	0.5	925	66.5	Top100	2025	94.1	Top100
	0.4	977	70.2		2067	96.0	
	0.3	1020	73.3		2074	96.3	
	Avg		70.0			95.5	
	0.5	963	69.2	Top150	2064	95.9	Top150
	0.4	1029	74.0		2098	97.4	
	0.3	1080	77.6		2107	97.9	
	Avg		73.6			97.1	

Table 2. Performance evaluation of the proposed FOD model for HSI images in comparison with a model following the selective search method.

Method	Validation set				Testing set			
	AP@			Avg	AP@			Avg
	0.5	0.4	0.3		0.5	0.4	0.3	
Selective search (3D-CNN)	26.2	40.3	53.1	39.9	31.7	52.2	67.9	50.6
RPN (3D-CNN)	57.2	61.6	63.7	60.8	75.9	82.1	85.1	81.0

selective search method, both on the validation and testing set of HSI images. The RPN network is more accurate both for FOD localisation and detection. Figure 6 provides a visual comparison between the two FOD models on selected HSI images from validation and testing sets.

We also analyse the run-time of the investigated models and methods; all methods and models are implemented on the same machine. Results show another efficiency of the RPN network; run-times (on average for all images in the datasets) are 0.06 s and 1.5 s for RPN and selective search, respectively. Run-times of complete FOD frameworks are 1.3 s and 4.6 s with RPN and selective search, respectively. These results show that RPN is much faster than selective search for FOD, which defines the RPN model as being more relevant for real-time applications in meat industry.

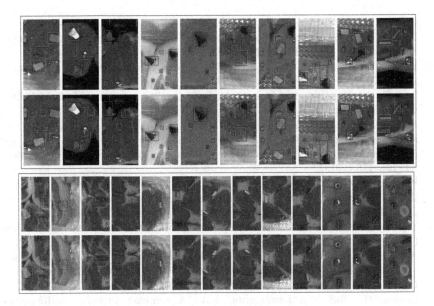

Fig. 6. Qualitative comparison between selective search and RPN-based models for FOD in HSI images. *First two rows*: Selected detection results of RPN-based model (*top*) and selective search (*bottom*) on validation dataset. *Last two rows*: Same comparison for selected results on testing dataset.

6   Conclusions

The paper shows that the use of HSI images for FOD in food products is an important opportunity for the food industry. The proposed framework consists of three modules in sequential order, including an RPN network, and a filtering and a classification module. The proposed FOD framework was designed for using both the spectral and spatial features of HSI images. Quantitative and qualitative results show that the proposed FOD framework outperforms state-of-the-art methods in terms of accuracy of detection, localisation of detected objects, and computation time. The proposed FOD framework is an efficient solution for completely portable HSI systems (mobile HSI systems) and FOD of video HSI.

References

1. Edwards, M.: Detecting Foreign Bodies in Food. Elsevier, Amsterdam (2004)
2. Graves, M., Smith, A., Batchelor, B.: Approaches to foreign body detection in foods. Trends Food Sci. Technol. **9**(1), 21–27 (1998)
3. Food recall statistics. www.foodstandards.govt.nz/industry/foodrecalls/recallstats/Pages/default.aspx. Accessed 25 Mar 2019
4. Nielsen, M., Lauridsen, T., Christensen, L., Feidenhans, R.: X-ray dark-field imaging for detection of foreign bodies in food. Food Control **30**(2), 531–535 (2013)

5. Chen, X., Jing, H., Tao, Y., Cheng, X.: High-resolution real-time x-ray and 3D imaging for physical contamination detection in deboned poultry meat. Monit. Food Saf. Agric. Plant Health **5271**, 108–118 (2004)
6. Einarsdóttir, H., et al.: Novelty detection of foreign objects in food using multi-modal X-ray imaging. Food Control **67**, 39–47 (2016)
7. Sun, D.-W.: Hyperspectral Imaging for Food Quality Analysis and Control. Elsevier, Amsterdam (2010)
8. Feng, C.-H., Makino, Y., Oshita, S., Martín, J.-F.: Hyperspectral imaging and multispectral imaging as the novel techniques for detecting defects in raw and processed meat products: current state-of-the-art research advances. Food Control **84**, 165–176 (2018)
9. Kamruzzaman, M., Makino, Y., Oshita, S.: Non-invasive analytical technology for the detection of contamination, adulteration, and authenticity of meat, poultry, and fish: a review. Analytica Chimica Acta **853**, 19–29 (2015)
10. Vejarano, R., Siche, R., Tesfaye, W.: Evaluation of biological contaminants in foods by hyperspectral imaging: a review. Int. J. Food Prop. **20**(2), 1264–1297 (2017)
11. Al-Sarayreh, M., Reis, M., Yan, W.Y., Klette, R.: Deep spectral-spatial features of snapshot hyperspectral images for red-meat classification. In: Proceedings of International Conference on Image Vision Computing New Zealand, pp. 1–6 (2018)
12. Geelen, B., Tack, N., Lambrechts, A.A.: A compact snapshot multispectral imager with a monolithically integrated per-pixel filter mosaic. In: Proceedings of Advanced Fabrication Technologies Micro/Nano Optics Photonics, p. 89740L (2014)
13. Cao, X., et al.: Region based CNN for foreign object debris detection on airfield pavement. Sensors **18**, 737 (2018)
14. Han, Z., Fang, Y., Xu, H., Zheng, Y.: A novel FOD classification system based on visual features. In: Proceedings of International Conference on Image and Graphics, pp. 288–296 (2015)
15. Xu, H., Han, Z., Feng, S., Zhou, H., Fang, Y.: Foreign object debris material recognition based on convolutional neural networks. EURASIP J. Image Video Process. **2018**(1), 21 (2018)
16. Sommer, C., Hoefler, R., Samwer, M., Gerlich, D.W.: A deep learning and novelty detection framework for rapid phenotyping in high-content screening. Mol. Biol. Cell **28**(23), 3428–3436 (2017)
17. Lowe, D.-G.: Distinctive image features from scale-invariant keypoints. Int. J. Comput. Vis. **60**(2), 91–110 (2004)
18. Dalal, N., Triggs, B.: Histograms of oriented gradients for human detection. In: Proceedings of IEEE Conference on Computer Vision Pattern Recognition, pp. 886–893 (2005)
19. Ojala, T., Pietikäinen, M., Mäenpää, T.: Multiresolution gray-scale and rotation invariant texture classification with local binary patterns. IEEE Trans. Pattern Anal. Mach. Intell. **7**, 971–987 (2002)
20. Simonyan, K., Zisserman, A.: Very deep convolutional networks for large-scale image recognition. arXiv, arXiv:1409.1556 (2014)
21. Girshick, R., Donahue, J., Darrell, T., Malik, J.: Rich feature hierarchies for accurate object detection and semantic segmentation. In: Proceedings of IEEE Conference on Computer Vision Pattern Recognition, pp. 580–587 (2014)
22. Girshick, R.: Fast R-CNN. In: Proceedings of IEEE International Conference on Computer Vision, pp. 1440–1448 (2015)

23. Ren, S., He, K., Girshick, R.-B., Sun, J.: Faster R-CNN: towards real-time object detection with region proposal networks. In: Proceedings of Advances Neural Information Processing Systems, pp. 91–99 (2015)
24. He, K., Gkioxari, G., Dollár, P., Girshick, R.: Mask R-CNN. In: Proceedings of the IEEE International Conference on Computer Vision, pp. 2961–2969 (2017)
25. Jiang, H., Learned-Miller, E.: Face detection with the faster R-CNN. In: Proceedings of the IEEE International Conference on Automatic Face Gesture Recognition, pp. 650–657 (2017)
26. Uijlings, J.-R., Van De Sande, K.-E., Gevers, T., Smeulders, A.-W.: Selective search for object recognition. Int. J. Comput. Vis. **104**(2), 154–171 (2013)
27. Redmon, J., Divvala, S.-K., Girshick, R.-B., Farhadi, A.: You only look once: unified, real-time object detection. In: Proceedings of the IEEE Conference on Computer Vision Pattern Recognition, pp. 779–788 (2016)
28. Liu, W., et al.: SSD: single shot multibox detector. In: Leibe, B., Matas, J., Sebe, N., Welling, M. (eds.) ECCV 2016. LNCS, vol. 9905, pp. 21–37. Springer, Cham (2016). https://doi.org/10.1007/978-3-319-46448-0_2

Transfer Learning for Improving Lifelog Image Retrieval

Fatma Ben Abdallah[1,2](✉), Ghada Feki[1], Anis Ben Ammar[1],
and Chokri Ben Amar[1]

[1] REGIM-Lab.: REsearch Groups in Intelligent Machines, University of Sfax,
National Engineering School of Sfax (ENIS), BP 1173, 3038 Sfax, Tunisia
{ben.abdallah.fatma,ghada.feki,anis.ben.ammar,chokri.benamar}@ieee.org
[2] Higher Institute of Technological Studies, ISET Kairouan, 3199 Raccada, Tunisia
http://www.regim.org,
http://www.isetkr.rnu.tn/

Abstract. With lifelogging devices; such as wearable camera, smart
watches, audio recorder or standalone smartphone applications; capturing daily moments becomes easier. In recent years, many workshops and
panels have emerged and proposed benchmarks to face challenges in organizing, analyzing, managing, indexing and retrieving specific moments in
the huge amount of multi-modal lifelog dataset. Recent advances in deep
neural networks have given rise to new approaches to deep learning-
based image retrieval. However, using deep neural networks in lifelog
context systems is continuously rising challenges: relying on a convolutional neural network which is trained on images not related to the
retrieval dataset reduced the performance to extract features. In this
paper, we propose a novel fine-tuned Convolutional Neural Network approach based on a Long Short Term Memory processing for improving
lifelog image retrieval. The experimental results show the feasibility and
effectiveness of our approach with encouraging performance by reaching
third place in the ImageCLEF Lifelog Moment Retrieval Task 2018.

Keywords: Lifelog · Image retrieval · Transfer-learning ·
Fine-tuning · Deep learning · Convolutional neural network

1 Introduction

Recently, with the widespread use of smart watches and other sensors to save
personal data, we have noticed the emergence of a new trend called lifelog also
known as egocentric-vision, self-tracking, quantified self and personal data. Several workshops and benchmarks were interested in this area like LTA[1], LSC[2],
NTCIR [13] and ImageCLEF [8]. The goal of the lifelog tasks in this kind of
competition is to create a system that allows to find specific moments in the

---

[1] https://fedcsis.org/2019/lta.
[2] http://lsc.dcu.ie/.

© Springer Nature Switzerland AG 2019
M. Vento and G. Percannella (Eds.): CAIP 2019, LNCS 11678, pp. 284–295, 2019.
https://doi.org/10.1007/978-3-030-29888-3_23

lifelogger's life. It can best be compared to a known-item search task with one or more relevant items per topic [13]. Moments are semantic events or activities that happened throughout one or several days. This kind of system offers many benefits: memory aid [6], diet monitoring [19] and dementia disease monitoring [16]. The major challenge is to find an automatic way to extract and analyze multi-modal data to retrieve relevant images for a query. The dataset provided by the organizers of these competition contains images with erroneous or no annotations, semantic content and biometric information. There is no precise structure or format for this huge amount of data. Therefore, it is difficult to practice conventional image retrieval methods like content-based image retrieval (CBIR) [9] and text-based image retrieval (TBIR) [28]. CBIRs are generally based on low-level features such as texture (Gabor filter or Discrete Wavelet transform), color (histogram) or shape (Fourier descriptor).

In TBIR, a text file is used to store the descriptive concepts for each and every image. It is important in lifelog image retrieval to associate both visual and textual content in a hybrid approach. Indeed, using low-level features is generally not suitable for complex image retrieval tasks due to the semantic gap between such features and high-level human perception.

Deep learning is a new approach that has gone beyond the classical approach of machine learning. Indeed, it allows building models that have shown superior performance in areas such as computer vision and natural language processing. Deep learning has become a must since 2012 after the success of Krizhevsky et al. [15] in the image classification task. In fact, investments in artificial intelligence (AI) technologies have climbed in recent years [7] and this is due to the availability of very large datasets, to a huge computing capacity (GPU) and to very flexible new learning models which are able to manage the dimensionality. In view of the efficiency of deep learning architectures like Convolutional Neural Network (CNN), Recurrent Neural Networks (RNN) or Deep Neural Network (DNN) in computer vision and natural language processing, we proposed in this paper a new deep learning-based approach for lifelog image retrieval using transfer learning also known as fine-tuning.

Our architecture consists of five phases. In the first phase, we use a fine-tuned CNN to classify the lifelog images. We then obtain the concepts and the scores for each image. In the second phase, we create an image inverted index for each lifelogger's day which contains an indexed list of concepts, including the image name and the corresponding score. Seeing that the dataset containing semantic and biometric information in XML format, we rely in the third phase on XQuery FLWOR expression to extract data related to location, activity and time. In the fourth phase, we analyze the query using word embedding and trained a Long Short Memory Term (LSTM) to be able to classify a given query. The last phase, which is online, consists in retrieving relevant images in the inverted index based on the trained LSTM network, the fine-tuned CNN and the XQuery results.

The remainder of this paper is divided into five sections. In Sect. 2, we present recent related works in the deep-learning-based image lifelog retrieval context. In Sect. 3, we detail our approach which is based on several categories of neural networks. Section 4 presents the experimental results of our implementation. Section 5 provides some concluding remarks and suggests future works.

2   Related Works: Lifelog Retrieval Architectures Using Deep Neural Network

Deep neural networks have been widely studied and applied for images classification, human actions recognition, scenes analysis, etc. They have demonstrated their effectiveness in reaching good performance comparable to the best state-of-the-art approaches. On the bases of this observation, we focused our study on existing works which used deep neural networks in their lifelog image retrieval architectures. In the following, firstly we will discuss works which rely only on CNN and DNN pre-trained on ImageNet or Places365 to extract features. Secondly, we will present fine-tuned approach for lifelog image retrieval.

Authors in [10, 20, 21, 23, 26] used Deep CNN Model (AlexNet, GoogleNet, VGGNet, ResNet and LSDA CNN) trained on ImageNet to recognize objects and extract features. Furthermore, Yamamoto et al. [26] exploited these models trained on Places365 to recognize scenes. Zhou et al. [31] utilize CAFFE-CNN visual concept detector to extract concepts from images. Tang et al. in [24] used two DenseNet (Dense Convolutional Network) pre-trained respectively on ImageNet1K and Places365, a DarkNet neural network [22] pre-trained on MSCOCO and a Fast Region-based Convolutional Network [12] pre-trained on Open Images Dataset to generate automatic concept tagging. They consider the fine-tuning as the removing of the useless terms from the query and the manually adding of additional concepts. The authors in [10, 25] also used Fast Region-based Convolutional Network but pre-trained on MSCOCO.

In [10], Dogariu et al. used the InceptionV3 architecture pre-trained on the ImageNet dataset and fine-tuned it on the Food101-dataset to build a food classifier network. Kavallieratou et al. in [14] chose manually true images then trained AlexNet and GoogleNet on it. The authors in [18] developed a general framework to translate lifelog images into features. They fine-tuned VGG-16 pre-trained on ImageNet1K by replacing the last layer which contains 1000 neurons with 634, followed by sigmoid activation instead of softmax function.

According to Babenko et al. [5] performance is improved on standard retrieval benchmarks when the network is re-trained with a dataset that is closer to the target task. The authors demonstrated a significant improvement in the search performance of the neural network when it is trained on a dataset which is similar to the one encountered during the test phase. This opinion is confirmed by the official results of NTCIR-13 [13] which placed the work of Lin et al. [18] first followed by the work of Yamamoto et al. [26] which did not use fine-tuning.

Previous works were carried out on large images datasets and used different CNNs. The choice of such CNNs is not justified by the authors. In this work, as a preliminary study, we chose to work with AlexNet and GoogleNet and to replace the last layers of these CNNs. In the near future, we intend to evaluate other methods of fine-tuning. Despite the manual effort required to construct training dataset, fine-tuning method outperforms those use only pre-trained CNN on ImageNet1K, Places365, MSCOCO or Open Images dataset.

3   Our Proposed Approach: Transfer Learning CNN for Image Lifelog Retrieval

Creating a network from scratch is expensive in terms of expertise, equipment and the amount of annotated data needed. First of all, we must fix the architecture of the network, the number of layers, their sizes and the matrix operations that connect them. The training then consists of optimizing the network coefficients to minimize the output classification error. This training can take several weeks for the best CNNs, with many Graphics Processing Unit (GPU) working on hundreds of thousands of annotated images. For practical purposes, it is possible to harness the power of CNNs without being an expert in the field, with accessible hardware and a reasonable amount of annotated data. The complexity of creating CNN can be avoided by adapting publicly available pre-trained networks. These techniques are called transfer learning because the knowledge acquired on a general classification problem is exploited to apply it again to a particular problem. Our proposed approach which is based on five phases is presented in Fig. 1: (1) the fine-tuned CNN, (2) the image inverted index generation, (3) the semantic data extraction, (4) the query analysis and (5) the retrieval of relevant images according to a specific query. This approach is an evolution of our previous works described in [1,3]. We detail each phase in the following.

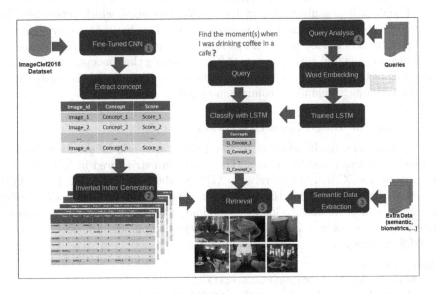

Fig. 1. Image lifelog retrieval architecture based on transfer learning CNN

3.1   Fine-Tuned CNN

Fine tuning involves using a pre-trained model as initialization for training on a new problem. The interest is twofold: we use an architecture carefully optimized by specialists, and we take advantage of features extraction capabilities learned on a publicly dataset. Fine Tuning on images consists of taking a visual system already well trained on a classification task to refine it on a similar task. To do this, we replace the last layer of the CNN by a layer with n neurons where n represents the number of categories. To avoid modifications on the ratios of sizes between successive layers, which correspond to reductions in the size of the information, we added an intermediate layer before the output and changed the size of the previous layers.

In our experimentation, we use Googlenet and Alexnet on 2184 images organized in 48 categories. For the training of the fine-tuned Googlenet, we froze the initial 110 layers and we only adapted the final layers for the new classification problem. Freezing all the convolutional layers gives as final classifier a pre-initialized multilayer perceptron. Indeed, the pre-trained network has already optimized coefficients carefully on a large dataset. We need to modify them weakly with each iteration, to adapt smoothly to the new problem, without aggressively crushing the knowledge already acquired. For this, we used a low learning rate in the order of 10^{-4}.

3.2   Image Inverted Index Generation

The inverted index is the mechanism used by the search engines. It is a compact structure effective and well-tried on which the search operations can be carried out. The data is organized in a matrix, called incidence, which represents the occurrence (or not) of each word in each document. The image inverted index is similar to the inverted index except that we no longer manipulate documents but images associated with concepts. After extracting the concepts' list from the last layer of the fine-tuned CNN, we generated for each day of the lifelogger, a matrix with images names as column and concepts as rows.

3.3   Semantic-Based Data Extraction

Lifelog data contains in addition to the images, semantic information describing human activity and biometrics. These data are structured in XML file. To navigate in the XML tree, we rely on XQuery which uses some of the XPATH language. For example, for the topic «Find the moments when I was having dinner at home», we need to intersect the images containing the concept dinner with the images taken at home between 6 pm and 10 pm with the above XQuery FLWOR expression:

```
xquery version "1.0";
let $doc := doc('lifelog_metadata.xml')
for $i in $doc//location[1]/name[1][contains(text(),'Home')]
let $minute :=$i//ancestor::minute[1][@id>=1080 and @id<=1320]
return $minute//images[1]/image[1]/image-id[1]
```

3.4 LSTM-Based Query Analysis

Generally, to answer the user query, the majority of retrieval models represent documents and queries in the form of «bag of words». Although widely used, this type of representation does not allow capturing the meaning of words and the potential relationships between these words, which are expressed more precisely by the structure and order in which the terms are presented. In order to capture better representations, we exploit deep learning based on neural networks. These networks, thanks to their multi-layer structuring, are able to generate abstract representations to capture the semantics of the document content. Particularly in the context of natural language processing [17], neural networks allow learning complex words representations and capture more complex relationships (other than the co-occurrence) between the terms. This model allows to model semantic relations between terms via mathematical expressions.

Our work is inspired by state-of-the-art approaches, particularly those that exploit words embeddings to improve retrieval results [4,11,27]. For that purpose, we build a document which contains labelled textual descriptions of queries moments. Then we convert the words to numeric vectors by training a word embedding with dimension 100 and 50 epochs. After that, we create and train an LSTM network based on the sequences of word vectors using the stochastic gradient descent with momentum (SGDM) optimizer with learning rate 0.05.

3.5 Doc2sequence-Based Retrieval

All the previous phases described above are offline. Only the retrieval is done online. The proposed approach for the retrieval process is based on the trained LSTM, the fine-tuned CNN and the XQuery FLWOR expression results. Firstly, we classify the query using the trained LSTM network. We then obtain the concepts that we are working on in the inverted index. Secondly, we search the concepts in the inverted index then we extract the relevant images with scores. After that, we realized an intersection between the results got from the fine-tuning and those obtained by XQuery FLWOR expression. Finally, we sort the results based on the highest scores.

4 Experimentation

4.1 Challenge Description

ImageCLEF Lifelog Moment Retrieval Task (LMRT) 2018 aims to provide comparative benchmarks to promote research into lifelogging by creating multimodal test collections [8]. The ImageCLEF Lifelog LMRT dataset contains 50 days of a lifelogger: 18.854 GB of data distributed in 80 440 images captured with OMG Autographer wearable camera and annotated using Microsoft Computer Vision API, semantic content (locations and activities), biometrics information and music listening history described in XML format. The goal of the lifelog tasks is to create a system that allows to find specific moments in the lifelogger's life.

4.2   Settings

We use Intel(R) Core(TM) i5-4430 CPU @3.00 Ghz with 16GB RAM. Our architecture is implemented using Neural Network, Parallel Computing Toolbox and GPU coder which generates CUDA from MATLAB.

For assessing performance, we used the metrics below:

- Cluster Recall at X (CR@X): a metric that assesses how many different clusters from the ground truth are represented among the top X results. The CR@X equation is done by (1).

$$CR@X = \frac{Number\,of\,detected\,cluster\,for\,top\,n\,images}{Number\,of\,estimated\,cluster\,for\,top\,n\,images} \tag{1}$$

- Precision at X (P@X): measures the number of relevant photos among the top X results. The P@X equation is done by (2)

$$P@X = \frac{Relevant\,extracted\,images\,at\,n}{n} \tag{2}$$

- F1-measure at X (F1@X): the harmonic mean of the previous two. The F1@X equation is done by (3)

$$F1@X = 2 * \frac{P@n*CR@n}{P@n+CR@n} \tag{3}$$

4.3   Retrieval Refinement with Fine-Tuned CNN

Alexnet is trained on more than one million images and can classify images into 1000 object categories. The network has five convolutional layers and three fully connected layers. The last three layers of the pre-trained network net are configured for 1000 classes.

In our work, we transfer the layers to the new classification task by replacing the last three layers with a fully connected layer, a softmax layer, and a classification output layer. We set the fully connected layer to have the same size as the number of classes in the new data. Our new dataset contains 2184 images organized in 48 categories. We divide these data into training and validation data sets. We use 70% of the images for training and 30% for validation. The network requires input images of size $227 \times 227 \times 3$, but the images in the dataset have different sizes. We use an augmentation on images to automatically resize the training images. Data augmentation helps prevent the network from overfitting and memorizing the exact details of the training images.

To perform the fine-tuning, we initialize by the convolutional layers of AlexNet. Then, we use a learning rate equal to 10^{-4} for 10 epochs with 912 iterations, momentum 0.9 and batch size 10.

We detailed in Fig. 2 (a, b, c and d) classic metrics that had been deployed. Various cut off points are considered: X = 5, 10, 20, 30, 40, 50. In our proposed approach, we try the fine-tuning using Alexnet and Googlenet. Despite that Googlenet obtained 6.67% at top-5 error rate in the ImageNet Large Scale Visual Recognition Challenge (ILSVRC) versus 15.3% for Alexnet, Alexnet gave best results in our participation at the ImageCLEFlifelog LMRT Task 2018. For our part, we speculate that this is because we freeze the weights of earlier layers in the network by setting the learning rates in those layers to zero. Indeed, Babenko et al. [5] observed that best performance is not on the upper layer, but rather at the layer that is two levels below the outputs. Furthermore, Zhi et al. [30] found that deleting higher pre-trained layers gives an improvement in performance. Specifically, Zheng et al. [29] find that the pooled Conv5 features produce better or competitive performance to fully connected features. Our future investigations will deal with the performance's improvement based on the analysis of the different layers. We will also consider designing a new deep learning network for lifelogging tasks.

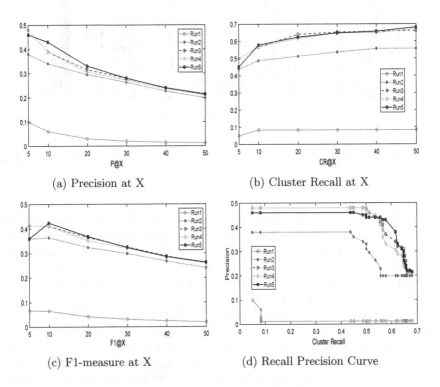

(a) Precision at X

(b) Cluster Recall at X

(c) F1-measure at X

(d) Recall Precision Curve

Fig. 2. Classic metrics: Precision, Cluster Recall and F1-measure

4.4 Comparison with the Other Architectures in the ImageCLEF LMRT 2018

We participated with our approach [2] in the ImageCLEF LMRT 2018 [8]. The participants have to retrieve 10 specific topics (LST001 to LST010 detailed in [8]) in a lifelogger life. Five other teams have participated: AILab-GTI [14], HCMUS [25], NLP-Lab [24], CAMPUS-UPB [10] and the Organizers team [32].

Official ranking metrics was the F1-measure@10, which gives equal importance to diversity (via CR@10) and relevance (via P@10). The Fig. 3 detail the official results based on F1@10 measure. As we can see, our approach was the only one to provide a result greater than zero for the 10 topics. We reached the third place with 0.424 behind AILabGTi Team [14] with 0.545 and HCMUS Team [25] with 0.479.

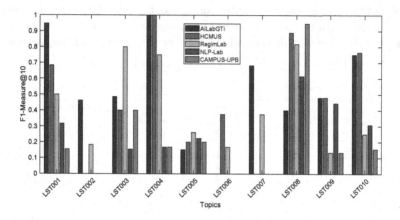

Fig. 3. ImageCLEF LMRT teams results comparison per topic in term of F1-measure@10

For the topic LST003: «Find the moment(s) when I was drinking coffee in a cafe», we obtained the best result. Indeed, the performance depends strongly on the number of examples provided during the fine-tuning. The details of this information is not given by the other teams. It would be interesting to compare this and to make a relationship between the number of examples to provide for transfer learning and the CNN performance.

We submitted 5 runs on the ImageCLEF LMRT subtask. The first run is exploiting only the concepts provided by the ImageCLEF LMRT organizers. The second run is using the fine-tuned Googlenet network. The third run is using the fine-tuned Alexnet network. In the fourth run, we cross the result of the two previous runs and sorted the scores. In the fifth run, we intersect the result of the best run with the result of XQuery FLWOR expression applied to the semantic XML file.

Best result was given by the fifth run which exploits metadata that contains location, activity and time information. The worst result was given by the first run which is based only on the concepts provided by the organizers. Indeed, the organizers Team [32] reached the last place in this challenge. As they say, without human intervention, the results can be near to zero. This demonstrated that the key challenge is to find advanced methods to translate the query to exploitable concepts by aggregate information from the multi-modal lifelog data.

The AILab-GTI Team [14] also used fine-tuning with Alexnet and Googlenet with various strategies (two-class, ten-class and eleven-class). By analyzing more in details the runs of this team, we found that Alexnet outstrip Googlenet for the ten-class strategy, from $X = 20$ for the two-class strategy and from $X = 40$ for the eleven-class strategy.

5 Discussions

AILabGTi Team [14] and HCMUS Team [25] have preceded us in the Image-CLEF LMRT Task thanks to the human in the loop method during the retrieval process. AILabGTi Team manually split the results into the classes after the fine-tuning. HCMUS Team implied the user to retrieve and then to filter the given results. In addition to that, they manually choose the best results to submit. Their systems were designed to assist the user and not to retrieve automatically the images. We have a doubt concerning the generalization of these approaches on another lifelog dataset with other topics. Our work didn't involve the user in the automatic retrieval phase. Our trained LSTM is able to find concepts related to any query for other unknown topics. Due to lack of time during the LMRT Task, we organized manually 2184 images in 48 categories for the fine-tuning. We also built manually a document which contains labeled textual descriptions of queries moments for training a word embedding. We expect to automate these procedures in the next ImageCLEF Lifelog 2019 competition. Thus, automatically transcribe the query concepts into the retrieval process is still a challenge which needs further investigations. The improvement and stabilization of our system could lead to the creation of a memory recall system for people with impairments and memory disorders such as people with Alzheimer's disease or focal epilepsy. It can be also used to analyze patterns to prevent depression, anxiety, anorexia or other psychological distress.

6 Conclusion

This paper has presented a new deep learning-based approach for improving lifelog image retrieval. Deep neural networks lifelog image retrieval architectures have been reviewed and limits highlighted. The experimental results on a publicly available dataset reflect the efficiency of the proposed solution. These results have demonstrated a significant improvement in the search performance of the neural network when it is trained on a dataset which is similar to the one encountered during the test phase.

As future works, we will investigate on the effect of varying the fine-tuned methods and parameters on the performance. Moreover, we will focus on pre-processing the noisy, blurred and uninformative lifelog images. In addition to that, we will work on training CNN from scratch to study the possibility of improvement.

Acknowledgments. The research leading to these results has received funding from the Ministry of Higher Education and Scientific Research of Tunisia under the grant agreement number LR11ES48.

References

1. Ben Abdallah, F., Feki, G., Ben Ammar, A., Ben Amar, C.: A new model driven architecture for deep learning-based multimodal lifelog retrieval. In: Poster Proceedings: International Conference WSCG, CSRN 2803, Czech Republic, pp. 8–17 (2018)
2. Ben Abdallah, F., Feki, G., Ezzarka, M., Ben Ammar, A., Ben Amar, C.: Regim lab team at ImageCLEF lifelog moment retrieval task 2018. In: Working Notes of CLEF 2018, France (2018)
3. Ben Abdallah, F., Feki, G., Ben Ammar, A., Ben Amar, C.: Multilevel deep learning-based processing for lifelog image retrieval enhancement. In: Proceedings of the IEEE International Conference SMC, Japan, pp. 1348–1354 (2018)
4. Ai, Q., Yang, L., Guo, J., Croft, W.B.: Improving language estimation with the paragraph vector model for ad-hoc retrieval. In: Proceedings of the 39th International ACM SIGIR, USA, pp. 869–872 (2016)
5. Babenko, A., Slesarev, A., Chigorin, A., Lempitsky, V.: Neural codes for image retrieval. In: Fleet, D., Pajdla, T., Schiele, B., Tuytelaars, T. (eds.) ECCV 2014. LNCS, vol. 8689, pp. 584–599. Springer, Cham (2014). https://doi.org/10.1007/978-3-319-10590-1_38
6. Browne, G., et al.: SenseCam improves memory for recent events and quality of life in a patient with memory retrieval difficulties. Memory **19**, 713–722 (2011)
7. Crawford, K., Calo, R.: There is a blind spot in AI research. Nature **538**(7625), 311 (2016)
8. Dang-Nguyen, D.-T., Piras, L., Riegler, M., Zhou, L., Lux, M., Gurrin, C.: Overview of ImageCLEFlifelog 2018: daily living understanding and lifelog moment retrieval. In: CLEF2018 Working Notes, CEUR-WS.org (2018)
9. Datta, R., Li, J., Wang, J.: Content-based image retrieval: approaches and trends of the new age. In: Multimedia Information Retrieval, pp. 253–262 (2005)
10. Dogariu, M., Ionescu, B.: Multimedia lab@ ImageCLEF 2018 lifelog moment retrieval task. In: Working Notes of CLEF 2018 - Conference and Labs of the Evaluation Forum, Avignon, France (2018)
11. Ganguly, D., Roy, D., Mitra, M., Jones, G.J.: Word embedding based generalized language model for information retrieval. In: Proceedings of the 38th International ACM SIGIR Conference on Research and Development in Information Retrieval, pp. 795–798. ACM (2015)
12. Girshick, R.: Fast R-CNN. In: Proceedings of the 2015 IEEE ICCV, Chile, pp. 1440–1448 (2015)
13. Gurrin, C., et al.: Overview of NTCIR-13 Lifelog-2 task. In: Proceedings of the Thirteenth NTCIR conference, Japan (2017)
14. Kavallieratou, E., del-Blanco, C.-R., Cuevas, C., Garcia, N.: Retrieving events in life logging. In: CLEF (Working Notes), CEUR-WS.org, France, vol. 2125 (2018)
15. Krizhevsky, A., Sutskever, I., Hinton, G.E.: ImageNet classification with deep convolutional neural networks. In: Proceedings of the 25th International Conference on Neural Information Processing Systems, NIPS 2012, USA, vol. 1, pp. 1097–1105 (2012)
16. Mégret, R., et al.: The IMMED project: wearable video monitoring of people with age dementia. In: Proceedings of the 18th ACM International Conference on Multimedia, pp. 1299–1302 (2010)

17. Mikolov, T., Yih, W.-T., Zweig, G.: Linguistic regularities in continuous space word representations. In: Proceedings of the 2013 Conference of the North American Chapter of the Association for Computational Linguistics: Human Language Technologies, pp. 746–751 (2013)
18. Lin, J., et al.: VCI2R at the NTCIR-13 Lifelog-2 lifelog semantic access task. In: Proceedings 13th NTCIR Conference, Japan (2017)
19. O'Loughlin, G., et al.: Using a wearable camera to increase the accuracy of dietary analysis. Am. J. Prev. Med. 44, 297–301 (2013)
20. Oliveira Barra, G., Ayala, A.C., Bolanos, M., Dimiccoli, M., Giro i Nieto, X., Radeva P.: LEMoRe: a lifelog engine for moments retrieval at the NTCIR-lifelog LSAT task. In: Proceedings of the 12th NTCIR Conference, Japan (2016)
21. Oliveira-Barra, G., Dimiccoli, M., Radeva, P.: Leveraging activity indexing for egocentric image retrieval. In: Alexandre, L., Salvador Sánchez, J., Rodrigues, J. (eds.) IbPRIA 2017. LNCS, vol. 10255, pp. 295–303. Springer, Cham (2017). https://doi.org/10.1007/978-3-319-58838-4_33
22. Redmon, J., Farhadi, A.: YOLO9000: better, faster, stronger. In: Proceedings of the IEEE Conference on CVPR, pp. 7263–7271 (2017)
23. Safadi, B., Mulhem, P., Quénot, G., Chevallet, J.-P.: LIG-MRIM at NTCIR-12 lifelog semantic access task. In: Proceedings of 12th NTCIR Conference, Japan (2016)
24. Tang, T., Fu, M., Huang, H., Chen, K., Chen, H.: Visual concept selection with textual knowledge for understanding activities of daily living and life moment retrieval. In: Working Notes of CLEF 2018, France (2018)
25. Tran, M., Truong, T., Duy, T.D., Vo-Ho, V., Luong, Q., Nguyen, V.: Lifelog moment retrieval with visual concept fusion and text-based query expansion. Working Notes of CLEF 2018, France (2018)
26. Yamamoto, S., Nishimura, T., Akagi, Y., Takimoto, Y., Inoue, T., Toda, H.: PBG at the NTCIR-13 lifelog-2 LAT, LSAT, and LEST tasks. In: Proceedings of the 13th NTCIR Conference, Japan (2017)
27. Zamani, H., Croft, W.B.: Estimating embedding vectors for queries. In: Proceedings of the 2016 ACM International Conference on the Theory of Information Retrieval, ICTIR 2016, New York, USA, pp. 123–132 (2016)
28. Zare, M.R., Woo, C.S., Ismail, J.N.: Comparative analysis of image retrieval approaches. In: Abu Osman, N.A., Ibrahim, F., Wan Abas, W.A.B., Abdul Rahman, H.S., Ting, H.N. (eds.) 4th Kuala Lumpur International Conference on Biomedical Engineering 2008. IFMBE Proceedings, vol. 21, pp. 847–850. Springer, Heidelberg (2008). https://doi.org/10.1007/978-3-540-69139-6_209
29. Zheng, L., Zhao, Y., Wang, S., Wang, J., Tian, Q.: Good Practice in CNN Feature Transfer, CoRR, abs/1604.00133 (2016)
30. Zhi, W., Chen, Z., Yueng, H.W.F., Lu, Z., Zandavi, S.M., Chung, Y.Y.: Layer removal for transfer learning with deep convolutional neural networks. In: Liu, D., Xie, S., Li, Y., Zhao, D., El-Alfy, E.S. (eds.) ICONIP 2017. LNCS, vol. 10635, pp. 460–469. Springer, Cham (2017). https://doi.org/10.1007/978-3-319-70096-0_48
31. Zhou, L., Piras, L., Riegler, M., Boato, G., Dang-Nguyen, D., Gurrin, C.: Organizer team at ImageCLEFlifelog 2017: baseline approaches for lifelog retrieval and summarization. In: Working Notes of CLEF 2017, Ireland (2017)
32. Zhou, L., Piras, L., Riegler, M., Lux, M., Dang-Nguyen1, D.T., Gurrin, C.: An interactive lifelog retrieval system for activities of daily living understanding. In: Working Notes of CLEF 2018, France (2018)

Data Sets and Benchmarks

Which Is Which? Evaluation of Local Descriptors for Image Matching in Real-World Scenarios

Fabio Bellavia[(✉)] and Carlo Colombo

CVG/DINFO, University of Florence, via di S. Marta 3, 50134 Firenze, Italy
{fabio.bellavia,carlo.colombo}@unifi.it,
http://cvg.dsi.unifi.it/wisw.caip2019

Abstract. Matching with local image descriptors is a fundamental task in many computer vision applications. This paper describes the WISW contest held within the framework of the CAIP 2019 conference, aimed at benchmarking recent descriptors in challenging planar and non-planar real image matching scenarios. According to the contest results, the descriptors submitted to the competition, most of which based on deep learning, perform significantly better than the current state-of-the-art in image matching. Nonetheless, there is still room for improvement, especially in the case of non-planar scenes.

Keywords: Local image descriptors · Image matching · Deep descriptors

1 Introduction

Local image descriptors [13] play a critical role in establishing reliable point correspondences among several images in many computer vision applications, such as image stitching [8], 3D reconstruction [32] and visual odometry [15]. Research on this topic is still very active today. Impressive advances have been obtained in the last few years both with handcrafted and data-driven descriptors, thanks to careful modeling and design strategies, deep learning architectures, big data and efficient hardware.

The "Which is Which? Evaluation of local descriptors for image matching in real-world scenarios" (WISW) contest, held within the framework of the CAIP 2019 conference, was aimed at benchmarking recent descriptors in challenging real image matching scenarios, facing with both planar and non-planar scenes. This paper reports the rationale, setup protocols and datasets employed in the contest, and comparatively analyzes the results achieved by the competing descriptors, also in relation to the state-of-the-art in the field. There were seven different submissions by four distinct research groups. The submitted descriptors were all brand new and in some cases still unpublished. According to the results, the competing local image descriptors, although designed as variants of

© Springer Nature Switzerland AG 2019
M. Vento and G. Percannella (Eds.): CAIP 2019, LNCS 11678, pp. 299–310, 2019.
https://doi.org/10.1007/978-3-030-29888-3_24

previous approaches, generally showed remarkable improvements with respect to the state-of-the-art. Descriptors based on deep learning showed to achieve the most important enhancements.

The paper is organized as follows. Motivation and related work on local image descriptor benchmarks are presented in Sect. 2. Datasets and setup protocols for both the planar and non-planar scenarios are defined in Sect. 3. Baseline and submitted descriptors are described in Sect. 4. Results are discussed in Sect. 5, and conclusions are outlined in Sect. 6, together with some directions for future work.

2   Motivation and Related Work

The factors that affect the matching accuracy and robustness of local image descriptors include the scene content, the image transformations involved, and the requirements in terms of computational efficiency (both in space and time). Adaptability to non-planar scene content and relevant viewpoint changes are the most important properties that a good descriptor must have in order to be used in general, real-world image matching applications.

The most consolidated benchmarks on local image descriptors contemplate planar scenes only and are based on the standard Oxford evaluation protocol [21,23]. The recent HPatches [2] is perhaps the most representative planar benchmark. In HPatches, ground-truth matches are estimated according to the overlap error, that can be obtained without ambiguity using image patches and their homography-based reprojections. Local patches are preferred over images as input, as they limit the influence of factors other than the descriptor itself on matching performance. Following such protocol, the planar evaluation case of the WISW benchmark also uses patches as input. On the other hand, differently from HPatches, custom patch orientations are allowed, since these are an integral part of the descriptor. Moreover, besides viewpoint transformations, typically considered by HPatches, their combinations with other illumination changes, blur and noise effects are also considered in WISW (illumination changes are also benchmarked by HPatches, but separately from viewpoint changes). At any rate, evaluation on planar scenes provides only a limited insight into descriptors since, for instance, it is not able to analyze and investigate the accuracy in the presence of self-occlusions in a real 3D scene.

In order to overcome the limitations of planar scenes, non-planar scenes have also been used in recent benchmarks. For this purpose, ground-truth was directly estimated (a) using stereo matching [16] or Structure-from-Motion [30], (b) through complex sensor-based system setups [12,33], or (c) according to some approximation scheme [6,26]. Alternative benchmarks were also proposed, that characterize indirectly matching robustness (d) by checking the correctness of the output for a given specific application task, such as object retrieval [14] or visual odometry [7]. However, none of these approaches is without drawbacks, since ground-truth may not be available for some image region (a, b), it can be erroneously estimated (a, c, d), or it can be biased towards the considered application (a, d). In WISW, the benchmark for non-planar scenes first introduced in [3], and based on a piecewise approximation of the overlap error, is used. As shown in Sect. 3.2, this benchmark is a natural extension of the planar benchmark, it can always provide ground-truth data with a low false positive rate, and it is not biased towards any specific application.

3   Benchmark Setup

Figure 1 shows the patch extraction pipeline adopted for WISW. There are several aspects that can influence the evaluation, including the keypoint detector employed, the patch normalization strategy, the distance used to compare the descriptors, and the matching strategy by which to assign putative correspondences. In order to have a fair comparison without ambiguities, for the contest most the above factors were fixed in advance. The HarrisZ [5] detector was used to extract affine patches (Fig. 1a), that were then normalized into circles with radius of $48 \times \sqrt{2} \approx 68$ pixels, extending by a factor of $\sqrt{2}$ the original normalized circular region of 48 pixels radius (Fig. 1b). Pixels outside the extended circular patch were masked. Contest participants could optionally assign their own orientation to the patch, by computing it on the 97×97 square patch (marked in white in Fig. 1b, $97 = 1 + 2 \times 48$) inside the extended patch. A default orientation for each patch was provided, computed by the deep learning approach described in [40] trained on EdgeFoci [41] patches. The extended and rotated circular patches (Fig. 1c) were then cropped into the final 97×97 square patches (Fig. 1d), and provided as input to descriptors.

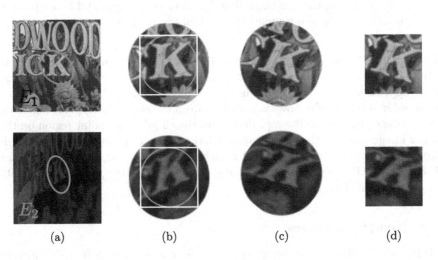

(a)   (b)   (c)   (d)

Fig. 1. Patch extraction process for two corresponding keypoints. Please refer to the text for details. (Best viewed in color, color figure online)

For a given pair of images, a matrix representing the distance between all the keypoint pairs of the two images was generated by the contest participants.

Such matrix reflects the kind of distance employed by the descriptor, but can also allow one to exploit descriptor distance statistics inside images, as done in [4]. Finally, the distance table was employed to extract the best matches according to their distance in a greedy way, so as to avoid that two matches share a common keypoint. The matches were then ordered according to the Nearest Neighbor Ratio (NNR) [19]. Since NNR is asymmetric and depends on which image is taken as reference, a symmetric version considering the average between the two possible choices was used. Using the proposed workflow, descriptor input is fixed as for HPatches [2] but, differently from it, the definition of custom orientations is allowed.

Notice that the WISW benchmark does not consider running times and computational efficiency, since these parameters are strongly dependent on the hardware and software implementations (e.g. CPU, SIMD, GPU). Moreover, emerging deep learning approaches to image matching that bind together keypoint detector and descriptor [9,28,39] are excluded from the comparison, since the proposed benchmark fixes the keypoint detector to focus only on local image descriptor behavior.

3.1 Planar Scenes

Dataset. The dataset employed consists of 15 different scenes of 6 images each, for a total of $15 \times (6-1) = 75$ image pairs. The scenes include "Bark", "Boat", "Graffiti" and "Wall" from the Oxford dataset [22], the whole Viewpoint dataset [40] and 6 new scenes (see Fig. 2). In addition to viewpoint changes, the new scenes also include at the same time illumination changes, blur and Moiré pattern noise, thus increasing the complexity of the image transformations at hand.

Evaluation Protocol. Planar scene evaluation follows the protocol described in [21]. The overlap error, computed according to [18] (i.e., without employing discrete approximations as in [21]), is used to define ground-truth matches. A match is considered correct if the overlap error between the elliptical keypoint region on the reference image and the reprojection of the elliptical keypoint region on the other image through the homography relating the viewpoint transformation is less than 50% (see Fig. 3). Finally, for each input image pair, the mean Average Precision (mAP) is computed from the precision/recall curve, interpolating data as described in [10].

3.2 Non-planar Scenes

Dataset. The dataset for the non-planar case contains images from 35 different scenes used in other works (19 having 3 images, the remaining 16 with 2 images only), for a total of $(19 \times 3) + 16 = 73$ image pairs. The dataset extends the one used in [3], which included only 42 image pairs (see the first two rows of Fig. 4 for some examples). Notice that in addition to the images to probe, this dataset contains reference matches that are employed both for computing the approximated overlap error and for refining correspondences according to their local flow [3].

(a) DD (b) OP

(c) Screen (d) Spidey

(e) Floor (f) Marilyn

Fig. 2. Sample image pairs from the new six planar scenes included in the benchmark. (Best viewed in color, color figure online)

Evaluation Protocol. Non-planar scene evaluation follows the protocol described in [3], employing the approximated overlap error defined in [6] for computing the ground-truth. Unlike other non-planar benchmarks, the approximated overlap relies on the whole local descriptor patch and not on the keypoint position only, thus being a natural extension of the overlap error to the non-planar case. This benchmark was shown to give a very low false positive rate (less than 5%), which does not affect descriptor ranking in unsupervised evaluations [6]. Similarly to the planar case, the approximated overlap error threshold was set to 50%. Unlike the planar case, the number of total correct matches employed to compute the recall denominator is not established by considering all the possible keypoint pair combinations, but only the union set of all the putative matches output by all the descriptors included in the contest. This is done to reduce false positive matches in the estimation of the total number of matches. It was verified that this way to compute the mAP does not change the relative rank between descriptors, when applied to the planar case, although mAP values may slightly differ when some descriptors are removed from or added to the evaluation (compare columns $\square$ and $\boxed{\mathbb{D}}$ in Table 1 later in the evaluation). Example of correct matches according to the approximated overlap error are shown in the last row of Fig. 4.

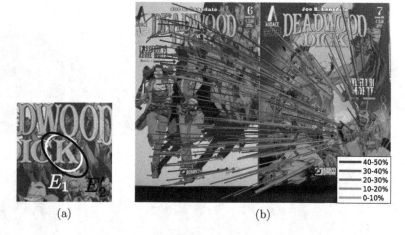

(a)   (b)

Fig. 3. Planar scene evaluation. (a) Overlap error computation for the two keypoints E_1 and E_2 in Fig. 1, belonging to the image pair in Fig. 2a. The elliptical keypoint region E_2 is reprojected into E_2' through the viewpoint homography and the overlap error is computed as $1 - (E_1 \cap E_2')/(E_1 \cup E_2')$. (b) Flow lines for correct matches among all those evaluated in the contest, different color intensities correspond to different overlap error values. (Best viewed in color and zoomed in, color figure online)

4   Local Image Descriptors Under Evaluation

Seven local image descriptors were submitted to WISW. These include **SOSNet** [35], still unpublished at contest time, the recent **HardNet$_A$** [29], obtained by training HardNet [24] on AMOS [29] and other datasets, **RalNet Shuffle** using the RalNet architecture [38] and additionally cropping and shuffling patches at training time, and **RsGLOH2**, "square rooting" sGLOH2 [4] according to RootSIFT [1]. Two variants of HardNet$_A$, exploiting the deep networks described in [25] either for custom orientation assignment or to accommodate patches before extracting the descriptor, were also submitted as **OriNet+HardNet$_A$** and **AffNet+HardNet$_A$**, respectively. The contest also included a variant of

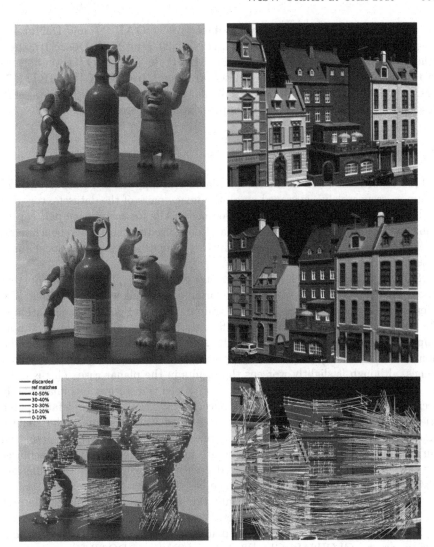

Fig. 4. (1st, 2nd rows) First and second images for two non-planar scene pairs included in the benchmark. (3th row) Flow lines for correct matches among all those evaluated in the contest, together with flow of reference matches and of matches discarded by local flow heuristic. Different color intensities correspond to different approximated overlap error values. (Best viewed in color and zoomed in, color figure online)

BisGLOH2 [4], named **BisGLOH2***, using more rotations at matching time than the default ones. With the exception of the handcrafted RsGLOH2 and BisGLOH2*, all the submitted descriptors were data-driven deep descriptors.

In addition to the descriptors submitted to the contest, several recent state-of-the-art descriptors were included as baseline, for a total of 22 descriptors. These include seven deep descriptors, i.e. **GeoDesc** [20], **DOAP** [17] and **L2Net** [34] together with their binary versions, **HardNet** [24], and **DeepDesc** [31], three other kinds of data-driven descriptors, i.e. **MIOP** [36] and **RFD** [11] (in both its two variants), and five handcrafted descriptors, i.e., **RootSIFT** [1], **MKD** [27], **LIOP** [37], **sGLOH2** [4] (in both its regular and binary versions). For baseline descriptors, their publicly available implementations were employed.

5   Evaluation Results

Table 1 reports the mAP in the case of planar and non-planar scenes ($\square$ and $\boxplus$ columns, respectively), averaged on all the image pairs of the datasets, together with the main descriptor properties. Detailed mAPs for each image pair can be found online[1], together with the code and data used in the WISW benchmark, freely available for reproducibility and further comparisons on future local image descriptors.

SOSNet is the best performing descriptor on both the planar and non-planar cases. The results of HardNet$_A$ and its variants, that follow in the ranking, also offer clear insights about the impact of training data and patch normalization in the matching process. HardNet$_A$ significantly improves on HardNet by simply employing a better training set. At the same time, affine patch accommodation thanks to AffNet preprocessing appears to be very suitable for non-planar scenes, although it slightly worsens the results in the planar case. This is quite reasonable, since being able to tolerate more patch transformations unavoidably decreases the discrimination power. Concerning OriNet [25], the default patch orientation system of the deep network detailed in [40] seems to be slightly better, possibly due to the difference between the keypoint detector employed during training and that used to generate input patches. RsGLOH2 achieves the best results among the handcrafted descriptors, while RalNet Shuffle and BisGLOH2* are comparable with average baseline descriptors.

Considering baseline descriptors only, the recent GeoDesc achieves the best results, followed by HardNet and L2Net. With our benchmark, HardNet obtains slightly better results than L2Net on planar scenes and slightly worse on non-planar scenes. sGLOH2, BisGLOH2, binary L2Net and DOAP follow next. As for L2Net and HardNet, sGLOH2 and BisGLOH2 are better than DOAP on non-planar scenes and worse on planar scenes. MKD and RootSIFT come next, followed by the remaining descriptors.

With respect to a recent evaluation using a very similar setup protocol [3], some differences in the descriptor relative rank can be noted (e.g. RootSIFT in WISW evaluation is better than RFD, as opposed to what reported in [3]). More than to the different number of image pairs evaluated (almost doubled in WISW), this is due to a better input patch registration and to the final matching strategy in the proposed benchmark (mAP results on the same planar and non-planar scene datasets of [3] are reported as columns $\boxplus$ and $\square$ in the

---

[1] https://drive.google.com/open?id=1P1easA8UwmFyAVYzu2K4tk4zu88Jg4Px.

Table 1, respectively). This underlines a critical issue when designing the matching pipeline, since descriptors more tolerant to inaccurate patch registration can be less discriminative. Finally, in order to consider possible inaccuracies in the ground-truth estimation due to false positives in the non-planar scenes, average mAP excluding scenes with very low mAP have been computed, but no relevant changes in descriptor rank were observed (compare columns 𝔼 and 𝔻 in the Table 1, where only two image pairs were removed).

Table 1. Contest evaluation results

		mAP (%)						info				
	▷	🗗	🔲	🗐	🗖	🗗	⚑	🛠	⟲	🔖	#	type
L_2	SOSNet	76.30	77.58	74.01	53.40	54.73	60.76	✓			[35]	128	float
	AffNet+HardNet$_A$	74.11	75.09	71.71	52.34	53.64	59.98	✓			[25,29]	128	uchar
	OriNet+HardNet$_A$	73.50	74.38	71.14	49.92	51.22	57.09	✓			[25,29]	128	uchar
	HardNet$_A$	74.29	75.22	72.14	50.08	51.38	57.47	✓			[29]	128	uchar
	GeoDesc	75.60	76.67	71.83	47.56	48.78	55.47				[20]	128	uchar
	HardNet	71.49	72.17	68.86	47.80	49.01	55.37				[25,29]	128	uchar
	L2Net	69.49	70.20	66.97	48.79	50.05	56.46				[34]	256	float
	RalNet Shuffle	65.51	66.50	62.76	41.53	42.62	49.75	✓			[38]	128	uchar
	DOAP	69.80	70.57	67.19	40.66	41.77	44.99				[17]	128	float
	MIOP	56.83	57.49	52.13	33.38	34.24	39.33			✓	[36]	128	float
	DeepDesc	53.24	53.90	56.32	37.03	38.02	44.93				[31]	128	float
L_1	RsGLOH2	70.68	72.50	67.84	48.19	49.48	56.11	✓	✓	✓	[4]	256	float
	sGLOH2	67.25	69.59	63.50	44.86	46.08	52.49		✓	✓	[4]	256	uchar
	RootSIFT	58.46	59.25	56.74	37.73	38.73	44.77		✓		[1]	128	uchar
	LIOP	54.51	54.97	49.50	32.05	32.91	37.93		✓	✓	[37]	144	uchar
H	BisGLOH2*	66.80	68.01	62.33	44.18	45.40	51.76	✓	✓	✓	[4]	1152	bit
	BisGLOH2	66.04	66.99	62.27	44.08	45.29	51.63		✓	✓	[4]	1152	bit
	Binary L2Net	63.11	63.96	61.06	43.33	44.47	50.86				[34]	256	bit
	Binary DOAP	54.24	54.82	52.74	34.57	35.49	41.41				[17]	128	bit
	RFD$_G$	53.58	53.99	50.75	34.17	35.06	40.40				[11]	406	bit
	RFD$_R$	52.62	53.22	50.28	32.96	33.85	39.31				[11]	293	bit
*	MKD	59.52	60.42	56.40	39.05	40.09	45.70				[27]	128	float

▷ planar 🗗 with alternative recall computation 🔲 "viewpoint only" dataset of [3]
🗐 non-planar 🗖 removing image pairs with mAP<5% 🗗 non-planar dataset of [3]
⚑ contest submission 🛠 hand-crafted ⟲ rotationally invariant 🔖 references # vector length
L_2 Euclidean distance L_1 Manhattan distance H Hamming distance * dot product

6 Conclusions and Future Work

This paper presented the results of the WISW contest, held within the framework of the CAIP 2019 conference, aimed at benchmarking recent local descriptors in challenging real image matching scenarios. For this purpose, descriptors were evaluated on both planar and non-planar scenes, since relevant viewpoint changes and adaptability to non-planar objects and self-occlusions in the scene represent the most general and significant real-world environments. The WISW contest extended existing datasets by adding more test images. In the case of planar scenes, viewpoints changes were combined with other image transformations such as illumination variations and blur, so as to achieve a more realistic and challenging complexity.

Evaluation results showed remarkable improvements of recent descriptors with respect to the state-of-the-art. These were particularly impressive for some of the descriptors based on deep learning, thanks to their smart architecture, combined to the ever increasing availability of big data and modern hardware capabilities. Nevertheless, there is still room for improvement, especially in the case of non-planar scenes.

The proposed benchmark evidenced the fact that, beside descriptors, other factors often overlooked, such as patch normalization and matching strategy, are critical for image matching and are worth to be better investigated in the future. Future work will also include the evaluation of novel descriptors in the benchmark. To this aim, **the WISW contest will remain permanently open.** Furthermore, image pairs with increased complexity combining more image transformations simultaneously will be added in the datasets and, in the case of non-planar scenes, refined extensions of the approximated overlap error will be investigated to further reduce the number of false positive matches.

Acknowledgment. The Titan Xp used for this research was generously donated by the NVIDIA Corporation.

This material is based on research partially sponsored by the Air Force Research Laboratory and the Defense Advanced Research Projects Agency under agreement number FA8750-16-2-0188. The U.S. Government is authorized to reproduce and distribute reprints for Governmental purposes notwithstanding any copyright notation thereon. The views and conclusions contained herein are those of the authors and should not be interpreted as necessarily representing the official policies or endorsements, either expressed or implied, of the Air Force Research Laboratory and the Defense Advanced Research Projects Agency or the U.S. Government.

References

1. Arandjelović, R., Zisserman, A.: Three things everyone should know to improve object retrieval. In: Proceedings of the IEEE Conference on Computer Vision and Pattern Recognition (CVPR), pp. 2911–2918 (2012)
2. Balntas, V., Lenc, K., Vedaldi, A., Mikolajczyk, K.: HPatches: a benchmark and evaluation of handcrafted and learned local descriptors. In: IEEE Conference on Computer Vision and Pattern Recognition (CVPR), pp. 3852–3861 (2017)
3. Bellavia, F., Colombo, C.: An evaluation of recent local image descriptors for real-world applications of image matching. In: Proceedings of the IAPR International Conference on Machine Vision Applications (MVA) (2019)
4. Bellavia, F., Colombo, C.: Rethinking the sGLOH descriptor. IEEE Trans. Pattern Anal. Mach. Intell. **40**(4), 931–944 (2018)
5. Bellavia, F., Tegolo, D., Valenti, C.: Improving Harris corner selection strategy. IET Comput. Vis. **5**(2), 86–96 (2011)

6. Bellavia, F., Valenti, C., Lupascu, C.A., Tegolo, D.: Approximated overlap error for the evaluation of feature descriptors on 3D scenes. In: Petrosino, A. (ed.) ICIAP 2013. LNCS, vol. 8156, pp. 270–279. Springer, Heidelberg (2013). https://doi.org/10.1007/978-3-642-41181-6_28

7. Bian, J., Zhang, L., Liu, Y., Lin, W.Y., Cheng, M.M., Reid, I.D.: MatchBench: an evaluation of feature matchers. arXiv (2018)

8. Brown, M., Lowe, D.G.: Automatic panoramic image stitching using invariant features. Int. J. Comput. Vis. **74**(1), 59–73 (2007)

9. DeTone, D., Malisiewicz, T., Rabinovich, A.: Superpoint: self-supervised interest point detection and description. In: Proceedings of the IEEE Conference on Computer Vision and Pattern Recognition (CVPR) Workshops (2018)

10. Everingham, M., Van Gool, L., Williams, C., Winn, J., Zisserman, A.: The Pascal visual object classes (VOC) challenge. Int. J. Comput. Vis. **88**, 303–338 (2010)

11. Fan, B., Kong, Q., Trzcinski, T., Wang, Z., Pan, C., Fua, P.: Receptive fields selection for binary feature description. IEEE Trans. Image Process. **26**(6), 2583–2595 (2014)

12. Fan, B., et al.: A performance evaluation of local features for image-based 3D reconstruction. IEEE Trans. Image Process. **28**, 4774–4789 (2019)

13. Fan, B., Wang, Z., Wang, F.: Local Image Descriptor: Modern Approaches. Springer, Heidelberg (2015). https://doi.org/10.1007/978-3-662-49173-7

14. Fan, B., Wu, F., Hu, Z.: Rotationally invariant descriptors using intensity order pooling. IEEE Trans. Pattern Anal. Mach. Intell. **34**(10), 2031–2045 (2012)

15. Fanfani, M., Bellavia, F., Colombo, C.: Accurate keyframe selection and keypoint tracking for robust visual odometry. Mach. Vis. Appl. **27**(6), 833–844 (2016)

16. Fraundorfer, F., Bischof, H.: A novel performance evaluation method of local detectors on non-planar scenes. In: IEEE Computer Society Conference on Computer Vision and Pattern Recognition (CVPR), p. 33 (2005)

17. He, K., Lu, Y., Sclaroff, S.: Local descriptors optimized for average precision. In: Proceedings of the IEEE Conference on Computer Vision and Pattern Recognition (CVPR) (2018)

18. Hughes, G.B., Chraibi, M.: Calculating ellipse overlap areas. Comput. Vis. Sci. **15**(5), 291–301 (2012)

19. Lowe, D.: Distinctive image features from scale-invariant keypoints. Int. J. Comput. Vis. **60**(2), 91–110 (2004)

20. Luo, Z.,et al.: GeoDesc: learning local descriptors by integrating geometry constraints. In: Proceedings of the European Conference on Computer Vision (ECCV) (2018)

21. Mikolajczyk, K., Schmid, C.: A performance evaluation of local descriptors. IEEE Trans. Pattern Anal. Mach. Intell. **27**(10), 1615–1630 (2005)

22. Mikolajczyk, K., et al.: A comparison of affine region detectors. Int. J. Comput. Vis. **65**(1–2), 43–72 (2005)

23. Miksik, O., Mikolajczyk, K.: Evaluation of local detectors and descriptors for fast feature matching. In: Proceedings of the International Conference on Pattern Recognition (ICPR), pp. 2681–2684 (2012)

24. Mishchuk, A., Mishkin, D., Radenovic, F., Matas, J.: Working hard to know your neighbor's margins: local descriptor learning loss. In: Advances in Neural Information Processing Systems 30: Annual Conference on Neural Information Processing Systems (NIPS), pp. 4829–4840 (2017)

25. Mishkin, D., Radenovic, F., Matas, J.: Repeatability is not enough: learning discriminative affine regions via discriminability. In: Proceedings of the European Conference on Computer Vision (ECCV) (2018)

26. Moreels, P., Perona, P.: Evaluation of features detectors and descriptors based on 3D objects. Int. J. Comput. Vis. **73**(3), 263–284 (2007)
27. Mukundan, A., Tolias, G., Chum, O.: Multiple-Kernel local-patch descriptor. In: British Machine Vision Conference (BMVC) (2017)
28. Ono, Y., Trulls, E., Fua, P., Yi, K.M.: Learning local features from images. In: Proceedings of the Conference on Neural Information Processing Systems (NIPS) (2018)
29. Pultar, M., Mishkin, D., Matas, J.: Leveraging outdoor webcams for local descriptor learning. In: Proceedings of the Computer Vision Winter Workshop (CVWW) (2019)
30. Schönberger, J.L., Hardmeier, H., Sattler, T., Pollefeys, M.: Comparative evaluation of hand-crafted and learned local features. In: IEEE Conference on Computer Vision and Pattern Recognition (CVPR) (2017)
31. Simo-Serra, E., Trulls, E., Ferraz, L., Kokkinos, I., Fua, P., Moreno-Noguer, F.: Discriminative learning of deep convolutional feature point descriptors. In: Proceedings of the IEEE International Conference on Computer Vision (ICCV) (2015)
32. Snavely, N., Seitz, S., Szeliski, R.: Modeling the world from internet photo collections. Int. J. Comput. Vis. **80**(2), 189–210 (2008)
33. Strecha, C., von Hansen, W., Gool, L.J.V., Fua, P., Thoennessen, U.: On benchmarking camera calibration and multi-view stereo for high resolution imagery. In: IEEE Conference on Computer Vision and Pattern Recognition (CVPR) (2008)
34. Tian, Y., Fan, B., Wu, F.: L2-Net: deep learning of discriminative patch descriptor in Euclidean space. In: IEEE Conference on Computer Vision and Pattern Recognition (CVPR), pp. 6128–6136 (2017)
35. Tian, Y., Yu, X., Fan, B., Wu, F., Heijnen, H., Balntas, V.: SOSNet: second order similarity regularization for local descriptor learning. In: Proceedings of the IEEE Conference on Computer Vision and Pattern Recognition (CVPR) (2019)
36. Wang, Z., Fan, B., Wang, G., Wu, F.: Exploring local and overall ordinal information for robust feature description. IEEE Trans. Pattern Anal. Mach. Intell. **38**(11), 2198–2211 (2016)
37. Wang, Z., Fan, B., Wu, F.: Local intensity order pattern for feature description. In: Proceedings of the IEEE International Conference on Computer Vision (ICCV), pp. 603–610 (2011)
38. Xu, Y., Gong, M., Liu, T., Batmanghelich, K., Wang, C.: Robust angular local descriptor learning. In: Proceedings of the Asian Conference on Computer Vision (ACCV) (2018)
39. Yi, K.M., Trulls, E., Lepetit, V., Fua, P.: LIFT: learned invariant feature transform. In: Leibe, B., Matas, J., Sebe, N., Welling, M. (eds.) ECCV 2016. LNCS, vol. 9910, pp. 467–483. Springer, Cham (2016). https://doi.org/10.1007/978-3-319-46466-4_28
40. Yi, K., Verdie, Y., Fua, P., Lepetit, V.: Learning to assign orientations to feature points. In: Proceedings of the IEEE Conference on Computer Vision and Pattern Recognition (CVPR), pp. 1–8 (2016)
41. Zitnick, C.L., Ramnath, K.: Edge foci interest points. In: IEEE International Conference on Computer Vision (ICCV), pp. 359–366 (2011)

How Well Current Saliency Prediction Models Perform on UAVs Videos?

Anne-Flore Perrin[1]([✉])(ID), Lu Zhang[2](ID), and Olivier Le Meur[1](ID)

[1] Univ Rennes, CNRS, IRISA, 263 Avenue Général Leclerc, 35000 Rennes, France
{anne-flore.perrin,olemeur}@irisa.fr
[2] Univ Rennes, INSA Rennes, CNRS, IETR - UMR 6164, 35000 Rennes, France
lu.ge@insa-rennes.fr

Abstract. It is exciting to witness the fast development of Unmanned Aerial Vehicle (UAV) imaging which opens the door to many new applications. In view of developing rich and efficient services, we wonder which strategy should be adopted to predict salience in UAV videos. To that end, we introduce here a benchmark of off-the-shelf state-of-the-art models for saliency prediction. This benchmark monitors two challenging aspects related to salience, namely the peculiar characteristics of UAV contents and the temporal dimension of videos. This paper enables to identify the strengths and weaknesses of current static, dynamic, supervised and unsupervised models for drone videos. Eventually, we highlight several strategies for the development of visual attention in UAV videos.

Keywords: Benchmark · Salience · Dynamic saliency models · Unmanned Aerial Vehicles (UAV) · Videos

1 Introduction

Unmanned Aerial Vehicles (UAVs) are propitious for a broad range of applications. Drone racing tournaments, new autonomous delivery services, wildfire detection, and private house surveillance is a sample of these highly promising services. However, we reach the point that service improvement lies in technology-, imagery- and context-based solutions. Indeed, UAV imagery presents specificities that could undermine the performance of current image processing algorithms.

Services mentioned above heavily rely on object detection, segmentation and even more on saliency detection. Salience expresses the extent of importance of an area, approximating perceptual processes of visual attention. It is represented as the prediction of the fixation probability density of a multimedia content [26]. Its prediction is essential in diverse fields, from content-aware re-targeting and

The presented work is funded by the ongoing research project ANR ASTRID DISSO-CIE (Automated Detection of SaliencieS from Operators' Point of View and Intelligent Compression of DronE videos) referenced as ANR-17-ASTR-0009.

M. Vento and G. Percannella (Eds.): CAIP 2019, LNCS 11678, pp. 311–323, 2019.
https://doi.org/10.1007/978-3-030-29888-3_25

compression to advertisement analyses. As UAV applications may further benefit from visual attention theory, we investigated whether state-of-the-art saliency models are suitable for predicting visual attention in UAV videos.

Several works already applied saliency prediction models in UAV services. An automatic salient object detection is implemented in [37] through mean-shift segmentation and edge-detection operators. In [38], the combination of frame alignment, forward/backward difference and blob detection creates a UAV video event summarization, tracking salient objects. Deep architectures are used for real-time autonomous indoor navigation [12,22] and for monitoring wildfire [44], among others. Such approaches build upon basic deep-learning models, namely AlexNet [25] and CaffeNet [19].

Let us stress that very few works address the temporal dimension in traditional and UAV videos. Methods that tackle the temporal dimension comprise hand-crafted motion features [11,36], network architecture fed with optical flow [1], in a two-layer fashion [1,8], or Long Short-Term Memory (LSTM) architectures [2,20,29,41] to benefit from their memory functionality.

Regarding conventional imaging, elegant, elaborate and efficient solutions have been developed for saliency prediction. However, we wonder whether typical schemes keep their promises when dealing with UAV video characteristics. Indeed, this new-born imagery field is distinct from typical imagery in many aspects, including the bird-point-of-view which modifies the semantic and size of objects [24], the loss of pictorial depth cues [16] i.e. the lack of horizontal line [10], and the presence of camera movements [24].

In this paper, we provide answers to the above questions by first introducing the saliency models under review in Sect. 2. In Sect. 3, we go through the details of the benchmark. Results are discussed in Sect. 4. Finally, key takeaways of this benchmark are given in Sect. 5.

2   Saliency Models

Tremendously different approaches have been developed throughout the years to reach high accuracy prediction of visual attention. We propose here a taxonomy to categorize existing salience solutions.

2.1   Taxonomy

With the introduction of temporal dimension in videos, Borji [3] classified models according to the use or not of motion features and deep learning architectures. We refine this taxonomy by focusing on all types of supervision and not only emphasizing deep-learning-based models. Accordingly, we define five model categories:

- **Static Unsupervised (SU):** Itti [18], LeMeur [28], GBVS [13], SUN [43], Judd [21], Hou [15], RARE2012 [35], BMS [42],
- **Static Deep learning (SD):** Salicon [17], DeepNet [34], ML-Net [7], SalGAN [33],
- **Dynamic Unsupervised (DU):** Fang [9], OBDL [14],

- **Dynamic Machine learning (DM):** PQFT [11], Rudoy [36],
- **Dynamic Deep learning (DD):** DeepVS [20], ACL-Net [41], STSconvNet [1], FGRNE [29].

Beyond the scope of this study, deep learning models could be further classified depending on their loss function(s) [4] or architecture attributes (e.g. Convolutional Neural Networks (CNN) design, multi-level features, encoder-decoder system, and LSTM(s)).

2.2 Models Under Study

Models under study were selected based on a study of the state of the art, exhibiting most used models for cross-model comparisons. Accordingly, we evaluate a total of 11 off-the-shelf models, including 8 static models and 3 dynamic models. They are briefly described hereinafter, following our taxonomy categorization.

Static Unsupervised Models

- **Itti:** One of the first and most used static models is referred to as Itti's model. In [18], authors got inspired from primates' visual systems, especially the center-surround analytic behavior of retina and cortical lateral inhibition mechanisms. They investigated three modalities, namely color, intensity, and orientation, through features on variable scales.
- **Graph-Based Visual Saliency (GBVS)** [13]: GBVS is a bottom-up visual saliency model, exploiting the real-time ability of graph algorithms. It implements a feature extraction using biologically inspired filters, an activation measure by subtracting features at different scales and finally a normalization, applied based on local maxima, convolution, and non-linear weighting.
- **Saliency Using Natural statistics (SUN)** [43]: SUN mimics the visual system behavior to find potential targets by means of a Bayesian probabilistic framework. It includes computation of self-information, likelihood and location prior to reach an estimation of pointwise mutual information, which expresses the overall salience.
- **SIM** [31]: First, a convolution of the image with a bank of filters using a multi-resolution wavelet transform yields to a scale-space decomposition. Then, a Gaussian Mixture Model (GMM), trained on eye-fixation data, simulates the inhibition mechanisms in visual cortex cells. Finally, multi-scale information is integrated using an inverse wavelet transform.
- **RARE2012** [35]: The key of RARE2012 is its multi-scale rarity mechanism applied on low-level colour and medium-level orientation features extracted beforehand. To emphasise both local contrasts and global rare regions, highly salient regions have the lowest occurrence probabilities of pixel at all scales.
- **Hou** [15]: Assuming that sparsity in spatial and frequential domains discriminate the foreground from the background, the foreground is represented by the sign of the discrete cosine transform of the signal. The inverse transform of the three color channels foregrounds are squared, summed up and smoothed to get the saliency map.

- **Boolean Map Saliency (BMS)** [42]: First, a set of Boolean maps is created by applying uniformly distributed thresholds on the image color channels. Attention maps are derived from this set through morphological dilatation and Gaussian blurring. The final saliency map is the average attention map.

Dynamic Machine Learning Model

- **PQFT** [11]: This model extends phase spectrum of Fourier transform models to a temporal approach. Chroma, luma and motion information form the quaternion of a frame. The quaternion symplectic form is converted to the frequency domain. Only the phase, which represents local information of the signal, is converted back to the spatial domain. Such information, after Gaussian filtering, produce the saliency map.

Static Deep Learning Model

- **ML-Net** [7]: This multi-level Fully Convolutional neural Network (FCN) combines low- and high-level features to predict saliency. However, the true ingenuity of this model lies in the defined loss function, which penalises more errors occurring on salient pixels, and the use of a learnt prior, which takes into account content characteristics.

Dynamic Deep Learning Models

- **DeepVS:** Jiang et al. [20] proposed an elegant architecture including two models applied sequentially. The Object-to-Motion CNN (OM-CNN) is encoding objectedness features through a complex and comprehensive network combining hierarchical spatial (coarse) and temporal saliency maps. To further compute dynamic salience of videos, a Saliency-Structured Convolutional LSTM (SS-ConvLSTM), is added. Its two successive LSTM networks leverage both short and long term correlations.
- **ACL-Net:** Wang et al. [41] implemented a CNN-LSTM architecture for video saliency. An attention module supervises the CNN, forcing it to learn static features and ensuring the LSTM to deal with dynamic characteristics.

3   Benchmark Design

3.1   Baselines

To include comparison points for the above models, we include six baselines. First, the average saliency map over all observers and all sequences (OHM) brings out an overall representation of **Human Mean** (HM). Also, average saliency maps over observers for a sequence (SHM), and over all observers for all sequences but the one under study (abSHM) examine content-dependencies. Then, the **Center Bias** (CB) map is a centered isotropic Gaussian stretched to video frame aspect ratio [5]. Last, we add two **chance** representations, inspiring from [32]. We split SHMs into 16 blocks, which are redistributed in the final map following two 4×4 magic squares. Thus, shuffled maps contain no salience information but deliver a similar cover ratio and dynamic range than the ground truth.

3.2 Dataset

Specific datasets are required to conduct saliency performance analyses. Indeed, eye movements of human beings or any substitute, collected during stimuli visualization, establish the Ground Truth (GT) essential to assess the validity of predicted saliency maps.

EyeTrackUAV dataset [24] is the only UAV salience dataset available, to the best of our knowledge. It includes 19 different videos extracted from the UAV123 database [30]. These video sequences were captured from a fully stabilized and manually controlled off-the-shelf professional-grade UAV (DJI S1000) flying at low-altitudes (varying between 5–25 m). Criteria for content selection were the diversity of environment, distance and angle to the scene, size of the principal object and presence of sky. Authors of [24] collected highly precise binocular gaze data (1000 Hz) from 14 subjects in free viewing conditions. Stimuli were videos with a resolution of 720p, 30 fps which represent overall 26599 frames and 887 s.

From data, two maps have been computed for evaluation purposes. Saliency maps were inferred directly from raw data gathered by the eye tracker. Binocular gaze recordings were averaged over all observers. These maps were then filtered using a Gaussian kernel and normalized [27]. Fixations were retrieved through a Dispersion-Threshold Identification (I-DT) algorithm [23]. Fixation points, in this spatiotemporal detection, are assumed to cluster together.

3.3 Metrics

To carry out the evaluation, we use six quality metrics included in the MIT benchmark [6,27]: Correlation Coefficient (CC) ($\in [-1, 1]$), Similarity (SIM) ($\in [0, 1]$) the intersection between histograms of saliency, Area Under the Curve (AUC) Judd and Borji ($\in [0, 1]$), Normalized Scanpath Saliency (NSS) ($\in]-\infty, +\infty[$), and Kullback Leibler divergence (KL) ($\in [0, +\infty[$). Details of these metrics can be found in [6,27] and a cross-comparison in [5].

4   Results and Discussion

4.1   Analyses

Static, dynamic, non-supervised, machine-learning and deep-learning models are compared here. We discuss our results qualitatively, overall and on a frame-by-frame basis.

Qualitative Analysis

The qualitative verification is done on the sequence *Person20*, which illustrates models efficiency in a typical scenario of UAV applications. By observing Fig. 1, one can note that deep learning and dynamic models detected less salient areas than unsupervised static models. This is in line with the assumed sparsity of video saliency.

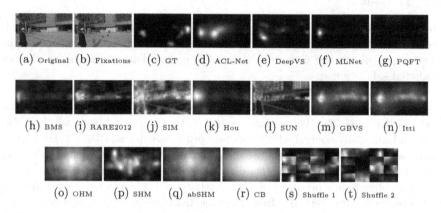

(a) Original (b) Fixations   (c) GT   (d) ACL-Net (e) DeepVS   (f) MLNet   (g) PQFT

(h) BMS   (i) RARE2012   (j) SIM   (k) Hou   (l) SUN   (m) GBVS   (n) Itti

(o) OHM   (p) SHM   (q) abSHM   (r) CB   (s) Shuffle 1 (t) Shuffle 2

Fig. 1. Saliency maps of the 11 models (1d–1n) and baselines (1o–1t) together with the ground truth (1c), fixations (1b) and source (1a) of frame 1035 in *person20*.

Overall Analysis

Overall results are presented in Table 1. The analysis relies on mean and standard deviation of raw results while Analysis of Variance (ANOVA) and multi-comparison studies have been conducted to verify the statistical significance of observed differences. We draw several observations.

Deep learning models present the best scores, especially for SIM for which differences with other models are statistically significant. This result was expected as the same behavior is observed since the development of deep learning techniques in saliency prediction [7,17,33,34,40].

Within static models, BMS model, followed closely by GBVS and Itti models, happens to be the most efficient static unsupervised model. SIM and SUN models are significantly less performing for CC, SIM, NSS and KL.

Regarding dynamic models, ACL-Net reaches the first and second position for all but AUC-Borji metric. DeepVS is also ranked high up behind the two other deep learning schemes. Contrarily, PQFT achieves statistically significantly the lowest performance of all models for all metrics and achieves similar performances as baselines.

Baselines statistically predict salience less efficiently than all models but PQFT - and SIM and SUN models with respect to KL and SIM. This emphasizes the potential of most current models for UAV saliency prediction. Despite being the most performing baseline, Center Bias results are quite low when compared

Table 1. Performance of saliency models in average over all videos and all frames. Best performances are in bold. (AUC-B = AUC-Borji; AUC-J = AUC-Judd)

		CC ↑	SIM ↑	AUC-J ↑	AUC-B ↑	NSS ↑	KL ↓
DD	ACL-Net [41]	0.4516	**0.3586**	0.8199	0.7717	1.9622	1.7803
	DeepVS [20]	0.3986	0.3204	0.8059	0.7384	1.7904	1.9063
SD	MLNet [7]	**0.4621**	0.3149	**0.8347**	**0.7866**	**2.1479**	**1.5857**
DM	PQFT [11]	0.1367	0.1817	0.7054	0.5591	0.7364	2.3282
SU	BMS [42]	0.3846	0.2482	0.8189	0.7855	1.8180	1.8053
	RARE2012 [35]	0.3422	0.2566	0.7946	0.7582	1.5093	1.8240
	Hou [15]	0.2811	0.2204	0.7565	0.7279	1.1529	1.9818
	SIM [31]	0.2213	0.1893	0.7511	0.7235	0.9899	2.1482
	SUN [43]	0.2065	0.1913	0.7361	0.7059	0.9593	2.1702
	GBVS [13]	0.3687	0.2431	0.8125	0.7854	1.5915	1.8115
	Itti [18]	0.3687	0.2431	0.8125	0.7855	1.5915	1.8115
Baselines	OHM	0.1889	0.1883	0.7208	0.6934	0.6881	2.3526
	SHM	0.1917	0.1944	0.7051	0.6790	0.6880	2.2463
	abSHM	0.1808	0.1868	0.7125	0.6840	0.6544	2.3539
	CB	0.2055	0.1980	0.7493	0.7172	0.7588	2.3776
	Shuffle 1	0.0282	0.1558	0.5724	0.5427	0.1315	2.4275
	Shuffle 2	−0.0085	0.1468	0.5323	0.5041	−0.0046	2.4745

to results on traditional contents. This raises suspicions about the suitability of this bias for UAV videos. We have indecisive results regarding overall image-dependent properties. Indeed, SHM is not statistically different from other HM baselines and is alternatively better (CC, SIM, KL) or worse (AUC-based and NSS).

From the above observations, UAV saliency models can be built upon static and dynamic deep learning models. Performances of today's solutions are fair and could reach better scores through fine-tuning or training on UAV-dedicated databases. Also, we recommend avoiding frequency-based solutions, even though this result must be replicated with other models and datasets for validation.

Sequence-Based Analysis

A challenge in video quality assessment is to design metrics that are representative of the entire sequence, considering the disparity in quality scores of video frames. Saliency prediction in videos presents the same challenge. In this benchmark, we tackled this issue by considering average and according standard deviation values of metrics over the entire sequence. To dig further in UAV video saliency, let us discuss the accuracy of predictions on a frame-by-frame basis. This in-depth investigation exhibits potential perspectives for metrics development in video saliency prediction.

In Figs. 2a to c, a comparison of averaged scores for models sorted by categories, following the above-defined taxonomy, is provided in terms of CC scores for sequence *bike3*. Also, overall CC results of all models and average baseline are reported in Fig. 2d for *wakeboard10*.

High Disparity. Overall, the disparity of standard deviation and mean values spreads out over a wide range among sequence frames. Hence, giving one score per video for saliency prediction may not be appropriate. Also, we claim that the lack of consideration of temporal continuity in performance estimation may prevent thorough assessments of predictions. Implementing temporal coherence metric for video saliency prediction may be a solution to reach highly accurate and constructive analyses.

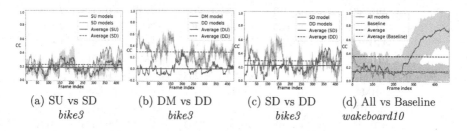

(a) SU vs SD	(b) DM vs DD	(c) SD vs DD	(d) All vs Baseline
bike3	*bike3*	*bike3*	*wakeboard10*

Fig. 2. Temporal comparison of model categories in *bike3* and results of all models in *wakeboard10* for metric CC for all sequence frames. Colored envelop represents standard deviation associated with mean results of models. (Color figure online)

Deep Learning Models Perform Better. Even on a frame-by-frame basis and amongst sequences presenting statistically different results, we can observe in Figs. 2a and b the clear advantage of deep learning architectures over unsupervised and machine learning schemes, for both dynamic and static models.

Static vs Dynamic Deep Learning Models. There is no evidence of significant over-performance of static deep learning over dynamic deep learning approaches, as illustrated in Fig. 2c. Actually, ANOVA has not rejected the null hypothesis when comparing the distributions of these two categories. We observe that results are content-dependent, hinting that the difference of performance between deep learning static and dynamic models lies in videos characteristics.

Event-Related Performance. We could not relate the varying features of Eye-TrackUAV videos (overall angle and distance to the scene, environment, presence of sky, and object size) to models' efficiency. Our intuition is that model performances are event-related. We further studied our results to identify causes of abrupt changes in metrics along video frames.

It turns out that a decrease in performance may be caused by the entry of new objects of potential interest or environments variations. However, a point of interest arises in that a sudden increase in prediction accuracy often follows camera movements towards reframing the content (change of camera angle, distance, speed or trajectory guided by an operator). Reframing reintroduces a center bias in the content. This explains the increase in prediction accuracy at the end of the scene *wakeboard10* in Fig. 2d. This shows the importance of understanding patterns and biases in the used imagery.

4.2 Challenges and Open Problems

Several aspects of our study must be examined and discussed, from the limitations due to the used dataset, to the "normalization" of metrics for better comparison and analyses of saliency prediction strategies.

Dataset
EyeTrackUAV presents a clear lack of non-natural videos. But most importantly, this dataset is not sufficient to train a deep model, even with data augmentation. To address the need of dedicated UAV video saliency prediction, one needs new larger databases with more videos, possibly with natural and non-natural images.

Likewise, the larger the population taking part in the gaze data gathering is, the more accurate should be the ground truth - on which rely performance analyses. Also, based on our results, event-related annotations, even though complicated to collect, can provide a valuable contribution.

Finally, this dataset has been designed to study bottom-up attention. However, multiple UAV applications, such as aerial surveillance, monitoring and observation with drone, require the study of top-down attention, which is task-related. Both bottom-up and top-down attention ground truth is necessary for the development of UAV services.

Center Bias. An additional UAV feature is that the center bias [39] is less significant in EyeTrackUAV sequences than in traditional video sequences, as seen in Fig. 3. It may explain, in part, the weak performance of existing saliency models. Further analyses are required to confirm this compelling finding.

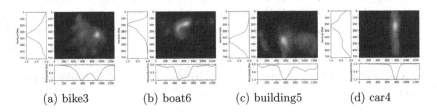

(a) bike3   (b) boat6   (c) building5   (d) car4

Fig. 3. Center bias for sequences *bike3*, *boat6*, *building5* and *car4*.

Metrics. As mentioned earlier, temporal metrics must be developed to correctly assess video saliency predictions. Our main point is that the averaged prediction performance over video frames may not be representative of the prediction along scenes in videos. It might be profitable to mimic the continuum of our visual gaze deployment. Several strategies may be deployed accordingly, possibly inspiring from event summarization [38].

With a slight shift of perspective, one may also consider to apply post-processing to predicted saliency maps to reach comparable metric results. To reduce metric biases, Kummerer et al. [26] proposed to turn a given fixation density into metric-specific saliency maps prior to metric computations.

5   Conclusion

UAV new services want to benefit from the substantial improvement in saliency prediction of this last decade. This benchmark reviews the ability of 11 state-of-the-art off-the-shelf prediction schemes to identify the direction to take toward the development of UAV imagery-dedicated models.

We studied qualitatively models performance over the EyeTrackUAV dataset which includes 19 natural UAV videos together with precise eye tracking information, collected from 14 subjects. Predicted maps have been assessed using typical metrics, namely CC, SIM, AUC-Judd, AUC-Borji, NSS and KL. Overall scores of models are reported through mean and standard deviation over the entire sequence. ANOVA and multi-comparison analyses have been included to detect if models differences are statistically significant.

Several insights are provided among which are three key takeaway messages:

(1) In line with studies on traditional contents, static and dynamic deep learning models, trained on conventional contents, show the most promising results. This outcome is highly encouraging, especially with the potential of reaching higher performance through fine-tuning or training on larger UAV databases.
(2) Yet there are no significant difference between static and dynamic deep learning. This outcome has been shown to be content-dependent. Although video characteristics (angle, distance to the scene, environment type and object size) were not sufficient to explain our results, it seems that event-related annotations could help to efficiently learn saliency on such contents.
(3) The need of dedicated UAV-centric models is hereby made clear. We need to go deeper in content specificities and better encode them for future high-quality UAV-based services. Also, we found out that the center bias does not necessarily apply to UAV videos, which needs deeper exploration. A broad investigation of typical biases of attention and cognition could be carried out.

Different challenges have also been discussed, including the need to develop video-based metrics in view to further investigate video prediction performance as well as to better represent the quality of prediction along the entire sequence, or the necessity to create large datasets for UAV imagery saliency prediction.

References

1. Bak, C., Kocak, A., Erdem, E., Erdem, A.: Spatio-temporal saliency networks for dynamic saliency prediction. IEEE Trans. Multimedia **20**(7), 1688–1698 (2018)
2. Bazzani, L., Larochelle, H., Torresani, L.: Recurrent mixture density network for spatiotemporal visual attention. arXiv preprint arXiv:1603.08199 (2016)
3. Borji, A.: Saliency prediction in the deep learning era: an empirical investigation. arXiv preprint arXiv:1810.03716 (2018)
4. Bruckert, A., Tavakoli, H.R., Liu, Z., Christie, M., Meur, O.L.: Deep saliency models: the quest for the loss function. arXiv preprint arXiv:1907.02336 (2019)
5. Bylinskii, Z., Judd, T., Oliva, A., Torralba, A., Durand, F.: What do different evaluation metrics tell us about saliency models? IEEE Trans. Pattern Anal. Mach. Intell. **41**(3), 740–757 (2019)
6. Bylinskii, Z., et al.: MIT saliency benchmark (2015)
7. Cornia, M., Baraldi, L., Serra, G., Cucchiara, R.: A deep multi-level network for saliency prediction. In: 2016 23rd International Conference on Pattern Recognition (ICPR), pp. 3488–3493. IEEE (2016)
8. Jain, S.D., Xiong, B., Grauman, K.: FusionSeg: learning to combine motion and appearance for fully automatic segmentation of generic objects in videos. In: Proceedings of the IEEE Conference on Computer Vision and Pattern Recognition, pp. 3664–3673 (2017)
9. Fang, Y., Wang, Z., Lin, W., Fang, Z.: Video saliency incorporating spatiotemporal cues and uncertainty weighting. IEEE Trans. Image Process. **23**(9), 3910–3921 (2014)
10. Foulsham, T., Kingstone, A., Underwood, G.: Turning the world around: patterns in saccade direction vary with picture orientation. Vis. Res. **48**(17), 1777–1790 (2008)
11. Guo, C., Zhang, L.: A novel multiresolution spatiotemporal saliency detection model and its applications in image and video compression. IEEE Trans. Image Process. **19**(1), 185–198 (2010)
12. Guo, X., Cui, L., Park, B., Ding, W., Lockhart, M., Kim, I.: How will humans cut through automated vehicle platoons in mixed traffic environments? A simulation study of drivers' gaze behaviors based on the dynamic areas-of-interest. In: Adams, S., Beling, P., Lambert, J., Scherer, W., Fleming, C. (eds.) Systems Engineering in Context. Springer, Cham (2019). https://doi.org/10.1007/978-3-030-00114-8_55
13. Harel, J., Koch, C., Perona, P.: Graph-based visual saliency. In: Advances in Neural Information Processing Systems, pp. 545–552 (2007)
14. Hossein Khatoonabadi, S., Vasconcelos, N., Bajic, I.V., Shan, Y.: How many bits does it take for a stimulus to be salient? In: The IEEE Conference on Computer Vision and Pattern Recognition (CVPR), June 2015
15. Hou, X., Harel, J., Koch, C.: Image signature: highlighting sparse salient regions. IEEE Trans. Pattern Anal. Mach. Intell. **34**(1), 194–201 (2012). https://doi.org/10.1109/TPAMI.2011.146
16. Howard, I.P., Rogers, B.: Depth perception. Stevens Handb. Exp. Psychol. **6**, 77–120 (2002)
17. Huang, X., Shen, C., Boix, X., Zhao, Q.: SALICON: reducing the semantic gap in saliency prediction by adapting deep neural networks. In: Proceedings of the IEEE International Conference on Computer Vision, pp. 262–270 (2015)
18. Itti, L., Koch, C., Niebur, E.: A model of saliency-based visual attention for rapid scene analysis. IEEE Trans. Pattern Anal. Mach. Intell. **20**(11), 1254–1259 (1998)

19. Jia, Y., et al.: Caffe: convolutional architecture for fast feature embedding. In: Proceedings of the 22nd ACM International Conference on Multimedia, MM 2014, pp. 675–678. ACM (2014)
20. Jiang, L., Xu, M., Liu, T., Qiao, M., Wang, Z.: DeepVS: a deep learning based video saliency prediction approach. In: Ferrari, V., Hebert, M., Sminchisescu, C., Weiss, Y. (eds.) Computer Vision – ECCV 2018. LNCS, vol. 11218, pp. 625–642. Springer, Cham (2018). https://doi.org/10.1007/978-3-030-01264-9_37
21. Judd, T., Ehinger, K., Durand, F., Torralba, A.: Learning to predict where humans look. In: 2009 IEEE 12th International Conference on Computer Vision, pp. 2106–2113. IEEE (2009)
22. Kim, D.K., Chen, T.: Deep neural network for real-time autonomous indoor navigation. arXiv preprint arXiv:1511.04668 (2015)
23. Krassanakis, V., Filippakopoulou, V., Nakos, B.: EyeMMV toolbox: an eye movement post-analysis tool based on a two-step spatial dispersion threshold for fixation identification. J. Eye Mov. Res. 7(1) (2014). https://doi.org/10.16910/jemr.7.1.1
24. Krassanakis, V., Perreira Da Silva, M., Ricordel, V.: Monitoring human visual behavior during the observation of unmanned aerial vehicles (UAVs) videos. Drones 2(4), 36 (2018)
25. Krizhevsky, A., Sutskever, I., Hinton, G.E.: ImageNet classification with deep convolutional neural networks. In: Pereira, F., Burges, C.J.C., Bottou, L., Weinberger, K.Q. (eds.) Advances in Neural Information Processing Systems, vol. 25, pp. 1097–1105. Curran Associates, Inc. (2012)
26. Kümmerer, M., Wallis, T.S.A., Bethge, M.: Saliency benchmarking made easy: separating models, maps and metrics. In: Ferrari, V., Hebert, M., Sminchisescu, C., Weiss, Y. (eds.) ECCV 2018. LNCS, vol. 11220, pp. 798–814. Springer, Cham (2018). https://doi.org/10.1007/978-3-030-01270-0_47
27. Le Meur, O., Baccino, T.: Methods for comparing scanpaths and saliency maps: strengths and weaknesses. Behav. Res. Method 45(1), 251–266 (2013)
28. Le Meur, O., Le Callet, P., Barba, D.: Predicting visual fixations on video based on low-level visual features. Vis. Res. 47(19), 2483–2498 (2007)
29. Li, G., Xie, Y., Wei, T., Wang, K., Lin, L.: Flow guided recurrent neural encoder for video salient object detection. In: Proceedings of the IEEE Conference on Computer Vision and Pattern Recognition, pp. 3243–3252 (2018)
30. Mueller, M., Smith, N., Ghanem, B.: A benchmark and simulator for UAV tracking. In: Leibe, B., Matas, J., Sebe, N., Welling, M. (eds.) ECCV 2016. LNCS, vol. 9905, pp. 445–461. Springer, Cham (2016). https://doi.org/10.1007/978-3-319-46448-0_27
31. Murray, N., Vanrell, M., Otazu, X., Parraga, C.A.: Saliency estimation using a non-parametric low-level vision model. In: CVPR 2011, pp. 433–440, June 2011
32. Ninassi, A., Le Meur, O., Le Callet, P., Barba, D.: Does where you gaze on an image affect your perception of quality? Applying visual attention to image quality metric. In: 2007 IEEE International Conference on Image Processing, vol. 2, p. II-169. IEEE (2007)
33. Pan, J., et al.: SalGAN: visual saliency prediction with generative adversarial networks. arXiv preprint arXiv:1701.01081 (2017)
34. Pan, J., Sayrol, E., Giro-i Nieto, X., McGuinness, K., O'Connor, N.E.: Shallow and deep convolutional networks for saliency prediction. In: Proceedings of the IEEE Conference on Computer Vision and Pattern Recognition, pp. 598–606 (2016)
35. Riche, N., Mancas, M., Duvinage, M., Mibulumukini, M., Gosselin, B., Dutoit, T.: RARE2012: a multi-scale rarity-based saliency detection with its comparative statistical analysis. Signal Process. Image Commun. 28(6), 642–658 (2013)

36. Rudoy, D., Goldman, D.B., Shechtman, E., Zelnik-Manor, L.: Learning video saliency from human gaze using candidate selection. In: Proceedings of the IEEE Conference on Computer Vision and Pattern Recognition, pp. 1147–1154 (2013)
37. Sokalski, J., Breckon, T.P., Cowling, I.: Automatic salient object detection in UAV imagery. In: Proceedings of the 25th International Unmanned Air Vehicle Systems, pp. 1–12 (2010)
38. Trinh, H., Li, J., Miyazawa, S., Moreno, J., Pankanti, S.: Efficient UAV video event summarization. In: Proceedings of the 21st International Conference on Pattern Recognition (ICPR 2012), pp. 2226–2229. IEEE (2012)
39. Tseng, P.H., Carmi, R., Cameron, I.G., Munoz, D.P., Itti, L.: Quantifying center bias of observers in free viewing of dynamic natural scenes. J. Vis. **9**(7), 4 (2009)
40. Vig, E., Dorr, M., Cox, D.: Large-scale optimization of hierarchical features for saliency prediction in natural images. In: Proceedings of the IEEE Conference on Computer Vision and Pattern Recognition, pp. 2798–2805 (2014)
41. Wang, Z., Ren, J., Zhang, D., Sun, M., Jiang, J.: A deep-learning based feature hybrid framework for spatiotemporal saliency detection inside videos. Neurocomputing **287**, 68–83 (2018)
42. Zhang, J., Sclaroff, S.: Exploiting surroundedness for saliency detection: a boolean map approach. IEEE Trans. Pattern Anal. Mach. Intell. **38**(5), 889–902 (2016)
43. Zhang, L., Tong, M.H., Marks, T.K., Shan, H., Cottrell, G.W.: SUN: a Bayesian framework for saliency using natural statistics. J. Vis. **8**(7), 32 (2008)
44. Zhao, Y., Ma, J., Li, X., Zhang, J.: Saliency detection and deep learning-based wildfire identification in UAV imagery. Sensors **18**(3), 712 (2018)

Place Recognition in Gardens by Learning Visual Representations: Data Set and Benchmark Analysis

María Leyva-Vallina$^{(\boxtimes)}$, Nicola Strisciuglio, and Nicolai Petkov

Bernoulli Institute for Mathematics, Computer Science and Artificial Intelligence,
University of Groningen, Groningen, The Netherlands
m.leyva.vallina@rug.nl

Abstract. Visual place recognition is an important component of systems for camera localization and loop closure detection. It concerns the recognition of a previously visited place based on visual cues only. Although it is a widely studied problem for indoor and urban environments, the recent use of robots for automation of agricultural and gardening tasks has created new problems, due to the challenging appearance of garden-like environments. Garden scenes predominantly contain green colors, as well as repetitive patterns and textures. The lack of available data recorded in gardens and natural environments makes the improvement of visual localization algorithms difficult.

In this paper we propose an extended version of the TB-Places data set, which is designed for testing algorithms for visual place recognition. It contains images with ground truth camera pose recorded in real gardens in different seasons, with varying light conditions. We constructed and released a ground truth for all possible pairs of images, indicating whether they depict the same place or not.

We present the results of a benchmark analysis of methods based on convolutional neural networks for holistic image description and place recognition. We train existing networks (i.e. ResNet, DenseNet and VGG NetVLAD) as backbone of a two-way architecture with a contrastive loss function. The results that we obtained demonstrate that learning garden-tailored representations contribute to an improvement of performance, although the generalization capabilities are limited.

Keywords: Benchmarking · Data set · Deep learning · Place recognition

1 Introduction

Visual place recognition is a widely studied problem in Computer Vision and concerns the recognition of a previously seen scene based on the analysis of visual features only [11,12]. The problem gained great interest among researchers in the fields of robotics and computer vision due to its applications to autonomous

© Springer Nature Switzerland AG 2019
M. Vento and G. Percannella (Eds.): CAIP 2019, LNCS 11678, pp. 324–335, 2019.
https://doi.org/10.1007/978-3-030-29888-3_26

driving [13], robot navigation [4,6,11,14,22], camera localization based on image retrieval [16] and loop-closure detection [23]. It is a key component for visual localization based on image retrieval algorithms. Given a query image, a reference image with known camera pose that depicts the same place has to be retrieved from a database. Subsequently, the relative pose between query and reference image can be calculated, and the camera pose in the reference system corresponding to the query image can be estimated. In this work, treat place recognition as distinguishing between pairs of similar and dissimilar images.

Visual place recognition algorithms face challenges when appearance changes occur due to variations of illumination, weather, season, camera viewpoint or when repetitive textures are present [24]. However, depending on the particular environments where place recognition algorithms are applied, the specific problem and challenges can vary. For instance, in outdoor environments, large changes in illumination (day and night) [14,17] and weather conditions (sun and rain) [22] are often present. In addition, urban scenes are subject to partial or total occlusions due to obstacles (i.e. vehicles or pedestrians), while countryside environments are affected by seasonal changes [3,22].

Holistic image descriptors were proposed to face these challenges, such as SeqSLAM [14,22] and NetVLAD [1]. The former performs place recognition by matching sequences of images, while the latter is a CNN-based method that employs a new orderless pooling VLAD layer, trained with weakly-labeled image triplets (one reference, a set of positive matches, and a set of negative matches). Outdoor environments are usually large, therefore high spatial precision for recognition or localization is not required. In contrast, indoor environments are typically smaller, and a more accurate localization is necessary. In addition, indoor place recognition methods are required to be able to recognize a scene even under substantial viewpoint variations, and are usually faced with repetitive patterns [18]. Algorithms based on local features like FAB-MAP have been successfully implemented for visual localization in indoor environments [4,5].

With the raise of interest in gardening and agricultural robotics [2,15,21,25], new challenges and problems have become relevant for place recognition algorithms. Gardens are affected by illumination and seasonal changes, and localization algorithms are required to also be robust to viewpoint variations, while faced with very similar and repetitive textures. Moreover, gardens have a lot of internal similarity, i.e. a bush can look similar to all the other bushes in the garden. Thus, for a localization algorithm to be successful, it is required to capture and describe the relevant parts of the scene and their relative arrangement, while ignoring irrelevant elements (i.e. the common background).

In [10], we released the first version of the TB-Places data set for benchmarking the performance of existing algorithms in garden environments, and recorded low recognition results. Existing algorithms and CNN-based models for place recognition are not robust to the challenges provided by garden-like environments. Thus, more data and garden-specialized place recognition methods are needed to advance the state-of-the-art of computer vision applied to gardening and agricultural robotics.

In this paper, we propose an extended version of the TB-Places data set, with more than 23K new images. We learn garden-specific feature descriptors by training several models of deep Convolutional Neural Networks as backbone for a siamese architecture with a contrastive loss function. We carried out experiments with ResNet [7], DenseNet [8] and a VGG [19] pre-trained with a VLAD [1] layer as backbone for the place recognition architecture. The results that we obtained demonstrate that learning garden-specific representations contributes better recognition, but the generalization capabilities are still limited.

The paper is structured as follows. We introduce the extended version of the TB-Places data set in Sect. 2. In Sect. 3, we explain the network architecture that we employ to compute the image descriptors and the training procedure, while in Sect. 4 we present and compare the results that we achieved. Finally, we draw conclusions in Sect. 5.

(a)   (b)

Fig. 1. (a) Robot platform in the Wageningen garden of TrimBot2020 project. (b) Camera rig employed for the recording sessions.

2   Data Set

We propose an extended version of the TB-Places data set [10], which consists of images recorded in the test gardens of the TrimBot2020 project [21]. The gardens are located at the campus of the Wageningen University and Research (Netherlands) and at the Bosch Research Center in Renningen (Germany). The original TB-Places data set is composed of three sub sets, corresponding to two recording sessions that took place in Wageningen in 2016 and 2017 (W16 and W17), and one recording session in the garden in Renningen in 2017 (R17). The data was recorded using a modified Bosch Indego lawn mower robot, with a camera rig with 5 pairs of stereo cameras, which have 360° field of view (see Fig. 1). The cameras in the rig are synchronized by means of an FPGA and record pictures at a resolution of 752×480 pixels [21]. Each image has an associated ground truth camera pose in the garden reference system, recorded with a TopCon laser tracker and an inertial measurement unit (IMU). Additionally, we constructed a place recognition ground truth, labelling all the possible pairs

Table 1. Details on the composition of the extended TB-Places data set with the new W18 set of images. We report, for each subset, the number of image pairs labelled as similar and their percentage among all the possible image pairs.

Garden	Set	# imgs	# similar pairs	% similar pairs
Wageningen	W16	40752	5.12M	0.6168
Wageningen	W17	10948	330K	0.5441
Wageningen	W18	23043	1.03M	0.3877
Renningen	R17	7999	150K	0.4822

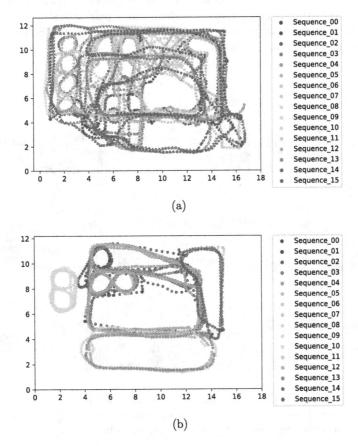

(a)

(b)

Fig. 2. Top-view of the trajectories followed by the robot during the recording sessions in the Wageningen garden in (a) 2018 (W18) and (b) 2017 (W17).

of images indicating whether they depict similar or dissimilar scenes. For details about the labelling process, we refer the reader to [10].

We expanded the TB-Places data set with a new subset of 23K images (which we name W18), corresponding to a new recording session that took place in the garden in Wageningen during the summer of 2018. In Table 1, we report details on the composition of the data set. For the recording of the new set of images, the camera lenses where setup with an exposure value that allows to capture clearer details in the lower part of the image (i.e. closer objects and possible reference points) rather than in the upper part of the image (mostly sky). This provides visual localization algorithms with landmarks of finer quality for more precise camera pose estimation. The W18 set consists of 16 sequences, the trajectories of which are shown in Fig. 2a. As displayed in Fig. 2a and b, W18 data set covers parts of the environment that are not recorded in W17. Similarly to the rest of the data set, these additional images are provided with an associated camera pose in the garden reference system and a pair-wise similarity ground truth, which we constructed with the method proposed in [10]. Some examples of images in the W18 set are included in Fig. 3.

Fig. 3. Examples of TB-Places W18 data set. The left column shows reference images, while the center shows positive matches (green squares), and the right column shows negative matches (dashed red squares). (Color figure online)

3   Evaluation

For the experiments, we used the W17 set as training set and the W18 set as test set. This setting allows to evaluate the robustness of image descriptors for place recognition against seasonal changes of the garden, color variations, as well as generalization to parts of the garden that are not seen during training.

We carried out experiments to evaluate the performance of state-of-the-art holistic image descriptors that we took as the baseline, and show that garden-specific descriptors can be developed by learning suitable representations using the garden images contained in the TB-Places data set. In the rest of the section, we provide details about the employed baseline descriptors and the learning process that we implemented.

3.1 Performance Measures

We evaluated the performance of the considered descriptors (see Sect. 3.2 for details) by computing the precision (P), recall (R) and F_1-score for the classification of pairs of images as depicting similar or dissimilar places:

$$P = \frac{TP}{TP + FP}, R = \frac{TP}{TP + FN}, F_1 = \frac{2 \times P \times R}{R + P}$$

where TP stands for true positives, TN is true negatives and FN means false negatives. A positive sample corresponds to a pair of images depicting the same scene. We present the results that we achieved in the form of a precision-recall curve, that we constructed by varying a threshold t on the Euclidean distance of the computed image descriptors. All pairs with distance lower or equal to t are classified as similar (positive).

Moreover, as an overall performance measure, we compute the Average Precision (AP), defined as:

$$AP = \sum_t (R_t - R_{t-1})P_n$$

3.2 Baseline

We selected three state-of-the-art holistic image descriptors as the baseline descriptors for evaluation of place recognition performance on the extended TB-Places data set. We considered the representation computed at the last layer of the ResNet-152 [7], DenseNet-161 [8] and NetVLAD [1] architectures. For NetVLAD, we also evaluated the feature vectors computed at two intermediate layers, namely relu5_2 and pool5. In the case of ResNet and DenseNet, the baseline models were trained on ImageNet [6], while the baseline NetVLAD model was trained on the Pittsburg30k data set [24]. When the output descriptor is three dimensional, we apply a *AvgPool* operation, which outputs the average of the activation of each kernel, and a *MaxPool*, which computes the maximum. In Table 2 we report further details about the dimensionality of the considered image descriptors.

3.3 Learning Garden-Specific Representations

We employed a siamese CNN architecture where two backbone networks that share their weights to compute the descriptors of two input images (see Fig. 4).

Table 2. Details on the descriptors that we considered in the benchmark analysis.

Model	Layer	Feature pooling	Descriptor size
NetVLAD	VLAD	-	4096
	AvgPool	-	$(512 \times 7 \times 7) = 25088$
		MaxPool	512
		AvgPool	512
	relu5_2	-	$(512 \times 7 \times 10) = 35840$
		MaxPool	512
		AvgPool	512
	pool5	-	$(512 \times 7 \times 10) = 35840$
		MaxPool	512
		AvgPool	512
ResNet	AvgPool	-	2048
DenseNet	norm5	-	$(2208 \times 7 \times 11) = 170016$
		MaxPool	2208
		AvgPool	2208

During training, the weights of the networks are updated so as to optimize a Contrastive Loss function $L(f_0, f_1)$ that compares the computed descriptors, f_0 and f_1. As initial conditions for the learning process, we selected the ResNet and DenseNet models pre-trained on ImageNet, which we consider good initialization for place recognition, and NetVLAD, which is pre-trained on the Pittsburgh30k data set. We learn garden-specific representations by training the considered models with images of the TB-Places data set.

For all models, we evaluate the descriptor that we compute by means of a *global AvgPool* layer that we add in the end of the network. We use these descriptors to optimize a Contrastive Loss function L, formally defined as:

$$L(f_0, f_1) = \frac{1}{2N} \sum_{n=0}^{N-1} \left(y^{(n)} d(f_0^{(n)}, f_1^{(n)})^2 + (1 - y^{(n)}) \cdot \max(\alpha - d(f_0^{(n)}, f_1^{(n)}), 0)^2 \right)$$

where $d(f_{n0}, f_{n1}) = ||f_{n0} - f_{n1}||_2$ is the Euclidean distance between the feature vectors f_0 and f_1, y_n is the ground truth label (0: dissimilar, 1: similar). The hyperparameter α is the loss margin, i.e. a threshold value of the descriptor distance above which a pair of images is not considered as depicting the same place. We set α as the value of the threshold that contributes to the highest F_1-score on the training set (W17). The selected values are reported in Table 3.

We trained the considered models, for 15 epochs, using the 10K images included in the W17 set, which contain 330K image pairs with positive class label. We set the batch size equal to 16 pairs and included in each training epoch the 330k positive pairs and an equal number of negative pairs, in order to avoid class unbalance while training. The total amount of training iterations is thus approximately 620k. We trained with Stochastic Gradient Descent, with one initial learning rate of 0.01, that was decreased by 10^{-1} every 5 epochs.

As stated in [1], fine-tuning all the convolutional kernels in a CNN is not necessary to learn effective descriptors for visual place recognition. Early layers of a CNN, indeed, learn low level visual features (i.e. gabor-like filters) [9], while upper deeper learn to detect more complex, task-specific features. We thus train the parameters of layers deeper layers, which compute semantically rich features. In particular, for the ResNet-152 and DenseNet-161 backbone CNNs, we train the last residual block (block5), and for the VGG network of NetVLAD, we trained the last convolutional block (conv5). This choice allows to learn the value of a reduced set of parameters, i.e. only those of the deeper convolutional layers, simplifying the optimization problem and reducing the training time.

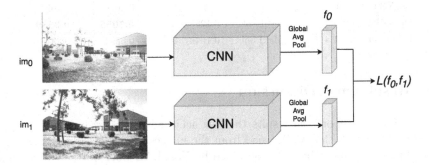

Fig. 4. Sketch of the employed architecture for learning garden-specific descriptors for place recognition. We feed a pair of images to a siamese CNN architecture and compute their representation with a Global Average Pool layer. The training is guided by optimizing a contrastive loss function $L(f_0, f_1)$.

Table 3. Details on the trained models. The second column displays the number of features of the learned holistic descriptors. The selected α values correspond to the threshold that produces the best F_1-score in the training set.

Model	Feature length	α
NetVLAD AvgPool + Global MaxPool	512	7.5
ResNet152 AvgPool	2048	12.7
DenseNet norm5 + Global AvgPool	2208	69.278

Table 4. Achieved performance (Average Precision) in W17 and W18 data sets before (Baseline) and after training the models.

Descriptor	Baseline		Trained	
	W17	W18	W17 (train)	W18 (test)
NetVLAD VLAD	0.1470	**0.1383**	-	-
NetVLAD AvgPool	0.1438	0.1018	0.4627	0.1921
NetVLAD AvgPool + Global AvgPool	0.1610	0.1264	0.7016	0.1230
NetVLAD AvgPool + Global MaxPool	0.1215	0.0844	0.4273	0.0893
NetVLAD relu5_2	0.1185	0.0812	0.4256	0.1470
NetVLAD relu5_2 + Global AvgPool	**0.1671**	0.1330	0.6978	0.1252
NetVLAD relu5_2 + Global MaxPool	0.1241	0.0894	0.4052	0.0879
NetVLAD pool5	0.1169	0.0899	0.4087	0.0996
NetVLAD pool5 + Global AvgPool	0.1590	0.1301	0.6749	0.1655
NetVLAD pool5 + Global MaxPool	0.1323	0.0972	0.4230	0.1011
ResNet152 AvgPool	0.0991	0.0891	0.6616	0.1605
DenseNet norm5 + Global AvgPool	0.1288	0.1078	**0.7055**	**0.2339**
DenseNet norm5 + Global MaxPool	0.1040	0.0724	0.6591	0.2318

4   Results and Discussion

In Table 4, we report the results that we achieved using the baseline descriptors and the ones that we learned from the images of the TB-Places data set. The highest value of the AP is obtained by NetVLAD both on the training set (W17) and on the test set (W18). More specifically, the descriptor computed with global average pooling on the relu5_2 layer of NetVLAD achieved the best performance results (AP = 0.1671) on the W17 set. On the W18 set, instead, the highest AP value (AP = 0.1383) was obtained by using as image descriptor the output of the VLAD layer of NetVLAD. After training the models using the siamese architecture described in Sect. 3, we observed an overall improvement of results as the networks are able to learn garden-specific features that contribute to improve the place recognition performance. The model that best performs after training is DenseNet, which achieves AP values of 0.7055 and 0.2339 on the train set (W17) and (W18) test set, respectively. In Fig. 5a and b, we show the Precision-Recall curves before and after training, respectively. All models improve their performance on the train and test set. The best results were obtained by DenseNet.

We observed that, although training the considered networks on the garden images contained in the TB-places data set contributes to improve place recognition results, the resulting models suffer from a certain degree of specialization. In Fig. 6, we show a plot that illustrate the effect of the training process on the specialization of the models. In the case of VGG NetVLAD, this happens right after the end of the first epoch, while for ResNet it happens after the second epoch (>80K iterations). The DenseNet model reaches its best performance in

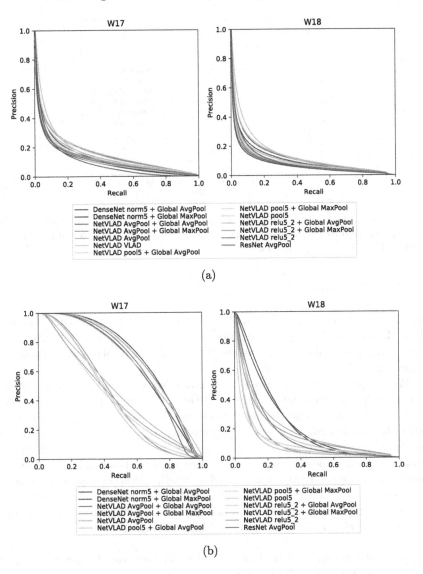

Fig. 5. Precision-recall curves achieved on train (W17) and test (W18) by the considered descriptors (a) before and (b) after training the models.

epoch six. This indicates that the methods, although able to learn effective garden descriptors, have a tendency to overfit after a certain number of iterations. We conjecture that this is due to the fact that the W18 data set images are captured with modified exposure setting of the camera, and CNNs are very sensitive to variations in the input, producing unstable outputs [20,26].

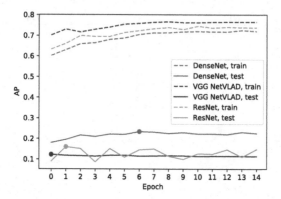

Fig. 6. Train and test performance vs training epoch. The bullet indicates the best test AP achieved by each method, corresponding to epoch 6 for DenseNet, epoch 0 for NetVLAD VGG, and epoch 1 for ResNet.

5   Conclusions

We proposed an extended version of the TB-Places data set, that includes more than 23k additional images recorded in a real garden of the Trimbot2020 project. The data set is designed to stimulate the benchmark of place recognition algorithms in garden environments.

We compared the performance of several CNN-based holistic image descriptors, namely those computed by ResNet, DenseNet and NetVLAD architecture, on the task of place recognition in garden scenes. We learned garden-specific image descriptors and demonstrated that garden-scene representations can be learned and improve the recognition results. However, their performance is affected by variations of the appearance of the environment due to changing light and weather conditions, or to color variations caused by modifications of exposure settings of the cameras. Thus, their generalization capabilities are limited. Therefore, the design of new robust image descriptors is required for effective visual localization or navigation systems for gardening and agricultural robotics.

Acknowledgements. This work was funded by the European Horizon 2020 program, under the project TrimBot2020 (grant No. 688007).

References

1. Arandjelovic, R., Gronat, P., Torii, A., Pajdla, T., Sivic, J.: NetVLAD: CNN architecture for weakly supervised place recognition. In: IEEE CVPR, pp. 5297–5307 (2016)
2. Bac, C.W., van Henten, E.J., Hemming, J., Edan, Y.: Harvesting robots for high-value crops: state-of-the-art review and challenges ahead. J. Field Robot. **31**(6), 888–911 (2014)
3. Badino, H., Huber, D., Kanade, T.: Visual topometric localization. In: 2011 IEEE Intelligent Vehicles Symposium (IV), pp. 794–799 (2011)

4. Cummins, M., Newman, P.: FAB-MAP: probabilistic localization and mapping in the space of appearance. Int. J. Robot. Res. **27**(6), 647–665 (2008)
5. Cummins, M., Newman, P.: Highly scalable appearance-only SLAM-FAB-MAP 2.0. Robot. Sci. Syst. **5**, 17 (2009)
6. Geiger, A., Lenz, P., Stiller, C., Urtasun, R.: Vision meets robotics: the KITTI dataset. Int. J. Robot. Res. **32**(11), 1231–1237 (2013)
7. He, K., Zhang, X., Ren, S., Sun, J.: Deep residual learning for image recognition. In: IEEE CVPR, pp. 770–778 (2016)
8. Huang, G., Liu, Z., Van Der Maaten, L., Weinberger, K.Q.: Densely connected convolutional networks. In: IEEE CVPR, pp. 4700–4708 (2017)
9. Krizhevsky, A., Sutskever, I., Hinton, G.E.: ImageNet classification with deep convolutional neural networks. In: NIPS, pp. 1097–1105 (2012)
10. Leyva-Vallina, M., Strisciuglio, N., López-Antequera, M., Tylecek, R., Blaich, M., Petkov, N.: TB-places: a data set for visual place recognition in garden environments. IEEE Access **7**, 52277–52287 (2019)
11. Lopez-Antequera, M., Gomez-Ojeda, R., Petkov, N., Gonzalez-Jimenez, J.: Appearance-invariant place recognition by discriminatively training a convolutional neural network. Pattern Recognit. Lett. **92**, 89–95 (2017)
12. Lowry, S., et al.: Visual place recognition: a survey. IEEE Trans. Robot. **32**(1), 1–19 (2016)
13. McManus, C., Churchill, W., Maddern, W., Stewart, A.D., Newman, P.: Shady dealings: robust, long-term visual localisation using illumination invariance. In: IEEE ICRA, pp. 901–906 (2014)
14. Milford, M.J., Wyeth, G.F.: SeqSLAM: visual route-based navigation for sunny summer days and stormy winter nights. In: IEEE ICRA, pp. 1643–1649 (2012)
15. Ohi, N., et al.: Design of an autonomous precision pollination robot. In: IEEE IROS (2018)
16. Sattler, T., et al.: Benchmarking 6DOF outdoor visual localization in changing conditions. In: IEEE CVPR, vol. 1 (2018)
17. Sattler, T., Weyand, T., Leibe, B., Kobbelt, L.: Image retrieval for image-based localization revisited. In: BMVC, vol. 1, p. 4 (2012)
18. Shotton, J., Glocker, B., Zach, C., Izadi, S., Criminisi, A., Fitzgibbon, A.: Scene coordinate regression forests for camera relocalization in RGB-D images. In: IEEE CVPR, pp. 2930–2937 (2013)
19. Simonyan, K., Zisserman, A.: Very deep convolutional networks for large-scale image recognition. arXiv preprint arXiv:1409.1556 (2014)
20. Strisciuglio, N., Lopez-Antequera, M., Petkov, N.: A push-pull layer improves robustness of convolutional neural networks. arXiv preprint arXiv:1901.10208 (2019)
21. Strisciuglio, N., et al.: TrimBot2020: an outdoor robot for automatic gardening. In: ISR (2018)
22. Sünderhauf, N., Neubert, P., Protzel, P.: Are we there yet? Challenging SeqSLAM on a 3000 km journey across all four seasons. In: IEEE ICRA, p. 2013 (2013)
23. Sünderhauf, N., Protzel, P.: BRIEF-Gist-closing the loop by simple means. In: IEEE IROS, pp. 1234–1241. IEEE (2011)
24. Torii, A., Sivic, J., Okutomi, M., Pajdla, T.: Visual place recognition with repetitive structures. IEEE Trans. Pattern Anal. Mach. Intell. **37**, 2346–2359 (2015)
25. Walter, A., et al.: Flourish-a robotic approach for automation in crop management. In: ICPA (2018)
26. Zheng, S., Song, Y., Leung, T., Goodfellow, I.: Improving the robustness of deep neural networks via stability training. In: IEEE CVPR, pp. 4480–4488 (2016)

500,000 Images Closer to Eyelid
and Pupil Segmentation

Wolfgang Fuhl$^{(\boxtimes)}$, Wolfgang Rosenstiel, and Enkelejda Kasneci

Eberhard Karls University Tübingen, 72076 Tübingen, Germany
{Wolfgang.Fuhl,Wolfgang.Rosenstiel,Enkelejda.Kasneci}@uni-tuebingen.de

Abstract. Human gaze behavior is not the only important aspect about
eye tracking. The eyelids reveal additional important information; such
as fatigue as well as the pupil size holds indications of the workload.
The current state-of-the-art datasets focus on challenges in pupil center
detection, whereas other aspects, such as the lid closure and pupil size,
are neglected. Therefore, we propose a fully convolutional neural network for pupil and eyelid segmentation as well as eyelid landmark and
pupil ellipsis regression. The network is jointly trained using the Log
loss for segmentation and L1 loss for landmark and ellipsis regression.
The application of the proposed network is the offline processing and
creation of datasets. Which can be used to train resource-saving and
real-time machine learning algorithms such as random forests. In addition, we will provide the worlds largest eye images dataset with more
than 500,000 images DOWNLOAD.

Keywords: Eye tracking · Eyelid segmentation · Eyelid opening ·
Pupil segmentation · Landmark detection · Landmark regression ·
Pupil ellipses regression · Eyelid regression

1 Introduction

Psychology, medicine, marketing research, computer graphics, car industry, and
many other disciplines are interested in the information contained in human
eyes. For instance computer graphics need a robust gaze signal for foveated
rendering [31,50] to be useful for the consumer market. With the upcoming of
autonomous driving, the interest in information contained in the eye is also rising for the car industry [6,44]. They not only regard the gaze signal alone. The
main interest is in the estimation of the drivers capability to take over the car in
critical situations [6,44]. Therefore, other features such as the eyelids are important to extract information about the cognitive state of a person [29,46]. This
information is also important for psychology and cognition science. Where the
workload of a person [40,48], movement processes which are predictable based on
the gaze [41], and also characteristic eye movements which identify diseases [5].
In medicine, eye tracking is not applied to disease classification [4,35]. Current
research also regards novice training and expertise level classification [14,28] as

© Springer Nature Switzerland AG 2019
M. Vento and G. Percannella (Eds.): CAIP 2019, LNCS 11678, pp. 336–347, 2019.
https://doi.org/10.1007/978-3-030-29888-3_27

well as surgical microscope steering [13]. Using the gaze signal as a control signal for human computer interaction is also used in virtual reality [12] and the eye is used as an identification characteristic [47]. Duchowski summarized most of the aforementioned application areas already in 2002 [11]. Further advancement in the field of eye tracking and its application areas is still limited by the amount of information that can be extracted out of the eye.

Current research in video based eye tracking mainly concerns a robust pupil signal [20, 26, 49]. The same is true for commercial systems [38] because robust gaze signal is the most important first step for eye tracking to be applicable. It needs to handle near infrared illuminated images containing heavy reflections, and rapid illumination changes trough sunlight etc. Stand alone algorithms for eyelid extraction and eyelid opening estimation were also proposed in [10, 23]. This separation of pupil and eyelid detection limits research and progress in application areas that use all the information contained in the eye. Machine learning based image processing have made huge progress through the invention of local stationary features as used in convolution neural networks (CNN) [42]. Together with the advances in hardware allowing GPUs as massive parallel programming device, CNNs are already applicable in real time. Further advances in CNN architectures, like residual [34] and inception modules [57], allow to train deeper networks and improve the accuracy and robustness further. The current state-of-the-art in computer vision tasks (detection, classification, segmentation, image generation) is taken by the above mentioned architectures. For semantic image segmentation, the invention of transposed convolutions [45] lead to a breakthrough. They can train a fully convolution neural network [45] in a way that the loss function also contains spatial information compared to fully connected layers. Another approach is the encoder and decoder architecture [3]. Here, the pooling information is shared between corresponding layers in the encoder and the decoder for up-sampling. Other approaches for image segmentation stem from generative adversarial networks (GAN) [30]. They have the disadvantage that the training is difficult because the discriminator is likely to overfit. While this issue was solved with the cycle loss function [65] and unpaired training samples, they have not yet achieved the accuracy of fully convolutional neural networks trained on training sample pairs.

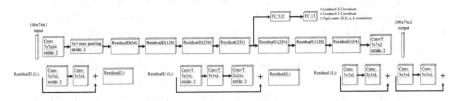

Fig. 1. The proposed architecture of the joint regression and segmentation CNN.

In this work, we propose a combined convolutional neural network architecture for eyelid landmark, pupil ellipse regression together with pupil area and eyelid area segmentation. Our architecture is based on residual blocks [34], which allow us to train a deep network. We used the L1 loss and the log loss function for regression and segmentation respectively. The idea behind a combined approach is that multiple tasks performed by the same network improve the accuracy [64]. Additionally, the results and the landmarks can be compared against each other to detect invalid segmentations and correct them. Furthermore, we contribute a large dataset containing more than 500,000 images with segmented pupil and eyelid areas. These images were annotated using the proposed architecture, which will be described with the training procedure in the following.

2   Related Works

Recent developments in video based eye tracking concern the improvement of the reliability of the pupil signal. Summarizations for head mounted and remote eye tracking can be found in [26,59] and [20,49] respectively. One difference between head and remote eye tracking is the resolution of the eye images and the necessity for remote eye tracking to detect the face of a person and estimate its head pose. In head mounted eye tracking, the most successful approaches are based on edge detection [21,25,54,56], which allows to extract the pupil ellipses. This process is important for the validation [25,54] as well as the precision, since the ellipsis allows sub pixel accuracy. While edge based approaches are continuously improving, other attempts based on thresholding also have their advantages if edge detection is not applicable, i.e. for blurred and out of focus images. These attempts range from adaptive thresholding [32] to segment selection and combination [36]. Multistage approaches based on CNNs where also applied already [2,24,60]. They have the advantage to be applicable for a wider variety of challenges with the drawback of higher computational demands. Other approaches out of the realm of machine learning are based on random ferns [19] and oriented edge boosting [18]. Currently, the main disadvantage of all machine learning approaches so far is the lack in available pupil outline annotations for segmentation.

In the field of eyelid segmentation, edge detection was one of the first applied methods [62]. After the eyelid edges where found, the structure was approximated using parabolas for the upper and lower lid. Another edge based approach was proposed in [9]. Here, the iris was initially detected and afterwards the eyelids based on their distortion of the circular structure of the iris. The final approximation of the eyelids was done using splines. Similar to first eyelid extraction approach, the largest edges were selected with the difference of an anisotropic diffusion preprocessing [1]. Since blurred and out of focus images affect edge detection, a thresholding approach was proposed in [55]. After the separation of the image into regions based on a threshold, a likelihood map was computed using texture patches [63]. This approach was further developed using additional statistics for the computation of the likelyhood map [16]. VASIR [43] uses a linear Hough transform for iris segmentation in the first step. In the second step, a third order polynomial is fitted to edges above and below the iris for eyelid approximation. Machine learning approaches where also applied for eyelid detection [53] as well as histograms of oriented gradients and support vector machines [17]. Similar to BORE [18], an optimization was formulated to extract the eyelids based on oriented edge values [23].

The field of computer vision also achieved considerable progress in image segmentation. On the one hand it comes by the further development of the CNN architecture [34,58] and on the other hand from the development of transposed convolution filters [45]. Other approaches where also developed using the pooling indices of an encoder for up sampling but with less success [3]. Both used the soft max loss function to train their networks. The fully convolution approach was further developed by applying a region loss function [8,33,51] to achieve a higher accuracy at the segmentation borders. Unpaired training of generative adversarial networks (GANs) [30] together with the cycle loss function [65] was also applied on image segmentation, but the current state-of-the-art is based on the fully convolution architecture together with conditional random fields for refinement [7].

In this work, we use fully convolutional neural networks which have been proven to be the best performers on image segmentation [7,27]. Our network is jointly trained for segmentation and landmark regression to further improve the accuracy [64]. This network was used to generate a huge dataset together with manual correction of the found segmentations.

3   Method

Figure 1 shows the architecture of our CNN. Our network starts with a convolution and pooling layer. Afterward, residual layers with downscaling (ResidualD(L)) are used for feature encoding. The parameter L is the amount of learned filters. For further feature encoding, we used a residual block without scaling (Residual(L)). Outgoing from the result of this block, we regress the landmarks and the parameters of the pupil ellipse. In addition, we use the results of the central residual block for segmentation. Therefore, we use transposed convolutions in residual blocks (ResidualU(L)). The "ConvT." is a transposed convolution and is computed by upscaling the input by the specified stride. The final transposed convolution outputs the segmentation in two separated layers.

The design of the architecture has two purposes. First it allows the usage of only the regression part of the CNN, which makes it real time capable on a GPU ($\approx$6 ms), this runtime can be further reduce using binarized weights. In addition, the segmentation using the transposed convolution layers allows to increase the loss for training due to the pixel-wise comparison. It allows longer training period and, therefore, more accurate results.

Since the pupil parameters are numerically in no relation to landmarks and the additional segmentation, the loss function of the ellipse was reformulated into landmark form. Therefore, one ellipse is interpreted as n points (eight in our implementation). It allows to calculate the euclidean distance for each point, which serves as a loss function and is equivalent to the eyelid landmarks. For this it is necessary that each landmark can be assigned to a different one, for which we have used the orientation to the elliptical center. It means that each landmark on the ellipse corresponds to an angle $(0°, 45°, 90°, 135°, 180°, \dots$ in our implementation).

Fig. 2. The pupil ellipse as landmark representation. Landmarks in the same color belong to the same orientation. (Color figure online)

Figure 2 shows the representation of the pupil ellipse as landmark. It means that our FC13 block in Fig. 1 contains an internal block with sixteen inputs (elliptical landmarks) and five outputs (ellipse parameters). For the final ellipse parameter estimation we used the geometrical ellipse fitting approach proposed in [52].

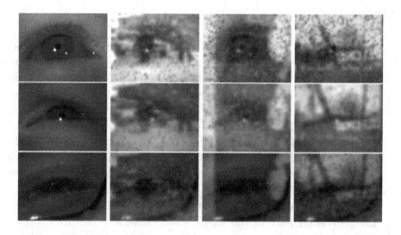

Fig. 3. Augmented training samples where the first column is the input image and the following rows are the image with added reflections, noise, adjusted contrast etc.

For training, we used a fixed learning rate of 10^{-8}. The loss function for the fully connected layers regressing the landmarks and the ellipse was an L1 norm and for the segmentation we used a logarithmic loss. We trained our network for ≈ 2000 epochs, whereby we augmented the data online so that our network could not see the same image twice. For data augmentation, we used image shifts of up to 40% in each direction to cover images where the entire eye is not present. Scaling each axis between 0.8 and 1.2 was applied to cover more camera perspectives than present in the training dataset together with a rotation between −30 and 30°. We also added random noise between 0 and 30% of the image. The contrast was changed between −30% and 30% of the intensity values. For occlusions, we added random patches which could cover up to 50% of the image. Reflections were added based on the approach from [61], where the reflection is assumed to be a blurred additive of a second image. Therefore, we used all the images from the PASCAL Visual Object Classes Challenge 2007 [15] as reflection pool from which we selected randomly. Those reflections were also shifted, rotated, and scaled with the same parameters as the original image. Examples of augmented data without shifting and scaling are shown in Fig. 3. For the training dataset, we used the one published in [17], which consists of 16,200 hand-labeled images, where the eyelids and the pupil ellipsis was annotated. The recording system was a near-infrared remote camera in a driving simulator setting with a resolution of 1280 × 752 pixels.

4   Data Set

The image source for our dataset was the same as for the ElSe [25] and ExCuSe [21] algorithm, which are the on-road recordings from [37]. The recording device during this study was a head-mounted camera system (Dikablis Mobile Eye Tracker by Ergoneers GmbH) with a frame rate of 25 Hz and a resolution of 384 × 288. Our dataset contains 20 subjects and 501,230 images. Figure 5 shows some exemplary images with drawn eyelids (red) as well as the pupils ellipse (green). The contained challenges are noise, illumination changes, closed eyes, reflections, eyelashes, makeup, pupil dilation, motion blur, contact lens, and physiological characteristics (e.g. additional black dot on the iris). For the annotation, we used the proposed network (Fig. 1). Afterwards, we used the Jaccard index ($\frac{A1 \cap A2}{A1 \cup A2}$) to evaluate the quality of the found annotations: 0.5 is common as a good value for segmentations. A1, in our case, is the area of the segmentation and A2 is the area segmented by our landmarks and pupil ellipses. For interpolation of the landmarks we used natural Bezier splines. Figure 4 shows a segmentation on the left, where white is the pupil area and grey the eyelid area. The central image in Fig. 4 shows the detected landmarks in red and the pupil

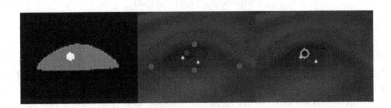

Fig. 4. Example result of our network with the segmentation, landmarks, and pupil ellipses in the same order. (Color figure online)

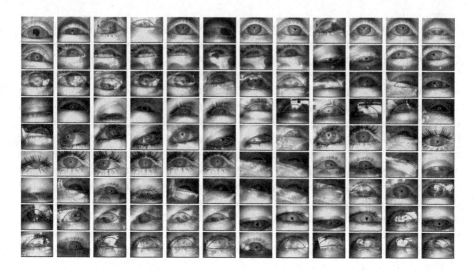

Fig. 5. Examples from the proposed dataset.

center in blue. The pupil ellipses is drawn in green on the right of Fig. 4. For
finding false detections and false segmentations, we used the averaged sum of the
Jaccard index of the segmented eyelid area and the area enclosed by the landmarks (red dots in Fig. 4) as well as the pupil segment (white) and the area of
the pupil ellipses. If the average Jaccard index was below 0.8, we inspected and
corrected the image. Afterwards, we analysed all frames as video for mistakes.
Overall, we had to correct ≈2% of the eyelid and ≈4% of the pupil annotations.
The manual annotation itself was done using a modified version of EyeLad [22],
which allows to annotate the pupil ellipses and the eyelids with many supporting
features like relative normalization, zooming, and tracking.

Table 1. Average Jaccard index per algorithm on the dataset from [25].

Algorithm	Eyelid	Pupil
[39]	41.45	-
[23]	52.89	-
Proposed	87.34	81.00

The runtime of our trained network is 30ms per image on an NVIDIA 1050Ti
for the entire architecture. Since our network is capable of regressing landmarks
and segment the image, the segmentation part can be omitted for a faster detection. It improves the runtime to 6ms per image, which allows a realtime usage
with 160 Hz using a GPU. The average Jaccard index per subject cross validated
on the dataset proposed in [17] is 87.34 for the eyelid area and 81.00 for the pupil

area (Table 1). The ExCuSe [21], ElSe [25], and PupilNet [24], Swirski [56], and Labeled Pupils in the Wild [59] datasets were recorded using a head mounted eye tracker, we reach 92%, 96%, and 92% respectively for the pixel error up to 5 pixels which is the suggested pixel tolerance by the authors to compensate for inaccurate annotations (Table 2).

Table 2. Average detection result over all subjects on the publicly available datasets [21,24,25,56,59].

Algo.	ElSe	ExCuSe	[56]	PURE	CBF	PNET	Prop.
[21,24,25]	0.67	0.54	0.30	0.72	0.91	0.76	**0.92**
[56]	0.81	0.86	0.77	0.78	-	-	**0.96**
[59]	0.54	0.50	0.49	0.73	-	-	**0.92**

5 Conclusion

We propose a dataset for eyelid and pupil detection wherein the pupil ellipse as well as the enclosed eyelid area is segmented. The dataset contains more than 500,000 images from challenging real world recordings. In addition, we proposed a combined architecture for landmark regression and segmentation with a novel ellipse-to-landmark loss transformation. This network can also be used partially with a runtime of 6ms on the GPU for real time usage of up to 160 Hz. In addition, it can be used for dataset generation and data post processing. The dataset itself will help training and evaluating pupil and landmark detection algorithms, such as [18,19,39], which use less computational resources.

Acknowledgments. Work of the authors is supported by the Institutional Strategy of the University of Tübingen (Deutsche Forschungsgemeinschaft, ZUK 63). This research was supported by an IBM Shared University Research Grant including an IBM PowerAI environment. We especially thank our partners Benedikt Rombach, Martin Mähler and Hildegard Gerhardy from IBM for their expertise and support.

References

1. Adam, M., Rossant, F., Amiel, F., Mikovikova, B., Ea, T.: Eyelid localization for iris identification. Radioengineering **17**(4), 82–85 (2008)
2. Anas, E.R., Henríquez, P., Matuszewski, B.J.: Online eye status detection in the wild with convolutional neural networks. In: VISIGRAPP (6: VISAPP), pp. 88–95 (2017)
3. Badrinarayanan, V., Kendall, A., Cipolla, R.: SegNet: a deep convolutional encoder-decoder architecture for image segmentation. arXiv preprint arXiv:1511.00561 (2015)
4. Benitezy, J.T.: Eye-tracking and optokinetic tests: diagnostic significance in peripheral and central vestibular disorders. Laryngoscope **80**(6), 834–848 (1970)

5. Boraston, Z., Blakemore, S.J.: The application of eye-tracking technology in the study of autism. J. Physiol. **581**(3), 893–898 (2007)
6. Braunagel, C., Rosenstiel, W., Kasneci, E.: Ready for take-over? A new driver assistance system for an automated classification of driver take-over readiness. IEEE Intell. Transp. Syst. Mag. **9**(4), 10–22 (2017)
7. Chen, L.C., Papandreou, G., Kokkinos, I., Murphy, K., Yuille, A.L.: DeepLab: semantic image segmentation with deep convolutional nets, atrous convolution, and fully connected CRFs. IEEE Trans. Pattern Anal. Mach. Intell. **40**(4), 834–848 (2017)
8. Dai, J., He, K., Li, Y., Ren, S., Sun, J.: Instance-sensitive fully convolutional networks. In: Leibe, B., Matas, J., Sebe, N., Welling, M. (eds.) ECCV 2016. LNCS, vol. 9910, pp. 534–549. Springer, Cham (2016). https://doi.org/10.1007/978-3-319-46466-4_32
9. Daugman, J.: How Iris recognition works. In: The Essential Guide to Image Processing, pp. 715–739. Elsevier (2009)
10. Dong, W., Qu, P.: Eye state classification based on multi-feature fusion. In: Chinese Control and Decision Conference, CCDC 2009, pp. 231–234. IEEE (2009)
11. Duchowski, A.T.: A breadth-first survey of eye-tracking applications. Behav. Res. Methods Instrum. Comput. **34**(4), 455–470 (2002)
12. Duchowski, A.T., Shivashankaraiah, V., Rawls, T., Gramopadhye, A.K., Melloy, B.J., Kanki, B.: Binocular eye tracking in virtual reality for inspection training. In: Proceedings of the 2000 Symposium on Eye Tracking Research & Applications, pp. 89–96. ACM (2000)
13. Eivazi, S., Bednarik, R., Leinonen, V., von und zu Fraunberg, M., Jääskeläinen, J.E.: Embedding an eye tracker into a surgical microscope: requirements, design, and implementation. IEEE Sens. J. **16**(7), 2070–2078 (2016)
14. Eivazi, S., Bednarik, R., Tukiainen, M., von und zu Fraunberg, M., Leinonen, V., Jääskeläinen, J.E.: Gaze behaviour of expert and novice microneurosurgeons differs during observations of tumor removal recordings. In: Proceedings of the Symposium on Eye Tracking Research and Applications, pp. 377–380. ACM (2012)
15. Everingham, M., Van Gool, L., Williams, C.K., Winn, J., Zisserman, A.: The PASCAL visual object classes (VOC) challenge. Int. J. Comput. Vis. **88**(2), 303 (2010)
16. Fuhl, W., Santini, T., Geisler, D., Kübler, T., Rosenstiel, W., Kasneci, E.: Eyes wide open? Eyelid location and eye aperture estimation for pervasive eye tracking in real-world scenarios. In: PETMEI, September 2016
17. Fuhl, W., Castner, N., Zhuang, L., Holzer, M., Rosenstiel, W., Kasneci, E.: MAM: transfer learning for fully automatic video annotation and specialized detector creation. In: Leal-Taixé, L., Roth, S. (eds.) ECCV 2018. LNCS, vol. 11133, pp. 375–388. Springer, Cham (2019). https://doi.org/10.1007/978-3-030-11021-5_23
18. Fuhl, W., Eivazi, S., Hosp, B., Eivazi, A., Rosenstiel, W., Kasneci, E.: BORE: boosted-oriented edge optimization for robust, real time remote pupil center detection. In: Proceedings of the 2018 ACM Symposium on Eye Tracking Research & Applications, p. 48. ACM (2018)
19. Fuhl, W., Geisler, D., Santini, T., Appel, T., Rosenstiel, W., Kasneci, E.: CBF: circular binary features for robust and real-time pupil center detection. In: Proceedings of the 2018 ACM Symposium on Eye Tracking Research & Applications, p. 8. ACM (2018)

20. Fuhl, W., Geisler, D., Santini, T., Rosenstiel, W., Kasneci, E.: Evaluation of state-of-the-art pupil detection algorithms on remote eye images. In: Proceedings of the 2016 ACM International Joint Conference on Pervasive and Ubiquitous Computing: Adjunct, pp. 1716–1725. ACM (2016)

21. Fuhl, W., Kübler, T., Sippel, K., Rosenstiel, W., Kasneci, E.: ExCuSe: robust pupil detection in real-world scenarios. In: Azzopardi, G., Petkov, N. (eds.) CAIP 2015. LNCS, vol. 9256, pp. 39–51. Springer, Cham (2015). https://doi.org/10.1007/978-3-319-23192-1_4

22. Fuhl, W., Santini, T., Geisler, D., Kübler, T., Kasneci, E.: EyeLad: remote eye tracking image labeling tool. In: 12th Joint Conference on Computer Vision, Imaging and Computer Graphics Theory and Applications (VISIGRAPP 2017), February 2017

23. Fuhl, W., Santini, T., Kasneci, E.: Fast and robust eyelid outline and aperture detection in real-world scenarios. In: 2017 IEEE Winter Conference on Applications of Computer Vision (WACV), pp. 1089–1097. IEEE (2017)

24. Fuhl, W., Santini, T., Kasneci, G., Kasneci, E.: PupilNet: convolutional neural networks for robust pupil detection. arXiv preprint arXiv:1601.04902 (2016)

25. Fuhl, W., Santini, T.C., Kübler, T., Kasneci, E.: ElSe: ellipse selection for robust pupil detection in real-world environments. In: Proceedings of the Ninth Biennial ACM Symposium on Eye Tracking Research & Applications, pp. 123–130. ACM (2016)

26. Fuhl, W., Tonsen, M., Bulling, A., Kasneci, E.: Pupil detection for head-mounted eye tracking in the wild: an evaluation of the state of the art. Mach. Vis. Appl. **27**(8), 1275–1288 (2016)

27. Garcia-Garcia, A., Orts-Escolano, S., Oprea, S., Villena-Martinez, V., Garcia-Rodriguez, J.: A review on deep learning techniques applied to semantic segmentation. arXiv preprint arXiv:1704.06857 (2017)

28. Gegenfurtner, A., Lehtinen, E., Säljö, R.: Expertise differences in the comprehension of visualizations: a meta-analysis of eye-tracking research in professional domains. Educ. Psychol. Rev. **23**(4), 523–552 (2011)

29. Gilzenrat, M.S., Nieuwenhuis, S., Jepma, M., Cohen, J.D.: Pupil diameter tracks changes in control state predicted by the adaptive gain theory of locus coeruleus function. Cogn. Affect. Behav. Neurosci. **10**(2), 252–269 (2010)

30. Goodfellow, I., et al.: Generative adversarial nets. In: Advances in Neural Information Processing Systems, pp. 2672–2680 (2014)

31. Guenter, B., Finch, M., Drucker, S., Tan, D., Snyder, J.: Foveated 3D graphics. ACM Trans. Graph. (TOG) **31**(6), 164 (2012)

32. Haro, A., Flickner, M., Essa, I.: Detecting and tracking eyes by using their physiological properties, dynamics, and appearance. In: Proceedings of the IEEE Conference on Computer Vision and Pattern Recognition, vol. 1, pp. 163–168. IEEE (2000)

33. He, K., Gkioxari, G., Dollár, P., Girshick, R.: Mask R-CNN. In: 2017 IEEE International Conference on Computer Vision (ICCV), pp. 2980–2988. IEEE (2017)

34. He, K., Zhang, X., Ren, S., Sun, J.: Deep residual learning for image recognition. In: Proceedings of the IEEE Conference on Computer Vision and Pattern Recognition, pp. 770–778 (2016)

35. Holzman, P.S., Proctor, L.R., Levy, D.L., Yasillo, N.J., Meltzer, H.Y., Hurt, S.W.: Eye-tracking dysfunctions in schizophrenic patients and their relatives. Arch. Gen. Psychiatry **31**(2), 143–151 (1974)

36. Javadi, A.H., Hakimi, Z., Barati, M., Walsh, V., Tcheang, L.: SET: a pupil detection method using sinusoidal approximation. Front. Neuroeng. **8**, 4 (2015)

37. Kasneci, E., et al.: Driving with binocular visual field loss? A study on a supervised on-road parcours with simultaneous eye and head tracking. PLoS ONE **9**(2), e87470 (2014)
38. Kassner, M., Patera, W., Bulling, A.: Pupil: an open source platform for pervasive eye tracking and mobile gaze-based interaction. In: Proceedings of the 2014 ACM International Joint Conference on Pervasive and Ubiquitous Computing: Adjunct Publication, pp. 1151–1160. ACM (2014)
39. Kazemi, V., Sullivan, J.: One millisecond face alignment with an ensemble of regression trees. In: Proceedings of the IEEE Conference on Computer Vision and Pattern Recognition, pp. 1867–1874 (2014)
40. Krumpe, T., Scharinger, C., Gerjets, P., Rosenstiel, W., Spüler, M.: Disentangeling working memory load—finding inhibition and updating components in EEG data. In: Proceedings of the 6th International Brain-Computer Interface Meeting: BCI Past, Present, and Future, p. 174 (2016)
41. Lappi, O.: Eye movements in the wild: oculomotor control, gaze behavior & frames of reference. Neurosci. Biobehav. Rev. **69**, 49–68 (2016)
42. LeCun, Y., et al.: Backpropagation applied to handwritten zip code recognition. Neural Comput. **1**(4), 541–551 (1989)
43. Lee, Y., Micheals, R.J., Filliben, J.J., Phillips, P.J.: VASIR: an open-source research platform for advanced iris recognition technologies. J. Res. Nat. Inst. Stand. Technol. **118**, 218 (2013)
44. Liu, X., Xu, F., Fujimura, K.: Real-time eye detection and tracking for driver observation under various light conditions. In: IEEE Intelligent Vehicle Symposium, vol. 2, pp. 344–351. IEEE (2002)
45. Long, J., Shelhamer, E., Darrell, T.: Fully convolutional networks for semantic segmentation. In: Proceedings of the IEEE Conference on Computer Vision and Pattern Recognition, pp. 3431–3440 (2015)
46. Marshall, S.P.: Identifying cognitive state from eye metrics. Aviat. Space Environ. Med. **78**(5), B165–B175 (2007)
47. Matsushita, M.: Iris identification system and Iris identification method, US Patent 5,901,238, 4 May 1999
48. Palinko, O., Kun, A.L., Shyrokov, A., Heeman, P.: Estimating cognitive load using remote eye tracking in a driving simulator. In: Proceedings of the 2010 Symposium on Eye-Tracking Research & Applications, pp. 141–144. ACM (2010)
49. Park, S., Zhang, X., Bulling, A., Hilliges, O.: Learning to find eye region landmarks for remote gaze estimation in unconstrained settings. In: Proceedings of the 2018 ACM Symposium on Eye Tracking Research & Applications, p. 21. ACM (2018)
50. Patney, A., et al.: Towards foveated rendering for gaze-tracked virtual reality. ACM Trans. Graph. (TOG) **35**(6), 179 (2016)
51. Pinheiro, P.O., Lin, T.-Y., Collobert, R., Dollár, P.: Learning to refine object segments. In: Leibe, B., Matas, J., Sebe, N., Welling, M. (eds.) ECCV 2016. LNCS, vol. 9905, pp. 75–91. Springer, Cham (2016). https://doi.org/10.1007/978-3-319-46448-0_5
52. Prasad, D.K., Leung, M.K., Quek, C.: ElliFit: an unconstrained, non-iterative, least squares based geometric ellipse fitting method. Pattern Recogn. **46**(5), 1449–1465 (2013)
53. Ren, S., Cao, X., Wei, Y., Sun, J.: Face alignment at 3000 FPS via regressing local binary features. In: Proceedings of the IEEE Conference on Computer Vision and Pattern Recognition, pp. 1685–1692 (2014)
54. Santini, T., Fuhl, W., Kasneci, E.: PuRe: robust pupil detection for real-time pervasive eye tracking. Comput. Vis. Image Underst. **170**, 40–50 (2018)

55. Suzuki, M., Yamamoto, N., Yamamoto, O., Nakano, T., Yamamoto, S.: Measurement of driver's consciousness by image processing-a method for presuming driver's drowsiness by eye-blinks coping with individual differences. In: SMC, vol. 4, pp. 2891–2896. IEEE (2006)

56. Świrski, L., Bulling, A., Dodgson, N.: Robust real-time pupil tracking in highly off-axis images. In: Proceedings of the Symposium on Eye Tracking Research and Applications, pp. 173–176. ACM (2012)

57. Szegedy, C., Ioffe, S., Vanhoucke, V., Alemi, A.A.: Inception-v4, Inception-ResNet and the impact of residual connections on learning. In: AAAI, vol. 4, p. 12 (2017)

58. Szegedy, C., et al.: Going deeper with convolutions. In: Proceedings of the IEEE Conference on Computer Vision and Pattern Recognition, pp. 1–9 (2015)

59. Tonsen, M., Zhang, X., Sugano, Y., Bulling, A.: Labelled pupils in the wild: a dataset for studying pupil detection in unconstrained environments. In: Proceedings of the Ninth Biennial ACM Symposium on Eye Tracking Research & Applications, pp. 139–142. ACM (2016)

60. Vera-Olmos, F.J., Malpica, N.: Deconvolutional neural network for pupil detection in real-world environments. In: Ferrández Vicente, J.M., Álvarez-Sánchez, J.R., de la Paz López, F., Toledo Moreo, J., Adeli, H. (eds.) IWINAC 2017. LNCS, vol. 10338, pp. 223–231. Springer, Cham (2017). https://doi.org/10.1007/978-3-319-59773-7_23

61. Wan, R., Shi, B., Duan, L.Y., Tan, A.H., Kot, A.C.: Benchmarking single-image reflection removal algorithms. In: Proceedings of ICCV (2017)

62. Wildes, R.P.: Iris recognition: an emerging biometric technology. Proc. IEEE 85(9), 1348–1363 (1997)

63. Yang, F., Yu, X., Huang, J., Yang, P., Metaxas, D.: Robust eyelid tracking for fatigue detection. In: ICIP, pp. 1829–1832, September 2012

64. Zhang, K., Zhang, Z., Li, Z., Qiao, Y.: Joint face detection and alignment using multitask cascaded convolutional networks. IEEE Signal Process. Lett. 23(10), 1499–1503 (2016)

65. Zhu, J.Y., Park, T., Isola, P., Efros, A.A.: Unpaired image-to-image translation using cycle-consistent adversarial networks. arXiv preprint (2017)

Structural and Computational Pattern Recognition

Blur Invariant Template Matching Using Projection onto Convex Sets

Matěj Lébl[1]([✉]), Filip Šroubek[1], Jaroslav Kautský[2], and Jan Flusser[1]

[1] Institute of Information Theory and Automation, The Czech Academy of Sciences,
Pod Vodárenskou věží 4, 182 08 Prague 8, Czech Republic
{lebl,sroubekf,flusser}@utia.cas.cz
[2] The Flinders University of South Australia, Adelaide, Australia

Abstract. Blur is a common phenomenon in image acquisition that negatively influences recognition rate if blurred images are used as a query in template matching. Various blur-invariant features and measures were proposed in the literature, yet they are often derived under conditions that are difficult to satisfy in practise, for example, images with zero background or periodically repeating images and classes of blur that are closed under convolution. We propose a novel blur-invariant distance that puts no limitation on images and is invariant to any kind of blur as long as the blur has limited support, non-zero values and sums up to one. A template matching algorithm is then derived based on the blur-invariant distance, which projects query images on convex sets constructed around template images. The proposed method is easy to implement, it is robust to noise and blur size, and outperforms other competitors in this area.

Keywords: Blur-invariant distance · Projection operator ·
Object recognition · Blurred image

1 Introduction

Image recognition covers a wide variety of practical and theoretical areas ranging from feature-based classification for product quality control to complex tasks such as video tracking used in forensics. The images themselves vary not only in captured information but also in quality. This paper focuses on a recognition of blurred templates. We introduce a method that can match a blurred query image against a database of clean templates. This task is very challenging as the templates may be fairly similar and some inputs can be severely degraded so that visual recognition is difficult. Presented results thus serve not only as automation of the recognition process but also help in cases when human visual classification fails.

This work was supported by the Czech Science Foundation (Grant No. GA18-07247S) and by the Praemium Academiae, awarded by the Czech Academy of Sciences.

© Springer Nature Switzerland AG 2019
M. Vento and G. Percannella (Eds.): CAIP 2019, LNCS 11678, pp. 351–362, 2019.
https://doi.org/10.1007/978-3-030-29888-3_28

A commonly used model of image acquisition is a simple convolution equation

$$g = f * h + n, \tag{1}$$

where f is the ideal original image, h is the blur kernel representing the degradation, and n is noise. Although this model is only an approximation of the real image formation process, it is a reasonable and mathematically tractable simplification of many real scenarios. In this paper, we assume the image degradation (blur and noise) to follow the model (1).

Since 1960's, a large number of papers have been devoted to image restoration, i.e. to estimation of f from its blurred version g. This is, however, superfluous for template matching purposes. One can avoid the time-consuming and ill-posed inversion of (1) by designing a matching algorithm, which is robust (or even totally invariant) to the blur. In this paper, we propose a new algorithm of this kind.

We show that all admissible blurred versions of an image form a convex set in the image space. We construct this set for each database template f_i. Given a query image g, we measure its distance to all these convex sets and g is then classified by a minimum distance rule. We show that the distance between an image and a convex set is a simple minimization problem which can be efficiently resolved numerically. This results in a blur-invariant matching algorithm, which outperforms state-of-the-art methods in most aspects. The performance of the algorithm is illustrated by experiments on standard datasets of human faces and handwritten digits.

The paper is organized as follows. First, we give an overview of related work in Sect. 2 and then we formulate the proposed blur-invariant distance formally in Sect. 3. The presented theory is used for developing a projection based method for blur-invariant template matching in Sect. 4. Sections 5 and 6 discuss the effect of noise and the blur size. Finally, the experimental Sect. 7 verifies the theory and provides a comparison with three reference methods.

2   Related Work

Methods performing the blur-invariant image recognition task can be categorized according to assumptions on the blur kernel properties. Most of the methods assume a particular shape of the blur and then construct invariants to convolution with the kernel of this kind. Classification is then performed in the space of invariants, usually by the minimum distance rule [8]. This approach was originally introduced by Flusser et al. [5,7] who proposed moment-based invariants w.r.t. centrosymmetric blur. Later on, their theory was extended to N-fold symmetric blur [6,15] and N-fold dihedral blur [16].

If a parametric form of the blur kernel is known, the invariants from the above group do not provide a maximum possible discrimination power because they do not employ the parametric form explicitly. In order to maximize the discriminability, some authors attempted to design special blur invariants w.r.t. rotation-symmetric Gaussian blur. First invariants of this kind were found heuristically [13,17] but recently a consistent theory of Gaussian blur invariants was presented in [4]. An interesting method, still limited to Gaussian blur, was published by Zhang et al. [20]. Instead of deriving blur invariants explicitly, the authors proposed a distance measure between two images which is independent of circular Gaussian blur. Their core idea is to estimate the blur level of images to be compared, bring them to the same blur level by blurring of the one which is less blurred, and then measure their similarity by the geodesic distance on a manifold.

Gopalan et al. [10] derived another blur-invariant distance measure without assuming the knowledge of the blur shape but imposed a limitation on its support size. From this point of view, their method is the closest one to our proposed technique, so we review their method in more detail.

Gopalan et al. established the correspondence between images and subspaces representing points on Grassmann manifold. Classification is then performed by minimizing the Riemannian distance of those points. This distance can be viewed as measuring angles between two subspaces. Gopalan et al. consider $\mathcal{H}$ to be a set of *arbitrary* blur kernels with fixed support $m \times n$, i.e.

$$\mathcal{H} = \left\{ h \in (\mathbb{R})^{m \times n} \right\}. \tag{2}$$

Then any blur $h \in \mathcal{H}$ can be written as a linear combination of "basis" blurs. Without loss of generality we can consider the standard basis

$$h_{ij}(x,y) = \begin{cases} 1, & \text{if } x = i, \, y = j, \\ 0, & \text{otherwise} \end{cases} \tag{3}$$

where $i = 1, \ldots, m$, $j = 1, \ldots, n$. The basis blurs are thus shifted delta functions.

Let us denote the set of all images resulting from the convolution of clear image f with the basis blurs h_{ij} as

$$\mathcal{S}_f = \{ f * h_{ij}, i = 1, \ldots, m, \, j = 1, \ldots, n \}. \tag{4}$$

Consequently, the blur invariance of $\text{Span}(\mathcal{S}_f)$ is proven, i.e. $\text{Span}(\mathcal{S}_f) = \text{Span}(\mathcal{S}_g)$. In theory, when g is a blurred version of f, both subspaces $\text{Span}(\mathcal{S}_f)$ and $\text{Span}(\mathcal{S}_g)$ are identical. Employing Grassmann manifold recognition is then performed by means of the minimum-distance classifier with metric defined by Riemannian distance $d_G(\text{Span}(\mathcal{S}_g), \text{Span}(\mathcal{S}_{f_i}))$.

3 Blur-Invariant Distance

Blur functions in standard acquisition scenarios have various shapes, yet typically they have three properties in common: limited support, non-negative values, and preservation of the mean image intensity. Let us define the set of admissible blurs with these properties as

$$\mathcal{H} := \left\{ h \in (\mathbb{R})^{m \times n} \, \middle| \, h(x,y) \geq 0, \sum_{x,y} h(x,y) = 1 \right\}. \tag{5}$$

where $D = m \times n$ is the maximal assumed blur size. Note that imposing the non-negativity and brightness-preservation constraints is a significant difference from the assumptions used in [10], which changes the geometry of blur-invariant sets. We will now derive a blur-invariant distance with respect to $\mathcal{H}$.

The set of blurs $\mathcal{H}$ in (5) is a convex set with D vertices. For every image f of size N, the set of all its blurred versions

$$\mathcal{C}_f := \left\{ f * h \,\middle|\, h \in \mathcal{H} \right\} \tag{6}$$

is also a convex set residing in the N dimensional space, which follows from linearity of convolution. The convex set is equivalent to a convex hull of $\mathcal{S}_f$ in (4). By definition, $g \in \mathcal{C}_f \Leftrightarrow g = h * f$ for some $h \in \mathcal{H}$. The blur invariant matching problem can be therefore seen as a task to find, for query image g, the closest set $\mathcal{C}_f$.

Let us denote the projection of g onto $\mathcal{C}_f$ as $P_f(g)$, then

$$I(f,g) := \|P_f(g) - g\| \tag{7}$$

is a blur-invariant distance with respect to $\mathcal{H}$ defined in (5). The projection $P_f(g)$ is a point in $\mathcal{C}_f$ with the shortest Euclidean distance from g. Then the blur-invariant distance can be formulated as minimization

$$I(f,g)^2 = \min_h \|f * h - g\|^2, \text{ s.t. } h \in \mathcal{H}, \tag{8}$$

which is a simple convex problem. If h^* denotes the minimizer of (8), then the projection to $\mathcal{C}_f$ is implemented as $P_f(g) = f * h^*$. The efficient computation of $I(f,g)$ is discussed in Sect. 4.

Due to sampling, quantization and additive noise, $I(f,g)$ might be non-zero even if g is a blurred version of f. In the case of multiple templates $\{f_i\}$, the distance $I(f_i,g)$ is used to determine the closest matching template f^*. The discriminability of this approach is influenced by mutual position and shape of convex sets $\mathcal{C}_{f_i}$'s, which are determined by the type of template images and the dimension D of $\mathcal{H}$. An illustration is provided in Fig. 1.

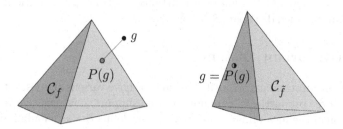

Fig. 1. Illustration of projection process with g not belonging to the convex set $\mathcal{C}_f$ (left) and g being in the set $\mathcal{C}_{\tilde{f}}$.

The proposed blur-invariant distance in (7) has a single parameter, which is the assumed blur size D. In many practical applications, the upper bound of the blur size is known or can be estimated. In addition, the distance is robust to size overestimation as discussed in Sect. 6 and to some extent also to underestimation as shown in Sect. 7.

Simple visualization of main differences between Zhang's, Gopalan's and ours blur invariant measures is illustrated in Fig. 2.

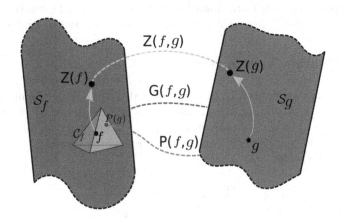

Fig. 2. Illustration of blur invariant distances: Zhang's (Z) image to image, Gopalan's (G) subspace to subspace and proposed (P) image to convex set.

4   Implementation Details

The computation of the proposed blur-invariant distance (8) can be formulated as a problem of quadratic programming. Having the given blur set $\mathcal{H}$ with the blur size $D = m \times n$, we first construct for each template image f_i of size $N = k \times l$ a matrix $\mathbf{U}_{f_i} \in \mathbb{R}^{N \times D}$ by vectorizing elements of $\mathcal{S}_{f_i}$ and concatenating them, i.e.

$$\mathbf{U}_{f_i} = [\mathbf{F}_i \mathbf{h}_{11}, \ldots, \mathbf{F}_i \mathbf{h}_{mn}], \tag{9}$$

where $\mathbf{F}_i \mathbf{h}_{(\cdot,\cdot)}$ is the column vectorized $f * h_{(\cdot,\cdot)}$. Matrices $\mathbf{U}_{f_i}$ are stored and used repeatedly for the same dataset and blur size D. The computational cost is fairly low. For example for the standard basis (3), the columns are just shifted versions of f_i.

The query image g in its vectorized form $\mathbf{g}$ is then used to solve the quadratic problem

$$I(f_i, g)^2 = \min_h \mathbf{h}^T \mathbf{U}_{f_i}^T \mathbf{U}_{f_i} \mathbf{h} - 2\mathbf{g}^T \mathbf{U}_{f_i} \mathbf{h} + \mathbf{g}^T \mathbf{g}, \tag{10}$$

subject to

$$\mathbf{h} \geq 0, \ \sum \mathbf{h} = 1. \tag{11}$$

The complete algorithm for blur invariant template matching can be described as follows:

1. Prepare the convex set $\mathcal{C}_{f_i}$ for each template image f_i by constructing $\mathbf{U}_{f_i}$ as in (9).
2. For the given query image g and every set $\mathcal{C}_{f_i}$, compute the blur-invariant distance $I(f_i, g)$ according to (10).
3. The best matching template f^* is $f^* = f_j$, where $j = \arg\min_i I(f_i, g)$.

Note that by solving (10), we obtain the estimated blur h^* as a byproduct, yet our goal is not to restore the query image g. Full recovery of image f is an ill-posed problem even with the knowledge of h; see e.g. [1,3,18,19]. Here the aim is to find the template, from which the query image was created by degradation.

5   Constraints Versus Noise

Let us consider a query image g that is a blurred version of some template image f, i.e. $g = \tilde{h} * f$, $\tilde{h} \in \mathcal{H}$. In the noiseless case, the minimizer h^* of (8) clearly corresponds to $\tilde{h}$. In the presence of noise, the acquisition model follows (1) and the minimizer h^* will partially compensate for the introduced noise.

Combining (1) and (8), we obtain

$$h^* = \min_h \|f_i * h - f_i * \tilde{h} - n\|^2 =$$
$$= \min_h \|f_i * (h - \tilde{h}) - n\|^2$$

and the optimal h^* can be written as

$$h^* = \tilde{h} + c, \tag{12}$$

where

$$c = \arg\min_h \|f_i * h - n\|^2, \quad \text{s.t.} \quad h \in \mathcal{H}$$

The element c serves as a compensation for noise n. The problem is, that noise is Gaussian-distributed, hence c and consequently h^* would be very likely a better minimizer if allowed to have negative values.

Solution to this is to ignore the constraints (11). The quadratic problem in (10) then simplifies to the classical least squares method that is solved by a system of linear algebraic equations as $I(f, g) = \|\mathbf{U}_f(\mathbf{U}_f^T\mathbf{U}_f)^{-1}\mathbf{U}_f^T\mathbf{g} - \mathbf{g}\|$.

Omitting the constraints of blur model (11) means, that we are projecting g onto $\mathrm{Span}(\mathcal{S}_f)$ instead of convex set $\mathcal{C}_f$. On one hand, this can improve classification of noisy images, on the other hand, we loose some discrimination power. As shown in Sect. 7, there are real-life inspired datasets where the constrained version outperforms the unconstrained one. Figure 3 illustrates the difference between projecting g onto $\mathcal{C}_f$ and $\mathrm{Span}(\mathcal{S}_f)$.

To combine benefits of both versions, we propose to relax the non-negativity constraint but still to keep the brightness-preservation constraint. There are many possibilities how to achieve that. One way is to introduce a penalization for attaining negative value in the minimization problem (10). Other option, which is even simpler, is to change $h \geq 0$ to $h > -\varepsilon$, where ε becomes a new parameter in the algorithm. During experiments, this approach proved to improve results though the change was not significant and choosing incorrect ε could worsen the recognition rate.

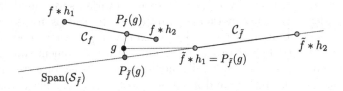

Fig. 3. Simple 2D schematic showing impact of constraints on classification. Convex sets C_f and $C_{\tilde{f}}$ are two line segments. With constraints in effect, $g = f * h + n$ is assigned to the template image f as $\|g - P_f\|^2 < \|g - P_{\tilde{f}}\|^2$. Without the non-negativity constraint, $\|g - P_{\tilde{f}}\|^2$ becomes smaller than $\|g - P_f\|^2$ and $\tilde{f}$ would be incorrectly selected.

Depending on the task we are solving and given set of templates, we have to decide, whether we want to solve unconstrained problem (10) and have better robustness to noise or if we employ constraints (11) and have potentially better results for templates whose convex sets are close together.

6 Blur Size

The main advantage of our method is its generality. We are not bound by any specific blur class and it does not require any input parameters except the blur size. We may attempt to estimate the blur size from given data as described, e.g., in [2] and [14]. This could lead to different blur size settings for each query image even though they were all acquired the same way and its safe to assume that the actual blur support is the same for all of them. Such case would mean unnecessary computational cost.

First, let us discuss the influence of overestimating blur size. It follows immediately from the construction of convex sets and the matrix form of the minimization problem (10) that estimated blur will be the original blur padded with zeroes. Overestimation thus has a negligible effect on the recognition rate and only increases the computational cost since blur size determines the dimension of the problem (10).

We conducted an experiment to quantify the effect of underestimating blur size. Results show (see Fig. 6), that even with over 30% underestimation, the classification still maintains good performance. For most cases it is sufficient to estimate the blur size only once for each given dataset of templates.

7 Experiments

We prepared two datasets, the first one consisting of handwritten binary digits (0–9) from MNIST database [12] and the second one consisting of 38 faces from

YaleB database [9]. We corrupted all images by blur of various sizes and two types – motion (M) and Gaussian blur (G) – and added Gaussian white noise with SNR ranging from 50 dB to 1 dB (see Fig. 4). We compared the proposed projection method (PM) with the method of Gopalan (GM), Zhang (ZM) and with moment-based blur invariants (MI). Two types of moment invariants were used depending on the considered blur. For motion blur, invariants to centrosymmetric blur [5] and for Gaussian blur, invariants to Gaussian blur [11] were used to ensure optimal performance. In all cases, the maximum order of moments was manually tuned to produce the best results. To mimic realistic usage of tested methods, we normalized both template and query images to have unit mean value. This makes recognition generally more difficult but it is necessary in practice.

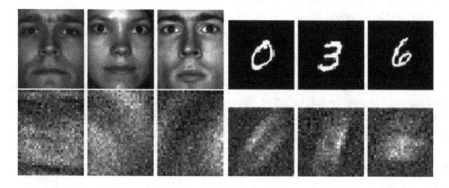

Fig. 4. Examples of the face and digit images used in experiments: clear database (top row) and corrupted query images (bottom).

Tables 1 and 2 summarize the success rate of the classification with changing SNR and blur size, respectively. Compared to the other methods, the proposed method shows excellent robustness to noise, type of the blur and also to the amount of blur. Only in the case of Gaussian blur, MI slightly outperforms the proposed method. This is probably because the MIs were designed specifically for Gaussian blur, while our projection method does not employ any assumption about the kernel parametric form. However in the case of motion blur, small discretization effects break the centrosymmetry assumption and the performance of MI starts to deteriorate. Zhang's method performs better for Gaussian blur as it is derived for this type of blur. Maybe surprisingly Gopalan's method shows a relatively poor recognition rate. By construction, it is less dependent on the type of blur compared to the Zhang and MI. Our hypothesis is that the Riemannian distance between often overlapping subspaces is not a good blur-invariant measure.

We compared the performance of all methods using regular desktop PC. Time required for one query-template comparison was measured, results are shown in Fig. 5. Gopalan's method was implemented based on the "Algorithm 1" in [10] using CS decomposition which is very slow. The time for computing

MI is affected also by the maximum order of moments computed. The highest order used in the previous experiment was used for measuring the computational time. Note that the moment-based algorithm is independent of blur size and the computational time is not affected by it. With increasing image and blur size, MI becomes more time efficient. It outperforms the Projection method for images 600×60 px with blur 50×50 px.

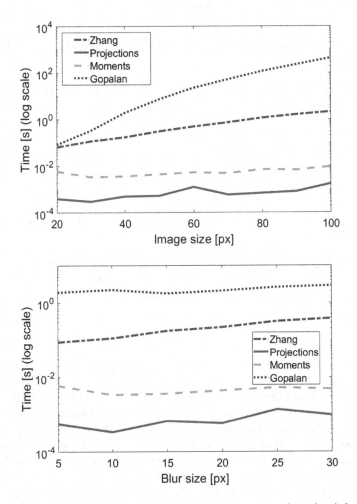

Fig. 5. Time [s] needed to compare one query image to one template: (top) dependency on image size with fixed blur size of 15×15 px and (bottom) dependency on blur size with fixed image size 40×40 px. The Y axis is shown in logarithmic scale.

The graph in Fig. 6 shows that even when we estimate the blur support to be less than 70% of the original one, we still achieve perfect accuracy with the proposed method. For this experiment we used uniform blur as it is the worst possible scenario for underestimated support.

We also tested our hypothesis from Sect. 5, that omitting the non-negativity constraint improves recognition results for noisy images and repeated the experiment for the projection method without the non-negativity constraint. For brevity, we refer to this method as the unconstrained variant and to the original projection method as the constrained variant. For low-level noise, both variants perform the same. However for SNR <5 dB, the constrained variant starts to misclassify query images slightly more often.

Table 1. The recognition rate [%], digits dataset was used with image size 28 × 28 px and blur size 15 × 15 px.

SNR [dB]	GM (G)	ZM (G)	MI (G)	PM (G)	GM (M)	ZM (M)	MI (M)	PM (M)
50	99	100	100	100	100	94	100	100
20	67	96	100	100	98	80	99	100
10	45	28	100	100	81	23	85	100
5	38	28	100	98	58	22	79	100
1	35	27	97	86	55	18	53	96

Table 2. The recognition rate [%], faces dataset was used with image size 40 × 35 px and SNR 20 dB.

Blur size	GM (G)	ZM (G)	MI (G)	PM (G)	GM (M)	ZM (G)	MI (M)	PM (M)
7 × 7	74	100	100	100	99	100	87	100
11 × 11	25	86	100	100	76	72	71	100
15 × 15	5	48	95	100	40	17	45	100

The second experiment demonstrates the opposite scenario when the constrained variant outperforms the unconstrained one. A special dataset was prepared that consists of the same handwritten digits as in the first experiment, but this time we added a frame – either a circle or a square. This was motivated by a problem of traffic-sign recognition where the actual shape of the frame changes the meaning of the sign and it is thus important to correctly match not only the symbol (number), but the frame as well. Sample images are shown in Fig. 7.

Images of size 41 × 41 px were degraded by motion blur of size 25 × 25 px and noise with SNR 5 dB was added. The constrained variant maintained 100% recognition accuracy while the unconstrained variant achieved only 85% accuracy. In all the failure cases, the unconstrained algorithm matched the query image with a template containing the correct symbol but a wrong frame. This is in accordance with the illustration in Fig. 3.

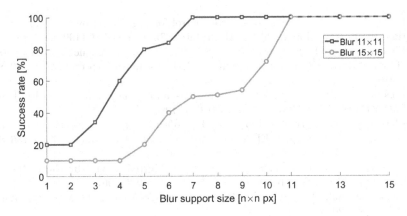

Fig. 6. The recognition rate [%] of projection method w.r.t. underestimation of blur support. Digits dataset was used with uniform blur of size 11×11 (blue) and 15×15 (yellow), both with SNR = 20 dB. (Color figure online)

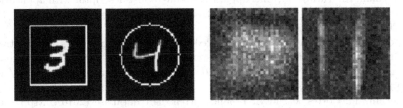

Fig. 7. Example of clean images (left) and their degraded versions (right) used to test the effect of the constrains in the projection method.

8 Conclusion

We showed that the projection onto a convex set representing the template image with its all admissible blurred variants can be used to construct blur-invariant measure for arbitrary blur of finite support. Experiments demonstrated high robustness and recognition rate on a par with the state-of-the-art method of moment invariants while providing better generality. The proposed method is easy to implement and requires only one parameter, which is the maximum expected blur size. A possible future improvement to the proposed method is to introduce regularization in the optimization problem.

References

1. Carasso, A.S.: The APEX method in image sharpening and the use of low exponent Lévy stable laws. SIAM J. Appl. Math. **63**(2), 593–618 (2003)
2. Chen, L., Yap, K.H.: Identification of blur support size in blind image deconvolution. In: Proceedings of the 2003 Joint Fourth International Conference on Information, Communications and Signal Processing and the Fourth Pacific Rim Conference on Multimedia, vol. 1, pp. 503–507. IEEE (2003)

3. Elder, J.H., Zucker, S.W.: Local scale control for edge detection and blur estimation. IEEE Trans. Pattern Anal. Mach. Intell. **20**(7), 699–716 (1998)
4. Flusser, J., Farokhi, S., Höschl IV, C., Suk, T., Zitová, B., Pedone, M.: Recognition of images degraded by Gaussian blur. IEEE Trans. Image Process. **25**(2), 790–806 (2016)
5. Flusser, J., Suk, T.: Degraded image analysis: an invariant approach. IEEE Trans. Pattern Anal. Mach. Intell. **20**(6), 590–603 (1998)
6. Flusser, J., Suk, T., Boldyš, J., Zitová, B.: Projection operators and moment invariants to image blurring. IEEE Trans. Pattern Anal. Mach. Intell. **37**(4), 786–802 (2015)
7. Flusser, J., Suk, T., Saic, S.: Recognition of blurred images by the method of moments. IEEE Trans. Image Process. **5**(3), 533–538 (1996)
8. Flusser, J., Suk, T., Zitová, B.: 2D and 3D Image Analysis by Moments. Wiley, Chichester (2016)
9. Georghiades, A., Belhumeur, P., Kriegman, D.: From few to many: illumination cone models for face recognition under variable lighting and pose. IEEE Trans. Pattern Anal. Mach. Intell. **23**(6), 643–660 (2001)
10. Gopalan, R., Turaga, P., Chellappa, R.: A blur-robust descriptor with applications to face recognition. IEEE Trans. Pattern Anal. Mach. Intell. **34**(6), 1220–1226 (2012)
11. Kostková, J., Flusser, J., Lébl, M., Pedone, M.: Image invariants to anisotropic Gaussian blur. In: Felsberg, M., Forssén, P.-E., Sintorn, I.-M., Unger, J. (eds.) SCIA 2019. LNCS, vol. 11482, pp. 140–151. Springer, Cham (2019). https://doi.org/10.1007/978-3-030-20205-7_12
12. LeCun, Y., Cortes, C.: MNIST handwritten digit database (2010). http://yann.lecun.com/exdb/mnist/
13. Liu, J., Zhang, T.: Recognition of the blurred image by complex moment invariants. Pattern Recogn. Lett. **26**(8), 1128–1138 (2005)
14. Liu, S., Wang, H., Wang, J., Cho, S., Pan, C.: Automatic blur-kernel-size estimation for motion deblurring. Vis. Comput. **31**(5), 733–746 (2015)
15. Pedone, M., Flusser, J., Heikkilä, J.: Blur invariant translational image registration for N-fold symmetric blurs. IEEE Trans. Image Process. **22**(9), 3676–3689 (2013)
16. Pedone, M., Flusser, J., Heikkilä, J.: Registration of images with N-fold dihedral blur. IEEE Trans. Image Process. **24**(3), 1036–1045 (2015)
17. Xiao, B., Ma, J.F., Cui, J.T.: Combined blur, translation, scale and rotation invariant image recognition by Radon and pseudo-Fourier-Mellin transforms. Pattern Recogn. **45**, 314–321 (2012)
18. Xue, F., Blu, T.: A novel SURE-based criterion for parametric PSF estimation. IEEE Trans. Image Process. **24**(2), 595–607 (2015)
19. Zhang, W., Cham, W.K.: Single-image refocusing and defocusing. IEEE Trans. Image Process. **21**(2), 873–882 (2012)
20. Zhang, Z., Klassen, E., Srivastava, A.: Gaussian blurring-invariant comparison of signals and images. IEEE Trans. Image Process. **22**(8), 3145–3157 (2013)

Partitioning 2D Images into Prototypes of Slope Region

Darshan Batavia[⊠], Jiří Hladůvka, and Walter G. Kropatsch

Pattern Recognition and Image Processing Group 193/03, TU Wien, Vienna, Austria
{darshan,jiri,krw}@prip.tuwien.ac.at

Abstract. A gray scale digital image can be represented as a 2.5D surface where the height of the surface corresponds to the gray value of the respective pixel. Analysis of the gray scale image can be efficiently done by exploiting the properties of the plane graph embedded in the 2.5D surface. The vertices of the graph can be easily categorized into critical and non-critical points by use of Local Binary Patterns (LBPs). Well defined graph operations such as contraction and removal of edges are used to eliminate the non-critical points and preserve the critical points thereby reducing the size of graph. In this process, it is important to preserve the structural and topological properties of the regions of a gray scale image. After analysing the topological properties of a well composed image, we provide two prototypes of the slope region and the necessary conditions for their existence. Also we prove that every slope region conforms to either of the two prototype. Conversely the prototypes may be used to generate an image with a required topological properties.

1 Introduction

Exploiting the surface properties by its representation using the surface elements (viz. local maximum, local minimum, etc.) and simultaneously preserving the structural (topological) properties has been a classical problem in pattern recognition and image processing. It has various applications like multi-resolution image segmentation, image compression and so on. The surface elements are broadly classified into two types: critical points (maximum, minimum, saddle) and non-critical points (slope point). Cayley [4] and Maxwell [14] explored the critical points and slope lines of a surface in terms of earth's topography. A century later, Lee [13] came up with a graphical representation of the surface and enumerated different possible configurations of the critical points in a Morse function.

Identifying the critical points in the neighborhood graph of a digital image was described in [5] using Local binary Patterns (LBPs) which eliminated the computation of differentiation. An extension, Cerman *et al.* [6] provided an algorithm for multi-resolution image segmentation using the graph pyramid which is a stack of reduced graphs. Wei in [15] uses an approach to construct a hierarchical structure similar to the graph pyramid called 'super-pixel hierarchy' for multi-resolution image segmentation. Edelsbrunner *et al.* [8] discuss the construction of

© Springer Nature Switzerland AG 2019
M. Vento and G. Percannella (Eds.): CAIP 2019, LNCS 11678, pp. 363–374, 2019.
https://doi.org/10.1007/978-3-030-29888-3_29

a hierarchy of increasingly smaller Morse-Smale complexes to decompose a piecewise linear 2-D manifold. In [11,12] authors provide definitions of slope regions and slope complex which generalizes Morse-Smale complexes and enumerates the different configurations of the slope regions formed by critical points. [2] deals with a prototype of a slope region and counts the number of slope regions at a given level of the graph pyramid. In [1] authors describe the necessary and sufficient conditions for merging slope regions in the region adjacency graph (RAG) and its dual the boundary adjacency graph (BAG).

After recalling basic definitions related to the topological aspects of digital images (Sect. 2), we extend our previous work [11] in several ways. In Sect. 3 we introduce a new prototype for the slope region. Section 4 is devoted to the description of holes and two different ways they are attached to the boundary of the slope region. In Sect. 5 we prove that any digital image can be partitioned into slope regions of one of the two prototypes. Finally, in Sect. 6 we explain the necessary conditions for the existence of a saddle point on the boundary of the slope region.

2   Basic Definitions and Formation of a Slope Region

A digital image P can be visually perceived as a sampled version of a geographical terrain model which is a continuous surface. The sampling frequency to choose the samples should satisfy the Nyquist criterion for the minimum distance between any two critical points. The digital image P can be efficiently represented by a dual pair of plane graphs. The region adjacency graph (RAG) $G = (V, E)$ is formed by vertices $v \in V$ corresponding to pixels $p \in P$ connected to the four adjacent neighbors by edges $e \in E$. The dual of the RAG is the boundary adjacency graph (BAG) $\overline{G} = (\overline{V}, \overline{E})$ where every vertex $\overline{v} \in \overline{V}$ of BAG corresponds to a face formed by the intersection of the boundary segments in the RAG G and edges $\overline{e} \in \overline{E}$ of the BAG correspond to the boundary separating the faces in the RAG G [7, Sect. 4.6]. The gray value of the pixel p is visually conceived as the height of the surface and it is denoted by $g(p) = g(v)$ where v is the vertex corresponding to p. There are two operations to build a graph pyramid [10]: contraction and removal of edges in the graph. Contraction of an edge [7, Sect. 1.7] in G will result in merging the corresponding two pixels connected by the respective edge. This is equivalent to the removal operation in the BAG $\overline{G}$. Duality imposes a one-to-one correspondence between the edges of the RAG G and of its dual the BAG $\overline{G}$. The removal of an edge $(v, w) \in E$ disconnects the two vertices v and w and merges the two faces which is equivalent to contract $\overline{e} \in \overline{E}$ in $\overline{G}$.

By successively contracting and removing edges, we form a stack of progressively reducing planar graphs $(G_k, \overline{G_k})$, $k \in \{0, 1, \ldots, n\}$ where each graph G_{k+1} is smaller than the graph G_k [3,9,10]. The base level of the graph pyramid is the neighborhood graph or RAG G_0.

Definition 1. *The **orientation of an edge** $(v, w) \in E$ in the **RAG** $G = (V, E)$ is directed from vertex $v \in V$ to vertex $w \in V$ iff $g(v) > g(w)$, otherwise edges are not oriented.*

The edge $e \in E$ connecting two vertices $v, w \in V$ with $g(v) = g(w)$ is non-oriented. Note that we define the orientation of edges by considering only the gray values as a feature of an image. The theory stated in this paper remains valid for higher dimensional feature vectors provided that their ordering is defined.

Now using the orientation of an edge incident to a vertex, we can categorize a vertex into a local maximum, local minimum, saddle or a slope point.

Definition 2. *A vertex $v \in V$ is a **local maximum** $\oplus$ if all the edges incident to v are oriented outwards.*

Definition 3. *A vertex $v \in V$ is a **local minimum** $\ominus$ if all the edges incident to v are oriented inwards.*

Definition 4. *A vertex $v \in V$ is a **saddle point** $\otimes$ if there are more than two changes in the orientation of edges when the edges incident on v are traversed circularly (clockwise or counter-clockwise direction).*

Definition 5. *A vertex $v \in V$ is a **slope point** if there are exactly two changes in the orientation of edges when traversed circularly (clockwise or counter-clockwise direction).*

Categorizing a vertex using orientation of edges incident to it is equivalent to that of LBP code. The LBP value of an outward oriented edges are encoded as 1 and inward orientated edges are encoded as 0. The LBP code of a vertex is formed by concatenating LBP values of the incident edges in clockwise or counter-clock wise direction. The LBP code of a maximum will consist of 1 only while the LBP code of a minimum will consist of 0 only. The LBP code of slope points will have exactly 2 bit switches and saddles will have more than 2 bit switches. By use of orientated edges, we avoid the calculation of derivatives and eigen-values of the Hessian matrix to categorize a vertex.

Definition 6. *A **path** π is a non empty sub-graph of G, consisting of an alternating sequence of vertices and edges $\pi = v_1, e(v_1, v_2), v_2, \ldots, e(v_{r-1}, v_r), v_r$. A path $\pi(v_1, v_r)$ is **monotonic** if all the oriented edges $(v_i, v_{i+1}), i \in [1, r-1]$ have the same orientation.*

Note: Paths with non-oriented edges are called *level curves*. A level curve can be part of a monotonic path.

A monotonic path $\pi(v_1, v_r)$ can be further extended by adding an edge oriented in the same direction as the direction of monotonic path $\pi(v_1, v_r)$. A monotonic path which cannot be further extended is called a **maximal monotonic path**. The end points of a maximal monotonic path will always be a local maximum and a local minimum. The definition of the monotonic paths is used to define the slope region which is the foundation for the rest of the paper.

Definition 7. *A face in a surface embedded plane graph G is a **slope region** $\mathbb{S}$ if all the pairs of points in the face can be connected by a continuous monotonic curve inside the face.*

Remark 1. The boundary $\delta\mathbb{S}$ of the slope region $\mathbb{S}$ is either a level curve or it can be decomposed into exactly two monotonic paths [11, Lemma 1].

Remark 2. **Property of a slope region:** Saddle points can only exist on the boundary $\delta\mathbb{S}$ of the slope region $\mathbb{S}$ and not in the interior $\mathbb{S} \setminus \delta\mathbb{S}$ [11, Lemma 2].

Contraction of the low contrast edges in the monotonic paths without eliminating the critical points, preserves the monotonicity of the path. A sequence of contractions may generate self-loops and multiple edges. In such cases, the slope region is difficult to analyze. The next section deals with the prototypes of the slope region in which the slope regions can be categorized.

3   Two Prototypes of the Slope Regions

A prototype of a slope region is a graphical representation including all the possible components that a slope region may consist of. In other words, a slope region conforming to a prototype will obey the properties of the prototype. In this section, we explain the two prototypes of the slope region i.e. horizontal and inclined, by analyzing the similarities and the differences between them. Prototype 1 - Inclined slope region prototype is the extended version of the slope region prototype mentioned in [11]. The graphical and 2.5D representation of the prototype 1 and the prototype 0 are showed in Figs. 1 and 2 respectively. Existence and properties of holes in slope regions are described in Sect. 4.

3.1   Components and Similarity Between the Two Prototypes

Figures 1(a) and 2(a) show all the components of prototype 1 - the inclined slope region and prototype 0 - the horizontal slope region respectively. Horizontal slope region prototype, in short is called as prototype 0 since it has zero inclination unlined the inclined slope region prototype. Both of them consists of at most two extrema (one local maximum $\oplus$ and one local minimum $\ominus$) geometrically inside the boundary of the slope region and are connected to the boundary via a monotonic path. All the elements such as $\oplus$, $\ominus$, holes are required to be connected to the boundary of the slope region to avoid generation of a disconnected graph. Therefore we have paths $(\oplus, m_1)$ and $(m_2, \ominus)$ connecting $\oplus$ and $\ominus$ to the boundary at vertex m_1 and m_2 respectively. The paths $(\oplus, m_1)$ and $(m_2, \ominus)$ must be monotonic to satisfy the Definition 7. A saddle point can only be present on the boundary of the slope region as stated in Remark 2. There might exist points (for example a local maximum or a local minimum disregarding $\oplus$ and $\ominus$) within the boundary which cannot be connected to either of the two extremum with a monotonic curve. Collections of all such points, geometrically inside the boundary of the slope region are classified as holes. Semantically, holes are not part of the slope region, since slope region is homeomorphic to the disk.

A hole in the slope region which do not lie on the monotonic path (for example: $Hole_3$ in Figs. 1 and 2) is surrounded by a self-loop and is connected to the boundary of the slope region by a level curve.

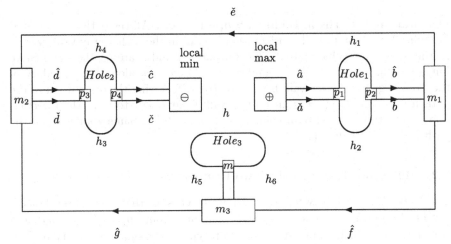

(a) Graphical representation of Prototype 1: inclined slope region

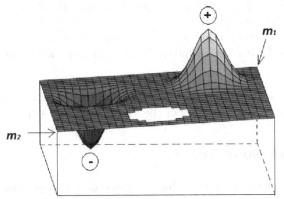

(b) Example of a mesh plot of prototype 1 without $Hole_1$ and $Hole_2$

Fig. 1. Prototype 1: inclined slope region.

A complete traversal of the *potentially folded boundary* of the inclined slope region is an alternating sequence of vertices and edges: $(\oplus, \hat{a}, p_1, h_1, p_2, \hat{b}, m_1, \breve{e}, m_2, \hat{d}, p_3, h_4, p_4, \hat{c}, \ominus, \breve{c}, p_4, h_3, p_3, \breve{d}, m_2, \breve{g}, m_3, h_5, m, h, m, h_6, m_3, \hat{f}, m_1, \breve{b}, p_2, h_2, p_1, \breve{a}, \oplus)$. Traversal of the folded boundary for horizontal slope region prototype can be worked out in similar fashion.

For a continuous case, all the gray values in the range $[g(\ominus), g(\oplus)]$ exist on the potentially folded boundary of the slope region. Any component, i.e., $\oplus$, $\ominus$ and holes may be excluded from the prototype to form a catalogue of all the possible slope regions conforming to the prototype 1 or prototype 0 respectively. An example of a mesh plot of prototype 1 and prototype 0 without $Hole_1$ and $Hole_2$ can be viewed in Fig. 1(a).

Orientation of Paths in Inclined Slope Region: All the paths are oriented following Definition 1 of edge orientation, i.e., from the higher gray-value vertex to the lower gray-value vertex. The two paths $\hat{a}$ and $\breve{a}$ are on the same curve but are defined separately to complete the closed walk along the boundary of the slope region. $\hat{a}$ is the walk from $\oplus$ to $Hole_1$ following the orientation of the path from $\oplus$ to $Hole_1$. $\breve{a}$ is an up-hill walk from $Hole_1$ to $\oplus$ in the direction opposite to the oriented path connecting $\oplus$ and $Hole_1$. Same applies to all the paths: $\hat{b}, \breve{b}, \hat{c}, \breve{c}, \hat{d}, \breve{d}, h_5, h_6$.

3.2 Difference Between the Two Prototypes

The only difference between the two prototypes is that, the outer boundary of Prototype 1 consists of exactly two monotonic paths $(m_1, \breve{e}, m_2)$ and $(m_1, \hat{f}, m_3, \hat{g}, m_2)$. In contrast to the Prototype 1, the outer boundary of Prototype 0 is made up of level curve $(m_1, e, m_2, g, m_3, h_5, m, h, h_6, f)$ i.e. all the points on the boundary have same gray value. Consequently, it is possible that the extrema and holes are connected to only one vertex on the level curve, which would be the result of contraction of edges connecting (m_1, m_2) and (m_2, m_3) forming a self-loop. Hence the boundary in the self-loop slope region is non-oriented.

Note 1. The outer boundary of the Prototype 1 consists of exactly two monotonic paths while the outer boundary of the Prototype 0 is a single level curve.

4   Holes in the Slope Region

Collections of all the points within the boundary of the slope region, which cannot be connected to the other points with a monotonic curve are classified as holes in the slope region and the points inside the hole do not belong to the slope region. Holes can be distinguished into two types depending on the connection of the hole with he boundary of the slope region. In Sect. 4.1 we describe the properties and condition for the hole connected to the boundary with a level curve and in Sect. 4.2 for the hole connected to the boundary with a monotonic path.

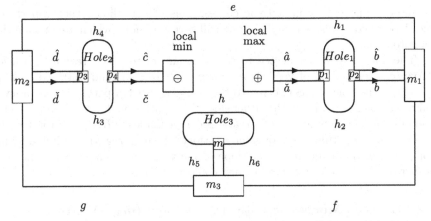

(a) Graphical representation of Prototype 0: horizontal slope region

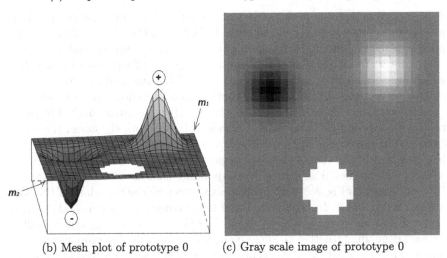

(b) Mesh plot of prototype 0   (c) Gray scale image of prototype 0

Fig. 2. Prototype 0: horizontal slope region.

4.1   Hole Outside the Monotonic Path ($Hole_3$)

Collection of points which do not appear on the monotonic paths ($\oplus$, m_1) and (m_2, $\ominus$) and which cannot be connected to either $\oplus$ and $\ominus$ by a monotonic curve will be classified as a hole: $Hole_3$.

In prototype 1, as all the gray values in the range $[g(m_1), g(m_2)]$ exist on the outer boundary. Every point in one of the two monotonic paths of the boundary will be connected via an isoline (level-curve) to its counterpart point (with the same gray value) on the other monotonic path. If the boundary of the hole intersects multiple isolines, it will generate pair of points which can not be anymore connected by monotonic curves. This will invalidate the property of the slope region. Hence a single isoline will surround holes which are outside the monotonic path.

The hole must be connected to the boundary of the slope region by a level curve (cf., connection of vertices m and m_3 in Figs. 1(a) and 2(a)). In contradiction, if the hole was connected to the boundary with a path other than level curve, the pair of points on the either side of this path would not be connected by a monotonic curve. Similarly observations can be made for $Hole_3$ in prototype 0.

In case of multiple holes of same category, all the holes will be individually connected to the boundary of the slope region with a level curve. Since the hole is surrounded by a level curve, it must conform to prototype 0.

4.2   Holes on Monotonic Paths ($\oplus$, m_1) and (m_2, $\ominus$): ($Hole_1$ and $Hole_2$)

A hole on a monotonic path needs to intersect at least two distinct points to invalidate the monotonicity of the path. Referring to Figs. 1(a) and 2(a), $Hole_1$ intersects the monotonic path ($\oplus$, m_1) at two distinct points p_1 and p_2.

Figure 3(a) and (b) shows the simplest example of existence of such hole which are formed by a local maximum and a local minimum (disregarding $\oplus$ and $\ominus$) respectively. In Fig. 3(a), the curve marked in yellow color will surround the hole with gray value $g(u)$. Similarly in Fig. 3(b), the curve marked in yellow color will surround the hole with gray value $g(l)$. In both the cases, the region between the range $[g(u), g(l)]$ (visible region between red and yellow curve) can be connected to the rest of the slope region with a monotonic curve, and hence will not be considered as a hole. Corresponding contour plots of Fig. 3(a) and (b) can be seen in Fig. 3(c) and (d) respectively where the boundary of the holes are marked in black. In prototype 1 and 0, referring to Figs. 1(a) and 2(a), the gray value of the path h_1 and h_2 connecting the two vertices p_1 and p_2 will be decided depending whether the hole is encapsulating a local maximum or a local minimum inside it. If the hole encapsulates a local maximum, the boundary of the hole equals to $g(u)$ and in case of minimum it equals to $g(l)$ as shown in Fig. 3. Same applies to the boundary of $Hole_2$ appearing on the monotonic path m_2, $\ominus$ in both the prototypes. Since the hole is surrounded by a level curve, it must conform to prototype 0.

4.3   Multiple Holes on Monotonic Paths

As we have already showed in the previous section that the boundary of the hole is a level curve, in Fig. 4 $g(p_1) = g(p_2)$ and $g(p_3) = g(p_4)$. In case of multiple holes appearing on the same monotonic path, the boundaries of different holes will be connected to each other either by a level curve or a monotonic path depending on the gray values of the level curve surrounding the holes. Referring to Fig. 4, if the gray values of the level curves surrounding the holes: $Hole_1$ and $Hole_2$ are the same, then the boundaries of the holes are connected by a level curve. Otherwise, they are connected by a monotonic path with orientation defined in Definition 1,

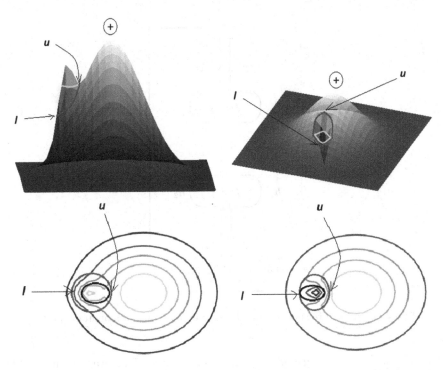

Fig. 3. Examples of mesh and contour plot of a hole on the monotonic path surrounding a local maximum (left) and a local minimum (right). (Color figure online)

i.e., from higher (p_2) to lower (p_3) gray value. The orientation will preserve the monotonicity of the path ($\oplus, m_1$) and ($m_2, \ominus$) in both the prototypes.

5 Partitioning of 2D Digital Image into Prototypes of Slope Region

Remark 3. A 2D image can be partitioned into the slope regions which can be categorized into one of the two prototypes: 1. inclined slope region and 2. horizontal slope region.

Proof. We already know that all the faces in the RAG G of a well-composed sampled surface are slope regions [2, Lemma 1]. The boundary of the slope region is composed by either a level curve or exactly two monotonic paths connecting the local maximum to the local minimum [11, Lemma 1]. The prototype of the *inclined slope region* (Sect. 3) corresponds to the slope region surrounded by exactly two monotonic paths. The prototype of *horizontal slope region* corresponds to the slope region surrounded by a level curve. Consecutively all the holes in both the enumerations follow the prototype 0 - *horizontal slope region*. The prototype satisfies the basic condition, that any pair of points inside the

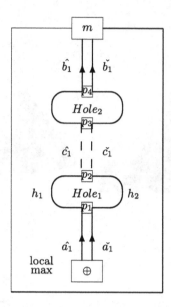

Fig. 4. Graphical representation of multiple holes on the monotonic path.

slope region can be connected by a monotonic curve. Thus we can span a 2D digital image with these two prototypes of slope regions. In other words, a 2D digital image can be partitioned into these two prototypes.   □

6   Slope Regions Connected to Saddle Point

Lemma 1. *Presence of a saddle point guarantees existence of at least two slope regions.*

Proof. We prove Lemma 1 by contradiction. We already know that a saddle point cannot exist inside the slope region. A saddle point can only occur on the boundary of the slope region (Remark 2). A saddle point requires a minimum of 4 edges and at least 4 bit switches in the LBP coding (cf. Definition 4). When a saddle point is on the boundary of the inclined slope, it has at least two oriented edges or at most three oriented edges (if either of u or l in Fig. 1 are saddle points) connected to it. The saddle point on the boundary with two incident edges: 1. oriented inwards from local maximum towards to saddle point and 2. oriented outward from saddle point towards the local minimum. Let us assume that the other two edges incident on the saddle are inside the slope region. Referring to Fig. 5, the saddle point will require two additional edges which are connected to s_{max} and s_{min}. Also we know that for every point on the monotonic path $\check{a}$ connecting u and l, there exists a point on another monotonic path $(\hat{f}, \hat{c})$ connecting u and l, which can be connected by a level curve. Thus we cannot connect $\ominus$ and s_{min} with a monotonic curve. Similarly we also cannot connect s_{max} and $\oplus$ with a monotonic curve. This results in contradiction to our Definition 7 of slope region. We can prove the same for the saddle point (on u and l) with three incident edges. In case of horizontal slope region, the point m in Fig. 2 can be a saddle point on the boundary of the slope region the proof by contradiction holds good. Hence the presence of a saddle point guarantees existence of at least two slope regions, as one slope region is insufficient to satisfy the conditions of a saddle point.

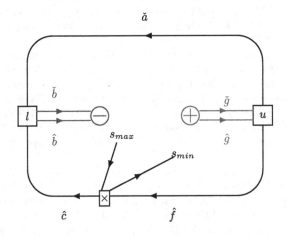

Fig. 5. Saddle on the boundary of a single slope region.

7 Conclusion

We introduced two prototypes of slope region: 1. inclined slope region and 2. horizontal slope region. We showed that a well composed 2D digital image can be partitioned into slope regions categorized into one of these two prototypes. We described the properties of the different types of holes which may appear inside a slope region and show that all holes follow prototype 0. We exploited the properties and connections incident to a saddle point on the boundary of the slope region. With the presence of a single saddle point, the property guarantees existence of at least two slope regions connected to the saddle point. The prototypes of the slope region along with the property of the saddle point introduced in this paper can form a grammar to generate digital images. We leave this topic and related questions for future research.

References

1. Batavia, D., Kropatsch, W.G., Casablanca, R.M., Gonzalez-Diaz, R.: Congratulations! Dual graphs are now orientated!. In: Conte, D., Ramel, J.-Y., Foggia, P. (eds.) GbRPR 2019. LNCS, vol. 11510, pp. 131–140. Springer, Cham (2019). https://doi.org/10.1007/978-3-030-20081-7_13
2. Batavia, D., Kropatsch, W.G., Gonzalez-Diaz, R., Casblanca, R.M.: Counting slope regions in surface graphs. In: Computer Vision Winter Workshop (2019)
3. Brun, L., Kropatsch, W.G.: Dual contraction of combinatorial maps. In: Kropatsch, W.G., Jolion, J.M. (eds.) 2nd IAPR-TC 2015 Workshop on Graph-based Representation, pp. 145–154. OCG-Schriftenreihe, Österreichische Computer Gesellschaft (1999). Band 126
4. Cayley, A.: XL. On contour and slope lines. Lond. Edinb. Dublin Philos. Mag. J. Sci. **18**(120), 264–268 (1859)
5. Cerman, M., Gonzalez-Diaz, R., Kropatsch, W.: LBP and irregular graph pyramids. In: Azzopardi, G., Petkov, N. (eds.) CAIP 2015. LNCS, vol. 9257, pp. 687–699. Springer, Cham (2015). https://doi.org/10.1007/978-3-319-23117-4_59
6. Cerman, M., Janusch, I., Gonzalez-Diaz, R., Kropatsch, W.G.: Topology-based image segmentation using LBP pyramids. Mach. Vis. Appl. **27**(8), 1161–1174 (2016)
7. Diestel, R.: Graph Theory. Graduate Texts in Mathematics (1997)
8. Edelsbrunner, H., Harer, J., Natarajan, V., Pascucci, V.: Morse-Smale complexes for piecewise linear 3-manifolds. In: Proceedings of the Nineteenth Annual Symposium on Computational Geometry, pp. 361–370. ACM (2003)
9. Haxhimusa, Y., Kropatsch, W.: Hierarchy of partitions with dual graph contraction. In: Michaelis, B., Krell, G. (eds.) DAGM 2003. LNCS, vol. 2781, pp. 338–345. Springer, Heidelberg (2003). https://doi.org/10.1007/978-3-540-45243-0_44
10. Kropatsch, W.G.: Building irregular pyramids by dual graph contraction. IEE-Proc. Vis. Image Signal Process. **142**(6), 366–374 (1995)
11. Kropatsch, W.G., Casablanca, R.M., Batavia, D., Gonzalez-Diaz, R.: Computing and reducing slope complexes. In: Marfil, R., Calderón, M., Díaz del Río, F., Real, P., Bandera, A. (eds.) CTIC 2019. LNCS, vol. 11382, pp. 12–25. Springer, Cham (2019). https://doi.org/10.1007/978-3-030-10828-1_2
12. Kropatsch, W.G., Casablanca, R.M., Batavia, D., Gonzalez-Diaz, R.: On the space between critical points. In: Couprie, M., Cousty, J., Kenmochi, Y., Mustafa, N. (eds.) DGCI 2019. LNCS, vol. 11414, pp. 115–126. Springer, Cham (2019). https://doi.org/10.1007/978-3-030-14085-4_10
13. Lee, R.N.: Two-dimensional critical point configuration graphs. IEEE Trans. Pattern Anal. Mach. Intell. **4**, 442–450 (1984)
14. Maxwell, J.C.: L. On hills and dales: to the editors of the philosophical magazine and journal. Lond. Edinb. Dublin Philos. Mag. J. Sci. **40**(269), 421–427 (1870)
15. Wei, X., Yang, Q., Gong, Y., Ahuja, N., Yang, M.H.: Superpixel hierarchy. IEEE Trans. Image Process. **27**(10), 4838–4849 (2018)

Homological Region Adjacency Tree for a 3D Binary Digital Image via HSF Model

Pedro Real[1]([⊠])(iD), Helena Molina-Abril[1](iD), Fernando Díaz-del-Río[1](iD),
and Sergio Blanco-Trejo[2](iD)

[1] H.T.S. Informatics' Engineering, University of Seville, Seville, Spain
{real,habril,fdiaz}@us.es
[2] Department of Aerospace Engineering and Fluid Mechanics, University of Seville,
Seville, Spain
sblanco1@us.es

Abstract. Given a 3D binary digital image I, we define and compute an edge-weighted tree, called *Homological Region Tree* (or Hom-Tree, for short). It coincides, as unweighted graph, with the classical Region Adjacency Tree of black 6-connected components (CCs) and white 26-connected components of I. In addition, we define the weight of an edge (R, S) as the number of tunnels that the CCs R and S "share". The Hom-Tree structure is still an isotopic invariant of I. Thus, it provides information about how the different homology groups interact between them, while preserving the duality of black and white CCs.

An experimentation with a set of synthetic images showing different shapes and different complexity of connected component nesting is performed for numerically validating the method.

Keywords: Binary 3D digital image · Region Adjacency Tree · Combinatorial topology · Homological Spanning Forest

1 Introduction

A classic scheme in most image understanding algorithms always includes two important initial steps: (a) [segmentation] partition into regions and (b) [region connectivity representation] data structure specifying the connectivity relationships between the regions of this segmentation.

The vast majority of the region connectivity representations used are based on the mathematical concept of graph. The most notorious example of this kind of representation is the region adjacency graph (RAG, for short) [23]. The reasoning used in RAG is based on two topological properties: adjacency and inclusion. In the case of 3D digital images, the most usual adjacency relationships

Work supported by the Spanish research projects TOP4COG:MTM2016-81030-P (AEI/FEDER, UE), COFNET (AEI/FEDER, UE) and the VPPI of University of Seville.

M. Vento and G. Percannella (Eds.): CAIP 2019, LNCS 11678, pp. 375–387, 2019.
https://doi.org/10.1007/978-3-030-29888-3_30

between cubical voxels employed to be extended in determining edges of the region adjacency graph are 6, 18 and 26-adjacencies. Two cubical voxels are 6, 18 or 26-adjacent if they share a common face, edge, or vertex. To prevent topological paradoxes and, at the same time, to benefit from strong topological duality properties, we specify 6-adjacency between black voxels and 26-adjacency between white voxels or, in other words, we use a $(6, 26)$-image.

In order to exclusively highlight the ambient isotopic property "to be surrounded by" (inclusion) as an adjacency relationship between regions or boundaries of regions, the notion of *Region-Adjacency Tree* (or RAG tree, for short) (also called *homotopy tree, inclusion tree* or *topological tree*) was created [23,24]. Restricted to binary 2D digital images, the RAG tree contains all the homotopy type information of the foreground (FG) (black object according to our convention) but the converse is, in general, not true [24]. Aside from image understanding applications [5], RAG trees have encountered exploitation niches in geoinformatics, computer aided design, rendering, dermatoscopics image, biometrics,... [1,4–6].

Focusing on homotopy-based representation models of digital objects and images, there are numerous works that arise from sources of digital topology (for instance, [14]), continuous or cellular topology [16] and nD shape search [3] with three clearly differentiated notions: Reeb graphs [7], skeletons [2,12] and boundary representations [17].

Given a binary 3D digital image I, an edge-weighted graph structure, called *Homological Region Tree* (Hom-Tree, for short), which, as unweighted graph, coincides with the classical Region Adjacency Tree of black 6-connected components and white 26-connected components of I I. The weight of an edge (R, S) is the number of tunnels that the CCs R and S of opposite color "share" (that is, those whose have a same root node).

The unique Hom-Tree representation is computed here from a complete and flexible homotopy model for I (considered as a cubical complex) called Homological Spanning Forest (or HSF, for short) [9,18,19]. Seen as segmentations, the Hom-Tree can be obtained from the topological "over-segmentation" HSF, via a suitable region merging. The elementary merging operation involves two cells of dimensions differing in one and can be redefined as homotopy operations on the cell complex analogous of I [15].

The contribution of this paper relies on the definition of the compact Hom-tree data structure and of its topological properties. In particular, following [13], two nD pictures are topologically equivalent iff their rooted RAG trees are isomorphic, where the background (BG) defines the root for both pictures. Within the context of 3D binary digital images, Hom-Tree appears to be one tool allowing to coherently define a new refined notion of nD topological equivalence.

The paper has the following sections. Section 2 is devoted to recall the machinery for computing the structures needed for HSF construction. Next, an algorithm for constructing a Hom-Tree from a HSF structure is showed in Sect. 3. Section 4 is devoted to an experimentation with a set of synthetic images showing different shapes and different complexity of connected component nesting for numerically validating the method. Finally, the conclusions are summarized.

2   HSF Structure Seen as an Over-Segmentation

In this section, we recall the constituting parts of a HSF representation of I and stress its close relationship with the Euler numbers of the CCs of I. For technical details of the algorithm for constructing a HSF structure, see [9,21].

From now on, when we refer to a digital image I or digital object $S \subset I$, it can be indistinctly understood as a spatial matrix linked to a cubical grid or as a finite abstract cubical complex (homotopically equivalent to the semi-continuous analog of I or S). Let us recall that an abstract cell complex (ACC) is a particular locally finite space in which a dimension is defined for each cell and each k-cell (cell of dimension k, $k \geq 1$) has a boundary set $Bd(c)$ of $(k-1)$-cells and a coboundary set $Cb(c)$ of $(k+1)$-cells. Usually, as is our case here, the coboundary set of the cells is completely determined by their boundary set (or viceversa). The cells of I live in its auto-dual cubical grid and they can be voxels, pair of voxels, 4-uples of voxels and 8-uples of voxels.

The goal of a topological graph-based data structure of a binary nD digital image is to save cells (given at inter-n-xel level) and incidence relationships between them, in such a way that, for correctly and efficiently retrieving global topological information of I (for example, connected components, region's Euler number,...), only graph transformations over the structure are needed. HSF data structures completely meet this objective. Roughly speaking, a HSF structure on a $(6,26)$-image is a graded set of graphs of cell-nodes, that appropriately extend to higher dimension the classical algorithm of labeling connected components of a digital image via a spanning forest covering all the voxels [20].

Given an binary image I with set of black 6-CCs $\{R_1, \ldots, R_m\}$ and set of white 26-CCs $\{S_1, \ldots, S_n\}$, the output of the HSF construction algorithm provides us for each black or white CC R, a set of graphs that, in a particular maximal and non-redundant way, cover all the cells of R at inter-voxel level. Each graph of this kind has as nodes k-cells and $(k+1)$-cells ($k \geq 0$) and it is denoted as $(k, k+1)$-graph. A $(k, k+1)$-graph G is essential (resp. inessential) if $\chi(G) = \sharp\{k$-cell nodes of $G\} \setminus \sharp\{(k+1)$-cell nodes of $G\}$ (where $\sharp$ means cardinality of a set) is different from zero (resp. zero). Anyway, for each CC R of I, there is exactly one essential $(0,1)$-tree and the Euler number $\chi(R)$ of R as cell complex (that is, $\chi(R) = \sharp\{0$-cells in $R\} - \sharp\{1$-cells in $R\} + \sharp\{0$-cells in $R\}$) agrees with the alternate sum

$$1 - \sum_{G \in (1,2)\text{-graph of } R} \chi(G) + \sum_{G \in (2,3)\text{-graph of } R} \chi(G).$$

Let us note that $\sum_{G \in (0,1)\text{-graph of } R} \chi(G) = 1$. Moreover, $\chi(R)$ can also be expressed in global topological terms as $\chi(R) = \sharp\{CC \text{ of } R\} - \sharp\{\text{tunnels of } R\} + \sharp\{\text{cavities of } R\} = 2 - \sharp\{\text{tunnels of } R\}$.

For representing the homological characteristics of the CCs of I in terms of simple cells, we need to place vectors (c, c') (c being a k-cell and c' being a neighbor $(k + 1)$-cell) on the HSF-graphs in a maximal way and satisfying that any cell is in one vector at most (see [10]). Hence, only in the essential HSF $(k, k + 1)$-graphs, there are k-cells, called *critical cells*, that remain unpaired. Let us limit to say here that the combinatorial homology classes of any region R are intimately associated to the critical cells of its essential HSF-graphs and, in particular, the number of tunnels of R agrees with the number of its critical 1-cells.

This particular region-growing strategy at inter-voxel level is sequentially guided by two criteria: (a) [merging through boundary] A k-cell c (cell of dimension k ($k \geq 1$) and all the $(k - 1)$-cells of $Bd(c)$ are included as nodes in an essential HSF-graph G of dimension $(k - 1, k)$ (composed of $(k - 1)$-cells and k-cells) if there is an odd number of cells of $Bd(c)$ belonging to G and (b) [region color similarity] We give to each cell a unique color and a color-dependant dimension. Then, region color similarity at inter-voxel level is prioritized. In the parallel version of the HSF construction algorithm of [21], the idea is different from the previous one and it is based in the cellular technique of crack transport [9].

3   Hom-Tree Seen as a Homological Segmentation

The underlying idea behind the RAG Tree of the binary 3D digital $(6, 26)$-image I is that I can be naturally segmented as a set of black 6-CCs $\{R_1, \ldots, R_m\}$ and a set of white 26-CCs $\{S_1, \ldots, S_n\}$, and any such region can have one or two 6-neighbor regions specified by the inclusion condition. In fact, given a 6-neighbor region of voxels R_i (for instance, a black 6-CC) and a S_j (a white 26-CC):

- R_i is surrounded by S_j or S_j is surrounded by R_i.
- its intersection $R_i \cap S_j$ is always a connected frontier cubical complex at inter-voxel level.
- As cubical complexes, if R_i is surrounded by S_j and S_j has a non-null number of tunnels, at least there is one tunnel of S_j that is shared with R_i.

Given a 3-tuple of regions, it is evident that its common intersection is always $\emptyset$. Taking into account that the topological Euler number of a segmented solid satisfy the inclusion-exclusion principle, we have in the contractile case of I:

$$1 = \sum_i \chi(R_i) \ + \ \sum_i \chi(S_i) \ - \ \sum_{i,j} \chi(R_i \cap S_j).$$

This last equality can be decomposed in terms of CCs, tunnels and cavities of the regions of $\{R_i\}$ and $\{S_j\}$ is as follows:

- In terms of CCs, we have:

$$\sum_{i,j} \sharp\{\text{CCs of } R_i \cap S_j\} = (m + n) - 1$$

– In terms of tunnels, we have:

$$\sum_i \#\{\text{tunnels of } R_i\} + \sum_i \#\{\text{tunnels of } S_i\} = \sum_{i,j} \#\{\text{tunnels of } R_i \cap S_j\}$$

– In terms of cavities, we have:

$$\sum_i \#\{\text{cavities of } R_i\} + \sum_i \#\{\text{cavities of } S_i\} = \sum_{i,j} \#\{\text{cavities of } R_i \cap S_j\}$$

In consequence,

$$\sum_i \#\{\text{tunnels of } R_i\} = \sum_i \#\{\text{tunnels of } S_i\}) = \frac{1}{2} \cdot \sum_{i,j} \#\{\text{tunnels of } R_i \cap S_j\}.$$

Then, taking advantage of the duality properties of the homological characteristics of the black 6-CCs and white 26-CCs, we can deduce a new isotopic invariant of I, by adding weights to the edges of the rooted classical RAG tree of I. This tree is called *Homological Region Tree* (or *Hom-Tree*, for short) and the weight of the edge (R, S) is given by the number of tunnels the CCs R and S share.

In order that an algorithm for computing a HSF structure of I could be correctly adapted to the computation of the Hom-Tree (see Fig. 1), we first need to work on the auto-dual cubical grid, specifying the contribution of each black and white set C of eight mutually 6-adjacent voxels to the global computation of an HSF for I and for its corresponding CCs. For instance, if we have a set C of this type with only one white voxel: (a) its contribution in terms of cells to a black 26-CC is of 1 0-cells, 6 1-cells, 11 2-cells and 7 3-cells; (b) its contribution in terms of cells to a white 6-CC is reduced to one 0-cell. In this way, each intervoxel element of the auto-dual cubical grid is endowed with a unique color and with a color-dependent dimension, before constructing an HSF for I.

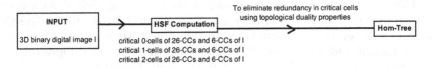

Fig. 1. Scheme of the Hom-Tree computation via HSF

Let us note that the cells of an inter-voxel frontier cubical complex between two regions R_i and S_j still belong to the auto-dual cubical grid. Let us note that it can be identified with a connected boundary surface (cubical complex) that is the intersection of the set of physical voxels of R_i with than that of S_j.

Finally, for obtaining the Hom-Tree from the set of critical 0, 1 and 2-cells of the different black 6-CCs and white 26-CCs of I, we need to apply boundary and coboundary operations to the critical cells in order to: (a) to pair by duality black critical 0-cells (CCs) with white critical 2-cells (cavities) and vice-versa; and (b) to pair by duality critical 1-cells (tunnels) of a black 6-CC with critical 1-cells of a white neighbor 26-CC. After Step (a), the edges of the RAG Tree of I are determined. After Step (b), the weights of the edges are defined (Fig. 2).

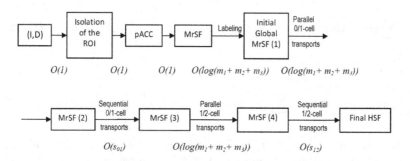

Fig. 2. Time orders for the different steps of HSF computation in [21], having $m_1 \times m_2 \times m_3$ computation processors. s_{01} and s_{12} are the number of sequential cancellations of remaining 0/1 and 1/2 cells respectively (after the parallel cancellation of these pairs).

4   Experimentation

Part of the experimentation of the new proposed method has been done using an automatic homotopy deformation (thinning-thickening) tool based on the notion of 3D simple point that has been developed for this purpose. For algorithmic details, see [2].

The idea is to corroborate with our HSF computation software that homotopically (in fact, isotopically) equivalent shape nestings return the same Hom-Tree.

Then, we use the thinning-thickening algorithm to randomly deform three synthetic image examples, and then use these modified shapes to validate the property of isotopy-invariance of the Hom-Tree. Up to 500 26-simple points have been randomly added/removed 100 times for each of these cases: Three concentric spheres, one torus with two spheres inside, and one sphere with two spheres inside (see Fig. 3).

In the rest of the section we present briefly the HSF tool that allows us to compute the Hom-tree of several binary 3D images. Previous version of our HSF software was presented in [9] for binary 2D images, and in [8] for color 2D images. Additionally, in [22] the scaffolding of tridimensional HSF and a unpretentious software was published. That preliminary version could not do support transports of cracks. We are now developing a complete HSF software with emphasis in its parallel computation of all of its stages.

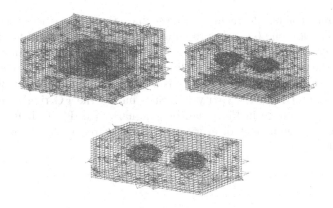

Fig. 3. Examples of deformed objects: Three concentric spheres, one torus with two spheres inside, and one sphere with two spheres inside.

In a nutshell, and as it is shown in Fig. 4, HSF software is based on an abstract cubical complex (ACC) of a 3D digital image. In this Figure, 0-cells, 1-cells, 2-cells and 3-cells are represented by circles, triangles, squares and stars respectively. At the left bottom of the figure there is a representation of a voxel as a light blue hexahedron, which is the minimal processing element (PE) of a real 3D digital image. Then, the way to produce an HSF is building the connections of all the cells in the ACC. More exactly, and in order to promote an efficient parallel computation, we built three trees: the (0, 1), (1, 2) and (2, 3) trees. More details about crack transports and time orders of parallel HSF computation can be consulted in [21].

In the present paper, some restrictions still remain on our HSF software, like considering only 6-adjacency for FG voxels. Whereas this restriction impedes us to present abundant testing with real images in order to capture their homotopy-based features, it is sufficient for distinguishing complex patterns from synthetic images.

According to the generation of a HSF structure, each critical 0-cell of a color has a link (vector of cells) that connects with the opposite color. Thus, the nesting of components (and then the classical Region-Adjacency Tree) can be easily found. Moreover, those critical cells of higher dimensions can be associated with the component of their border cells. In the case of 3D, tunnels add a valuable information when relating each tunnel with a pair of a FG and a BG components. In addition, cavities (represented by critical 2-cells) have a dual relation with critical 0-cells. From now on, these relations are expressed in the Hom-trees of the processed images, using dashed arcs to enclose related cells. Once the 1 and 2 related cells have been identified, Hom-tree can be simply reduced to the edges that connects the 0-cells (black and white little circles in e.g. Fig. 6) plus a weight indicating the number of tunnels that hang from a component.

A simple but clarifying object is first presented: a foreground ring normal to Z axis (see Fig. 5). In this figure, all the HSF trees for this ring are depicted using different colors. Meanwhile, thickest lines represent critical cells. For the FG ring, they are one 0-cell (representative of the FG component) and one 1-cell (representative of the FG tunnel). Correspondingly, the BG ambiance that surrounds the ring contains one 0-cell (represented by the most upper right 0-cell), one 1-cell (because the FG ring is seen like a tunnel for the BG) and a 2-cell, representative of the cavity (which is indeed the FG ring). Finally, the Hom-tree of the image in Fig. 5 can be summarized in Fig. 6, Left. Note that each connected component of every color is associated with its corresponding critical cells.

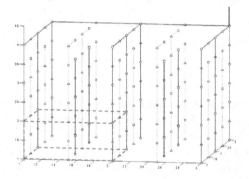

Fig. 4. A visual representation of the scenario where the digital image will be "embedded". 0-cells, 1-cells, 2-cells and 3-cells are represented by circles, triangles, squares and stars respectively. At the left bottom of the figure there is a representation of a voxel as a light blue hexahedron, which is the minimal processing element (PE) of a real 3D digital image. (Color figure online)

More complicated images can be topologically classified with the Hom-tree representation. In Fig. 6, right, we depict the Hom-tree of a binary image containing a FG sphere surrounding a FG torus. From top to bottom for the 0-cells, we distinguish the following: (1) Firstly the 0-cell of the BG canvas that has no dual correspondence; (2) Secondly, the FG sphere representative (which is related to the cavity of previous 0-cell); (3) A new BG 0-cell related to the cavity of the FG sphere; (4) the 0-cell of the torus that is linked with the previous BG component. Between these two previous 0-cells there is interface (a red edge in this Fig. 6) weighted with 1, because the outer tunnel of the torus can be delineated using a line that resides in the sphere cavity. And finally, (5) the last BG component is the cavity of the torus, with hold the delineation of the inner tunnel of the torus (thus the last red edge is also weighted with 1. The fact that each critical cell has its corresponding dual (except the BG component of the canvas) means that the Euler number of the whole 3D image is simply 1.

Finally, Hom-Tree is able to distinguishing non-isotopic patterns. An interesting example occurs for spheres with handles. In Fig. 7 a HSF of a FG sphere with two external handles is completely drawn to distinguish that the borders

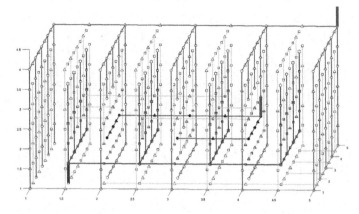

Fig. 5. A foreground ring normal to Z axis is depicted along with the computation of a HSF structure. $(0, 1)$-HSF-trees are displayed in red, $(1, 2)$-HSF-trees in yellow and $(2, 3)$-HSF-trees in blue. The thickest line of every tree represents the critical cell of its corresponding tree. (Color figure online)

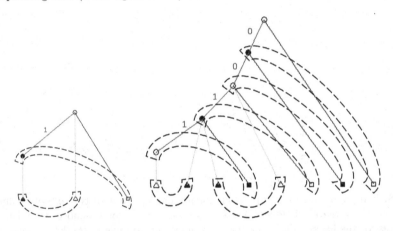

Fig. 6. Left: Hom-tree for the previous foreground ring of Fig. 5. Same color convention is followed. Solid symbols are for foreground cells and hollow symbols for the background ones. An example of the duality of the HSF is showed pairing every critical cell of the FG with its corresponding BG counterpart (excepting the BG critical cell of the canvas, which is the root of the tree). These associations are shown with dashed arcs. In this case, the BG canvas has only one cavity that is associated to the FG component, and the FG tunnel is directly associated with the BG tunnel. Right: Hom-tree for an image containing a FG sphere that in turn surrounds a FG torus. Note that each critical cell has its corresponding dual (except the BG component of the canvas). (Color figure online)

of its two critical 1-cells (marked with thickest yellow lines at $Z = 2$, $Y = 2$, $X = 2.5$ and $X = 6.5$) fall into the FG component. Moreover, there are two additional tunnels for the BG external component (ahead of the two previous ones

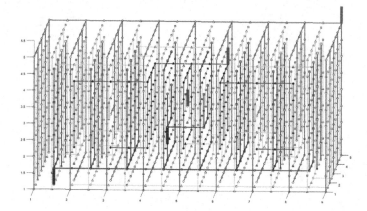

Fig. 7. HSF of a sphere with two external handles. The colors code is the same as the employed for the previous figures. All trees are being displayed along with their corresponding critical cells. In the upper right part of the figure, a red link represents the BG CC of the image. (Color figure online)

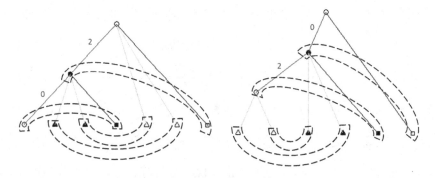

Fig. 8. Left: Hom-tree for the previous foreground sphere with two external handles. Same color convention is followed. Solid symbols are for foreground cells and hollow symbols for the background ones. The root node corresponds to the BG critical 0-cell of the canvas in which the image in embedded. Every critical cell will have a dual nature, i.e. for every FG critical cell can be associated a BG critical cell (these parings are shown with dashed arcs), excepting the critical cell corresponding to the canvas. Right: Hom-Tree for a foreground sphere with two inner handles. Although the FG component has the same Hom-Tree, the most inner BG component contains now the two tunnels that was associated to the BG canvas on the left Hom-Tree. (Color figure online)

at $Y = 1.5$). As a result, its condensed Hom-tree (see Fig. 8, left) is composed by three connected components whose edges from top to bottom have weights 2 and 0. On the other hand, for the sphere with two internal handles, (see Fig. 8, right), its RAG coincides with the previous one, but the tunnels are delineated here within the sphere cavity. That means that the weights for the Hom-tree edges are now (from top to bottom) 0 and 2.

Nevertheless, it is worth to mention that some dissimilar nesting of digital objects cannot be distinguished using the Hom-tree representation: this is the case of a torus versus a sphere with an inner tunnel and an external one. Both of them result with the same Hom-tree representation and edge weights.

5 Conclusions

We present Hom-tree as an compressed representation of a 3D binary digital image I. It is an edge-weighted RAG Tree of black 6-CCs and white 26-CCs, with weights measured in terms of "common" tunnels of neighbors CCs. An algorithm for computing a Hom-Tree via a HSF model of I is presented and its isotopic invariance is validated with several synthetic images. This concept surpasses the classical RAG Tree with regard to topological classification tasks. Moreover, this representation allows to define graph-based operations for modifying it [25] (e.g. splitting and merging of regions,...) in order to develop a Solid Constructive Topology theory. Also, potential applications of the Hom-Tree structure (possibly, with weights representing geometrical and analytic properties, like area, volume, delineations lengths,...) can be explored for retrieval, classification, recognition and registrations tasks on biomedical digital images.

In a near future, we plan:

(a) To implement a fully parallel algorithm for computing the Hom-Tree from an HSF model.
(b) To extend this notion to grey-level and color images (extending the classical Region-Adjacency-Graph notion) and to higher dimension (3D+t, 4D, nD) and to mimic the Hom-Tree parallel computation via HSF model to these more complex contexts.

In the longer term, we will try to enrich the Hom-Tree structure with more complex topological (mainly, homological) characteristics of the CCs of I, in order to distinguish, for example, a torus from a sphere with an internal and an external handle.

References

1. Ansaldi, S., De Floriani, L., Falcidieno, B.: Geometric modeling of solid objects by using a face adjacency graph representation. In: ACM SIGGRAPH Computer Graphics, vol. 19, no. 3, pp. 131–139. ACM, July 1985
2. Bertrand, G.: Simple points, topological numbers and geodesic neighborhoods in cubic grids. Pattern Recogn. Lett. **15**, 1003–1011 (1994)
3. Cardoze, D.E., Miller, G.L., Phillips, T.: Representing topological structures using cell-chains. In: Kim, M.-S., Shimada, K. (eds.) GMP 2006. LNCS, vol. 4077, pp. 248–266. Springer, Heidelberg (2006). https://doi.org/10.1007/11802914_18

4. Costanza, E., Robinson, J.: A region adjacency tree approach to the detection and design of fiducials. In: Video, Vision and Graphics, pp. 63–99 (2003)
5. Cucchiara, R., Grana, C., Prati, A., Seidenari, S., Pellacani, G.: Building the topological tree by recursive FCM color clustering. In: Object Recognition Supported by User Interaction for Service Robots, vol. 1, pp. 759–762. IEEE, August 2002
6. Cohn, A., Bennett, B., Gooday, J., Gotts, N.: Qualitative spacial representation and reasoning with the region connection calculus. GeoInformatica 1(3), 275–316 (1997)
7. Delgado-Friedrichs, O., Robins, V., Sheppard, A.: Skeletonization and partitioning of digital images using discrete Morse theory. IEEE Trans. Pattern Anal. Mach. Intell. 37(3), 654–666 (2015)
8. Díaz-del-Río, F., Real, P., Onchis, D.: Labeling color 2D digital images in theoretical near logarithmic time. In: Felsberg, M., Heyden, A., Krüger, N. (eds.) CAIP 2017. LNCS, vol. 10425, pp. 391–402. Springer, Cham (2017). https://doi.org/10.1007/978-3-319-64698-5_33
9. Díaz-del-Río, F., Real, P., Onchis, D.M.: A parallel homological spanning forest framework for 2D topological image analysis. Pattern Recogn. Lett. 83, 49–58 (2016)
10. Forman, R.: Morse theory for cell complexes. Adv. Math. 134, 90–145 (1998)
11. Klette, R., Rosenfeld, A.: Digital Geometry Geometric: Methods for Digital Picture Analysis. Morgan Kaufmann, San Francisco (2004)
12. Klette, G.: Skeletons in digital image processing. CITR, The University of Auckland, New Zealand (2002)
13. Klette, R., Rosenfeld, A.: Digital Geometry: Geometric Methods for Digital Picture Analysis. Elsevier, Amsterdam (2004)
14. Kong, T.Y., Rosenfeld, A.: Topological Algorithms for Digital Image Processing, vol. 19. Elsevier, Amsterdam (1996)
15. Kong, T.Y., Roscoe, A.W.: A theory of binary digital pictures. Comput. Vis. Graph. Image Process. 32(2), 221–243 (1985)
16. Kovalevsky, V.: Algorithms in digital geometry based on cellular topology. In: Klette, R., Žunić, J. (eds.) IWCIA 2004. LNCS, vol. 3322, pp. 366–393. Springer, Heidelberg (2004). https://doi.org/10.1007/978-3-540-30503-3_27
17. Lienhardt, P.: Topological models for boundary representation: a comparison with n-dimensional generalized maps. Comput. Aided Des. 23(1), 59–82 (1991)
18. Molina-Abril, H., Real, P., Nakamura, A., Klette, R.: Connectivity calculus of fractal polyhedrons. Pattern Recogn. 48(4), 1150–1160 (2015)
19. Molina-Abril, H., Real, P.: Homological spanning forest framework for 2D image analysis. Ann. Math. Artif. Intell. 64(4), 385–409 (2012)
20. Pavlidis, T.: Algorithms for Graphics and Image Processing. Springer, Heidelberg (1997)
21. Real, P., Molina-Abril, H., Díaz-del-Río, F., Blanco-Trejo, S., Onchis, D.: Enhanced parallel generation of tree structures for the recognition of 3D images. In: Carrasco-Ochoa, J., Martínez-Trinidad, J., Olvera-López, J., Salas, J. (eds.) MCPR 2019. LNCS, vol. 11524, pp. 292–301. Springer, Cham (2019). https://doi.org/10.1007/978-3-030-21077-9_27
22. Real, P., Diaz-del-Rio, F., Onchis, D.: Toward parallel computation of dense homotopy skeletons for nD digital objects. In: Brimkov, V.E., Barneva, R.P. (eds.) IWCIA 2017. LNCS, vol. 10256, pp. 142–155. Springer, Cham (2017). https://doi.org/10.1007/978-3-319-59108-7_12

23. Rosenfeld, A.: Adjacency in digital pictures. Inf. Control **26**(1), 24–33 (1974)
24. Serra, J.: Image Analysis and Mathematical Morphology. Academic Press, Cambridge (1982)
25. Stell, J., Worboys, M.: Relations between adjacency trees. Theoret. Comput. Sci. **412**(34), 4452–4468 (2011)

Poster Session

Reliability of Results and Fairness in the Comparison of Rates Among 3D Facial Expression Recognition Works

Gilderlane Ribeiro Alexandre[(⊠)] [iD], George André Pereira Thé[iD], and José Marques Soares[iD]

Departamento de Engenharia de Teleinformática, Centro de Tecnologia, Campus do Pici, Universidade Federal do Ceará, Fortaleza, CE 60455-970, Brazil
`gilderlane.ribeiro@gmail.com`,`{george.the,marques}@ufc.br`

Abstract. The capability of replicating experiments and comparing results is a basic premise for scientific progress. Thus, it is imperative that the conduction of validation experiments follow transparent methodological steps and be also reported in a clear way to allow accurate replication and fair comparison between results. In 3D facial expression recognition, the presented results are estimates of performance of a classification system and, therefore, have an intrinsic degree of uncertainty. Because of that, the reliability of a measure for evaluation is directly related to the concept of stability. In this work, we examine the experimental setup reported by a set of 3D facial expression recognition studies published from 2013 to 2018. This investigation revealed that the concern with stability of mean recognition rates is present in only a small portion of studies. In addition, it demonstrates that the highest rates in this domain are also, potentially, the most unstable. Those findings lead to a reflection on the fairness of comparisons in this domain.

Keywords: 3D facial expression recognition ·
Stability of recognition rates · Fairness of comparisons

1 Introduction

The concern with some fundamental methodological aspects in scientific works allows the community for its continuation, eventual improvement and proposition of alternatives, which has been the foundation of the scientific advance. Properly following and reporting a methodological process are basic conditions expected from a contribution that is intended to impact science.

Different research areas have particular characteristics that generate specific demands to improve the methodological decisions. For example, the proposed

This study was financed in part by the Coordenação de Aperfeiçoamento de Pessoal de Nível Superior - Brasil (CAPES) - Finance Code 001.

© Springer Nature Switzerland AG 2019
M. Vento and G. Percannella (Eds.): CAIP 2019, LNCS 11678, pp. 391–401, 2019.
https://doi.org/10.1007/978-3-030-29888-3_31

solutions for the 3D facial expression recognition (3D FER) problem are elaborated by means of a combination of computer vision and machine learning techniques. In this context, the object of study are 3D expressive facial images, available in a very limited number of public databases.

A common pipeline followed on 3D FER studies involves the steps of preprocessing, face representation decisions, classification and evaluation of results, as illustrated in Fig. 1. Certainly, preprocessing and face representation procedures have an influence on the results achieved by classification and are, indeed, intended to have. However, more subtly, the experiment design itself has an impact and may compromise the reliability of the presented results, affecting the evaluation of their generality.

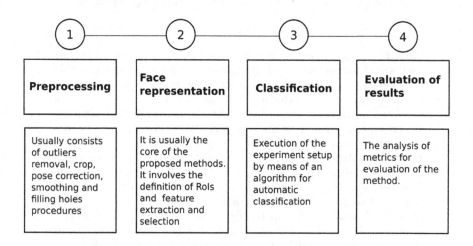

Fig. 1. Usual pipeline followed in 3D FER studies.

In pattern classification, stability of classifiers is a key concept associated with the generality of a model and depends on the quantity of data (n) available for learning [5]. That is, the greater the amount of data $(n \to \infty)$, the better. In practice, however, there is no infinite data available. In fact, important limitations in n are frequent and thus the result of the presentation of infinite data to the classifier is estimated by means of resampling techniques. That estimate is utilized as the measure for the evaluation of the model and, therefore is the main criterion of comparison between similar scenarios. As all estimates, however, those measures have an intrinsic uncertainty and their reliability increases with the count of trials that gives rise to them. That aspect should not be disregarded, specially for the purposes of comparison.

Due to the evident relevance of the systematic concern with stability, in this work, we investigate a number of 3D FER studies by means of a rigorous examination of the experimental design reported. That investigation aims to contribute with the understanding of how stability is approached in this domain and how that aspect affects the measures of evaluation, main criteria of comparison.

The remainder of this paper is organized as follows. In Sect. 2, we present the theoretical basis for the concept of stability of learning algorithms. In Sect. 3 we present the method of examination of the studies. In Sect. 4 the results are presented. We discuss the outcomes of the investigation in Sect. 5 and, finally, Sect. 6 concludes with general considerations.

2 Theoretical Foundation

Stability of learning algorithms has been approached in the specialized literature for decades [4]. Unstable classifiers are sensitive to changes in the training data and, therefore, lead to models of low generality.

The measures of bias and variance quantify the goodness of a given model to the training data, regarding its accuracy and precision, respectively. A low biased classifier fits well the particularities of the training data, while a low variance classifier is consistent across variations of the training set. Ideally, the classifiers should have low bias and low variance. However, those measures are not independent and increasing flexibility to adapt to the training set generally leads to lower bias but higher variance [5]. Figure 2 illustrates that phenomenon. It is, indeed, another manifestation of the well-known trade-off between simplifying the model and fitting the data.

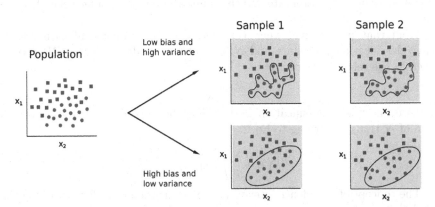

Fig. 2. The bias-variance trade-off. A low bias classifier fits well each variation of the training set and, therefore has high variance; while a high bias classifier does not capture some particularities of data, but is consistent across variations.

Additionally, the size of the training set plays an important role in the adjustment of the variance as, for a given bias, the increased number of patterns leads to lower and stable generalization error. Often, machine learning problems lack a very large training set available and, therefore, resort to resampling methods to achieve informative estimates to evaluate the classifier's performance (e.g. accuracy).

Specifically, in the 3D FER domain there is a very limited number of 3D face databases available, of which the BU-3DFE [15] and Bosphorus face database [13] are the most widely employed. The former is composed of 2,500 scans of 100 subjects, each reproducing an equal set of conditions: a neutral pose and facial expressions of the six basic emotions (anger, disgust, fear, happiness, sadness and surprise) distributed in four levels of intensity. In spite of that, frequently only the scans of the highest levels of intensity of a subset of subjects are actually considered in the experiments. In turn, Bosphorus face database has 4,666 scans of 105 subjects in varied conditions of pose, occlusion and expression. In this database, not all subjects reproduce all scenarios. Accordingly, only a subset of the complete database is composed of subjects performing facial expressions of all the six basic emotions, and therefore, employed for 3D FER.

In this scenario of very limited data, multiple executions of classification experiments with resampling methods are performed and the average measure of accuracy of all runs is often used as the classifier's performance estimate and reported as the mean recognition rate (RR). There is, however, a known relation between the number of repetitions of the classification strategy and the stability of the measure for evaluation. That relation has been empirically demonstrated by Gong et al. in [3], in which classification experiments performed only a few times presented highly unstable results. Indeed, that is an expected behavior that finds its theoretical basis in the connection between the confidence intervals for the estimate of recognition rate and the count of repetitions of face classification trials.

From that perspective, when considering k, the outcome of each resampling/classification procedure and N, the total of trials, the mean RR can be taken as the relative frequency

$$\hat{p} = \frac{k}{N}, \tag{1}$$

of the event "right classification", which has the binomial distribution over a total of N trials, according to Eq. 2.

$$P(k) = \binom{N}{k} p^k (1 - p)^{N-k}. \tag{2}$$

The concept of confidence interval (CI) gives us the means for describing the reliability of a given measure, as it evidence a range of potential true values for an estimate at a level of confidence. By fixing the confidence level at 99% and varying N, we end up with a series of possible true values p for a given estimate $\hat{p}$ and observe that the uncertainty associated with a given $\hat{p}$ is smaller for greater values of N, as shown in Fig. 3.

3   Method

In order to aggregate evidences of how stability is addressed in 3D FER field, a number of studies in this domain was searched and selected. Naturally, some

99% Confidence intervals for different N

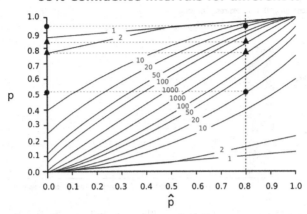

Fig. 3. The 99% confidence intervals for different counts of N. Highlighted, the uncertainty margins of the predicted RR 0.8 when derived from 20 repetitions (represented by dots) and 1000 repetitions (represented by triangles). Notice that, the more far apart the margins, more uncertainty associated with the measure $\hat{p}$.

selection criteria for candidate studies were applied and a sample of the initially retrieved works was actually considered. The establishment of these criteria aims to reduce the bias of the researchers when selecting studies, avoiding the decision making based on purely subjective aspects. The first two selection criteria restrict the scope of the study, that is, it assures that the candidate study proposes a solution for the automatic 3D FER problem and that they include in their investigation the six basic emotions: Anger, Disgust, Fear, Happiness, Sadness and Surprise, since the universe of facial expressions is large and not all of them are emotional expressions. That definition is important for the purposes of comparing studies, since the number of classes has an impact in the classification performance.

In addition, it is necessary that the study be available in an accessible language for later extraction of data. Data from Scopus[1] and the Web of Science[2] (former ISI Web of Knowledge), two well reputed databases that index important journals and conference proceedings in the fields of technology and science, endorse English as being the main language for publication in this field (see Fig. 4). For that reason, English was taken as the third selection criterion, followed by a time limiting aspect. Table 1 summarizes the four characteristics found in all selected studies.

We have finally examined 34 3D FER research papers. That collection of studies undergone the extraction of data regarding the reported experimental designs. A total of 50 classification experiments were identified and their key characteristics were registered. The data extraction fields are detailed in Table 2.

---

[1] https://www.scopus.com/search/form.uri?display=basic.
[2] https://www.webofknowledge.com/.

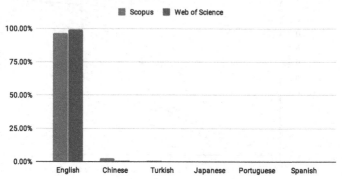

Fig. 4. Languages of published works in 3D FER indexed by Scopus and WoS by employing the search topic: 3D facial expression recognition

Table 1. The four basic characteristics found in the all selected studies

Criteria	Description
1	The study proposes a solution to the automatic 3D FER problem
2	The study appraises all six basic emotions (may or not include the neutral expression)
3	Available in English
4	Date of publication: from 2013 to 2018

Table 2. Key characteristics extracted from the collection of 3D FER studies.

Extracted data	Description
3D face database	The 3D face database used to validate the method proposed in the study
Data sample	The subset of the database actually employed (i.e. number of subjects, levels of intensity, whether neutral samples are included)
Training/test split	e.g. 90%/10%, 10-CV
Repetition	How many times the classifier ran over the training/test split
Classifier	The algorithm for classification e.g. SVM, k-NN
Results	The recognition accuracy achieved

4   Results

Considering the discussion about the relationship between the uncertainty associated with the RRs and the number of repetitions of the resampling/classification procedures presented in Sect. 2, it follows that although there is no strict threshold separating stable estimates from unstable ones, it is possible to compare their degrees of stability.

Among the surveyed studies, we observed a huge gap between the group of studies reporting more than 100 rounds of classification and the group of studies reporting only a few repetitions (up to 20). There is no reported result from an intermediate number of rounds. For that reason, we used a threshold of 100 repetitions to categorize the mean RRs derived from the 50 experiments under evaluation as stable or non stable.

We found a proportion of 35% of studies that mention the concern about stability of the achieved RRs. Those studies employ and report a count of rounds of classification superior to 100. The remaining studies[3] either employed less than 100 repetitions or did not mention any repetition in their classification strategy. We refer to the measures for evaluation derived from the first group of experiments as stable and to the ones derived from the latter as non stable. In Fig. 5, the histograms of both groups of RRs are presented, while Table 3 shows their statistics. The details of the experiments reported in those studies are presented in Table 4 categorized by the database and the count of classes of emotions utilized. The highest mean RR of each category is highlighted.

Density of RRs of 3D FER experiments

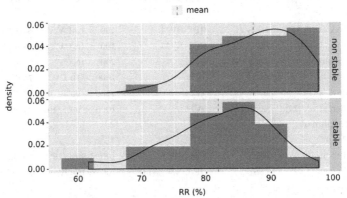

Fig. 5. Densities of RRs categorized into stable experiments and unstable experiments, regarding the count of repetitions of the classification experiment reported.

---

[3] For the complete list of those studies, please see the supplementary material available in https://goo.gl/JUP1cM.

Table 3. Main statistics of RRs of groups of experiments categorized as non stable and stable

	Non stable	Stable
Min	72.25%	61.69%
Median	87.67%	84.33%
Mean	87.31%	81.84%
Max	97.3%	94.56%

Table 4. 3D FER classification experiments performing a minimum of 100 repetitions for stability. In bold, the highest recognition rates of each category.

Study	Data sample	Classifier	Strategy	RR
6 basic expressions				
BU-3DFE				
2D+3D				
Zeng et al. [16]	60S+2L	SRC	100 × 90%/10%	70.93%
Li et al. [9]	60S+2L	RBF-SVM	100 × 90%/10%	86.32%
Li et al. [12]	60S+2L	RBF-SVM	100 × 90%/10%	**94.56%**
Li et al. [8]	100S+2L	DF-CNN (svm)	100 × 10-CV	86.86%
	100S+4L	DF-CNN (softmax)	100 × 10-CV	81.33%
Azazi et al. [2]	60S	k-NN	100 × 10-CV	61.69%
	60S	NB	100 × 10-CV	74.08%
	60S	RBF-NN	100 × 10-CV	71.56%
	60S	RBF-SVM	100 × 10-CV	79.36%
Jan and Meng [6]	60S+2L	SVM	100 × 10-CV	90.04%
Azazi et al. [1]	60S	SVM with EPE	100 × 10-CV	85.81%
3D				
Yang et al. [14]	60S+2L	RBF-SVM	100 × 10-CV	84.8%
Li et al. [10]	60S+2L	RBF-SVM	100 × 10-CV	88.32%
Lemaire et al. [7]	100S+2L	SVM	200 × 10-CV	78.13%
	60S+2L	SVM	1000 × 10-CV	76.6%
An et al. [11]	60S	SVM	1000 × 90%/10%	**91.3%**
Zhen et al. [17]	60S+2L	SVM	1000 × 90%/10%	84.5%
Bosphorus				
2D+3D				
Li et al. [9]	60S	RBF-SVM	100 × 90%/10%	**84.33%**
Li et al. [8]	60S	DF-CNN (svm)	100 × 10-CV	80.28%
6 basic expressions + 1 neutral				
BU-3DFE				
2D+3D				
Jan and Meng [6]	60S+2L	SVM	100 × 10-CV	**88.32%**
Bosphorus				
2D+3D				
Jan and Meng [6]	Unknown	SVM	100 × 10-CV	**79.46%**

5   Discussion

The comparison of performance of different methods proposed for 3D FER must be carefully handled. The RR, held as the main measure for evaluation, is affected by a number of factors distributed over the whole experimental pipeline until the evaluation of the classification results. That effect is exemplified in Table 4, in which the RRs of classification experiments performing a minimum of 100 repetitions are grouped by the number of classes of emotions, the 3D face database and the type of data employed, in order to facilitate the comparison of results from much alike scenarios. Clearly, many decisions contribute to the final outcomes; even more than the few categories presented. Naturally, the interventions designed to intentionally diminish difficulties and improve the capability of description, such as the specific feature extraction and selection procedures, have an impact in the classification performance. Those interventions are usually the core of the proposed method and, therefore, it is their effectiveness that is subject to comparison by means of the RR.

However, in addition to those interventions, the experimental setup might influence the final result in not so explicit ways, affecting for example the certainty associated with it. The RRs derived from an average of few resampling/classification experiments carry, potentially, a poor representative measure of performance of a given method, once they are also more unstable. Therefore, it is a concerning finding that only a small portion of the examined 3D FER studies presents a clear interest about the stability of the presented results. This directly impacts the capability of replicating those results even when performing the very same experiment. It also raises the question of fairness of comparisons between results when neglecting that aspect. In fact, the 99% confidence intervals of the mean RRs reported, illustrated in Fig. 6, evidence the differences of the levels of uncertainty associated with the measures of both groups.

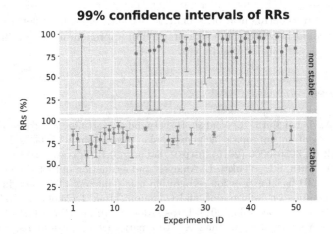

99% confidence intervals of RRs

Fig. 6. The 99% confidence intervals for the RRs derived from the analyzed studies. The experiments that have not explicitly mentioned the count of repetitions of their classification strategy were assumed to perform a unique round.

Moreover, we have presented in Fig. 5 the histograms of the RRs achieved by experiments grouped into stable and non stable, which points to an association between higher RRs and non stable experiments. Indeed, complementary to it, the statistics of the RRs presented in Table 3 indicate that scenarios with more rigid criteria of stability have lower performance. In practice, that means that, currently, the experiments in 3D FER field with the highest RRs have also a higher chance of having unstable ones. That phenomenon should be carefully taken into account when comparing results, once it may lead the community to, inadvertently, pursue results that could actually be unattainable under certain circumstances or incomparable under other.

6 Conclusion

In this work, we examined the experiment designs of a sample of 3D facial expression recognition research papers, on the subject of the uncertainty associated with the measures for evaluation. For this purpose, we have considered the number of independent classifications that originated the mean recognition rates reported, once those measures are frequently the final estimates of classification performance in those studies.

This investigation revealed that the concern with the stability of those measures is recently a neglected aspect in this domain, once only a small portion of 35% of the examined studies have reported performing a number of repetitions of the resampling/classification procedure that allows the assumption of stability, and therefore reliability, of the measures reported. Moreover, it revealed that there is a correlation between the mean recognition rates and its stability, in such manner that the highest values are also, on average, the most unstable.

We call attention to the direct implications of those findings in the capability of replicating experiments and therefore, in the fairness of comparisons between results. Although it is our understanding that it is not feasible to establish absolutely rigid experimentation scenarios, we have shown evidences that this community could benefit from a more regardful approach in the conduction and reporting of classification experiments.

References

1. Azazi, A., Lebai Lutfi, S., Venkat, I., Fernández-Martínez, F.: Towards a robust affect recognition: automatic facial expression recognition in 3D faces. Expert Syst. Appl. **42**(6), 3056–3066 (2015). https://doi.org/10.1016/j.eswa.2014.10.042
2. Azazi, A., Lutfi, S.L., Venkat, I.: Analysis and evaluation of SURF descriptors for automatic 3D facial expression recognition using different classifiers. In: 2014 4th World Congress on Information and Communication Technologies, WICT 2014, pp. 23–28. IEEE, December 2014. https://doi.org/10.1109/WICT.2014.7077296
3. Gong, B., Wang, Y., Liu, J., Tang, X.: Automatic facial expression recognition on a single 3D face by exploring shape deformation. In: ACM International Conference on Multimedia, pp. 569–572 (2009)

4. Bousquet, O., Elisseeff, A.: Stability and generalization. J. Mach. Learn. Res. **2**(3), 499–526 (2002). https://doi.org/10.1162/153244302760200704
5. Duda, R.O., Hart, P.E., Stork, D.G.: Algorithm-independent machine learning. In: Pattern Classification, pp. 453–516. Wiley, New York (2012). Chap. 9
6. Jan, A., Meng, H.: Automatic 3D facial expression recognition using geometric and textured feature fusion. In: 2015 11th IEEE International Conference and Workshops on Automatic Face and Gesture Recognition (FG), vol. 05, pp. 1–6. IEEE, May 2015. https://doi.org/10.1109/FG.2015.7284860
7. Lemaire, P., Ardabilian, M., Chen, L., Daoudi, M.: Fully automatic 3D facial expression recognition using differential mean curvature maps and histograms of oriented gradients. In: 2013 10th IEEE International Conference and Workshops on Automatic Face and Gesture Recognition (FG). pp. 1–7. IEEE, April 2013. https://doi.org/10.1109/FG.2013.6553821. http://ieeexplore.ieee.org/document/6553821/
8. Li, H., Sun, J., Xu, Z., Chen, L.: Multimodal 2D+3D facial expression recognition with deep fusion convolutional neural network. IEEE Trans. Multimed. **19**(12), 2816–2831 (2017). https://doi.org/10.1109/TMM.2017.2713408
9. Li, H., et al.: An efficient multimodal 2D + 3D feature-based approach to automatic facial expression recognition. Comput. Vis. Image Underst. **140**(C), 83–92 (2015). https://doi.org/10.1016/j.cviu.2015.07.005
10. Li, Q., An, G., Ruan, Q.: 3D Facial expression recognition using orthogonal tensor marginal fisher analysis on geometric maps. In: 2017 International Conference on Wavelet Analysis and Pattern Recognition (ICWAPR), vol. 35, pp. 65–71. IEEE, July 2017. https://doi.org/10.1109/ICWAPR.2017.8076665
11. Li, X., Ruan, Q., An, G.: 3D facial expression recognition using delta faces. In: 5th IET International Conference on Wireless, Mobile and Multimedia Networks (ICWMMN 2013), pp. 234–239. Institution of Engineering and Technology (2013). https://doi.org/10.1049/cp.2013.2415
12. Li, X., Ruan, Q., An, G., Jin, Y., Zhao, R.: Multiple strategies to enhance automatic 3D facial expression recognition. Neurocomputing **161**(C), 89–98 (2015). https://doi.org/10.1016/j.neucom.2015.02.063
13. Savran, A., et al.: Bosphorus database for 3D face analysis. In: Schouten, B., Juul, N.C., Drygajlo, A., Tistarelli, M. (eds.) BioID 2008. LNCS, vol. 5372, pp. 47–56. Springer, Heidelberg (2008). https://doi.org/10.1007/978-3-540-89991-4_6
14. Yang, X., Huang, D., Wang, Y., Chen, L.: Automatic 3D facial expression recognition using geometric scattering representation. In: 2015 11th IEEE International Conference and Workshops on Automatic Face and Gesture Recognition (FG), pp. 1–6. IEEE, May 2015. https://doi.org/10.1109/FG.2015.7163090
15. Yin, L., Wei, X., Sun, Y., Wang, J., Rosato, M.J.: A 3D facial expression database for facial behavior research. In: FGR 2006: Proceedings of the 7th International Conference on Automatic Face and Gesture Recognition 2006, pp. 211–216 (2006). https://doi.org/10.1109/FGR.2006.6
16. Zeng, W., Li, H., Chen, L., Morvan, J.M., Gu, X.D.: An automatic 3D expression recognition framework based on sparse representation of conformal images. In: 2013 10th IEEE International Conference and Workshops on Automatic Face and Gesture Recognition (FG), pp. 1–8. IEEE, April 2013. https://doi.org/10.1109/FG.2013.6553749
17. Zhen, Q., Huang, D., Wang, Y., Chen, L.: Muscular movement model-based automatic 3D/4D facial expression recognition. IEEE Trans. Multimed. **18**(7), 1438–1450 (2016). https://doi.org/10.1109/TMM.2016.2557063

On the Null-Space of the Shape-Color Moment Invariants

Jitka Kostková$^{(\boxtimes)}$ⓘ and Jan Flusser

The Czech Academy of Sciences, Institute of Information Theory and Automation,
Pod Vodárenskou věží 4, 182 08 Prague 8, Czech Republic
{kostkova,flusser}@utia.cas.cz

Abstract. In this paper, we extend the theory of the combined Shape-Color Affine Moment Invariants (SCAMIs) for recognition of color images, proposed originally by Gong et al. in [3]. Since in the real pictures the shape deformation is always accompanied by the color deformation, it is not sufficient to use the shape invariant or color invariant descriptors only and the use of combined invariants is needed. However, the SCAMIs are not able to recognize images, the color channels of which are linearly dependent or highly correlated. This situation is not rare in practice and is of particular importance in hyper-spectral image analysis, where the spectral bands are highly correlated. We analyze why the SCAMIs fail in such situations, correct the theory and propose a solution to overcome such drawback. Unlike the SCAMIs, the new invariants have in the null-space the constant-zero images only, which leads to a better discrimination power, as demonstrated also on various pictures.

Keywords: Color image recognition · Affine transformation ·
Channel mixing · Moment invariants · Null-space

1 Introduction

Image descriptors, which are invariant with respect to certain group of spatial and/or color transformations, have been a topic of much research in image analysis. In the recent paper [3], Gong et al. proposed invariants of 2D color images, represented by their RGB channels, with respect to affine transformation of the spatial coordinates and simultaneously to affine transformation of the RGB space. Their invariants are based on classical theory of moments (see, for instance, [1,2] for a survey). The paper [3] was on one hand inspired by the work of Suk and Flusser [7], who proposed a general framework based on graph theory, allowing a systematic construction of affine moment invariants (AMIs) of graylevel images. Suk and Flusser extended their theory to color images, too, by incorporating a between-channel bond and introducing so-called joint affine

---

This work was supported by the Czech Science Foundation (Grant No. GA18-07247S), by the *Praemium Academiae,* and by the Grant Agency of the Czech Technical University (Grant No. SGS18/188/OHK4/3T/14).

M. Vento and G. Percannella (Eds.): CAIP 2019, LNCS 11678, pp. 402–408, 2019.
https://doi.org/10.1007/978-3-030-29888-3_32

invariants [6]. On the other hand, another motivation came from the work of Mindru et al. [4,5], where also the color changes (called "photometric changes" in their work) of RGB images were considered along with spatial transformations. Gong et al. put these two approaches together but also added a significant novelty. While in [7] and [6] only a spatial affine transform is considered and in [5] the main part is devoted to affine transformation of the RGB space with no transformation of the coordinates, Gong et al. [3] considered for the first time these two transformation groups acting jointly (actually, such joint model was mentioned already in [5] but was considered to be too complicated and was left without any invariants being derived.) Gong et al. succeeded in derivation of *shape-color affine moment invariants* (SCAMIs). However, they missed an important issue. Their SCAMIs do not form a complete set of invariants and their recognition power is limited. There exists a relatively large class of images, totally different from each other visually, which all lie in the joint null-space of the SCAMIs and cannot be distinguished by means of them.

In this paper, we analyze why this happens, show what images are in the SCAMIs null-space, and propose an extension of the Gong's theory which makes the invariants complete. The null-space of the new invariants contains just a constant zero image. Simple experiments demonstrate the advantages of the extended SCAMIs (ESCAMIs).

2   Recalling the SCAMIs

To show where is the weak point of the paper [3] and to explain how it can be corrected, we have to start with a very brief summary of the main idea of [3].

Gong et al. assumed the following transformation model

$$\mathbf{c}'(\mathbf{x}) = M\mathbf{c}(A\mathbf{x}) \tag{1}$$

where $\mathbf{x} = (x, y)^T$, $\mathbf{c}(\mathbf{x}) = (R(\mathbf{x}), G(\mathbf{x}), B(\mathbf{x}))^T$ is a color RGB image, A is a regular 2×2 matrix of affine spatial transformation, and M is a regular 3×3 matrix describing a linear color mixing. Gong et al. claimed this model describes the change of viewpoint and illumination in outdoor scenes (for indoor scenes, M is supposed to have a diagonal form, which brings us back to the work by Mindru et al. [5]). For the model (1), it is reasonable to try to construct invariants, because this transformation forms a group which is known to be a necessary condition for the existence of invariants [2].

The problem of finding invariants w.r.t. A was treated correctly in [3] (the authors followed the theory from [7]) and no modification is necessary. The null-space problem is caused solely by the way how the invariance w.r.t. M is achieved. To focus on that, we will from now on assume that $A = I$. This simplifies the reasoning but all our conclusions stay valid for arbitrary regular matrix A.

Consider arbitrary three points $\mathbf{x}_i, \mathbf{x}_j, \mathbf{x}_k$ and construct the determinant

$$V(i, j, k) \equiv |C_{ijk}| = \begin{vmatrix} R(\mathbf{x}_i) & R(\mathbf{x}_j) & R(\mathbf{x}_k) \\ G(\mathbf{x}_i) & G(\mathbf{x}_j) & G(\mathbf{x}_k) \\ B(\mathbf{x}_i) & B(\mathbf{x}_j) & B(\mathbf{x}_k) \end{vmatrix}. \tag{2}$$

In the color space, $V(i, j, k)$ can be understood as a volume of the pyramid with vertices in the three points $(R(\mathbf{x}_i), G(\mathbf{x}_i), B(\mathbf{x}_i))$, $(R(\mathbf{x}_j), G(\mathbf{x}_j), B(\mathbf{x}_j))$, and $(R(\mathbf{x}_k), G(\mathbf{x}_k), B(\mathbf{x}_k))$, respectively, and in the origin $(0, 0, 0)$. $V(i, j, k)$ is a relative invariant w.r.t. M. If $\mathbf{c}'(\mathbf{x}) = M\mathbf{c}(\mathbf{x})$, then $V'(i, j, k) = |M| V(i, j, k)$.

If we use $n > 3$ points $\mathbf{x}_1, \mathbf{x}_2, \ldots, \mathbf{x}_n$, we can construct m point triplets (m could be arbitrary high because the same triplet can be used many times) and multiply the corresponding determinants as

$$E(n, m) = V(1, 2, 3) V(g, h, i) \cdots V(r, s, n). \tag{3}$$

$E(n, m)$ is also a relative invariant w.r.t. M since $E'(n, m) = |M|^m E(n, m)$.

Gong proposed to multiply $E(n, m)$ by so-called *shape primitives* that eliminate the influence of A. Since here we assume $A = I$, the shape primitives are just powers of spatial coordinates. Finally, the product is integrated n-times over the entire image plane

$$E_{\mathbf{p}, \mathbf{q}} = \int \int \cdots \int x_1^{p_1} y_1^{q_1} \cdots x_n^{p_n} y_n^{q_n} E(n, m) \, \mathbf{dx}_1 \cdots \mathbf{dx}_n. \tag{4}$$

Doing so, they obtained relative invariant $E'_{\mathbf{p}, \mathbf{q}} = |M|^m E_{\mathbf{p}, \mathbf{q}}$ which depends on the number of chosen points and on the selected triplets but does not depend on particular positions of the points $\mathbf{x}_1, \mathbf{x}_2, \ldots, \mathbf{x}_n$. It is worth noting that $E_{\mathbf{p}, \mathbf{q}}$ can be expressed in terms of *generalized color moments* μ_{pq} which are defined as

$$\mu_{pq}^{abc} = \int \int x^p y^q R^a(x, y) G^b(x, y) B^c(x, y) \, dx \, dy. \tag{5}$$

That is why we can consider $E_{\mathbf{p}, \mathbf{q}}$ to be a member of a family of *moment invariants*.

Absolute invariants are then obtained by an obvious normalization as a ratio of two appropriate relative invariants. At this point, the authors of [3] considered the theory complete.

3   Where Is the Problem?

Let us imagine what happens if matrix C_{ijk} is singular for any triplet (i, j, k) used in Eq. (3). (Note that the rank of C_{ijk} is in no way linked with the rank of M, which is assumed to be regular, and that the rank of C_{ijk} does not change if the image undergoes transformation (1).) In that case, $V(i, j, k) = 0$ for arbitrary (i, j, k). Consequently, any $E(n, m)$ vanishes and also $E_{\mathbf{p}, \mathbf{q}} = 0$ regardless of $n, \mathbf{p}, \mathbf{q}$ and of the choice of the triplets.

Let us explain what the singularity of C_{ijk} means for the image $\mathbf{c}(\mathbf{x})$. It happens if and only if its R,G,B channels are linearly dependent. Hence, the nullspace of the SCAMIs is formed by all images with linearly dependent channels. This conclusion is not violated even if we admit an arbitrary regular A, as is clearly apparent from Eq. (26) of [3]. In other words, images with linearly dependent channels cannot be distinguished by the SCAMIs, although they may be visually quite different (see Fig. 1 for some examples) and easy-to-distinguish by some other methods. Since the numerical experiments in [3] apparently did not included such images, this phenomenon has remained unrevealed.

4 The Proposed Solution

Fortunately, there is an easy and elegant solution to the problem. We simply disregard one color channel (for instance B) and work with R and G only. Instead of the triplets, we use only pairs of points. Instead of $V(i, j, k)$ we have

$$V(i,j) \equiv |C_{ij}| = \begin{vmatrix} R(\mathbf{x}_i) & R(\mathbf{x}_j) \\ G(\mathbf{x}_i) & G(\mathbf{x}_j) \end{vmatrix}, \tag{6}$$

which is again a relative invariant. We proceed to the construction of $E(n, m)$ and $E_{\mathbf{p},\mathbf{q}}$ similarly to the previous case.

If the rank of C_{ijk} equals two, then C_{ij} is regular (at least for some point configurations, which is sufficient for $E_{\mathbf{p},\mathbf{q}}$ to be non-zero). In the joint null-space of these invariants, we find all images whose rank of C_{ijk} equals one (see Fig. 2 for some examples). These images are still not distinguishable. To distinguish among them, we have to create yet another set of invariants.

It is sufficient to consider just a single color channel (the other two are its linear transformations). There is in fact no true "channel mixing", matrix M (even if it is not diagonal) only makes a contrast stretching of the channels. We can treat the selected channel as a graylevel image. We take graylevel affine moment invariants from [7] and normalize them to contrast stretching. This completes our solution. In the joint null-space of the extended invariants we can find just a constant-zero image.

When designing an image recognition system, we of course need not to check for each image the rank of C_{ijk} for all possible point triplets. That would be extremely time consuming. We can start with the calculation of SCAMIs. If at least one of them is non-zero, we do not calculate any other invariants and use the SCAMIs directly. If all of them are zero (in practice, the term "all of them" means up to our maximum order and the term "they are zero" means they are within a user-defined interval around zero), then we remove one color band and calculate the invariants from two other color bands. If they all are still zero, we take a single channel and calculate the graylevel AMIs. This extended set, which we call ESCAMIs, can discriminate any two images (modulo the action of the transformation group given by Eq. (1)).

5 Discussion

The null-space problem is a general problem of any features designed for object recognition. The images laying in the null-space are in principle not distinguishable by these features because all features are zero. In general, the smaller null-space the better recognition power. In an ideal case, the null-space should contain only images equivalent (modulo the considered transformation group) to the zero image. The reasons why an image falls into the null-space depend on the nature of the features. We showed that in the case of SCAMIs, the necessary and sufficient condition is a linear dependence among the color channels.

Fig. 1. Examples of images that are not distinguishable by the SCAMIs from [3]. The rank of C_{ijk} equals two in all cases. The images are clearly distinguishable by the proposed ESCAMIs using two channels. This figure should be viewed in colors.

One might feel that such images are rare in practice but it is not the case. Color bands of many real images are not exactly dependent but are highly correlated, which leads to "almost vanishing" SCAMIs. The SCAMI values are not zero but they are comparable to noise. This effect becomes more apparent as the number of color bands increases. All the theory can be easily modified for hyper-

Fig. 2. Examples of images that are neither distinguishable by the original SCAMIs nor by ESCAMIs from Eq. (6), but are clearly distinguishable by the grayscale AMIs [7] applied to a single channel. The rank of C_{ijk} equals one in all cases. This figure should be viewed in colors.

spectral images with arbitrary number of bands (current hyperspectral sensors use to have several hundreds of them). Those bands are very narrow and close to each other in terms of the wavelength. Hence, they are highly correlated and matrix C is quite often close to be singular. Without the extension presented in this paper, application of SCAMIs on hyperspectral images would be useless.

Another class of images, where the SCAMIs vanish completely, are some artificially colored pictures, that often contain linearly dependent channels.

6   Conclusion

In this paper, we extended the theory of the SCAMI invariants for recognition of color images, presented originally in [3]. The proposed solution not only corrects the theory from [3] but it is also important for practical image classification.

Our extension can handle a special case of images with linearly dependent or highly correlated channels, for which the original method fails. The efficiency of the proposed extension is in the fact that it not only improves the recognition power but also in its fast calculation. It can be applied directly after the original SCAMIs have been calculated and have vanished. The new method does not require any preliminary testing or pre-classification of the images.

References

1. Flusser, J., Suk, T., Zitová, B.: Moments and Moment Invariants in Pattern Recognition. Wiley, Chichester (2009)
2. Flusser, J., Suk, T., Zitová, B.: 2D and 3D Image Analysis by Moments. Wiley, Chichester (2016)
3. Gong, M., Hao, Y., Mo, H., Li, H.: Naturally combined shape-color moment invariants under affine transformations. Comput. Vis. Image Underst. **162**(Suppl. C), 46–56 (2017). https://doi.org/10.1016/j.cviu.2017.07.003
4. Mindru, F., Moons, T., Gool, L.V.: Color-based moment invariants for viewpoint and illumination independent recognition of planar color patterns. In: Singh, S. (ed.) International Conference on Advances in Pattern Recognition ICAPR 1999, pp. 113–122. Springer, London (1999). https://doi.org/10.1007/978-1-4471-0833-7_12
5. Mindru, F., Tuytelaars, T., Gool, L.V., Moons, T.: Moment invariants for recognition under changing viewpoint and illumination. Comput. Vis. Image Underst. **94**(1–3), 3–27 (2004)
6. Suk, T., Flusser, J.: Affine moment invariants of color images. In: Jiang, X., Petkov, N. (eds.) CAIP 2009. LNCS, vol. 5702, pp. 334–341. Springer, Heidelberg (2009). https://doi.org/10.1007/978-3-642-03767-2_41
7. Suk, T., Flusser, J.: Affine moment invariants generated by graph method. Pattern Recogn. **44**(9), 2047–2056 (2011)

Variational Optical Flow: Warping and Interpolation Revisited

Georg Radow$^{(\boxtimes)}$ and Michael Breuß

Brandenburg University of Technology Cottbus-Senftenberg,
03046 Cottbus, Germany
{radow,breuss}@b-tu.de

Abstract. One of the fundamental problems in computer vision is to attain the apparent motion in image sequences, the optical flow. As evaluations at hand of recent benchmarks show, this field is highly competitive. High ranking variational methods often consist of a combination of techniques, where frequently the presentation in the literature focuses on novel contributions in modelling.

In this paper we investigate the warping technique and related algorithmic design choices that are fundamental for practical implementation. At hand of a detailed yet straightforward derivation we discuss different warping variations. These are evaluated in numerical experiments, and furthermore we investigate the impact of a variety of interpolation methods that can be used.

Keywords: Optical flow · Variational methods · Warping · Interpolation · B-splines

1 Introduction

Optical flow (OF) is one of the fundamental problems in computer vision and there is a rich literature on corresponding models and computational approaches, see *e.g.* [8] for an overview. A very successful class of OF methods is based on variational approaches where the flow field is determined as the minimiser of a suitable energy functional, see *e.g.* [15] for a recent survey comparing this approach to convolutional neural networks. In this paper we focus on the class of variational OF methods.

Most of the top ranking variational OF methods on recent benchmarks involve highly sophisticated models. As these methods usually involve a combination of algorithmic components, it is a difficult task to keep track of all beneficial aspects that contribute in making a particular method successful. There are not too many attempts in the literature that are dedicated to analysing the building blocks of successful algorithms and that focus on the main tools in this respect. The probably most influential work concerned with variational OF algorithms is the article of Sun, Roth and Black [14], as it covers many details and variants on important techniques like especially, the warping technique, or the filtering of the flow field during computation. The latter computational aspect has been given some attention in [9] by taking into account that variational OF may be realised by either optimisation methods or by employing the Euler-Lagrange equations equivalent to the necessary optimality condition.

© Springer Nature Switzerland AG 2019
M. Vento and G. Percannella (Eds.): CAIP 2019, LNCS 11678, pp. 409–420, 2019.
https://doi.org/10.1007/978-3-030-29888-3_33

Possibly one of the most significant concepts in modern variational OF algorithms is to employ a coarse-to-fine (CTF) scheme in combination with image warping, see e.g. [2,4,6,11] for some milestones on this technique. In particular in [12] the design of the warping algorithm and many corresponding details have been given a high attention. Let us also mention the fundamental discussion in [1] relating warping to the scale space concept.

With this paper we aim to elaborate on technical issues that are still open to some discussion after the above mentioned seminal works, namely we focus on the design choices when implementing the CTF method combined with image warping. Let us note that, concerning the underlying OF method, we consider here a relatively simple model. This serves two purposes. Firstly, we can give more details on the techniques that are actually used within the algorithmic approach, which makes the whole discussion more tractable. Secondly, we can evaluate the impact of a single ingredient in our approach, as it is not directly linked to many other algorithmic parameters. Namely we vary the interpolation scheme used within our warping and CTF frameworks. Also we have a detailed look on multiple design choices for the warping strategy.

2   Variational Optical Flow

The general task in OF is to derive the motion of objects in a sequence of images I alongside the image domain $\Omega \in \mathbb{R}^2$. In this work we consider the most simple setting given by two grey value images $I(x,y,0)$ and $I(x,y,1)$, and the aim is to find the flow field $(u,v)^\top : \Omega \to \mathbb{R}^2$ that describes the motion of an object at time $t_0 = 0$ and location $(x,y)^\top \in \Omega$ to the location $(x+u(x,y),y+v(x,y))^\top \in \mathbb{R}^2$ at time $t_1 = 1$.

To find a reasonable flow field one usually infers one or more constancy assumptions on the objects in a given image sequence. The most fundamental one is grey value constancy. This holds true if there are no illumination changes:

$$\rho(x,y,u,v,I) := I(x+u(x,y),y+v(x,y),1) - I(x,y,0) = 0, \tag{1}$$

where we let ρ denote the difference of grey values at (x,y) induced by the flow field (u,v). If in the above expression we substitute the second image with a first order Taylor approximation at $(x,y,0)$, i.e.

$$I(x+u,y+v,1) \approx I(x,y,0) + I_x(x,y,0)u + I_y(x,y,0)v + I_t(x,y,0), \tag{2}$$

then ρ can be approximated as

$$\rho(u,v,I) \approx I_x(x,y,0)u + I_y(x,y,0)v + I_t(x,y,0), \tag{3}$$

where we omitted the dependencies on (x,y) in ρ, u and v, and lowercase variables denote partial derivatives. Let us note that in the two image case the only possible finite difference approximation of I_t is $I(x,y,1) - I(x,y,0)$.

The grey value constancy assumption is not sufficient to determine the flow field, as it induces one equation for two unknowns (u,v) at each location (x,y). This is also known as the aperture problem. Therefore a regulariser is employed. As rigid objects tend to move in the same direction, it is natural to penalise differences in the flow, *i.e.* ∇u and ∇v should be small with ∇ denoting the spatial gradient. Here we consider the models

$$\min_{u,v} \iint_{\Omega} \left\| \begin{pmatrix} \nabla u \\ \nabla v \end{pmatrix} \right\|_2^q + \lambda \,|\rho(u,v,I)|^q \mathrm{d}x\mathrm{d}y, \qquad q \in \{1,2\}, \tag{4}$$

where $\lambda > 0$ denotes the weight of the data term. For $q = 2$ we obtain the classical model of Horn and Schunck [10]. In the case $q = 1$ we gain the more robust combination of a total variation (TV) regulariser with a data term based on the L_1 norm. This model is similar to the one discussed in [17], but for the regulariser we follow [7] and employ the integrand $\sqrt{u_x^2 + u_y^2 + v_x^2 + v_y^2}$.

Although the models in (4) with the linearisation (3) can lead to satisfactory results for a given image sequence, there are two techniques usually employed to enhance optic flow algorithms significantly. These techniques are discussed in the remainder of this section.

Warping. To deal with large motions the so-called warping technique was proposed, *cf.* [4, 12]. To evaluate the impact of this technique in OF, we will actually discuss three warping variations. As a byproduct, we investigate the underlying linearisations more explicitly than as it was done *e.g.* in the recent works [14, 18].

We will discuss some variations of the approximation (3). Alternatively to $t_0 = 0$, one may also linearise the second image in $(x,y,1)$, leading to

$$I(x+u, y+v, 1) \approx I(x,y,1) + I_x(x,y,1)u + I_y(x,y,1)v. \tag{5}$$

Inserting the average of (2) and (5) into (1) gives us the following approximation, where no warping is used:

$$\tilde{\rho}_0(u,v,I) := I(x,y,1) - I(x,y,0)$$
$$+ \frac{1}{2}\left(I_x(x,y,0) + I_x(x,y,1)\right)u + \frac{1}{2}\left(I_y(x,y,0) + I_y(x,y,1)\right)v. \tag{6}$$

However we can also linearise at $(x+u_0, y+v_0, 1)$ with some initial flow field (u_0, v_0), leading to

$$I(x+u, y+v, 1) \approx I(x+u_0, y+v_0, 1)$$
$$+ I_x(x+u_0, y+v_0, 1)(u-u_0) + I_y(x+u_0, y+v_0, 1)(v-v_0). \tag{7}$$

This enables us to incorporate the current estimate of our flow field into the linearisation. For a fixed pair (u_0, v_0) the optimisation problem derived from (4) with linearisation (7) can be solved with efficient solvers like [7] under mild assumptions. In the case $q = 2$ the objective function is strictly convex and the unique solution is found as the solution of a linear system of equations. The warping strategy consists of alternatingly finding a solution of (4) and updating the current estimate (u_0, v_0) used in (7). If the approximation (7) is substituted in (1), we get the approximator

$$\tilde{\rho}_1(u,v,I) := I(x+u_0, y+v_0, 1) - I(x,y,0)$$
$$+ I_x(x+u_0, y+v_0, 1)(u-u_0) + I_y(x+u_0, y+v_0, 1)(v-v_0). \tag{8}$$

In (8) only the spatial derivatives in the second image are used. For this reason usually some averaging process of the spatial derivatives similar to (6) is applied. In a first attempt we can linearise the second image at $(x + u_0, y + v_0, 0)$, which similarly to (2) leads to

$$I(x+u,y+v,1) \approx I(x+u_0,y+v_0,1)$$
$$+ I_x(x+u_0,y+v_0,0)(u-u_0) + I_y(x+u_0,y+v_0,0)(v-v_0). \qquad (9)$$

If we substitute the average of (7) and (9) into (1), we get

$$\tilde{\rho}_2(u,v,I) := I(x+u_0,y+v_0,1) - I(x,y,0) + \bar{I}_x(x,y)(u-u_0) + \bar{I}_y(x,y)(v-v_0) \qquad (10)$$

where

$$\bar{I}_x(x,y) := \frac{1}{2}\left(I_x(x+u_0,y+v_0,1) + I_x(x+u_0,y+v_0,0)\right) \qquad (11)$$

and $\bar{I}_y$ is defined analogously.

The approximator $\tilde{\rho}_2$ includes the warped derivatives of the first image, which appears somewhat unnatural. Another approach would be to substitute the average of (2) and (7) into (1), leading to the usage of the non-warped second image. We tested this model and found it to deliver worse results than all other approximators of ρ where warping was used. Therefore we omit this model in our further presentation.

However we can reuse (2) by substituting u with u_0 and v with v_0 on both sides, and then reorganising the approximation into

$$I(x,y,1) \approx I(x+u_0,y+v_0,1) - I_x(x,y,0)u_0 - I_y(x,y,0)v_0. \qquad (12)$$

Substituting the average of (2) and (7) into (1) and approximating the non-warped second image through (12) finally leads to

$$\tilde{\rho}_3(u,v,I) := I(x+u_0,y+v_0,1) - I(x,y,0) + \hat{I}_x(x,y)(u-u_0) + \hat{I}_y(x,y)(v-v_0) \qquad (13)$$

where

$$\hat{I}_x(x,y) := \frac{1}{2}\left(I_x(x+u_0,y+v_0,1) + I_x(x,y,0)\right) \qquad (14)$$

and $\hat{I}_y$ is defined analogously.

The warping strategy needs to rely on interpolation for finding values of I and its derivatives. As interpolation schemes are discussed in the next section, we conclude this paragraph with two rather general notes on the design choices arising from interpolation in the context of warping. If the spatial derivatives I_x and I_y are computed with finite differences, there are two possibilities. One could compute the differences with the warped image, which has grey values $I(x+u_0,y+v_0,1)$ for all $(x,y) \in \Omega$. In [14] similar results are reported when the differences obtained from the original image $I(x,y,1)$ are interpolated afterwards. As is also pointed out there, the results achieved with the second approach are more consistent with interpolation methods, where the derivatives are computed analytically, cf. Sect. 3. For this reason we use the second approach.

Since (4) also includes a regulariser, there may arise flow fields pointing outside of the image domain, i.e. $(x+u_0,y+v_0) \notin \Omega$. Actually this usually happens in computations. Therefore the question arises, if one can extrapolate image values to $\mathbb{R}^2 \setminus \Omega$.

Although this can be done *e.g.* by assuming Neumann boundary conditions, we follow another strategy [14]. If $(x + u_0, y + v_0) \notin \Omega$, we deactivate the data term for the corresponding pixel. Thereby the optimisation of $(u(x,y), v(x,y))$ relies only on the regulariser.

Coarse-to-Fine. The original problem (4) is severely ill-posed. Without a linearisation of ρ there might be multiple local minima where an algorithm may be trapped, even if a warping strategy is employed. A typical remedy encountered in many OF algorithms is to combine a CTF scheme with the warping strategy, see again *e.g.* [12]. Thereby the images and its dervatives are evaluated on different scales, typically observed through a convolution with a Gaussian.

On a coarser scale, the OF problem is typically easier to solve, since only large scale objects remain in the image sequence. As a byproduct any linearisation of the images, as *i.e.* in (2), is valid for a larger range of flow fields. Generally speaking, the flow fields are estimated at the coarsest scale and then updated at finer scales to better solve the original problem (4).

For efficient computations, the CTF scheme is usually realised through downsampling. In this way it can be described as follows: If the original image has the resolution $M \times N$, then the CTF pyramid consists of downsampled images with resolution $(\xi^n M) \times (\xi^n N)$ rounded towards $\mathbb{N}^2$, where $n = 0, 1, \ldots, n_{\max}(\xi)$ and $\xi \in (0,1)$. The initial flow is computed with $n = n_{\max}(\xi)$. The flow field obtained at a coarse level $n > 0$ is upsampled, scaled by ξ^{-1} and then used as initial flow field for the next finer level $n - 1$. The final flow field is computed at $n = 0$ with the original resolution. The choice of the downsampling factor ξ may depend on the practical implementation, *cf.* [9, 14]. The CTF scheme is typically combined with a warping strategy, such that there are multiple warping steps performed at each pyramid level.

To prevent aliasing, the images are convoluted with a Gaussian before downsampling. For the standard deviation we choose $\sigma(\xi, n) = -8n \ln \xi$, motivated by the semigroup property of the convolution operator and the fact that, for different ξ_1, ξ_2 and n_1, n_2 with $(\xi_1)^{n_1} = (\xi_2)^{n_2}$, the identity $\sigma(\xi_1, n_1) = \sigma(\xi_2, n_2)$ should hold. The factor -8 was chosen manually. In contrast, often the standard deviation for downsampling between two pyramid levels is reported as *e.g.*, $\sqrt{2}/(4\xi)$ in [18] or $1/\sqrt{2\xi}$ in [14].

3 Interpolation

The impact of interpolation techniques for the warping procedure was discussed in [14] at hand of bilinear and bicubic (spline) interpolation. Here, to include interpolation techniques of higher order, we also discuss b-splines. Since bilinear and bicubic spline interpolation are well known techniques, *cf.* [5, 13], we only discuss the principles behind them and focus on the less commonly used b-spline interpolation.

The general interpolation idea is to find some function $p : \Omega \to \mathbb{R}$ that resembles the image $I : \Omega \to \mathbb{R}$. In this section we omit the time variable and denote with $I(x,y)$ the grey values of some image I. The interpolated function p can then be evaluated at any $(x_0 + \delta_x, y_0 + \delta_y)$ where usually the sample coordinates x_0, y_0 are integers and $(\delta_x, \delta_y)^\top \in [0,1]^2$.

Bilinear Interpolation. During bilinear interpolation, the image I is approximated with a linear spline, *i.e.* p is piecewise linear. For every $(x_0 + \delta_x, y_0 + \delta_y)$ the corresponding value of p is determined by the values of I at the four surrounding pixel locations (x_0, y_0), $(x_0 + 1, y_0)$, $(x_0, y_0 + 1)$ and $(x_0 + 1, y_0 + 1)$.

The interpolator p is continuous but only piecewise differentiable. Therefore I_x and I_y in (8) are computed from the original image and then interpolated separately from I.

Bicubic/Bicubic Spline Interpolation. In the case of bicubic interpolation the interpolator is a piecewise cubic function, *i.e.* within $[x_0, x_0 + 1] \times [y_0, y_0 + 1]$ it can be described as

$$p(x_0 + \delta_x, y_0 + \delta_y) = \sum_{i=0}^{3} \sum_{j=0}^{3} a_{i,j} (\delta_x)^j (\delta_y)^i. \tag{15}$$

The 16 coefficients $a_{i,j}$ can be determined by evaluating I in a neighbourhood of 4×4 pixel, which is referred to as bicubic interpolation.

In contrast, for bicubic spline interpolation, only the surrounding locations are considered, similar to bilinear interpolation. However besides the image I also the derivatives I_x, I_y and I_{xy} are utilised. These can be derived from one dimensional cubic splines by considering only a single row or column of a digital image. In our application we used Neumann boundary conditions, as they are a common choice for image processing applications.

By design the interpolator p is in C^1 everywhere. Therefore the spatial image derivatives can be approximated by p_x and p_y.

B-Spline Interpolation. We will now discuss the construction of an interpolating spline with b-splines. For more details on the fundamentals of b-splines – which for the most part we omit in this paper – see also [5, 16].

Let us at first discuss b-splines in a one dimensional setting. To this end, we assume to have some spline knots $t_j \leq t_{j+1}$ with some indices $j \in J \subset \mathbb{Z}$. From these spline knots, b-splines $B_{j,k} : \mathbb{R} \to \mathbb{R}$ with order $k \in \mathbb{N}$ can be constructed in the following way: First-order b-splines are piecewise constant functions of the form

$$B_{j,1}(t) := \begin{cases} 1, & t_j \leq t < t_{j+1}, \\ 0, & \text{otherwise.} \end{cases} \tag{16}$$

B-splines of higher order $k = 2, 3, \ldots$ are then defined recursively through

$$B_{j,k}(t) := \omega_{j,k}(t) B_{j,k-1}(t) + (1 - \omega_{j+1,k}(t)) B_{j+1,k-1}, \tag{17}$$

where

$$\omega_{j,k}(t) := \begin{cases} \frac{t - t_j}{t_{j+k-1} - t_j}, & t_j < t_{j+k-1}, \\ 0, & \text{otherwise.} \end{cases} \tag{18}$$

A spline of order k with spline knots t_j and spline coefficients a_j can now be defined as

$$s(t) := \sum_{j \in J} a_j B_{j,k}(t) \tag{19}$$

We assume to have m function values $f(\tau_j)$ at locations with $\tau_j < \tau_{j+1}$ for all $j = 1,\ldots,m-1$. To find an interpolating spline we have to choose the order k, fix spline knots t_ℓ and compute spline coefficients a_ℓ subject to

$$f(\tau_j) = s(\tau_j) = \sum_{\ell=1}^{m} a_\ell B_{\ell,k}(\tau_j), \qquad j = 1,\ldots,m. \tag{20}$$

Here we already made the choice of modelling f with m b-splines, so that (20) is a linear system of m equations with m unknowns a_ℓ. A condition for the regularity gives the theorem of Schoenberg and Whitney, cf. [5].

It is straightforward to extend one dimensional interpolation with b-splines to the two dimensional case for images. We assume to be given image intensities $I(x,y)$ for all $(x,y)^\top \in \{\mu_1,\ldots,\mu_N\} \times \{v_1,\ldots,v_M\} \subset [0,N] \times [0,M] = \Omega$. A two dimensional (tensor product) spline can be formulated as

$$p(x,y) := \sum_{i=1}^{M} \sum_{j=1}^{N} a_{i,j} B_{j,k}^{x}(x) B_{i,k}^{y}(y) \tag{21}$$

with (one dimensional) b-splines $B_{j,k}^{x}$ induced by spline knots $x_1,\ldots,x_{N+k}$ and $B_{i,k}^{y}$ induced by spline knots $y_1,\ldots,y_{M+k}$. Again, with properly chosen spline knots (x_j,y_i), the coefficients $a_{i,j}$ are the unique solution of a linear system induced by the restraints $p(\mu_j,v_i) = I(\mu_j,v_i)$ for all $j = 1,\ldots,N$ and $i = 1,\ldots,M$. Let us note that, due to the compact support of b-splines, only k^2 coefficients $a_{i,j}$ need to be considered when evaluating (21) at some location, e.g with de Boor's algorithm, cf. [5], Chap. X, which is readily extended to the 2D case.

Let us note that there is some freedom in choosing the spline knots (x_j,y_i). We consider b-spline interpolation with even order $k = 2,4,\ldots$, and choose the spline knots as follows. Since every sample $I(\mu_j,v_i)$ should represent an equal amount of the image domain $\Omega = [0,N] \times [0,M]$ we assume that the sample coordinates are $(\mu_j,v_i) = (j - 0.5, i - 0.5)$ for all $j = 1,\ldots,N$ and $i = 1,\ldots,M$. Since we want to evaluate p for any[1] location in Ω, we set

$$x_1 = \cdots = x_k = 0, \quad x_{k+j} = \mu_{\frac{k}{2}+j} \text{ for } j = 1,\ldots,N-k, \quad x_{N+1} = \cdots = x_{N+k} = N \tag{22}$$

and the coordinates y_i are set analogously. By this choice we have a symmetric distribution of spline knots, the inner spline knots coincide with the sample locations, and we ensure the fundamental property

$$\sum_{i=1}^{M} \sum_{j=1}^{N} B_{j,k}^{x}(x) B_{i,k}^{y}(y) = \begin{cases} 1, & (x,y) \in \Omega, \\ 0, & \text{otherwise.} \end{cases} \tag{23}$$

Since b-splines are $k-2$ times continuously differentiable, we may approximate image derivatives by p_x and p_y if we choose some $k > 2$. If we evaluate derivatives at the boundary $\partial\Omega$ we get the limit from the interior $\overset{\circ}{\Omega}$, i.e.

$$\nabla p(\mu,v) = \lim_{\overset{\circ}{\Omega} \ni (x,y)^\top \to (\mu,v)^\top} \nabla p(x,y), \quad \text{for all } (\mu,v)^\top \in \partial\Omega. \tag{24}$$

---

[1] To have a meaningful representation of I at the boundary (with $x = N$ or $y = M$) we change the last b-splines of order 1 in our construction to $B_{N+k-1,1}^{x}(x_{N+k}) = 1$ and $B_{M+k-1,1}^{y}(y_{M+k}) = 1$, cf. (16).

4   Numerical Evaluation

We now want to test the different modelling choices discussed previously. After discussing the remaining details of our experimental setup we evaluate the approximations of ρ presented in (6), (8), (10) and (13). Then we discuss the different interpolation methods in terms of quality and efficiency.

Experimental Setup. For evaluation we use data from the Middlebury benchmark[2] presented in [3]. This benchmark is somewhat characterised by laboratory conditions. Effects like motion blur, illumination changes and large occlusions do not occur in the images. This favours the aim of our experiments, namely to focus on basic design choices. In detail we use the following eight data sets with publicly available groundtruth: *RubberWhale, Hydrangea, Dimetrodon, Grove2, Grove3, Urban2, Urban3* and *Venus*.

We convolve the input images with a Gaussian, as this is a usual step in OF algorithms for making the images differentiable (in theory) and addressing noise. This is done before and independently of the CTF scheme. For the standard deviation we choose $\sigma_0 = 0.75$.

For each of the two models in (4) we investigate two practical realisations. For the case $q = 2$, which is usually referred to as the model of Horn and Schunck [10], we solve the linear system directly with the backslash operator in Matlab. This realisation is denoted by HS_{dir}. In some cases we use the conjugate gradient method (through the pcg routine in Matlab 2018b) with the tolerance on the relative residual set to 10^{-6}, which is referred to as HS_{cg}. Here the maximum number of iterations was set to 500. For $q = 1$, the combination of an L_1 data term with a TV regulariser, we employ the standard realisation of the primal-dual algorithm from [7]. Usually the number of iterations was set to 200 for each warping step, resulting in the realisation $L_1\text{TV}_{fix}$. Sometimes the maximum number of iterations was set to 500 and the algorithm was stopped if after some iteration m the relation

$$\frac{1}{M(n)N(n)} \sum_{i=1}^{M(n)} \sum_{j=1}^{N(n)} \left\| \begin{pmatrix} u_{i,j}^{(m+1)} \\ v_{i,j}^{(m+1)} \end{pmatrix} - \begin{pmatrix} u_{i,j}^{(m)} \\ v_{i,j}^{(m)} \end{pmatrix} \right\|_2^2 \leq \xi^n 10^{-6} \qquad (25)$$

held true. Here $M(n) \times N(n)$ is the resolution of the current CTF level n, $u_{i,j}^{(m)}$ is the i,jth pixel of u in the mth iteration and other components are denoted likewise. This realisation is denoted by $L_1\text{TV}_{var}$.

An example with manually chosen data weight *OF* is shown in Fig. 1. As usual the flow field is colour coded where the hue is derived from the angle of (u,v) and the saturation depicts the absolute value. The hue for each angle is depicted on the image boundary. Full saturation is used if the absolute value is higher or equal to the maximum in the groundtruth. Black is used for locations where no groundtruth is given, *e.g.* due to occlusions. For all other images and listed error measures weights of the data term were optimised for minimal average endpoint error (AEE) through the fminsearch routine in Matlab 2018b.

---

[2] http://vision.middlebury.edu/flow/.

Fig. 1. *RubberWhale* sequence: *(top)* left-to-right: frame 10 of the sequence and groundtruth flow; *(bottom)* solution of (4) with $\tilde{\rho}_3$ approximator and bicubic spline interpolation; left-to-right: $L_1 \text{TV}_{fix}$ with $\lambda = 20$ and HS_{dir} with $\lambda = 400$

The spatial derivatives in the regulariser in (4) were approximated with standard forward differences, *e.g.* with the stencil $[0, -1, 1]$ and Neumann boundary conditions for u_x. The image derivatives in the linearised data term were computed analytically for the experiments with b-spline interpolation or bicubic spline interpolation. For the experiments with bilinear interpolation the image derivatives were computed with fourth order central differences, *i.e.* $\frac{1}{12}[1, -8, 0, 8, -1]$ with Neumann boundary conditions led to I_x. The results were then interpolated in the same way as I.

The CTF parameter was set to $\xi = 0.5$, a typical choice for image pyramids. The coarsest level n_{max} was usually chosen to at least have resolution 4×4 for bilinear and bicubic spline interpolation and $k \times k$ for b-spline interpolation with order k. The number of warping steps at each level was usually set to 10.

When using the approximator $\tilde{\rho}_0$ without warping, the number of 'warping steps' was set to 1 and computations were only done at the level $n_{max} = 0$. In this case the number of iterations for $L_1 \text{TV}_{fix}$ was changed to 500.

For all experiments we report only the AEE due to spatial constraints. In our experiments we also observed the angular error, the results were virtually the same.

Choice of the Approximator of ρ. We want to evaluate the influence of the approximation of ρ in (4). Since we have three possible choices in (8), (10) and (13) with warping and (6) without warping, the question of the best approximator naturally arises.

For this experiment the results with bicubic spline interpolation are displayed in Table 1. The evaluation of the AEE shows that the final approximator $\tilde{\rho}_3$ works best on most data sets. However the approximator $\tilde{\rho}_1$, where only the spatial derivatives in the second image are used, delivers only slightly worse results. The approximator $\tilde{\rho}_2$, where the warped derivatives in the first image are used, performs worse than $\tilde{\rho}_3$ and $\tilde{\rho}_1$ on almost all data sets. Unsurprisingly the original approximation $\tilde{\rho}_0$ without warping leads to worse results than the other approximators, especially for the synthetic *Urban* data sets, which are characterised by relatively large motions and occlusions. Nevertheless the error values show that $\tilde{\rho}_0$ can be used to estimate flow fields quite reliably.

Table 1. Average endpoint error for all data sets depending on the choice of the approximator of ρ. $L_1\text{TV}_{fix}$ in the upper half and HS_{dir} in the lower half. For some data sets $\tilde{\rho}_1$ gives slightly better results than $\tilde{\rho}_3$. Overall $\tilde{\rho}_3$ gives the best results.

Data set	Avg.	Rubber.	Hydran.	Dimetr.	Grove2	Grove3	Urban2	Urban3	Venus
$\tilde{\rho}_0$	2.8135	0.2633	2.0359	0.5474	1.6389	2.5182	7.2904	5.9060	2.3082
$\tilde{\rho}_1$	0.3369	0.1687	**0.2082**	**0.1375**	0.1547	0.7223	**0.3796**	0.5228	0.4013
$\tilde{\rho}_2$	0.4236	0.2094	0.2624	0.2042	0.1869	0.8762	0.5327	0.7286	0.3888
$\tilde{\rho}_3$	**0.3112**	**0.1629**	0.2095	0.1389	**0.1450**	**0.6834**	0.3796	**0.4210**	**0.3496**
$\tilde{\rho}_0$	2.7837	0.3185	1.8626	0.4776	1.4144	2.6250	7.3205	6.0501	2.2015
$\tilde{\rho}_1$	0.4921	0.2275	0.3005	**0.1360**	0.2187	0.9651	**0.7262**	0.9249	0.4375
$\tilde{\rho}_2$	0.6435	0.2569	0.4187	0.2045	0.2621	1.1706	0.9057	1.3630	0.5666
$\tilde{\rho}_3$	**0.4725**	**0.2158**	**0.2999**	0.1369	**0.2137**	**0.8879**	0.7292	**0.8823**	**0.4146**

As the results suggest, we view $\tilde{\rho}_3$ as the best approximator, where linearisations in the non-warped first image and the warped second image are employed.

Besides bicubic spline interpolation, we repeated the discussed experiment with bilinear interpolation and b-spline interpolation of order $k = 4, 6, 8$. The resulting relations between $\tilde{\rho}_0$, $\tilde{\rho}_1$, $\tilde{\rho}_2$ and $\tilde{\rho}_3$ were the same, therefore we omitted the error values here.

Choice of the Interpolation Method. As we have now found $\tilde{\rho}_3$ to deliver the best results, we continue by evaluating the different interpolation methods when using this approximator. For the downsampling and warping of the images as well as for the upscaling of the flow field due to the CTF framework, we tested bilinear, bicubic spline and b-spline interpolation. The latter, denoted by b-spline$k$, was carried out with order $k = 4$, $k = 6$ and $k = 8$. For each interpolation method the average error values across all eight data as well as the individual error values can be found in Table 2. Here we focus on AEE, for which the data weight λ is optimised.

The reported error values are very similar. The largest differences are between bilinear interpolation and the other methods. Due to its lower modelling order and relatively low complexity, bilinear interpolation is usually employed in the literature.

The results of bicubic spline interpolation and 4th order b-spline interpolation are almost identical. This can be expected, since in both methods splines of polynomials with degree 3 are constructed. The main difference is the distribution of spline knots near the boundary of the interpolated image. Differences between these two methods mostly occur for *Grove3* and *Urban2*, which exhibit relatively large motions and occlusions.

In terms of average error values, the best results are achieved with bicubic spline interpolation, closely followed by 4th order b-splines and then 6th order b-splines. The

Table 2. Average endpoint error for all data sets and interpolation methods. $L_1\text{TV}_{fix}$ in the upper half and HS_{dir} in the lower half.

Data set	Avg.	Rubber.	Hydran.	Dimetr.	Grove2	Grove3	Urban2	Urban3	Venus
Bilinear	0.3302	0.1779	0.2159	0.1566	0.1646	0.7001	0.4026	0.4549	0.3692
Bicubic	0.3112	0.1629	0.2095	**0.1389**	0.1450	0.6834	**0.3796**	**0.4210**	0.3496
B-spline4	**0.3110**	0.1629	0.2098	0.1393	**0.1443**	**0.6806**	0.3802	0.4210	0.3501
B-spline6	0.3121	**0.1622**	0.2083	0.1412	0.1451	0.6827	0.3836	0.4245	0.3491
B-spline8	0.3147	0.1622	**0.2073**	0.1444	0.1469	0.6854	0.3944	0.4284	**0.3485**
Bilinear	0.4874	0.2303	0.3175	0.1502	0.2338	0.9019	**0.7214**	0.9005	0.4433
Bicubic	**0.4725**	0.2158	0.2999	**0.1369**	**0.2137**	**0.8879**	0.7292	**0.8823**	0.4146
B-spline4	0.4742	0.2155	0.3001	0.1375	0.2142	0.8910	0.7363	0.8835	0.4156
B-spline6	0.4752	**0.2149**	**0.2985**	0.1413	0.2150	0.8966	0.7349	0.8911	**0.4091**
B-spline8	0.4805	0.2155	0.3000	0.1455	0.2175	0.9003	0.7424	0.9058	0.4168

interpolation with 8th order b-splines results in slightly higher error measures, which might be due to stronger oscillations when modelling with polynomials of degree 7.

Up to now we used a direct solver for the linear system in HS_{dir} or a fixed number of iterations for the optimiser in $L_1\text{TV}_{fix}$. This may not be practical for other OF applications, therefore we want to evaluate the influence of the interpolation method in the context of iterative solvers with a stopping criterium, e.g. $L_1\text{TV}_{var}$ and HS_{cg}. The achieved results are displayed in Table 3. Especially for $L_1\text{TV}_{var}$ the algorithms based on b-splines need fewer iterations to fulfill the stopping criterium. We conjecture that this is due to faster 'convergence' across the warping steps. In this case it would be reasonable that there are fewer iterations needed especially within the later warping steps at some fixed CTF level. With HS_{cg} the algorithms based on b-splines mostly need fewer iterations, but the average number of iterations increases with the order k.

Table 3. Average of error values and number of iterations per warping level across all data sets for different interpolation methods. $L_1\text{TV}_{var}$ in the upper half and HS_{cg} in the lower half. B-spline and bicubic spline interpolation deliver similar error values. B-spline interpolation often leads to faster convergence of the average warping step.

Interpolation	Bilinear	Bicubic	B-spline4	B-spline6	B-spline8
AEE	0.3333	0.3154	0.3153	**0.3150**	0.3176
Avg. iter.	89.0	86.4	59.4	**59.0**	62.4
AEE	0.4878	**0.4730**	0.4742	0.4772	0.4814
Avg. iter.	125.3	125.7	**111.5**	120.1	133.2

5 Summary and Conclusions

The best warping results are achieved when combining the image values and derivatives of the non-warped first and warped second image. This approach is theoretically justified by actually using three linearisations, whereas the intuitive choice would be to use only one linearisation in the first and second image, respectively.

Although the general procedure is very similar for all three discussed warping variations, the results show that it is beneficial to consider the details of the implementation. Regarding the choice of the interpolation method with respect to the quality of computed flow fields, b-splines and bicubic splines are comparable. However b-splines may offer better efficiency, if iterative solvers are employed.

Acknowledgement. This publication was funded by the Graduate Research School (GRS) of the Brandenburg University of Technology Cottbus – Senftenberg. This work is part of the Cluster »StochMethod«.

References

1. Alvarez, L., Weickert, J., Sánchez, J.: Reliable estimation of dense optical flow fields with large displacements. Int. J. Comput. Vis. **39**(1), 41–56 (2000)
2. Anandan, P.: A computational framework and an algorithm for the measurement of visual motion. Int. J. Comput. Vis. **2**, 283–310 (1989)
3. Baker, S., Scharstein, D., Lewis, J.P., Roth, S., Black, M.J., Szeliski, R.: A database and evaluation methodology for optical flow. Int. J. Comput. Vis. **92**(1), 1–31 (2011)
4. Black, M.J., Anandan, P.: The robust estimation of multiple motions: parametric and piecewise-smooth flow fields. Comput. Vis. Image Underst. **63**(1), 75–104 (1996)
5. de Boor, C.: A Practical Guide to Splines, revised edn. Springer, New York (2001)
6. Bruhn, A., Weickert, J., Schnörr, C.: Lucas/Kanade meets Horn/Schunck: combining local and global optic flow methods. Int. J. Comput. Vis. **61**(3), 211–231 (2005)
7. Chambolle, A., Pock, T.: A first-order primal-dual algorithm for convex problems with applications to imaging. J. Math. Imaging Vis. **40**(1), 120–145 (2011)
8. Fortun, D., Bouthemy, P., Kervrann, C.: Optical flow modeling and computation: a survey. Comput. Vis. Image Underst. **134**, 1–21 (2015)
9. Hoeltgen, L., Setzer, S., Breuß, M.: Intermediate flow field filtering in energy based optic flow computations. In: Boykov, Y., Kahl, F., Lempitsky, V., Schmidt, F.R. (eds.) EMMCVPR 2011. LNCS, vol. 6819, pp. 315–328. Springer, Heidelberg (2011). https://doi.org/10.1007/978-3-642-23094-3_23
10. Horn, B.K., Schunck, B.G.: Determining optical flow. Artif. Intell. **17**(1–3), 185–203 (1981)
11. Mémin, E., Pérez, P.: Hierarchical estimation and segmentation of dense motion fields. Int. J. Comput. Vis. **46**(2), 129–155 (2002)
12. Papenberg, N., Bruhn, A., Brox, T., Didas, S., Weickert, J.: Highly accurate optic flow computation with theoretically justified warping. Int. J. Comput. Vis. **67**(2), 141–158 (2006)
13. Press, W.H., Teukolsky, S.A., Vetterling, W.T., Flannery, B.P.: Numerical Recipes: The Art of Scientific Computing, 3rd edn. Cambridge University Press, Cambridge (2007)
14. Sun, D., Roth, S., Black, M.J.: A quantitative analysis of current practices in optical flow estimation and the principles behind them. Int. J. Comput. Vis. **106**(2), 115–137 (2014)
15. Tu, Z., Xi, W., Zhang, D., Poppe, R., Veltkamp, R.C., Lie, B., Yuan, J.: A survey of variational and CNN-based optical flow techniques. Sig. Process. Image Commun. **72**, 9–24 (2019)
16. Unser, M.: Splines: A perfect fit for signal and image processing. IEEE Signal Process. Mag. **16**(6), 22–38 (1999)
17. Zach, C., Pock, T., Bischof, H.: A duality based approach for realtime TV-L^1 optical flow. In: Hamprecht, F.A., Schnörr, C., Jähne, B. (eds.) DAGM 2007. LNCS, vol. 4713, pp. 214–223. Springer, Heidelberg (2007). https://doi.org/10.1007/978-3-540-74936-3_22
18. Zimmer, H., Bruhn, A., Weickert, J.: Optic flow in harmony. Int. J. Comput. Vis. **93**(3), 368–388 (2011)

Robust Histogram Estimation Under Gaussian Noise

Jitka Kostková(✉)(iD) and Jan Flusser

The Czech Academy of Sciences, Institute of Information Theory and Automation,
Pod Vodárenskou věží 4, 182 08 Prague 8, Czech Republic
{kostkova,flusser}@utia.cas.cz

Abstract. We present a novel approach to description of a multidimensional image histogram insensitive with respect to an additive Gaussian noise in the image. The proposed quantities, although calculated from the histogram of the noisy image, represent the histogram of the original clear image. Noise estimation, image denoising and histogram deconvolution are avoided. We construct projection operators, that divide the histogram into non-Gaussian and Gaussian part, which is consequently removed to ensure the invariance. The descriptors are based on the moments of the histogram of the noisy image. The method can be used in a histogram-based image retrieval systems.

Keywords: Gaussian additive noise · Multidimensional histogram · Invariant characteristics · Moments · Projection operator

1 Introduction

Real images are often corrupted by noise, which not only degrades their visual appearance but also significantly changes all quantitative descriptors. If the signal-to-noise ratio is low, the corruption may be so heavy that it is very difficult to deduce anything about the original scene from the acquired image.

In this paper, we pay attention to the influence of the noise on the image histogram. Histogram provides statistics of graylevel/color frequencies and has become a simple, yet powerful descriptor for image classification. Histogram has established itself as a meaningful image characteristic for content-based image retrieval (CBIR) [8,12,14] because histogram similarity is a salient property for human vision. Two images with similar histograms are mostly perceived as similar even if their actual content may be very different from each other. On the other hand, those images that have substantially different histograms are rarely rated by observers as similar. Another attractive property of the histogram is

---

This work has been supported by the Czech Science Foundation (Grant No. GA18-07247S), by the *Praemium Academiae*, and by the Grant SGS18/188/OHK4/3T/14 provided by the Ministry of Education, Youth, and Sports of the Czech Republic (MŠMT ČR).

© Springer Nature Switzerland AG 2019
M. Vento and G. Percannella (Eds.): CAIP 2019, LNCS 11678, pp. 421–432, 2019.
https://doi.org/10.1007/978-3-030-29888-3_34

that it does not depend on image translation, rotation and (if normalized to the image size) on scaling. Simple preprocessing can also make the histogram insensitive to linear changes of the contrast and brightness of the image.

The CBIR methods based on comparing histograms are sensitive to noise in the images. Additive noise leads to a histogram smoothing, the degree of which is proportional to the amount of noise (see Fig. 1 for illustration). This follows from the well-known theorem from probability theory. Given a random variable X (which represents the pixel values of the image) with probability density function (PDF) h_X (which is now the normalized histogram of the image) and additive noise N with PDF/histogram h_N, then for the PDF h_Z of noisy random variable $Z = X + N$ holds

$$h_Z(x) = (h_X * h_N)(x) = \int h_X(x - s) h_N(s)\, ds, \tag{1}$$

assuming that the noise is independent of the image. The histogram smoothing immediately results in a drop of the retrieval performance because different histograms tend to be more and more similar to each other.

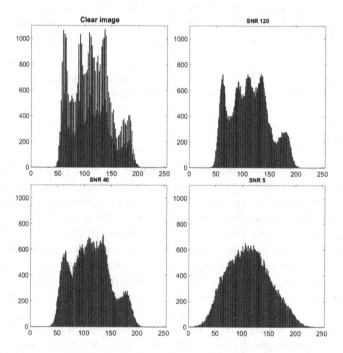

Fig. 1. Histogram smoothing due to image noise. Histogram of clear Lena image (top left). Histograms of noisy images: SNR = 120 (top right), SNR = 40 (bottom left), SNR = 5 (bottom right). For low SNR the histogram becomes unimodal and hard to distinguish from other smoothed histograms.

In digital photography, when using a CCD chip, the noise is unavoidable. It is apparent especially when taking a picture in low light using high ISO and/or long exposure time (see Fig. 2). The noise has several components. Photon shot noise, thermal noise, readout noise and background noise are the main ones. Additive noise component can be reasonably modelled by a Gaussian random variable uncorrelated with the image values. The signal-dependent component follows Poisson distribution. The method presented in this paper can handle only the former one.

Fig. 2. A low-light scene (left). On the close-up, the noise is clearly apparent (right).

Although the noise in digital imaging is an issue we cannot ignore even in consumer photography, very little attention has been paid to developing noise-resistant histogram representation. The authors of the papers on CBIR have either skipped this problem entirely or rely on denoising algorithms applied to all images before they enter the database. A pioneer work on this field was published by Höschl and Flusser [3] who proposed a kind of *convolution moment invariants*. Their work was motivated by blur invariants applied to a different problem in the image domain [1,2,6,9,15]. The authors presented invariants w.r.t. convolution, calculated from the histogram moments. These invariants were, however, defined only for 1D histogram of a graylevel image and cannot be easily extended to multidimensional histograms of color and multispectral images.

In this paper, we present a new histogram representation, based on its moments, which is totally resistant (at least theoretically) to additive Gaussian noise. This histogram representation could be implemented in CBIR systems in the case of noisy database and/or noisy query images (see Fig. 3 for the method outline). Our method does not perform any denoising and cannot replace it in the applications where the noise should be suppressed in order to improve the visual quality of the image. Unlike [3], the proposed method works with *multidimensional* histograms, which makes it suitable for color images. Another remarkable feature is that the method does not assume an independent noise in individual channels/spectral bands.

The main idea of this paper is the following one. We introduce *projection operators*, acting on the histogram space, that divide each histogram into two

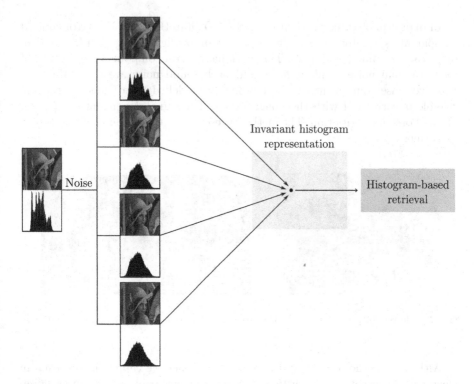

Fig. 3. The outline of the proposed method. From left to right: original image and its histogram, noisy images with smoothed histograms, representation of the histograms by invariant features (the core of the method), potential usage for noise-robust image retrieval. The actual implementation works with color images and the histograms are multidimensional.

components. Based on the known parametric form of h_N, we show that one of the components can be used to compute quantities, which are invariant with respect to convolution in Eq. (1). These quantities can be used directly to characterize h_X regardless of the amount of noise present.

2 Problem Formulation

Let $\mathbf{X}$ be an r-band original clear image with histogram $h_{\mathbf{X}}$ and $\mathbf{N} \sim \mathcal{N}(\mathbf{0}, \Sigma)$ be a normally distributed random noise, independent of $\mathbf{X}$, with regular covariance matrix Σ. The r-D noise histogram $h_{\mathbf{N}}$ has the well-known Gaussian shape

$$h_{\mathbf{N}}(\mathbf{x}) = \frac{1}{\sqrt{(2\pi)^r |\Sigma|}} \exp\left\{ -\frac{1}{2}\mathbf{x}^T \Sigma^{-1} \mathbf{x} \right\}, \tag{2}$$

where $\mathbf{x} = (x_1, \ldots, x_r)^T$ is the vector of intensities. Under the above assumptions, histogram $h_{\mathbf{Z}}$ of the noisy image $\mathbf{Z} = \mathbf{X} + \mathbf{N}$ is given as

$$h_{\mathbf{Z}} = h_{\mathbf{X}} * h_{\mathbf{N}}. \tag{3}$$

Our aim is to design a histogram descriptor I, which is invariant with respect to the noise, i.e. we require

$$I(h_{\mathbf{X}}) = I(h_{\mathbf{Z}}) = I(h_{\mathbf{X}} * h_{\mathbf{N}}) \qquad (4)$$

for any normally distributed zero-mean random noise $\mathbf{N}$ with arbitrary (unknown) covariance matrix Σ.

Complying with Eq. (4) is, however, not the only desirable property of I. At the same time, I must be *discriminable*, which means

$$I(h_{\mathbf{X}}) \neq I(h_{\mathbf{Y}}) \qquad (5)$$

for any two images $\mathbf{X}$ and $\mathbf{Y}$ such that $\mathbf{Y}$ is not a noisy version of $\mathbf{X}$.

3   Construction of the Invariant

The main idea of constructing invariants to Gaussian convolution is based on projections of a histogram onto the set of all Gaussian functions and on its complement. In this way, we decompose any histogram into Gaussian and non-Gaussian components. We show that the ratio of these two components possesses the desired invariant property. In the sequel, we introduce the necessary mathematical background.

Let us denote the set of all probability density functions (normalized histograms) as $\mathcal{D}$ and the set of all zero-mean Gaussian probability density functions (including Dirac δ-function) as $\mathcal{S}$.

Lemma 1. $\mathcal{S}$ *is closed under convolution.*

Proof. It holds for any two Gaussian PDFs $h_{\mathbf{N}_1}$ and $h_{\mathbf{N}_2}$ with covariance matrices Σ_1 and Σ_2 that the result of convolution is again a Gaussian PDF

$$h_{\mathbf{N}_1} * h_{\mathbf{N}_2} = h_{\mathbf{N}}$$

with covariance matrix $\Sigma = \Sigma_1 + \Sigma_2$.

The set $\mathcal{S}$ with the operation convolution $(\mathcal{S}, *)$ is a commutative semi-group. However, $\mathcal{S}$ is not a vector space.

Let us define projection operator P that projects arbitrary PDF $h \in \mathcal{D}$ on the "nearest" Gaussian PDF in the sense of having the same covariance matrix. In other words, $P : \mathcal{D} \mapsto \mathcal{S}$ is defined as

$$P(h) = h_{\mathbf{N}}, \qquad (6)$$

where $h_{\mathbf{N}}$ has the same covariance matrix as h. The operator P is well defined for all PDFs with a regular covariance matrix. It is idempotent, i.e. $P^2 = P$ and every $h \in \mathcal{D}$ can be uniquely written in the form $h = Ph + h_a$, where h_a is defined as $h - Ph$. In this way, the set $\mathcal{D}$ can be expressed as a direct sum $\mathcal{D} = \mathcal{S} \oplus \mathcal{A}$, where $\mathcal{S}$ is the range of P and $\mathcal{A}$ is the kernel. Note that P is not a projector in the common sense known from linear algebra because it is not a linear operator. Still, we call it projector because it keeps the above mentioned key properties of "algebraic" projection operators.

For our purposes, the crucial property of operator P is that it commutes with the convolution with functions from $\mathcal{S}$. This property is necessary for the construction of the invariant descriptors, as we demonstrate later.

Lemma 2. Let $h \in \mathcal{D}$ and $h_N \in \mathcal{S}$. Then

$$P(h * h_N) = Ph * h_N. \tag{7}$$

Proof. First, we investigate the right-hand side, where we have a convolution of two Gaussians with covariance matrices Σ_h and Σ_{h_N}, respectively. Thanks to Lemma 1, this is also a Gaussian with covariance matrix $\Sigma_h + \Sigma_{h_N}$. On the left-hand side, $P(h * h_N)$ is by definition a Gaussian with covariance matrix Σ_{h*h_N}. It is well known that central second-order moments of any PDF, which is a convolution of two other PDFs, are sums of the same moments of the factors. The same is true for entire covariance matrix. Hence, on the left-hand side we have $\Sigma_{h*h_N} = \Sigma_h + \Sigma_{h_N}$, which completes the proof.

Now we formulate the principal theorem of the paper that introduces the invariant descriptor of a probability density function as a ratio of certain characteristic functions. Characteristic function of a random variable is in fact the Fourier transform of its density [5].

Theorem 1. Let $h \in \mathcal{D}$ and let P be the projector onto $\mathcal{S}$ defined above. Then the ratio of characteristic functions Φ of the densities h and Ph

$$I(h)(\mathbf{u}) = \frac{\Phi(h)(\mathbf{u})}{\Phi(Ph)(\mathbf{u})} \tag{8}$$

is an invariant to convolution with a Gaussian probability density function: $I(h) = I(h * h_N)$ for any $h_N \in \mathcal{S}$.

Proof. First of all, note that $I(h)$ is well defined for any h because both $\Phi(h)$ and $\Phi(Ph)$ exist and $\Phi(Ph)(\mathbf{u}) \neq 0$ for any $\mathbf{u}$. The proof of invariance follows from the fact that P commutes with the convolution (see Lemma 2). If $h_N \in \mathcal{S}$, then

$$I(h * h_N) = \frac{\Phi(h * h_N)}{\Phi(P(h * h_N))} = \frac{\Phi(h * h_N)}{\Phi(Ph * h_N)} = \frac{\Phi(h)\Phi(h_N)}{\Phi(Ph)\Phi(h_N)} = \frac{\Phi(h)}{\Phi(Ph)} = I(h).$$

The following theorem claims that the invariant I is a complete description of h modulo convolution with a Gaussian.

Theorem 2. Let $h_1, h_2 \in \mathcal{D}$ and let I be the invariant defined in Theorem 1. Then $I(h_1) = I(h_2)$ if and only if there exist $h_{N_1}, h_{N_2} \in \mathcal{S}$ such that $h_{N_1} * h_1 = h_{N_2} * h_2$.

Proof.

$$I(h_1) = I(h_2) \Leftrightarrow \frac{\Phi(h_1)}{\Phi(Ph_1)} = \frac{\Phi(h_2)}{\Phi(Ph_2)} \Leftrightarrow \Phi(h_1)\Phi(Ph_2) = \Phi(h_2)\Phi(Ph_1)$$

$$\Leftrightarrow \Phi(h_1 * Ph_2) = \Phi(h_2 * Ph_1) \Leftrightarrow h_1 * Ph_2 = h_2 * Ph_1,$$

which implies that $h_{\mathbf{N}_1}, h_{\mathbf{N}_2} \in \mathcal{S}$ exist and are defined as $h_{\mathbf{N}_1} = Ph_2$, $h_{\mathbf{N}_2} = Ph_1$.

Theorems 1 and 2 show that invariant I entirely and uniquely describes any normalized histogram modulo convolution with a Gaussian.

Consider the equivalence relation on $\mathcal{D}$: $h_1 \sim h_2$ if and only if there exist functions $h_{\mathbf{N}_1}, h_{\mathbf{N}_2} \in \mathcal{S}$ such that $h_{\mathbf{N}_1} * h_1 = h_{\mathbf{N}_2} * h_2$. The factor set $\mathcal{D}/\!\sim$ is the same as the orbit set of the semi-group action with $(\mathcal{S}, *)$. Invariant I is constant within each orbit but has distinct values for any two different orbits. In particular, for the Gaussian orbit $\mathcal{S}$ we have $I(h) = 1$.

4   Invariants from Moments

Although theoretically the invariant $I(h)$ fully describes the orbit, several problems may occur when dealing with finite-precision arithmetic. The division by small numbers leads to the precision loss. To speed up the computation, it would be better to avoid the explicit construction of $\Phi(h)$ and $\Phi(Ph)$. In this Section, we show that it can be accomplished by constructing moment-based invariants equivalent to $I(h)$. The idea of describing a histogram by its moments is reasonable. Moment-based representation yields an additional feature – the number of the moments used is a user-defined parameter by means of which we may control the trade-off between a high compression on one hand and an accurate histogram representation on the other hand [7].

We rewrite Eq. (8) as

$$\Phi(Ph)(\mathbf{u}) \cdot I(h)(\mathbf{u}) = \Phi(h)(\mathbf{u}). \tag{9}$$

If the characteristic function is n-times differentiable, then the nth derivative is a moment of the PDF up to a multiplicative constant. Assuming that both $\Phi(h)$ and $\Phi(Ph)$ have a Taylor expansion, then we can write, using a multi-index notation,

$$\sum_{\substack{\mathbf{k}=0 \\ |\mathbf{k}| \neq 0,\ \text{even}}}^{\infty} \frac{\mathrm{i}^{|\mathbf{k}|}}{\mathbf{k}!} m_{\mathbf{k}}^{(Ph)} \mathbf{u}^{\mathbf{k}} \cdot \sum_{\mathbf{p}=0}^{\infty} \frac{\mathrm{i}^{|\mathbf{p}|}}{\mathbf{p}!} A_{\mathbf{p}} \mathbf{u}^{\mathbf{p}} = \sum_{\mathbf{q}=0}^{\infty} \frac{\mathrm{i}^{|\mathbf{q}|}}{\mathbf{q}!} m_{\mathbf{q}}^{(h)} \mathbf{u}^{\mathbf{q}}, \tag{10}$$

where

$$m_{\mathbf{k}}^{(h)} = \int \mathbf{x}^{\mathbf{k}} h(\mathbf{x})\, \mathrm{d}\mathbf{x}. \tag{11}$$

By comparing coefficients of the same power of $\mathbf{u}$ we get

$$\sum_{\substack{\mathbf{l}=0 \\ |\mathbf{l}|\ \text{even}}}^{\mathbf{k}} \frac{\mathrm{i}^{|\mathbf{l}|}}{\mathbf{l}!} m_{\mathbf{l}}^{(Ph)} \frac{\mathrm{i}^{|\mathbf{k}|-|\mathbf{l}|}}{(\mathbf{k}-\mathbf{l})!} A_{\mathbf{k}-\mathbf{l}} = \frac{\mathrm{i}^{|\mathbf{k}|}}{\mathbf{k}!} m_{\mathbf{k}}^{(h)}, \tag{12}$$

which is equivalent to

$$\sum_{\substack{l=0 \\ |l| \text{ even}}}^{k} \binom{k}{1} m_1^{(Ph)} A_{k-1} = m_k^{(h)}.$$

(13)

Each A_k, being a Taylor coefficient of $I(h)$, must be an invariant. Rearranging the previous equation, we obtain a recursive formula for A_k

$$A_k = m_k^{(h)} - \sum_{\substack{l=0 \\ |l| \neq 0, \text{ even}}}^{k} \binom{k}{1} m_1^{(Ph)} A_{k-1}.$$

(14)

The intuitive meaning of invariants A_k is the following one. If the "mother PDF" h_r exists, then $I(h)$ is its characteristic function and A_k's are its moments. The invariants A_k can be, however, applied even if h_r does not exist. Another noteworthy point is that generally we have to calculate moments of both h and Ph in order to evaluate Eq. (14). In the next Section, we show how the construction of Ph and calculation of its moments can be avoided.

5   Invariants in One and Two Dimensions

Histogram is a function of either a single variable when working with graylevel images or of multiple variables for color/multispectral images. In this Section, we show how Eq. (14) can be further simplified in 1D and 2D cases.

In 1D, the invariants (14) obtain the form

$$A_p = m_p^{(h)} - \sum_{\substack{k=2 \\ k \text{ even}}}^{p} \binom{p}{k} (k-1)!! \, m_2^{k/2} A_{p-k}.$$

(15)

This simplification follows from the fact that the odd-order moments of a 1D Gaussian with standard deviation σ vanish and the even-order ones are given as $m_p = \sigma^p (p-1)!!$. Furthermore, $\sigma^2 \equiv m_2^{(Ph)} = m_2^{(h)}$ which allows to express all moments of Ph in terms of moments of h.

In 2D, simplification of Eq. (14) is much more difficult. First, we need to express the moments of 2D Gaussian explicitly. If we assume that the two components of our random variable $\mathbf{N}$ are independent, then we can constraint the covariance matrix of Ph to be diagonal. Then the moments of Ph are simply

$$m_{pq}^{(Ph)} = m_{20}^p m_{02}^q (p-1)!!(q-1)!!$$

(16)

and we obtain similar formula as in 1D case

$$A_{mn} = m_{mn}^{(h)} - \sum_{\substack{l=0 \\ l+k \neq 0, \\ l+k \text{ even}}}^{m} \sum_{k=0}^{n} \binom{m}{l}\binom{n}{k} (l-1)!!(k-1)!! \, m_{20}^{l/2} m_{02}^{k/2} A_{m-l,n-k}.$$

(17)

However, the assumption of independent noise components and hence of the diagonal covariance matrix is not always realistic in practice. In Fig. 4 we can see 2D histogram of red and green channels of the noise, extracted from a real RGB photograph. The noise is actually a background and thermal noise of the camera; the noise extraction was done by subtracting a time-averaged image. A correlation about 0.33 was found (and is also apparent visually) between the noise acting in the red and the green channel (the correlation was probably introduced by an in-built postprocessing/interpolation on the chip). So, to make our method applicable in practice, we have to assume a general covariance matrix of Ph.

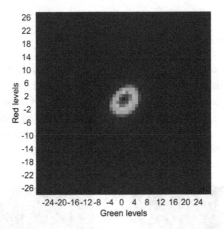

Fig. 4. 2D histogram of the noise extracted from red and green channels of a real digital image. The on-chip postprocessing introduced a correlation about 0.33 between the noise in both channels. (Color figure online)

For the general covariance matrix, the formula for moments of a Gaussian is not commonly cited in the literature.[1] Therefore we derived an explicit formula for 2D zero-mean case, which is very useful in the sequel:

$$
m_{mn}^{(Ph)} = \sum_{\substack{i=0 \\ j \geq \frac{m-n}{2}}}^{\lfloor \frac{m}{2} \rfloor} \sum_{j=0}^{i} (-1)^{i-j} \binom{m}{2i} \binom{i}{j} (m+n-2i-1)!!(2i-1)!! \cdot
$$

$$
\cdot m_{11}^{m-2j} m_{20}^{j} m_{02}^{\frac{n-m}{2}+j}.
$$

(18)

---

[1] The reader is usually referred to the classical Isserlis' paper [4] or to some more recent papers [10,11,13] but no simple explicit formula can be found there.

If we use Formula (18), the recurrence (14) turns to the form

$$
A_{mn} = m_{mn}^{(h)} - \sum_{\substack{l=0 \\ l+k\neq 0, \\ l+k\ \text{even}}}^{m} \sum_{k=0}^{n} \binom{m}{l}\binom{n}{k} \sum_{i=0}^{\lfloor \frac{k}{2} \rfloor} \sum_{\substack{j=0 \\ j\geq \frac{k-l}{2}}}^{i} (-1)^{i-j} \binom{k}{2i}\binom{i}{j} \cdot
$$

$$
\cdot (l+k-2i-1)!!(2i-1)!!\, m_{11}^{k-2j}\, m_{20}^{\frac{l-k}{2}+j}\, m_{02}^{j}\, A_{m-l,n-k} \,.
$$

(19)

Note that the formula contains only the moments of h. Neither the character-istic functions $\Phi(h)$ and $\Phi(Ph)$ nor the projection Ph itself are necessary to be constructed.

6 Experiment

In this experiment, we show the invariance property if the noise follows the Gaussian model. We used blue and green channels of a real RGB image as "clear" test data. We corrupted the image 100 times with a Gaussian noise generated according to Eq. (2), the covariance matrix of which was randomly generated in each realization. As one can see in Fig. 5, the histogram of noisy image is actually a smoothed version of the histogram of the clear image.

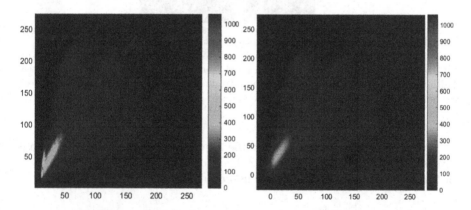

Fig. 5. 2D histogram of the blue and green channels of the original clear image (left) and of the same image corrupted by additive Gaussian noise (right). Note that the "noisy" histogram is actually a smoothed version of the original histogram. (Color figure online)

We calculated more than 300 invariants (19) of each noisy image histogram. In Fig. 6 left, we can see a cumulative graph of the ratio between the invariants of noisy and clear histograms (each invariant order is represented by a single cumu-lative value). The ratio is almost perfectly equal to one, even for higher orders. To show the advantage of the proposed invariants over the plain moments, we calculated the same for histogram moments, see Fig. 6 right. The errors of the moments are much higher since the moments do not posses the invariance property and are heavily influenced by noise. The error grows with the increasing moment order. This experiment clearly shows the quality of the proposed histogram descriptors.

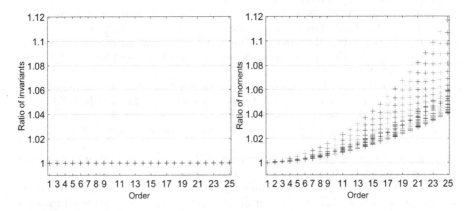

Fig. 6. Ratio of the invariants (left) and of the moments (right) between the 2D histograms of noisy and clear images. The invariants/moments of the same order have been cumulated. Black crosses denote the median of the invariants.

7   Conclusion

We proposed a new method for description of multidimensional histogram, which is robust to additive Gaussian noise in the source image. The method employs the fact that the histogram of noisy image is a convolution of the original histogram and the histogram of the noise. We proposed moment-based descriptors, which characterize the original histogram but can be computed directly from the histogram of the noisy image. The method does not require any denoising or estimation of the noise parameters, which makes it attractive for practical usage. Potential applications are in noise-robust histogram-based image retrieval and also in some areas outside image processing.

References

1. Flusser, J., Suk, T.: Degraded image analysis: an invariant approach. IEEE Trans. Pattern Anal. Mach. Intell. **20**(6), 590–603 (1998)
2. Flusser, J., Suk, T., Boldyš, J., Zitová, B.: Projection operators and moment invariants to image blurring. IEEE Trans. Pattern Anal. Mach. Intell. **37**(4), 786–802 (2015)
3. Höschl IV, C., Flusser, J.: Robust histogram-based image retrieval. Pattern Recogn. Lett. **69**(1), 72–81 (2016)

4. Isserlis, L.: On a formula for the product-moment coefficient of any order of a normal frequency distribution in any number of variables. Biometrika **12**(1/2), 134–139 (1918)
5. Lukacs, E.: Characteristic Functions Griffin books of Cognate Interest. Hafner Publishing Company, New York (1970)
6. Makaremi, I., Ahmadi, M.: Wavelet domain blur invariants for image analysis. IEEE Trans. Image Process. **21**(3), 996–1006 (2012)
7. Mandal, M.K., Aboulnasr, T., Panchanathan, S.: Image indexing using moments and wavelets. IEEE Trans. Consum. Electron. **42**(3), 557–565 (1996)
8. Pass, G., Zabih, R.: Histogram refinement for content-based image retrieval. In: Proceedings 3rd IEEE Workshop on Applications of Computer Vision WACV 1996, pp. 96–102. IEEE (1996)
9. Pedone, M., Flusser, J., Heikkilä, J.: Blur invariant translational image registration for N-fold symmetric blurs. IEEE Trans. Image Process. **22**(9), 3676–3689 (2013)
10. Schott, J.R.: Kronecker product permutation matrices and their application to moment matrices of the normal distribution. J. Multivar. Anal. **87**(1), 177–190 (2003)
11. Song, I., Lee, S.: Explicit formulae for product moments of multivariate gaussian random variables. Stat. Probab. Lett. **100**, 27–34 (2015)
12. Swain, M.J., Ballard, D.H.: Color indexing. Int. J. Comput. Vis. **7**(1), 11–32 (1991)
13. Triantafyllopoulos, K.: On the central moments of the multidimensional gaussian distribution. Math. Sci. **28**(2), 125–128 (2003)
14. Wang, L., Healey, G.: Using Zernike moments for the illumination and geometry invariant classification of multispectral texture. IEEE Trans. Image Process. **7**(2), 196–203 (1998)
15. Zhang, H., Shu, H., Han, G.N., Coatrieux, G., Luo, L., Coatrieux, J.L.: Blurred image recognition by Legendre moment invariants. IEEE Trans. Image Process. **19**(3), 596–611 (2010)

A Discrete Approach for Polygonal Approximation of Irregular Noise Contours

Phuc Ngo$^{(\boxtimes)}$

Université de Lorraine, LORIA, UMR 7503,
54506 Vandoeuvre-lès-Nancy, France
hoai-diem-phuc.ngo@loria.fr

Abstract. Polygonal approximation is often involved in many applications of computer vision, image processing and data compression. In this context, we are interested in digital curves extracted from contours of objects contained in digital images. In particular, we propose a fully discrete structure, based on the notion of blurred segments, to study the geometrical features on such curves and apply it in a process of polygonal approximation. The experimental results demonstrate the robustness of the proposed method to local variation and noise on the curve.

Keywords: Discrete structure · Polygonal representation · Dominant point

1 Introduction

Image processing applications often involve in computing, analyzing and studying objects contained in digital images. In this context, objects are usually extracted by a process of image segmentation. Due to the discrete nature of data to process, contours of these objects are digital curves whose points have integer coordinates. Then, a polygonal approximation of a digital object usually refers to a discrete representation of its contour by a finite number of segments joining two adjacent vertices. It should be mentioned that this discrete modeling of digital objects is required in many applications of computer vision, graphics, image processing and data compression (*e.g.*, [5,23]). Furthermore, noise robustness is also an important constraint in the applications.

In the field of digital geometry, new mathematical definitions of basic geometric objects, such as lines or circles, are introduced to better fit these discrete data. In particular, the notion of blurred segment [7,8] was proposed to deal with digital curves containing noise or other sources of imperfections from the real data by using a fixed thickness parameter ν. The sequence of blurred segments of thickness ν along a digital curve C is called a ν-*tangential cover* of C and can be computed in quasi-linear time [6]. It is used in many different contexts to study and analyze the geometrical characteristics of noisy curves such as length, tangent, curvature estimators (*e.g.*, [14,18]).

© Springer Nature Switzerland AG 2019
M. Vento and G. Percannella (Eds.): CAIP 2019, LNCS 11678, pp. 433–446, 2019.
https://doi.org/10.1007/978-3-030-29888-3_35

The present paper aims at designing a fully discrete framework to approximate a digital curve extracted from contour object in a digital image using the notion of blurred segment. More precisely, the proposed method composes of two steps. Firstly, we compute an *adaptive tangential cover* of the input curve (see Sect. 4). The particularity of this structure is that it contains a sequence of blurred segments with diffrent thicknesses varying in function of noise present along the curve. Such adaptive thicknesses are computed thanks to the local noise estimator of *meaningful thickness* [11]. Using this structure of adaptive tangential cover, we detect the points of local maximum curvature, called *dominant points*, on the digital curve (see Sect. 5). In brief, dominant points are located in the smallest common zones induced by successive blurred segments. Then, by using a simple measure of angle, we can identify the dominant point as point having the smallest angle. The sequence of dominant points forms a polygonal representation of the curve. However, due to the nature of the tangential cover, dominant points usually stay very close to each others. This is sometimes undesirable as the goal of polygonal approximation is to reduce the amount of necessary information to store a curve, and improve its processing. Therefore, we propose to perform a simplification on the obtained polygon in order to achieve a higher compression while preserving important features of the input curve. The experimental results on both simulated and real data in Sect. 6 show that the proposed method, based on the structure of adaptive tangential cover, allows an effective representation of noisy digital curves.

2   Background Notions

We recall hereafter some basic notions in the digital geometry literature [12] for analyzing digital curves, particularly the noisy ones.

2.1   Digital Line and Blurred Segment

A digital line D is defined as the set of integer points satisfying:

$$D = \{(x, y) \in \mathbb{Z}^2 : 0 \leq ax + by + c < \omega\}$$

with $a, b, c \in \mathbb{Z}$, $gcd(a, b) = 1$, and $\omega \in \mathbb{Z}$ is a constant indicating the *thickness* of D. We denote such a digital line by $D(a, b, c, \omega)$. In particular, when $\omega = \max(|a|, |b|)$ then D is the narrowest 8-connected line and called *naif digital line*, and $\omega = |a| + |b|$ then D is 4-connected line and called *standard digital line*. A *digital straight segment* is a finite subset of D. Figure 1(a-b) show some examples of digital straight lines and segments.

In this work, we consider digital curves, i.e., a finite sequence of discrete points in a predefined order, either counterclockwise or anticlockwise. Such digital curves are generally extracted from contours of objects in digital images.

Definition 1 ([7]). *A finite sequence of discrete points S is a* blurred segment *of thickness ν iff (i) $\forall (x, y) \in S$, $(x, y) \in D(a, b, c, \omega)$, and (ii) the vertical*

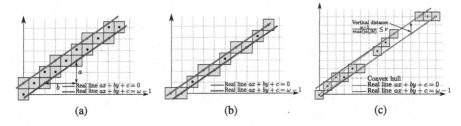

Fig. 1. Examples of (a) a standard segment belongs to the 4-connected digital line $D(2, -3, 3, 5)$, (b) a naif segment belongs to the 8-connected digital line $D(2, -3, 0, 3)$ and (c) a blurred segment of thickness $\nu = 1.5$ belongs to the digital line $D(3, -4, 3, 7)$.

(or horizontal) distance $d = \frac{\omega - 1}{\max(|a|, |b|)}$ equals to the vertical (or horizontal) thickness of the convex hull of S such that $d \leq \nu$.

Let consider a digital curve $C = (C_i)_{0 \leq i \leq n-1}$ of n points. Let $C_{i,j}$ denote the sub-sequence of points from C_i to C_j in C. Let us consider the predicate of a blurred segment of thickness ν for $C_{i,j}$ such that

$$B(i, j, \nu) = \begin{cases} True \text{ if } C_{i,j} \text{ is a blurred segment of thickness } \nu \\ False \text{ otherwise} \end{cases}$$

Then, we define a *maximal blurred segment (MBS)* of a sequence of points, not necessarily connected, as follows.

Definition 2 ([7]). *A blurred segment $C_{i,j}$ of C is said to be* maximal *iff* $B(i, j, \nu)$, $\neg B(i - 1, j, \nu)$ *and* $\neg B(i, j + 1, \nu)$.

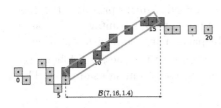

Fig. 2. Maximal blurred segment (in green) $\mathcal{B}(7, 16, 1.4)$ on a disconnected curve. (Color figure online)

The maximal blurred segment $C_{i,j}$ of thickness ν is denoted by $\mathcal{B}(i, j, \nu)$. The blurred segment and maximal blurred segment are respectively illustrated in Fig. 1(c) and Fig. 2. The sequence of maximal blurred segments of a fixed thickness ν along C is called ν-*tangential cover* of C. In [6], an optimal algorithm is proposed to compute this structure with a complexity of $O(n \log n)$ where n is the number of points of C.

2.2 Noise Estimator: Meaningful Thickness

Hereafter, we briefly explain a method of noise detection based on the above notions. In [9,10], a notion, called *meaningful scale* (MS), was proposed to locally estimate the best scale – grid size – to analyze a digital curve. The method is based on the asymptotic properties of the discrete length L of maximal segments.

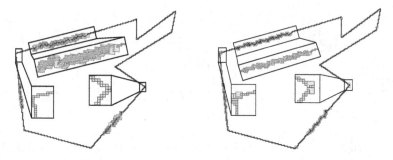

Fig. 3. Comparison between MS (left) and MT (right) estimators. The blue box sizes represent the MS and MT values of each point. Both estimators allow to prevent the local noise perturbation along the curve. However, MT is more sensible at corners than MS. (Color figure online)

Theorem 1 ([13]). *Let $\mathfrak{S}$ be a simply connected shape in $\mathbb{R}^2$ with a smooth C^3-boundary. Let p be a point on the boundary of $\mathfrak{S}$. Let L^h be the mean discrete length of maximal segments covering p along the digitized boundary of $\mathfrak{S}$; i.e., $\mathfrak{S} \cap h\mathbb{Z} \times h\mathbb{Z}$ (where h represents the grid size). Then, L^h is between $\Omega(h^{-1/3})$ and $O(h^{-1/2})$ if p is located on a strictly concave or convex part and near $O(h^{-1})$ elsewhere.*

Roughly speaking, the MS method consists in analyzing each point p on a curve at different grid sizes by sub-sampling and reporting the maximal scale of p for which the mean lengths of maximal segments covering p follow the previous theoretical behavior.

This method of MS estimator has been extended to the detection of *meaningful thickness* (MT) [11] by using maximal blurred segment primitive together with its thickness parameter. Such a strategy presents an advantage to be easier to implement without any sub-sampling. In particular, the length variation of the maximal blurred segments $\overline{\mathcal{L}}^{t_i}$ obtained at different thicknesses t_i follows the equivalent properties to the maximal segment defined from sub-sampling. This has been experimentally verified in [11].

Conjecture 1 ([11]). The ratio $\mathcal{L}_j^{t_i}/t^i$ in log-scale are approximately affine with negative slopes s located between $-\frac{1}{2}$ and $-\frac{1}{3}$ for a curved part and around -1 for a flat part.

As suggested in [11], an analysis on the log-scale $(\log(t_i), \log(\overline{\mathcal{L}}^{t_i}/t_i))_{i=1,\dots,n}$ at each point p of the contour is performed to determine an indication of local variation at p. The graph of log-scale of p is called *multi-thickness profile* and the first thickness at which the mean length of maximal blurred segments covering p follows the asymptotic behavior is called *meaningful thickness* of p. In other words, the meaningful thickness permits a local estimation of the noise level at each point of a digital contour and provides the thickness of blurred segments should be used to analyze the point. It is worth noting that the MT estimator is slightly more sensitivity than MS at the corners. In particular, high noise level can be detected at corners as illustrated in Fig. 3. However, MT has the advantage to be able to process non-integer coordinates, non-connected curves, and more efficient in term of computation comparing to MS.

3 Previous Works

In the digital geometry field, several attempts have been proposed to handle digital curves containing noise, such as the tangential cover based on maximal blurred segments with a fixed thickness ν, named ν-*tangential cover* [14] (see Fig. 4(c)). Then, the user can manually adjust the parameter ν as in [17,21]. This is however a difficult task to select appropriate thickness. Another solution is to set it as the average of the meaningful thicknesses detected overall the points of the studied curve as in [22]. As the thickness ν is globally set for all maximal blurred segments of the ν-tangential cover, this approach works well when noise is uniformly distributed on the curve, but it is not adapted to local noise. In other words, ν-tangential cover is inadequate in case of noise varying differently on the curve. To over come this issue, a discrete structure, called *adaptive tangential cover* (ATC), is presented in [18]. Such a structure is designed to capture the local noise on curve by adjusting the thickness of maximal blurred segments in accordance with the amount of noise present along the curve.

Definition 3 ([18]). *Let* $C = (C_i)_{0 \leq i \leq n-1}$ *be a digital curve. Let* $\eta = (\eta_i)_{0 \leq i \leq n-1}$ *be the vector of MT associated to each* C_i *of* C. *Let* $\mathcal{B}(C) = \{\mathcal{B}_{\nu_k}(C)\}$ *be the set of* ν_k-*tangential covers for* $\nu_k \in \eta$. *An adaptive tangential cover (ATC) of* C *is the sequence of the MBS that* $ATC(C) = \{\mathcal{B}_j = \mathcal{B}(B_j, E_j, \nu) \in \mathcal{B}(C) \mid \nu = \max\{\eta_t \mid t \in [\![B_j, E_j]\!]\}\}$ *such that* $\mathcal{B}_j \not\subseteq \mathcal{B}_i$ *for* $i \neq j$, *where* $[\![a, b]\!]$ *is the integer interval between* a *and* b, *including both.*

In order to prevent the local perturbation, the MT estimator is integrated in the construction of ATC as a noise detector at each point of the curve. More precisely, the ATC is composed of MBS with thicknesses varying in function of detected perturbations, by the presence of noise or corners, with the MT estimator. In particular, the MBS has bigger thickness at noisy zones, and smaller thickness in zones with less or no noise, as illustrated in Fig. 4(d).

Still in [18], an algorithm is proposed to build the ATC of a given curve based on Definition 3. The algorithm is divided into two steps: (1) labeling the points with thickness values from MT estimator, and (2) building the ATC with the MBS of thickness from the obtained labels. It should be noted that, in the labeling step, the method uses the maximal strategy; i.e., the label associated to the points of a MBS is the maximal meaningful thicknesses detected by MT estimator in the MBS.

The ATC is a good tool for analyzing noisy digital curves [18]. However, when using ACT, we often observe that there are the MBS of big thickness encompassing the significant details of the curve; See Figs. 4(d) and 5(a) as examples

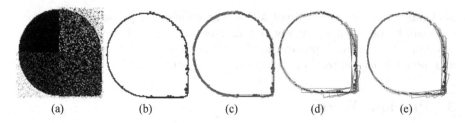

Fig. 4. Digital contour (b) extracted from noisy image (a) with its 2-tangential cover (c) and its adaptive tangential cover (d) and its modified adaptive tangential cover (e) with MBS of different thickness transmitted from local noise detector of meaningful thickness.

of this behavior. This is due to the strategy of labeling the point with the maximal meaningful thickness values. As mentioned in Sect. 2.2, the MT detector is sensible at corners, and provides a less frequent and big thickness at these points. Then, using maximal strategy of meaningful thickness will propagate the improper thicknesses, and generate the big MBS. More importantly, the polygonal representation of a digital curve based on ATC does not fit well the curve, in particular at the corners as illustrated in Fig. 5(a) and (b).

4   Modified Adaptive Tangential Cover

As MT estimator may detect a big value of thickness at corners, using the maximal values of meaningful thickness of points in a MBS is not a relevant strategy. To tackle this limitation, we propose a new decision-making of labeling points of the digital curve from the thicknesses detected by the MT estimator.

More precisely, instead of using maximal meaningful thickness, we consider the most frequent thickness for labeling points of MBS constituting the ATC. This is based on the observation that high meaningful thickness at corner is mostly appeared as a singular value while the one caused by noise is a repetitive value. In other words, a more frequent meaningful thickness means a higher probability of presence of noise.

Definition 4. *Let $C = (C_i)_{0 \le i \le n-1}$ be a digital curve. Let $\eta = (\eta_i)_{0 \le i \le n-1}$ be the vector of MT associated to each C_i of C. Let $\mathcal{B}(C) = \{\mathcal{B}_{\nu_k}(C)\}$ be the set of ν_k-tangential covers for the different values ν_k in η. A modified adaptive tangential cover (MATC) of C is defined as the sequence of the MBS $\{\mathcal{B}_j = \mathcal{B}(B_j, E_j, \nu) \in \mathcal{B}(C) \mid \nu = \max\{count(\eta_t) \mid t \in [\![B_j, E_j]\!]\}\}$ such that $\mathcal{B}_j \nsubseteq \mathcal{B}_i$ for $i \neq j$, where $count(\eta_t)$ is the function that counts the occurrences of η_t in the vector of MT.*

By definition, the MATC possesses the following property.

Property 1. Let $C = (C_i)_{0 \le i \le n-1}$ be a digital curve and $\mathcal{B}_i = \mathcal{B}(B_i, E_i, .), \mathcal{B}_j = \mathcal{B}(B_j, E_j, .)$ be two distinct MBS of the modified adaptive tangential cover of C. If $i < j$, then $B_i < B_j$ and $E_i < E_j$.

Algorithm 1. Calculation of modified adaptive tangential cover associated to meaningful thickness.

Input   : $C = (C_i)_{0 \le i \le n-1}$ digital curve,

$\eta = (\eta_i)_{0 \le i \le n-1}$ vector of MT to each C_i,

$\nu = \{\nu_k \mid \nu_k \in \eta\}$ ordered set of η, and $\mathcal{B}(C) = \{\mathcal{B}_{\nu_k}(C)\}_{k=0}^{m-1}$ sets of MBS of C for each thickness value $\nu_k \in \nu$

Output   : $TC(C)$ modified adaptive tangential cover

Variables : $\gamma = (\gamma)_{0 \le i \le n-1}$ vector of labels to each C_i

1 **begin**

2      $TC(C) = \emptyset$;

3      $\gamma_i = \eta_i$ for $i \in [\![0, n-1]\!]$;

     // Step 1: Label each point C_i of C

4   **foreach** $\nu_k \in \nu$ **do**

5   **foreach** $\mathcal{B}(B_i, E_i, \nu_k) \in \mathcal{B}_{\nu_k}(C)$ **do**

6            $count_i = \#~\eta_i$ for $i \in [\![B_i, E_i]\!]$;   // count the occurrences of η_i

7            $\alpha = \max\{count_i \mid i \in [\![B_i, E_i]\!]\}$;

8   **if** $\alpha = \nu_k$ **then**

9               $\gamma_i = \nu_k$ for $i \in [\![B_i, E_i]\!]$;

     // Step 2: Calculate the MATC of C with MBS of thickness issued from the labels γ

10   **foreach** $\nu_k \in \nu$ **do**

11   **foreach** $\mathcal{B}(B_i, E_i, \nu_k) \in \mathcal{B}_{\nu_k}(C)$ **do**

12   **if** $\exists \gamma_i$, *for* $i \in [\![B_i, E_i]\!]$, *such that* $\gamma_i = \nu_k$ **then**

13              $TC(C) = TC(C) \cup \{\mathcal{B}(B_i, E_i, \nu_k)\}$;

From Definition 4, the high thicknesses at corners will not be spread along the curve but only those of noise detected by MT estimator. Thus, the MATC allows to produce a better fitting with MBS along the curve (see Fig. 5(c) and (d)). The principle for computing the MATC is described in Algorithm 1. It is similar to the one in [18] except for the labeling step as described above. It should be mentioned that the computation of MATC has no parameter to set, or only two values related to MT estimator [10]. In particular, the algorithm has $O(kn \log n)$ complexity where k is the number of noise levels detected by MT estimator and $O(n \log n)$ is the complexity for computing ν-tangential cover [6] of each meaningful thickness detected on a digital curve of n points. In practice, k is much smaller than n.

Figure 5 shows a comparison between the ATC and the MATC on a same digital curve. One can observe that the modified ATC contains of MBS that fit better the shape than those of the former ATC. Furthermore, the polygonal approximation (see Sect. 5) based on the modified ATC archives a more accuracy of the digital curve than this with the ATC. More comparisons are given in Sect. 6.

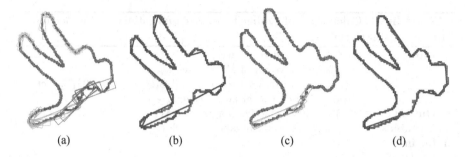

| (a) | (b) | (c) | (d) |

Fig. 5. Comparison between ATC (a) and MATC (c). The polygonal approximations (red lines) of the contour based on ATC and MATC are respectively (b) and (d). (Color figure online)

5   Polygonal Approximation Using MATC

Polygonal approximation is often involved in many applications of computer vision, graphics, image processing and data compression. In [18,20], ATC is used as a tool to study digital curves as the sequence of MBS composing ATC provides important information about the geometrical structure of the curve. In particular, it is involved in detecting points of local maximum curvature, called *dominant points* [3]. Since MATC has the same properties as ATC, we can use the same algorithm in [20] for detecting the dominant point with the proposed structure of MATC.

Let us recall the main idea of the detection method. Firstly, the candidates of dominant points are located in the smallest common zones induced by successive MBS of the tangential cover. Then, a simple measure of angle, as a *pseudo-curvature*, is estimated for each candidate in the same zone to determine the dominant point in the zone. Such an angle is calculated as the acute angle from the candidate point to the two extremities of the left and right of the MBS composing the zone. Finally, the dominant point is identified as the point with the smallest angle value as the local maximum curvature (see Fig. 6(a)). It should be noticed that, from Property 1, the common zone can be detected by simply verifying the extremities of MBS composing the MATC. By joining the straight line segments bounded by two consecutive dominant points, we obtain a polygon $\mathcal{P}$ representing the digital curve. However, due to the nature of the tangential cover, $\mathcal{P}$ usually contains vertices being very close to each others. In the context of polygonal simplification, it is sometimes undesirable as the goal is to reduce the amount of necessary information to store a curve, and improve its processing. Therefore, a reduction on $\mathcal{P}$ is needed to eliminate certain vertices in order to achieve a higher compression of the polygonal approximation and a more effective representation of the original curve. For this, we associate to each vertex of $\mathcal{P}$ a score indicating its importance w.r.t the simplified polygon $\mathcal{P}'$. In particular, the score is calculated as the ratio of two factors: (1) an error metric

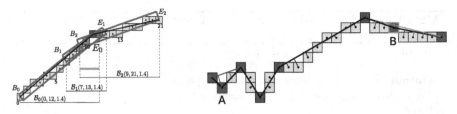

Fig. 6. Left: selection of dominant point (in blue) in the smallest common zone (in green) by the three successive MBS. The angle at C_9, C_{10}, C_{11} and C_{12} are 2.802, 2.733, 2.653 and 2.717 respectively. Then, dominant point is C_{11} which has the smallest angle. Right: Score calculation for dominant points (in red). The point A has a score of $2/1.57^2 = 0.812$ which is greater than the point B of $2.59/3.02^2 = 0.284$. Therefore, A is more important than B. (Color figure online)

of the approximating polygon and the shape and (2) the angular relationship with the two neighboring vertices on $\mathcal{P}$.

More precisely, we would like to remove the *nearly* collinear vertices of the polygon. Thus, we consider the angle measure of the vertex to its two neighbours on $\mathcal{P}$, and suppress the vertices with big angle measure; *i.e.*, angle closes to 2π. Besides, we consider the integral sum of square errors (ISSE) as the sum of squared distances of the curve points from the approximating polygon. This error metric evaluates how much the approximated polygon is similar to a curve. In particular, smaller ISSE means better descriptive of the curve by the approximated polygon. For an equivalence of power, the score is computed as $\frac{ISSE}{angle^2}$. An illustration is given in Fig. 6(b).

In order to determine the number of dominant points to eliminate during simplification process, we consider the criterion *figure of merit*, defined as

$$FOM_2 = CR^2/ISSE$$

where $CR = n/V$ refers to *compression ratio* which is defined as the ratio of the number of curve points n and of polygon vertices V. It is shown in [4,17] that this function is a performance measure to evaluate the approximation of a curve by a polygon as the compression ratio (CR) describes the effective data reduction, while ISSE describes the discrepancy between the approximating polygon and the curve. In other words, FOM_2 with the numerator and the denominator being of equal power represents a compromise between the low approximation error and the benefit of the high data reduction. Therefore, we use FOM_2 as objective function in the optimization (maximization) process of polygonal simplification. The algorithm is described in Algorithm 2. Roughly speaking, the polygonal simplification removes incrementally one by one dominant point of highest score until reaching the maximum value of FOM_2.

6 Experimental Results and Evaluation

In this section, we present results of the polygonal simplification algorithm using the proposed structure MATC and other recent methods in the literature. In

---

Algorithm 2. Polygonal approximation of digital curves using tangential cover.

Input   : $C = (C_i)_{0 \le i \le n-1}$ digital curve,
$TC(C) = \{\mathcal{B}(B_j, E_j, .)\}_{j=0}^{m-1}$ (modified) adaptive tangential cover

Output : $\mathcal{P}'$ vertices of the approximating polygon of C

Variables: $\mathcal{P}$ sequence of dominant points of C

1 **begin**

// Step 1: Detect dominant points (DP)

2   $q = 0;\ p = 1;\ \mathcal{P} = \emptyset$;

3   **while** $p < m$ **do**

4   **while** $E_q > B_p$ **do** $p + +$;

5     $\mathcal{P} = \mathcal{P} \cup \min\{Angle(C_{B_q}, C_i, C_{E_{p-1}}) \mid i \in [\![B_{p-1}, E_q]\!]\}$;

6     $q = p - 1$;

// Step 2: Simplify polygon of the DP

7   $\mathcal{P}' = \mathcal{P}$;

8   **for** $i := 0$ to $|\mathcal{P}| - 1$ **do**

9     $score(p_i) = ISSE(p_{i-1}, p_i, p_{i+1})/Angle^2(p_{i-1}, p_i, p_{i+1})$;

10 $F = FOM_2(\mathcal{P}')$;

11 **repeat**

12    $F' = F$;

13    $p_i = \arg\min\{score(p_j) \mid p_j \in \mathcal{P}'\}$;

14    $score(p_{i-1}) = ISSE(p_{i-2}, p_{i-1}, p_{i+1})/Angle^2(p_{i-2}, p_{i-1}, p_{i+1})$;

15    $score(p_{i+1}) = ISSE(p_{i-1}, p_{i+1}, p_{i+2})/Angle^2(p_{i-1}, p_{i+1}, p_{i+2})$;

16    $\mathcal{P}' = \mathcal{P}' \setminus \{p_i\}$;

17    $F = FOM_2(\mathcal{P}')$;

18 **until** $F < F'$;

---

order to evaluate the goodness of a method, we consider the standard evaluation metrics in the literature [16,24] such as compression ratio (CR), the integral sum of square errors (ISSE), the maximum error (L_∞) and the figure of merit (FOM, computed by $FOM_n = \frac{CR^n}{ISSE}$ with $n = 1, 2, 3$).

6.1   Polygonal Simplification Using ATC and MATC

This section shows the experimental results of the polygonal simplification using the two structures ATC and MATC on the curves with and without noise. The first tests visually compare the results on the curves in Figs. 5 and 7, and Table 1 quantifies these results with the evaluation criteria. Further experiments are carried out on KIMA216 database [2]. This database contains 216 shapes, grouped in 18 classes with 12 shapes in each. The quantitative results are shown in Fig. 8. From the experimental results, we observe a performance improvement of the polygonal simplification using the MATC comparing to the ATC. In particular, the results with MATC provides a better fitting of the curve than those with ATC.

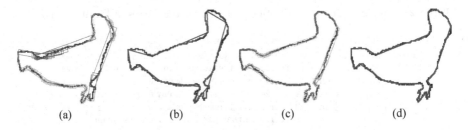

(a)   (b)   (c)   (d)

Fig. 7. Comparison between ATC (a) and MATC (c) on a digital contour. The polygonal approximations of the contour based on ATC (b) and MATC (d).

Table 1. Comparisons of polygonal simplification (Algorithm 2) on the curves in Fig. 5 and Fig. 7 using the structures ATC and MATC.

Curve	Algorithm 2	$V \downarrow$	$CR \uparrow$	$ISSE \downarrow$	$L_\infty \downarrow$	$FOM \uparrow$	$FOM_2 \uparrow$	$FOM_3 \uparrow$
Figure 5	ATC	**17**	**26.706**	1047.426	4.919	0.025	0.681	18.184
$n = 454$	MATC	23	16.814	**213.764**	**2.354**	**0.071**	**1.393**	**27.491**
Figure 7	ATC	**11**	**49.818**	2280.26	6.434	0.022	1.088	**54.222**
$n = 548$	MATC	24	22.833	**449.214**	**2.71**	**0.051**	**1.161**	26.501

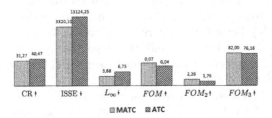

Fig. 8. Comparisons of polygonal simplification (Algorithm 2) on the KIMA216 database [2] using the structures ATC and MATC.

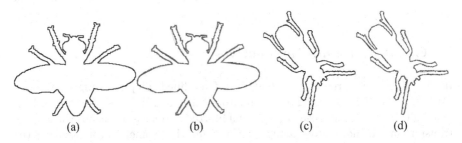

(a)   (b)   (c)   (d)

Fig. 9. (a)–(c): input curves of polygonal simplification. (b)–(d): the polygonal results using the proposed method (Algorithm 2 with the ATC (in blue) and MATC (in red) structures) and the methods of Sivignon [25] (in green) and Liu *et al.* [15] (in yellow). (Color figure online)

Table 2. Comparing results with other methods for the curves in Fig. 9 (a) and (c).

Curve	Methods	V ↓	CR ↑	ISSE ↓	L_∞ ↓	FOM ↑	FOM_2 ↑	FOM_3 ↑
Figure 9(a)	Algorithm 2 using ATC	125	15	935.088	2.575	0.016	0.241	3.609
$n = 1990$	Algorithm 2 using MATC	126	15.794	**931.422**	2.405	**0.017**	**0.268**	**4.23**
	Liu [15], s = 0.16	**124**	**16.048**	2588.09	4.953	0.006	0.1	1.597
	Sivignon [25], e = 2.5	124	16.048	1203.97	**2.057**	0.013	0.214	3.433
Figure 9(c)	Algorithm 2 using ATC	127	22.583	1950.001	2.861	0.0116	0.262	5.906
$n = 2868$	Algorithm 2 using MATC	**126**	**22.762**	**1924.778**	3.113	**0.0118**	**0.269**	**6.127**
	Liu [15], s = 0.021	126	22.762	5712	5.16	0.004	0.091	2.065
	Sivignon [25], e = 2.9	128	22.406	2360.35	**2.043**	0.009	0.213	4.766

6.2 Comparisons with Other Methods

The comparisons are also performed with two other recent methods whose source code was made publicly available by the authors: Liu *et al.* [15] and Sivignon [25]. More precisely, the method proposed by Liu *et al.* in [15] is a polygonal reconstruction from the visual curvature using a parameter s associated to the scale of the contour analysis. The method by Sivignon in [25] computes a simplification of the curve such that the Fréchet distance between the original and the simplified curve is less than the error e. The experiments are performed on the curves in Fig. 9(a) and (c). For a fair comparison, we choose the value of scale s in [15] and error e in [25] such that the resulting polygon has the number of vertices V being closed to this detected by Algorithm 2 using MATC. The results are given in Table 2 and Fig. 9(b) and (d).

The proposed method – in particular with MATC – provides, as expected, the best values of FOM_n for $n = 1, 2, 3$ but also good values of ISSE. The results by Sivignon's method [25] have the best L_∞, it is normal as this method minimizes the distance between the curve and the simplified polygon. Yet, our methods provide competitive results of L_∞ as they are very close to the best values.

7 Conclusion and Perspectives

In this paper, we present the structure of modified adaptive tangential cover (MATC) deduced from the noise estimator of meaningful thickness. The MATC of a digital curve is composed of maximal blurred segments of various thicknesses transmitting the noise levels along the curve and the geometrical structure of the given curve. An algorithm of polygonal simplification is then proposed using this structure of MATC. This parameter-free method permits to obtain good results on the contour of digital shapes with or without noise. The implementation of polygonal simplification, based on the DGtal [1] library, is available for testing from an online demonstration and a *GitHub* source code repository: http://ipol-geometry.loria.fr/~phuc/ipol_demo/PAMATC_IPOLDemo.

The proposed method can be involved in contour-based corner detection which consists in extracting planar curves from images then find local curvature maximal points on the curves. Furthermore, the obtained polygon of the contour of a shape can be applied in a classification process. On the other hand, the MATC can be used to study the geometric estimators of digital curves [18], the decomposition of curves into arcs and segments [19]. In this paper, we only compare the results of the proposed method with two methods [15,25]. In future, we would like to conduct more comparisons with the state-of-the-art methods on the more real data.

References

1. DGtal: Digital geometry tools and algorithms library. http://libdgtal.org
2. Kima216 database. http://classif.ai/dataset/kima216
3. Attneave, E.: Some informational aspects of visual perception. Psychol. Rev. **61**(3), 183–193 (1954)
4. Carmona-Poyato, A., Fernández-García, N.L., Medina-Carnicer, R., Madrid-Cuevas, F.J.: Dominant point detection: a new proposal. Image Vis. Comput. **23**(13), 1226–1236 (2005)
5. Prasad, D.K., Leung, M.L.: Polygonal representation of digital curves. In: Digital Image Processing (2012)
6. Faure, A., Buzer, L., Feschet, F.: Tangential cover for thick digital curves. Pattern Recogn. **42**(10), 2279–2287 (2009)
7. Isabelle, D.R., Fabien, F., Jocelyne, R.D.: Optimal blurred segments decomposition of noisy shapes in linear time. Comput. Graph. **30**(1), 30–36 (2006)
8. Isabelle, D.R., Rémy, J.L., Jocelyne, R.D.: Segmentation of discrete curves into fuzzy segments. Discrete Math. **12**, 372–383 (2003)
9. Kerautret, B., Lachaud, J.-O.: Multi-scale analysis of discrete contours for unsupervised noise detection. In: Wiederhold, P., Barneva, R.P. (eds.) IWCIA 2009. LNCS, vol. 5852, pp. 187–200. Springer, Heidelberg (2009). https://doi.org/10.1007/978-3-642-10210-3_15
10. Kerautret, B., Lachaud, J.O.: Meaningful scales detection along digital contours for unsupervised local noise estimation. IEEE Trans. Pattern Anal. Mach. Intell. **34**(12), 2379–2392 (2012)
11. Kerautret, B., Lachaud, J.O., Said, M.: Meaningful thicknes detection on polygonal curve. In: International Conference on Pattern Recognition Applications and Methods, pp. 372–379 (2012)
12. Klette, R., Rosenfeld, A.: Digital Geometry - Geometric Methods for Digital Picture Analysis. Morgan Kaufmann, Burlington (2004)
13. Lachaud, J.O.: Espaces non-euclidiens et analyse d'image: modèles déformables riemanniens et discrets, topologie et géométrie discrète. Habilitation à Diriger des Recherches, Université Bordeaux 1, Talence, France (2006). (in French)
14. Lachaud, J.-O.: Digital shape analysis with maximal segments. In: Köthe, U., Montanvert, A., Soille, P. (eds.) WADGMM 2010. LNCS, vol. 7346, pp. 14–27. Springer, Heidelberg (2012). https://doi.org/10.1007/978-3-642-32313-3_2
15. Liu, H., Latecki, L.J., Liu, W.: A unified curvature definition for regular, polygonal, and digital planar curves. Inter. J. Comput. Vis. **80**(1), 104–124 (2008)
16. Marji, M., Siy, P.: Polygonal representation of digital planar curves through dominant point detection - a nonparametric algorithm. Pattern Recogn. **37**(11), 2113–2130 (2004)

17. Nasser, H., Ngo, P., Debled-Rennesson, I.: Dominant point detection based on discrete curve structure and applications. J. Comput. Syst. Sci. **85**, 177–192 (2018)
18. Ngo, P., Debled-Rennesson, I., Kerautret, B., Nasser, H.: Analysis of noisy digital contours with adaptive tangential cover. J. Math. Imaging Vis. **59**(1), 123–135 (2017)
19. Ngo, P., Nasser, H., Debled-Rennesson, I.: A discrete approach for decomposing noisy digital contours into arcs and segments. In: Chen, C.-S., Lu, J., Ma, K.-K. (eds.) ACCV 2016. LNCS, vol. 10117, pp. 493–505. Springer, Cham (2017). https://doi.org/10.1007/978-3-319-54427-4_36
20. Ngo, P., Nasser, H., Debled-Rennesson, I.: Efficient dominant point detection based on discrete curve structure. In: Barneva, R.P., Bhattacharya, B.B., Brimkov, V.E. (eds.) IWCIA 2015. LNCS, vol. 9448, pp. 143–156. Springer, Cham (2015). https://doi.org/10.1007/978-3-319-26145-4_11
21. Nguyen, T.P., Debled-Rennesson, I.: A discrete geometry approach for dominant point detection. Pattern Recogn. **44**(1), 32–44 (2011)
22. Nguyen, T.P., Kerautret, B., Debled-Rennesson, I., Lachaud, J.-O.: Unsupervised, fast and precise recognition of digital arcs in noisy images. In: Bolc, L., Tadeusiewicz, R., Chmielewski, L.J., Wojciechowski, K. (eds.) ICCVG 2010. LNCS, vol. 6374, pp. 59–68. Springer, Heidelberg (2010). https://doi.org/10.1007/978-3-642-15910-7_7
23. Ray, K.S., Ray, B.K.: Polygonal Approximation and Scale-Space Analysis of Closed Digital Curves. CRC Press, Boca Raton (2013)
24. Sarkar, D.: A simple algorithm for detection of significant vertices for polygonal approximation of chain-coded curves. Pattern Recogn. Lett. **14**(12), 959–964 (1993)
25. Sivignon, I.: A near-linear time guaranteed algorithm for digital curve simplification under the fréchet distance. Image Process. Line **4**, 116–127 (2014)

Learning the Graph Edit Distance Parameters for Point-Set Image Registration

Shaima Algabli, Pep Santacruz, and Francesc Serratosa[(✉)]

Universitat Rovira i Virgili, Tarragona, Catalonia, Spain
shaima.ahmed@estudiants.urv.cat,
{joseluis.santacruz,francesc.serratosa}@urv.cat

Abstract. Alignment of point sets is frequently used in pattern recognition when objects are represented by sets of coordinate points. The idea behind this problem is to be able to compare two objects regardless of the effect of a given transformation on their coordinate data. This paper presents a method to align point sets based on the graph edit distance. The main idea is to learn the edit costs (in a learning step) and then apply graph edit distance (in a pattern recognition step) with the learned edit costs. Thus, the edit cost would have to incorporate the transformation parameters. In the experimental section, we show that the method is competitive if the graph edit distance parameters are automatically learned considering the learning set. These parameters are the insertion and deletion costs and also the weights on the substitution costs.

Keywords: Point set alignment · Graph edit distance · Learning edit costs · Graph-matching algorithm

1 Introduction

The core of many object recognition applications, in which objects are defined by coordinate data, is the point set alignment. For instance, medical image analysis or reconstructing a scene from various views [11]. The idea behind it is to be able to compare two objects regardless of the effects of a given transformation on their coordinate data. The aim of this paper is to present a method for point set alignment based on the graph edit distance. Recently, Deep learning techniques have been used to perform image registration. Nevertheless, it has to be considered that these techniques can only be properly used in huge databases, which it is not always the case. For this reason, we consider it is worth analysing old methods and presenting new ones based on point-set alignment.

Given that the point correspondences are known, some years ago, there was an extensive work done towards the goal of finding the alignment parameters that minimise some error measure. To cite a few, [14] and [13] deal with isometries and

© Springer Nature Switzerland AG 2019
M. Vento and G. Percannella (Eds.): CAIP 2019, LNCS 11678, pp. 447–456, 2019.
https://doi.org/10.1007/978-3-030-29888-3_36

similarity transformations; [2] and [29] deal with Euclidean transformations (i.e. excluding reflections from isometries); [10] deals with similarity and projective transformations; and [11] deals exclusively with projective transformations.

However, the point-set alignment problem is often found in the more realistic setting of unknown point-to-point correspondences. This problem becomes then a registration problem, that is, one of jointly estimating the alignment and correspondence parameters. Although non-iterative algorithms exist for specific types of transformation models [12], this problem is usually solved by means of non-linear iterative methods that, at each iteration, estimate correspondence and alignment parameters. Despite being more computationally demanding, iterative methods are more appealing to us than the direct ones due to its superior tolerance to noise and outliers.

We distinguish between two families of approaches to solve this problem. Ones are based on the Expectation Maximization (EM) algorithm [5], and the others use Softassign [7,8,18]. The former ones have the advantage of offering statistical insights of such decoupled estimation processes while the latter ones benefit from the well-known robustness and convergence properties of the Softassign embedded within deterministic annealing procedures.

Coherent Point Drift (CPD) [17] is a point-set registration method that uses the EM algorithm that is defined for rigid, affine and non-rigid transformations. Moreover, Robust Point Matching (RPM) [8,18] is a method that uses Softassign that is defined for affine and rigid transformations. Later, TPS-RPM [3] was presented, which is an extension to non-rigid transformations of RPM.

Graph matching approaches allow for neighbouring relations between points to be considered into the point-set registration problem. Graduated Assignment [7] and Bipartite graph matching [6,20,23–25] are remarkable graph matching methods that use Softassign and Least Sum Assignment solvers. An approach for graph matching and point-set alignment using the EM algorithm that was defined for affinities and projectivities was presented in [4]. One limitation of this approach is the high computational demand of the dictionary-based structural model. In [15], it was proposed an EM-like approach for graph matching and point-set alignment based on a cross-entropy measure. They proposed a model of structural errors based on a Bernoulli distribution. This model was defined as rigid-body transformations. Finally, [21] proposed a joint structural graph matching and point-set registration method whose main contribution was to bridge the gap between the EM-based and the Softassign-based approaches by formulating the graph matching problem within a principled statistical framework, while benefiting from the desirable properties of the Softassign and deterministic annealing ensemble.

The aim of this paper is to present an image registration method based on the graph edit distance [19,28]. That is, we present a classical graph matching approach based on a well-known distance between graphs. The novelty of the method is not the transformation of the image into an attributed graphs neither the graph edit distance itself. Contrarily, the novelty is to show a method that has the capability of learning the parameters of the graph edit distance such that the image registration is properly carried out. In the past, any paper was presented that learned the graph edit distance parameters and directly applied the graph edit distance to deduce the salient points correspondences. We assume it was due to the graph edit distance parameters were manually tuned and then, the deduced graph correspondence was far away from the optimal one. This was the reason why other mechanisms were presented that, in the process itself, somehow related the graphs into the images, for instance methods [4,15,21]. Note that the information on the salient points (and thus, on the nodes of the graphs) is usually composed of a vector larger or equal to 60 elements. This feature makes impossible to manually tune the weights on each vector element.

The outline of the paper is as follows. In the next section, we define attributed graphs and graph edit distance. In Sect. 3, we present the learning strategy applied to image registration. In Sect. 4, we show the experimental validation and finally, in Sect. 5, we conclude the article.

2 Graph Edit Distance

The Graph Edit Distance (GED) [27] between two attributed graphs is defined as the transformation from one graph into another, through the edit operations, which obtains the minimum cost. These edit operations are: Substitution, deletion and insertion of nodes and also edges. Every edit operation has a cost depending on the attributes on the involved nodes or edges. This graph transformation can be defined through a node-to-node mapping f between nodes of both graphs.

Having a pair of graphs, G and G', a correspondence f between these graphs is a bijective function that assigns one node of G to only one node of G'. We suppose both graphs have the same number of nodes since they have been expanded with new nodes that have a concrete attribute. We call these new nodes as $Null$. Note that the mapping between edges is imposed by the mapping of the nodes whose edges are connected.

We define G_i as the ith node in G, G'_a as the ath node in G', $G_{i,j}$ as the edge between the ith node and the jth node in G, $G'_{a,b}$ as the edge between the ath node and the bth node in G'. Nodes and edges have N and M attributes, which are Real numbers, respectively. Moreover, γ_i^t is the tth attribute of node G_i and $\beta_{i,j}^t$ is the tth attribute of edge $G_{i,j}$. We also define the mapping $f(i) = a$ from G_i to G'_a, we say that it represents a node substitution if both nodes are not $Null$. Contrarily, if node G'_a is a $Null$ and G_i is not, we say that it represents a deletion. Finally, if node G_i is a $Null$ and G'_a is not, we say that it represents an insertion. Similarly happens with the edges. The case that both nodes or both edges are null is not considered since the cost is always zero.

We define the GED as follows:

$$GED(G, G') = \min_{\forall f: G \to G'} \left\{ \sum_{\forall G_i} C^n(i,a) + \sum_{\forall G_{i,j}} C^e(i,j,a,b) \right\} \tag{1}$$

Where, $f(i) = a$, $f(j) = b$, functions $C^n(i, a)$ and $C^e(i, j, a, b)$ represent the cost of mapping a pair of nodes (G_i and G'_a) and a pair of edges ($G_{i,j}$ and $G'_{a,b}$), respectively, and they are defined through the cost functions in Eqs. 2 and 3.

$$C^n(i, a) = \begin{cases} C^n_S(i, a) & \text{if } G_i \neq Null \wedge G'_a \neq Null \\ C^n_D(i) & \text{if } G_i \neq Null \wedge G'_a = Null \\ C^n_I(a) & \text{if } G_i = Null \wedge G'_a \neq Null \end{cases} \quad (2)$$

$$C^e(i, j, a, b) = \begin{cases} C^e_S(i, j, a, b) & \text{if } G_{i,j} \neq Null \wedge G'_{a,b} \neq Null \\ C^e_D(i, j) & \text{if } G_{i,j} \neq Null \wedge G'_{a,b} = Null \\ C^e_I(a, b) & \text{if } G_{i,j} = Null \wedge G'_{a,b} \neq Null \end{cases} \quad (3)$$

Where $C^n_S(i, a)$ is the cost of substituting node G_i by node G'_a, $C^n_D(i)$ is the cost of deleting node G_i and $C^n_I(a)$ is the cost of inserting node G'_a. Similarly, $C^e_S(i, j, a, b)$ is the cost of substituting edge $G_{i,j}$ by edge $G'_{a,b}$, $C^e_D(i, j)$ is the cost of deleting edge $G_{i,j}$ and $C^e_I(a, b)$ is the cost of inserting edge $G'_{a,b}$.

The learning method used in this paper, [1], assumes the deletion and insertion costs of nodes and edges are constant and also that the substitution costs are a weighted Euclidean distance between the attributes of the nodes. In our case, it means that deleting any salient point or edge is independent of the features of the involved salient points and also that the cost of substituting a pair of salient points depends on the points' attributes. More concretely, the restrictions on the insertion and deletion operations are $C^n_I(a) = C^n_D(i) = K^n$ and $C^e_I(a, b) = C^e_D(i, j) = K^e$, where $K^n, K^e \in R$. And the restrictions on the node substitutions are $C^n_S(i, a) = \sum_{t=1}^{N} w^n_t \left\| \gamma^t_i - \gamma'^t_a \right\|$, where $w^n = (w^n_1, ..., w^n_N)$ is the vector of node attributes' weights, in which $\sum_{t=1}^{N} w^n_t = 1$. In our application, edges do not have attributes, thus $C^e_S(i, j, a, b) = 0$.

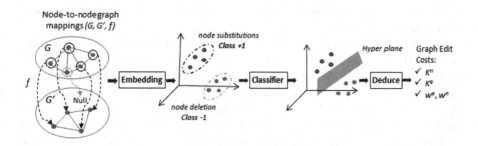

Fig. 1. Basic scheme of the off-line learning method.

3   Learning the Graph Edit Costs for Image Registration

In this section, we first plainly summarise the method presented in [1] since it is the method applied to learn the image registration parameters. Note in [1], the

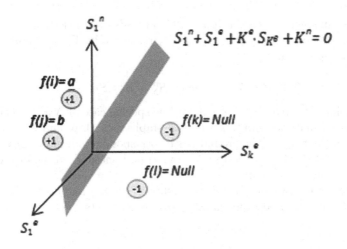

Fig. 2. Hyper-plane obtained in the learning process when $N = 1$.

learning method was presented in a general form, that is, independently of the application at hand and therefore what the attributed graphs represent. In this paper, attributed graphs represent images in which nodes are salient points and edge relations between them (as commented in Sect. 1), and for this reason, the summary has been adapted to our application.

The algorithm is composed of four main steps (Fig. 1):

- In the first step (Feature extraction), the system receives a set of images in which salient points and correspondences are selected either manually of using an algorithm. Then, these sets of points and their correspondences are transformed into triplets composed of two graphs and a ground-truth correspondence between them, $\{(G, G', f)_1, (G, G', f)_2, ...\}$. Figure 1 only shows one triplet composed of two graphs that have five and four nodes, respectively. The ground-truth correspondence is represented through the dashed arrows. Four nodes are substituted and one node is deleted.
- In the second step (Embedding), the ground-truth node-to-node mappings are embedded into a Euclidean space S, $S = (S_1^n, ..., S_N^n, S_{K^e})$ of dimension $N + 1$. Each node substitution is transformed into a point in this space and it is assigned the "$+1$" class. Moreover, each node deletion is transformed into $\tilde{N}$ points, which are assigned the "-1" class. $\tilde{N}$ is the number of substituted nodes in the ground-truth correspondence. The ground-truth correspondence in Fig. 1 makes the embedding step to generate four points that represent the four node substitution operations (one point per substitution) and four points that represent the only one node deletion (the number of points that generate each deletion is the number of substituted nodes).
- In the third step (Classifier), a linear hyper-plane is computed that has to be the best linear border between both classes. Authors in [1] describe that any known linear classifier that return the hyper-plane can be used. Equation 4 defines this border, as described in [1]. Note the constants in this hyper-plane

are the substitution weights $w_2^n, ..., w_N^n$ and also the insertion and deletion costs on nodes and edges K^n and K^e, respectively. Finally, note that w_1^n does not appear in Eq. 4.

$$S_1^n + w_2^n \cdot S_2^n + ... + w_N^n \cdot S_N^n + K^e \cdot S_{K^e} + K^n = 0 \qquad (4)$$

For explanatory reasons, Fig. 2 shows the specific case of $N = 2$, where S is a 3D dimensional space. In this example, graphs have three and two nodes (not shown in the figure). The ground-truth correspondence imposes two nodes to be substituted (they generate two points) and one node to be deleted (that also generates two points).

– Finally, in the last step (Deduce), weights $w_1^n, ..., w_N^n$ and also constants K^n, and K^e are extracted from the hyper-plane constants.

Table 1. Mean projection error on each database.

	Boat	East park	East south	Residence
Sanromà	48	49	25	25
Unified	150	130	120	135
Dual step	54	35	28	28
Graduated assignment	175	120	126	120
Matching by correlation	185	130	130	150
Neural network	36	30	19	27
Graph edit distance	0	0	0	0

4   Experimental Validation

Four databases have been used to test the proposed method and compare it to known image registration methods: *Boat, East park, South park* and *Residence*. These databases are composed of sequences of images, in which there is the same object but the point of view has been slightly modified (www.featurespace.org). From these databases, we have extracted 50 salient points per each image using the *SURF* extractor. Moreover, we have generated attributed graphs that nodes are the salient points and edges have been deduced by Delaunay triangulation. The attributes on the nodes are the information deduced by the *SURF* extractor (a vector of 60 elements) and edges are unattributed. Finally, a ground-truth correspondence between the salient points of adjacent images in the sequences have been manually deduced, for testing purposes. Not all the 50 salient points are present in all the images in the sequence, for this reason, the ground-truth correspondences have substitutions (a salient point of the first image is mapped to a salient point of the second image), deletions (the salient point of the second image is not present) and insertions operations (the salient point of the first image is not present). The databases composed of these sequence of graphs are available at [26] and an extended explanation of the databases were published in [16]. Figure 3 shows an image of each database with their attributed graph.

BOAT   EAST_PARK

EAST_SOUTH   RESID

Fig. 3. An example of an image per database

Using these databases, the learning algorithm in [1] was able to learn the substitution costs C^S, the insertion costs C^I and the deletion costs C^D. Then, we analysed the ability of the graph edit distance to deduce the salient point correspondence between pair of images, given these costs. Recall that the point correspondence is the first step to perform image registration. The point correspondence deduced by the graph edit distance was compared to classical methods, such as Sanroma [21], Unified [15], Dual step [4], Graduated assignment [9], Matching by correlation [4], Neural Network [22] and Algabli [1].

The quality of the point correspondences has been set through two metrics: The mean projector error and the number of mapped points. The mean projector error is a quality measure that informs of the mean Euclidean distance between the receiving pixel of the ground truth and the receiving pixel of the correspondence deduced by the matching algorithm, given all the mapped points of all pairs of images. The number of mapped points is a simpler measure, which informs of how many points on the first image are mapped to points on the second image. Note that in this case, the ground-truth correspondence does not influence on this measure.

Table 1 shows the mean projector error deduced by each algorithm using the previously commented databases. We realise there are extreme values. For instance, the graph edit distance with the edit costs learned by Algabli [1] (the method we wanted to analyse) generates zero error but Matching by correlation [4] generates an error between 130 and 185. Having seen these results, it is important also to have a look at Table 2, which shows the mean number of mapped points per pair of images. Note that the last row refers to this measure given the ground truth correspondence. Thus, if an algorithm returns a mean number of mapped points lower than the ground truth number, it means that the algorithm tends to map too few points or discard good ones. Conversely, if an algorithm returns a mean number higher than the ground truth number, it means that the algorithm tends to map too much points, and thus, it maps points that would not have to be mapped.

Comparing the selected algorithms, on the one side, we realise that the graph edit distance generates a zero mean projection error but it also generates few number of mapped points. Thus, this algorithm only returned the mapped points with a high confidence. On the other side, Unified [15], Graduated assignment [9] and Matching by correlation [4] mapped all the points and, for this reason, they generated the highest mean projection error.

We conclude the quality of these matching algorithms cannot be analysed without considering the mean projection error and also the mean number of mapped points. Moreover, it is usually preferable to return a low number of mapped points but having a good quality (low mean projection error) than to return a larger number of mapped points but increasing the number of wrong ones. This is because, only some mapped points is enough to deduce the image transformation. Besides, the algorithms that approximate the image transformations usually return better results with few non-noisy points than with a larger number of points, which some of them being noisy.

Table 2. Mean number of mapped points on each database.

	Boat	East park	East south	Residence
Sanromà	29	38	37	35
Unified	50	50	50	50
Dual step	35	32	33	35
Graduated assignment	50	50	50	50
Matching by correlation	50	50	50	50
Neural network	18	23	17	22
Graph edit distance	9.24	9.6	9.48	10
Ground truth	17.44	16.16	12.80	17.56

5   Conclusions

We have presented a method to perform point set alignment based on transforming the point sets in attributed graphs and then deducing the distance between attributed graphs by the graph edit distance. Point set alignment is an old problem and several methods have been presented to solve it. Some of them only make use of the information of the points but other ones convert the point set into an attributed graph, through considering the value around the pixel and also the pixel position. The main difference between our method and the methods based on graphs is that we do not specifically introduce any mechanism related to the fact that graphs represent point sets. The novelty of this paper is to show that properly tuning the graph edit distance (learning them through an automatic method) is enough to achieve competitive results in some public databases. In this paper, we have used an specific learning algorithm but other ones could be used.

The experimental section corroborates our theory, since the classical graph edit distance, in which the weights on the edit costs have been automatically learned, returns competitive results with regard to the algorithms devoted to perform image alignment.

Acknowledgements. This research is supported by projects TIN2016-77836-C2-1-R and DPI2016-78957-R. And also the European projects AEROARMS (H2020-ICT-2014-1-644271).

References

1. Algabli, S., Serratosa, F.: Embedding the node-to-node mappings to learn the graph edit distance parameters. Pattern Recogn. Lett. **112**, 353–360 (2018)
2. Berge, J.M.F.: The rigid orthogonal procrustes rotation problem. Psychometrika **71**(1), 201–205 (2006). https://doi.org/10.1007/s11336-004-1160-5
3. Chui, H., Rangarajan, A.: A new algorithm for non-rigid point matching. In: CVPR (2000)
4. Cross, A.D.J., Hancock, E.E.: Graph matching with a dual-step EM algorithm. IEEE Trans. Pattern Anal. Mach. Intell. **20**, 1236–1253 (1998)
5. Dempster, A.P., Laird, N.M., Rubin, D.B.: Maximum likelihood from incomplete data via the EM algorithm. Statist. Soc. Ser. B (Methodol.) **39**, 1–22 (1977)
6. Ferrer, M., Serratosa, F., Riesen, K.: Improving bipartite graph matching by assessing the assignment confidence. Pattern Recogn. Lett. **65**, 29–36 (2015). https://doi.org/10.1016/j.patrec.2015.07.010
7. Gold, S., Rangarajan, A.: A graduated assignment algorithm for graph matching. IEEE Trans. Pattern Anal. Mach. Intell. **18**, 377–388 (1996)
8. Gold, S., Rangarajan, A., Lu, C.P., Pappu, S., Mjolsness, E.: New algorithms for 2D and 3D point matching: pose estimation and correspondence. Pattern Recogn. **31**, 1019–1031 (1998)
9. Gold, S., Rangarajan, A.: A graduated assignment algorithm for graph matching. IEEE Trans. Pattern Anal. Mach. Intell. **18**(4), 377–388 (1996). https://doi.org/10.1109/34.491619
10. Haralick, R.M., Joo, H., Lee, C., Zhuang, X., Vaidya, V.G., Kim, M.B.: Pose estimation from corresponding point data. IEEE Trans. Syst. Man Cybern. **19**(6), 1426–1446 (1989)
11. Hartley, R.I., Zisserman, A.: Multiple View Geometry in Computer Vision, 2nd edn. Cambridge University Press, Cambridge (2004). ISBN: 0521540518

12. Ho, J., Yang, M.H.: On affine registration of planar point sets using complex numbers. Comput. Vis. Image Underst. **115**, 50–58 (2011)

13. Kendall, D.: Shape manifolds, procrustean metrics, and complex projective spaces. Lond Math. Soc. **16**, 81–121 (1984)

14. Dryden, I.L., Mardia, K.V.: Statistical Shape Analysis, Wiley Series in Probability and Statistics: Probability and Statistics. Wiley, Hoboken (1998). ISBN: 9780470699621

15. Luo, B., Hancock, E.: A unified framework for alignment and correspondence. Comput. Vis. Image Underst. **92**, 26–55 (2003)

16. Moreno-García, C.F., Cortés, X., Serratosa, F.: A graph repository for learning error-tolerant graph matching. In: Robles-Kelly, A., Loog, M., Biggio, B., Escolano, F., Wilson, R. (eds.) S+SSPR 2016. LNCS, vol. 10029, pp. 519–529. Springer, Cham (2016). https://doi.org/10.1007/978-3-319-49055-7_46

17. Myronenko, A., Song, X.: Point set registration coherent point drift. IEEE Trans. Pattern Anal. Mach. Intell. **32**, 2262–2275 (2010)

18. Rangarajan, A., Chui, H., Bookstein, F.L.: The softassign procrustes matching algorithm. In: Duncan, J., Gindi, G. (eds.) IPMI 1997. LNCS, vol. 1230, pp. 29–42. Springer, Heidelberg (1997). https://doi.org/10.1007/3-540-63046-5_3

19. Riesen, K.: Structural Pattern Recognition with Graph Edit Distance. ACVPR. Springer, Cham (2015). https://doi.org/10.1007/978-3-319-27252-8

20. Riesen, K., Bunke, H.: Approximate graph edit distance computation by means of bipartite graph matching. Image Vis. Comput. **27**(7), 950–959 (2009)

21. Sanroma, G., Alquézar, R., Serratosa, F., Herrera, B.: Smooth point-set registration using neighboring constraints. Pattern Recogn. Lett. **33**(15), 2029–2037 (2012)

22. Santacruz, P., Serratosa, F.: Learning the sub-optimal graph edit distance edit costs based on an embedded model. In: Bai, X., Hancock, E.R., Ho, T.K., Wilson, R.C., Biggio, B., Robles-Kelly, A. (eds.) S+SSPR 2018. LNCS, vol. 11004, pp. 282–292. Springer, Cham (2018). https://doi.org/10.1007/978-3-319-97785-0_27

23. Serratosa, F.: Fast computation of bipartite graph matching. Pattern Recogn. Lett. **45**, 244–250 (2014)

24. Serratosa, F.: Speeding up fast bipartite graph matching through a new cost matrix. Int. J. Pattern Recogn. Artif. Intell. **29**, 1550010 (2014). https://doi.org/10.1142/S021800141550010X

25. Serratosa, F.: Computation of graph edit distance: reasoning about optimality and speed-up. Image Vis. Comput. **40**, 38–48 (2015)

26. Serratosa, F.: Graph databases (2015). http://deim.urv.cat/~francesc.serratosa/databases/

27. Serratosa, F.: Graph edit distance: restrictions to be a metric. Pattern Recogn. **90**, 250–256 (2019). https://doi.org/10.1016/j.patcog.2019.01.043

28. Serratosa, F., Cortés, X.: Interactive graph-matching using active query strategies. Pattern Recogn. **48**(4), 1364–1373 (2015). https://doi.org/10.1016/j.patcog.2014.10.033

29. Umeyama, S.: Least squares estimation of transformation parameters between two point patterns. IEEE Trans. Pattern Anal. Mach. Intell. **13**, 376–380 (1991)

An Explainable AI-Based Computer Aided Detection System for Diabetic Retinopathy Using Retinal Fundus Images

Adrian Kind[1](✉) and George Azzopardi[2](✉)

[1] University of Malta, Msida, Malta
kindadrian@gmail.com
[2] University of Groningen, Groningen, The Netherlands

Abstract. Diabetic patients have a high risk of developing diabetic retinopathy (DR), which is one of the major causes of blindness. With early detection and the right treatment patients may be spared from losing their vision. We propose a computer-aided detection system, which uses retinal fundus images as input and it detects all types of lesions that define diabetic retinopathy. The aim of our system is to assist eye specialists by automatically detecting the healthy retinas and referring the images of the unhealthy ones. For the latter cases, the system offers an interactive tool where the doctor can examine the local lesions that our system marks as suspicious. The final decision remains in the hands of the ophthalmologists. Our approach consists of a multi-class detector, that is able to locate and recognize all candidate DR-defining lesions. If the system detects at least one lesion, then the image is marked as unhealthy. The lesion detector is built on the faster R-CNN ResNet 101 architecture, which we train by transfer learning. We evaluate our approach on three benchmark data sets, namely Messidor-2, IDRiD, and E-Ophtha by measuring the sensitivity (SE) and specificity (SP) based on the binary classification of healthy and unhealthy images. The results that we obtain for Messidor-2 and IDRiD are (SE: 0.965, SP: 0.843), and (SE: 0.83, SP: 0.94), respectively. For the E-Ophtha data set we follow the literature and perform two experiments, one where we detect only lesions of the type micro aneurysms (SE: 0.939, SP: 0.82) and the other when we detect only exudates (SE: 0.851, SP: 0.971). Besides the high effectiveness that we achieve, the other important contribution of our work is the interactive tool, which we offer to the medical experts, highlighting all suspicious lesions detected by the proposed system.

Keywords: Computer-aided detection · Diabetic retinopathy · Object detection · Convolutional neural networks · ResNet

© Springer Nature Switzerland AG 2019
M. Vento and G. Percannella (Eds.): CAIP 2019, LNCS 11678, pp. 457–468, 2019.
https://doi.org/10.1007/978-3-030-29888-3_37

1   Introduction

Diabetic retinopathy (DR) is responsible for the visual loss and blindness of millions of people world-wide. Statistics show that such diabetic retinal diseases are on the increase [16]. The early diagnosis and treatment of ocular diseases reduces progression of such illnesses and provides better quality of life. Currently, mass-screening programs are very expensive to conduct and are laborious and prone to error. Ophthalmologists and trained specialists are hard pressed to keep up with the large demands imposed by such a labour-intensive procedure.

Globally, it was estimated that in 2017 there were 451 million people with diabetes worldwide. These figures were expected to increase to 693 million by 2045 [4], Fig. 1a. As a consequence, the number of people with DR will grow from 126.6 million in 2010 to 191.0 million by 2030 [18], Fig. 1b. Such statistics indicate that diabetic retinopathy cases are on the increase and that it is difficult to have enough medical specialists running mass screening programs.

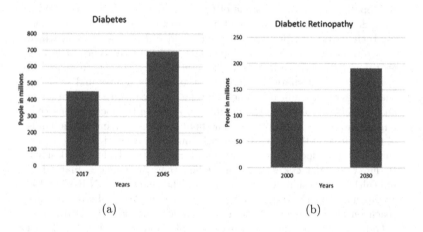

(a)   (b)

Fig. 1. Worldwide projections of (a) diabetes and (b) diabetic retinopathy [18].

Most vision problems are often asymptomatic at the early stages, and the affected persons only realize there may be a problem when their conditions worsen. Such pathology may lead to visual impairment and even to blindness in just a few years. More effort is required to address these issues in order to reduce the unacceptable amount of unnecessary blindness.

There is, therefore, a growing need to semi-automate mass-screening programs for the identification of diabetic retinopathy at an early stage followed by regular monitoring. Automating such a diagnostic system would reduce waiting lists and would also result in mass-screening that is more efficient, more effective and financially feasible. The current lengthy process delays any intervention that needs to be performed to prevent or slow down the disease, the effects of which may lead to vision impairment or even blindness.

We propose a computer-aided detection system that automatically classifies retinal images into healthy and unhealthy. The system draws bounding boxes around lesions that define diabetic retinopathy and provides an interactive tool to the medical experts that allows them to conduct a further in-depth examination. Ultimately, it is the ophthalmologist who makes the decision of whether the concerned retina is healthy or not. For each processed image, the system that we propose generates a report including the list of lesions detected and an image showing the location of the detected lesions. This allows medical experts understanding the reason for the healthy and unhealthy classification and taking better informed decisions. This software is presented as an online web solution and can be easily used from a browser.

1.1 Related Work

Deep learning is a term coined for data driven learning mechanisms composed of multiple layers to learn representations of data with numerous levels of abstraction [10]. Convolutional Neural Networks (CNNs) are special types of networks that learn vision-based and data-driven classification models by means of deep learning. AlexNet [9] was the winning CNN in the image classification and object recognition competition called ImageNet Large Scale Visual Recognition Challenge [15] for the first time in 2012. The error rate was nearly cut in half from the previous year. From then onwards new and more sophisticated architectures have been introduced. Such architectures include GoogLeNet [17], and ResNet (Deep Residual Learning for Image Recognition) by He et al. [8], among others.

There are various state-of-the-art works that propose automatic methods for the detection of DR from retinal fundus images and the best results have been achieved from those that are based on deep learning. Image classification using convolutional neural networks is the main architecture used to diagnose fundus images and detect DR. Some of the best works published using these techniques include that of Gulshan et al. [7]. They applied deep learning to develop an algorithm for automated detection of diabetic retinopathy and diabetic macular edema in retinal fundus images. A deep convolutional neural network was trained using a data set of 128,175 retinal images, which were graded three to seven times by a panel of 54 US licensed ophthalmologists and ophthalmology senior residents. The final algorithm was validated using two separate data sets (EyePACS-1 and Messidor-2), both graded by at least seven US board-certified ophthalmologists.

Abramoff et al. [12] presented the IDx-DR commercial product providing a fully autonomous system capable of making the medical decisions safely and effectively. They provided an automated diabetic retinopathy diagnostic solution which has been authorised by the US Food Drug Administration (FDA) for use in clinics. IDx-DR is a commercializing partnership with IBM Watson Health Europe. It consists of a hybrid screening algorithm using both supervised and unsupervised deep learning techniques. That work is developed to detect referable DR (RDR), defined as moderate and worse diabetic retinopathy.

Gargeya et al. [6] developed a data-driven deep learning algorithm for the problem at hand. Their algorithm processes colour retinal fundus images and classifies them as healthy (no retinopathy) or having DR. A total of 75,137 publicly available fundus images were used to train and test their model. Their method was evaluated on the Messidor-2 and E-Ophtha data sets.

The highest sensitivity from automatic DR detection algorithms on public data sets has been measured by Rakhlin et al. [13]. In 2017 they obtained a sensitivity of 0.99 at a specificity of 0.71. They made use of CNNs to diagnose retinal fundus images. For the evaluation, they used the Kaggle and Messidor-2 data sets.

Desbiens et al. [5] also proposed a CNN-based solution for the diagnosis of DR from retinal images. They achieved a sensitivity of 0.93 at a specificity of 0.99. In particular, they built a multi-phase automatic grading system for diabetic retinopathy.

Most of the papers on automated DR detection use deep learning image classifiers, which are trained to give a label to a retinal fundus image as a whole; healthy or unhealthy. In this respect, such systems are considered as black boxes, in that it is difficult to interpret why a given image is labelled in a certain way. The system that we propose is more interpretable, in that it outputs bounding boxes around each suspicious lesion that are characteristic of diabetic retinopathy. As a result, our system allows the medical experts to take better-informed decisions on the images that the system marks as unhealthy.

2   Methods

2.1   Overview

In the following we describe in detail the new approach that we propose. The novelty component of our work is based on learning a multi-lesion detector that can localize the DR-defining lesions. Figure 2 illustrates an overview of the proposed pipeline. The software runs on a browser, and the whole process is initiated on the upload of a retinal fundus image. The system crops the field-of-view (FOV) and performs other pre-processing steps to enhance features and to reduce noise. The resulting image is then processed by an object detection model, which provides the classification, bounding boxes and confidence scores for the detected lesions. A decision function considers the scores of all detected lesions and classifies the given fundus image as Healthy or Unhealthy. Finally, the result is presented to the user on the browser where an interactive tool allows the user to zoom in and to examine both the pre-processed and the original images.

2.2   Pre-processing

We apply a couple of pre-processing steps before analysing the images for diabetic retinopathy. Firstly, we crop the FOV of the retina from the background. This is achieved by first applying contrast-limited adaptive histogram equalization

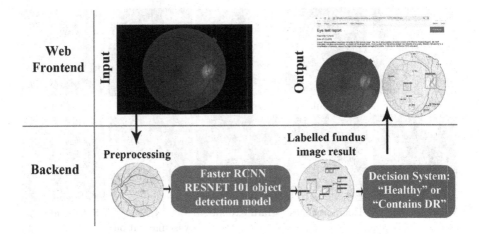

Fig. 2. A high-level overview of the proposed pipeline.

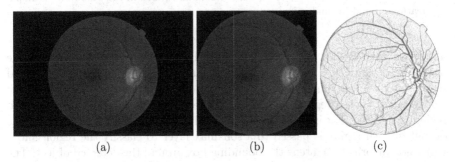

Fig. 3. Pre-processing steps. (a) Input image, (b) segmentation of the field-of-view (FOV), and (c) the Retinex result.

(CLAHE) followed by Gaussian blurring in order to improve the contrast and to smoothen out noise in the given images, respectively. Finally, we consider the outer edges detected by the Canny edge operator [3] in order to delineate the FOV from the background, Fig. 3b.

Secondly, we use the Retinex algorithm with four iterations for further enhancement of the segmented coloured retinal fundus images [11], Fig. 3c. This step provides a means of sharpening the fundus images, improves their colour consistencies regardless of variations in illumination and achieves dynamic range compression.

2.3 Classification Model

The classification model that we propose is one that can distinguish between various retinal healthy and unhealthy features. In particular, we use the Faster R-CNN ResNet 101 COCO as it is very robust in the localization and recognition of patterns of interest [8]. The Faster R-CNN [14] is an object detection

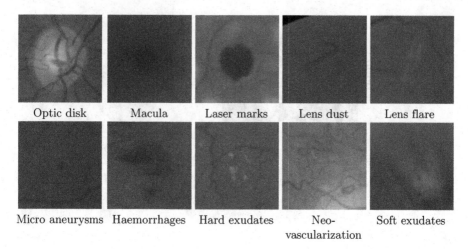

Optic disk   Macula   Laser marks   Lens dust   Lens flare

Micro aneurysms   Haemorrhages   Hard exudates   Neo-   Soft exudates
                                              vascularization

Fig. 4. Examples of all (top row) retinal features and (bottom row) diabetic retinopathy features found in fundus images.

algorithm with Region Proposal Networks (RPN). The RPN process uses the last layer of the CNN and slides a 3 × 3 window across the feature map and maps it to a lower dimension. For each window multiple possible regions are generated. If such a region has a score above a certain threshold the proposed region is selected. For each of these rectangular regions, a CNN is applied. The output of each region is passed to a soft-max layer to classify the region and a regression algorithm tightens the bounding box around the detected object. The architecture of the pre-trained model consists of 101 layers and it was originally trained on the COCO data set. In our work we use transfer learning by using the publicly available pre-trained model[1] as a feature extractor and only re-learn the last layer of the neural network. We also change the output classes of the network with the following 10 labels: optic disk, Macula, laser marks, lens dust and lens flare and the other five are DR-defining lesions, namely microaneurysms (Ma), haemorrhages (H), hard exudates (HE), soft exudates (SE), and neovascularization (NVE). The first five labels are retinal features that are commonly found in healthy retinas and the remaining labels are DR-defining features. Figure 4 shows examples of each of these 10 classes. We identify the DR lesion classes from the study in [2].

For the transfer learning of our model we use the retinal and DR features from 590 images, which we first preprocess using the above mentioned steps and then we manually extract (by cropping) and label 5,243 retinal and DR-defining features. Figure 5 illustrates the output of our system to an image of unhealthy retina.

---

[1] https://tinyurl.com/yxlmyq38.

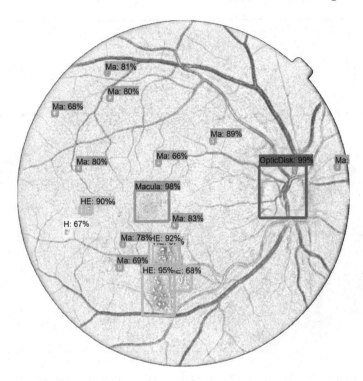

Fig. 5. Example of the output of our system to a retinal image with signs of DR. Each bounding box shows the name of the detected feature along with the confidence score.

2.4 Decision Criteria

A retinal image is marked as unhealthy if the classification model detects at least one DR feature out of the five mentioned above. Such a strict decision criteria is implemented in order to refer all images to the medical experts that contain even very small signs of DR.

2.5 System-Generated Report

For each processed image, our system generates a report containing whether the image is healthy or abnormal, the retinal image and the detected lesions, if any, along with some descriptive text for the medical expert. An example of such a report is shown in Fig. 6. It contains some descriptive text along with both the input image and the pre-processed image with the detected features indicated by bounding boxes and confidence scores.

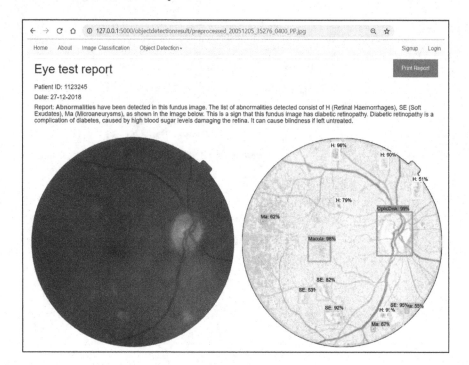

Fig. 6. The final report for a single image generated by our system.

3   Data Sets

We evaluate the proposed system on the retinal fundus images of three public benchmark data sets found online, namely Messidor-2[2] (1748 images), IDRiD[3] test set (103 images) and E-Ophtha[4] (463 images). In total, they contain 2,314 images. We do not use the EyePACS-1 data set mentioned above as it is not publicly available.

The training data, which we used to learn our classification model described above, consist of the retinal and DR features, which we manually labelled from 590 images. We obtained these training images from the public data sets IDRID (training set), KAGGLE[5], DiaRetDB1 V2.1[6] and STARE[7] data sets. Each training fundus image contains between 1 to 30 labelled retinal and DR features, which in total add up to 5,243 samples.

The Messidor-2 data set contains 1,748 images, which are divided into five grades. Grade 0 contains images with No DR, and the remaining grades represent

---

[2] http://www.adcis.net/en/Download-Third-Party/Messidor.html.
[3] https://idrid.grand-challenge.org/.
[4] http://www.adcis.net/en/Download-Third-Party/E-Ophtha.html.
[5] https://www.kaggle.com/c/diabetic-retinopathy-detection/data.
[6] http://www.it.lut.fi/project/imageret/diaretdb1_v2_1/.
[7] http://cecas.clemson.edu/~ahoover/stare/.

images with mild, moderate, severe and proliferative DR, respectively. Of the 1,748 images, 1,017 are grade 0 (i.e. healthy), 270 are grade 1, and the remaining ones have what are known as referable diabetic retinopathy (RDR) with a total of 457 images.

The IDRiD data set is also separated into the same five grades. It contains 103 fundus images where 34 are healthy images and 69 images contain DR.

E-Ophtha contains two sub data sets namely E-Ophtha-MA (Micro aneurysms), and E-Ophtha-EX (Exudates). The two data sets are separated in other two subsets: the first containing the fundus images without DR lesions and the other containing the ones with lesions. There are 381 fundus images labelled with micro aneurysms. Therefore the complete E-Ophtha data set consists of 463 images. The Micro aneurysms data set consists of 148 fundus images and 233 fundus images without Micro aneurysms but may contain other lesions, such as Exudates. On the other hand, the Exudates subset contains 47 images with Exudate lesions and 35 images without Exudates lesions but possibly containing other DR lesions, such as Micro aneurysms and Hemorrhages.

4   Experiments and Results

In the following we describe the experiments that we carried out and report the obtained results. Similar to the related works, for each experiment we count the number of true positives (TP), false positives (FP), true negatives (TN) and false negatives (FN), and subsequently we quantify our results in terms of sensitivity (SN) and specificity (SP).

$$SN = \frac{TP}{FN + TP}, \quad SP = \frac{TN}{TN + FP} \tag{1}$$

An image is counted as TP if the system correctly marks it as unhealthy, while it is counted as FP if the system incorrectly marks it as unhealthy. A TN is counted when the system correctly marks an image as healthy. If the system incorrectly marks an image as healthy then it is counted as FN. Sensitivity and specificity measure the abilities of our method in detecting the truly unhealthy images (aka true positive rate), and the truly healthy ones, respectively.

In Table 1 we report the results that we achieve for the concerned data sets. Similar to the related works we eliminate the mild DR (grade 1) and treat the remaining grades of unhealthy retinas as one unhealthy class.

5   Discussion

We compare our results on the Messidor-2 data set to those of related works in Table 2. The large size and its popularity motivate our decision to focus our comparison on Messidor-2. We compare our results with the best performing methods in the literature. The fundamental difference between our approach and the others lies in the interpretability of the output. Our approach uses an object

Table 1. Experimental results in terms of sensitivity and specificity.

		Predicted healthy	Predicted unhealthy	Sensitivity	Specificity
Messidor-2 1474 images	Healthy	TN: 857	FP: 160	0.965	0.843
	Unhealthy	FN: 16	TP: 441		
IDRiD 103 images	Healthy	TN: 32	FP: 2	0.830	0.940
	Unhealthy	FN: 11	TP: 53		
E-Ophtha-MA 381 images	Healthy	TN: 191	FP: 42	0.939	0.820
	Unhealthy	FN: 9	TP: 139		
E-Ophtha-EX 82 images	Healthy	TN: 34	FP: 1	0.851	0.971
	Unhealthy	FN: 7	TP: 40		

Table 2. Comparison of our results to those of the related works on the Messidor-2 data set. The ground truths labelled as **Grades** and **Ophthalmologists** refer to the standard grades as provided by the Messidor-2 data set, and to proprietary ground truth labelled by ophthalmologists, respectively.

Author	Year	Ground truth	Sensitivity	Specificity
Ours	**2019**	**Grades**	**0.965**	**0.843**
Desbiens et al. [5]	2018	Ophthalmologists	0.929	0.989
Gargeya et al. [6]	2017	Grades	0.930	0.870
Rakhlin et al. [13]	2017	Grades	0.990	0.710
Abramoff et al. [1]	2016	Grades	0.968	0.870
Gulshan et al. [7]	2016	Ophthalmologists	0.961	0.939

detection model, which locates the DR-defining features in a given image and determines their confidence scores. This is in contrast to the other approaches, which address the problem from an image classification point of view and label a given image as healthy or unhealthy without indicating the involved features. Our method, therefore, provides more information - in terms of bounding boxes, labels and confidence scores - to the medical experts as to why the referred images are flagged as unhealthy. The application of the retinex preprocessing algorithm is also a novel introduction to automatic DR detection, which was not encountered in the related work. It provides colour enhancement and makes retinal features much more visible from the background.

For future works we aim to involve medical experts in order to have a bigger and more accurate labelled training set, which will contribute in achieving a more robust data driven classification model. Moreover, we aim to investigate the fusion of our object detection approach with an image classification method. By combining local and global decisions we expect to improve the results even more. Another direction for future work is to investigate a computational model that can also identify the extent (i.e. the grade) of diabetic retinopathy detected in the given images. Such an approach would further improve the efficiency of a mass screening program as the flagged images could then be referred to specific ophthalmologists based on the grade that would be predicted by the system.

6 Conclusion

The proposed computer-aided detection system for the detection of diabetic retinopathy from retinal fundus image is very effective. The novel component of our work is the application of an object detection faster R-CNN ResNet model that is able to localize and recognize all features related to diabetic retinopathy. In this way, our approach assists the medical experts to take better-informed decisions on the referred images.

References

1. Abràmoff, M.D., et al.: Improved automated detection of diabetic retinopathy on a publicly available dataset through integration of deep learning. Invest. Ophthalmol. Vis. Sci. **57**(13), 5200–5206 (2016)
2. Agurto, C., et al.: Multiscale AM-FM methods for diabetic retinopathy lesion detection. IEEE Trans. Med. Imaging **29**(2), 502–512 (2010)
3. Bao, P., Zhang, L., Wu, X.: Canny edge detection enhancement by scale multiplication. IEEE Trans. Pattern Anal. Mach. Intell. **27**(9), 1485–1490 (2005)
4. Cho, N., et al.: IDF diabetes atlas: global estimates of diabetes prevalence for 2017 and projections for 2045. Diab. Res. Clin. Pract. **138**, 271–281 (2018)
5. Desbiens, J., Gupta, S., Stevenson, J., Alderman, A., Trivedi, A., Buehler, P.: Deep annotated learning, harmonic descriptors and automated diabetic retinopathy detection (2018)
6. Gargeya, R., Leng, T.: Automated identification of diabetic retinopathy using deep learning. Ophthalmology **124**(7), 962–969 (2017)
7. Gulshan, V., et al.: Development and validation of a deep learning algorithm for detection of diabetic retinopathy in retinal fundus photographs. JAMA **316**(22), 2402–2410 (2016)
8. He, K., Zhang, X., Ren, S., Sun, J.: Deep residual learning for image recognition. In: Proceedings of the IEEE Conference on Computer Vision and Pattern Recognition, pp. 770–778 (2016)
9. Krizhevsky, A., Sutskever, I., Hinton, G.E.: ImageNet classification with deep convolutional neural networks. In: Advances in Neural Information Processing Systems, pp. 1097–1105 (2012)
10. LeCun, Y., Bengio, Y., Hinton, G.: Deep learning. Nature **521**(7553), 436 (2015)
11. McCann, J.: Lessons learned from mondrians applied to real images and color gamuts. In: Color and Imaging Conference, vol. 1999, pp. 1–8. Society for Imaging Science and Technology (1999)
12. Michael, D.A., Renato, A., Michael, F.C., Peter, A.K., Ursula, S.E.: IDx transforming healthcare through automation. https://www.eyediagnosis.net. Accessed 30 May 2018
13. Rakhlin, A.: Diabetic retinopathy detection through integration of deep learning classification framework. bioRxiv, p. 225508 (2018)

14. Ren, S., He, K., Girshick, R., Sun, J.: Faster R-CNN: towards real-time object detection with region proposal networks. In: Advances in Neural Information Processing Systems, pp. 91–99 (2015)
15. Russakovsky, O., et al.: ImageNet large scale visual recognition challenge. Int. J. Comput. Vis. (IJCV) **115**(3), 211–252 (2015). https://doi.org/10.1007/s11263-015-0816-y
16. Shah, S.: Blindness and visual impairment due to retinal diseases. Commun. Eye Health **22**(69), 8 (2009)
17. Szegedy, C., et al.: Going deeper with convolutions. In: CVPR (2015)
18. Zheng, Y., He, M., Congdon, N.: The worldwide epidemic of diabetic retinopathy. Indian J. Ophthalmol. **60**(5), 428 (2012)

An Adaptive Copy-Move Forgery Detection Using Wavelet Coefficients Multiscale Decay

Vittoria Bruni[1,2], Giuliana Ramella[2(✉)], and Domenico Vitulano[3]

[1] Department of SBAI, University of Rome La Sapienza, Rome, Italy
vittoria.bruni@sbai.uniromal.it
[2] Institute for the Applications of Calculus, CNR, Naples, Italy
giuliana.ramella@cnr.it
[3] Institute for the Applications of Calculus, CNR, Rome, Italy
d.vitulano@iac.cnr.it

Abstract. In this paper, an adaptive method for copy-move forgery detection and localization in digital images is proposed. The method employs wavelet transform with non constant Q factor and characterizes image pixels through the multiscale behavior of corresponding wavelet coefficients. The detection of forged regions is then performed by considering similar those pixels having the same multiscale behavior. The method is pointwise and the length of pixel features vector is image dependent, allowing for a more precise and fast detection of forged regions. The qualitative and quantitative evaluation of the experimental results reveals that the proposed method outperforms some existing transform-based methods in terms of performance and execution time.

Keywords: Image Forensics · Copy-move forgery detection · Wavelet transform · Lipschitz exponents

1 Introduction

In recent years, the authentication of visual documents for their validation in the forensic field has gained considerable importance because of the expansion and ubiquity of communication networks and the massive dissemination of smart devices. At the same time, due to the development of current acquisition systems and sophisticated photographic editing software, the manipulation of digital images has become a simple and widespread operation. Therefore, image forgery identification, within the broader scope called Image Forensics, has become a large area of research that boast many methods for the authentication of digital data [1–3].

Traditionally image forgery detection methods are divided into two main groups: Active methods and Passive (Blind) methods. Active methods incorporate sub-data into the image that are a mark/signature of authenticity [4, 5]. Passive methods mainly rely on the fact that manipulations can bring specific and detectable alterations in the image (also called traces) that are considered tamper indicators such as they cannot be found simply by a visual inspection, especially in case of high quality falsifications [6–8]. Traces of interest occur during the creation/processing/storing of digital images. Passive detection techniques can also be split into three branches; image splicing, image

© Springer Nature Switzerland AG 2019
M. Vento and G. Percannella (Eds.): CAIP 2019, LNCS 11678, pp. 469–480, 2019.
https://doi.org/10.1007/978-3-030-29888-3_38

retouching, copy-move. Owing to its simplicity, the copy-move forgery (CMF) is one of the most common forgery attacks. In CMF a part of the image (patch) is copied and pasted in another part of the same image usually with the intention of hiding or duplicate an object or a region. In order to make forgery attack more convincing, post-processing operations such as blurring, noise, rotation, and so on are often applied to duplicated regions. This paper focuses on passive CMF detection methods.

The pioneering works on this topic are [9, 10]. In [9] the authors discussed the main requirements for the detection algorithm, including the possibility of detecting tampering even in image areas of limited size and the possibility of having few false alarms, an acceptable processing time and limited complexity. The CMF detection method proposed in [9] is based on block matching. The image is divided into overlapping blocks, and specific features are extracted from each block. Pair of blocks having very similar features in the spatial domain are considered as forgery regions. In [10], Principal Component Analysis (PCA) is used to extract blocks features. The computational complexity of [9, 10] is mainly due to lexicographical sorting applied to features vectors of image blocks. Beside the high computational burden, these methods may not get good results when duplicated area is resized or rotated considerably. In [11], a method based on polar logarithmic coordinates and the wavelet transform has been proposed. The use of polar logarithmic coordinates allows for an efficient exhaustive search to identify similar blocks using correlation as a similarity criterion. The application of the wavelet transform to the input image allows to obtain a reduction of the dimensionality. Recently, in [12] Zandi et al. proposed an adaptive approach which selects a threshold for each image content while in [13], Mahmood et al. proposed a method based on the stationary wavelet transform (SWT) where discrete cosine (DCT) transform is used for reducing the number of block features. Refinement to this work have been presented based on the use of different implementations of the wavelet transform.

Overall, at present, passive methods for detecting CMF provide high detection accuracy at the cost of higher computational complexity and require the interpretation of the results by a human expert. In addition, these methods can lead to a number of high false positives or fail when the area of the manipulated region is small with respect to the size of the input image. One of the main motivation is the fact that most of existing methods are block-based; hence, block dimension limits the size of detectable regions. In addition, the number of features per block is fixed. As a result, if a block contains only a part of the forged region, very fine details could be lost if the number of selected features is too high and not forged pixels in two corresponding blocks are very different; on the contrary, false alarms are more likely if it is too small.

The aim of this work is to define a pointwise adaptive method based on wavelet transform that provides results at least comparable with those existing in the literature but is more effective and efficient computationally. Local features are determined on the basis of local image regularity which is derived from the decay of wavelet coefficients along scales. The local nature of this measure is such that no block subdivision is needed. To increase the robustness of the method, the number of features is chosen depending on the overall image visual content which is computed using a multiscale contrast measure. As a result, the method is fully image adaptive and does not require to set absolute thresholds.

The paper is organized as follows. Section 2 presents the proposed method while experimental results are provided in Sect. 3. Last section draws the conclusions.

2   The Proposed Method

CMF detection problem mainly consists of the detection of non-local image similarities. To this aim, it is necessary to: define the domain for similarities search; select few and distinctive features in order to allow a fast but successful search; tune a suitable threshold for assessing similarities.

In this paper image pixels are characterized through the pointwise behavior of the modulus of the detail component of image wavelet transform computed at few different consecutive scales; two pixels are then defined similar if they have the same multiscale behavior within a tolerance which depends on image self-similarities. The use of wavelet transform is twofold advantageous: it provides a local (pointwise) characterization of image pixels, allowing for the detection of very small forged regions; it allows a fast implementation, thanks to the use of a directional filter bank.

2.1   Multiscale Features

Wavelet transform is a multiscale differential operator having several nice properties which made it one of the most common and powerful signal analysis tools [14]. One of the main reason of its widespread use is the possibility of implementing its discrete version as a perfect reconstruction filter bank, even for the 2D case, while preserving many of the properties of the continuous case. One of them is the characterization of local signal singularities. In particular, as proved by a wide literature concerning this topic, the decay of wavelet coefficients with respect to the scale is strictly related to the local Lipschitz exponent of the analyzed function which, in turn, characterizes the type of singularity in a given domain. One of the main result in this sense is the following [14], which can be easily extended to the 2D case:

Theorem 1. If $f \in L^2(R)$ is uniformly Lipschitz α over an interval $[a, b]$, there exists $A > 0$ such that:

$$\forall (u, s) \in [a, b] x R^+, \quad |Wf(u, s)| \leq As^{\alpha + 1/2} \tag{1}$$

where $Wf(u, s)$ is the wavelet transform of f at time u and scale s.

Conversely, if f is bounded and $Wf(u, s)$ satisfies Eq. (1) for $\alpha < n$, where n is the number of wavelet vanishing moments, then f is uniformly Lipschitz α on $[a + \varepsilon, b - \varepsilon]$, for any $\varepsilon > 0$.

As it can be observed, the decay, or more in general, the way wavelet coefficients change along scales depends on: (i) singularity type in the original image (Lipschitz exponent); (ii) local content (wavelet support at scale s). Hence, if we look at this behavior, we can gather some information concerning the original signal in terms of relationships with neighbors. The behavior of interest is substantially given by the ratio of corresponding coefficients at successive scales, computed in regions proportional to the wavelet support (resolution of analysis).

In addition, the correspondence between points as s increases depends on singularities interactions, as proved in [15] and the parameters of this behavior can define a similarity index [16]. In particular, if the decay is regular, the exact singularity type is described and we expect an almost stationary curve; on the contrary, if the behavior is not regular, it means that the local point neighborhood greatly changes, i.e. pixels belong to a not homogeneous region, as, for example, a textured region. As a result, if two image points belong to two identical image regions, they have the same neighborhood and then they have to show a similar multiscale behavior.

However, in case of forged regions, we expect that those behaviors have much in common just for a limited number of scales since, from a given s on, pixel neighborhoods change with high probability, as they are located in different areas of the image. An example is shown in Fig. 1.

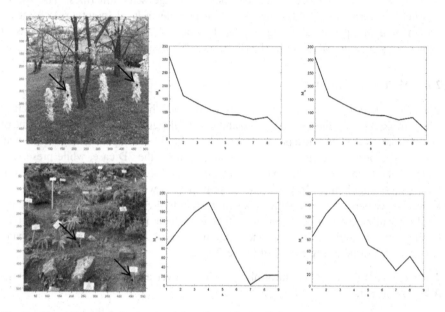

Fig. 1. The multiscale behavior (modulus of wavelet coefficients versus scale) corresponding to two image pixels belonging to corresponding forged regions having large size (top) and small size (bottom)—corresponding points are indicated in the original images using black arrows.

As a result, the best domain to use for comparing image pixels depends on the size of forged region, which unfortunately is a priori unknown. In addition, in order to capture subtle differences, a continuous scale should be employed.

In order to overcome these two problems, in this paper we select a number of pixel features which depends on global image characteristics; specifically, the global image contrast is used and it still is measured in a multiscale fashion. Multiscale contrast [17] defines a visual rate-distortion curve which quantifies the loss of image details as the resolution decreases. Hence, according to results in [18, 19], the scale at which image contrast does not considerably change indicates the resolution, i.e. the viewing distance, from which significant visually image changes are not perceived. More precisely, the optimal scale is defined as:

$$\hat{s} = argmin_s\, C_s + \lambda s \tag{2}$$

where C_s is the multiscale contrast [17] and λ is a proper parameter which balances the two terms. $\hat{s}$ corresponds to the largest frequency resolution step (inverse of scale parameter) which provides the minimum perceivable loss of contrast between two consecutive frequency bands (Fig. 2a). As a result, it guarantees that two consecutive detail bands in the corresponding wavelet decomposition retain visible and distinguishable image details. Hence, scales belonging to the interval $[1, \hat{s}]$ are the best candidates from which extracting the features that better characterize image pixels.

In order to have an enough dense set of scales, integer values for the scale parameter s have been considered. Hence, by denoting with M_s the absolute value of detail bands at scale s of the 2D wavelet transform of the image I, the feature vector for the pixel at location (i, j) is defined as

$$F(i,j) = [L_1(i,j), L_2(i,j), \ldots, L_N(i,j)] \tag{3}$$

where:

$$L_s(i,j) = log_2\left(\frac{M_s(i,j)}{M_{s-1}(i,j)}\right), \quad s = 1,\ldots,\hat{s} \tag{4}$$

while

$$L_1(i,j) = log_2\left(\frac{M_1(i,j)}{I(i,j)}\right) \tag{5}$$

is the local image contrast and represents a sort of DC component.

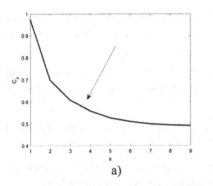
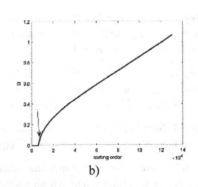

a)   b)

Fig. 2. (a) Multiscale Peli's contrast curve. The arrow indicates the selected optimal scale. The curve refers to the image in Fig. 1 bottom; (b) Sorted distance of consecutive features vectors of each image pixel. Forged pixels are in the first part of the curve. The arrow indicates the selected optimal threshold value.

2.2 Similarities Assessment Threshold

The threshold T to use for assessing pixel similarities is selected in adaptive manner. More precisely, the lexicographic order of the rows of the matrix F in Eq. (3) is considered and the vector D, whose components are the distances between consecutive feature vectors in the sorted F, is built. The optimal threshold is then defined as the first point realizing the maximum curvature of the sorted version of D. Figure 2b shows a typical behavior of such a curve.

As it can be observed we expect that candidate points are those providing the least values of the sorted distance vector: most of them are zero and they mainly correspond to the central parts of forged regions; on the contrary, points at the border of image regions, provide values close to zero due to the influence of a neighborhood that can slightly change, according to image local context. On the other hand, distance values cannot be too much large as they can be confused with natural image self-similarities. As a result, even in this case, the best trade off is realized by the point of maximum curvature of the first part of the distance curve, as in Fig. 2b.

The detailed algorithm is presented in the following section.

2.3 Algorithm

Step 1. Extract the luminance component I from the input RGB image.

Step 2. Compute the multiscale wavelet transform of I using Haar wavelet with integer and increasing scale s and let A_s, V_s, H_s respectively be the approximation component, the vertical and horizontal detail bands at scale s. Let M_s be the absolute value of detail components at scale s: $M_s(i,j) = \sqrt{H_s^2(i,j) + V_s^2(i,j)}$.

Step 3. For each $s > 1$ and for each position (i, j) compute the local Lipschitz coefficients as in Eq. (4) and the pointwise contrast in Eq. (5).

Step 4. For each s compute the mean value of the multiscale Peli's contrast [17] $C_s(i,j) = \frac{M_s(i,j)}{A_s(i,j)}$ and store it in the vector U.

Step 5. Set the number of features $N = \lceil \hat{s} \rceil$, according to Eq. (2), i.e. the component index realizing the maximum curvature of U, and define the feature vector F for each pixel position (i, j) as in Eq. (3).

Step 6. For each position (i, j), sort $F(i, j)$ in lexicographic order and build the feature matrix F_{sort}. For each pair of rows of F_{sort} compute the Euclidean distance among the N elements and store it in the vector D.

Step 7. Sort D in increasing order and determine the point of maximum curvature. Let m be the corresponding index. Set T equal to $D(m)$.

Step 8. Store in the forged map the consecutive elements in F_{sort} whose features vector distance is less than T and whose spatial distance is less than a threshold d.

Step 9. Remove noisy regions having area less than 3% of the largest region, then fill hollows and dilate the image.

3   Experimental Results

To evaluate the proposed method, we considered the publically available standard image collections namely CoMoFoD [20]. CoMoFoD image collection contains 200 images of size 512×512 pixels grouped in 5 subsets according to applied manipulation: translation, rotation, scaling, combination and distortion. Different types of post-processing methods: JPEG compression (JC), brightness change (BC), image blurring (IB), noise adding (NA), color reduction (CR), contrast adjustments (CA), are applied to all forged and original images. In this paper, we limit ourselves to consider only the first forty forged images (shift) to which any geometric manipulation has been applied. The only predefined threshold employed is the value of the spatial distance d, set equal to 10 in this paper. Ten integer scale values have been used for computing image wavelet transform in all tests.

3.1   Qualitative Evaluation

Figures 3, 4, 5 and 6 show some examples that demonstrate the strength as well as the limits of the proposed method. Figures 3 and 4 show respectively a good and an intermediate example of CMF detection where only few detail are disregarded.

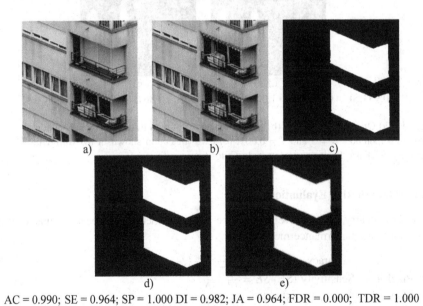

AC = 0.990; SE = 0.964; SP = 1.000 DI = 0.982; JA = 0.964; FDR = 0.000; TDR = 1.000

Fig. 3. (a) Original image #35; (b) forged image; (c) ground truth; (d) CMF detection using the proposed method—$N = 3$ and $T = 0.008$; (e) CMF detection shown in (d) with True Positive (green) - no False Positive are detected. (Color figure online)

As it can be observed, the proposed method is able to correctly detect and locate forged regions without introducing false alarms. As pointed out in the previous section, the only critical parts are pixels at the border of the forged region, due to the different neighborhood of corresponding points. More interesting examples are in Figs. 5 and 6 where forged regions include fine details that could be difficult to detect, as the legs of the girl in Fig. 5 and the thin supports of the signs in Fig. 6. The proposed method is able to detect those fine details thanks to its pointwise and adaptive nature. Even in this case any false alarm is introduced.

a)   b)   c)

d)   e)

AC = 0.993; SE = 0.864; SP = 1.000; DI = 0.927; JA = 0.864; FDR = 0.000; TDR = 1.000

Fig. 4. (a) Original image #27; (b) forged image; (c) ground truth; (d) CMF detection using the proposed method—$N = 3$ and $T = 0.001$; (e) CMF detection shown in (d) with True Positive (green) - no False Positive are detected. (Color figure online)

3.2   Quantitative Evaluation

In order to carry comparative studies, the proposed method has been evaluated using the following performance metrics [21]:

- Pixel-level Accuracy (AC) $AC = \frac{TP + TN}{TP + FP + TN + FN}$
- Pixel-level Sensitivity (SE) $SE = \frac{TP}{TP + FN}$
- Pixel-level Specificity (SP) $SP = \frac{TN}{TN + FP}$
- Dice Coefficient or F-measure (DI) $DI = \frac{2 * TP}{2 * TP + FN + FP}$
- Jaccard Index (JA) $JA = \frac{TP}{TP + FN + FP}$

where TP, TN, FP and FN respectively denote true positive, true negative, false positive and false negative assessments.

Table 1 reports the performance values achieved by the proposed method on the considered image of the Comofod dataset, as well as by transform-based methods in

[9, 13]. As it can be observed, the proposed method outperforms competing methods thanks to a well balance between correct assessments and missing forged pixels. In addition, it is robust to post processing operations like contrast adjustment, brightness change and color reduction.

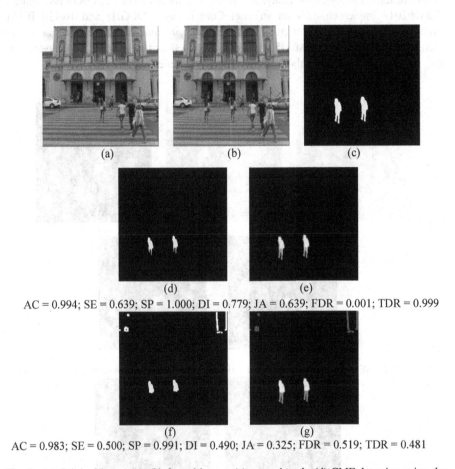

(a)   (b)   (c)

(d)   (e)

AC = 0.994; SE = 0.639; SP = 1.000; DI = 0.779; JA = 0.639; FDR = 0.001; TDR = 0.999

(f)   (g)

AC = 0.983; SE = 0.500; SP = 0.991; DI = 0.490; JA = 0.325; FDR = 0.519; TDR = 0.481

Fig. 5. (a) Original image #1; (b) forged image; (c) ground truth; (d) CMF detection using the proposed method—$N = 3$ and $T = 0.020$; (e) CMF detection shown in (d) with True Positive (green) - no False Positive are detected; (f) CMF detection using [13]; (g) CMF detection shown in (f) with False Positive (red) and True Positive (green). (Color figure online)

Similar conclusions can be drawn if comparative studies involve True Discovery Rate (TDR) and False Discovery Rate (FDR), i.e. $FDR = \frac{FP}{FP + TP}$ and $TDR = 1 - FDR$. The proposed method significantly improves the method in [13] thanks to the reduced number of false positive assessments, even if a smaller number of features N is employed on average for each image (see Table 1) ranging from 3 to 8. The advantage of the proposed method is demonstrated in Figs. 5 and 6: the method in [13] misses fine details due to the reduced number of features and the block dimension with respect to the forged area.

To complete the quantitative evaluation of the results, Table 1 contains the execution times (in seconds) of analyzed methods. Timings have been obtained using a Matlab2018 implementation on an Intel Core i7 with 2.8 GHz and 16 GB RAM, running Win7 operating system. It is worth noticing that the execution time of the method is reduced of at least 1/5 with respect to [13] and at least 1/25 with respect to [9]; on average it requires about 4 s for processing one image.

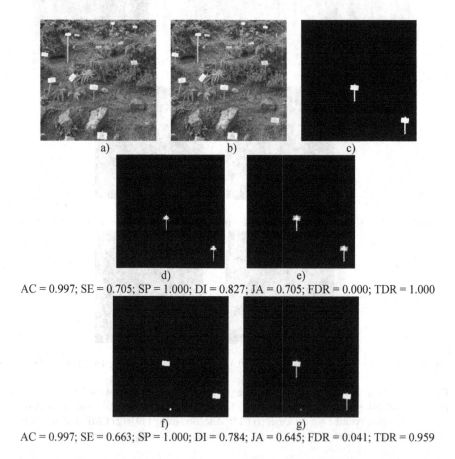

a)   b)   c)

d)   e)

AC = 0.997; SE = 0.705; SP = 1.000; DI = 0.827; JA = 0.705; FDR = 0.000; TDR = 1.000

f)   g)

AC = 0.997; SE = 0.663; SP = 1.000; DI = 0.784; JA = 0.645; FDR = 0.041; TDR = 0.959

Fig. 6. (a) Original image #18; (b) forged image; (c) ground truth; (d) CMF detection using the proposed method—$N = 3$ and $T = 0.001$; (e) CMF detection shown in (d) with True Positive (green) - no False Positive are detected; (f) CMF detection using [13]; (g) CMF detection shown in (f) with False Positive (red) and True Positive (green). (Color figure online)

Table 1. Average performance results on the selected dataset – best results are in bold.

Method	AC	SE	SP	DI	JA	FDR	TDR	N	Computing time
[9] (all)	*0.919*	*0.782*	*0.919*	*0.572*	*0.489*	*0.411*	*0.589*	*256*	*82,01*
(shift)	0.918	0.782	0.918	0.562	0.477	0.423	0.577	256	81,33
(shift + CA)	0.905	0.787	0.903	0.553	0.472	0.431	0.569	256	81,04
(shift + BC)	0.927	0.772	0.928	0.579	0.496	0.401	0.599	256	81,98
(shift + CR)	0.926	0.786	0.925	0.580	0.494	0.406	0.594	256	80,99
[13] (all)	*0.986*	*0.807*	*0.990*	*0.778*	*0.704*	*0.161*	*0.839*	*6*	*18,00*
(shift)	0.986	0.813	0.990	0.797	0.731	0.116	0.884	6	17,46
(shift + CA)	0.988	0.813	0.992	0.803	0.735	0.112	0.888	6	17,50
(shift + BC)	0.982	0.799	0.987	0.745	0.665	0.220	0.780	6	17,59
(shift + CR)	0.987	0.813	0.991	0.795	0.725	0.126	0.874	6	17,30
Proposed (all)	*0.995*	*0.836*	*0.999*	*0.884*	*0.818*	*0.034*	*0.966*	*3*	*4,00*
(shift)	0.996	0.856	1.000	0.908	0.845	0.014	0.986	3	3,59
(shift + CA)	0.996	0.855	1.000	0.903	0.838	0.020	0.980	3	3,49
(shift + BC)	0.993	0.817	0.999	0.864	0.798	0.048	0.952	3	4,01
(shift + CR)	0.996	0.846	1.000	0.896	0.832	0.024	0.976	3	3,39

4 Conclusions

In this paper a method for CMF detection based on the decay of wavelet coefficients along scales has been presented. This measure is referred to each pixel but it also takes into account pixel neighborhood since wavelet details measure the local variation of the function in a neighborhood proportional to the scale. As a consequence, block image subdivision is avoided making the method independent of the choice of block size. Moreover, the measure of decay involves multiple levels of resolution and only depends on the variation of absolute intensity, making the method robust to post processing operations like brightness change, contrast adjustments, color reduction. The method is fully adaptive since the required parameters are image dependent.

As preliminary tests have shown, the main advantage of the proposed method is the ability in detecting fine details due to the pointwise nature of the adopted features. In addition, the method benefits from the fast implementation of the transform; as a result execution times are low enough for its use in the forensics routine practice.

In the future investigations there is room to improve in different directions this preliminary version of the proposed wavelet-based method. In particular, the next step will be devoted to more extensive comparative studies with the existing methods and to a generalization of the method in order to make it robust to geometric manipulations.

Acknowledgments. This research has been supported by the GNCS (Gruppo Nazionale di CalcoloScientifico) of the INdAM (IstitutoNazionale di Alta Matematica) and partially funded by Regione Lazio, POR FESR Aerospace and Security Programme, Project COURIER - COUntering RadIcalism InvEstigation platform - CUP F83G17000860007.

References

1. Farid, H.: A survey of image forgery detection. IEEE Sig. Proc. Mag. **26**, 16–25 (2009)
2. Piva, A.: An overview on image forensics. ISRN Sig. Process. **2013**, 1–22 (2013)
3. Farid, H.: Photo Forensics. MIT Press, Cambridge (2016)
4. Kumar, C., Kumar Singh, A., Kumar, P.: A recent survey on image watermarking techniques and its application in e-governance. Multimed. Tools Appl. **77**, 3597–3622 (2018)
5. Arnold, M., Schmucker, M., Wolthusen, S.D.: Techniques and Applications of Digital Watermarking and Content Protection. Artech House Inc., Norwood (2003)
6. Lin, X., Li, J., Wanga, S., Liew, A., Cheng, F., Huang, X.: Recent advances in passive digital image security forensics: a brief review. Engineering **4**, 29–39 (2018)
7. Birajdar, G.K., Mankar, V.H.: Digital image forgery detection using passive techniques: a survey. Digit. Invest. **10**(3), 226–245 (2013)
8. Panda, S., Mishra, M.: Passive techniques of digital image forgery detection: developments and challenges. In: Kalam, A., Das, S., Sharma, K. (eds.) Advances in Electronics, Communication and Computing. LNEE, vol. 443, pp. 281–290. Springer, Singapore (2018). https://doi.org/10.1007/978-981-10-4765-7_29
9. Fridrich, A.J., Soukal, B.D., Lukas, A.J.: Detection of copy-move forgery in digital images. Int. J. **3**(2), 652–663 (2003)
10. Popescu, A.C., Farid, H.: Exposing digital forgeries by detecting duplicated image regions. Technical report. Department of Computer Science, Dartmouth College, Hanover, No. TR2004-515 (2004)
11. Myna, A., Venkateshmurthy, M., Patil, C.: Detection of region duplication forgery in digital images using wavelets and log-polar mapping. In: Proceedings of the International Conference on Computational Intelligence and Multimedia Applications (ICCIMA 2007), pp. 371–377 (2007)
12. Zandi, M., Mahmoudi-Aznaveh, A., Mansouri, A.: Adaptive matching for copy-move forgery detection. In: Proceedings of IEEE International Workshop on Information Forensics and Security, pp. 119–124 (2014)
13. Mahmood, T., Mehmood, Z., Shah, M., Sabad, T.: A robust technique for copy-move forgery detection and localization in digital images via stationary wavelet and discrete cosine transform. J. Vis. Commun. Image Represent. **53**, 202–214 (2018)
14. Mallat, S.: A Wavelet Tour of Signal Processing. Academic Press, Cambridge (1998)
15. Bruni, V., Piccoli, B., Vitulano, D.: A fast computation method for time-scale signal denoising. Sig. Image Video Process. **3**(1), 63–83 (2009)
16. Bruni, V., Vitulano, D.: Time scale similarities for robust image denoising. J. Math. Imaging Vis. **44**(1), 52–64 (2012)
17. Peli, E.: Contrast in complex images. J. Opt. Soc. Am. **7**(10), 2032–2040 (1990)
18. Basile, M.C., Bruni, V., Vitulano, D.: A CSF-based preprocessing method for image deblurring. In: Blanc-Talon, J., Penne, R., Philips, W., Popescu, D., Scheunders, P. (eds.) ACIVS 2017. LNCS, vol. 10617, pp. 602–614. Springer, Cham (2017). https://doi.org/10.1007/978-3-319-70353-4_51
19. Bruni, V., Salvi, A., Vitulano, D.: A wavelet based image fusion method using local multiscale image regularity. In: Blanc-Talon, J., Helbert, D., Philips, W., Popescu, D., Scheunders, P. (eds.) ACIVS 2018. LNCS, vol. 11182, pp. 534–546. Springer, Cham (2018). https://doi.org/10.1007/978-3-030-01449-0_45
20. Tralic, D., Zupancic, I., Grgic, S., Grgic, M.: CoMoFoD—new database for copy-move forgery detection. In: 55th International Symposium, ELMAR 2013, pp. 49–54 (2013)
21. Al-Qershi, O.A., Khoo, B.E.: Evaluation of copy-move forgery detection: datasets and evaluation metrics. Multimed. Tools Appl. **77**, 31807–31833 (2018)

Real Time Object Detection on Aerial Imagery

Raghav Sharma[1,2(✉)], Rohit Pandey[2], and Aditya Nigam[1]

[1] Indian Institute of Technology Mandi, Mandi, India
t17132@students.iitmandi.ac.in, aditya@iitmandi.ac.in
[2] Hughes Systique Corporation, Gurugram, India
rohit.pandey@hsc.com

Abstract. Aerial images usually are huge (around 2K resolution). Such high-resolution images contain thousands of small objects, and detecting all of them is a very challenging problem. The complexity of detection and classification in real-time is much higher than the usual images (<1K with high Object to Image Ratio OIR). Deep learning has many algorithms for object detection, but they are not designed for handling aerial images, and these algorithms are often sub-optimal for small scale object detection and their precise localization. In this work, a novel technique based on a modified SSD architecture OIR-SSD has proposed for real-time object detection on aerial images attaining high mean Average Precision (mAP). OIR-SSD has two approaches. The approach-I proposed for higher mAP, whereas the approach-II proposed to achieve real-time object detection. The approach-I has improved mAP from 0.72 to 0.92 (28% improvement) on Stanford data-set while from 0.04 to 0.44 (1100% improvement) on Visedrone2018 at 4 Frames Per Second (FPS) whereas the approach-II has improved mAP from 0.72 to 0.82 at 42 FPS.

Keywords: Aerial Imagery · SSD · OIR-SSD · Object detection · UAV · Surveillance

1 Introduction

According to GMI [1] and ITR [2] report, Aerial Imaging market size was 1.7B in 2017, as a project it will grow with 12–14% CAGR from 2018–2024. Object detection on aerial images is a key ingredient of automated UAV. Object detection [3,4] is the algorithm that can localize and classify each desire object present in an image. Each object class has its unique feature which helps to classify and localize the object. Human can easily extract that feature to identify object in an image, but in case of machine first it need to identify probable region for object, then extract feature like SIFT [5], HOG [6], Haar-like [7] to represent them and then classify using classifier like SVM [8], AdaBoost [9], DPM [3]. These procedures are complex and difficult to design. To reduce the complexity and improve object detection many other algorithms were introduced based on

© Springer Nature Switzerland AG 2019
M. Vento and G. Percannella (Eds.): CAIP 2019, LNCS 11678, pp. 481–491, 2019.
https://doi.org/10.1007/978-3-030-29888-3_39

deep learning framework [10–12] like R-cnn [13], YOLO [14], SSD [15]. Deep learning-based algorithms can automatically learn object features by training. That is why it is not necessary to design feature selection and classifier, so it is easy to detect the object in an image using deep learning. Object detection has various application in the industry like self-driving vehicles [16], identify group activities, guarantees appropriate quality control of parts in assembling. These are simply beginning that object detection can do. This work focused on object detection using aerial images. Because it has a wide range of application like surveillance, disaster management, object tracking, resource management, product delivery, destructive weapon and many more. Figure 1 shows the overall idea of this work.

Fig. 1. Overall scope of this work.

Aerial Imagery is taken from high altitudes to cover large geometrical regions and thousands of objects, so aerial images have a resolution of around $2K \times 2K$ to $6K \times 6K$. The computational complexity of object detection algorithm is directly related pixel density and number of bounding boxes, as an example for the case of SSD computed output tensor is 8732×25 for 300×300 images and 24528×25 for 512×512. So it can be deduced that processing such high-resolution images for object detection based on existing deep learning algorithms is an NP-hard problem. To perform optimal object detection on such high-resolution images, either improve existing algorithms or innovate new techniques. A new architecture based on SSD called OIR-SSD has proposed to solve high-resolution aerial images object detection. Proposed OIR-SSD algorithm discussed in the Sect. 5.

2   Dataset

The following two different aerial data sets used to evaluate OIR-SSD along with other state-of-art object detection algorithms. Stanford Aerial Pedestrian Dataset [17] provided by Computational Vision and Geometry Lab Stanford. Sample images of the data set shown in Fig. 2a.

Table 1. Comparison of dataset with respect to data size, view.

Data-set	Images	Categories	Average number of labels/categories	Resolution	View	Camera
Stanford	929.5K	6	1769.4K	1424 × 1088	Top	Fixed
Visdron	10.2K	10	54.2K	2000 × 1500	Lateral	Moving

Table 2. Comparison of dataset with respect to object and object size.

Data-set	10–60 pixel	60–300 pixel	Above 300 pixel	Average number of objects/image
Pascal voc	0.14	0.61	0.25	≈03
Stanford	.90	.10	0	≈15
Visdron	0.57	0.41	0.02	≈70

Visdrone2018 data set [18] collected from 14 different cities of China. It contains 6471 training images and 548 validation images for the object detection task. These are high-resolution images captured via drone based imaging technique. Sample images of the data set shown in Fig. 2b.

With the help of Tables 1 and 2 it can infer that Visrone2018 dataset is more complex then Stanford aerial object detection. As well as Table 2 shows that aerial data (Stanford, Visdrone) are much more complex than normal data (Pascal VOC), which we have discussed in Sect. 4.

(a) Sample image of aerial data of Stanford. (b) Sample image of Visdrone2018 Dataset.

Fig. 2. Sample images of datasets.

3 Related Work

There are already many algorithms based on CNN published for object detection. These algorithms can be divided into two classes, (a) Multi-stage Network and (b) Single-stage Network. The multi-stage algorithm in which object detection needs more than one stage is more accurate because of multiprocessing on the single image but slows the algorithm hence not suitable for real-time application (such as R-CNN [13], Fast R-CNN [19], and Faster R-CNN [20]). In the single-stage network, object detection need only one stage. It is faster than the multi-stage network but less accurate like YOLO (You Only Look Once) [14], SSD (Single Shot multi-box Detector) [15], Retina Net [21].

3.1 Multi-stage Network

In developing stage of object detection, a sliding window has used, but in this case, for the object localization, we need to feed thousands of patches in classifier for just one image. It was too expensive from a computational point of view. R-CNN [13] proposed by Ross B. Girshick et al. in 2013 was the path-breaking technique, in this work Region proposal network was introduced to find out the probable areas where an object can be present, and only those patches will feed into the classifier for detection and localization. However, it was still slow for the real-time application then fast R-CNN [19] and faster R-CNN [20] were introduced as an improved version of R-CNN.

3.2 Single-Stage Network

To achieve real-time object detection, many algorithms have proposed which can use for the real-time application. These algorithms processed image only once for detection. First proposed an algorithm in this series was YOLO [14] proposed in 2015. It was using 24 convolution layer for feature detection followed by two fully connected layers for the object detection, But its accuracy was not good. To improve efficiency, the YOLO version2 [22] was proposed. This version was using two feature map at a different scale to handle the small object present in the image. After this work SSD, retina net and YOLO version 3 [23] was introduced to handle the various problem related to object scales and efficiency.

4 Incompatibility of Existing Methods for Aerial Images

Discussed methods were proposed for front view images. The object present in the front view images is sufficiently large as compared to aerial images. As shown in Fig. 3 it can infer that child riding horse, but it is hard to recognize an object in the aerial image. Green patch present in Fig. 3 indicate the object to identify whereas red spot in the image suggests an area where the object is not present, but it looks like same as an object which cannot be differentiated from the correct object.

(a) Front view image taken from VOC data set.   (b) Aerial image taken Stanford aerial data set.

Fig. 3. Sample images of datasets.

The second challenge was the number of objects present in images. Most of the existing algorithm detect a limited number of object efficiently, which is only suitable for front view images because aerial images cover lots of area in a single image like (0.12 to 0.36 km^2 area per image) such area can cover thousands of object, as shown in Fig. 4 from Inria data-set [24].

Fig. 4. Sample image of The Inria Aerial Image Labeling data-set [24].

The third challenge is the resolution of images. Exiting algorithm designed for the low-resolution image (300–600) but aerial images are a high-resolution image (2K–4K). Now if the size of the image reduced, then it will lose the vital information which will help to detect the desired object. On the other hand, exist algorithm is not able to process an image without making its low resolution.

5 Methodology

Three significant problems to handle aerial data have discussed in Sect. 4 that is several objects, the scale of object and size or the resolution of the image. These problems can adequately address if Object to Image Ratio (OIR) is in a specific range.

5.1 Object to Image Ratio (OIR)

With the help of multiple experiments, it has found that SSD has a limit to detect the specific size of the object with respect to the image. Below that limit, SSD could not perform optimally. Similarly, this limit can be different for different object detector algorithms. To define this limit with respect to object size and image size, the term called OIR has used.

$$OIR = \frac{Area\ of\ Smallest\ Object}{Area\ of\ Image}$$

For example, consider an object detector that can detect the object of minimum size (60×60) in the image of size (300×300) then OIR for that object detector will $((60 \times 60)/(300 \times 300) = 0.04)$. OIR of SSD with some hyperparametric tuning is approximately 0.015, but in the aerial images object of size (64×64) presents in the image of size (1024×1024) which means $IOR = 0.004$. So SSD cannot perform well directly on this data. Now to improve performance either change the network so it can work well on lower OIR or increase OIR of the image. Now if somehow image size decreases without a change in object size, then OIR of the image will increase. To achieve this image patching is a right way. The suitable size of the patch can determine with the help of OIR $\left(\frac{Area\ of\ smallest\ object}{OIR}\right)$.

5.2 Hyper-parameter Tuning

SSD initially was designed for the front view images where object size large as compare to aerial images. Because of this default boxes size, the scale of layer everything was large, which was not suitable for aerial images. So the size of anchor boxes and scale of the layers have modified which was best suitable for aerial images in-place of front view images. Like the minimum scale in original SSD was 0.2. It has changed to 0.05 so SSD can able to detect the small scale object. This modification gives the improvement in mAP form 25.8 to 31.2 on the Visdrone2018 data set.

5.3   OIR-SSD Approach-I - Image in the Form of Patch at Train and Test

It has discussed in the Sect. 4 that re-sizing of the image is not the right solution because it will lead to loss of information. SSD can not process high-resolution images directly; instead, it would re-size the image as per the configuration. However, it has discussed in the Sect. 5.1 image patching can be a right approach for handling high resolution. We need to find the valid optimal value of OIR for the desired object detection algorithm. The desired patch size of the image can find With the help of OIR. Now, these patches will use to train the desired object detection algorithm in place of the full image, as shown in Fig. 5. OIR-SSD object detection algorithm based on SSD. Image overlapping can use at the time of image patching to handle the corner object present in the patch.

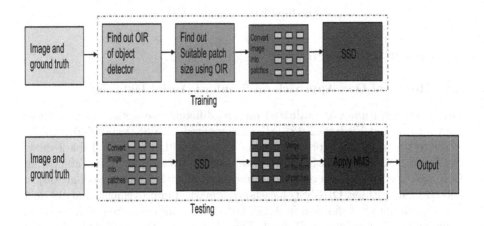

Fig. 5. OIR-SSD Approach-I - Image in the form of patch at train and test.

5.4   OIR-SSD Approach-II - Image in the Form of Patch at Train for Efficiency

The modified approach to handle the aerial images has discussed in the Sect. 5.3. According to this modification images patching will use for training as well as testing. This approach will slow down the speed of the object detector because, for the single image, it will process multiple patches. To handle this problem, approach-II has proposed. In this approach, image patching used only at the time of training because of this image will not lose information due to re-sizing of image and object detector will learn the required feature need to detect the object. With the help of this feature, the object detector will able to recognize the object even though without patching at testing time. This approach gives less mAP as compare to the first approach, but speed will not degrade, so this approach is a trade-off between mAP and speed (Fig. 6).

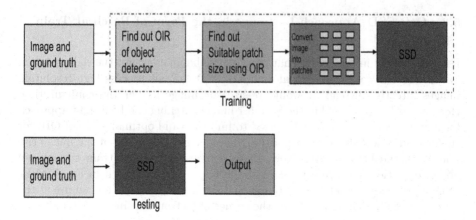

Fig. 6. OIR-SSD Approach II.

6 Result and Discussion

6.1 Result of Our Approach on Stanford Aerial Data Set

OIR-SSD algorithm was evaluated on two different datasets. Stanford aerial data set [17] and Visdrone2018 [18] and compared with SSD and YOLOV3. To evaluate the proposed approach, Nvidia Titan X GPU was used. Table 3 shows the result of OIR-SSD on Stanford data set [17]. It can infer from Table 3 that OIR-SSD is optimal for aerial images in caparison with other state-of-art object detection algorithms. OIR-SSD has shown a marked improvement of about 28% in comparison to SSD for Stanford [17]. OIR-SSD result compared with the other approaches [25] as shown in Table 4. This table shows that OIR-SSD gives the highest mAP and FPS.

Table 3. Comparison of mAP.

Object	mAP when image apply directly	mAP using OIR-SSD Approach II	mAP using OIR-SSD Approach I
Pedestrian	0.2269	0.6272	0.8569
Skater	0.6642	0.6382	0.9142
Cart	0.9033	0.8982	0.9401
Car	0.9286	0.9700	0.9633
Bus	0.9644	0.9989	0.9911
Biker	0.5938	0.7917	0.8394
mAP	0.71	0.8207	0.9175

Table 4. Comparison with other approach.

Algorithm	Frame per second	mAP
SSD (ResNet-50)	23.26	80.42
Faster R-CNN (ResNet-50)	13.18	83.64
RetinaNet (ResNet-50)	24.45	85.17
SSD (ResNet-101)	21.52	81.92
Faster R-CNN (ResNet-101)	11.27	85.33
RetinaNet (ResNet-101)	22.23	86.58
OIR-SSD Approach1	4.66	**91.75**
OIR-SSD Approach2	**42**	82.75

6.2   Result on Visdrone2018 Data Set

Result of OIR-SSD on Visdrone2018 dataset shown in Table 5. It has discussed in Sect. 2 that Visdrone2018 dataset is more complex then Stanford data set, so the maximum mAP on this dataset is much lower as compared to others. OIR-SSD has shown a marked improvement of about 1100% in comparison to SSD for Visdrone2018 [18].

Table 5. Comparison of mAP.

Object	mAP using OIR-SSD Approach I with SSD	mAP using OIR-SSD Approach I and hyperparameter tuning with SSD	mAP using OIR-SSD Approach I with YOLOv3
Ignoredregions	0.021	0.025	0.0467
Pedestrian	0.282	0.336	0.4848
People	0.230	0.274	0.3473
Bicycle	0.131	0.179	0.2004
Car	0.628	0.675	0.7603
Van	0.384	0.437	0.4070
Truck	0.278	0.35	0.3244
Tricycle	0.228	0.264	0.2739
Awningtricycle	0.170	0.205	0.1490
Bus	0.426	0.515	0.4008
Motor	0.307	0.366	0.4302
Others	0.25	0.120	0.0124
mAP	0.257	0.312	0.447

References

1. Global Market Insights. Aerial Imaging Market Share - Industry Size, Outlook Report 2018–2024, May 2018. https://www.gminsights.com/industry-analysis/aerial-imaging-market. Accessed 12 Mar 2018
2. IndustryARC. Aerial Imaging Market, December 2018. https://industryarc.com/Report/16300/aerial-imaging-market.html. Accessed 12 Mar 2018
3. Felzenszwalb, P.F., Girshick, R.B., McAllester, D., Ramanan, D.: Object detection with discriminatively trained part-based models. IEEE Trans. Pattern Anal. Mach. Intell. **32**(9), 1627–1645 (2010)
4. Viola, P., Jones, M., et al.: Robust real-time object detection. Int. J. Comput. Vis. **57**(2), 137–154 (2001)
5. Lowe, D.G.: Distinctive image features from scale-invariant keypoints. Int. J. Comput. Vis. **60**(2), 91–110 (2004)
6. Dalal, N., Triggs, B.: Histograms of oriented gradients for human detection. In: International Conference on Computer Vision & Pattern Recognition (CVPR 2005), vol. 1, pp. 886–893. IEEE Computer Society (2005)
7. Lienhart, R., Maydt, J.: An extended set of Haar-like features for rapid object detection. In: Proceedings of the International Conference on Image Processing, vol. 1, p. I. IEEE (2002)
8. Cortes, C., Vapnik, V.: Support vector machine. Mach. Learn. **20**(3), 273–297 (1995)
9. Freund, Y., Schapire, R.E.: A decision-theoretic generalization of on-line learning and an application to boosting. J. Comput. Syst. Sci. **55**(1), 119–139 (1997)
10. Hinton, G.E., Osindero, S., Teh, Y.-W.: A fast learning algorithm for deep belief nets. Neural Comput. **18**(7), 1527–1554 (2006)
11. Hinton, G.E., Salakhutdinov, R.R.: Reducing the dimensionality of data with neural networks. Science **313**(5786), 504–507 (2006)
12. LeCun, Y., Bengio, Y., Hinton, G.: Deep learning. Nature **521**(7553), 436 (2015)
13. Girshick, R.B., Donahue, J., Darrell, T., Malik, J.: Rich feature hierarchies for accurate object detection and semantic segmentation. CoRR, abs/1311.2524 (2013)
14. Redmon, J., Divvala, S.K., Girshick, R.B., Farhadi, A.: You only look once: unified, real-time object detection. CoRR, abs/1506.02640 (2015)
15. Liu, W., et al.: SSD: single shot multibox detector. CoRR, abs/1512.02325 (2015)
16. Bojarski, M., et al.: End to end learning for self-driving cars. CoRR, abs/1604.07316 (2016)
17. Robicquet, A., Sadeghian, A., Alahi, A., Savarese, S.: Learning social etiquette: human trajectory understanding in crowded scenes. In: Leibe, B., Matas, J., Sebe, N., Welling, M. (eds.) ECCV 2016. LNCS, vol. 9912, pp. 549–565. Springer, Cham (2016). https://doi.org/10.1007/978-3-319-46484-8_33
18. Zhu, P., Wen, L., Bian, X., Ling, H., Hu, Q.: Vision meets drones: a challenge. arXiv preprint arXiv:1804.07437 (2018)
19. Girshick, R.B.: Fast R-CNN. CoRR, abs/1504.08083 (2015)
20. Ren, S., He, K., Girshick, R.B., Sun, J.: Faster R-CNN: towards real-time object detection with region proposal networks. CoRR, abs/1506.01497 (2015)
21. Lin, T., Goyal, P., Girshick, R.B., He, K., Dollár, P.: Focal loss for dense object detection. CoRR, abs/1708.02002 (2017)
22. Redmon, J., Farhadi, A.: YOLO9000: better, faster, stronger. CoRR, abs/1612.08242 (2016)

23. Redmon, J., Farhadi, A.: YOLOv3: an incremental improvement. CoRR, abs/1804.02767 (2018)
24. Maggiori, E., Tarabalka, Y., Charpiat, G., Alliez, P.: Can semantic labeling methods generalize to any city? The Inria aerial image labeling benchmark. In: 2017 IEEE International Geoscience and Remote Sensing Symposium (IGARSS), pp. 3226–3229. IEEE (2017)
25. Wang, X., Cheng, P., Liu, X., Uzochukwu, B.: Fast and accurate, convolutional neural network based approach for object detection from UAV. CoRR, abs/1808.05756 (2018)

Comparison of Deep Learning-Based Recognition Techniques for Medical and Biomedical Images

Tomáš Majtner$^{(\boxtimes)}$ and Esmaeil S. Nadimi

Group of Machine Learning and AI, The Maersk Mc-Kinney Moller Institute,
University of Southern Denmark, Odense, Denmark
tomaj@mmmi.sdu.dk

Abstract. The recognition and classification of medical and biomedical images typically suffer from the problem of a low number of annotated samples. This comes along with the problem of efficient training of the current deep learning frameworks. Therefore, many researchers opt for various techniques which could substitute the traditional training of convolutional neural networks (CNN) from scratch. In this article, we are comparing multiple of these methods, including transfer learning and using the CNNs as feature extractors. The paper contains results on two datasets with different modalities and three different CNN architectures. We demonstrate the high effectiveness of transfer learning and suggest that, in some cases, it is worth retraining more layers at the end of the network for achieving higher accuracy.

Keywords: Image recognition · GoogLeNet · VGG-16 · ResNet-50 · Transfer learning · Polyp detection · HEp-2 image classification

1 Introduction

The recent progress in machine learning algorithms has a significant impact on all domains where image analysis is present. New recognition methods, typically based on convolutional neural networks (CNN) and so-called *deep learning* approach, are presented in the literature with high frequency. The domains of medical and biomedical image analysis are typical examples. Only since last year, we can find a guide to deep learning in healthcare [9], applications in biomedicine [4,33], medical image analysis [18], biomedical data science [2], and many others.

Image recognition methods and applications based on deep learning in these domains are easily accessible, and they are still attracting a lot of attention. However, many questions regarding their optimal usage remain open. One of them, which is of our interest in this paper, relates to the training process. To design and train any accurate deep learning recognition framework, a large amount of training samples is required. Depending on the network architecture, we need a certain minimal number of input images to set all the weights in network layers for precise categorisation of test images.

© Springer Nature Switzerland AG 2019
M. Vento and G. Percannella (Eds.): CAIP 2019, LNCS 11678, pp. 492–504, 2019.
https://doi.org/10.1007/978-3-030-29888-3_40

In a real-world image recognition scenario, networks are typically trained on ImageNet [7], where millions of images are hand-annotated. However, in medical and biomedical domains, we must deal with a lack of annotated images. There are some specific methods based on the reduction of annotation effort by making judicious suggestions on the most effective annotation areas [34], or based on image augmentation [28], or generative adversarial networks (GANs) [26] that could be used to increase the size of our datasets. However, even these methods will not properly simulate the quality and variability of large real-world datasets.

Therefore, many researchers in medical and biomedical domains are not training networks from scratch, but they rather use a transfer learning approach [35]. In this scenario, networks pretrained on real-world images are used, with only the last layers of the network modified to classify new images to desired categories. All the weights from the original network are simply copied. However, one can also opt for retraining more layers at the end of the network and transfer/copy only those weights that correspond to the first layers.

Another popular option is to use the CNN as a feature extractor [19], where values from the last layers, typically fully-connected ones, are used together with an external classifier like the discriminant analysis (LDA) or the k-nearest neighbour classifier (k-NN). This approach often leads to overlooking the curse of dimensionality [17, 22].

Because of the variability of above-mentioned methods, we decided to compare all of these options for two particular datasets. The first one is medical and consists of images from colon capsule endoscopy, where we aim to detect polyps. The second one is biomedical and contains images of human epithelial (HEp-2) cells. These images are used in indirect immunofluorescence tests to detect autoimmune diseases. Even though both datasets are visually very different (compare Figs. 1 vs. 2) and come from different domains, in both cases the sample categorisation is currently mostly done by humans. This approach is often subjective, too dependent on the experience of the expert, and with the increasing number of new samples also expensive. Thus, computer-aided systems in both cases aim to assist doctors with correct and fast diagnosis.

Our motivation is to provide a fair comparison for both datasets to see if we can find any patterns which could be later generalised also for other medical and biomedical datasets. For this purpose, we are using three different network architectures, namely GoogLeNet [31], VGG-16 [30], and ResNet-50 [12].

In the next section, we will shortly describe the recent related work in the field and recent progress in polyp detection and HEp-2 image recognition. Subsequently, we will introduce our datasets, pre-processing methods, and an overview of all compared configurations. At the end of the article, we present the results together with a detailed discussion, conclusions, and suggested future work.

2   Related Work

The comparison between transfer learning and training the network from scratch for medical image analysis was covered by Tajbakhsh et al. [32]. Based on their experiments, transfer learning is more robust. A similar comparison was made by Shin et al. [29] who focused on thoraco-abdominal lymph node detection and interstitial lung disease, and they also came to a similar conclusion. The study on the dependence of the detection performance on the extent of transfer for kidney images was done by Ravishankar et al. [27].

In the domain of polyp detection, Mamonov et al. [23] presented an automated method with 81% sensitivity per polyp at a specificity level of 90%. A review of polyp detection and segmentation from video capsule endoscopy was published in 2017 [24]. Many successful methods can be found that are still relying on the traditional recognition approach that is based, for example, on the Gabor texture features and the K-means clustering [14] or the scale-invariant feature transform and the complete local binary pattern [37]. However, the translation of information technology research to clinical practice is still limited [15].

The recent progress in the HEp-2 image analysis has been covered by a special issue of Pattern Recognition Letters [11]. Novel techniques including those examining the role of Gaussian Scale Space theory as a pre-processing approach [25], a superpixel-based classification method calculating the sparse codes of image patches [8], a multi-process system based on an ensemble of 15 support vector machines [5], and many others were introduced. More recently, Gao et al. [10] analysed the impact of hyper-parameter settings of proposed fully-connected CNN on the classification accuracy. The influence of several pre-processing techniques on HEp-2 image classification was studied by Bayramoglu et al. [3].

Our contribution differs from the previous similar comparative studies by direct evaluation of multiple transfer learning options together with the training from scratch strategy and with the usage of CNNs as feature extractors. We are also offering a comparison between two different image modalities trained on the same conditions using three different network configurations. The previous studies usually focused only on a specific domain and/or particular network configuration and/or comparison of the particular two training strategies.

3   Datasets

In this paper, we are using two different datasets. The POLYP DATASET consists of 854 individual frames that were acquired using PillCam^{TM} COLON 2 System, extracted from the videos, and annotated at Odense University Hospital. This dataset consists of 613 polyp images and 241 non-polyps. Because the original images contain text information near the corners, we used a Chan-Vese segmentation via graph cuts [6] to extract the binary mask and segment the relevant information from the image (see Fig. 1 for illustration).

We randomly split the original dataset into 70% for training, 10% for validation, and 20% for testing. Some researchers rather opt for N-fold cross-validation over all available images, especially when the dataset is small. However, this approach leads to biased results [1], where the performance tends to drop significantly when the algorithm is applied to new, previously unseen data. Therefore,

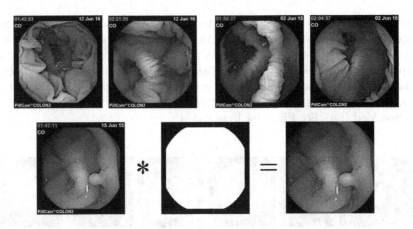

Fig. 1. The top row: examples of the images from the POLYP DATASET. First two from the left contain polyps, while the remaining two do not contain polyps. The bottom row: illustration of the pre-processing for one particular sample.

we use a separate validation part to evaluate the performance during the training of deep learning and independent testing part to report the final performance.

Because the number of samples in our dataset is small, we decided to augment the training and validation part of the dataset. The most natural technique to augment these images is to use image rotation around the image centre and the flipping or reversing operation, where the image is generated as mirror-reversal of an original one across a horizontal axis. First, we rotated each training and validation image by 90°, 180°, and 270°. Since the dataset is unbalanced, we decided to further augment each image from the non-polyp class of training dataset by 30° and 60°. Together with the flipping operation, this augmentation leads to the significant increase of dataset images. The total number of samples in the POLYP DATASET after above specified augmentation of training and validation dataset is summarized in Table 1.

Table 1. The total number of images in the POLYP DATASET after augmentation.

	Polyp	Non-polyp	Total
Training after augm.	3,424	4,032	7,456
Validation after augm.	488	192	680
Testing	124	49	173
Total	4,036	4,273	8,309

The HEP-2 DATASET is a publicly available dataset that was used for benchmarking [13]. The original dataset contains 13,596 pre-segmented and annotated cell images with their ground truth classes. The specimens, one for each patient serum, were automatically photographed using a monochrome high dynamic range cooled microscopy camera. Since the brightness and contrast of the images vary a lot, we performed intensity adjustment by linear stretching, where 1% of the pixels are saturated at the low and the high end of the intensity range in order to maximize the contrast. This dataset is divided into six categories: Centromere (Ce), Golgi (Go), Homogeneous (Ho), Nuclear Membrane (Nm), Nucleolar (Nu), and Speckled (Sp). See Fig. 2 for illustration.

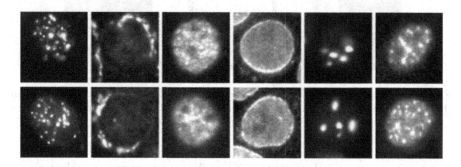

Fig. 2. Examples of images from the HEP-2 DATASET. Each column represents a different image class in order: Ce, Go, Ho, Nm, Nu, Sp.

Also here we used the same random split into 70% for training, 10% for validation, and 20% for testing. Since we have more samples here, we decided to further augment only training part of this dataset. We used the rotation around the image centre by 90°, 180°, and 270° plus the flipping operation, as for the previous dataset. The HEP-2 DATASET is also unbalanced with one class (Golgi) having $3 - 4\times$ lower number of images than the remaining five classes. Therefore, we additionally rotated each Golgi image by angles of size $23° \times i$, where $i \in \{1, 2, 3\}$, where these rotated images were cropped to the size of the largest rectangle within the input image. After this step, Golgi class has similar size than the remaining classes. The total number of samples in each class after the augmentation is summarised in Table 2.

Table 2. The total number of images in the HEP-2 DATASET after augmentation.

	Ce	Go	Ho	Nm	Nu	Sp	Total
Training after augm.	15,344	16,192	13,960	12,368	14,552	15,848	88,264
Validation	274	72	249	220	259	283	1,357
Testing	549	146	500	442	520	567	2,724
Total	16,167	16,410	14,709	13,030	15,331	16,698	92,345

4   Overview of Compared Configurations

As it was mentioned before, we are considering three different approaches for image recognition that are connected to deep leaning. The first one is based on extracting features and using external classifier. This methodology is common for medical image analysis [16,19,21], and its main advantage is that it does not require high computational resources. The idea is that we only download the pretrained model of the network, typically fine-tuned for the real-world images, and use it as a feature extractor for each image from our dataset. These features are subsequently used as an input to a classifier, as it is depicted in Fig. 3.

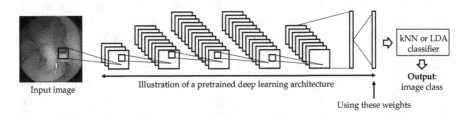

Fig. 3. Illustration of the principle, where a deep learning architecture is used as a feature extractor.

We employed two different classifiers, namely the k-nearest neighbours classifier (k-NN) and the discriminant analysis (LDA). Features extracted from the training dataset were used to train the classifiers and features from validation dataset to set the hyper-parameters. For better comparison, we extracted features from two different layers from each of the pretrained networks. Table 3 offers the summary of used layers for each network architecture together with the size of the feature vector length.

Table 3. Names and sizes of layers that are used to extract features for each architecture.

GoogLeNet	pool5-7x7_s1 (1024)	VGG-16	fc7 (4096)	ResNet-50	avg_pool (2048)
	loss3-classifier (1000)		fc8 (1000)		fc1000 (1000)

Because the dimensionality of extracted features, specified in brackets in Table 3, is very high in comparison with our test dataset, we employed principal component analysis (PCA) to reduce it. Using this approach, we were able to decrease the number of used features down to 20 for k-NN classifier with achieving the same classification accuracy. For LDA classifier, we reduced the dimensionality to approximately 200, while keeping the same accuracy. The exact numbers will be presented in the next section.

The second approach for image recognition used in this study is based on training the deep learning architecture from scratch. In this scenario, we consider only the architecture, but we ignore the pretrained weights. As it was pointed out in previous studies [36], this approach is common for computer vision, where large datasets are available. For the medical and biomedical image processing, its usability and effectiveness are, however, limited [32]. Often the dataset is not large enough to train these networks and researchers tend to design smaller architecture. In this study, we are comparing only three predefined architectures, we are not attempting to design new ones. Therefore, we will only report the results on those configurations, where the training was possible due to the dataset size restrictions.

The last approach is based on transfer learning [35], which is generally very popular for medical and biomedical image recognition [20,29,32]. Here, all three network architectures were pretrained on ImageNet [7], and we replaced/retrained their last layers to classify images directly to our two categories for the POLYP DATASET and six categories for the HEP-2 DATASET.

We also decided to test how far we can go with retraining the pretrained layers. In traditional transfer learning, we typically only replace layers responsible for classification to specified categories. However, researchers could retrain also some convolutional layers (CONV) to better capture the specific fine characteristics of their dataset. In theory, this should be important especially when we are transferring the knowledge between image modalities. Specifically in our case, in GoogLeNet we replaced last 8 layers (incl. 1 CONV), last 19 layers (incl. 6 CONV), and last 33 layers (incl. 12 CONV); in VGG-16 we replaced last 16 layers (incl. 3 CONV) and last 23 layers (incl. 6 CONV); in ResNet-50 we replaced last 8 layers (incl. 1 CONV), last 14 layers (incl. 3 CONV), and last 30 layers (incl. 8 CONV).

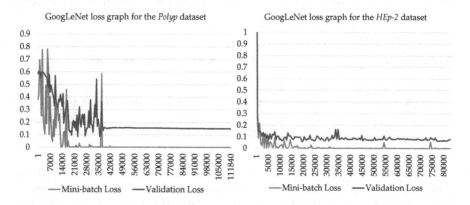

Fig. 4. Graphs depicting the loss for transfer learning using GoogLeNet on both datasets. The x-axis shows the number of iterations.

All images were resized to 224 × 224 to fit the input size of networks. The experiments were performed using MATLAB R2018b, and hyper-parameters were fine-tuned using validation dataset. For the training of each CNN, either from scratch or via transfer learning, we utilised stochastic gradient descent with momentum optimiser. The HEP-2 DATASET was trained for 30 epochs with a learning rate of 10^{-3} and a mini-batch size of 32 images. Since the POLYP DATASET is much smaller, we used a mini-batch size of 4 images, and after we trained them for 30 epochs with a learning rate of 10^{-3}, we added 30 more epochs with a learning rate of 10^{-4}. This decrease in learning rate had a positive effect on convergence towards minimum validation loss. We did not observe this effect for the HEP-2 DATASET. We cannot provide here all the graphs from the training process, but the illustration of the loss development for transfer learning using GoogLeNet is depicted in Fig. 4.

5   Results and Discussion

The evaluation of classification performance is done using various metrics. In the POLYP DATASET, we have a binary classification problem, where the most commonly used metrics include classification accuracy (ACC), sensitivity (TPR), and specificity (SPC). They are defined as follows:

$$ACC = \frac{\text{true positives} + \text{true negatives}}{\text{number of samples}}, \tag{1}$$

$$TPR = \frac{\text{true positives}}{\text{true positives} + \text{false negatives}}, \tag{2}$$

$$SPC = \frac{\text{true negatives}}{\text{true negatives} + \text{false positives}}. \tag{3}$$

For the evaluation of the HEP-2 DATASET, we use the classification accuracy (ACC), which is defined here as the overall correct classification rate of all images. The second evaluation metric is the mean class accuracy (MCA), which is defined as

$$MCA = \frac{1}{K} \sum_{k=1}^{K} CCR_k \tag{4}$$

where CCR_k is the classification accuracy of a particular cell class k and K is the number of cell classes.

The comparison of all tested variants for the POLYP DATASET is summarized in Table 4 and for the HEP-2 DATASET in Table 5. In all cases, extracting the features from deep learning and using them with external classifier performed worse when compared to methods based on transfer learning. As it was expected, even the training from scratch was not performing well. In many cases, it was not possible to train the network at all, due to the limited number of samples but even when the training was successful, the performance was low.

The most interesting result, however, is the comparison between transfer learning strategies. From the results, we can see that retraining last layers can have a positive effect on the final performance of the recognition framework. This was observed especially for GoogLeNet and ResNet-50 architectures, and we see this effect on both datasets, which means that it is not specific for one domain or one type of images. We can also observe the trend that with retraining more layers, the performance typically starts to decline, which could be ascribed to low number of samples.

Table 4. The summary of results for the POLYP DATASET. The number of nearest neighbours in k-NN classifier is specified in brackets. In transfer learning, *end* represents the retraining of layers responsible for classifying, while the *lastX* variants represent the retraining of last X layers. Presented values are in %.

GoogLeNet									
Features				Scratch	Transfer learning				
pool5-7x7_s1		loss3-classifier							
	k-NN(10)	LDA	k-NN(11)	LDA		end	last 8	last 19	last 33
ACC	77.46	75.72	75.14	76.88	–	91.33	**93.06**	89.02	90.75
TPR	91.94	87.10	93.55	87.90	–	96.77	**98.39**	96.77	95.16
SPC	40.82	46.94	28.57	48.98	–	77.55	**79.59**	69.39	79.59

VGG-16								
Features				Scratch	Transfer learning			
fc7		fc8						
	k-NN(10)	LDA	k-NN(10)	LDA		end	last 16	last 23
ACC	76.30	79.19	76.88	78.03	–	**94.22**	90.17	89.59
TPR	91.94	87.10	92.74	90.32	–	**96.77**	95.97	95.97
SPC	36.73	59.18	36.73	46.94	–	**87.76**	75.51	73.47

ResNet-50									
Features				Scratch	Transfer learning				
avg_pool		fc1000							
	k-NN(11)	LDA	k-NN(10)	LDA		end	last 8	last 14	last 30
ACC	78.61	84.39	79.19	84.97	74.57	**94.22**	90.75	90.75	80.34
TPR	90.32	87.10	91.94	88.71	83.87	**97.58**	91.93	94.35	87.09
SPC	48.98	77.55	46.94	75.51	51.02	85.71	**87.76**	81.63	63.26

The results on the POLYP DATASET are not comparable with the literature since the dataset is private, but the comparison of our top performing results for the HEP-2 DATASET with the methods from the literature is presented in Table 6. We included only those results that are using a similar split technique for training and testing dataset. The method presented by Shen et al. [28] proposed

Table 5. The summary of results for the HEp-2 DATASET. The number of nearest neighbours in k-NN classifier is specified in brackets. In transfer learning, *end* represents the retraining of layers responsible for classifying, while the *lastX* variants represent the retraining of last X layers. Presented values are in %.

GoogLeNet

	Features				Scratch	Transfer learning			
	pool5-7x7_s1		loss3-classifier						
	k-NN(10)	LDA	k-NN(12)	LDA		end	last 8	last 19	last 33
ACC	88.77	90.05	87.26	86.78	–	**98.53**	98.49	98.38	98.05
MCA	87.67	89.34	85.74	85.18	–	**98.64**	98.62	98.44	98.21

VGG-16

	Features				Scratch	Transfer learning			
	fc7		fc8						
	k-NN(8)	LDA	k-NN(15)	LDA		end	last 16	last 23	
ACC	88.91	91.37	87.11	86.23	94.38	**98.16**	97.61	97.54	
MCA	87.06	90.53	84.84	84.24	94.89	**98.22**	97.53	97.62	

ResNet-50

	Features				Scratch	Transfer learning			
	avg_pool		fc1000						
	k-NN(10)	LDA	k-NN(9)	LDA		end	last 8	last 14	last 30
ACC	94.68	94.09	92.84	91.89	96.29	97.91	**98.42**	97.87	98.27
MCA	94.01	93.84	91.88	91.29	96.28	97.84	**98.57**	97.79	98.31

a deep cross residual network (DCRNet) for HEp-2 cell classification, and it was the winner of the most recent HEp-2 image recognition contest.

Table 6. The comparison with other approaches on the same dataset and with the same division of publicly available part of HEp-2 images. Presented values are in %.

	ACC	MCA
Gao et al. [10]	97.24	96.76
Shen et al. [28]	**98.82**	98.62
Our top performing method	98.53	**98.64**

6   Conclusion

In this article, we presented a comparison of three different techniques for image recognition, where all of them are based on deep learning. We used three different network configurations to capture the effect of architecture choice on final results, and we tested two different image modalities, which currently share the same problem with manual annotation. Our results demonstrate the high performance of our solutions, which are demonstrated especially on the HEp-2 DATASET. We also observed that the retraining of the last layers can be very efficient in terms of the final performance. Moreover, this conclusion was observed on both datasets, which means that it is not domain dependent.

The future work should be concentrated on the improvement of performance on the POLYP DATASET. It is always challenging to build a framework for a domain with very few samples, and therefore we would like to explore more the possibilities of increasing the number of samples by using generative adversarial networks.

Acknowledgement. This research was supported by a research grant from the University of Southern Denmark, Odense University Hospital, Danish Cancer Society, and Region of Southern Denmark through the Project EFFICACY.

References

1. Babyak, M.: What you see may not be what you get: a brief, nontechnical introduction to overfitting in regression-type models. Psychosom. Med. **66**(3), 411–421 (2004)
2. Baldi, P.: Deep learning in biomedical data science. Ann. Rev. Biomed. Data Sci. **1**, 181–205 (2018)
3. Bayramoglu, N., Kannala, J., Heikkilä, J.: Human epithelial type 2 cell classification with convolutional neural networks. In: 15th International Conference on Bioinformatics and Bioengineering, pp. 1–6. IEEE (2015)
4. Cao, C., et al.: Deep learning and its applications in biomedicine. Genomics Proteomics Bioinform. **16**(1), 17–32 (2018)
5. Cascio, D., Taormina, V., Cipolla, M., Bruno, S., Fauci, F., Raso, G.: A multiprocess system for HEp-2 cells classification based on SVM. Pattern Recognit. Lett. **82**, 56–63 (2016)
6. Daněk, O., Matula, P., Maška, M., Kozubek, M.: Smooth Chan-Vese segmentation via graph cuts. Pattern Recognit. Lett. **33**(10), 1405–1410 (2012)
7. Deng, J., Dong, W., Socher, R., Li, L.J., Li, K., Fei-Fei, L.: ImageNet: a large-scale hierarchical image database. In: IEEE Conference on Computer Vision and Pattern Recognition, pp. 248–255. IEEE (2009)
8. Ensafi, S., Lu, S., Kassim, A.A., Tan, C.: Accurate HEp-2 cell classification based on sparse coding of superpixels. Pattern Recognit. Lett. **82**, 64–71 (2016)
9. Esteva, A., et al.: A guide to deep learning in healthcare. Nat. Med. **25**(1), 24–29 (2019)
10. Gao, Z., Wang, L., Zhou, L., Zhang, J.: HEp-2 cell image classification with deep convolutional neural networks. IEEE J. Biomed. Health Inform. **21**(2), 416–428 (2017)
11. Harandi, M., Lovell, B., Percannella, G., Saggese, A., Vento, M., Wiliem, A.: Executable thematic special issue on pattern recognition techniques for indirect immunofluorescence images analysis. Pattern Recognit. Lett. **82**, 1–2 (2016)

12. He, K., Zhang, X., Ren, S., Sun, J.: Deep residual learning for image recognition. In: IEEE Conference on Computer Vision and Pattern Recognition, pp. 770–778 (2016)
13. Hobson, P., Lovell, B., Percannella, G., Vento, M., Wiliem, A.: Benchmarking human epithelial type 2 interphase cells classification methods on a very large dataset. Artif. Intell. Med. **65**(3), 239–250 (2015)
14. Hwang, S., Celebi, M.E.: Polyp detection in wireless capsule endoscopy videos based on image segmentation and geometric feature. In: 2010 IEEE International Conference on Acoustics, Speech and Signal Processing, pp. 678–681. IEEE (2010)
15. Iakovidis, D.K., Koulaouzidis, A.: Software for enhanced video capsule endoscopy: challenges for essential progress. Nat. Rev. Gastroenterol. Hepatol. **12**(3), 172 (2015)
16. Kawahara, J., BenTaieb, A., Hamarneh, G.: Deep features to classify skin lesions. In: 13th International Symposium on Biomedical Imaging (ISBI), pp. 1397–1400. IEEE (2016)
17. Keogh, E., Mueen, A.: Curse of dimensionality. In: Sammut, C., Webb, G.I. (eds.) Encyclopedia of Machine Learning and Data Mining, pp. 314–315. Springer, Boston (2017). https://doi.org/10.1007/978-1-4899-7687-1_192
18. Ker, J., Wang, L., Rao, J., Lim, T.: Deep learning applications in medical image analysis. IEEE Access **6**, 9375–9389 (2018)
19. Lai, Z., Deng, H.: Medical image classification based on deep features extracted by deep model and statistic feature fusion with multilayer perceptron. Comput. Intell. Neurosci. **2018**, 1–13 (2018)
20. Liu, A., Gao, Z., Tong, H., Su, Y., Yang, Z.: Sparse coding induced transfer learning for HEp-2 cell classification. Bio-Med. Mater. Eng. **24**(1), 237–243 (2014)
21. Majtner, T., Yildirim-Yayilgan, S., Hardeberg, J.Y.: Combining deep learning and hand-crafted features for skin lesion classification. In: 6th International Conference on Image Processing Theory, Tools and Applications, pp. 1–6. IEEE (2016)
22. Majtner, T., Yildirim-Yayilgan, S., Hardeberg, J.Y.: Optimised deep learning features for improved melanoma detection. Multimed. Tools Appl. **78**(9), 11883–11903 (2019)
23. Mamonov, A.V., Figueiredo, I.N., Figueiredo, P.N., Tsai, Y.H.R.: Automated polyp detection in colon capsule endoscopy. IEEE Trans. Med. Imaging **33**(7), 1488–1502 (2014)
24. Prasath, V.: Polyp detection and segmentation from video capsule endoscopy: a review. J. Imaging **3**(1), 1–15 (2017)
25. Qi, X., Zhao, G., Chen, J., Pietikäinen, M.: HEp-2 cell classification: the role of gaussian scale space theory as a pre-processing approach. Pattern Recognit. Lett. **82**, 36–43 (2016)
26. Radford, A., Metz, L., Chintala, S.: Unsupervised representation learning with deep convolutional generative adversarial networks. arXiv preprint arXiv:1511.06434 (2015)
27. Ravishankar, H., et al.: Understanding the mechanisms of deep transfer learning for medical images. In: Carneiro, G., et al. (eds.) LABELS/DLMIA-2016. LNCS, vol. 10008, pp. 188–196. Springer, Cham (2016). https://doi.org/10.1007/978-3-319-46976-8_20
28. Shen, L., Jia, X., Li, Y.: Deep cross residual network for HEp-2 cell staining pattern classification. Pattern Recognit. **82**, 68–78 (2018)
29. Shin, H.C., et al.: Deep convolutional neural networks for computer-aided detection: CNN architectures, dataset characteristics and transfer learning. IEEE Trans. Med. Imaging **35**(5), 1285–1298 (2016)

30. Simonyan, K., Zisserman, A.: Very deep convolutional networks for large-scale image recognition. arXiv preprint arXiv:1409.1556 (2014)
31. Szegedy, C., et al.: Going deeper with convolutions. In: Proceedings of the IEEE Conference on Computer Vision and Pattern Recognition, pp. 1–9 (2015)
32. Tajbakhsh, N., et al.: Convolutional neural networks for medical image analysis: full training or fine tuning? IEEE Trans. Med. Imaging **35**(5), 1299–1312 (2016)
33. Wainberg, M., Merico, D., Delong, A., Frey, B.J.: Deep learning in biomedicine. Nat. Biotechnol. **36**(9), 829 (2018)
34. Yang, L., Zhang, Y., Chen, J., Zhang, S., Chen, D.Z.: Suggestive annotation: a deep active learning framework for biomedical image segmentation. In: Descoteaux, M., Maier-Hein, L., Franz, A., Jannin, P., Collins, D.L., Duchesne, S. (eds.) MICCAI 2017. LNCS, vol. 10435, pp. 399–407. Springer, Cham (2017). https://doi.org/10.1007/978-3-319-66179-7_46
35. Yosinski, J., Clune, J., Bengio, Y., Lipson, H.: How transferable are features in deep neural networks? In: Advances in Neural Information Processing Systems, pp. 3320–3328 (2014)
36. Yu, Y., Lin, H., Meng, J., Wei, X., Guo, H., Zhao, Z.: Deep transfer learning for modality classification of medical images. Information **8**(3), 91 (2017)
37. Yuan, Y., Li, B., Meng, M.Q.H.: Improved bag of feature for automatic polyp detection in wireless capsule endoscopy images. IEEE Trans. Autom. Sci. Eng. **13**(2), 529–535 (2016)

Retrieved Image Refinement
by Bootstrap Outlier Test

Hayato Watanabe[1], Hideitsu Hino[2,3]([✉]) [iD], Shotaro Akaho[4] [iD],
and Noboru Murata[1] [iD]

[1] Waseda University, Tokyo 169-0072, Japan
[2] The Institute of Statistical Mathematics, Tokyo 190-8562, Japan
hino@ism.ac.jp
[3] RIKEN AIP, Tokyo 103-0027, Japan
[4] National Institute of Advanced Industrial Science and Technology,
Ibaraki 305-8568, Japan

Abstract. Outlier detection is used to identify data points or a small number of subsets of data that are significantly different from most other data in a given dataset. It is challenging to detect outliers using an objective and quantitative approach. Methods that use the framework of statistical hypothesis testing are widely used by assuming a specific parametric distribution as a data generation model, but there is no guarantee that the distribution of data can be adequately approximated by a parametric distribution in practical problems. In this paper, a simple method is proposed to objectively detect outliers by hypothesis testing without assuming a specific distribution of outlier scores. By using an arbitrary outlier score function, hypothesis testing is used to determine whether each given sample is an outlier. The distribution of the test statistics is needed for the hypothesis test, and is estimated based on the given data using the bootstrap method. The effectiveness of the proposed outlier test was verified by applying it to outlier detection for text-based image retrieval, where it improved the quality of image searches by removing irrelevant images.

Keywords: Outlier removal · Image retrieval · Hypothesis testing

1 Introduction

According to Hawkins [16], an outlier is defined as *a point suspected to have been caused by a different mechanism because it is far from other data points*. Outliers often have important meanings, and detecting them is important in various scenarios. Therefore, many methods have been proposed to detect outliers in given data. Of them, the method that employs hypothesis testing [2,4,15] and one based on k-nearest neighboring distances [5,28] are most commonly used.

Partly supported by JST CREST JPMJCR1761, JSPS KAKENHI 17H01748,17H02953 and 19H04113.

M. Vento and G. Percannella (Eds.): CAIP 2019, LNCS 11678, pp. 505–517, 2019.
https://doi.org/10.1007/978-3-030-29888-3_41

Other approaches have also been developed, e.g., methods based on probability density [9] or one-class SVM [30]. For detailed and comprehensive surveys, see [1, 8, 19, 27]. The method that uses the hypothesis test for outlier detection is the most natural way to determine whether the data points of interest (hereinafter referred to as *inspection points*) are outliers. When determining an outlier based on data with stochastic fluctuation, probabilistic errors cannot be avoided. The framework of hypothesis testing has the advantage whereby we can objectivity control the probability of errors. On the contrary, as a distribution of the generation of data is assumed in standard statistical tests, it cannot be applied when the given data significantly deviate from this assumption, where this is common in practical problems.

In the method based on the distance between a given point and the k-nearest neighbors, there is no need to assume the generative distribution of the data. In many outlier detection methods, including the k-nearest neighbor distance-based method, angle-based outlier detection method [20], and isolation forest [22], the outlier score for each sample is calculated instead of directly judging whether it is an outlier. On the contrary, there are practical scenarios where we want to know whether a given sample is an outlier, and the outlier score is not the focus of interest. For example, in case we want to identify defective items as outliers at a manufacturing site, we want to identify the defective product rather than the extent to which it is suspected to be defective. Similarly, if we want to identify people who are ill as outliers in a medical examination, we want to determine whether a given subject is ill rather than the degree to which he or she is thought to be ill.

In the context of outlier detection based on the k-nearest neighbor distance, one method to identify outliers involves regarding κ samples with the highest outlier scores as outliers [28]. However, the number of outliers κ is not known in general. Therefore, when determining whether an inspection point is an outlier based on the outlier score, we typically determine a threshold and compare the outlier score of the given point with it. This method has two major drawbacks. The first is that the interpretability of the outlier score is poor and empirical rules are inevitable to set a threshold. The second is that there may be outliers that cannot be detected using a single threshold. Because of these problems with the threshold-based approach, it has been accorded little consideration in research. The few exceptions include the local correlation integral [26], which determines the threshold automatically but uses the three-σ rule for outlier scores to determine outliers. The three-σ rule is an empirical rule whereby a data item exceeding (average) $+ 3 \times$ (standard deviation) is regarded as an outlier [21]. The local outlier probability [18] generates the probability of *outlierness* based on a local outlier factor (LOF) proposed in [7], which is based on the k-nearest neighbor distance. Although the method is based on LOF, the statistic for deriving outlierness probability is different from that used in LOF.

In this paper, we propose a method that combines the objectivity of the hypothesis test and the flexibility of the k-nearest neighbor distance. Using an arbitrary outlier score function based on the k-nearest neighbor distance, the hypothesis test is used to determine whether a given inspection point is an outlier. Our method is based on the statistical test, and has the advantage whereby a threshold value can be determined by considering the risk of overlooking an outlier (significance level α). The framework of statistical test allows us to adaptively determine appropriate *threshold* for judging whether the inspection point is an outlier, which is difficult in conventional score based methods (See Fig. 2 in next section for details). The distribution of the test statistic is needed to perform the hypothesis test, and conventional outlier test assumes Gaussian or other simple distribution. On the contrary, we estimate it based on the data given using the bootstrap method [6]. We consider an application of the proposed method to text-based image retrieval (TBIR). Most search engines can provide images in response to text queries, but a large number of the search results are irrelevant to the intended query. See Fig. 1, for example, which shows the search results of the query *tower of Pisa*, where the upper half is occupied by relevant results but the bottom half contains irrelevant ones. Thus, the text information may fail to capture the contents of images [23–25].

Fig. 1. Example of the results of image retrieval on the INRIA Web queries dataset [17]. For the query *tower of Pisa*, there were 187 relevant and 34 irrelevant outputs. The top four images are relevant and the bottom four irrelevant to the *tower of Pisa*.

2   Problem Formulation

The problem of outlier detection can be formally stated as follows:

Problem 1. *Let $\mathcal{X}$ be the domain of the observed data, and suppose a dataset $D = \{x_i; i = 1, \ldots, n\} \subset \mathcal{X}$ is given. Then, the problem of outlier detection is one of unsupervised learning: to determine whether a certain data item $x \in D$, which is called the inspection point, is an outlier based on a given outlier score $s_k(x; D)$.*

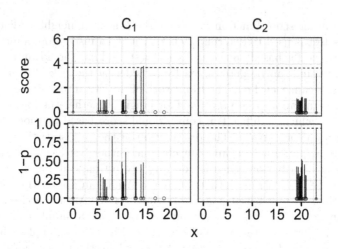

Fig. 2. An example of data with outliers that cannot be detected when a single threshold value is used. The single threshold tuned for chunk C_1 (top left) is inappropriate for detecting the outlier in chunk C_2 (top right).

In the above, $s_k : \mathcal{X} \to \mathbb{R}$ is a given outlier score function with a parameter k. The function $s_k(\,\cdot\,; D)$ gives the degree of outlierness of its input based on the locality parameter k. Note that the output of the conventional outlier detection problem involves calculating the outlier score of the inspection point $s_k(x; D)$, and it is left to the user to determine whether point x with score $s_k(x; D)$ is an outlier or an inlier.

To determine whether a given inspection point is an outlier based on outlier scores, in the conventional approach, a single threshold is set, and the inspection point is considered an outlier if its score exceeds the threshold value. However, this fixed-threshold approach has two major drawbacks. First, it is difficult to interpret the degree of the outlier obtained, and it is difficult for the user to set the threshold in a subjective manner that is nonetheless principled. For example, the LOF [7] tends to return an outlier score of around one if the inspection point is not an outlier and a score greater than one if it is. It is challenging to know how different this is from a point with an outlier score of two or three. With regard to the LOF, a value between 1.2 and two is set as threshold [14], although it is nothing more than a rule of thumb and does not offer objectivity. Moreover, even if we can tentatively determine a threshold using an annotated dataset, i.e., for which the outlier label is given, the meaning of the outlier scores changes if we consider a different dataset. Thus, using the same threshold over different datasets is inappropriate. The second problem is that, even if we can obtain the *best* single threshold value, there would be some data points with lower outlier scores than the threshold that should nevertheless be treated as outliers. For example, suppose we have two chunks. The first chunk C_1 shown in left panels is $\{x_{1,1}, \ldots, x_{1,20}\}$ uniformly sampled from the interval $[5, 15]$, plus an outlier $x_{1,0} = 0$. The second chunk C_2 shown in right panels is $\{x_{2,1}, \ldots, x_{2,20}\}$, uniformly sampled from the interval $[19, 21]$ plus an outlier $x_{2,0} = 23$. The result of calculating outlier scores by LOF is shown in Fig. 2. Vertical axis of top panels show the LOF scores and that of bottom panels show $1 - p$ value.

From the values of LOF scores in Fig. 2, it is clear that if the threshold value is set so that the only outlier $x_{1,0}$ among the chunk C_1 can be detected, the outlier in C_2 is missed. On the other hand, when the threshold is set to detect the outlier $x_{2,0}$, large amount of inliers in C_1 are mistakenly detected as outliers. Imagine if we observe the union of the two chunks C_1 and C_2. Conventional methods of outlier detection would miss outlier $x_{2,0}$ or, in the worst case, if tuned to detect $x_{2,0}$, would consider many points in chunk 1 as outliers. On the contrary, our proposed method based on the bootstrap statistical test successfully identifies outliers in both chunks as shown in bottom panels.

Despite the problem with a single fixed threshold, little consideration has been accorded to it in the literature on outlier and novelty detection. In this paper, we propose a method to determine whether inspection point x is an outlier based on the given outlier score function $s_k(\cdot)$. The problem to be solved in this work is as follows:

Problem 2. *Given the dataset $D \subset \mathcal{X}$ and the outlier score function $s_k(\,\cdot\,; D)$, perform a statistical test to determine whether the inspection point $x \in D$ is an outlier.*

3   Statistical Test for Outlier Detection

In the situation shown in Fig. 2, there exist outliers that cannot be detected regardless of how the threshold value is determined. Therefore, we propose to adaptively determine threshold values. To formulate the proposed approach, we consider the following assumption:

Assumption 1. *If inspection point $x \in D$ is not an outlier, its outlier score $s_k(x; D)$ and the average outlier score of its neighborhood are almost identical.*

Let $\mathcal{N}_k(x)$ be the k-nearest neighbors of the inspection point x. Then, the average outlier score in $\mathcal{N}_k$ is defined as

$$\bar{s}_k(x; D) = \frac{1}{k} \sum_{y \in \mathcal{N}_k(x)} s_k(y; D). \tag{1}$$

Let the means of $s_k(x; D)$ and $\bar{s}_k(x; D)$ over an unknown population distribution be μ and $\bar{\mu}$, respectively. Based on Assumption 1, we can construct a statistical test by considering the following hypotheses:

$$\begin{aligned} &\text{Null hypothesis } H_0 : \mu = \bar{\mu} \\ &\text{Alternative hypothesis } H_1 : \mu > \bar{\mu} \end{aligned} \tag{2}$$

As our concern is whether the inspection point is an outlier, we consider the one-sided test. For test statistic t, we use

$$t = s_k(x; D) - \bar{s}_k(x; D). \tag{3}$$

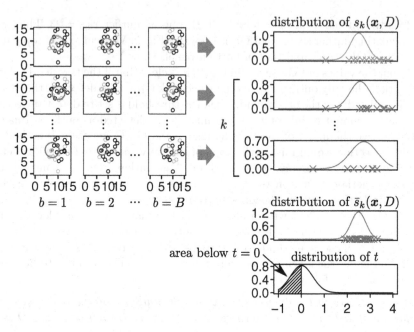

Fig. 3. Schematic diagram of how to calculate the p value of the outlier test based on bootstrap sampling. The shaded area corresponds to the p value for the null hypothesis.

To perform the statistical test, it is sufficient to know the probability distribution of test statistic t. The probability distributions of the given dataset D and that of the corresponding set of outlier scores are unknown. In the next section, the probability distribution of test statistic t is approximated using the bootstrap method.

The bootstrap method is a general framework to evaluate the properties of statistics based only on an observed dataset. In the bootstrap test, we calculate the bootstrap test statistic $\hat{t}^*$ by the following formula:

$$\hat{t}^* = s_k(\boldsymbol{x}; \mathcal{N}_k^*(\boldsymbol{x})) - \bar{s}_k(\boldsymbol{x}; \mathcal{N}_k^*(\boldsymbol{x})), \qquad (4)$$

where $\mathcal{N}_k^*(\boldsymbol{x})$ is the set of points constructed by k resamplings from the k-nearest neighbors $\mathcal{N}_k(\boldsymbol{x})$ of inspection point $\boldsymbol{x}$. Many methods are available to estimate the distribution of test statistics based on bootstrap test statistics $\{\hat{t}^{*b}; b = 1, \ldots, B\}$ obtained by B bootstrap sampling. Some common ones include the percentile method, normal approximation method, and the BC_a method. The details of each can be found in [11]. In an examination of various methods in our preliminary experiments, the percentile method yielded the best results. It is one of the most intuitive and flexible ways to estimate the summary statistics of test statistics. Figure 3 shows how the distribution and p value are estimated by bootstrap sampling. We compute B copies of test statistics $\hat{t}^{*b}$, sort the statistics in ascending order, and calculate the empirical percentile based on the sorted statistics. The concrete procedure for the bootstrap outlier test for our

---

Algorithm 1. Bootstrap Outlier Detection Test

Require: Observed dataset D, outlier score function s_k with locality parameter k, the inspection point $x \in D$, number of bootstrap samples B, and significance level α for statistical test.

1: Set counter $n = 0$.
2: **for** $b = 1$ to B **do**
3:    Calculate the bootstrap test statistics

$$\hat{t}^{*b} = s_k(x; \mathcal{N}_k^{*b}(x)) - \bar{s}_k(x; \mathcal{N}_k^{*b}(x)).$$

4:    Increase the counter n by one if $\hat{t}^{*b}$ is less than or equal to zero.
5: **end for**
6: **return** Test result: if $n/B < \alpha$, the inspection is judged to be an outlier. Otherwise, the inspection point is not regarded as an outlier.

---

problem is very simple. Under the null hypothesis H_0, the distribution of test statistic t should be concentrated around zero. The p value of the statistical test is estimated as the ratio of the realizations of test statistics smaller than or equal to zero. The p value is the probability that statistic t ($t = 0$ in this case) is realized under the null hypothesis, and a small p value implies that the given inspection point is likely to be an outlier. As in the statistical test, we set the significance level before performing outlier detection. Then, if the estimated p value is under the predefined significance level (typically set to 0.05 or 0.01, but these values do not have any theoretical meaning), the inspection point is considered an outlier. The concrete procedure for the proposed outlier test algorithm is given in Algorithm 1. In our experiments, the number of bootstrap replicate B is set to 10^5.

4   Experiments

We applied the proposed bootstrap outlier test to the problem of refinement of the results of image retrieval. The outlier score was calculated as the k-th nearest neighbor distance (we investigated cases where $k = 5$ and $k = 10$). We used the INRIA Web queries dataset [17] containing 71,478 images and metadata retrieved by 353 Web queries. For each retrieved image, the relevance label was manually assigned. We note that the proposed method can be used with arbitrary method which outputs an outlier score. We only show the results with k-th nearest neighbor distance and the proposed method to avoid obscuring the point we want to stress, namely, the bootstrap outlier test can improve the raw outlierness score.

Table 1. List of queries related to tourist attractions with outlier ratios smaller than 50%.

Id	Query_string	Outlier (%)	Data size
0	Arc de triomphe	0.38	221
1	Eiffel tower	0.484	223
20	Mont saint michel	0.349	215
22	Colosseum rome	0.485	97
23	Victor emmanuel II	0.25	16
24	Pantheon rome	0.266	256
25	Trevi fountain	0.361	72
30	Piazza san marco	0.401	237
34	Tower of pisa	0.152	224
36	Sagrada familia	0.232	224
41	Tower bridge	0.214	248
42	Big ben	0.25	212
45	Buckingham palace	0.34	244
50	Brandenburg gate	0.373	51
53	Omar jerusalem	0.36	25
56	Empire state building	0.346	237
57	Times square	0.494	249
58	Guggenheim museum	0.389	234
59	Statue of liberty	0.494	241
61	White house	0.496	252
62	Capitol	0.311	206
63	Lincoln memorial	0.213	211
65	Grand canyon	0.309	204
73	Pearl tower	0.437	238
77	Moscow basilica	0.263	19
82	Machu picchu	0.152	224
87	Tikal	0.415	224
91	Opera sydney	0.154	246
92	Pyramids egypt	0.35	200
93	Taj mahal	0.322	208

In the standard problem setting of outlier detection, it is often implicitly or explicitly assumed that the number of outliers is very small relative to that of the inliers. However, when we consider the image retrieval refinement problem, a considerable amount of irrelevant data can be included in the responses to a query. We assumed that the *outliers are not majorities*, and selected the queries for which the ratio of outliers (irrelevant outputs) was smaller than 50% from the INRIA Web queries dataset. The number of queries selected by this criterion was still over 130, and it was unrealistic to visually inspect the results of query refinement. To reduce the number of queries (datasets to be applied), we limited queries to those related to tourist attractions, which were 30, as listed in Table 1.

Evaluation Measure. We used the area under the ROC curve (AUC) as a measure to assess the refinement of the retrieved images. For the raw score-based method, we gradually changed the threshold for the outlier and calculate the AUC value. For the proposed method, we used $1-p$ as the normalized outlier score and calculated the AUC by changing the threshold from zero to one in the same manner as in the raw score-based method.

Computation of Outlier Score for Images. To calculate the outlier score, it is necessary to calculate the distance between images. For this purpose, we entered each image into the Xception V1 model [10] trained using ImageNet [29], and obtained a 2,048-dimensional in the final layer that was used as the feature vector of the image. The Euclidean distance between images was calculated for this feature vector. In this example, Euclidean distance was used in Xception, which is a popular and efficient tool to extract features from images. If the outlier score can be calculated, the distance between the images is arbitrary.

4.1   Results

In Fig. 4, we show AUCs of the score-based method and the proposed method for 30 queries. We also show box plots of the paired t-test with the null hypothesis whereby there was no difference between the methods shown in Fig. 5. The p values of the paired t-test indicate that the AUCs of the proposed method were significantly larger than those of the score-based method on average.

From the experimental results and visual inspection, the proposed method outperformed the raw score-based method when the density of data depended significantly on location and required adaptive thresholding, as was the case shown in Fig. 2. The proposed method selected appropriate *thresholds* depending on each location of the inspection point via the evaluation of the p value through bootstrap sampling. There are cases in which the proposed method deteriorate the results. The true reason for this phenomenon is unknown, but we conjecture that the proposed method does not improve the raw score based method when the distribution of the data points is simple and raw score is already good enough for outlier detection.

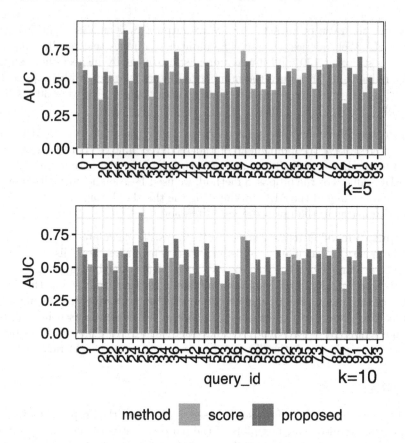

Fig. 4. AUCs for 30 queries obtained using the score-based method and the proposed method. Top: score was calculated with $k = 5$. Bottom: with $k = 10$

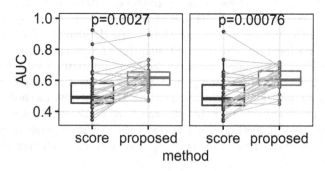

Fig. 5. Paired t-test for two samples: $k = 5$-th (left) and $k = 10$-th (right) nearest scores vs. those of the proposed method. We see only minor impact on the choice of k.

5   Conclusion and Future Work

This paper proposed an outlier test based on arbitrary outlier scores. A hypothesis test was constructed based only on the assumption that the outlier score of a given inspection point and the average outlier score around its local neighbors are equal. The p value was calculated by a simple bootstrap method, i.e., the percentile method. Using the INRIA Web query dataset, we showed that the proposed method can improve the method based on the raw outlier scores in terms of refining images retrieved through text-based queries.

The disadvantage of the proposed outlier test is its computational complexity. The number of bootstrap replicates B should be sufficiently large to stably perform statistical tests. The appropriate number of bootstrap samplings can depend on the characteristics of the given data and the method used to calculate outlier score. Methods to reduce the number of the bootstrap samplings B have been proposed in [12,13], and can be used to reduce computational complexity without reducing the accuracy of outlier detection.

There are two directions of our future research based on the work here. The first is further investigation of Assumption 1 used here. In Assumption 1, we used the average $\bar{s}_k(x; D)$ of the outlier score of the k-nearest neighbors of the inspection point x, but there is no strong theoretical reason to use the average. We calculated the bootstrap replicate of the outlier scores of the k-nearest neighbors of inspection point x only to average the scores. We may not have made full use of the bootstrapping method in our method.

The second is the proposal of an ensemble method with many outlier scores. In the data mining community, the ensemble method for the unsupervised calculation of outlier scores has been extensively studied in recent years [3,31]. The difficulty that arises when ensembling a large number of outlier scores is standardizing and combining outlier scores with different meanings. By estimating the distribution of outlier scores, as was done in this study, it is possible to absorb the differences in outlier scores, which makes it easier to develop an ensemble method using the estimated distribution.

References

1. Aggarwal, C.C.: Outlier Analysis. Springer, New York (2013). https://doi.org/10.1007/978-1-4614-6396-2
2. Aggarwal, C.C., Philip, S.Y.: Outlier detection with uncertain data. In: SDM, vol. 8, pp. 483–493. SIAM (2008)
3. Aggarwal, C.C., Sathe, S.: Theoretical foundations and algorithms for outlier ensembles. ACM SIGKDD Explor. Newsl. 17(1), 24–47 (2015)
4. Barnett, V., Lewis, T.: Outliers in Statistical Data. Wiley Series in Probability and Statistics. Wiley, Chichester (1994)
5. Bay, S., Schwabacher, M.: Mining distance-based outliers in near linear time with randomization and a simple pruning rule. In: ACM SIGKDD International Conference on Knowledge Discovery and Data Mining, pp. 29–38 (2003). https://doi.org/10.1145/956750.956758

6. Bøvelstad, H.M., Holsbø E., Bongo, L.A., Lund, E.: A standard operating procedure for outlier removal in large-sample epidemiological transcriptomics datasets. BioRxiv (2017)

7. Breunig, M.M., Kriegel, H.P., Ng, R.T., Sander, J.: LOF: identifying density-based local outliers. ACM SIGMOD Rec. 29(2), 93–104 (2000)

8. Chandola, V., Banerjee, A., Kumar, V.: Anomaly detection: a survey. ACM Comput. Surv. (CSUR) 41(3), 15 (2009)

9. Chen, Y., Dang, X., Peng, H., Bart Jr., H.L.: DOutlier detection with the kernelized spatial depth function. IEEE Trans. Pattern Anal. Mach. Intell. 31(2), 288–305 (2009)

10. Chollet, F.: Xception: deep learning with depthwise separable convolutions. In: Proceedings - 30th IEEE Conference on Computer Vision and Pattern Recognition, CVPR 2017 pp. 1800–1807 (2017). https://doi.org/10.1109/CVPR.2017.195

11. Davison, A., Hinkley, D.: Bootstrap Methods and Their Application, vol. 1. Cambridge University Press, Cambridge (1997)

12. Dvison, A., Hinkley, D.V., Schechtman, E.: Efficient bootstrap simulation. Biometrika 73(3), 555–566 (1986)

13. Efron, B.: More efficient bootstrap computations. J. Am. Stat. Assoc. 85(409), 79–89 (1990)

14. Goldstein, M.: FastLOF: an expectation-maximization based local outlier detection algorithm. In: 2012 21st International Conference on (ICPR) (2012)

15. Grubbs, F.E.: Procedures for detecting outlying observations in samples. Technometrics 11(1), 1–21 (1969)

16. Hawkins, D.: Identification of Outliers. Springer, Dordrecht (1980). https://doi.org/10.1007/978-94-015-3994-4

17. Krapac, J., Allan, M., Verbeek, J., Juried, F.: Improving web image search results using query-relative classifiers. In: 2010 IEEE Conference on Computer Vision and Pattern Recognition (CVPR), pp. 1094–1101. IEEE (2010)

18. Kriegel, H.P., Kröger, P., Schubert, E., Zimek, A.: Loop: local outlier probabilities. In: Proceedings of the 18th ACM Conference on Information and Knowledge Management, pp. 1649–1652. ACM (2009)

19. Kriegel, H.P., Kröger, P., Zimek, A.: Outlier detection techniques. In: Tutorial at the 16th ACM International Conference on Knowledge Discovery and Data Mining (SIGKDD), Washington, DC (2010)

20. Kriegel, H.P., Zimek, A., et al.: Angle-based outlier detection in high-dimensional data. In: Proceedings of the 14th ACM SIGKDD International Conference on Knowledge Discovery and Data Mining, pp. 444–452. ACM (2008)

21. Lehmann, R.: 3 σ-rule for outlier detection from the viewpoint of geodetic adjustment. J. Surv. Eng. 139(4), 157–165 (2013)

22. Liu, F.T., Ting, K.M., Zhou, Z.H.: Isolation-based anomaly detection. ACM Trans. Knowl. Discov. Data (TKDD) 6(1), 3 (2012)

23. Liu, W., Hua, G., Smith, J.R.: Unsupervised one-class learning for automatic outlier removal. In: Proceedings of the IEEE Conference on Computer Vision and Pattern Recognition, pp. 3826–3833 (2014)

24. Lu, J., Zhou, J., Wang, J., Mei, T., Hua, X.S., Li, S.: Image search results refinement via outlier detection using deep contexts. In: 2012 IEEE Conference on Computer Vision and Pattern Recognition (CVPR), pp. 3029–3036. IEEE (2012)

25. Ng, H.W., Winkler, S.: A data-driven approach to cleaning large face datasets. In: 2014 IEEE International Conference on Image Processing (ICIP), pp. 343–347. IEEE (2014)

Retrieved Image Refinement by Bootstrap Outlier Test 517

26. Papadimitriou, S., Kitagawa, H., Gibbons, P.B., Faloutsos, C.: LOCI: Fast outlier detection using the local correlation integral. In: 2003 Proceedings of the 19th International Conference on Data Engineering, pp. 315–326. IEEE (2003)
27. Pimentel, M.A., Clifton, D.A., Clifton, L., Tarassenko, L.: A review of novelty detection. Signal Process. **99**, 215–249 (2014)
28. Ramaswamy, S., Rastogi, R., Shim, K.: Efficient algorithms for mining outliers from large data sets. ACM SIGMOD Rec. **29**, 427–438 (2000). https://doi.org/10.1145/342009.335437
29. Russakovsky, O., et al.: ImageNet large scale visual recognition challenge. Int. J. Comput. Vis. **115**(3), 211–252 (2015). https://doi.org/10.1007/s11263-015-0816-y
30. Schölkopf, B., Platt, J.C., Shawe-Taylor, J., Smola, A.J., Williamson, R.C.: Estimating the support of a high-dimensional distribution. Neural Comput. **13**(7), 1443–1471 (2001)
31. Zimek, A., Campello, R.J., Sander, J.: Ensembles for unsupervised outlier detection: challenges and research questions a position paper. ACM SIGKDD Explor. Newsl. **15**(1), 11–22 (2014)

MDAD: A Multimodal and Multiview in-Vehicle Driver Action Dataset

Imen Jegham[1](✉) ⓘ, Anouar Ben Khalifa[2] ⓘ, Ihsen Alouani[3] ⓘ,
and Mohamed Ali Mahjoub[2] ⓘ

[1] Institut supérieur de l'informatique et des techniques de communication,
LATIS-Laboratory of Advanced Technology and Intelligent Systems,
Université de Sousse, 4011 Sousse, Tunisia
imen.jegham@isitc.u-sousse.tn
[2] Ecole Nationale d'Ingénieurs de Sousse,
LATIS-Laboratory of Advanced Technology and Intelligent Systems,
Université de Sousse, 4023 Sousse, Tunisia
[3] IEMN-DOAE, Université polytechnique Hauts-de-France, Valenciennes, France

Abstract. "Driver's distraction is deadly!". Due to its crucial role in saving lives, driver action recognition is an important and trending topic in the field of computer vision. However, a very limited number of public datasets are available to validate proposed methods. This paper introduces a new public, well structured and extensive dataset, named Multiview and multimodal in-vehicle Driver Action Dataset (MDAD). MDAD consists of two temporally synchronised data modalities from side and frontal views. These modalities include RGB and depth data from different Kinect cameras. Many subjects with various body sizes, gender and ages are asked to perform 16 in-vehicle actions in several weather conditions. Each subject drives the vehicle on multiple trip routes in Sousse, Tunisia, at different times to describe a large range of head rotations, changes in lighting conditions and some occlusions. Our recorded dataset provides researchers with a testbed to develop new algorithms across multiple modalities and views under different illumination conditions. To demonstrate the utility of our dataset, we analyze driver action recognition results from each modality and every view independently, and then we combine modalities and views. This public dataset is of benefit to research activities for humans driver action analysis.

Keywords: Distracted driving · Public dataset ·
Driver action recognition · Multimodal · Multiview · Fusion

1 Introduction

By 2030, road accidents are estimated to become the seventh leading cause of death without sustained actions, compared to 2000 (tenth) and 2016 (eighth) [32]. Road traffic injuries cause considerable economic losses to individuals, families, and nations as a whole [5,14]. Distraction, wrong maneuver, drunkenness

M. Vento and G. Percannella (Eds.): CAIP 2019, LNCS 11678, pp. 518–529, 2019.
https://doi.org/10.1007/978-3-030-29888-3_42

are major causes. Recently, driver distraction has been acknowledged as one of the leading causes of death. It claimed alone 3,450 lives in 2016, in USA [31]. Distracted driving is generally defined as a form of driver carelessness or inattention. It is a deviation of attention away from activities that are critical to safe driving toward a secondary activity [19]. There are two kinds of sources of distraction [26]: The first one is internal or in-vehicle, which occurs when the driver source of distraction is internal (inside the vehicle). The second source is external, which happens when the driver's distraction comes from outside the vehicle. Consequently, the driving performance and situational consciousness of a driver are impaired. There are many types of driver distractions that can be clustered into four groups [28]:

- Physical or biomechanical distraction: For a long time, one or both driver's hands are taken off the steering wheel to manipulate an object.
- Visual distraction: For an extended period, the driver neglects looking at areas they should concentrate on while driving, focusing instead for some period of time on another visual target.
- Cognitive distraction: The visual field of the driver is blocked where they have to be looking at while driving, such as the front, rear or sides of the vehicle. Therefore, the driver's attention is absorbed to the point that they cannot focus anymore on the act of driving.
- Auditory distraction: The driver is prevented by sounds from making the best use of their hearing, since their attention is drawn to whatever causes the sound.

To avoid this dangerous behavior, many efforts have been made to detect and identify driver's distraction. Proposed approaches can be grouped into three categories [2]: In the first approach that aims to monitor the surroundings of a vehicle, information is obtained from multiple sensors mounted on a vehicle [12,26]. These latter assist in autonomous cruising, collision avoidance, and lane changing. In the second approach, information is collected from sensors mounted inside the cabin [4,15,16]. The study of driver's in-vehicle actions on the road in real-life can provide a deeper understanding of common distractions during driving. On the other hand, the last approach fuses information from both the vehicle surroundings and the cabin [11]. In this paper, we focus mainly on studying different body parts of the driver using sensors mounted in the cabin.

The choice of the most appropriate acquisition device is fundamental. In the literature several physiological and physical signals have been captured [13,29] such as electrocardiogram, electroencephalogram, electrooculogram, facial electromyogram, interstitial fluid, plethysmogram, respiration, electrodermal activity, glucose and motion sensors (accelerometers and gyroscopes) [1,25]. However, the complexity of their installation and their high cost have led us to the use of robust vision sensors. In this study, we focus primarily on vision-based systems.

To effectively validate and compare proposed vision-based distracted driving recognition methods, public datasets play an important role. Thus, several datasets have been recorded and employed in the validation of new approaches. Yet, most of them are private and publically unavailable [6,22,33].

To facilitate research activities in distracted driver action recognition, we put forward a new public, multimodal and extensive dataset that highlights the issues observed in simulated environments of driving from multiple users, illumination settings, cluttered background, and viewpoints employing a Kinect depth camera, named MDAD. Our dataset covers a more comprehensive set of distracted actions reported by the WHO [31]. It provides temporally synchronized RGB frames and depth frames at daytime. Such a dataset is of benefit to researchers working in different fields such as computer vision, image processing and sensor fusion.

This paper is organized as follows: In Sect. 2, main publically available datasets are briefly reviewed. Our dataset is described in Sect. 3. Section 4 demonstrates the utility of our dataset in recognizing driver's in-vehicle actions by reporting several experiments based on the features extracted from Spatio Temporal Interest Points (STIPs). The conclusion is finally stated in Sect. 5.

2   Existing Public Datasets

Driver distraction detection is a challenging computer vision and machine learning task. The work in this field can be categorized into three groups: driver hand detection and tracking [3,27], driver face detection and analysis [6,16] and information interpretation from both the face and the hands [2]. Distraction detection in itself is not enough for good driver assistance. For example, assisting the driver when writing a message is not the same when they rub their eyes and hide their mouth yawning. For this reason, distraction recognition and classification become crucial. To effectively work in this field, several datasets have been recorded. However, only few of them are publically available. As for our multiple attempts to obtain it, we know that the authors of these datasets have not made it publically available [6,22,33]. In this section, up to our knowledge, we have reviewed the public existing datasets.

2.1   State Farm Dataset

To improve the success of the American insurance group "State Farm", they launched a competition on Kaggle to automatically detect drivers engaging in secondary activities using dashboard cameras. State Farm introduced the first publically available dataset [10] of 2D dashboard camera images to challenge Kagglers to classify driver's behaviors. The dataset described ten postures to be classified: safe driving, texting using right hand, talking on the phone using right hand, texting using left hand, talking on the phone using left hand, talking to passengers, drinking, operating the radio, doing hair and makeup, and reaching behind. Twenty-six subjects with different body sizes, ages and gender, in varying illumination, performed actions in the dataset. The State Farm dataset was restricted for competition.

2.2   AUC Distracted Driver Dataset

The American university in Cairo, Egypt, collected the AUC distracted driver dataset [9] in a parked vehicle using an ASUS ZenPhone rear camera fixed using an arm strap to the car roof handle on top of the passenger's seat. The same postures, as the State Farm dataset, were simulated by 31 participants from seven countries.

2.3   EBDD Video Database

With a view to facilitate the work on driver distraction recognition, the EBDD video dataset [2] was captured by a camera mounted on the front windshield inside a vehicle. It was developed by considering diversity in driving environments as well as expertise of drivers. EBDD was released publically.

3   MDAD Dataset

By proposing a new multiview and multimodal dataset we are addressing several drawbacks of the aforementioned datasets, for example the lack of multiview and multimodal synchronized data, the diversity of drivers, and the number of distracted actions. Table 1 gives a comparative summary of multiple existing public datasets as well as our introduced one.

3.1   Dataset Acquisition

For our multimodal driver's action dataset, two Microsoft Kinect cameras [24] are used. The first Kinect is mounted on the car handle on the top of the passenger window, and the second is placed on the dashboard in front of the driver. This is intentional due to the practicality or relative non-intrusiveness aspect of using this varied modality sensor. The latter is widely available, low cost, easy to operate, and does not require much computational power for the real-time manipulation of its generated data. Each Kinect camera captures a color image with a resolution of 640*480 pixels and a 16-bit depth image, both with an acquisition rate of 30 Hz. Although the color and depth acquisition inside the Kinect are not perfectly synchronized, the temporal difference is not noticeable in the output due to the relatively high frame rate. Figure 1 shows the layout of the sensors used.

3.2   Dataset Description

Our MDAD dataset includes real-world driving scenarios in which 50 participants (38 males and 12 females) aged between 19 and 41 were asked to drive a Volkswagen Polo 4 in naturalistic driving settings. Every driver was asked to perform one safe driving and 15 various common secondary tasks under different route segments. Prior to each recording, the participants were given instructions

Table 1. Comparison of MDAD to existing public datasets.

Research study	Sensor	Activity classes	Drivers	Camera perspectives	Experimental settings	Content type
State Farm dataset [10]	One color camera	10	26		Naturalistic driving	102,151 images
AUC distracted driver dataset [9]	One color camera	10	31		Parked vehicle	17,310 images
EBDD video database [2]	One color camera	13 4			Naturalistic driving	59 video sequences (40 min)
MDAD (ours)	Two Kinect cameras	16	50		Naturalistic driving	800 video sequences (367 min) X 2 view X 2 modality

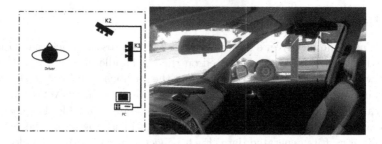

Fig. 1. Diagram of data acquisition system.

on what action to perform, and no specific detail was given on how the action had to be performed, e.g. the performance style. The subjects have therefore incorporated different styles in performing some of the actions. Table 2 describes the selected actions that are commonly executed by individuals while driving. The choice of these activities has been proved by the study of the fatal accident reporting system database collected by the U.S. Department of Transportation [26].

Figure 2 shows the snapshots from all the performed tasks taken from the side view. All the drivers performed each task for a range of 20 to 35 seconds, yielding about 800 sequences that correspond to about 367 min of the total recording

Table 2. Tasks considered in this study

Task name	Description
A1: Safe driving	Driver keeps both hands in the steering wheel according to the technique recommended by the National Highway Traffic Safety Administration (NHTSA) known as 9 and 3: considering the wheel as a clock, the left hand on the left portion of the steering wheel in a location approximate to where 9 would be and the right hand on the right portion of the wheel where 3 would be located
A2: Doing hair and makeup	Driver looks to interior mirror to do their hair or to put make up
A3: Adjusting radio	Driver tunes the radio until obtaining predetermined radio station
A4: GPS operating	Driver inputs the destination address into GPS and then follows the GPS instructions
A5: Writing message using right hand	Driver dials a message using their right hand
A6: Writing message using left hand	Driver dials a message using their left hand
A7: Talking phone using right hand	Driver interacts with the phone call and use their right hand to hold the phone
A8: Talking phone using left hand	Driver interacts with the phone call and use their left hand to hold the phone
A9: Having picture	Driver uses their cell phone to have picture: they take selfie or take pictures of road surroundings
A10: Talking to passenger	Driver is fully engaged in the speech with the passengers
A11: Singing or dancing	Driver interacts with the music by singing and moving rhythmically
A12: Fatigue and somnolence	Driver feels tired and exhausted. They generally yawn and barely open their eyes
A13: Drinking using right hand	Driver takes a cup using their right hand and drink a liquid
A14: Drinking using left hand	Driver takes a cup using their left hand and drink a liquid
A15: Reaching behind	Driver stretches out their arms in different directions in order to touch or grasp something
A16: Smoking	Driver smokes a cigarette if they are smoker or they imitate this action using an electronic cigarette

time. The data were collected during the day under varying illumination due to the changing natural conditions. Some occlusion of hands by other objects and self occlusion as well as the occlusion of eyes with sunglasses is presented. A snapshot of the distracted action "drinking using right hand" from the different modalities of the Kinect cameras is presented in Fig. 3. The high amount of

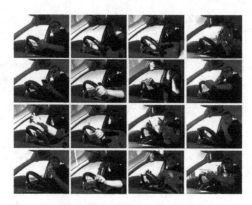

Fig. 2. Snapshots from all tasks available in dataset.

Fig. 3. Drinking using right hand action displayed from two Kinect cameras.

information that can be obtained from multiview and multimodal observations are demonstrated. The dataset is publically available[1].

4   Distracted Action Recognition Experiments

To highlight the utility of various views and modalities included in our dataset, we perform driver activity recognition experiments based on STIP features. In this section, we provide the result of every modality independently and then we provide the results of the data fusion approach for driver action recognition using MDAD. In all experiments, we divide the dataset into 75% for training and 25% for test data.

Space-time features are one of the most popular video representations for action recognition [21,23]. In the literature, multiple methods for spatio-temporal feature detection and description have been introduced, and promising recognition rates have been demonstrated. Wang *et al.* [30] evaluated and compared several proposed space-time features across several databases in a common experimental setup. They proved that Histograms of Gradients (HOG) [7] and Histograms of Optic Flow (HOF) [8] features extracted from STIPs [17], introduced by Laptev *et al.* in [18], tended to give the best results even for the most challenging datasets. For that, for each action sequence, we extract HOG/HOF features

---

[1] https://sites.google.com/site/benkhalifaanouar1/6-datasets.

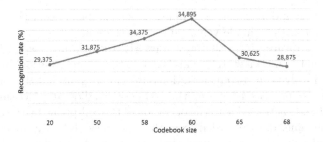

Fig. 4. Codebook size variation according to recognition rate of RGB data

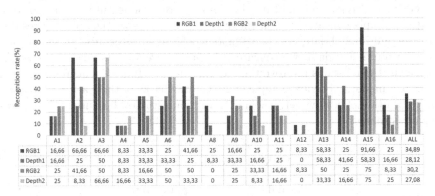

	A1	A2	A3	A4	A5	A6	A7	A8	A9	A10	A11	A12	A13	A14	A15	A16	ALL
■ RGB1	16,66	66,66	66,66	8,33	33,33	25	41,66	25	16,66	25	25	8,33	58,33	25	91,66	25	34,89
■ Depth1	16,66	25	50	8,33	33,33	33,33	25	8,33	33,33	16,66	25	0	58,33	41,66	58,33	16,66	28,12
■ RGB2	25	41,66	50	8,33	16,66	50	50	0	25	33,33	16,66	8,33	50	25	75	8,33	30,2
▨ Depth2	25	8,33	66,66	16,66	33,33	50	33,33	0	25	8,33	16,66	0	33,33	16,66	75	25	27,08

Fig. 5. Class specific recognition rate and overall recognition rate of 16 MDAD actions involving different modalities of each sensor.

from detected STIPs. After that, we quantize these features into 60 codebooks using k-means to finally represent each sequence as a histogram of codebooks. The choice of the size of codebooks is made after several experiments, as depicted in Fig. 4. Finally, we perform the classification process via the Support Vector Machine (SVM) with a polynomial kernel. The obtained results are displayed in Fig. 5, where A1, A2, ... represent the actions mentioned in Table 2.

As it can be seen in the latter figure, the results are fairly acceptable due to the amount of challenges present in our dataset. In fact, while performing an action, each driver has their own comfort zone, body size proportion and action performance style. In our dataset, the driver is not engaged only in performing the in-vehicle action, they principally drive the car. For this reason, depending on the situation, they perform other tasks related to driving such as turning the steering wheel to change direction, respecting and looking at traffic signs, supervising vehicle surroundings, etc. Therefore, a high intraclass variability and a high interclass similarity are present and make a high confusion. In addition, MDAD is recorded in a naturalistic driving setting at different daytimes and different weather conditions. The complex background comes from two sources: an internal one where a moving passenger appears in the field of view of the camera, and a dynamic external one appears from the car window. An illumination variation and a change in complex background can occur even in a single video sequence with a simple vehicle direction changing.

The data captured from the front view (K2) give worse results than those captured from the side view (K1). This is due to the Kinect position. In fact, some body parts involved in in-vehicle actions are partially occluded. For example, a confusion was produced between the "adjusting radio" and "writing message using right hand" actions due to the occlusion of the cell-phone by the dashboard. At the same time, data recorded from the side view (K1) are mixed with the dynamic and cluttered background appearing from the window in depth data. Thus, recognition rates from both Kinects are almost similar.

Given multiview and multimodal data, we opt for feature fusion [20]. For that, we simply concatenate feature vectors. Table 3 shows the obtained results. For the multimodal data, we concatenate the feature vectors accross modalities. For the multiview data, we concatenate the feature vectors accross views. As expected, these fusions improve the recognition rate. Indeed, features extracted from one modality or view complement the drawbacks of the features extracted from the other one. However, recognition rates are still low because of the recording environment.

Table 3. Data fusion results.

Fused data	Recognition rate
Multiview RGB	42.45%
Multiview depth	37.45%
Multi modal K1	39.41%
Multi modal K2	33.64%

5   Conclusion

Distracted driving is one of the major problems conducted for a huge number of accidents worldwide. Hence, researchers have made big efforts to detect and identify this dangerous behavior using several sensors particularly vision sensors, due to their reduced costs and ease of installation. To effectively validate and compare the proposed methods, several datasets have been recorded. However, only few of them are publically available. These public datasets do not describe all the challenges in the field of vision-based driver activity recognition and are recorded with a unique modality from a single view. Motivated by this research need, we introduce a new extensive multiview multimodal public dataset, named MDAD. Our dataset allows the evaluation and comparison of different driver and human activity recognition methods, especially those involving multimodal and multiview data fusions. The dataset can be considered one of the largest dataset with more than 367 min of data captured over various weather conditions from 50 subjects performing 16 in-vehicle actions. Our driver action recognition experiments based on the features extracted from STIPs and classified with SVM have shown the difficulty to overcome the high amount of challenges present in our dataset. Nevertheless, these performances dramatically decrease in low illumination conditions, hence the importance of finding a solution for the recognition of driver actions at night.

References

1. Ameur, S., Khalifa, A.B., Bouhlel, M.S.: A comprehensive leap motion database for hand gesture recognition. In: 2016 7th International Conference on Sciences of Electronics, Technologies of Information and Telecommunications (SETIT), pp. 514–519, December 2016. https://doi.org/10.1109/SETIT.2016.7939924
2. Billah, T., Rahman, S.M.M., Ahmad, M.O., Swamy, M.N.S.: Recognizing distractions for assistive driving by tracking body parts. IEEE Trans. Circ. Syst. Video Technol. **29**(4), 1048–1062 (2019). https://doi.org/10.1109/TCSVT.2018.2818407
3. Borghi, G., Frigieri, E., Vezzani, R., Cucchiara, R.: Hands on the wheel: a dataset for driver hand detection and tracking. In: 2018 13th IEEE International Conference on Automatic Face Gesture Recognition (FG 2018), pp. 564–570, May 2018. https://doi.org/10.1109/FG.2018.00090
4. Botta, M., Cancelliere, R., Ghignone, L., Tango, F., Gallinari, P., Luison, C.: Real-time detection of driver distraction: random projections for pseudo-inversion-based neural training. Knowl. Inf. Syst. 1–16 (2019). https://doi.org/10.1007/s10115-019-01339-0
5. Chebli, K., Khalifa, A.B.: Pedestrian detection based on background compensation with block-matching algorithm. In: 2018 15th International Multi-Conference on Systems, Signals Devices (SSD), pp. 497–501, March 2018. https://doi.org/10.1109/SSD.2018.8570499
6. Craye, C., Karray, F.: Driver distraction detection and recognition using RGB-D sensor. arXiv preprint arXiv:1502.00250 (2015)
7. Dalal, N., Triggs, B.: Histograms of oriented gradients for human detection. In: 2005 IEEE Computer Society Conference on Computer Vision and Pattern Recognition (CVPR 2005), vol. 1, pp. 886–893, June 2005. https://doi.org/10.1109/CVPR.2005.177
8. Danafar, S., Gheissari, N.: Action recognition for surveillance applications using optic flow and SVM. In: Yagi, Y., Kang, S.B., Kweon, I.S., Zha, H. (eds.) ACCV 2007. LNCS, vol. 4844, pp. 457–466. Springer, Heidelberg (2007). https://doi.org/10.1007/978-3-540-76390-1_45
9. Eraqi, H.M., Abouelnaga, Y., Saad, M.H., Moustafa, M.N.: Driver distraction identification with an ensemble of convolutional neural networks. J. Adv. Transp. **2019**, 1–12 (2019)
10. State Farm: state farm distracted driver detection. https://www.kaggle.com/c/state-farm-distracted-driver-detection/
11. Filtness, A., et al.: Safety implications of co-locating road signs: a driving simulator investigation. Transp. Res. Part F: Traffic Psychol. Behav. **47**, 187–198 (2017). https://doi.org/10.1016/j.trf.2017.04.007
12. Gillmeier, K., Schuettke, T., Diederichs, F., Miteva, G., Spath, D.: Combined driver distraction and intention algorithm for maneuver prediction and collision avoidance. In: 2018 IEEE International Conference on Vehicular Electronics and Safety (ICVES), pp. 1–6, September 2018. https://doi.org/10.1109/ICVES.2018.8519520

13. Jafarnejad, S., Castignani, G., Engel, T.: Non-intrusive distracted driving detection based on driving sensing data. In: VEHITS, pp. 178–186 (2018)
14. Jegham, I., Ben Khalifa, A.: Pedestrian detection in poor weather conditions using moving camera. In: 2017 IEEE/ACS 14th International Conference on Computer Systems and Applications (AICCSA), pp. 358–362, October 2017. https://doi.org/10.1109/AICCSA.2017.35
15. Jegham, I., Ben Khalifa, A., Alouani, I., Mahjoub, M.A.: Safe driving: driver action recognition using SURF keypoints. In: 2018 30th International Conference on Microelectronics (ICM), pp. 60–63, December 2018. https://doi.org/10.1109/ICM.2018.8704009
16. Knapik, M., Cyganek, B.: Driver's fatigue recognition based on yawn detection in thermal images. Neurocomputing **338**, 274–292 (2019). https://doi.org/10.1016/j.neucom.2019.02.014
17. Laptev, I., Lindeberg, T.: Space-time interest points. In: Proceedings Ninth IEEE International Conference on Computer Vision, vol. 1, pp. 432–439, October 2003. https://doi.org/10.1109/ICCV.2003.1238378
18. Laptev, I., Marszalek, M., Schmid, C., Rozenfeld, B.: Learning realistic human actions from movies. In: 2008 IEEE Conference on Computer Vision and Pattern Recognition, pp. 1–8, June 2008. https://doi.org/10.1109/CVPR.2008.4587756
19. Lee, J.D., Young, K.L., Regan, M.A.: Defining driver distraction. In: Driver Distraction: Theory Effects and Mitigation, vol. 13, no. 4, pp. 31–40 (2008)
20. Lejmi, W., Ben Khalifa, A., Mahjoub, M.A.: Fusion strategies for recognition of violence actions. In: 2017 IEEE/ACS 14th International Conference on Computer Systems and Applications (AICCSA), pp. 178–183, October 2017. https://doi.org/10.1109/AICCSA.2017.193
21. Lejmi, W., Mahjoub, M.A., Ben Khalifa, A.: Event detection in video sequences: challenges and perspectives. In: 2017 13th International Conference on Natural Computation, Fuzzy Systems and Knowledge Discovery (ICNC-FSKD), pp. 682–690, July 2017. https://doi.org/10.1109/FSKD.2017.8393354
22. Li, N., Busso, C.: Analysis of facial features of drivers under cognitive and visual distractions. In: 2013 IEEE International Conference on Multimedia and Expo (ICME), July 2013. https://doi.org/10.1109/ICME.2013.6607575
23. McNally, W., Wong, A., McPhee, J.: STAR-Net: action recognition using spatiotemporal activation reprojection. arXiv preprint arXiv:1902.10024 (2019)
24. Microsoft: Kinect for windows. http://www.microsoft.com/en-us/kinectforwindows/
25. Mimouna, A., Khalifa, A.B., Ben Amara, N.E.: Human action recognition using triaxial accelerometer data: selective approach. In: 2018 15th International Multi-Conference on Systems, Signals Devices (SSD), pp. 491–496, March 2018. https://doi.org/10.1109/SSD.2018.8570429
26. Qin, L., Li, Z.R., Chen, Z., Bill, M.A., Noyce, D.A.: Understanding driver distractions in fatal crashes: an exploratory empirical analysis. J. Saf. Res. **69**, 23–31 (2019)
27. Rangesh, A., Ohn-Bar, E., Trivedi, M.M.: Hidden hands: tracking hands with an occlusion aware tracker. In: 2016 IEEE Conference on Computer Vision and Pattern Recognition Workshops (CVPRW), pp. 1224–1231, June 2016. https://doi.org/10.1109/CVPRW.2016.155
28. Regan, M.A., Hallett, C., Gordon, C.P.: Driver distraction and driver inattention: definition, relationship and taxonomy. Accid. Anal. Prev. **43**(5), 1771–1781 (2011). https://doi.org/10.1016/j.aap.2011.04.008

29. Reyes-Muñoz, A., Domingo, M., López-Trinidad, M., Delgado, J.: Integration of body sensor networks and vehicular ad-hoc networks for traffic safety. Sensors **16**(1), 107 (2016)
30. Wang, H., Ullah, M.M., Klaser, A., Laptev, I., Schmid, C.: Evaluation of local spatio-temporal features for action recognition. In: British Machine Vision Conference, BMVC 2009, p. 124–1. BMVA Press (2009)
31. WHO: distracted   driving.   https://www.who.int/violence-injury-prevention/publications/road-traffic/distracted-driving-en.pdf
32. WHO: The top 10 causes of death. https://www.who.int/news-room/fact-sheets/detail/the-top-10-causes-of-death
33. Zhao, C., Zhang, B., Lian, J., He, J., Lin, T., Zhang, X.: Classification of driving postures by support vector machines. In: 2011 Sixth International Conference on Image and Graphics, pp. 926–930, August 2011. https://doi.org/10.1109/ICIG.2011.184

Robust Classification of Head Pose from Low Resolution Images

Mohammad Khaki[1], Issa Ayoub[1], Abbas Javadtalab[2],
and Hussein Al Osman[1(✉)]

[1] University of Ottawa, Ottawa, ON, Canada
{mkhak052,iayou005,halosman}@uottawa.ca
[2] Concordia University, Montreal, QC, Canada
abbas.javadtalab@concordia.ca

Abstract. We propose a method for the coarse classification of head pose from low-resolution images. We devise a mechanism that uses a cascade of three binary Support Vector Machines (SVM) classifiers. We use two sets of appearance features, Similarity Distance Map (SDM) and Gabor Wavelet (GW) as input to the SVM classifiers. For training, we employ a large dataset that combines five publicly available databases. We test our approach with cross-validation using the eight databases and on videos we collected in a lab experiment. We found a significant improvement in the results achieved by the proposed method over existing schemes. In the cross-validation test, we achieved a head pose detection accuracy of 98.60%. Moreover, we obtained a head pose detection accuracy of 93.76% for high-resolution and 89.81% for low-resolution videos collected in the lab under loosely constrained conditions.

Keywords: Head pose classification · Cascade classification · Appearance template method

1 Introduction

Digital Out Of Home (DOOH) advertisement screens have become a ubiquitous feature in airports, shopping malls, medical clinics, bus and gas stations, among others. By analyzing the gaze direction of each person viewing a public advertisement, we can infer the level of interest of the receiving audience.

There are two factors that must be analyzed to deduce information about the gaze direction: (1) head pose and (2) eye direction [1]. Various existing computer vision methods estimate one or both factors. However, detecting eye direction can be difficult and sometimes not feasible for low-resolution images since eyes' information can be of low quality or not available at all [2]. An eye direction detector also fails if the subject in the frame covers her/his eyes with sunglasses or other artifacts. Hence, relying on the calculation of head pose for gaze direction estimation can be a viable solution for DOOH advertising systems, especially that head pose has been shown to accurately reflect the gaze direction [3]. Moreover, if a person wants to pay attention to an object in the environment, he/she typically turns his/her head towards it [4]. Hence, in this paper we propose head pose detection method.

© Springer Nature Switzerland AG 2019
M. Vento and G. Percannella (Eds.): CAIP 2019, LNCS 11678, pp. 530–541, 2019.
https://doi.org/10.1007/978-3-030-29888-3_43

The human head pose has three degrees of freedom: pitch, yaw, and roll. In this work, we are interested in yaw of the head. The objective of our scheme is to approximate the head pose of roaming people by considering angles from −90 to +90°, where 0° corresponds to the frontal post (staring directly at the camera). We design a coarse head pose classifier as it has been shown to be a more robust solution for low-resolution images compared to fine head pose classifiers [5–8].

The design has two components: feature extractor and classifier; we make contributions regarding each component:

- We combine two sets of appearance features, SDM [5] and GW [9, 10], to train the SVM classifiers. We fuse these feature sets to realize a method that can better discriminate between classes.

- We devise a mechanism that uses a cascade of three binary SVM classifiers instead of a single multi-class classifier to allow for better fine-tuning of the classifiers.

The rest of this paper is organized as follows: Sect. 2 discusses relevant background and related work. Section 3 describes the proposed method. Section 4 presents and discusses the results for the cross-validation and lab experiment we conduct to compare the performance of the proposed method to existing ones. Section 5 summarizes the paper's findings.

2 Related Work

We divide head pose approaches into two general types: feature-based and appearance-based head detectors [11].

Feature-based approaches of pose detection use geometric features to detect head pose [11]. Fanelli et al. [12] proposes a feature-based scheme that treats the head pose detection problem as a random regression forest exercise and show that their method can handle extreme poses and partial occlusion, two challenging issues for most head pose detection methods, especially feature-based ones. They compare their method to that of [13]. They obtain an accuracy of 90.4% while the method in [13] reaches an accuracy of 80.8% with ±10° of error tolerance. Amos et al. [14] present OpenFace which is a recent image processing library that extracts face landmarks using a Deep Neural Network. The library supports a function for estimating head pose based on the landmarks. Since there are no reported results on the accuracy of the OpenFace head pose detector, we perform our own evaluation of this method as a representative feature-based approach in Sect. 5 and compare the results to our proposed method.

Appearance-based methods employ appearance facial features and consider the face as a whole without finding the location of particular face landmarks. Patacchiola and Cangelosi [15] consider a Convolutional Neural Network (CNN) along with deep learning techniques to tackle the problem of head pose estimation from real-world images. The authors conclude that a CNN with dropout and adaptive gradients produces an accuracy of 62.33%. Robertson and Reid [16] fuse body direction and head pose through Bayes' Rule to estimate gaze direction. First, a mean shift tracker is used to detect the body and head. Second, the method uses the colour-based tracking to estimate the velocity of the body. Third, they employ a fast pseudo-probabilistic binary search [17] based on Principal Components to search the exemplar database to make a probabilistic head pose estimation. Fourth, they estimate gaze direction by fusing head pose and body direction information. For the head pose detection, Robertson and Reid [16] use a texture descriptor based on skin colour to feed the fast pseudo-probabilistic binary search. The texture descriptor scheme is challenged by Orozco et al. [5] that state that there is no clear cut between hair and skin texture especially for low-resolution images. In fact, Orozco et al. [5] extract pose related features using SDM (described below). They estimate head pose by comparing the input image to templates representing each head pose. Using a multi-class SVM classifier [18], they assess which template is the closest to the input image. They use 100 images for each pose from the iLIDS dataset [19] to train the method that works for low-resolution images. The method achieves 80% average accuracy rate for 10 fold cross-validation results on the training dataset while Robertson and Reid [16] achieve 32.25%.

SDM is a method to extract a discriminative facial appearance descriptor for input images. This technique was presented in [5] to extract features for pose classification. To apply this method, we compute a Mean Appearance Template (MAT) using all the images in the training dataset. The MAT corresponds to the mean intensity of each pixel across all images in the dataset for a particular pose [5]. Then, to obtain the SDM for an input image, the method calculates the distance between each pixel in the latter image and the MAT for the Red, Green, and Blue (RGB) channels. The distance between pixels is calculated using the Kullback Leibler (KL) coefficient. The maximum of the three values obtained in the previous step is assigned to the corresponding SDM pixel.

The approaches for head pose detection described above exhibit a variety of granularities. Fine head pose estimation methods calculate the head pose continuously or classify it into a large number of discrete classes (large enough to be considered near continuous) [20]. Obviously, the higher the number of supported classes is, the more complex the system will be since it requires a much larger training dataset to satisfactorily train the classifier. Conversely, coarse head pose classification refers to head pose estimation methods which classify head pose into a small number of possible classes [20]. Coarse pose detection is a better fit for our application as we intend to roughly find out if a subject is looking in the direction of an advertisement or, which advertisement she/he consumes in the case where there are multiple advertising screens in the same setting.

3 Proposed Method

The proposed head pose detector is composed of two components: feature extractor and classifier. The feature extractor calculates two kinds of features, SDM and GW with 8 filters in a variety of orientations ranging from 0 to 180°. Then, the extracted features are fed to a three-stage classifier.

3.1 Feature Extractor

We apply two methods of feature extraction: SDM and GW. SDM is originally presented by Orozco et al. [5]. The method is designed to deemphasize the information carried in the background while accentuating the features of the foreground. The output of SDM also has information from all three RGB channels [5]. The general concept of SDM is described in Sect. 2.

As opposed to SDM, GW features are robust against illumination changes [21]. However, GW captures information from the background as well as the foreground, as opposed to SDM that mostly captures information from the foreground.

GW detects edges of an image in the orientation of the applied filter. We collect edge features through the application of 8 GW filters in various orientations. The filters range from 0 to 180° by a step of 22.5°. We also apply histogram equalization on the output of the GW filters to further reduce the effect of lighting variation [10]. Histogram equalization [22] is a process which equalizes and enhances the contrast of an image.

We fuse GW and SDM to obtain facial appearance descriptors that are more robust in the presence of local disturbance. Therefore, each one of these two methods extracts 2500 features from a 50 × 50 pixels image, which results in a total of 5000 features after fusion at the feature level.

3.2 Classifier

Instead of using the Multi-class Classifier (MC) (in particular, a five-class one-vs-all SVM classifier) used by Orozco et al. [5], we employ a Cascaded Classifier (CC) composed of a series of binary SVM classifiers (Fig. 1). In a five-class classifier setup, the SDM of an input image will be based on the MAT of all five poses. Nevertheless, the three-stage CC classifies the input image in three stages; (1) frontal and non-frontal pose, (2) left or right if it is non-frontal, and (3) +45 or +90 for the left pose and −45 or −90 for the right pose, as it is shown in Fig. 1. In each stage, the SDM of the input image or the output of the prior stage is calculated with only two MATs, which are extracted from the training images of each class.

The overall training dataset (described in the next section) is not balanced. Hence, the number of images used to train each classifier is not the same. That is due to the difference in the number of images available for each pose in the overall training dataset. We tried to balance the dataset by eliminating some images corresponding to more frequently occurring poses. Nonetheless, we allowed for a certain level of imbalance in the goal of maintaining a large training set. That imbalance applies to the classifiers at each stage, including the third one which discriminates between +45 and +90 for left side poses, and −45 and −90 for right side poses.

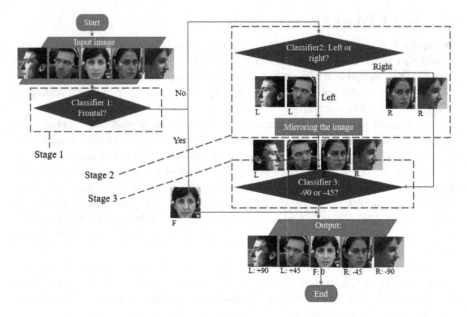

Fig. 1. Flow chart of three stage classifiers.

3.3   Training

Orozco et al. [5] extracted 100 images per pose from iLIDS dataset [19] to train their MC classifier.

We combined the iLIDS dataset [19] with seven other datasets [23–29] to train a robust classifier for different lighting conditions, various distances from the camera, presence and absence of facial hair and accessories, and diverse facial expressions. We applied the face detector of [30] on all training images and used the output to train the classifiers. We trained the classifiers of stages 1, 2 and 3 using approximately 79000, 32000 and 11000 images respectively.

Figure 2 shows the relationship between the sets of images that we use to train each stage of classifiers. We combine the datasets of [19, 23–29] to obtain a total of approximately 79000 images (Set U in Fig. 2). Although the proposed method only considers the yaw of the head, we used images that deviate from the $0°$ for the pitch and roll to have more variation in the input training images. This helps us extract robust features which can enable the classifier to better discriminate between classes. The sets of G and $\acute{G}$ in Fig. 2 are frontal and non-frontal images that we utilize to train the stage 1 classifier.

For the stage 2 classifier, we use datasets $\left(\acute{G} - J\right)$ (depicts left poses) and J (depicts right poses) to discriminate between left and right poses. For the stage 3 classifier(s), we further utilize subsets of J (D and E). Not all the images in J are labeled as -90 and -45, some are simply labeled as right. Therefore, not all of them are used to train the third stage classifier.

Every dataset used to compile the overall dataset has distinctive characteristics that are useful to train robust classifiers. The Columbia Gaze Dataset [31] presents a rich diversity of subjects in terms of their gender and ethnicity. It considers different eyes' direction for each head pose from −30 to +30 and head poses from −30 to +30. UPNA [24] and HPEG [25] are head images from close view videos. The dataset [24] also contains pitch and roll head orientation in addition to yaw, and dataset [25] provides diverse backgrounds that may contain other human faces. They do not provide balanced datasets for the five poses addressed in this work. PIE [26] contains different illumination, facial expression, and head poses for all subjects. Also, some of the subjects are talking in some images. Dataset [26] does not balance left and right poses.

Prima [27] has all possible poses (from −90 to +90) for both yaw and pitch for each subject. UcoHead [28] includes low-resolution images with different head poses and camera angles for each subject. The dataset contains only gray-scale images.

Yale Face Dataset [29] collects images of subjects with different facial expressions and accessories. It contains only grayscale images. iLIDS [19] contains images captured in the wild.

We have three major limitations regarding the datasets:

1. Not all datasets cover all possible head pose orientations (yaw, pitch and roll).
2. Not all datasets cover all the poses for the yaw orientation from −90 to +90.
3. Not all datasets provide balanced sets for all poses.

The CC gives us the chance of using all available datasets even the ones that label some of their images only as left and right pose, or the ones which support a limited range or number of poses.

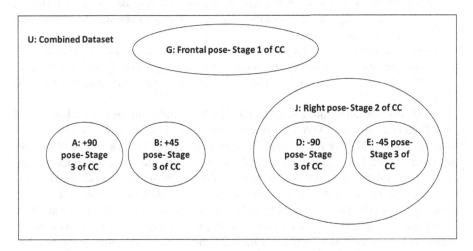

Fig. 2. Venn diagram shows the sets of images that are used to train each classes of CC. $\acute{G}$ is the set of non-frontal poses for stage 1. $\left(\acute{G} - J\right)$ is the set of left poses for stage 2.

We make two main assumptions in our work; first, based on [3], we conclude that it is possible to estimate gaze direction by detecting head pose as eye information is not accessible for some scenes with low-resolution images or in the presence of facial accessories. Second, although the head can rotate on three axes (yaw, pitch, and roll) and we use all kinds of rotated images to train the classifiers, we consider only yaw as it simplifies the problem as pitch and roll are not nearly as important for our application.

4 Evaluation and Results

In this section, we evaluate our proposed method and compare it to related recent work. In the first sub-section, we present a cross-validation of the classifiers of the three stages of the proposed method. We also compare our results to those of the multi-class SVM method presented in [5]. In the second sub-section, we describe a lab experiment we designed to compare the proposed method to other prominent ones. Hence, we describe the experimental procedure and apparatus and present the obtained results while comparing our method to the existing ones proposed in [5, 14, 15].

4.1 Cross-Validation on the Stages of CC

We perform cross-validation to find the best overall configuration for the CC. We use a 25% hold out cross-validation and sort the images randomly before the evaluation.

Orozco et al. [5] use a kernel of polynomial order three (cubic) with the strategy of one-vs-all to train their SVM classifier. We test several kernels to find the best one for our problem. For the CC, we have three stages of classifiers, for each classifier we consider three sets of features, namely SDM, GW, and GWSDM. GWSDM refers to the fusion of SDM and GW. For each feature set we consider 6 kernels (linear, polynomial order 2 [quadric], polynomial order 3 [cubic], Gaussian fine, Gaussian medium and Gaussian coarse).

Table 1 presents the accuracy of each stage of classifiers for all of the configurations. The classifiers perform significantly worse when the GW feature set is used. The GWSDM feature set performs slightly better than the SDM feature set for all classifiers.

SDM and GW affect images differently. SDM contains information related to all three RGB channels while GW uses gray scale images. However, GW is robust against lighting changes [21]. We further apply histogram equalization to the output of the GW to reduce the effect of lighting artifacts. GW does not discriminate between foreground and background and therefore detects edges in the background. However, SDM is less susceptible to capturing background information given that the training set used to calculate the MATs present a variety of backgrounds. Consequently, by fusing both feature sets, we compile relevant information from two complementary sources, which allows us to achieve better accuracy. Figure 3a shows the architecture of the best CC configurations (which combine the best performing classifiers according to Table 1):

Table 1. The results of different combinations of the CC and MC.

Feature set	SVM kernel		Stage 1 (%)	Stage 2 (%)	Stage 3 (%)
SDM	Linear		94.5	97.7	98.4
	Quadratic		99.1	99.3	99.0
	Cubic		99.3	99.2	99.3
	Gaussian	Fine	99.2	99.5	99.0
		Medium	95.3	98.0	97.9
		Coarse	91.7	97.1	84.5
GWSDM	Linear		94.5	95.3	98.5
	Quadratic		99.0	99.1	99.4
	Cubic		99.5	99.7	99.0
	Gaussian	Fine	98.9	99.1	98.8
		Medium	94.4	97.5	98.2
		Coarse	91.7	97.3	50.3
GW	Linear		94.7	99.0	97.2
	Quadratic		97.2	98.8	97.7
	Cubic		97.8	99.1	97.7
	Gaussian	Fine	65.8	66.6	74.2
		Medium	97.0	98.6	96.6
		Coarse	93.2	97.9	91.0

- SDM CC (SCC): Three staged classifier that uses the SDM feature set with cubic, Gaussian fine, and cubic SVM kernels for the first, second and third stage classifier respectively.
- GWSDM CC (GSCC): three staged classifier that uses the GWSDM feature set with cubic, cubic, and quadratic SVM kernels for the first, second and third stage classifier respectively.

In the cross-validation, SCC and GSCC achieved an accuracy of 98.31% and 98.60% respectively. CC allows us to use more images from the combined dataset even the ones that are not symmetric or precisely labeled. This allows us to train classifiers that better model the problem at hand. Since we gathered a dataset from a wide variety of subjects with different appearance characteristics including a variety of glasses, hair styles, facial hair, and facial expressions, the method has a better chance to work well for subjects in the wild.

In Table 2, we show the results for the MC with three different feature sets and six kernels. Therefore, the table shows that the cubic kernel works best for all cases and GWSDM with cubic kernel produces the best results among all other configurations. Figure 3b shows the architecture of the best CC and MC configurations:

- SDM MC (SMC): Multi-class classifier that uses the SDM feature set.
- GWSDM MC (GSMC): Multi-class classifier that uses the GWSDM feature set.

Table 2. The results regarding MC for all kernels and feature sets.

		SDM	GWSDM	GW
Linear		94.9	96.2	93.2
Quadratic		97.3	97.5	94.3
Cubic		97.9	98.4	97.0
Gaussian	Fine	97.3	97.3	40.1
	Medium	94.1	93.9	93.4
	Coarse	89.3	54.4	89.4

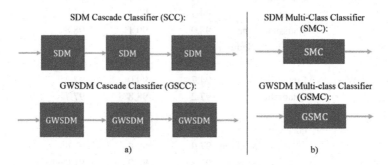

Fig. 3. The fastest and most accurate combination of CC and MC.

4.2 Video Experiments

In Sect. 4.1, we show that CC performs better than MC in a cross-validation assessment. In this experiment, we test the SCC, GSCC, SMC, and GSMC approaches (Fig. 3) on videos captured in a lab experiment of roaming subjects.

Experimental Setup. We test two combinations of our proposed method, two combinations of the MC method (Fig. 3), OpenFace [14], and the CNN-based method presented in [15]. We evaluate the OpenFace [30] method as a representative feature-based approach. Also, we assess the CNN-based approach as a representative neural network based solution, as these classifiers are gaining attention in resolving computer vision problems.

We recruited 4 female and 6 male subjects with ages ranging from 23 to 57. We set up a camera in front of a subject who walks forward until he/she reaches a line marked on the floor close to the camera. Then, he/she walks backwards away from the camera and stops at the original point of departure at the beginning of the experiment. By doing this back and forth trip, the distance between the camera and the subject is ranging between 120 and 540 inches. Each time the subject goes forward or backward, he/she holds their head in one of the possible five poses. To help the subject orient their head, we placed a marker on the room walls for each pose. The subject turns his/her head towards the marker corresponding to the desired pose before walking. The back-and-forth trips end after the subject adopts all possible five poses while walking.

We record all videos with KODAK Zi8 Pocket Video Camera, F2.8/f = 6.34 mm, 30 frames/sec at the resolution of 1920 × 1080. We process recorded videos in two different resolutions of 1920 × 1080 (high-resolution) and 960 × 540 (low-resolution). To estimate head pose, we apply the face detector of [30] on the high-resolution and low-resolution images, and in the next step, we apply the classifiers on the detected faces.

Results. Table 3 shows the accuracy of the tested methods on the high and low resolution images. GSCC performs the best among all methods. SMC ranks second and SCC ranks third. OpenFace, which is a feature-based method, does not work well for low-resolution images and its performance drops dramatically when the head has more than ±30° deviation from the frontal pose. That is due to its failure to detect the landmarks of a face as it deviates significantly from the frontal pose and some landmarks become occluded. Hence, for the +90 and −90° classes, the accuracy of OpenFace is 0%. Therefore, to convey more meaningful numbers, we report the accuracy of OpenFace for only 3 poses instead of 5 (we eliminate −90 and +90).

Our method deviates from that of [5] by making two major changes; First, we fuse GW features with those of SDM to emphasize edges and reduce the effect of illumination. Second, we split the MC into three cascaded binary classifiers. To show the contribution of each change, we need to consider the design with and without that change. A comparison of SCC to GSCC and SMC to GSMC shows the effect of merging the SDM and GW features into a combined set. The results show that the GWSDM feature set increases the accuracy of the CC and multi-class SVM schemes. GW features increase the method's robustness against lighting variation. Furthermore, a comparison of SCC to SMC and GSCC to GSMC shows the increased accuracy achieved by cascading the classifiers and decomposing the problem into three stages.

Table 3. Results of the video test on the four combinations, OpenFace and CNN.

	High resolution accuracy (%)	Low resolution accuracy (%)
SCC	91.82	85.98
GSCC	93.76	89.81
SMC [5]	84.51	76.79
GSMC	92.67	84.55
CNN [15]	80.70	74.20
OpenFace [14]	<71.89*	<25.65*

*The reported numbers for OpenFace is based on only three poses of −45, 0 and 45.

5   Conclusion

We propose an appearance-based method to detect the head pose from low-resolution images. We distinguish our work from existing ones, such as Orozco et al. [5], as follows: First, we improve the feature extraction process. Thus, we combine GW with SDM to create the GWSDM feature set. GWSDM is more robust against light changes and less sensitive to unhelpful information in the background. Second, we replace MC with a three-stage CC to increase the prediction accuracy. Third, we combine eight databases of images to create a comprehensive and diverse dataset that allows us to train classifiers that can tolerate changes in illumination and subjects' visual features.

Cross-validation results on the training dataset show that the proposed GSCC method performs better than SMC [5]. GSCC achieves a cross-validation accuracy of 98.60%. Moreover, we perform a video test under loosely constrained conditions. The proposed method performs better in the video experiments than [5], OpenFace [14] and CNN [15].

References

1. Langton, S., Honeyman, H., Tessler, E.: The influence of head contour and nose angle on the perception of eye-gaze direction. Percept. Psychophys. **66**(5), 752–771 (2004)
2. Stiefelhagen, R., Finke, M., Yang, J., Waibel, A.: From gaze to focus of attention. In: Huijsmans, D.P., Smeulders, A.W.M. (eds.) VISUAL 1999. LNCS, vol. 1614, pp. 765–772. Springer, Heidelberg (1999). https://doi.org/10.1007/3-540-48762-X_94
3. Stiefelhagen, R., Zhu, J.: Head orientation and gaze direction in meetings. In: CHI 2002 Extended Abstracts on Human Factors in Computing Systems (2002)
4. Stiefelhagen, R.: Tracking focus of attention in meetings. In: 4th IEEE International Conference on Multimodal Interfaces. IEEE Computer Society (2002)
5. Orozco, J., Gong, S., Xiang, T.: Head pose classification in crowded scenes. In: British Machine Vision Conference, pp. 120.1–120.11. BMVA Press (2009). https://doi.org/10.5244/C.23.120
6. Benfold, B., Reid, I.: Colour invariant head pose classification in low resolution video. In: British Machine Vision Conference, pp. 1–10 (2008)
7. Voit, M., Nickel, K., Stiefelhagen, R.: Multi-view head pose estimation using neural networks. In: The 2nd Canadian Conference on Computer and Robot Vision (CRV 2005), pp. 347–352. IEEE (2005). https://doi.org/10.1109/CRV.2005.55
8. Voit, M., Nickel, K., Stiefelhagen, R.: A Bayesian approach for multi-view head pose estimation. In: 2006 IEEE International Conference on Multisensor Fusion and Integration for Intelligent Systems, pp. 31–34. IEEE (2006). https://doi.org/10.1109/MFI.2006.265627
9. Tan, X., Triggs, B.: Fusing Gabor and LBP feature sets for kernel-based face recognition. In: Zhou, S.K., Zhao, W., Tang, X., Gong, S. (eds.) AMFG 2007. LNCS, vol. 4778, pp. 235–249. Springer, Heidelberg (2007). https://doi.org/10.1007/978-3-540-75690-3_18
10. Ba, S., Odobez, J.: A probabilistic framework for joint head tracking and pose estimation. In: 2004 Proceedings of the 17th International Conference on Pattern Recognition, ICPR 2004, vol. 4 (2004)
11. Smith, K., Ba, S., Odobez, J.: Tracking the visual focus of attention for a varying number of wandering people (2008)
12. Fanelli, G., Gall, J., Van Gool, L.: Real time head pose estimation with random regression forests. In: Conference on Computer Vision and Pattern Recognition, pp. 617–624. IEEE (2011). https://doi.org/10.1109/CVPR.2011.5995458
13. Breitenstein, M.D., Kuettel, D., Weise, T., van Gool, L., Pfister, H.: Real-time face pose estimation from single range images. In: 2008 IEEE Conference on Computer Vision and Pattern Recognition, pp. 1–8. IEEE (2008). https://doi.org/10.1109/CVPR.2008.4587807

14. Amos, B., Ludwiczuk, B., Satyanarayanan, M.: OpenFace: a general-purpose face recognition library with mobile applications. CMU School of Computer Science (2016)
15. Patacchiola, M., Cangelosi, A.: Head pose estimation in the wild using convolutional neural networks and adaptive gradient methods. Pattern Recogn. **71**, 132–143 (2017). https://doi.org/10.1016/j.patcog.2017.06.009
16. Robertson, N., Reid, I.: Estimating gaze direction from low-resolution faces in video. In: Leonardis, A., Bischof, H., Pinz, A. (eds.) ECCV 2006. LNCS, vol. 3952, pp. 402–415. Springer, Heidelberg (2006). https://doi.org/10.1007/11744047_31
17. Comaniciu, D., Meer, P.: Mean shift analysis and applications. In: 1999 Proceedings of the Seventh IEEE International Conference on Computer Vision (1999)
18. Debnath, R., Takahide, N., Takahashi, H.: A decision based one-against-one method for multi-class support vector machine. Pattern Anal. Appl. **7**, 164–175 (2004). https://doi.org/10.1007/s10044-004-0213-6
19. Branch, H.: Imagery library for intelligent detection systems (i-LIDS). In: 2006 Institution of Engineering and Technology Conference on Crime and Security. IET (2006)
20. Murphy-Chutorian, E., Trivedi, M.M.: Head pose estimation in computer vision: a survey. IEEE Trans. Pattern Anal. Mach. Intell. **31**(4) (2009). https://doi.org/10.1109/TPAMI.2008.106
21. Shen, L., Bai, L.: A review on Gabor wavelets for face recognition. Pattern Anal. Appl. **9**, 273–292 (2006). https://doi.org/10.1007/s10044-006-0033-y
22. Pizer, S.M., et al.: Adaptive histogram equalization and its variations. Comput. Vis. Graph. Image Process. **39**, 355–368 (1987). https://doi.org/10.1016/S0734-189X(87)80186-X
23. Smith, B., Yin, Q., Feiner, S., Nayar, S.: Gaze locking: passive eye contact detection for human-object interaction. In: Proceedings of the 26th Annual ACM Symposium on User Interface Software and Technology (2013)
24. Ariz, M., Bengoechea, J.J., Villanueva, A., Cabeza, R.: A novel 2D/3D database with automatic face annotation for head tracking and pose estimation. Comput. Vis. Image Underst. **148**, 201–210 (2016). https://doi.org/10.1016/j.cviu.2015.04.009
25. Asteriadis, S., Soufleros, D., Karpouzis, K.: A natural head pose and eye gaze dataset. In: Proceedings of the International Workshop on Affective-Aware Virtual Agents and Social Robots (2009)
26. Sim, T., Baker, S., Bsat, M.: The CMU pose, illumination, and expression (PIE) database. In: Automatic Face Gesture (2002)
27. Gourier, N., Hall, D., Crowley, J.: Estimating face orientation from robust detection of salient facial structures. In: FG Net Workshop on Visual Observation of Deictic Gestures (2004)
28. Muñoz-Salinas, R., Yeguas-Bolivar, E., Saffiotti, A.: Multi-camera head pose estimation. Mach. Vis. Appl. **23**(3), 479–490 (2012)
29. Samaria, F., Harter, A.: Parameterisation of a stochastic model for human face identification. In: 1994 Proceedings of the Second IEEE Workshop on Applications of Computer Vision. IEEE (1994)
30. Liao, S., Jain, A., Li, S.: A fast and accurate unconstrained face detector. IEEE Trans. Pattern Anal. **38**(2), 211–223 (2016)
31. Smith, B.A., Yin, Q., Feiner, S.K., Nayar, S.K.: Gaze locking: passive eye contact detection for human-object interaction. In: Proceedings of the 26th Annual ACM Symposium on User Interface Software and Technology, UIST 2013, pp. 271–280. ACM Press, New York (2013). https://doi.org/10.1145/2501988.2501994

Forecasting of Meteorological Weather Time Series Through a Feature Vector Based on Correlation

Mery Milagros Paco Ramos[1]($\boxtimes$)(iD), Cristian López Del Alamo[2](iD),
and Reynaldo Alfonte Zapana[1](iD)

[1] Universidad Nacional de San Agustín, Arequipa, Peru
{mpacor,ralfonte}@unsa.edu.pe
[2] Universidad La Salle, Arequipa, Peru
clopez@ulasalle.edu.pe

Abstract. Nowadays, the impacts of climate change are harming many countries around the world. For this reason, the scientific community is interested in improving methods to forecast weather events, so it is possible to avoid people from being injured. One important thing in the development of time series forecasting methods is to consider the set of values over time that facilitates the prediction of future value. In this sense, we propose a new feature vector based on the correlation and autocorrelation functions. These measures reflect how the observations of a time series are related to each other. Then, univariate forecasting is performed using Multilayer Perceptron (MLP) and Long Short-Term Memory (LSTM) deep neural network. Finally, we compared the new model with linear and non-linear models. Reported results exhibit that MLP and LSTM models using the proposed feature vector, they show promising results for univariate forecasting. We tested our method on a real-world dataset from the Fisher weather station (Harvard Forest).

Keywords: Forecasting of time series · Non-linear forecast models · Weather forecast · Feature vector · Correlation · Deep Learning

1 Introduction

Forecasting of time series are of fundamental importance in various fields, such as medicine, finance, marketing, meteorology, entertainment, among others; where the temporal component predominates [1,3]. By analyzing the temporal evolution, it is possible to predict the future of the series using different forecast models.

Historically, time series forecasting has been mainly studied in econometrics and statistics. However, solving analytical equations which only contain a minimum number of non-linear operations cannot describe the high-dimensionality and noise of time series [15].

© Springer Nature Switzerland AG 2019
M. Vento and G. Percannella (Eds.): CAIP 2019, LNCS 11678, pp. 542–553, 2019.
https://doi.org/10.1007/978-3-030-29888-3_44

Currently, a field of explosive expansion for the modeling of systems that exhibit non-linear behaviors is Deep Learning [4,23]. Deep Learning is a subset of specialized Machine Learning techniques based on neural networks and inspired by the functioning of the human brain. Its success is due to outstanding performance in various areas such as voice recognition [8], natural language processing [7], object detection [10,24], machine translation, among others. However, much of the focus in the Deep Learning community has been on developing learning algorithms for static data, and not so much on time series data [14].

The present paper proposes a feature vector based on the autocorrelation and correlation of meteorological signals. Then, we use Deep Learning model for prediction tasks. This work is structured as follows. Section 2 describes the related research works. In Sect. 3 introduces previous concepts to understand the proposed model. In Sect. 4 describes the proposed methodology. In Sect. 5 presents the experiments and results obtained. Finally, in Sect. 6 presents the main conclusions and future work.

2   Related Works

In the literature, many models have been proposed to improve the accuracy and efficiency of time series forecasting [1]. Linear models have attracted attention due to their simplicity and ease of application. However, most real-world forecasting applications do not fall into this category. Instead, they are characterized by non-linear models [1,22].

Two popular models for the univariate forecast of time series are the Exponential Smoothing (Holt-Winters) and Autoregressive Integrated Moving Average (ARIMA) [1]. ARIMA model uses Autoregressive models (AR), Moving Average (MA), and initial differencing steps to eliminate non-stationarity [18].

The underlying process used in both above mentioned models is linear and therefore does not capture the nonlinear patterns in time series [1]. To overcome this drawback, several nonlinear stochastic models have been proposed in the literature. Some of them are Non-linear Autoregressive (NAR) [17], Support Vector Regression (SVR) [22], K-Nearest Neighbor Regression (KNN) [2], Artificial Neural Networks (ANN) [9], Recurrent Neural Networks (RNN), among others.

3   Background

3.1   Time Series

Time series is a sequence of observations $\{\phi_1, ..., \phi_t\}$ recorded over time on the behavior of a variable of interest. Each observation $\{\phi_t\}$ is recorded at a particular timestamp t, usually in equally spaced intervals (annual, monthly, weekly, daily or even fraction of a second) [6,19].

3.2   Correlation and Autocorrelation Function

The correlation coefficient measures the degree or strength of the linear relationship between two random variables X and Y, and it is between $-1 \leq \rho_{x,y} \leq +1$. The correlation coefficient between X and Y is defined as [25]:

$$\rho_{x,y} = \frac{Cov(X,Y)}{\sqrt{Var(X)Var(Y)}} \tag{1}$$

Where $Cov(X,Y)$ is the covariance of X and Y, $Var(X)$ and $Var(Y)$ are the variance of X and Y respectively and $\rho_{x,y} = \rho_{y,x}$.

The autocorrelation of time series reflects the degree of linear dependence between the values over time $\{\phi_t\}$ and $\{\phi_{t+h}\}$, where h is the number of lags. The autocorrelation coefficient measures how past values of time series $\{\phi_t\}$ influence the present values. Consequently, there are two ways to measure this dependence: autocorrelation and partial autocorrelation.

Autocorrelation Function (ACF). The correlation coefficient between $\{\phi_t\}$ and $\{\phi_{t+h}\}$ is called autocorrelation of order h ($h > 0$), which is represented by the symbol ρ_h. Specifically, it is defined as:

$$\rho_h = \frac{Cov(\phi_t, \phi_{t+h})}{\sqrt{Var(\phi_t)Var(\phi_{t+h})}} \tag{2}$$

Partial Autocorrelation Function (PACF). The correlation between $\{y_t\}$ and $\{y_{t+h}\}$ is conditioned by the intermediate observations between them.

$$\rho_h = \frac{Cov(\phi_t, \phi_{t+h}|\phi_{t+1},...,\phi_{t+h-1})}{\sqrt{Var(\phi_t|\phi_{t+1},...,\phi_{t+h-1})Var(\phi_{t+h}|\phi_{t+1},...,\phi_{t+h-1})}} \tag{3}$$

3.3   Multilayer Perceptron (MLP)

MLP is an artificial neural network which its neurons are grouped in layers of different levels: an input layer, a hidden layer or various hidden layers and an output layer [12], as shown in the Fig. 1. The input layer represents a vector of regressors $[x_{t-1}, x_{t-2}, ..., x_{t-p}]$, which feed the hidden layer of n neurons through linear or non-linear activations $g_i = h(\mathbf{w_i}\mathbf{x} + b_i)$.

3.4   Recurrent Neural Networks (RNNs)

Recurrent connections are a characteristic of RNNs. Through these connections, the model can retain information from previous entries, enabling it to discover temporal correlations between events that are far away from each other [20].

In Fig. 2 shows an RNN where the output of the previous time step is used as input for the current timestep. This allows to develop a forecasting model

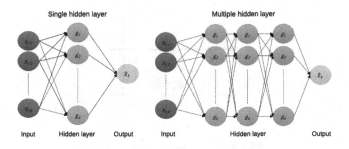

Fig. 1. Multilayer perceptron [21].

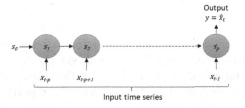

Fig. 2. Recurrent neural network with p steps of time [21].

where the input is the series $[x_{t-1}, x_{t-2}, ..., x_{t-p}]$ and the output from the last timestep is the prediction $\hat{x}_t$.

RNNs are notoriously difficult to be trained, mainly due to the problems of vanishing and exploding gradients that give erratic results during training. As a result, RNNs have difficulty in learning long-range dependencies. [20,21]. To solve this problem were created the LSTM networks.

Long Short-Term Memory (LSTM). These networks are explicitly designed to mitigate the problem vanishing gradient, which prevents standard RNNs from learning long-term dependencies [11,16]. The basic component of the model is the memory block (see Fig. 3), which contains one or more memory cells, an input gate i_t, forget gate f_t and output gate o_t. In addition, every timestep also has an internal hidden state h_t and internal memory C_t. These new units are calculated as follows [13]:

$$
\begin{aligned}
i_t &= \sigma\left(W_{xi}x_t + W_{hi}h_{t-1} + b_i\right)\\
f_t &= \sigma\left(W_{xf}x_t + W_{hf}h_{t-1} + b_f\right)\\
\tilde{C}_t &= \tanh\left(W_{xc}x_t + W_{hC}h_{t-1} + b_C\right)\\
C_t &= f_t \odot C_{t-1} + i_t \odot \tilde{C}_t\\
o_t &= \sigma\left(W_{xo}x_t + W_{ho}h_{t-1} + b_o\right)\\
h_t &= \tanh(C_t) \odot o_t
\end{aligned}
\tag{4}
$$

where σ is the sigmoid function, W_* are parameter matrices to be learned, b_* is the bias vectors and the $\odot$ operator denotes element-wise multiplication of two vectors.

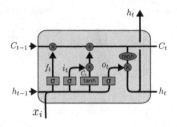

Fig. 3. LSTM memory block [11].

4   Proposal

In this article, we propose a new feature vector based on autocorrelation and correlation of meteorological signals. Once we get the feature vector from the meteorological signal, we proceed to train with Deep Learning models. Figure 4 shows a diagram that summarizes the workflow of the proposed methodology.

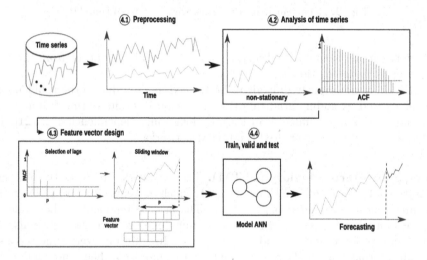

Fig. 4. The proposed method for univariate time series forecasting.

4.1   Data Preprocessing

With the goal to eliminate noise, filling missing values and to improve the convergence of the algorithm, the following steps were taken on the data set:

Data Cleaning. To estimate missing and outlier values we used linear interpolation between adjacent values.

$$y_t = y_{t-1} + \frac{y_{t+1} - y_{t-1}}{x_{t+1} - x_{t-1}} (x_t - x_{t-1}) \tag{5}$$

Data Standardization. To normalize the values of the weather series, we perform the following transformation:

$$\hat{x}_t = \frac{x_t - \mu_{train}}{\sigma_{train}} \tag{6}$$

Where μ_{train} is the mean and σ_{train} is the standard deviation of the training set.

4.2 Analysis of Time Series

Previous to the feature vector design, we need to make sure that the series is stationary because it affects the identification of the number of lags. If non-stationarity is detected, we will have to use methods to make the series stationary such as differentiation.

4.3 Feature Vector Design

To train Deep Learning models, we transform time series into sequences. In general, suppose we have time series ϕ_t, we embedded the original series into a dataset D made up of N input-output pairs as follows:

$$D = \left\{ (x_t, y_t) \in \left(\mathbb{R}^p \times \mathbb{R}^H \right) \right\}_{t=p}^N$$
$$x_t \subset \{\phi_t, .., \phi_{t-p+1}\}, \ y_t = \{\phi_{t+1}, .., \phi_{t+h}\} \tag{7}$$

Where $h \in \{1, .., H\}$, p is the number of lags and h is the forecast horizon. In this article, we will focus on one-step forecasting ($h = 1$).

The following explains the method to obtain the number of lags p to predict y_t and the formation of the feature vectors.

Lag Selection Criteria. To determine the number of lags p needed to predict y_t, we get significant values other than 0 that exceed the 95% confidence interval given by $\left(-1.96/\sqrt{N}, +1.96/\sqrt{N} \right)$ of the PACF correlogram.

Sliding Window. For the feature vectors design, we use a sliding window of length $p + h$ across the time series ϕ_t (see Fig. 5). Each instance of the sliding window corresponds to a record of the D training set. The X input corresponds to the first p lags in the window, while the Y output corresponds to the remaining h values.

Below is the result of sliding window where the forecast horizon h is equal to 1.

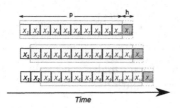

Fig. 5. An example of the sliding window approach.

Using a Signal

$$X = \begin{bmatrix} \phi_1 & \phi_2 & \cdots & \phi_p \\ \phi_2 & \phi_3 & \cdots & \phi_{p+1} \\ \vdots & \vdots & \cdots & \vdots \\ \phi_p & \phi_{p+1} & \cdots & \phi_{n+p-1} \end{bmatrix} = \begin{bmatrix} \phi_{p+1} \\ \phi_{p+2} \\ \vdots \\ \phi_{n+p} \end{bmatrix} \tag{8}$$

Using Multiple Signals

$$X = \begin{bmatrix} \phi_1^1 & \phi_2^1 & \cdots & \phi_{p'}^1 & \cdots & \phi_1^i & \phi_2^i & \cdots & \phi_p^i \\ \phi_2^1 & \phi_3^1 & \cdots & \phi_{p'+1}^1 & \cdots & \phi_2^i & \phi_3^i & \cdots & \phi_{p+1}^i \\ \vdots & \vdots & \cdots & \vdots & \cdots & \vdots & \vdots & \cdots & \vdots \\ \phi_{p'}^1 & \phi_{p'+1}^1 & \cdots & \phi_{n+p'-1}^1 & \cdots & \phi_p^i & \phi_{p+1}^i & \cdots & \phi_{n+p-1}^i \end{bmatrix} = \begin{bmatrix} \phi_{p+1}^i \\ \phi_{p+2}^i \\ \vdots \\ \phi_{n+p}^i \end{bmatrix} \tag{9}$$

4.4   Training, Validation, and Model Testing

The models to be used will be MLP and LSTM. Consequently, the data matrix obtained in Sect. 4.3 will be partitioned into three sets: 70% for training, 15% for validation, and 15% for testing. Therefore the procedure has been divided into 3 phases.

Training Phase. The training set is used to determine the parameters of the network, and the training algorithm is backpropagation.

Validation Phase. To find the optimal hyperparameters of the model, we will make use of the cross-validation for time series of K iterations. Table 1 shows the hyperparameters grid that is used throughout the experiments, in the form of minimum and maximum values for each hyperparameters.

Test Phase. The test set is used to estimate the generalization error of the model with the purpose to finally calculate the forecast accuracy using the MSE, RMSE and MAE metrics.

Table 1. Grid search used throughout the MLP and LSTM learning process. The range of values used in each parameter is represented by the respective minimum and maximum values.

Hyperparameter	Minimum value	Maximum value
Number of epochs	50	300
Size of batch	20	128
Number of hidden layers	1	8
Number of units per hidden layer	10	150
Number of recurring layers	1	8
Number of neurons per recurrent layer	10	100
Activation function	ReLU	
Optimizer	Adam	

5   Experiments and Results

5.1   Data

In this study, we used the data set from the Fisher weather station located in an open field in Prospect Hill (Harvard Forest), state of Massachusetts, EE. UU. (alt. 342 m, lat. 42.53311, long. −72.18968) [5].

The time interval of the data set is 17 years, 8 months, 2 weeks, 6 days, covering the period from February 11, 2001, to October 31, 2018. The data includes daily records of meteorological conditions such as air temperature (°C), relative humidity (%), precipitation (mm), barometric pressure (mb), solar radiation (MJ/m^2), wind speed (m/s), wind direction (sexagesimal degrees) and soil temperature (°C).

5.2   Analysis of Time Series

In Fig. 6(a), we observe that maximum air temperature exhibits a seasonal variation which is annual period. Moreover, ACF correlogram shows resistance to decrease to 0 (see Fig. 6(b)). Consequently, as we said before we proceed to remove the seasonal effects so that transform the series into stationary and finally, obtain the lags through the PACF correlogram.

Prediction Using a Signal. To evaluate the performance of MLP and LSTM models, we made a comparison between our proposal and ARIMA, SVR and KNN methods. Figure 7 show the comparison with the other methods for the series: maximum air temperature and maximum soil temperature. According to Table 3, we show that MLP and LSTM models provide a better performance than other models that we consider in the present analysis. However, in the vast majority of cases, LSTM model exceeds an MLP model with a minimum difference (Table 2).

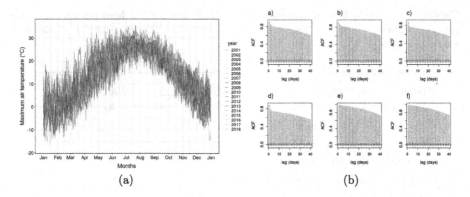

(a)   (b)

Fig. 6. (a) Seasonal plot for maximum air temperature (b) ACF correlogram of the first 40 lags of the meteorological variables. (a) Maximum air temperature (b) Minimum air temperature (c) Maximum dew point (d) Minimum dew point (e) Maximum soil temperature (f) Minimum soil temperature.

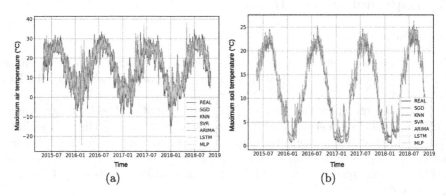

(a)   (b)

Fig. 7. Comparison of forecasting methods (a) Maximum air temperature (b) Maximum soil temperature.

Table 2. Forecasting evaluation measures for univariate models.

Weather variable	MLP		LSTM		ARIMA		SVR		KNN		SGD	
	RMSE	MAE	RMSE	MAE	RMSE	MAE	RMSE	MAE	RMSE	MAE	RMSE	MAE
Average air temperature	3.286	2.494	**3.283**	**2.515**	3.457	2.623	3.343	2.528	3.669	2.801	3.360	2.563
Maximum air temperature	4.191	3.291	**4.171**	**3.272**	4.261	5.064	4.930	3.724	4.661	3.659	4.217	3.280
Minimum air temperature	3.434	2.592	**3.433**	**2.574**	3.709	2.764	3.777	2.741	3.776	2.911	3.542	2.709
Average dew point	4.462	3.487	**4.456**	**3.436**	4.843	4.792	4.961	3.649	4.979	3.823	4.526	3.518
Maximum dew point	4.657	3.487	**4.650**	**3.466**	5.092	3.815	6.721	4.339	5.139	3.883	4.712	3.542
Minimum dew point	**4.743**	**3.652**	4.749	3.671	5.104	3.877	5.034	3.830	5.417	4.212	4.806	3.713
Average soil temperature	**0.615**	**0.442**	0.615	0.457	1.117	0.928	0.737	0.490	0.740	0.542	0.854	0.641
Maximum soil temperature	0.704	0.527	**0.698**	**0.530**	1.281	1.074	0.726	0.582	0.904	0.679	0.882	0.648
Minimum soil temperature	0.676	0.515	**0.673**	**0.510**	1.204	0.794	0.692	0.550	0.849	0.634	0.841	0.624

Prediction Using Multiple Signals. In our forecast model we include only the signals with high correlation with the target variable.

Table 3 shows the average errors with all the four forecasting methods. It was determined that the MLP is the model that obtains better forecast results, than the SVR, KNN and SGD models. Also, it is observed that the errors have decreased because the meteorological variables are strongly correlated with the variables under study.

Table 3. Forecasting evaluation measures for univariate models that use information from series correlated with the objective variable.

Weather variable	MLP		SVR		KNN		SGD	
	RMSE	MAE	RMSE	MAE	RMSE	MAE	RMSE	MAE
Average air temperature	**0.622**	**0.480**	1.422	0.922	1.900	1.464	0.708	0.524
Maximum air temperature	**4.101**	**3.217**	5.148	4.101	5.017	3.945	4.156	3.240
Minimum air temperature	**1.852**	**1.452**	2.242	1.678	2.837	2.164	2.241	1.682
Average dew point	**1.629**	**1.230**	2.203	1.532	3.313	2.568	1.819	1.272
Maximum dew point	**4.445**	**3.354**	5.380	4.030	5.349	4.079	4.517	3.399
Minimum dew point	**1.493**	**1.145**	2.110	1.527	3.201	2.489	1.836	1.391
Average soil temperature	**0.148**	**0.113**	0.723	0.526	0.655	0.508	0.234	0.177
Maximum soil temperature	**0.469**	**0.370**	0.721	0.536	0.888	0.680	0.604	0.461
Minimum soil temperature	**0.420**	**0.322**	0.656	0.494	0.744	0.574	0.541	0.428

Finally, Fig. 8, we present the comparison of the forecasting methods for the average air temperature and maximum soil temperature.

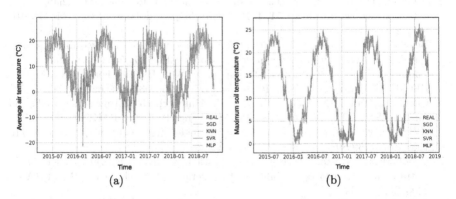

(a)   (b)

Fig. 8. Comparison of forecasting methods (a) Average air temperature (b) Maximum soil temperature.

6   Conclusions and Future Work

In this paper, we introduced the design of a new feature vector for the univariate forecasting, using the MLP and LSTM models. We demonstrated that MLP sometimes presented better or equal forecast approximation to LSTM. Likewise, both models surpass the ARIMA, SVR, SGD and KNN models.

One of the main drawbacks with LSTM model is that it implies a higher computational cost than the MLP model, as the number of recurrent neurons and layers increases. On the other hand, it has been possible to improve the accuracy of the forecast by including in the model strongly correlated time series with the time series to be predicted.

Among future works, a mutual information theory could be used for the selection of lags because the correlation coefficient assumes that the relationship between two variables is linear. In contrast, mutual information is a general measure of association between variables that detects both linear and non-linear relationships. Therefore, it represents an alternative for those time series that could present non-linear relationships. In addition, feature vectors obtained can be used to train other models of Machine Learning or Deep Learning.

Acknowledgments. The authors would like to express their sincere gratitude to FONDECYT, which is an initiative of the National Council of Science, Technology and Technological Innovation (CONCYTEC), for promoting and financing collaborative research through the research circle N° 148-2015-FONDECYT.

References

1. Adhikari, R., Agrawal, R.K.: An introductory study on time series modeling and forecasting (2013). https://doi.org/10.13140/2.1.2771.8084
2. Alavi, S.E., Sinaei, H., Afsharirad, E.: Predict the trend of stock prices using machine learning techniques. Int. Acad. J. Econ. **2**(12), 1–11 (2015)
3. Aminikhanghahi, S., Cook, D.J.: A survey of methods for time series change point detection. Knowl. Inf. Syst. **51**, 1–29 (2016). https://doi.org/10.1007/s10115-016-0987-z
4. Bengio, Y., Courville, A.C., Vincent, P.: Unsupervised feature learning and deep learning: a review and new perspectives. CoRR, abs/1206.5538 1 (2012)
5. Boose, E.: Fisher meteorological station (since 2001). Harvard Forest Data Archive: HF001 (2001). https://doi.org/10.6073/pasta/04076dfd30b286c6c29301b6345a63f5
6. Cheng, H., Tan, P.-N., Gao, J., Scripps, J.: Multistep-ahead time series prediction. In: Ng, W.-K., Kitsuregawa, M., Li, J., Chang, K. (eds.) PAKDD 2006. LNCS (LNAI), vol. 3918, pp. 765–774. Springer, Heidelberg (2006). https://doi.org/10.1007/11731139_89
7. Collobert, R., Weston, J., Bottou, L., Karlen, M., Kavukcuoglu, K., Kuksa, P.: Natural language processing (almost) from scratch. J. Mach. Learn. Res. **12**(Aug), 2493–2537 (2011)
8. Deng, L., et al.: Recent advances in deep learning for speech research at microsoft. In: 2013 IEEE International Conference on Acoustics, Speech and Signal Processing, pp. 8604–8608. IEEE (2013)
9. Doucoure, B., Agbossou, K., Cardenas, A.: Time series prediction using artificial wavelet neural network and multi-resolution analysis: application to wind speed data. Renew. Energy **92**, 202–211 (2016). https://doi.org/10.1016/j.renene.2016.02.003. http://www.sciencedirect.com/science/article/pii/S0960148116301045

10. Erhan, D., Szegedy, C., Toshev, A., Anguelov, D.: Scalable object detection using deep neural networks. In: Proceedings of the IEEE Conference on Computer Vision and Pattern Recognition, pp. 2147–2154 (2014)
11. Hu, F., Li, L., Xu, X., Wang, J., Zhang, J.: Opinion extraction by distinguishing term dependencies and digging deep text features. NeuralComputing and Applications, February 2018. https://doi.org/10.1007/s00521-018-3372-x
12. Isasi Viñuela, P., Galván León, I.: Redes de neuronas artificiales. Un Enfoque Práctico, Editorial Pearson Educación SA Madrid España (2004)
13. Jozefowicz, R., Zaremba, W., Sutskever, I.: An empirical exploration of recurrent network architectures. In: Proceedings of the 32nd International Conference on International Conference on Machine Learning, ICML 2015, vol. 37, pp. 2342–2350, JMLR.org (2015). http://dl.acm.org/citation.cfm?id=3045118.3045367
14. Längkvist, M.: Modeling time-series with deep networks (2014)
15. Längkvist, M., Karlsson, L., Loutfi, A.: A review of unsupervised feature learning and deep learning for time-series modeling. Pattern Recogn. Lett. **42**, 11–24 (2014)
16. LeCun, Y., Bengio, Y., Hinton, G.: Deep learning. Nature **521**(7553), 436–444 (2015)
17. Lydia, M., Kumar, S.S., Selvakumar, A.I., Kumar, G.E.P.: Linear and nonlinear autoregressive models for short-term wind speed forecasting. Energy Convers. Manag. **112**, 115–124 (2016). https://doi.org/10.1016/j.enconman.2016.01.007. http://www.sciencedirect.com/science/article/pii/S0196890416000236
18. Mahalakshmi, G., Sridevi, S., Rajaram, S.: A survey on forecasting of time series data. In: 2016 International Conference on Computing Technologies and Intelligent Data Engineering, ICCTIDE 2016, pp. 1–8, January 2016. https://doi.org/10.1109/ICCTIDE.2016.7725358
19. Mauricio, J.A.: Introducción al análisis de series temporales. Universidad complutense de Madrid (2003)
20. Pascanu, R., Mikolov, T., Bengio, Y.: On the difficulty of training recurrent neural networks. ICML **3**(28), 1310–1318 (2013)
21. Prakash, P., Pal, A.: Practical Time Series Analysis. Packt Publishing, Birmingham (2017)
22. Sapankevych, N.I., Sankar, R.: Time series prediction using support vector machines: a survey. IEEE Comput. Intell. Mag. **4**(2), 24–38 (2009). https://doi.org/10.1109/MCI.2009.932254
23. Schulz, H., Behnke, S.: Deep learning. KI-Künstliche Intelligenz **26**(4), 357–363 (2012)
24. Szegedy, C., Toshev, A., Erhan, D.: Deep neural networks for object detection. In: Advances in Neural Information Processing Systems, pp. 2553–2561 (2013)
25. Tsay, R.S.: Analysis of financial time series, vol. 543. Wiley, Hoboken (2005)

Smart Monitoring of Crops Using Generative Adversarial Networks

Hamideh Kerdegari[✉], Manzoor Razaak, Vasileios Argyriou,
and Paolo Remagnino

The Robot Vision Team (RoViT), Kingston University, London, UK
{h.kerdegari,manzoor.razaak}@kingston.ac.uk

Abstract. Unmanned aerial vehicles (UAV) are used in precision agriculture (PA) to enable aerial monitoring of farmlands. Intelligent methods are required to pinpoint weed infestations and make optimal choice of pesticide. UAV can fly a multispectral camera and collect data. However, the classification of multispectral images using supervised machine learning algorithms such as convolutional neural networks (CNN) requires a large amount of training data. This is a common drawback in deep learning. Our method makes use of a semi-supervised generative adversarial networks (GAN), providing a pixel-wise classification for all the acquired multispectral images. It consists of a generator network to provide photorealistic images as extra training data to a multi-class classifier acting as a discriminator and trained on small amounts of labeled data. The performance of the proposed semi-supervised GAN is evaluated on the weedNet dataset consisting of multispectral crop and weed images collected by a micro aerial vehicle (MAV). Results indicate high classification accuracy can be achieved and show the potential of GAN-based methods for the challenging task of multispectral image classification.

Keywords: Generative adversarial networks (GAN) ·
Semi-supervised GAN · Multispectral images · Classification ·
Unmanned aerial vehicles (UAV)

1 Introduction

Weed infestation is a major challenge for the agriculture sector. Early detection and removal of weed can greatly improve crop yield. Traditional methods of weed removal are time consuming: they require farmers to physically survey, identify and treat infested areas. UAV are used by farmers with cameras (RGB, multi or hyper spectral) to obtain a better view of their farm and identify specific weed infestations. Ultimately, the goal is to implement more effective treatment measures and reduce if not eliminate entirely weed infestation [1].

RGB cameras and multispectral sensors flown by UAV have proven to be useful in early weed detection. Figure 1 illustrates an example with spectral images of a farm. Captured data is then analyzed by computer vision algorithms

© Springer Nature Switzerland AG 2019
M. Vento and G. Percannella (Eds.): CAIP 2019, LNCS 11678, pp. 554–563, 2019.
https://doi.org/10.1007/978-3-030-29888-3_45

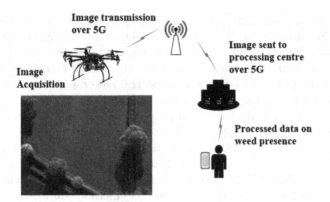

Fig. 1. A weed detection system: a UAV with a mounted multispectral camera, 5G transmission system, and a data processing centre hosting the captured image data and weed detection algorithms.

to detect the presence of weed. Studies that utilize RGB cameras mainly apply feature extraction techniques for the detection and classification of weed from crop. Hung et al. [2] proposed a feature learning based approach with a bank of image filters to draw image statistics and feed them to a linear classifier to be able to detect presence of weed from images captured by a RGB camera mounted on a UAV. In [3], the authors used a commercial camera that operates in the visible spectrum for a ultra-high resolution image acquisition over wheat fields. Their study calculated six different vegetation indices based on the RGB spectrum and achieved a high accuracy of above 85% in the detection and classification of vegetation. Although RGB image analysis methods can be successfully used for weed identification and classification [4], RGB images captured by UAV have few limitations in crop-weed disambiguation. Results in [5] showed that better performance for weed detection via RGB images was obtained for larger size of weed plants. To achieve high accuracy feature detection and learning, an expensive high resolution camera is necessary to capture sufficient details of the crop and weed. Further, RGB images capture less information at higher altitudes and it was observed that vegetation indices decrease as altitude increases [6].

Due to the limitations of the visible spectrum (RGB band), use of additional spectral bands, in the infrared side of the spectrum, have shown to provide detailed information that enables accurate calculation of vegetation indices and crop-weed classification [7]. Therefore, multispectral cameras are increasingly used for crop growth monitoring. Health analysis can be implemented through extraction of vegetation indices, such as the normalized difference vegetation index (NDVI), green normalized difference vegetation index (GNDVI) and soil adjusted vegetation index (SAVI) [8]. These indices are computed from different spectral bands captured by the multispectral camera and can be further utilized to analyze vegetation conditions.

Studies employing multispectral cameras apply different approaches for weed detection. For instance, in [9], an object detection based image analysis method was proposed that identifies objects in crop rows and applies classification techniques to discriminate crop and weed from the spectral images. Spectral index variation is an approach that considers spectral reflectance variation to discriminate between crop and weed [6]. Various statistical methods for weed detection from multispectral images have been proposed and include approaches such as Mahalanobis distance computation between vegetation rates [10] and partial least squares discriminant analysis classification models [11] that have shown detection accuracy in range over 80%. Machine learning approaches such as support vector machine (SVM) method was found to show better accuracy performance [12], compared to the decision tree (DT) method [13] where multispectral images were classified along with the use of NDVI thresholding.

More recently, deep learning methods have been explored for crop-weed disambiguation. In particular, the basic convolutional neural network (CNN) has gained ground in the analysis and classification of remote sensing data such as multispectral images [14]. For instance, Sa et al. [15] applied cascaded CNN, Segnet, on multispectral image datasets for classifying sugar beet crop from weed. They trained six models on different spectral channels and achieved a classification F1 score of 0.8. The study was further extended to include a sliding window approach on orthomosaic maps of the farm to apply a deep neural network and achieved improved performance accuracy [16]. Similarly, several other studies applied CNN based methods for weed classification with images captured from both UAV and ground based vehicles and achieved a high performance accuracy [17,18].

However, a large amount of training data for learning is an inherent requirement of deep learning methods. The lack of large corpora of specific labeled data is a challenge in general and for multi-spectral data in particular. Furthermore, collecting large corpora of multispectral image data with UAV platforms for crop-weed classification system is time consuming and expensive. To address this challenge, this paper utilizes a semi-supervised version of the generative adversarial networks (GAN) [19]. This method generates photo-realistic crop-weed images and can be employed to augment training data. In the presented GAN based semi-supervised classification method, a generator creates large realistic images, in turn, forcing a discriminator to learn better features for more accurate pixel classification. To the best of our knowledge, application of GAN methods for multispectral image classification is not well explored and our work addresses this research gap. The main contributions of this paper are:

- first application of semi-supervised GAN for classification of multispectral images acquired by UAV,
- investigation of limited annotated data for multispectral image classification task.

Section 2 presents the proposed approach by providing a brief background of GAN and semi-supervised GAN, then the design and structure of the proposed model for semi-supervised learning is described in system overview. Section 3 deals with experimental results, where results on the weedNet dataset [15] are presented, finally Sect. 4 concludes the paper.

2 Proposed Approach

This section presents a brief background about GAN, semi-supervised GAN and then describes the proposed network architecture for semi-supervised pixel-wise classification of multispectral crop/weed imaging data.

2.1 Semi-supervised Generative Adversarial Network

The GAN framework was first introduced by Goodfellow et al. [19] to train deep generative models. A GAN usually contains two networks: a generative (G) network and a discriminative (D) network. Both networks G and D are trained simultaneously in an adversarial manner, where G tries to generate fake inputs as real as possible, and D tries to disambiguate between real and fake data. The following formulation shows G and D competition in a two-player minmax game with value function $V(D, G)$:

$$\min_{G} \max_{D} V(D, G) = E_{x \sim P_x}[log D(x)] + E_{z \sim P_z}[log(1 - D(G(z)))] \tag{1}$$

Where symbol E represents the expected value. G transforms a noise variable z into $G(z)$, that is a sample from distribution p_z, and distribution p_z should converge to distribution p_x. D is trained to minimize $log(D(x))$ while G is trained to minimize $log(1 - D(G(z)))$.

Unlike typical GAN, where the discriminator is a binary classifier for discriminating real and fake images, semi-supervised GAN implements a multiclass classifier. In semi-supervised learning, where class labels are not available for all training images, it is convenient to leverage unlabeled data for estimating a proper prior to be used by a classifier for enhancing performance. This paper extends typical GAN by replacing the traditional discriminator D with a fully convolutional multiclass classifier, which, instead of predicting whether a sample x belongs to the data distribution (real or fake), it assigns to each input image pixel a label y from the n classes (i.e. crop, weed or background) or mark it as a fake sample (extra $n + 1$ class). More specifically, D network predicts the confidence for n classes of image pixels and softmax is employed to obtain the probability of sample x belonging to each class.

Figure 2 presents a schematic description of the semi-supervised GAN architecture that three inputs such as generated multispectral data, unlabeled data and a small number of labeled data are fed into the discriminator. Note that our GAN formulation is different from the typical GAN, where the discriminator is a binary classifier for discriminating real/fake images, while our discriminator performs multiclass pixel categorization.

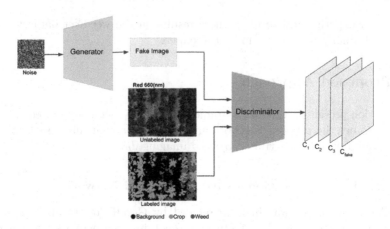

Fig. 2. The semi-supervised GAN architecture. Random noise is used by the Generator to generate an image. The Discriminator uses generated data, unlabeled data and labeled data to learn class confidences and produces confidence maps for each class as well as a label for a fake data.

2.2   System Overview

The details of our semi-supervised GAN architecture including both generator and discriminator are presented in this section.

The generator network, shown in Fig. 3, takes a uniform noise distribution as input, followed by a series of four convolution layers and generates a fake image resembling samples from real data distribution. The discriminator network processes the generated images, unlabeled images and a small number of labeled multi-spectral images to learn class confidence, producing a confidence map for each class as well as a label for fake data.

The underlying idea is that adding large fake multispectral images forces real samples to be close in the feature space, which, in turn, improves classification accuracy. Our semi-supervised GAN formulation extends the canonical GAN, where the discriminator is a binary classifier for real/fake images, implementing a pixel-wise multiclass classifier.

Note that the proposed semi-supervised GAN adopts the DCGAN [20] architecture with a modification in the last layer of the discriminator, replacing the sigmoid activation function with the softmax to enable pixel-wise multiclass classification. All the networks are implemented using the Keras library with a Tensorflow backend. The standard Adam optimizer with momentum is used for the discriminator and the generator optimization with learning rate and momentum ($\beta 1$) set to 0.0002 and 0.5, respectively. A batch size of 32 and batch normalization are utilized for both networks. The ReLU activation function is applied in the generator for all layers except for the output, which uses the Tanh and the LeakyReLU activation in the discriminator for all layers. In the experiments, no data augmentation or post-processing is performed.

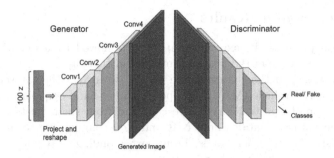

Fig. 3. The network architecture of our semi-supervised GAN. The noise is a vector of size 100 sampled from a uniform distribution and is used as input to the generator. The number of feature maps in the four different convolutional layers, respectively, are 256, 128, 64, 32 and 1 (Here 1 shows the number of channels).

During the testing process, the discriminator network is only used as pixelwise multiclass classifier network. Given a test image, the softmax layer of the discriminator outputs a set of probabilities for each pixel belonging to semantic classes, and accordingly, the label with the highest probability is assigned to the pixel. Figure 4 shows some generated images in different channels. Interestingly, these images indicate that the semi-supervised GAN framework is able to learn spatial object patterns, for example, crop shape and weed shape.

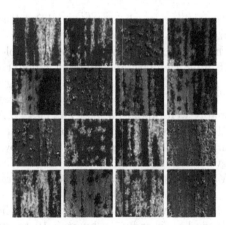

Fig. 4. Images generated by the generator of the semi-supervised GAN on the weedNet dataset. Interestingly, patterns related to crops and weeds from NDVI, Red and NIR channel can be observed that highlights the effectiveness of the approach.

3   Experimental Results

This section presents the experimental setup, followed by a quantitative and qualitative evaluation of the proposed method in this paper.

The proposed method is evaluated on the weedNet [15] dataset collected by a micro aerial vehicle (MAV) equipped with a 4-band Sequoia multispectral camera. The multispectral images are captured from sugar beets field at 2 m height. The dataset contains only NIR and Red channel due to difficulties in image registration of other bands. From corresponding NIR and Red channel images, the Normalized NDVI, given by:

$$NDVI = \frac{NIR - Red}{NIR + Red} \tag{2}$$

is extracted indicating the difference between soil and plant. Therefore, each training/test image consists of the 790 nm NIR channel, the 660 nm Red channel, and NDVI imagery. The dataset contains only crop, or weed, or crop-weed combination along with their corresponding pixel-wise annotated data. For semi-supervised training, different percentages of pixel-wise annotated images (such as 50%, 40% and 30%) are used as labeled data to the discriminator and the rest of images are without pixel-wise annotations. As metric, F1 score measure that is a harmonic average of precision and recall is employed:

$$F1 = 2 * \frac{precision * recall}{precision + recall} \tag{3}$$

Where precision is $\frac{TP}{TP+FP}$, recall is $\frac{TP}{TP+FN}$, TP, FP and FN indicate the number of true positive, false positive and false negative, respectively. Quantitative results of our method on weedNet are shown in Table 1. F1 measure with a varying number of input channels and different amount of labelled data are used as evaluation metric in this experiment. Considering the difficulty of the dataset, all models (including different channels + different amount of labeled data) perform reasonably well (about 80% for all classes). As shown in Table 1, two input channels (Red and NIR) yield higher performance compared to single channels as they contain more useful features to be used by the semi-supervised GAN network. However, using 3 channels (NDVI + Red + NIR) did not improve performance as NDVI depends on NIR and Red channels rather than capturing new information.

Furthermore, the network was evaluated by reducing the amount of labeled data starting at 50% and then reducing by step 10 to 30% to find out how it affects the classification performance. It is expected that higher amount of labeled data result in better performance. It can be seen by comparing the results of the 50%, 40% and 30% in Table 1.

Results of decoder-encoder cascaded CNN on weedNet dataset [15] is shown in the last column of Table 1. As compared with our semi-supervised GAN, it achieved higher accuracy using fully labeled data. However, we showed that semi-supervised GAN with limited training data ables to achieve a good accuracy about 80%.

Table 1. Results on the weedNet dataset using 50%, 40% and 30% of labeled data with different number of channels for semi-supervised GAN, and cascaded CNN [15] with fully labeled data. Higher F1 values indicate better classification performance.

F1 score	Semi-supervised GAN						Cascaded CNN	
Amount of labeled data	50%		40%		30%		Fully labeled	
Channel	Crop	Weed	Crop	Weed	Crop	Weed	Crop	Weed
Red	0.831	0.814	0.822	0.813	0.792	0.813	0.923	0.845
NIR	0.839	0.823	0.80	0.821	0.782	0.733	0.942	0.839
NDVI	0.826	0.803	0.817	0.79	0.788	0.812	0.952	0.849
Red + NIR	**0.857**	**0.865**	0.837	0.834	0.823	0.815	0.971	0.851
Red + NIR + NDVI	0.852	0.831	0.847	0.821	0.816	0.812	0.979	0.816

Qualitative results on some sample images are depicted in Fig. 5. As it is shown, each row contains original Red channel, NIR channel, NDVI imagery, semi-supervised GAN probability output and the corresponding ground truth. The probability of each class is mapped to the red, green and black color representing weed, crop and background, respectively. There are some noticeable weed and crop misclassification areas in the images that occur mostly when crop and weed are surrounded by each other. This misclassification shows that network can capture high-level features such as shape and texture in addition to the low-level features.

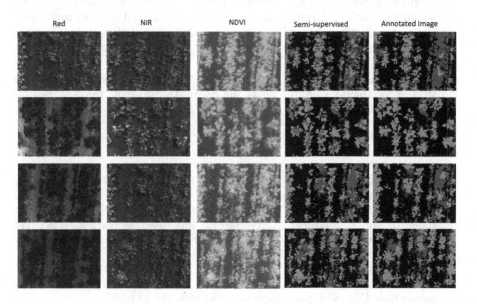

Fig. 5. Qualitative results of some sample images from the weedNet test set. The first three columns are input data to the semi-supervised GAN, the fourth is the results of semi-supervised GAN using 30% of labeled data and the last column is ground truth. (Color figure online)

4   Conclusion

This paper presents a semi-supervised framework, based on Generative Adversarial Networks (GAN), for the classification of multi-spectral images. The semi-supervised GAN network is trained on the weedNet dataset captured by an MVA from a sugar beet field. The performance of the system was evaluated using F1 score metric by varying the number of input channels and the amount of the labeled data. Results showed the F1 score of about 0.85 for two channels with 50% labeled data. Compared with weedNet paper [15] that utilized all the labeled data for training their decoder-encoder cascaded CNN for crop/weed classification, this paper demonstrated that even with limited labeled data the semi-supervised GAN network can classify the crop and weed with a relatively good accuracy. Additionally, the presented model generates synthetic images that could be used as additional multispectral data for other classifiers.

Future work includes adapting the algorithm for a near real-time application involving the transmission of aerial farm images from UAV to a processing server over 5G wireless network. Our semi-supervised GAN algorithm was only tested on one multispectral dataset with two channels (To the best of our knowledge, weedNet dataset is the only publicly available multispectral plant/weed dataset) that is one drawback of this work. To overcome this limitation, future work will involve collecting multispectral imagery with multiple channels using UAV from fields that contain both plant and weed. Therefore, we would be able to test the proposed method with the collected multispectral dataset that will contain more channels such as Infrared, Red edge, Red, Green and Blue to investigate the effect of each channel separately and in combination with each other on the classification performance.

Acknowledgement. This work is part of the 5GRIT project supported by the Department for Digital, Culture, Media and Sport (DCMS), UK, through their 5G Testbeds Program.

References

1. Lottes, P., Khanna, R., Pfeifer, J., Siegwart, R., Stachniss, C.: UAV-based crop and weed classification for smart farming. In: IEEE International Conference on Robotics and Automation (ICRA), pp. 3024–3031 (2017)
2. Hung, C., Xu, Z., Sukkarieh, S.: Feature learning based approach for weed classification using high resolution aerial images from a digital camera mounted on a UAV. Remote Sens. **6**(12), 12037–12054 (2014)
3. Torres-Sánchez, J., Peña, J.M., de Castro, A.I., López-Granados, F.: Multi-temporal mapping of the vegetation fraction in early-season wheat fields using images from UAV. Comput. Electron. Agric. **103**, 104–113 (2014)
4. Herrera, P.J., Dorado, J., Ribeiro, A.: A novel approach for weed type classification based on shape descriptors and a fuzzy decision-making method. Sensors **14**(8), 15304–15324 (2014)

5. Peña, J.M., Torres-Sánchez, J., Serrano-Pérez, A., de Castro, A.I., López-Granados, F.: Quantifying efficacy and limits of unmanned aerial vehicle (UAV) technology for weed seedling detection as affected by sensor resolution. Sensors **15**(3), 5609–5626 (2015)
6. Samseemoung, G., Soni, P., Jayasuriya, H.P., Salokhe, V.M.: Application of low altitude remote sensing (LARS) platform for monitoring crop growth and weed infestation in a soybean plantation. Precision Agric. **13**(6), 611–627 (2012)
7. López-Granados, F., Torres-Sánchez, J., Serrano-Pérez, A., de Castro, A.I., Mesas-Carrascosa, F.J., Peña, J.M.: Early season weed mapping in sunflower using UAV technology: variability of herbicide treatment maps against weed thresholds. Precision Agric. **17**(2), 183–199 (2016)
8. Bannari, A., Morin, D., Bonn, F., Huete, A.R.: A review of vegetation indices. Remote Sens. Rev. **13**(1–2), 95–120 (1995)
9. Pena, J.M., Torres-Sánchez, J., de Castro, A.I., Kelly, M., López-Granados, F.: Weed mapping in early-season maize fields using object-based analysis of unmanned aerial vehicle (UAV) images. PLoS ONE **8**(10), e77151 (2013)
10. Louargant, M., Villette, S., Jones, G., Vigneau, N., Paoli, J.N., Gée, C.: Weed detection by UAV: simulation of the impact of spectral mixing in multispectral images. Precision Agric. **18**(6), 932–951 (2017)
11. Herrmann, I., Shapira, U., Kinast, S., Karnieli, A., Bonfil, D.J.: Ground-level hyperspectral imagery for detecting weeds in wheat fields. Precision Agric. **14**(6), 637–659 (2013)
12. Ishida, T., et al.: A novel approach for vegetation classification using UAV-based hyperspectral imaging. Comput. Electron. Agric. **144**, 80–85 (2019)
13. Natividade, J., Prado, J., Marques, L.: Low-cost multi-spectral vegetation classification using an Unmanned Aerial Vehicle. In: IEEE International Conference on Autonomous Robot Systems and Competitions (ICARSC), pp. 336–342 (2017)
14. Mahdianpari, M., Salehi, B., Rezaee, M., Mohammadimanesh, F., Zhang, Y.: Very deep convolutional neural networks for complex land cover mapping using multispectral remote sensing imagery. Remote Sens. **10**(7), 1119 (2018)
15. Sa, I., et al.: weedNet: dense semantic weed classification using multispectral images and MAV for smart farming. IEEE Robot. Autom. Lett. **3**(1), 588–595 (2016)
16. Sa, I., et al.: WeedMap: a large-scale semantic weed mapping framework using aerial multispectral imaging and deep neural network for precision farming. Remote Sens. **10**(9), 1423 (2018)
17. Bah, M.D., Dericquebourg, E., Hafiane, A., Canals, R.: Deep learning based classification system for identifying weeds using high-resolution UAV imagery. In: Arai, K., Kapoor, S., Bhatia, R. (eds.) SAI 2018. AISC, vol. 857, pp. 176–187. Springer, Cham (2019). https://doi.org/10.1007/978-3-030-01177-2_13
18. Lottes, P., Behley, J., Milioto, A., Stachniss, C.: Fully convolutional networks with sequential information for robust crop and weed detection in precision farming. In: arXiv preprint, arXiv:1806.03412 (2018)
19. Goodfellow, I., et al.: Generative adversarial nets. In: Advances in neural information processing systems, pp. 2672–2680 (2014)
20. Radford, A., Metz, L., Chintala, S.: Unsupervised representation learning with deep convolutional generative adversarial networks. In: arXiv preprint, arXiv:1511.06434 (2015)

A CNN Based HEp-2 Specimen Image Segmentation and Identification of Mitotic Spindle Type Specimens

Krati Gupta[✉], Arnav Bhavsar, and Anil K. Sao

School of Computing and Electrical Engineering,
Indian Institute of Technology Mandi, Mandi, HP, India
krati_gupta@students.iitmandi.ac.in, {arnav,anil}@iitmandi.ac.in

Abstract. In the proposed work, an effective framework for identification of mitotic type staining patterns is demonstrated, integrated with a segmentation approach, in order to detect the autoimmune disorders using HEp-2 based cell substrates. It is shown that the segmentation approach obviates the requirement of DAPI channels in Indirect Immuno-Fluorescence (IIF) imaging process. Moreover, the segmentation is required for cell-based processing of staining patterns, which is in turn required, due to the rare appearance and occurrence of mitotic type cell patterns. The segmentation involves a pixel labeling strategy, using U-Net, a Deep Convolutional Neural Network (D-CNN) based approach. The effectiveness of such segmentation approach is shown by the subsequent performance for detection of Mitotic Spindle (MS) type staining patterns, framed as mitotic v/s non-mitotic/interphase classification problem. This classification task is effectively addressed using features extracted from a traditional filter bank and CNN based feature representation. After identification of individual MS cells in specimens, a threshold-based MS detection criteria has been used specifically for declaration of specimens, consisting of MS patterns. The current study demonstrates a comparative analysis of proposed segmentation masks, with given DAPI-based masks with encouraging results for segmentation, as well as classification, over a publicly available dataset.

Keywords: Computer-Aided Detection (CAD) system ·
Convolutional Neural Networks (CNN) · HEp-2 cells ·
Mitotic cells and segmentation

1 Introduction

Indirect ImmunoFluorescence (IIF) imaging technique is considered as a 'gold standard' test to detect the presence of autoimmune disorders and responsible auto/anti-nuclear antibodies (ANA) in patient blood sample [1,2]. Autoimmune disorders are the chronic conditions, characterized by inflammatory process on different organs, due to the false identification and striking on healthy blood

© Springer Nature Switzerland AG 2019
M. Vento and G. Percannella (Eds.): CAIP 2019, LNCS 11678, pp. 564–575, 2019.
https://doi.org/10.1007/978-3-030-29888-3_46

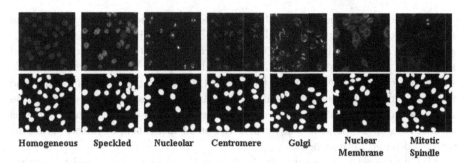

Fig. 1. Different interphase and mitotic (Mitotic Spindle) type staining patterns. First and second row represent FITC channel and DAPI channel images, respectively.

cells and tissues by human immune response. Here, HEp-2 (Human Epithelium Type-2) cells are used as a cell substrate, on which fluorescent dye labeled patient blood sample is added and seen under the microscope. The process results in different staining patterns, which are essentially the indicators of different types of ANA and associated disorders [3].

Though the IIF test is effective and accurate manual protocol, yet it is very time & labour intensive, tedious and erroneous task [1,2]. Hence, the test needs to be integrated with a Computer Aided Diagnostic/Detection (CADx/CADe) based system, that can aid to the medical experts and pathologists to make the decision-making process more efficient and less time complex.

In the diagnostic protocol, the staining patterns are identified in a specimen or whole slide image (WSI) of patient samples. Every cell is analyzed and final decision-making is done from the entire specimen. The images acquired through IIF is the Fluorescein Isothiocyanate (FITC) image channel that carries pattern information [2] and their binary masks are acquired through 4', 6-diaminidino-2-phenylindole (DAPI) image channels [1,2]. The analysis of individual cell and nuclear pattern requires localization of cells, which are typically derived using DAPI based channel images.

These staining patterns are broadly classified into interphase and mitotic phase patterns [4–7] (refer Fig. 1). To the best of our knowledge, most approaches have explored the classification schemes on interphase patterns [1,2]. However, mitotic patterns detection is an important and principal step in complete HEp-2 images screening framework [7], as these are the indicators of some lethal diseases and also the indicator of similar type of interphase patterns. Moreover, the presence of atleast one mitotic pattern per slide image demonstrates the correctness of slide preparation [4]. The main challenge of detecting mitotic patterns in specimens is their rare appearance and intra-class variations. Hence, the present study focuses on proposing an appropriate segmentation scheme, followed by a classification framework for mitotic v/s interphase patterns classification, with the following important aspects:

(I) In literature, the identification of a specimen is done, on the basis of the maximally occurred pattern in a slide image, known as 'majority rule for pattern declaration' [8]. Since, the mitotic type patterns represent the patterns visualized at mitotic phase of cell cycle (also a transition phase), hence very few cells undergo such transformation and thus manifest mitotic type patterns. Here, the majority-rule for patterns declaration also may not be applied for mitotic type patterns, and one needs to decide, whether each cell is of the mitotic patterns or not. Hence, the present study will focus on identification of mitotic patterns using cell-based approaches.

(II) As stated in literature, typically the DAPI channel is used to localize cells. However, the use of DAPI is an expensive, time-consuming protocol and the addition of DAPI may complicate the diagnostic work flow, and it may not even possible to perform in some pathological laboratories [2]. Some literature also suggests about the carcinogenic properties of this chemical [9]. As the Region-of-Interest for individual cell nuclei are typically required for a good quality classification, the current study suggests the computation of segmentation masks of FITC image channels. Thus, the work aims to avoid the requirement of secondary DAPI channel and to generate the binary segmentation maps, using only the primary FITC channel.

(III) Here, the pixel-based segmentation strategy has been proposed, using Deep Convolutional Neural Networks (D-CNN). The use of D-CNN is motivated by its efficiency in several segmentation and object detection tasks, including biomedical image segmentation [10]. Such segmentation strategy has been applied across all types of staining patterns, i.e., interphase as well as mitotic type staining patterns.

(IV) The work focuses on the identification of most prominent pattern among mitotic type staining patterns, i.e., Mitotic Spindle (MS) type pattern, which is characterized by the presence of two bright blob like structure, around the two extreme sides of nuclear periphery. Such a trait is consolidated, using an effective traditional feature representation, consisting of the responses acquired from Leung-Malik (LM) filter bank [11], which is further treated using Bag of Words (BoW) [12] representation, along with the appropriate binary classifiers. The CNN based features representation has also been explored in the work.

(V) We also perform a comparative analysis of the automatic segmentation, with the DAPI-based segmentation masks, using same features and classifiers. In this way, the efficacy of proposed approach can be fairly analyzed and compared. Moreover, the segmentation and classification framework are also compared with some existing approaches. A fair comparative analysis has also been done between traditional and CNN based learned feature representation, along with a traditional and baseline classifier.

1.1   Related Work

There are few works present on HEp-2 single cell or specimen segmentation tasks [13–15]. All of them use spatial and morphological features to extract the

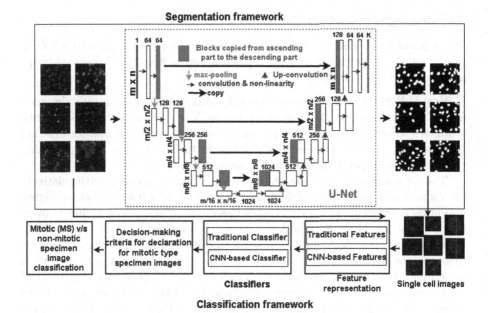

Fig. 2. Block diagram of the proposed approach of MS v/s non-MS specimen segmentation & classification.

cells, while in [13], the authors use a residual network. To the best of our knowledge, no other papers have used the D-CNN based segmentation framework, that we propose in our work. Moreover, for mitotic pattern identification task, the already existing papers [4,6,7] show classification approaches on single cell images, but not for specifically mitotic patterns present in specimens.

The works, which consider both interphase and mitotic patterns classification task [13,16–18], the rare occurrence of mitotic patterns are not considered and the detection of mitotic patterns are done, using the majority rule, that apply for interphase type patterns. Hence, the classification performance of mitotic v/s non-mitotic specimens are not very considerable [13,16–18]. In the proposed study, we propose a segmentation as well as classification framework for identification of mitotic patterns, specifically identification of Mitotic Spindle (MS) type patterns.

2   Proposed Approach

We discuss a pixel-based segmentation approach and its impact on classification tasks. Figure 2 shows a block diagram for the same. Thus, the entire strategy is divided into segmentation and classification framework, described as:

2.1   Segmentation Framework

For segmentation, first the images are pre-processed using gamma-transform at $\gamma = 0.4$ [19]. For the pixel-level segmentation, a well-known deep network architecture, U-Net is used.

U-Net: U-Net [10] is an end-to-end convolutional network, specifically designed for the segmentation of the biomedical images. The architecture consists of two symmetric contracting & expanding paths, to capture context and localization information respectively (refer Fig. 2). The features from the down-sampling path are also merged with those in the up-sampling path [10].

The advantages of the network include the efficient training with relatively less number of samples (only 390 images for training), with integration of higher resolution layers. The strategy yields seamless segmentation by applying an over-lap tile strategy. Moreover, the loss function is adjusted to give larger weights to the separating background labels between overlapping cells in the images. In this task, the standard U-Net architecture is used. The network is trained from scratch and DAPI masks are used for training, hence there is no requirement of manual ground truth labeling here. Note that, the DAPI masks are used only to train the U-Net. In the overall system with a trained U-Net, the DAPI channel will not be used, for further classification.

2.2   Classification Framework

Following the segmentation, the individual cells are extracted from pixel-based masks, as the classification strategy is based on cell-based approach. The classification framework can be defined in three important steps, i.e., feature representation, classifiers and decision making criteria for MS specimen declaration, described as below:

Feature Representation: Texture-Based Features: The used feature representations in this work, are as follows:

a. Traditional Filter-Bank Based Features:

Considering the visual distinctive characteristics for MS patterns, we employ the well-known LM filter bank features [11], which is a collection of 84 different filters that vary in parameters and orientations (first and second order derivatives of Gaussian with Laplacian of Gaussians (LoG)). After applied on single cell images, the output of filters are a set of features for each image. Such raw filter responses are compactly represented using the Bag-of-Words (BoW) approach, wherein each image is represented as a vector of the frequency of occurrences of visual words and then, in form of a histogram, which also help in addressing the intra-class variations. After this, the final feature representation for each image would be defined in form of a fixed-dimensional (64 in this case) histograms. The main challenge for such classification task is the data imbalance between the mitotic and non-mitotic/interphase cell images. Here, the majority class is undersampled and few samples are randomly removed from the interphase classes. However, one may explore different techniques to address the same.

b. CNN Based Features:

Other features used are D-CNN based features, wherein the features extracted from last pooling layer of a CNN architecture is explored. The motivation behind using such features is to use the context-specific learned information, that specifically works at different levels of abstraction and arguably capture more variations present in the images. For this particular task, the AlexNet [20] architecture is used, consisting of five convolutional layers and three fully connected (Fc) layers. In this work, this simple architecture is used, importantly to show and analyze the effectiveness of learned feature representation, however any other complex and sophisticated architecture may be explored in future studies.

Classification: Identification of Individual Cells: Two different types of classifier have been used here, defined as:

a. Support Vector Machines: For classification purpose, the well-known binary classifier, i.e., Support Vector Machine (SVM) is used with Gaussian kernel and the labels are predicted for individual test cells, extracted from specimen images. In this case, both traditional and CNN-based feature representations are classified with this classifier.

b. CNN Based Baseline Classifier: For a fair comparative analysis, CNN is used as feature extractor as well as baseline classifier also. In baseline classifier, the Fc layers are used for classification. The traditional feature representation is also classified using a neural network based classifier. In this way, both the traditional and CNN-based feature representation is classified using both neural network as well as SVM based classifier.

Decision-Making Criteria for Specimens: After acquiring the labels for each test cell image, extracted from sub-images (portion of specimen) or specimens, a threshold-based decision [5] is applied to declare a specimen as MS type, i.e., minimum number of MS cells should be present in a MS specimen. The threshold values are a-priori decided based on the images provided. Note that the majority rule for pattern declaration can not be applied here, which is done for interphase patterns where all present cells are of similar type.

3 Experiments and Results

3.1 Dataset Description

The proposed approach is validated using a public dataset, i.e., I3A Task-2 specimen dataset, that contains 7 classes [2], Homogeneous (H), Speckled (S), Nucleolar (N), Centromere (C), Golgi (G) and Nuclear Membrane (NM) and Mitotic Spindle (MS). Only MS type is associated with the mitotic cell cycle stage. The

Table 1. Dataset description. H = Homogeneous, S = Speckled, N = Nucleolar, C = Centromere, G = Golgi, NM = Nuclear Membrane and MS = Mitotic Spindle. Pos and Int refer to positive and intermediate images respectively.

Pattern type	Interphase													Mitotic Phase
Classes	H		S		N		C		G		NM		MS	
Type	Pos	Int	Pos	Int	Pos	Int	Pos	Int	Pos	Int	Pos	Int	Pos	Int
No. of specimens	26	27	25	27	26	25	17	33	7	14	4	6	5	10
No. of sub-images	102	108	100	108	104	100	68	132	28	56	16	24	20	40

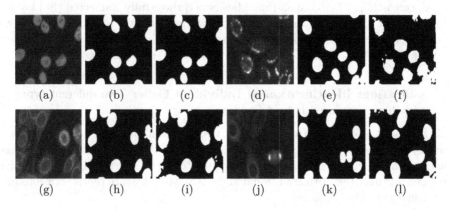

(a)   (b)   (c)   (d)   (e)   (f)

(g)   (h)   (i)   (j)   (k)   (l)

Fig. 3. (a, d, g, j) Original specimen images (cropped version), (b, e, h, k) Ground truth DAPI masks and (c, f, i, l) Proposed masks.

segmentation task for same dataset is available as a challenge, named as I3A challenge Task-4 [14]. The extracted MS cells (from specimens) are manually labeled painstakingly, using expert & domain knowledge [21]. Each specimen is associated with four sub-images (Table 1). Hence, the declaration of a particular specimen is done, considering all the associated sub-images.

3.2   Evaluation Protocol

For the segmentation, we use random cross-validation (RV) with three different sets of the data with 40% for training, 10% for validation and remaining for testing, with three different random sets and an average performance is reported. For classification, we use Leave-One-Out (LOO) protocol, as well as the random cross-validation protocol. In LOO, the proposed model is trained using N-1 specimens, out of total N specimens and remaining one is used for testing, in each round. For MS case, out of total 15 specimens, 11 are used for training, 3 (20%) for validation and 1 for testing in each trial. The LOO protocol was used only for traditional features (LM), as the implementation of LOO on CNN based features is quite extensive. Essentially, the LOO implementation is provided primarily for fair comparisons.

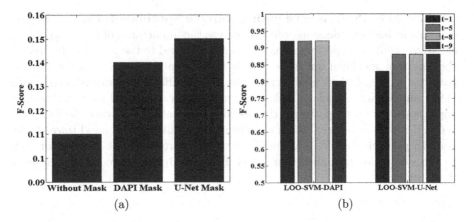

Fig. 4. (a) Classification results for mitotic v/s interphase complete specimen images and (b) LM features based results, using LOO approach, with cell-based strategy.

For segmentation, we measure the dice-index (similar to F1-score), using the DAPI based ground-truth. For classification, the mitotic class is considered as positive class. True-Positives (TP), False-Positive (FP) accuracies and F1-score [5] are reported for different value of thresholds t, for both the cases, i.e., classification using DAPI and proposed mask. For calculating FP, the specimens consisting of only interphase type cells are used.

3.3   Experimental Results for Segmentation

For U-Net based segmentation, the images are resized to 1024×1024 and divided into 256×256 size sub-images for better processing. The dice ratio is calculated with re-training of architecture with used data. In all the experiments, the best parameters are chosen, using validation data. The average dice-ratio for all random sets is 0.96, while the best result in previous works is around 0.89 [13,14]. This is a clear indication of the efficacy of the U-Net segmentation suggested in this work (also refer Table 2). Figure 3 shows few original images, DAPI masks and corresponding proposed masks. It is observed that the proposed mask is very close to the DAPI masks for interphase patterns (Fig. 3(a, b, c)). Indeed, in some cases for extra-nuclear (Golgi & NM) and mitotic patterns, the U-Net based masks appear better than the DAPI masks, where the latter seems to suffer from some underestimation (Fig. 3(d to l)).

3.4   Experimental Results for Classification

Here, four different threshold values are chosen to evaluate TP, FP and F-score. As already mentioned that the values indicate the minimum number of MS cells present in each specimen to declare that specimen as MS type. The evaluations are done for DAPI and proposed segmentation masks.

Classification Performance with Complete Specimen Images: The first experiment has been done in order to analyze the importance of cell-based strategy. Here, complete specimen images has been passed to the network, to predict the complete specimen image as mitotic type, even if it consists of few mitotic patterns. In Fig. 4(a), it is observed that the classification performance of both DAPI and U-Net masks are not good, hence it is concluded that due to rare appearance of mitotic patterns, the network is not able to capture the MS characteristics well and a traditional classification paradigm gets biased towards the non-MS patterns. Hence, such specimen based approach is not suitable for such patterns detection task and separate cell-based strategies are required to address these problems.

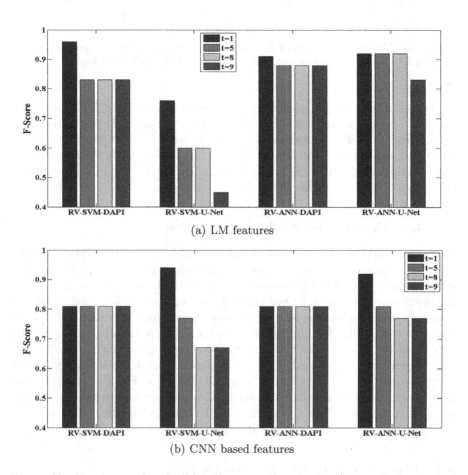

(a) LM features

(b) CNN based features

Fig. 5. Classification results of cell-based strategy for mitotic v/s interphase specimen images. RV refers to random cross-validation.

Classification Performance with Cell-Based Strategy: The classification performance of cell-based strategy is shown using different feature representations, defined as:

(a) Traditional Feature Representation: The traditional LM based feature representation has been used with SVM as well as Artificial Neural Network (ANN) based classifiers, using both LOO (Fig. 4(b)) and RV (Fig. 5(a)). It is observed that

- LOO and RV protocols yield almost similar performance with LM features, but the RV shows slightly better performance at two threshold values. Hence, the other performance evaluations can be done using RV.
- LM features perform good, with DAPI based patterns, i.e., F-score 0.96, but the performance with U-Net masks are also comparable. Indeed, the U-Net shows better performance than DAPI at two different threshold values.
- With respect to the classifiers, the ANN performs better than the SVM, both in DAPI and U-Net based cases. Hence, the considerably good results using LM features are obtained with ANN classifier, at different threshold values.

(b) CNN-based Feature Representation: For CNN based features, we note that (refer Fig. 5(b))

- At some thresholds, the U-Net masks are performing better than the DAPI based masks, specifically at $t = 1$.
- Both the SVM and ANN classifiers perform similar with the DAPI masks but for the U-Net masks, largely ANN performs better than the SVM classifier. Like LM based, here also, the U-Net masks should be considered for the system.
- The performance of CNN-based features are less than the LM based features. The reason of less performance of CNN might be the improper intermediate clustering step (refer Sect. 1) in feature representation, due to the less amount of data. Moreover, last convolutional and pooling layers of CNN architecture represent high-level information, which might not represent the data well.

Overall, the performance of proposed masks is close to the performance with DAPI mask at mid-level thresholds and even better at some threshold values. This indicates that a good segmentation approach can replace the DAPI channel in an overall system.

4   Comparison with Prior Approaches

The comparison of the proposed strategy to some existing approaches are reported in Table 2. No prior work has explicitly discussed the threshold based strategy as done in this work. Hence, the reported results are taken from their respective papers, from a 7 class confusion matrix but F-scores are calculated according to the binary class classification problem, for a fairer comparison. The

Table 2. Comparison of segmentation & classification with some prior approaches.

Segmentation	F-score	Classification	F-score
Otsu [13]	0.70	Ensafi [22]	0.89
FCN [13]	0.88	Ponomarev [23]	0.76
RF [14]	0.84	Manivannan [21]	0.67
FCRN [13]	0.89	Li [17]	0.65
Proposed	**0.96**	**Proposed**	**0.96**

first 2 columns show the results for the segmentation methods, and last 2 compare the classification results. Due to space constraint, we only highlight the best results of the approaches. It is noted that the proposed segmentation and classification approaches (best results quoted) outperform other methods.

5   Conclusion and Future Aspects

In the proposed work, a combined segmentation and MS specimen detection framework is presented. We demonstrate state-of-the-art segmentation using the U-Net approach which targets possibly obviating the DAPI channel. The MS specimen detection task is also handled effectively using the LM filter bank and CNN-based features, SVM and ANN classifiers and a threshold based decision criteria, and yields state-of-the-art results. In future, the analysis among features extracted from different layers of CNN and more sophisticated CNN architectures are planned to be explored. Additionally, we mean to propose an overall classification criteria for mitotic as well as interphase type patterns.

References

1. Foggia, P., Percannella, G., Soda, P., Vento, M.: Benchmarking HEp-2 cells classification methods. IEEE Transact. Med. Imaging **32**(10), 1878–1889 (2013)
2. Hobson, P., Lovell, B.C., Percannella, G., Vento, M., Wiliem, A.: Classifying anti-nuclear antibodies HEp-2 images: a benchmarking platform. In: Proceedings of ICPR-2014, pp. 3233–3238 (2014)
3. Hobson, P., Lovell, B.C., Percannella, G., Saggese, A., Vento, M., Wiliem, A.: Computer aided diagnosis for anti-nuclear antibodies HEp-2 images: progress and challenges. Pattern Recogn. Lett. **82**(1), 3–11 (2016)
4. Foggia, P., Percannella, G., Soda, P., Vento, M.: Early experiences in mitotic cells recognition on HEp-2 slides. In: Proceedings of International Symposium on Computer-Based Medical Systems, pp. 38–43 (2010)
5. Gupta, K., Bhavsar, A., Sao, A.K.: Mitotic cells detection for HEp-2 specimen images using threshold-based evaluation scheme. In: Proceedings of SPIE Medical Imaging, pp. 105810F (2018)
6. Iannello, G., Percannella, G., Soda, P., Vento, M.: Mitotic cells recognition in HEp-2 images. Pattern Recogn. Lett. **45**, 136–144 (2014)

7. Miros, A., Wiliem, A., Holohan, K., Ball, L., Hobson, P., Lovell, B.C.: A benchmarking platform for mitotic cell classification of ANA IIF HEp-2 images. In: Proceedings of International Conference on Digital Image Computing: Techniques and Applications, pp. 1–6 (2015)

8. Li, J., Tseng, K.K., Hsieh, Z.Y., Yang, C.W., Huang, H.N.: Staining pattern classification of antinuclear autoantibodies based on block segmentation in indirect immunofluorescence images. PLoS ONE **9**(12), e113132 (2014)

9. Chazotte, B.: Labeling nuclear DNA using DAPI. Cold Spring Harbor Protocols, 2011(1):pdb-prot5556, (2011)

10. Ronneberger, O., Fischer, P., Brox, T.: U-net: convolutional networks for biomedical image segmentation. CoRR, abs/1505.04597 (2015)

11. Leung, T., Malik, J.: Representing and recognizing the visual appearance of materials using three-dimensional textons. Int. J. Comput. Vis. **43**(1), 29–44 (2001)

12. Yang, J., Jiang, Y.G., Hauptmann, A.G., Ngo, C.W.: Evaluating bag-of-visual-words representations in scene classification. In: Proceedings of the International Workshop on Workshop on Multimedia Information Retrieval, pp. 197–206 (2007)

13. Li, Y., Shen, L., Yu, S.: HEp-2 specimen image segmentation and classification using very deep fully convolutional network. IEEE Transact. Med. Imaging **36**(99), 1561–1572 (2017)

14. Prasath, V.B.S., et al.: HEp-2 cell classification and segmentation using motif texture patterns and spatial features with random forests. In: Proceedings of International Conference on Pattern Recognition (ICPR), pp. 90–95, December 2016

15. Tonti, S., Di Cataldo, S., Bottino, A., Ficarra, E.: An automated approach to the segmentation of HEp-2 cells for the indirect immunofluorescence ana test. Comput. Med. Imaging Graph. **40**, 62–69 (2015)

16. Hobson, P., Lovell, B.C., Percannella, G., Saggese, A., Vento, M., Wiliem, A.: HEp-2 staining pattern recognition at cell and specimen levels: datasets, algorithms and results. Pattern Recogn. Lett. **82**(1), 12–22 (2016)

17. Li, H., Huang, H., Zheng, W.S., Xie, X., Zhang, J.: HEp-2 specimen classification via deep CNNs and pattern histogram. In: 2016 23rd International Conference on Pattern Recognition (ICPR), pp. 2145–2149 (2016)

18. Wiliem, J., Hobson, P., Lovell, B.C.: Discovering discriminative cell attributes for HEp-2 specimen image classification. In: IEEE Winter Conference on Applications of Computer Vision, pp. 423–430 (2014)

19. Gonzalez, R.C., Richard, E.: Digital Image Processing. Prentice Hall, Upper Saddle River (2008)

20. Krizhevsky, A., Sutskever, I., Hinton, G.E.: ImageNet classification with deep convolutional neural networks. In: Advances in Neural Information Processing Systems, vol. 25, pp. 1097–1105 (2012)

21. Manivannan, S., Li, W., Akbar, S., Wang, R., Zhang, J., McKenna, S.J.: An automated pattern recognition system for classifying indirect immunofluorescence images of HEp-2 cells and specimens. Pattern Recogn. **51**, 12–26 (2016)

22. Ensafi, S., Lu, S., Kassim, A.A., Tan, C.L.: Accurate HEp-2 cell classification based on sparse coding of superpixels. Pattern Recogn. Lett. **82**(1), 64–71 (2016)

23. Ponomarev, G.V., Kazanov, M.D.: Classification of ANA HEp-2 slide images using morphological features of stained patterns. Pattern Recogn. Lett. **82**(1), 79–84 (2016)

Unsupervised Routine Discovery in Egocentric Photo-Streams

Estefania Talavera[1,2(✉)], Nicolai Petkov[1], and Petia Radeva[2]

[1] Bernoulli Institute for Mathematics, Computer Science and Artificial Intelligence,
University of Groningen, Groningen, The Netherlands
estefania.tama@gmail.com
[2] Department of Mathematcis and Computer Science, University of Barcelona,
Barcelona, Spain

Abstract. The routine of a person is defined by the occurrence of activities throughout different days, and can directly affect the person's health. In this work, we address the recognition of routine related days. To do so, we rely on egocentric images, which are recorded by a wearable camera and allow to monitor the life of the user from a first-person view perspective. We propose an unsupervised model that identifies routine related days, following an outlier detection approach. We test the proposed framework over a total of 72 days in the form of photo-streams covering around 2 weeks of the life of 5 different camera wearers. Our model achieves an average of 76% Accuracy and 68% Weighted F-Score for all the users. Thus, we show that our framework is able to recognise routine related days and opens the door to the understanding of the behaviour of people.

Keywords: Routine discovery · Lifestyle · Egocentric vision ·
Behaviour analysis

1 Introduction

Health professionals are continuously working not only to cure but also to prevent diseases of people. Looking for an answer on how the life of people can be improved, promoting good routine lifestyles, a natural question is how can the automatic analysis of people's routines help to improve their lives? [3,8]. Routine discovery is a challenging task due to the wide range of combinations of image sequences that can describe our days. Describing routine goes hand in hand with mentioning performed activities by people. For instance, routine related days for a person whose job is to teach will be represented by 'commute to work', 'teach' or 'talk in front of an audience', 'meetings', 'eating', or similar. In contrast, the day of a policeman patrolling during the day could be described by 'driving', 'walking outside', 'talking to people', 'eating', 'meeting', among others. Some of the activities that describe a routine related day will be shared by most people, such as 'eating', or 'meeting', or 'talking to people'. However, many of them will

© Springer Nature Switzerland AG 2019
M. Vento and G. Percannella (Eds.): CAIP 2019, LNCS 11678, pp. 576–588, 2019.
https://doi.org/10.1007/978-3-030-29888-3_47

depend on their job or responsibilities. Routine differs per person, and it has proven to be difficult to define a standard routine pattern for all people. The automatic classification of routine related scenes can represent a valuable tool for many stakeholders, such as psychologists, who would be able to automatically understand and monitor the behaviour of their patients or clients. This automatic tool will allow them to infer how the detected routines affect the life of people and to develop personalized strategies for a change of behaviour.

Fig. 1. Stream of images recorded by one of the camera wearers.

Our aim is to recognize routine related days where a person performs common activities of his or her daily living. If we can help people to measure their daily routine, they can try to make changes to their daily habits and the long-term consequences they have on their life. By routine related days, we refer to the days that represent the majority of the days of a person. In consequence, non-routine related days will be described by the basic activities of a daily basis and some other novel activities that are not commonly performed. In this work, we propose a personalized and automatic tool for the discovery of routine related days within recorded photo-streams by a camera wearer. We hypothesize that discovering routine related days can be addressed as a clustering problem where methods such as k-means with, for instance, $k = 2$ could potentially classify the days in terms of the behaviour they represent.

However, some days present abnormal behaviour. These days correspond to non-routine related days. Most of the time they are not related to each other, which can be interpreted as outliers within the user's recorded photo-streams. Experience has shown that it is difficult to describe what non-routine related days are for a given photo-stream collection. In the context of outlier detection, samples considered as outliers do not form the cluster with higher density when representing the days in a feature space. We propose an unsupervised classification method that assumes that outliers are situated in low-density areas. Outlier detection methods are commonly used in data mining to indicate variability in measurements, errors or novel samples [6,12]. Among their applications are fraud detection [9] and satellite image analysis [1]. However, up to our knowledge for first-time routine detection is defined through an outlier detection approach.

Within the available outlier detection algorithms, we propose Isolation Forest algorithm [13]. This method has shown a good performance when detection outliers in multidimensional space, not seeking normal data points but identifying anomalies. Our model is unsupervised because routine differs per person and our aim is to propose a generic model able to discover routine of unknown users. However, since we have the labels of the recorded photo-streams that compose our dataset, we use them to validate if we are able to discover their routine related days.

The closest approaches in computer vision to our aim focus either on scene or activity recognition. However, we cannot characterize a given day as routine related by solely classifying single images from the photo-stream. We observed that information about the patterns of behaviour of a person can be obtained by keeping track of his or her *Activities of Daily Living* (ADLs). These activity patterns can help us expose what is common in the life of the camera wearer. Routine can be inferred when many sample days are recorded since it describes what is common. When aiming to determine a perfect classifier for routine related days, we would need an infinite amount of day samples. Therefore, we think that there is a need for defining a methodology that analyses a collection of images as a group, allowing to compare with other days. We then propose to look for correlation and occurrence of activities throughout the day, and the set of recorded days.

Hence, the contributions of the paper are three-fold:

- We address for the first time the problem of routine extraction from egocentric data.
- We propose an unsupervised and automatic model for the analysis of a routine within recorded egocentric photo-steams. This model is based on the aggregation of the descriptors of the images within the photo-stream.
- We test our proposed model over a home-made collected egocentric dataset. This dataset describes the daily life of the camera wearers. It is composed of a total of 73000 images, from 72 recorded days by 5 different users. We call it EgoRoutine dataset.

The rest of the paper is organized as follows: in Sect. 2, we highlight some relevant works related to this topic. Then, in Sect. 3 we describe the approach proposed for routine discovery. In Sect. 4, we describe our newly created EgoRoutine dataset and outline the experiments performed and the obtained results. Finally, in Sect. 5, we present our conclusions.

2   Related Works

People's routines have been studied in several approaches aiming to characterize patterns of behaviour. Before the emergence of static and wearable sensors, people's daily habits were manually recorded. For instance, ADLs were manually annotated by either individual users and/or specialists, as in [2,17]. In [2], manually recorded information about the ability of someone's ADLs performance was examined, with the aim of classifying the patients' dependence, as either dependent or independent. From another perspective, in [17], the authors studied diaries from 70 undergraduate students, who rated the assiduity of activity during the previous month through a questionnaire. The authors highlighted the high standard deviation of the number of behaviours per person. Thus, we conclude that behavioural patterns can be characterized per individual.

Besides activity recognition, scene recognition has been widely studied from conventional images. In [11] some of the challenges that the recognition of scenes presents were commented; recognizing concurrent activities (same activities performed at the same time), recognizing activities that are shortly interrupted, interpretation when classifying the activity and multiple residents per environment, among others. Nowadays, the incremental use of Convolutional Neural Networks (CNNs) for learning high-level features has shown huge progress in object recognition tasks, mainly due to the availability of large datasets like ImageNet [5]. However, the performance at the scene recognition level is still a challenging task due to the huge range of environments surrounding us and how diverse they can appear.

3   Routine Discovery

In this section, we propose an innovative and unsupervised routine discovery method. Its application scheme is given in Fig. 2.

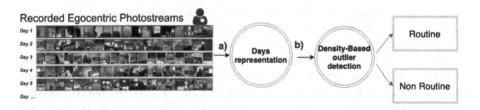

Fig. 2. The pipeline of the proposed model. Given a set of recorded days, (a) they are translated to a set of global or semantic features. Later, (b) days are considered as routine or non-routine based on their resemblance.

Our proposed method is based on an outlier detection algorithm. For outlier detection models, an outlier sample is known as a sample outside the 'boundary' of the known classes. In our case, these samples relate to non-routine related days. Hence, we assume that routine related days define a class, of which the samples are close to each other within the feature space. The proposed model indicates routine of the person by detecting the sample days that can be clustered together. In the following subsections, we describe the steps in the proposed pipeline as shown in Fig. 2.

(a) **From Days to Feature Vectors.** As mentioned above, a day is described by a collection of images and takes the form of photo-stream. We address the day classification by translating the recorded photo-streams into feature vectors for their later analysis and comparison.

Based on the high accuracy recently achieved for the classification of daily activities in egocentric images in [4], we use their proposed network for the characterization of the recorded days. Given an image, this network classifies it into 21 Activities of Daily Living. A day of the user is represented by $Day = \sum_i^N \frac{image_i}{N}$, where N is the number of images within a day, and $image$ represents the feature vector of the recorded images.

We consider the following descriptors obtained from the collected photo-streams:

1. Activity occurrence within the day: We consider the occurrence of activities throughout the day for the characterization of routine, i.e. bag-of-activities. This feature vector gives an overview of the activities the user performs in a day. However, it does not include temporal information.
2. Global descriptors: We use the ResNet CNN model [10] to extract global descriptors from the images. We use the activation over the entire image given by the last fully connected layer. Given an image, we obtain a 2048 features vector.
3. We concatenate the mentioned features in (1) and (2).

(b) **Routine Related Days Recognition.** More specifically, we rely on the unsupervised outlier detection *Isolation Forest* [13] algorithm, and use its available implementation in Scikit-learn [14]. It is a tree ensemble method that analyses the density of the space to 'isolate' outliers. The algorithm works as follows:

First, it randomly selects a feature. Then, for the selected feature, it randomly selects a split value between its maximum and minimum value. By recursive partitioning, it can be represented by a tree structure. As the number of trees increases, the algorithm reaches the convergence. The length of the path from the root to the end node can be considered as the number of splittings needed to isolate a sample. By randomly partitioning the data, the paths for anomalies become shorter. Therefore, samples with shorter path lengths are likely to be anomalies. Later, the anomaly score is calculated per sample based on the averaged and normalized distance of the path. Finally, samples considered as outliers have an anomaly score of 1, while samples with values close to 0 are considered as regular.

The *Isolation Forest* algorithm, given a set of n samples and an observation x, computes the anomaly score $s(x)$ as follows:

$$s(x, n) = 2^{-\frac{E(h(x))}{c(n)}}, \tag{1}$$

where h(x) is the path length of a point (x) measured by the number of edges that the point traverses from the root node until the last external node. E(h(x)) corresponds to the average of h(x) from a collection of isolation trees. c(n) is the average path length, and it is defined as follows:

$$c(n) = 2H(n-1) - (2(n-1)/n), \tag{2}$$

where H(i) is the harmonic number and it can be estimated by ln(i) + 0.5772156649 (Euler's constant).

To *summarize*, given a collection of photo-streams recorded by a camera wearer, our proposed personalized and automatic tool will detect the non-routine related days by computing the density within the feature space. The proposed *Isolation Forest* algorithm considers as routine related days if their samples are in a dense region of samples. In contrast, samples that represent non-routine related days correspond to points in a low-density area. This will have as an output the distinction among days, giving insight into the daily habits and lifestyle of the person.

4 Experiments

In this section, we describe the experimental setup, the metrics used to evaluate the analysis, and the obtained results.

4.1 Dataset

We collected data from 5 different subjects who were asked to record their daily life during at least a week. To this end, the users worn the *Narrative Clip* camera[1] fixed to their chest, with a resolution of 2 fpm. The introduced dataset consists of 100k images, from a total of 72 recorded days, see Table 1. They captured information about their daily routine, such as the people with whom they interacted, the activities they performed or how often they walked outside. Since there is no training involved in this approach, the whole dataset is analysed by our proposed model. Moreover, in order to show the variance among collected days, Fig. 3 shows the average number of images per day. We can observe how the amount of images differs per day and user.

Table 1. Description of the collected Egoroutine dataset by 5 users.

User ID	#1	#2	#3	#4	#5	Total
Num days	14	10	16	19	13	72
Images per day	20k	8k	21k	13k	11k	73k

---

[1] http://getnarrative.com/.

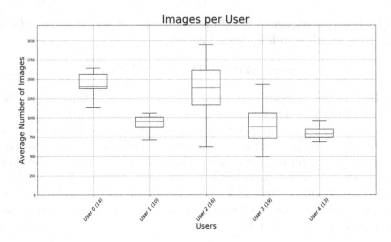

Fig. 3. Average number of images per recorded egocentric photo-stream. We give the number of collected days per user between parenthesis.

Process of Creating the Ground-Truth. The annotators got the following definition of *"Life routine; a sequence of actions which are followed regularly, or at specific intervals of time, daily or weekly"*. Next, they were shown mosaics of images representing days of the user. They were asked to first have a look at all the mosaics to get an impression of how routine looks like for that specific user. Later, they gave a binary label: routine or non-routine related.

In Table 2, we present the summary of the labels given by the different annotators. From the labelling results, we can deduce that defining what is routine and non-routine is not an easy task. Routine can be easily described in general terms, but it becomes challenging when sequences of images describing a long time period are classified. We can observe how in the majority of cases, the annotators agreed when it comes to label days as routine. However, the non-routine related days are more difficult to perceive leading to disagreement among the annotators. Finally, we have considered as routine related days when >4 of the labels agreed. In case of a draw, the day is labelled as non-routine related. Therefore, from a total of 72 recorded days, 51 days are routine related, and 21 are non-routine related. If we extrapolate to a common life scenario, 72 days correspond to almost 15 recorded weeks. If the users followed what could be considered common routine (a week has 5 working days and 2 weekend days or holiday), in 10 weeks we have 20 weekend days and 50 working days.

Table 2. Summary of the labelling results for the Egoroutine dataset.

Class	Six agree	Five agree	At least four agree	At least three agree	Total
All	34	21	11	6	72
Routine	28	16	7	0	51
Non-routine	6	5	4	6	21

4.2 Validation

We evaluate the performance of the proposed model and compare it with the baseline models by computing the *Accuracy* (Acc), *Recall* (R), *Precision* (P), and *F-Score* metrics, where: $F - Score = 2 \cdot \left(\frac{P \cdot R}{P + R}\right)$ *Precision* computes the ratio between True Positive (TP) samples and False Positive (FP) samples following: $TP/(TP + FP)$. *Recall* evaluates the ratio of TP and False Negative (FN), showing the ability of the model to find the positive samples, the formula is $TP/(TP + FN)$. Due to the unbalanced dataset we calculate and compare their 'macro' and 'weighted' mean. The 'weighted' mean evaluates the true classification per label, while 'macro' calculates the unweighted mean per label. The weighted measures provide the strength of the classifier when applied to unbalanced data.

4.3 Experimental Setup

To the best of our knowledge, no previous works have addressed the recognition of routine discovery from egocentric photo-streams. Therefore, we evaluate the performance of the proposed model and compare it with what we introduced as baseline methods. We select several outlier detection algorithms namely: Robust Covariance, and One-class SVM. Moreover, we propose to apply unsupervised clustering techniques that allow the identification of outliers or isolation of samples outside the high-density space. These methods allow the recognition of non-similar samples or with non-convex boundaries within the sample collection. Specifically, we evaluate the performance of DBSCAN and Spectral clustering.

Here we give a brief explanation of how these baseline methods work:

- Robust Covariance [16], also called elliptic envelope, assumes that the data follow Gaussian distribution and learns an ellipse. Its drawback is that it degrades when the data is not uni-modal.
- One-class SVM [15] is an unsupervised algorithm that estimates the support of the dimensional distribution.
- DBSCAN [7], short for Density-Based Spatial Clustering of Applications with Noise, finds samples with high density and defines them as the centre of a cluster. From the center, it expands the cluster. Its *eps* parameter determines the maximum distance between samples to be considered as in the same cluster. Outliers are samples that lie alone in low-density regions.
- Spectral Clustering [18] works on the similarity graph between samples. It computes the first k eigenvectors of its Laplacian matrix and defines a feature vector per sample. Later, k-Means is applied to these feature vectors to separate them into k classes. In our case, we set $k = 2$, so we evaluate its performance when addressing routine vs non-routine classification.

For the last two proposed unsupervised model, DBSCAN and Spectral Clustering, the closeness among the recorded days is computed based on their shared similarities, following an all-vs-all strategy. To do so, we use the well-known

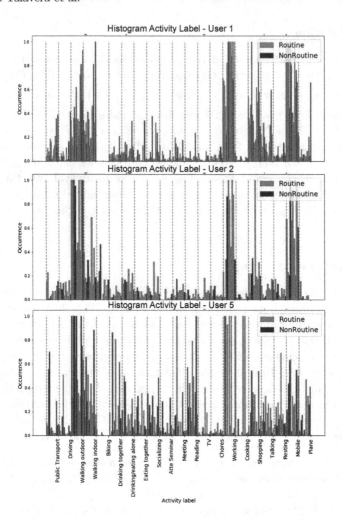

Fig. 4. Histograms showing the occurrence of activities throughout the days of 3 of the 5 users that worn the camera. As we can appreciate, some activities are more related to non-routine related days, while 'working' and 'walking indoor' characterizes routine related days. (Color figure online)

Euclidean metric. The computed similarity matrix is fed to the unsupervised classifier algorithm for the detection of outliers within the set samples. The outlier detection methods are fed with the feature matrix describing the samples.

4.4 Results

We present the obtained classification accuracy at day level for the performed experiments in Table 3. The proposed model, based on the Isolation Forest algorithm and with global features as descriptors of the recorded days, achieved the best performance with respect to the rest of the tested baseline methods. Our model achieves an average of 76% Accuracy and 68% Weighted F-Score for all the users, outperforming the rest of the tested methods. The highest performance is when analysing global features, which cover most of the possible present activities.

Table 3. Performance of the different methods implemented for the discovery of routine and non-routine days.

Methods	Feature vector	All users						
		Weighted				Macro		
		Acc	F-Score	P	R	F-Score	P	R
Robust covariance	Activity occurrence (Act)	0.61	0.49	0.50	0.50	0.59	0.59	0.61
	Global features (Glo)	0.71	0.60	0.63	0.60	0.69	0.70	0.71
	Act - Glo	0.54	0.39	0.39	0.41	0.52	0.51	0.54
One-Class SVM	Activity occurrence (Act)	0.72	0.65	0.69	0.65	0.70	0.70	0.72
	Global features (Glo)	0.67	0.56	0.60	0.57	0.64	0.67	0.67
	Act - Glo	0.65	0.58	0.59	0.58	0.64	0.64	0.65
DBSCAN	Activity occurrence (Act)	0.61	0.51	0.55	0.55	0.57	0.60	0.61
	Global features (Glo)	0.69	0.41	0.34	0.50	0.56	0.48	0.69
	Act - Glo	0.63	0.56	0.57	0.60	0.60	0.62	0.63
SpectralClustering	Activity occurrence (Act)	0.66	0.48	0.50	0.51	0.61	0.61	0.66
	Global features (Glo)	0.66	0.55	0.64	0.62	0.63	0.72	0.66
	Act - Glo	0.62	0.46	0.50	0.50	0.57	0.61	0.62
Isolation forest	Activity occurrence (Act)	0.69	0.61	0.62	0.62	0.68	0.67	0.69
	Global features (Glo)	**0.76**	**0.68**	0.71	0.68	**0.74**	0.75	0.76
	Act - Glo	**0.76**	**0.68**	0.71	0.68	**0.74**	0.75	0.76

Moreover, in Fig. 5 we visualize the days as points in the feature space drawn by the first two principal components of the dataset. We can see the Ground-truth indicated with the boundaries of the circles and the prediction of the model, for both cases red corresponds to routine related days and blue to non-routine related. As it can be observed, our model is the one that obtains the best results.

In Fig. 4 we can observe the occurrence of activities per day in the form of a histogram. This representation allows us to better infer and understand how routine (orange) and non-routine (blue) related days vary for the different camera wearers. From this representation we can confirm our initial assumptions: (i) the set of activities performed as routine and non-routine related days differs per person, (ii) a subset of activities is commonly shared when it comes to routine, such as 'working', which is mostly described by a laptop/pc as central object in the scene, or 'using mobile'. In contrast, some activities are specific per user: The routine of *User 5* is characterized by 'cooking', 'reading', and 'meeting'. In

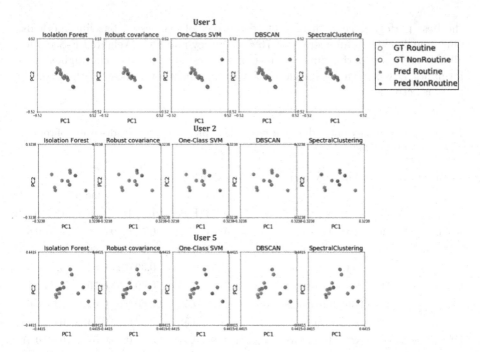

Fig. 5. Visualization of the obtained classification results based on the analysis of the histogram of activities occurring throughout the day for User1, User2 and User5. We show the classification per user and per studied method. Each dot in the graph corresponds to one day recorded by the user. Each of the 4 subplots shows the classification into routine or non-routine by the baseline methods. The colour of the boundaries of the dots represents the given Ground-truth and the filling the classification label; Red routine and Blue non-routine. (Color figure online)

contrast, for *User 2* 'walking outdoor', 'shopping', and 'mobile' are the more representative activities.

5   Conclusions

In this work, we propose a new unsupervised routine recognition model from egocentric photo-streams. To our knowledge, this is the first work on the field. Our proposed model achieves an average of 76% Accuracy and 69% Weighted F-Score for all the users. The results demonstrate the goodness of the proposed model and selected features. Moreover, it opens the door to the desired and personalized behavioural analysis.

The presented analysis can be improved in several directions as by augmenting the number of subjects and the amount of collected data. We believe this is a good starting point for this new field of unsupervised routine analysis from a first-person perspective. Moreover, and even though in this work we consider that there exists one routine per person, future lines will address the discovery of several routines. However, for that, it is needed a bigger amount of data. Currently, we are working on building a larger dataset with more users recording for larger periods of time. In future research, we will explore how the information of performed activities, and their temporal relation and context, can be integrated into the description of a day. The obtained information about routine related days and activities can have a direct positive impact on the lifestyle and health of the camera wearer. In addition, these findings provide additional information about how active a person is, which can be correlated to his or her emotional state.

Acknowledgment. This work was partially founded by projects RTI2018-095232-B-C21, 2017 SGR 1742, CERCA, Nestore Validithi, 20141510 (La MaratoTV3) and CERCA Programme/Generalitat de Catalunya. P. Radeva is partially supported by ICREA Academia 2014. We acknowledge the support of NVIDIA Corporation with the donation of Titan Xp GPUs.

References

1. Alvera-Azcárate, A., Sirjacobs, D., Barth, A., Beckers, J.M.: Outlier detection in satellite data using spatial coherence. Remote Sens. Environ. **119**, 84–91 (2012)
2. Andersen, C.K., Wittrup-Jensen, K.U., Lolk, A., Andersen, K., Kragh-Sørensen, P.: Ability to perform activities of daily living is the main factor affecting quality of life in patients with dementia. Health Qual. Life Outcomes **2**(1), 52 (2004)
3. Bar-On, R.: Emotional intelligence and self-actualization. Emotional intelligence in everyday life: a scientific inquiry, pp. 82–97 (2001)
4. Cartas, A., Marín, J., Radeva, P., Dimiccoli, M.: Batch-based activity recognition from egocentric photo-streams revisited. Pattern Anal. Appl. **21**(4), 953–965 (2018)
5. Deng, J., Dong, W., Socher, R., Li, L.J., Li, K., Fei-Fei, L.: ImageNet: a large-scale hierarchical image database. In: IEEE Conference on Computer Vision and Pattern Recognition, pp. 248–255 (2009)
6. Ding, Z., Fei, M.: An anomaly detection approach based on isolation forest algorithm for streaming data using sliding window. Int. Fed. Autom. Control **46**(20), 12–17 (2013)
7. Ester, M., Kriegel, H.P., Sander, J., Xu, X., et al.: A density-based algorithm for discovering clusters in large spatial databases with noise. ACM Transact. Knowl. Discovery Data **96**(34), 226–231 (1996)
8. Gardner, B.: A review and analysis of the use of 'habit'in understanding, predicting and influencing health-related behaviour. Health Psychol. Rev. **9**(3), 277–295 (2015)
9. Ghosh, S., Reilly, D.L.: Credit card fraud detection with a neural-network. In: 27th Hawaii International Conference on System Sciences, vol. 3, pp. 621–630 (1994)
10. He, K., Zhang, X., Ren, S., Sun, J.: Deep residual learning for image recognition. In: IEEE Conference on Computer Vision and Pattern Recognition, pp. 770–778 (2016)
11. Helal, S., Kim, E., Cook, D.: Human activity recognition and pattern discovery. IEEE Pervasive Comput. **9**, 48–53 (2010)
12. Hodge, V., Austin, J.: A survey of outlier detection methodologies. Artif. Intell. Rev. **22**(2), 85–126 (2004)

13. Liu, F.T., Ting, K.M., Zhou, Z.H.: Isolation forest. In: 8th IEEE International Conference on Data Mining, pp. 413–422 (2008)
14. Pedregosa, F., et al.: Scikit-learn: machine learning in Python. J. Mach. Learn. Res. **12**, 2825–2830 (2011)
15. Platt, J., et al.: Probabilistic outputs for support vector machines and comparisons to regularized likelihood methods. Adv. Large Margin Classif. **10**(3), 61–74 (1999)
16. Rousseeuw, P.J., Driessen, K.V.: A fast algorithm for the minimum covariance determinant estimator. Technometrics **41**(3), 212–223 (1999)
17. Wood, W., Quinn, J., Kashy, D.: Habits in everyday life: thought, emotion, and action. J. Pers. Soc. Psychol. **83**(6), 1281–1297 (2002)
18. Yu, S.X., Shi, J.: Multiclass spectral clustering. In: Proceedings of the 9th IEEE International Conference on Computer Vision, p. 313 (2003)

Color Visual Cryptography with Completely Randomly Coded Colors

Arkadiusz Orłowski[iD] and Leszek J. Chmielewski[(✉)][iD]

Department of Informatics, Warsaw University of Life Sciences–SGGW,
Nowoursynowska 159, 02-775 Warsaw, Poland
{arkadiusz_orlowski,leszek_chmielewski}@sggw.pl
http://www.wzim.sggw.pl

Abstract. The concept of visual cryptography with two completely random shares is applied to color images. In the classic coding the shares are not correlated with the coded image, but are not totally random. We apply a completely random coding, proposed previously for the case of black and white images, to color images. This improves the security of the process. The proposed method has similar properties to those of the majority of purely visual cryptographic methods, including reduced contrast and loss of minor details. In the decoding process no calculations are necessary so the decoding can be done by an unarmed human eye. Using the completely random coding of colors introduces some noise into the results, but its level is moderate. The RGB color model is used and the $(2, 2)$ cryptography scheme is considered.

Keywords: Visual cryptography · Color images · Random coding

1 Introduction

Since its beginnings, visual cryptography has experienced an important advancement. Besides the basic coding of two-level, black and white images [7,8], new concepts including grey-level and color coding were presented (see [1,6] for literature). In this paper, we shall investigate the applicability of the visual cryptography method with totally random shares, previously proposed in [9,10], to the coding of color images. We shall present the results of truly *random* coding in a comparison to the Naor-Shamir coding [7,8], which will be called here the *classic* coding. From the number of codings presented in our previous papers, only the version called simply *random* will be used; the other versions presented in those publications will not be considered.

The fact that the shares are truly random, and not only uncorrelated with the coded secret image, can be important as far as the security as well as the secrecy of the information transfer process is considered. The randomness of the shares has its price, that is, in the reconstructed image there is additional noise with respect to the case of the classic coding. Consequently, some minor details can be lost. This deterioration of quality is not severe, however.

© Springer Nature Switzerland AG 2019
M. Vento and G. Percannella (Eds.): CAIP 2019, LNCS 11678, pp. 589–599, 2019.
https://doi.org/10.1007/978-3-030-29888-3_48

The concept of presenting the color image with the RGB model which we use here is similar to that proposed in [12], where the pixel expansion is claimed to be just three. However, in the case of our methodology, where the color is coded in the truly random way, such a small expansion will not be possible. In some publications the CMY model is used, with [2,4] as examples.

The field of visual cryptography is constantly active and viable; new publications appear, like for example [2,3]. In [2] the CMY color scheme is used and very good image quality is attained. In [3] the RGB model is used, and the pixel expansion is 5 × 5, slightly less than in our case (but much more than three claimed in [12]). In one version, three shares contain the information for three color components separately; in another version, each two of three shares for color pairs RG, GB and BR are enough to show the secret image.

We shall consider the (2, 2) visual cryptography scheme, in which there are two shares of similar appearance, each containing information in three colors, and both of them are necessary to reveal the secret. We shall use the RGB model, and we shall represent the image in such a way that the classic coding for binary images is applicable. The pixel expansion in our method is 6 × 6.

The remaining part of this paper is organized as follows. In the next Section the general methodology used in visual cryptography is shortly reminded. The coding of binary images, including the use of truly random shares, is outlined in Sect. 2.1. The transformation of color images to the format in which binary coding is applicable is presented in Sect. 2.2. The process is illustrated with an example in Sect. 2.3. The results of application of the concept to natural images are shown in Sect. 3. In Sect. 4 the conclusions are given.

2   The Method

Let us shortly remind the notions used in visual cryptography. The image to be encoded is called the *secret*. The majority of encoding methods work on two-level images. We shall show later in which way the color image will be transformed into the two-level format. The image is encoded in two images called the *shares*. Any one of them contains no information on the secret, but the secret is revealed to a human eye when the shares are precisely overlaid on one another. This is called the *decoding*. In purely visual cryptography, for the decoding no technical devices should be necessary except the two shares printed on a transparent medium.

2.1   Coding a Two-Level Image

For the process of coding and decoding, each pixel of the secret is represented in each share by a square of $n \times n$ pixels, called the *tile*. We shall assume $n = 2$. The tile is two-level; hence, there are 16 tiles possible, shown in Fig. 1.

The coding process consists in generating one share, called the *basic share*, according to some rules independently of the secret, and in forming the other share, called the *coding share*, as the function of the basic share and the secret. The simplest and the most frequently used method for this is as follows. If the

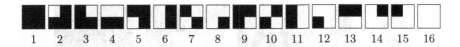

Fig. 1. All possible 2 × 2 tiles and their indexes.

pixel in the secret image is black, the coding tile is set to the negative of the basic tile (for example, tiles 8 and 9 of Fig. 1); hence, by overlaying the two tiles, a black tile corresponding to this pixel is received. If the pixel of the secret is white, the respective coding tile is set to equal to the basic tile; hence, by overlaying the two tiles, a region is received having as many white pixels as the basic tile (as well as the coding tile) has (for example, for tile 6 this is two).

In the classic coding [7,8], for the basic share the tiles from among the set of tiles no. 4, 6, 7, 10, 11, 13 are drawn at random. It is easy to see that, as a consequence, the tiles in the coding share belong to the same set of tiles. A bright pixel in the secret is always decoded as a 1/2-bright one in the decoded image. In the random coding [9,10], where the basic share is drawn totally at random from among the set of all 16 tiles, the brightness of the decoded bright pixel can differ from this value and can be black (if tile 1 is drawn), 1/4-bright (if tile 2, 3, 5, or 9 is drawn), 1/2-bright (if tile 4, 6, 7, 10, 11, or 13 is drawn), 3/4-bright (in case of tile 8, 12, 14 or 15), or white (tile 16). In [10] the brightness 1/2 characteristic for the classic coding was taken as a reference, which gave rise to the concept of -2, -1, $+1$ and $+2$ pixel errors. The probabilities of their occurrence in the case of a bright pixel in the secret is 1/16, 4/16, 4/16 and 1/16, respectively, according to the number of tiles with respective numbers of white pixels. The fact that these errors appear is the cost for having totally random pixels in both shares. As we shall see further, the errors make the decoded image look noisy to some extent.

It is important not to change the rule of choosing the coding tile depending on the brightness of the pixel in the secret. In [9] it has been shown, how resigning from choosing the tiles having less than two bright pixels when the corresponding pixel of the secret was white, was the direct reason of the leak of information on the secret into the coding share. This leak was due to that these darker tiles were chosen only where the secret was dark, so a darker region appeared also in the coding share. The implication of this consideration is that the coding tile should always be chosen at random. The true randomness of the shares results not only from that the drawing is random, but from that all the possible 16 types of the tiles are drawn with equal probability.

2.2   Transforming A Color Image into A Two-Level Format

A gray-level image can be encoded with the same scheme as a binary one is, by transforming a gray-level image into a binary one by dithering. In the case of a color image, dithering can be viewed as transforming a full-color image into a color image with a restricted palette. This palette image will be represented

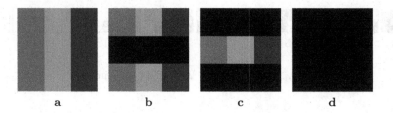

Fig. 2. Variants of a 3×3 pixel segment which encodes a single color pixel (in this case, in four levels of gray). (**a**) Full brightness – white pixel; (**b**) brightness 2/3 – bright gray; (**c**) brightness 1/3 – dark gray; (**d**) brightness 0 – black pixel. (Color figure online)

by an image with columns in the basic colors. In this way, the single pixel will be either black, or bright. The bright pixel will be in one of the basic colors – red, green or blue.

In order to do this, we shall represent each pixel in the image with a 3×3 segment in the dithered image. Columns in this segment will be red, green and blue, in sequence. In each column, the pixels can be either color or black. Four of the possible segments are shown in Fig. 2. To preserve the aspect ratio of the image it is convenient to have square segments, so according to the number of columns the number of rows is three. This makes it possible to represent four brightnesses of each color: 0, 1/3, 2/3 and 3/3 of the maximum brightness, by setting 0, 1, 2 or 3 pixels to bright (in the case of one byte per color, the corresponding brightnesses are 0, 85, 170 and 255). The detailed position of bright pixels, that is in the upper, middle or lower row of the segment, is negligible, due to small dimensions of a segment with respect to the image. We shall use only the positions as shown in Fig. 2.

Three colors, with four levels of brightness each, form a 64-color palette. Before coding, the secret is dithered with this palette. The standard function dither() from Matlab [11] is used. Then, each pixel of the secret is represented as a respective 3×3 pixel segment, like one of these shown in Fig. 2, according to the values of three basic colors in the respective palette entry. In this way, the number of pixels in the image becomes three times larger in each direction.

Now, each pixel of the dithered secret is either black, or bright: R, G or B. Such image can be coded, with either the classic or random coding, as described above. The coding results in replacing each pixel of the 3×3 segment by a 2×2 tile, which further increases the number of pixels in the image, by multiplication by two in each direction. In total, the pixel expansion in the methods used in this paper is $3^2 \times 2^2 = 36$.

The numerical complexity of the proposed method (besides the dithering process, which is performed in both the classic and the random coding) is $O(n)$, where n is the number of pixels of the original image, because all the operations are made on each pixel independently of the others.

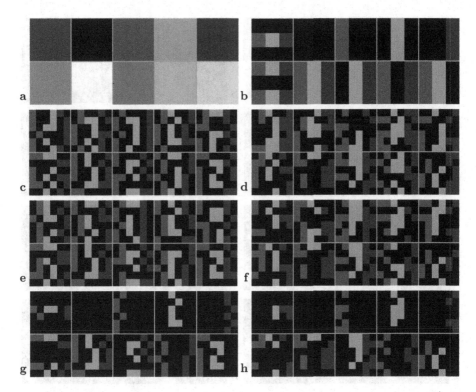

Fig. 3. Illustration of coding and decoding for an example image. (**a**) Secret (5 × 2), the dithered image is the same; (**b**) decomposed into color stripes for coding (15 × 6); (**c, e**) shares of classic coding (30 × 12); (**d, f**) shares of random coding (30 × 12); (**g**) decoded from classic coding (30 × 12); (**h**) decoded from random coding (30 × 12). Regions corresponding to single pixels of the secret are marked with overlaid gray lines. (Color figure online)

As written before, in the random coding the layout of the black and bright pixels is truly random. However, in the present implementation the setup of color columns is fixed, thus not random at all; still, the pixels which form these columns are generated in a truly random way. This can be managed by further randomizing the locations of the specific pixels of the shares within each segment, which is related to one pixel in the coded secret (segments like those shown in Fig. 2 are meant). This operation was not implemented within the present study.

2.3   Example

Let us now look at the process of coding and decoding of an example minimalistic image presented in Fig. 3. The image contains 10 pixels, in basic and complementary colors, and in the four shades of gray. All these colors are representable in the palette used, so the palette image is exactly the same as the input image,

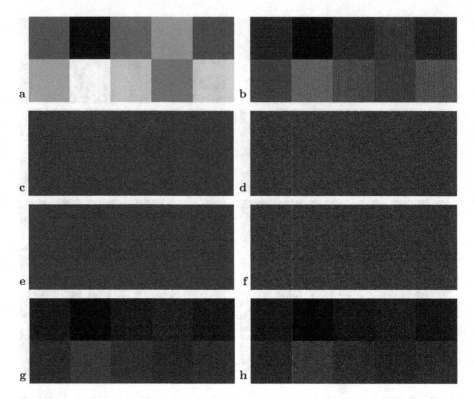

Fig. 4. Illustration of coding and decoding. (**a**) Secret (250 × 100), the dithered image is the same; (**b**) decomposed into color stripes for coding (750 × 300); (**c, e**) shares of classic coding (1500 × 600); (**d, f**) shares of random coding (1500 × 600); (**g**) decoded from classic coding (1500 × 600); (**h**) decoded from random coding (1500 × 600). (Color figure online)

Fig. 3a. The pixels are replaced by 3 × 3 segments with only the necessary pixels set to on, which forms the decomposed image in Fig. 3b. The image contains 90 pixels. See that in the white pixel of the secret all the pixels of the corresponding segment are on, while in the red (green, blue, respectively) pixel only the pixels of the segment in the red (green, blue) column are on. Inevitably, the dithered palette image represented in this way is darker than the original. The decomposed image is coded, with the classic coding (Figs. 4c, e, g) and random coding (Figs. 4d, f, h), where both shares and the result of decoding are shown. These images contain 360 pixels each.

In the example with such a small number of pixels the human eye sees each color separately and the colors of the original are lost. The corresponding example with 50^2 times more pixels is shown in Fig. 4. In this example the colors become visible. It is recommended to look at this Figure with a display of good quality and in proper magnification, to avoid the interference of the grid of pixels in the images with that of the display.

It can be seen that the decoded images are significantly darker than the original. The major decrease of quality can be noticed in the process of decomposing the dithered image into the two-level image, between the images **a** and **b**. The loss in brightness and contrast pertains to the processes of the classic as well as the random coding to the same extent. The brightness and color of the image **h** coded with the random coding are less uniform than those of the image **g** coded with the classic coding, due to the presence of differences, or errors, mentioned in one of the previous paragraphs. Nevertheless, the difference in quality of the images **g** and **h** does not preclude the random coding from being applied, should it be necessary, for example for the security reasons. In both codings, the colors can be discerned and properly attributed.

3   Examples for Natural Images

The classic and random coding has been applied to the examples of natural images. Some benchmark images generally used in color image analysis, chosen from numerous images available in data bases accessible from the historical Computer Vision Homepage [5], were used. The images "baboon", Fig. 5, and "peppers", Fig. 6, were chosen for their popularity and due to the moderate amount of detail in them. The size of the images was reduced, by interpolation, to make the results more visible in the screen as well as in print.

In both images the same observations can be made as those written down in the comments to Fig. 4. The major part of the quality deterioration is related to coding the image as a two-level image, which is necessary for coding, and as such, unavoidable to a large extent, as far as decoding with bare human eye is considered. Besides this quality loss, the objects in the image can be seen and recognized, as well as the colors of the objects can be noticed.

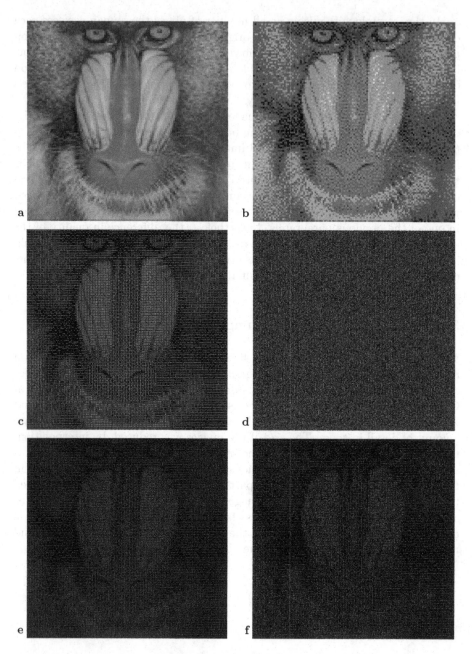

Fig. 5. Example for image "baboon" (reduced 4 times w.r.t. the original). (**a**) Secret (125 × 120); (**b**) dithered into the 64 color palette (125 × 120); (**c**) decomposed into color stripes for coding (375 × 360); (**d**) one share of random coding (750 × 720); (**e**) decoded from classic coding (750 × 720); (**f**) decoded from random coding (750 × 720). (Color figure online)

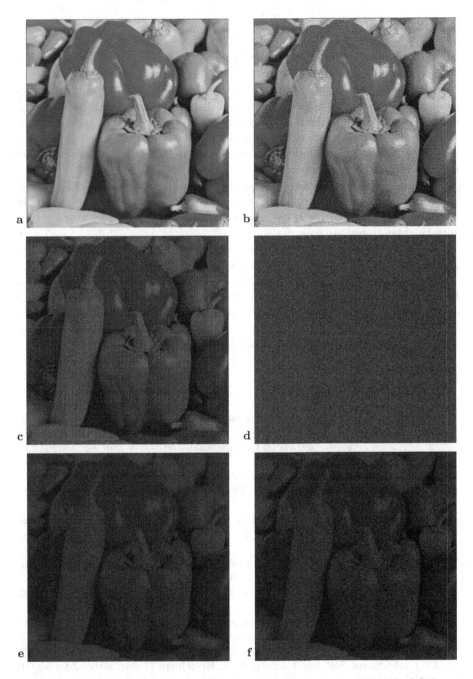

Fig. 6. Example for image "peppers" (reduced twice w.r.t. the original). (a) Secret (256 × 256); (b) dithered into the 64 color palette (256 × 256); (c) decomposed into color stripes for coding (768 × 768); (d) one share of random coding (1536 × 1536); (e) decoded from classic coding (1536 × 1536); (f) decoded from random coding (1536 × 1536). (Color figure online)

4 Conclusions and Perspective

In this preliminary study the concept of visual coding with completely random shares was applied to coding color images. The results were presented in comparison to classic coding. The applicability of the random coding appeared to be comparable to that of the classic coding, although the unavoidable existence of differences, or errors, in the random coding makes the decoded images look more noisy than in the case of classic coding. Besides the truly random choice of black and bright pixels in the shares, the red, green and blue pixels were organized into columns in a fixed way.

The major problems found to influence the results was the loss of brightness and contrast. These features are typical for the majority of visual cryptography methods, as far as the methods in which the decryption is performed merely with the human eye are considered.

The pixel expansion is 36 and belongs to the range of higher values, in comparison with the numbers attained in the other methods.

It could be expected that both the large pixel expansion and the loss of brightness could be reduced if the subtractive color model CMY was used. It could also be interesting to see what would be the influence of changing the layout of colors in the shares, from the structured column-wise one into a random one. These will be the directions of our future research in this field.

References

1. Cimato, S., Yang, C.N.: Visual Cryptography and Secret Image Sharing (Digital Imaging and Computer Vision). CRC Press Inc., Boca Raton (2011). https://www.crcpress.com/Visual-Cryptography-and-Secret-Image-Sharing/Cimato-Yang/9781439837214
2. Dahat, A.V., Chavan, P.V.: Secret sharing based visual cryptography scheme using CMY color space. Proc. Comput. Sci. **78**, 563–570 (2016). https://doi.org/10.1016/j.procs.2016.02.103
3. Dhiman, K., Kasana, S.S.: Extended visual cryptography techniques for true color images. Comput. Electr. Eng. **70**, 647–658 (2018). https://doi.org/10.1016/j.compeleceng.2017.09.017
4. Hou, Y.C.: Visual cryptography for color images. Pattern Recognit. **36**(7), 1619–1629 (2003). https://doi.org/10.1016/S0031-3203(02)00258-3
5. Huber, D.: The Computer Vison Homepage (2004). https://www.cs.cmu.edu/~cil/vision.html. Accessed Apr 2019
6. Liu, F., Yan, W.Q.: Visual Cryptography for Image Processing and Security. Springer, Cham (2014). https://doi.org/10.1007/978-3-319-09644-5
7. Naor, M., Shamir, A.: Visual cryptography. In: De Santis, A. (ed.) EUROCRYPT 1994. LNCS, vol. 950, pp. 1–12. Springer, Heidelberg (1995). https://doi.org/10.1007/BFb0053419
8. Naor, M., Shamir, A.: Visual cryptography II: Improving the contrast via the cover base. In: Lomas, M. (ed.) Security Protocols, pp. 197–202. Springer, Berlin, Heidelberg (1997). https://doi.org/10.1007/3-540-62494-5_18

9. Orłowski, A., Chmielewski, L.J.: Generalized visual cryptography scheme with completely random shares. In: Petkov, N., Strisciuglio, N., Travieso, C.M. (eds.) Proceedings of 2nd International Conference on Applications of Intelligent Systems APPIS 2019. ACM International Conference Proceeding Series, vol. 1869, pp. 33:1–33:6. ACM, New York (2019). https://doi.org/10.1145/3309772.3309805
10. Orłowski, A., Chmielewski, L.J.: Randomness of Shares versus quality of secret reconstruction in black-and-white visual cryptography. In: Rutkowski, L., Scherer, R., Korytkowski, M., Pedrycz, W., Tadeusiewicz, R., Zurada, J.M. (eds.) ICAISC 2019. LNCS (LNAI), vol. 11509, pp. 58–69. Springer, Cham (2019). https://doi.org/10.1007/978-3-030-20915-5_6
11. The MathWorks Inc.: MATLAB. Natick (2018). https://www.mathworks.com
12. Yang, C.N., Chen, T.S.: Colored visual cryptography scheme based on additive color mixing. Pattern Recogn. 41(10), 3114–3129 (2008). https://doi.org/10.1016/j.patcog.2008.03.031

Using the Properties of Primate Motion Sensitive Neurons to Extract Camera Motion and Depth from Brief 2-D Monocular Image Sequences

John A. Perrone[1]([✉]) [iD], Michael J. Cree[2] [iD], and Mohammad Hedayati[1,2] [iD]

[1] School of Psychology, University of Waikato, Hamilton 3240, New Zealand
john.perrone@waikato.ac.nz
[2] School of Engineering, University of Waikato, Hamilton 3240, New Zealand
{michael.cree,hedi.hedayati}@waikato.ac.nz

Abstract. Humans and most animals can run/fly and navigate efficiently through cluttered environments while avoiding obstacles in their way. Replicating this advanced skill in autonomous robotic vehicles currently requires a vast array of sensors coupled with computers that are bulky, heavy and power hungry. The human eye and brain have had millions of years to develop an efficient solution to the problem of visual navigation and we believe that it is the best system to reverse engineer. Our brain and visual system appear to use a very different solution to the visual odometry problem compared to most computer vision approaches. We show how a neural-based architecture is able to extract self-motion information and depth from monocular 2-D video sequences and highlight how this approach differs from standard CV techniques. We previously demonstrated how our system works during pure translation of a camera. Here, we extend this approach to the case of combined translation and rotation.

Keywords: Biologically-based motion sensor · Visual odometry · Monocular visual sensor · Optical flow · Image motion · Depth-from-motion

1 Introduction

It has long been known that the motion occurring on the back of our eyes (optic flow) provides a rich source of information regarding our own movement through the world ('self-motion') as well as the 3-D layout of the scene in front of us [10,18,19]. We are able to extract this information from just the motion projected on the retina of a single eye. Hence, we often perceive depth while viewing 2-D movies and can navigate and avoid obstacles while playing 2-D video games. This 3-D from 2-D motion extraction process occurs within fractions of a second which grants us the ability to run/drive through complex environments at speed while avoiding obstacles in our way.

© Springer Nature Switzerland AG 2019
M. Vento and G. Percannella (Eds.): CAIP 2019, LNCS 11678, pp. 600–612, 2019.
https://doi.org/10.1007/978-3-030-29888-3_49

Many animals share this amazing skill with us and there is a large industry dedicated to emulating this biological navigational ability in software/hardware in order to solve the visual odometry problem [9, 35]. However, the disparity between what animals and machines can achieve is currently still wide and attempts to map out of the environment in front of a moving robot or vehicle tend to rely on active sensors (e.g., LIDAR) or binocular systems [9, 35]. The former tend to be bulky and power hungry and the latter require the simultaneous processing of dual video streams and often require careful camera calibration to be able to exploit epipolar geometry to simplify feature matching. A passive sensor that worked with standard monocular video inputs would have many advantages.

The primate visual system seems to have taken a very different approach to most computer vision techniques for extracting odometry and depth information. The majority of computer vision methods either find corresponding pixels (indirect) [17, 22, 33, 36] or minimise photometric error (direct) [5, 6, 15] between two frames to estimate the camera displacement and depth information. These models can be further categorised as sparse, which only consider a set of independent points to solve the correspondence problems [17, 22], and as dense which use all pixels in the frame to estimate camera motion [6, 33, 36]. In contrast, the primate visual system has a series of stages ('the visual motion pathway' [3, 23]) where the image motion is first registered using banks of spatiotemporal filters, and after a series of integration stages [3, 21], produces a signal proportional to the image speed [14]. The brain then recovers self-motion (odometry) information at a relatively late stage of processing [3]. What are the advantages to be gained from this long chain of computational steps? Some of the motion processing steps seem to provide an economical use of neural hardware [25] but other potential advantages are currently unknown.

Discovering the benefits of neural-based approaches to odometry and depth estimation would be very useful in the design of smart sensors for robots and autonomous vehicles. Unfortunately, we do not yet have a full understanding of how the human or non-human primate visual systems are able to recover depth from 2-D video sequences. Some motion processing areas of the brain have been well studied [2] but many aspects of how visual motion is analyzed remain a mystery.

We have recently implemented a scheme based on the properties of neurons in the primate visual system that is able to solve the depth estimation problem [27]. This technique is able to derive 3-D scene depth estimates from the 2-D image motion generated during pure forward translation of the camera. Here we extend this system to work with a combined translation and rotation of the camera. We present a 'proof of principle' test that demonstrates that a system based on primate neuron properties is able to extract camera motion information as well as 3-D depth information from a brief 2-D video sequence. We see this as a first step in the process of comparing biologically-based methods with conventional computer vision approaches to odometry and depth recovery. We eventually hope to discover and highlight the advantages that the brain has developed through millions of years of evolution.

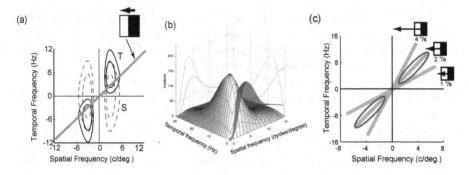

Fig. 1. Frequency space representations of the model early stage motion sensor filters and the representation of edge motion in spatial frequency (f_s)–temporal frequency (f_t) space. (a) Plan view of two types of model filters. A moving edge has a spectrum that falls on an oriented line with the slope proportional to the speed [38,39]. (b) 3-D surface plot of the upper right quadrant of $f_t - f_s$ space with the amplitude spectrum of the sustained type (S) of spatiotemporal filter shown in blue and the transient type (T) in red. (c) Representation of multiple edge speeds in the frequency domain. The red ovals represent a speed tuned filter tightly tuned to a particular edge speed. (Color figure online)

2   Extracting Velocity Vector Flow Fields (optic flow) from Image Sequences

Our approach to the visual odometry/obstacle avoidance problem makes use of measurements of the image motion occurring in a video input and these measurements are based on intensity changes in the images rather than on feature matching [9,17,22,35]. Figure 1 shows the early stage filtering used in our system for deriving image velocity estimates from an 8-frame video sequence.

2.1   Early Stage Motion Sensors Based on Neurons in Primate Primary Visual Cortex (V1)

In a plot of spatial frequency versus temporal frequency, a moving edge has a spectrum that falls along a line (grey line in Fig. 1a) with the slope of the line proportional to the edge speed [38,39]. The first stage in determining the slope of the spectrum (speed of the edge) in our system is to use two spatiotemporal frequency tuned filters, one with low pass temporal frequency tuning (dashed curve in Fig. 1 marked S for 'sustained') and one with bandpass tuning (solid lines in Fig. 1a marked T for 'transient').

The S filters are separable and made up of separate spatial and temporal frequency functions as given below. The T filters are one-quadrant separable and are constructed from individual non-directional spatiotemporal filters using the combination rules specified by Watson and Ahumada [39].

The temporal frequency amplitude response function of the S-type filter is given by:

$$\tilde{f}_{\text{sust}}(f_t) = e^{-f_t^2 \sigma^2/2}\, e^{-i2\pi f_t \theta}. \tag{1}$$

where f_t is the temporal frequency measured in Hz and $i = \sqrt{-1}$. The θ term (phase) controls the temporal delay (lag) of the response and σ controls the spread of the Gaussian.

The T-type filter temporal frequency tuning function is band-pass in shape and is given by:

$$\tilde{f}_{\text{trans}} = 0.25\tilde{f}_{\text{sust}}(f_t) f_t i. \tag{2}$$

The magnitude part of both of these functions are good matches [25] to the temporal frequency tuning functions often observed in primate V1 neurons [8, 12]. The two functions (S = blue, T = red) can be seen on the right wall of Fig. 1b and the parameter values can be found in [25].

The spatial frequency tuning functions of the front-end spatiotemporal filters (Fig. 1a, b) are based on the difference of difference of Gaussians with separation (dDOGs) function used by Hawken and Parker [11] to fit their primate V1 spatial frequency tuning data. (see [24]). The two S & T spatial frequency functions can be seen on the back wall of Fig. 1b. Only one size of filter is shown in the figure. The full model uses four different sizes in $\log_2$ steps [26].

2.2   Gradient Optical Flow Models Versus the Introduction of Tight Speed Tuning

In the space domain (inverse Fourier transformed versions), the S and T spatial filters look similar to standard Gabor or Difference of Gaussian (DoG) functions often used in computer vision. They come in both even and odd (quadrature) versions and the latter can act as a 1st derivative spatial operator over space (x). The T-type temporal bandpass filter is biphasic in time and can also be considered to be a 1st derivative operator over time (t). Therefore the ratio of the T and S filter outputs (T/S) is equal to $\Delta x / \Delta t = V$ (the image speed). The common gradient-based optical flow methods used in computer vision [7,13,40] use this operation inside the optical flow energy function to find V. Therefore an indication of the speed of a moving image feature is available at the very earliest stage of filtering in the primate visual system yet, for some reason, the estimation of the actual speed is delayed. The electrophysiological evidence points to speed-tuned sensors prior to the direct estimation of speed. Subsequent to the S&T filter stage (Fig. 1a), there are filters (Middle Temporal or MT neurons) that are precisely tuned to a particular image speed and their output is not linear with input speed [20,29]. It is only at a post-MT stage (see below) that an output proportional to input speed is found in the primate visual system [14].

We follow this primate motion processing pathway design and introduce tight speed tuning after the spatiotemporal filtering stage. The spatial filters in our model look superficially like standard Gabor functions but they differ in important ways [24,25]. The spatial and temporal frequency tuning functions used in the model motion sensor have been especially designed to create a filter that is very selective to a particular spectrum orientation (edge speed) and to be precisely tuned to a narrow range of image speeds (red oval outline in Fig. 1c). This is done via a type of AND operation whereby the speed tuned filter gives a large response whenever both the sustained and transient filter outputs are high and equal. For the S and T spectra profiles shown in Fig. 1b, this occurs along a locus that forms a straight line and is oriented relative to the two axes.

It has been shown that the slope of the line of intersection can be altered (and hence the speed tuning of the filter) by simply changing the weight of either the S or T energy output [25]. The speed tuned mechanism is therefore referred to as a 'Weighted Intersection Mechanism' (WIM) and is given by:

$$\text{WIM} = \frac{S + T}{|S - T| + \delta} \qquad (3)$$

where δ is a constant that controls the bandwidth of the speed tuning (set to 12 in the model tests reported here).

This design is based on theoretical work using frequency representations of visual motion [25,30,38] and the model filters mimic the oriented spectral receptive fields of neurons found in the Middle Temporal (MT) region of the primate brain [29]. This speed tuning stage is an important and unique feature of our flow field estimation scheme.

2.3   Image Velocity Estimation from Three Separate MT Unit Outputs

The MT unit sensors in our optic flow estimation system do not output a signal proportional to the stimulus speed of the feature passing over them; they are speed and direction tuned only. In the primate visual system evidence for cells that respond in a linear fashion to the input speed only appear at a stage after MT, namely the dorsal Medial Superior Temporal area (MSTd) [14]. Based on a theory that outlines a possible velocity code used by the primate visual system [26], our velocity estimation stage replicates this MT to MSTd transition and derives a velocity signal from the outputs of a 'triad' of MT units that come in two spatial scales.

This system uses competition (via a 2nd derivative stage) between two different sized MT units tuned to speed MTv and MT2v as well as a unit tuned to $V/2$. The latter input has the same spatial size as the MTV unit. In frequency space (see Fig. 1c) the $2V$ and $V/2$ units sit on either side of the ridge occupied by the main MTv unit (see red oval in Fig. 1c). They therefore isolate the correct location of the oriented line spectrum generated by an edge moving at speed V to a single velocity 'channel'. A precise speed signal is calculated using a centroid operation on the three triad unit outputs, which interpolates between the discrete MT unit speed tuning values $1, 2, 4, \ldots$ pixels/frame. The direction is similarly found with greater precision by using vector addition to estimate the direction from the output of multiple velocity sensors tuned to different directions [26].

3   Heading Estimation and Depth Extraction

The direct approach to deriving camera motion (odometry) and depth from the optical flow field is to directly input the velocity vectors (or image brightness changes) into the equations for observer motion [19] and solving for the camera parameters and depth. Again, the primate visual system seems to have taken a slightly different approach and has neural processing units designed to extract information about the observer's heading direction separately from information regarding depth [3]. The mechanism used seems to be based around a population of heading tuned units rather than a single neuron coding for all of the observer self-motion parameters and scene depth.

We follow this design and our approach makes use of a well-known property of flow fields that occurs during pure forward translation of an observer/camera; the image motion radiates out from a single point in the image (the focus of expansion or FOE) and this coincides with the heading direction [10]. The location of the FOE can be found using special 'heading detectors' or radial templates based on the properties of primate MSTd neurons [31,32]. In our model an array of detectors tuned to a range of heading azimuth and elevation values ($-50°$ to $50°$ in $2.5°$ steps for azimuth and elevation) is used to search for the FOE location in the image sequence.

A major problem encountered while attempting to estimate image motion is the aperture problem [41]; when just an edge is located in a motion sensor aperture, only the motion orthogonal to the edge direction can be detected and the estimated motion direction and speed are perturbed away from the true optic flow values. Our heading estimation units are very tolerant of noise in the flow field vector directions. As long as there are a sufficient number of vectors distributed across the field and the edge orientations causing the aperture problem are randomly distributed around the radial direction out from the putative FOE locations, the heading can still be estimated accurately [4,27]. Once the FOE has been determined, the true direction of the image motion is constrained to lie along the radial direction (α) of a line joining the derived FOE location to the vector location. The corrected magnitude of the vector can be found from $V_c = V/\cos(\alpha - \beta)$ where β is the vector direction and V is the magnitude. This correction is only applied to vector locations where $\alpha - \beta < 70°$.

3.1   Heading Estimation in the Presence of Camera Rotation

Most camera motion scenarios with a moving vehicle or aerial platform include rotation of the camera, which adds a rotation component (R) to the vector flow field created via pure translation of the camera (T). The resultant flow vectors (T + R) produce a flow field that no longer has a focus of expansion that coincides with the heading direction [34,37]. The flow is no longer purely radial and so the depth cannot be easily recovered from the image motion. This is known as the 'rotation problem' and somehow the T vectors need to be recovered from the T + R flow in order to determine the heading direction and depth. A biologically feasible method for this has been proposed [28]. Rotation activity is removed from the heading detector map distribution that is equivalent to vector subtraction at the local level (T + R − R = T). We use this same mechanism in our model.

3.2 Depth Extraction from Heading and Radial Flow

If heading direction (α, β) is known, and the position of two points w_1, w_2 are fixed in the world, the ratio of the distances to the two points D_1/D_2 can be found from s_1 and s_2, the image velocity vector magnitudes in the radial flow pattern. If the camera/observer's forward speed (V_O) is known, it is possible to obtain absolute values of D_1 and D_2. Therefore, our system first determines the heading direction (with rotation removed), derives the radial optic flow field and then estimates the depth of the points. An overall plan of the system can be found in [27] (see Fig. 2). This system is very different from the majority of computer vision approaches to the structure from motion problem [9,15,35]. After introducing a number of radically different approaches to the standard structure-from-motion estimation problem one may well ask if our system works? Are we able to estimate 3-D depth from a 2-D video sequence using these biologically-based motion filters? We next present a proof of principle that our system can solve the depth from 2-D motion problem.

4 Testing Methodology

We used a computer-controlled camera (Basler acA1920-150um) mounted on a Pan-Tilt unit attached to an X-Y translation table (Newmark CS Series XY Gantry-1500-1500-1). The camera (field of view = 42° horizontal and 26.3° vertical) moved towards a laboratory scene containing identifiable target objects (Fig. 2). The camera forward speed was 0.25 m/s while rotating to the left (from straight ahead) about a vertical axis at 2.5°/s. This scene contained a range of object sizes, contrasts and intensity distributions similar to what is commonly found in both indoor and outside environments. A series of eight frames (1984 × 1264 pixels) was extracted from the video stream at a 100 Hz sample rate. The output of the velocity code model develops over the eight-frame sequence and we use the output from the fourth frame as an estimate of the vector flow field. The current Matlab implementation is not capable of 'real-time' analysis but many of the model stages could be run in parallel.

Figure 2 shows the first and last frames of the eight-frame movie sequence with some of the objects that will be used to assess the depth extraction stage of the model. We used the blue zone (grid on left side of image) as a reference object and compared the depth estimates of other objects (each at a different distance) against the reference to see if the model could distinguish the depth location of the different objects. The far wall (red zone) was close to 4 m further than the reference object (true distances were 6 m and 2.1 m respectively). The yellow zone (middle card) was 0.6 m closer than the reference object (true yellow zone distance = 1.5 m) and the green zone object (card on extreme right) was

Fig. 2. Test input images. Frames 1 and 8 from the video sequence. (Color figure online)

0.4 m in front of the standard (true green zone distance $= 1.7$ m). The distance between the green and yellow zone objects was 0.2 m.

5   Results

The raw vector flow field output from the velocity estimation stage is shown in Fig. 3a. This vector field was passed through the heading detector array and the activity distribution from the array is plotted in Fig. 3b. Without the rotation being removed the heading estimate was $(-35.3°, -.75°)$. The rotational flow vectors produced by the known camera rotation ($2.5°$/s to left) was removed from this raw flow field. The rotation-free heading detector distribution is shown in Fig. 3c. After rotation removal the estimated heading was $(2.51°, -0.75°)$ which is very close to the true heading $(2.5°, 0°)$.

Given the estimated heading direction (and associated expansion point in the image), the actual radial direction of each vector was determined and the vector magnitude was corrected. The resulting radial flow field is shown in Fig. 3d. The radial flow was used to estimate the distance to each point occupied by a vector in the output field. The estimated point cloud from each zone is noisy because slight variations in the vector magnitudes can result in large depth variations given the small projection angles involved. In order to quantify the depth estimation performance of the model we binned the estimates along the Z dimension (using the histogram function in Matlab) and the resulting frequency histograms are shown in Fig. 4.

The means (and standard deviations) for the blue and red depth distributions were 2.7 m (0.5) and 5.5 m (1.7). A t-test indicated that these two distributions are significantly different, $t(1, 164) = 15.0$, $p < .001$. Therefore, the model was able to extract depth from the monocular video sequence and successfully identified that the two zones were at different distances from the camera. For the yellow zone object (middle card) the actual separation from the reference object was $-.6$ m. The mean of the depth estimates was 2.1 m (0.9) and this was significantly different from the estimated standard distance (2.7 m), $t(1, 209) = 6.5$, $p < .001$. For the green zone object (Fig. 2 right card) the mean depth estimate

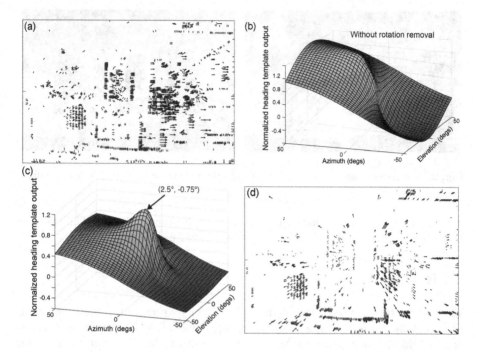

Fig. 3. (a) Initial vector flow field output from the velocity estimation stage of the model in response to the eight-frame test sequence. (b) Output of heading estimation stage of the model when the rotation is not removed from the flow field. The 3-D graph shows the activity of each heading detector (tuned to a particular azimuth and elevation value) in response to the vector flow field shown in a. (c) Heading template distribution after rotation removal. (d) Radial vector flow field output from the velocity estimation stage of the model in response to the eight-frame test sequence.

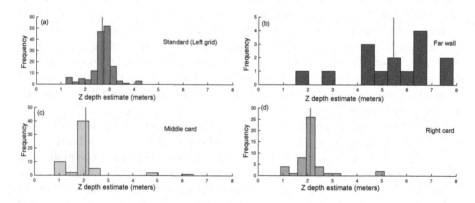

Fig. 4. Frequency histograms of the estimated distances (x-axis) found in each of the four image zones with the reference object at the top. The red vertical lines are the means of the distributions. (Color figure online)

was also 2.1 m (.71) and this was also significantly different from the standard, $t(1, 196) = 6.4$, $p < .001$. The separation distance from the standard was -0.4 m. A test to see if the model was able to distinguish the average depth of the yellow and green zone objects (separated by 0.2 m) was non-significant, $t(1, 105) = .2$, $p = .8$. The means were different in the right direction (yellow, 2.08 m closer than green, 2.11 m) but the spreads of the two distributions were too high to detect the difference. It should be noted that human observers also cannot distinguish the depth of these two objects while viewing the eight-frame movie sequence.

6   Discussion

Our test demonstrates that camera motion (heading direction) and 3-D depth information can be recovered from an eight frame, monocular video sequence using a model based on the properties of neurons in the primate visual system. In order to be effective for obstacle avoidance the detection of objects along the path of travel needs to occur very quickly if evasive action is to be executed in time. The temporal filters in the early stage of our velocity detection algorithm have an epoch of around 200 ms and the timeline for the extraction of depth is not much longer than this because the later stages mainly involve integration of the first stage motion signals. We use a feedforward pipeline only and we argue that this gives it an advantage over schemes that rely on iterative searches for solving the velocity or odometry stages [1]. However, we recognize that the output from the later stages of the model could be used to refine the depth estimates over time. The depth distributions could be used to refine future estimates of the extracted depth signals and implement some form of Kalman filtering [16].

7   Conclusion

The primate visual system uses a different series of steps and stages from standard computer vision approaches in its attempt to derive information about self motion (odometry) and depth. The computation of the visual flow field is delayed in the biological system relative to computer vision methods with the inclusion of a speed-tuned sensor stage (see Sect. 2.2 above). This speed tuning stage could be part of a system for determining the overall direction of an object from its separate edge components [2,24] but this is not known for certain. Once the flow field is determined, the estimation of depth and 3-D information from the visual motion occurring in a monocular video stream is still very difficult because the image motion is hard to measure accurately. The aperture problem perturbs the velocity vectors away from the true direction. We have taken a novel approach (based on knowledge of primate neuron properties) whereby we determine the heading direction using detectors tuned to radial motion that make use of redundant information distributed across the full visual field and which are therefore tolerant of the image motion noise introduced by the aperture problem. Once the heading direction is established it becomes relatively easy to derive the depth from the radial flow field. This is a different method to how depth from motion is usually estimated using computer vision approaches. We plan next to examine what these additional stages add to the depth and odometry recovery process and what advantages they provide.

References

1. Anandan, P.: A computational framework and an algorithm for the measurement of visual motion. Int. J. Comput. Vis. **2**(3), 283–310 (1989)
2. Born, R.T., Bradley, D.: Structure and function of visual area MT. Ann. Rev. Neurosci. **28**, 157–189 (2005)
3. Britten, K.H.: Mechanisms of self-motion perception. Ann. Rev. Neurosci. **31**, 389–410 (2008)
4. Cree, M.J., Perrone, J.A., Anthonys, G., Garnett, A.C., Gouk, H.: Estimating heading direction from monocular video sequences using biologically-based sensors. In: Proceedings of the 2016 International Conference on Image and Vision Computing New Zealand (IVCNZ), pp. 116–121 (2016)
5. Engel, J., Koltun, V., Cremers, D.: Direct sparse odometry. IEEE Transact. Pattern Anal. Mach. Intell. **40**(3), 611–625 (2018)
6. Engel, J., Schöps, T., Cremers, D.: LSD-SLAM: large-scale direct monocular SLAM. In: Fleet, D., Pajdla, T., Schiele, B., Tuytelaars, T. (eds.) ECCV 2014. LNCS, vol. 8690, pp. 834–849. Springer, Cham (2014). https://doi.org/10.1007/978-3-319-10605-2_54
7. Fortun, D., Bouthemy, P., Kervrann, C.: Optical flow modeling and computation: a survey. J. Comput. Vis. Image Underst. **134**, 1–21 (2015)
8. Foster, K.H., Gaska, J.P., Nagler, M., Pollen, D.A.: Spatial and temporal frequency selectivity of neurones in visual cortical areas V1 and V2 of the Macaque monkey. J. Physiol. **365**, 331–363 (1985)
9. Fraundorfer, F., Scaramuzza, D.: Visual odometry part II: matching, robustness, optimization, and applications. IEEE Robot. Autom. Mag. **19**(2), 78–90 (2012)
10. Gibson, J.: The Perception of the Visual World. Houghton Mifflin, Boston (1950)
11. Hawken, M., Parker, A.: Spatial properties of neurons in the monkey striate cortex. Proc. Royal Soc. London B. **231**, 251–288 (1987)
12. Hawken, M., Shapley, R., Grosof, D.: Temporal frequency selectivity in monkey visual cortex. J. Neurosci. **13**, 477–492 (1996)
13. Horn, B.K.P., Schunk, B.G.: Determining optic flow. Artif. Intell. **17**, 185–203 (1981)
14. Inaba, N., Shinomoto, S., Yamane, S., Takemura, A., Kawano, K.: MST neurons code for visual motion in space independent of pursuit eye movements. J. Neurophysiol. **97**(5), 3473–3483 (2007)
15. Irani, M., Anandan, P.: About direct methods. In: Triggs, B., Zisserman, A., Szeliski, R. (eds.) IWVA 1999. LNCS, vol. 1883, pp. 267–277. Springer, Heidelberg (2000). https://doi.org/10.1007/3-540-44480-7_18
16. Kalman, R.E.: A new approach to linear filtering and prediction problems. J. Basic Eng. **82**(1), 35–45 (1960)
17. Klein, G., Murray, D.: Parallel tracking and mapping for small AR workspaces. In: 6th IEEE and ACM International Symposium on Mixed and Augmented Reality, pp. 1–10. Nara, Japan (2007)

18. Koenderink, J.J., van Doorn, A.: Invariant properties of the motion parallax field due to the movement of rigid bodies relative to an observer. Optica Acta **22**(9), 773–791 (1975)
19. Longuet-Higgins, H.C., Prazdny, K.: The interpretation of moving retinal images. In: Proceedings of the Royal Society of London B. B 208, 385–387 (1980)
20. Maunsell, J., Van Essen, D.: Functional properties of neurons in the middle temporal visual area of the Macaque monkey. I. selectivity for stimulus direction, speed, orientation. J. Neurophysiol. **49**, 1127–1147 (1983)
21. Movshon, J.A., Adelson, E., Gizzi, M.S., Newsome, W.T.: The analysis of visual moving patterns. In: Chagas, C., Gross, C. (eds.) Pattern Recognition Mechanisms, pp. 117–151. Springer, New York (1985)
22. Mur-Artal, R., Montiel, J.M.M., Tardos, J.D.: ORB-SLAM: a versatile and accurate monocular SLAM system. IEEE Transact. Robot. **31**(5), 1147–1163 (2015)
23. Nakayama, K.: Biological image motion processing: a review. Vision. Res. **25**(5), 625–660 (1984)
24. Perrone, J.A.: A visual motion sensor based on the properties of V1 and MT neurons. Vis. Res. **44**(15), 1733–1755 (2004)
25. Perrone, J.A.: Economy of scale: A motion sensor with variable speed tuning. J. Vis. **5**(1), 28–33 (2005)
26. Perrone, J.A.: A neural-based code for computing image velocity from small sets of middle temporal (MT/V5) neuron inputs. J. Vis. **12**(8), 1 (2012)
27. Perrone, J.A., Cree, M.J., Hedayati, M., Corlett, D.: Testing a biologically-based system for extracting depth from brief monocular 2-D video sequences. In: International Conference on Image and Vision Computing New Zealand. Auckland, New Zealand, November 2018
28. Perrone, J.A., Krauzlis, R.: Vector subtraction using visual and extraretinal motion signals: a new look at efference copy and corollary discharge theories. J. Vis. **8**(14), 1–14 (2008)
29. Perrone, J.A., Thiele, A.: Speed skills: measuring the visual speed analyzing properties of primate MT neurons. Nat. Neurosci. **4**(5), 526–532 (2001)
30. Perrone, J.A., Thiele, A.: A model of speed tuning in MT neurons. Vis. Res. **42**(8), 1035–1051 (2002)
31. Perrone, J.: Model for the computation of self-motion in biological systems. J. Opt. Soc. Am. **9**, 177–194 (1992)
32. Perrone, J., Stone, L.: A model of self-motion estimation within primate extrastriate visual cortex. Vis. Res. **34**, 2917–2938 (1994)
33. Ranftl, R., Vineet, V., Chen, Q., Koltun, V.: Dense monocular depth estimation in complex dynamic scenes. In: Proceedings of the IEEE Conference on Computer Vision and Pattern Recognition (CVPR), pp. 4058–4066 (2016)
34. Regan, D., Beverley, K.I.: How do we avoid confounding the direction we are looking and the direction we are moving? Science **215**(8), 194–196 (1982)
35. Scaramuzza, D., Fraundorfer, F.: Visual odometry part I: the first 30 years and fundamentals. IEEE Robot. Autom. Mag. **18**(4), 80–92 (2011)
36. Valgaerts, L., Bruhn, A., Mainberger, M., Weickert, J.: Dense versus sparse approaches for estimating the fundamental matrix. Int. J. Comput. Vis. **96**(2), 212–234 (2012)
37. Warren, W.: Optic flow. In: Chalupa, L., Werner, J. (eds.) The Visual Neurosciences, vol. 2, pp. 1247–1259. Bradford, Cambridge (2003)
38. Watson, A., Ahumada, A.: A look at motion in the frequency domain. In: Tsotsos, J. (ed.) Motion: Perception and representation, pp. 1–10. Association for Computing Machinery, New York (1983)

39. Watson, A., Ahumada, A.: Model of human visual-motion sensing. J. Opt. Soc. Am. A: **2**, 322–342 (1985)
40. Weinzaepfel, P., Revaud, J., Harchaoui, Z., Schmid, C.: Deepflow: Large displacement optical flow with deep matching. In: Proceedings of the IEEE International Conference on Computer Vision, pp. 1385–1392 (2013)
41. Wuerger, S., Shapley, R., Rubin, N.: On the visually perceived direction of motion by Hans Wallach: 60 years later. Perception **25**(11), 1317–1367 (1996)

Refined Deep Learning for Digital Objects Recognition via Betti Invariants

Darian M. Onchis[1]([⊠]), Codruta Istin[2], and Pedro Real[3]

[1] West University of Timisoara, Timisoara, Romania
darian.onchis@e-uvt.ro
[2] Politehnica University of Timisoara, Timisoara, Romania
istin.codruta@cs.upt.ro
[3] University of Seville, Seville, Spain
real@us.es

Abstract. In this paper, we make use of the topological invariants of 2D images for an accelerated training and an improved recognition ability of a deep learning neural network applied to digital image objects. For our test images, we generate the associated simplicial complexes and from them we compute the Betti numbers which for a 2D object are the number of connected components and the number of holes. These information are used for training the network according to the corresponding Betti number. Experiments on the MNIST databases are presented in support of the proposed method.

Keywords: Deep learning · Betti numbers · Handwritten digits

1 Introduction

The intelligent classification of data objects with human eye precision and speed or if possible even more accurate, is one of the current ambitions in computer analysis of images and patterns. From quantum algorithms to topological data analysis to the state of the art deep learning architecture, the human mind is trying to overcome the condition of the machines and if possible his own native condition [2–5,12].

In this context, the search for refined methods of classification involves designing new algorithms that could make use of the research developments in scientific cross-fields. In here, we merge the use of Betti numbers from computational topology with the training of a deep learning network to enhance the speed and the accuracy of the recognition for the handwritten digits.

Similar merges have been proposed in [4–6], but the areas of application are different from our approach. For example in [4], the authors propose a Topology-Net for biomolecular property predictions. In [5], the topological characteristics of digital models were employed for geological core and in [6] a geometric data analysis for image understanding is proposed and this analysis is based on manifold learning.

© Springer Nature Switzerland AG 2019
M. Vento and G. Percannella (Eds.): CAIP 2019, LNCS 11678, pp. 613–621, 2019.
https://doi.org/10.1007/978-3-030-29888-3_50

Our method is based on designing a first layer of the deep learning net used to feeding the data to the network. So the network will be trained with extra-information on the object to be discovered. As a concrete example, instead of training the network for the entire MNIST database, we train three networks for the corresponding three Betti numbers 0, 1 and 2 characterizing the number of holes. The digits 1, 2, 3, 4, 5, 7, have 0 holes then 0, 6 and 9 have 1 hole, and respectively the digit 8 has 2 holes. Smaller networks allow a more flexible and faster training and possibly even more accurate results.

We evaluate our constructive model on the MNIST database which contains 60,000 training and 10,000 test examples of handwritten digit images, each of which is 28×28 pixels (784-dimensional) and belong to one of 10 classes [1]. We randomly partition the original training set into training and validation sets with a ratio of $5 : 1$.

Neural networks are widely used nowadays, but they have some drawbacks. A major one consists of the time spent to train the network, that is directly proportional to the accuracy of the results. We present in this work a different and novel approach that improves the accuracy and decreases the time spent for training the network. In order to do this, we make use of deep learning feed forward networks in which we alter the first layer of the network to act like a filter for the other layers that keep their standard role. The filtering is necessary for maintaining only the useful information in the database, such that the training will be performed optimally. For this, in the first step, we compute the boundaries of the objects and their holes and afterwards, we eliminate the impossible matching from the database that is not in our recognition interest.

The structure of the paper is the following: in the next section we introduce a theoretical brief about homology, topological spaces and Betti numbers, followed by a section with the presentation of the algorithm. In the last section, the final performances of our approach will be presented on the MNIST database, to emphasize the benefits stated by the theoretical algorithm.

2   Theoretical Brief

We describe briefly in this section the basis of the computational topology theory before applying them to the deep learning network.

We begin with homology which provides valuable information about topological spaces, by observing sets that intuitively have no boundary, but are on the boundary of other sets [13]. These sets are representative cycles of a homology hole, seen as an equivalence class. Algebraic homology information with coefficients in a field could be defined as the set of processed and structured linear algebraic data describing in some sense its (co)homology classes and the relations between them. We talk about homology and cohomology information as a whole due to the fact that homology and cohomology classes are measured using, up to dimension, the same algorithmic strategy of connectivity clustering over the initial topological data and they both provide the same measurable information quantities, up to "duality" [9,11]. A simple example of (co)homology information is provided by the numerical topological invariants called Betti numbers. If

X is a cell complex embedded in $\mathbf{R}^3$, Betti numbers β_0, β_1 and β_2 respectively measure the number of different connected components, (co)homological tunnels and cavities of X.

Roughly speaking, "homotopy holes" of objects (those related to generalized "parametrized and oriented closed curves") are theoretically attainable from homology's ones [10], but these methods have an enormous complexity in time and space [8]. An easier relation is given by the Euler-Poincaré characteristic (see [7]), defined in local terms as the alternate sum of the number of cells in each dimension. This number is the most simple example of homotopy invariant that can also be obtained from global homological information (Betti numbers).

A simplicial complex consists of a set of *vertices* and a set of *simplices* (over that set of vertices) satisfying some simple conditions that we now describe. We make no requirement on vertices other than that they admit a total order. An *n-dimensional ordered simplex*, or just *n-simplex*, over a set V of vertices is an $(n + 1)$-tuple of distinct vertices from V. (An ordered triangle is thus a 2-simplex.) An ordered simplex is *oriented* iff we do not distinguish between two orderings that differ by an even permutation (one that can be expressed as an even number of swaps). Oriented simplices therefore have a well-defined notion of "inside" and "outside".

An *n-dimensional, oriented, pure simplicial complex*, or just *n-complex* for short, is a pair $K = (V, S)$ where V is a set of vertices and S is a set of oriented simplices satisfying the following conditions:

1. Every vertex in V determines a 0-simplex in S. We usually do not distinguish between a vertex v and its associated 0-simplex (v).
2. Every sub-simplex of a simplex in K is also a simplex of K. That is, if $s \in S$ and $t \leq s$, then $t \in S$ (where $\leq$ is the ordered sub-simplex relation).
3. Every simplex $s \in S$ is a sub-simplex of some n-simplex in S. That is, there are no n'-simplices with $n' < n$ other than those that are faces of an n-simplex in S.

A *closed surface* is a 2-complex in which the link of every 0-simplex is a simple, closed polygon having the vertex as an interior point.

Now, we can build a continuous object out of the point cloud, hoping to get a good approximation of the original object. One way to do that is by centering a ball of fixed radius on each sample point. There are some smart techniques based on this idea: e.g., the construction of Vietoris-Rips or alpha complexes [14]. Out of these constructions, we can compute topological invariants; typically they are the dimensions of the homology modules at various dimensions k, called Betti numbers. Substantially, they count the numbers of k-cycles, i.e. connected components and voids in the object. The Betti numbers that one obtains depend on the radius of the balls. While varying the radius, there may be k-cycles which persist, and a good guess is that those may correspond to the true k-cycles of the sampled object.

3   Algorithm Description

The proposed algorithm makes use of the concrete relation between the computation of Betti numbers and the training of the neural network. Betti numbers already shown their use in computational topology, graphs theory and even in the determination of a neural network capacity [4–6]. But their use in the training of the deep learning networks was less explored. Therefore, we are considering in here the context in which a neural network is trained for object recognition in a 2D image. With the use of Betti numbers we can quickly discriminate during the training phase between the wheels of a car or bike and other objects with less or more number of holes. This information is useful for training as it does a separation of the objects to be recognized in smaller and more lighter neural networks.

We present below a complete and exhaustive algorithm description as we have implemented it.

---

1. Loading database
2. Dataset normalization of size $s \times (m \times n)$, image by image
3. Extract a point set from an image given as $m \times n$ matrix
4. Compute 2D simplicial complexes
5. Compute Betti numbers and determine the number of holes
   (a) Compute plot points
   (b) Compute vertices to form triangles
   (c) Determinate the number of unconnected elements
   (d) Determinate the number of holes
6. Send the image to the network corresponding to training the image with the same Betti number as the number of holes determined
7. Set beginning time for each network
8. Train the network
9. Set and compute end time for each network

For the MNIST database the maximum number of holes is 2 for number 8, so in order to have a concrete exemplification, we designed a network with 3 sub networks. We have designed and implemented a neural network as seen in Fig. 1. The first layer of the network computes the Betti numbers and depending on the number of holes determined, the image is sent to the corresponding network for training. The number of networks has to be equal to the number of holes that training images might have.

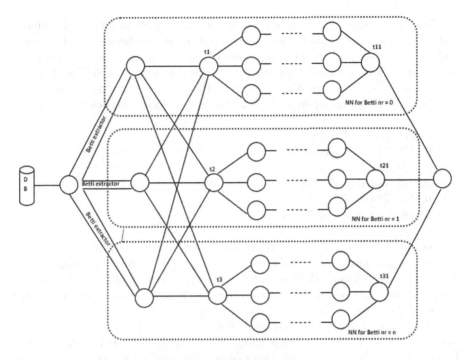

Fig. 1. Network architecture

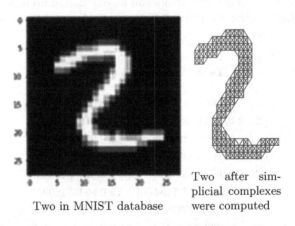

Two in MNIST database

Two after simplicial complexes were computed

The experiment must compare the accuracy of each network after training therefore we performed multiple sets of independent trainings i.e. training one time each of the 3 networks is an element of the set. Each set of training can have a number of epochs that can vary between the set elements.

On our way to compute the Betti numbers, we determine the simplicial complexes, the number of unconnected components and the number of holes from an image.

Considering the image representing a 2 in the MNIST database, the simplicial complexes were computed and the output image can be seen in the second picture. As mentioned in the description of the algorithm, first, the points of every vertex were computed and then the triangles were formed. For this particular example, there are 314 points and 157 vertices. An example of points coordinates as they result from the PYTHON code looks like below:

```
[[ 0.14285714  0.42857143]
 [ 0.14285714  0.46428571]
 [ 0.14285714  0.5 ]
 [ 0.14285714  0.53571429]
 [ 0.14285714  0.57142857]
 [ 0.17857143  0.32142857], etc].
```

For this image we get the Betti number 0 because we do not have any hole and we get the number of unconnected components 0, because the image has all the components connected. From the fact that the number has no holes, we can conclude that the possible numbers can be only 2, 3, 4, 5 and 7, because all the other numbers have at least one hole.

This topological computation is performed on the first layer of the neural network, due to the fact that depending on the result of the Betti numbers, the images are sent to the corresponding training sub network so both the accuracy and the training time are improved. The accuracy is enhanced and sometimes, as can be seen from Table 1, the errors can be eliminated even before the neural network training and the compilation time can be diminished by more than half, as the tests will show.

Table 1. Recognition percent

[7.] 7 0.99588446515	[0.] 0 0.961333326967
[2.] 2 0.865965937884	[6.] 6 0.619316634394
[1.] 1 0.988815228181	[9.] 9 0.955976339534
[0.] 0 0.985114050493	[0.] 0 0.989992193154
[4.] 4 0.989545536094	[1.] 1 0.994334666874
[1.] 1 0.993095777184	[5.] 5 0.894572800157
[4.] 4 0.968422037592	[3.] 3 0.89274171303
[9.] 9 0.809672938457	[9.] 9 0.964876201986
[5.] 6 0.376798989843	[7.] 7 0.995512296425
[9.] 9 0.935884560644	[4.] 4 0.996539732474

As it can be seen on line 9 of the recognition test, on a regular neural network, there is a mistake. It should have been five, but the network recognized a 6. By computing the Betti numbers first, this mistake would not have been possible to appear because five has ho hole, while 6 has one hole.

The Fig. 2 shows the initial picture from MNIST and the image after the topological computation of the simplicial complexes. Also the computation time for the simplicial complexes of each picture is shown.

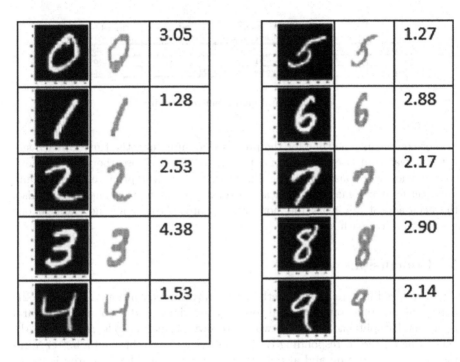

Fig. 2. Computational timings simplicial complexes

As it can be seen, the computation time for this images varies between 1.53 s and 4.38 s. The variation of time computation with respect to the number of vertices determined, will be discussed at Testing.

4 Testing

Experiments showed that by determining, for example the boundaries and number of holes from numbers, if a hole is found, than the number can be only 0, 6 or 9, so the training of the network could be done only with these numbers.

Integrating the topological computation to the first layer of the neural network has two important parts: the first one is actually computing the simplicial complexes and the second one is to send the picture to the corresponding sub network for training.

The tests were performed on a standard PC with Intel core I7 processor and 8G RAM. The comparison was made between a standard deep feed forward neural network trained with backpropagation and on the network showed in Fig. 1. Both time and accuracy were tested. For the consistency of the comparison we restricted the number of hidden layers to 3 in both the standard network and the proposed network on all the three sub networks. The results can be observed in Fig. 3.

	Betti 0 (numbers 1,2,3,4,5,7)	Betti 1 (numbers 0,6,9)	Betti 2 (number 8)	Classical network (whole mnist training)
Accuracy	No mistake	No mistake	No mistake	1 mistake
Time	45.933 s	31.395 s	20.861 s	313.809 s
Total	98.189+24.13(Betti computation) = 122.319 s			313.809 s

Fig. 3. Total neural network timing

For computing the time for the proposed architecture, the time for each sub network was computed (see t1-t11, t2-t21, t3-t31) and also the time for Betti computation was considered. The difference between the proposed method and architecture overcomes the classical network by reducing the time to half. Also, the accuracy of our work did not give any mistakes, while the classical one misplaced a five with a six.

5   Conclusions

We introduced in here a novel method for improved recognition of objects in 2D images by merging computational topology invariants and deep learning neural networks. By splitting the full network into several small deep learning networks depending on the corresponding Betti numbers we have obtained a better accuracy in the recognition and also a faster training time. The next step is to try different numbers of layers for the small networks architecture and to validate the procedure also on noisier data sets.

Acknowledgement. The second author acknowledges the support of the Project HPC-EUROPA3 (INFRAIA- 2016-1-730897), with the support of the EC Research Innovation Action under the H2020 Programme.

References

1. http://yann.lecun.com/exdb/mnist/
2. Lloyd, S., Garnerone, S., Zanardi, P.: Quantum algorithms for topological and geometric analysis of data. Nat. Commun. **7**, 10138 (2016)
3. Cang, Z., Mu, L., Wei, G.W.: Representability of algebraic topology for biomolecules in machine learning based scoring and virtual screening. PLoS Comput. Biol. **14**(1), e1005929 (2018)
4. Cang, Z., Wei, G.: TopologyNet: topology based deep convolutional and multi-task neural networks for biomolecular property predictions. PLoS Comput. Biol. **13**(7), e1005690 (2017)

5. Gilmanov, R.R., Kalyuzhnyuk, A.V., Taimanov, I.A., Yakovlev, A.A.: Topological characteristics of digital models of geological core. In: Holzinger, A., Kieseberg, P., Tjoa, A.M., Weippl, E. (eds.) CD-MAKE 2018. LNCS, vol. 11015, pp. 273–281. Springer, Cham (2018). https://doi.org/10.1007/978-3-319-99740-7_19
6. Miranda Jr., G.F., Thomaz, C.E., Giraldi, G.A.: Geometric data analysis based on manifold learning with applications for image understanding. In: 2017 30th SIB-GRAPI Conference On Graphics, Patterns and Images Tutorials (SIBGRAPI-T), SIBGRAPI - Brazilian Symposium on Computer Graphics and Image Processing, Niteroi, Brazil, 17–20 October, pp. 42–62 (2017). Brazilian Comp Soc; UFRJ; PUC Rio; NVIDIA; IBM; Univ Fed Fluminense, Inst Computacao; Univ Fed Rio Janeiro, Programa Engn Sistemas Computacao; Pontificia Univ Catolica Rio aneiro, Dept Informatica; Univ Fed Rio Janeiro; ACM SIGGRAPH; CAPES; CNPq; SIBGRAPI 2017
7. Alexandroff, P.S.: Combinatorial Topology. Dover, New York (1998)
8. Cadek, M., Krcal, M., Matousek, J., Vokrinek, L., Wagner, U.: Polynomial-time computation of homotopy groups and Postnikov systems in fixed dimension. SIAM J. Comput. 43(5), 1728–1780 (2014)
9. Díaz-del-Río, F., Real, P., Onchis, D.: A parallel homological spanning forest framework for 2D topological image analysis. Pattern Recogn. Lett. 83, 49–58 (2016)
10. Hurewicz, W.: Homology and homotopy theory. In: Proceedings of the International Mathematical Congress of, p. 344 (1950)
11. Real, P., Diaz-del-Rio, F., Onchis, D.: Toward parallel computation of dense homotopy skeletons for nD digital objects. In: Brimkov, V.E., Barneva, R.P. (eds.) IWCIA 2017. LNCS, vol. 10256, pp. 142–155. Springer, Cham (2017). https://doi.org/10.1007/978-3-319-59108-7_12
12. Feichtinger, H.G., Onchis, D.M., Wiesmeyr, C.: Construction of approximate dual wavelet frames. Adv. Comput. Math. 40(1), 273–282 (2014)
13. https://pi.math.cornell.edu/~hatcher/AT/AT.pdf
14. https://geometrica.saclay.inria.fr/team/Fred.Chazal/papers/CGLcourseNotes/main.pdf

Real-Time Micro-expression Detection in Unlabeled Long Videos Using Optical Flow and LSTM Neural Network

Jing Ding[1,3], Zi Tian[2,3], Xiangwen Lyu[2,3(✉)], Quande Wang[1],
Bochao Zou[2,3], and Haiyong Xie[2,3]

[1] School of Electronic Information, Wuhan University, Wuhan 430072, China
[2] Advanced Innovation Center for Human Brain Protection,
Capital Medical University, Beijing 100054, China
xwlyu@innovations.center
[3] National Engineering Laboratory for Public Safety Risk Perception
and Control by Big Data (PSRPC), China Academy of Electronics
and Information Technology, Beijing 100041, China

Abstract. Micro-expressions are momentary involuntary facial expressions which may expose a person's true emotions. Previous work in micro-expression detection mainly focus on finding the peak frame from a video sequence that has been determined to have a micro-expression, and the amount of computation is usually very large. In this paper, we propose a real-time micro-expression detection method based on optical flow and Long Short-term Memory (LSTM) to detect the appearance of micro-expression. This method takes only one step of data preprocessing which is less than previous work. Specifically, we use a sliding window with fixed-length to split a long video into several short videos, then a new and improved optical flow algorithm with low computational complexity was developed to extract feature curves based on the Facial Action Coding System (FACS). Finally, the feature curves were passed to a LSTM model to predict whether micro-expression occurs. We evaluate our method on CASMEll and SAMM databases, and it achieves a new state-of-the-art accuracy (89.87%) on CASMEll database (4.54% improvement). Meanwhile our method only takes 1.48 s to detect the micro-expression in a video sequence with 41 frames (the frame rate is about 28fps). The experimental results show that the proposed method can achieve better comprehensive performances.

Keywords: Micro-expression detection · Real-time · Optical flow ·
Long Short-term memory · Sliding window · Feature curves

1 Introduction

Facial expression is one of the main ways for human beings to express their feelings. There is a kind of difficultly-detected expressions, called micro-expressions. Micro-expressions are brief and involuntary facial expressions that are triggered to hide real emotions. In contrast to macro facial expressions, micro-expressions typically last 1/25

© Springer Nature Switzerland AG 2019
M. Vento and G. Percannella (Eds.): CAIP 2019, LNCS 11678, pp. 622–634, 2019.
https://doi.org/10.1007/978-3-030-29888-3_51

to 1/5 s [1], but the precise length definition varies [2] and the intensity of the muscle movement involved is subtle [3].

The use of micro-expressions detection and recognition for automatic identification of lies has great potential applications in many fields such as clinical security, crime survey, business, etc. For instance, doctors can identify symptoms by detecting the patient's suppressed emotions when additional reassurance is needed. Police officers can recognize potential criminals by analyzing the abnormal expression of suspects. With the help of micro-expression, business negotiators can determine whether the other party is satisfied with the plan.

For the detection of spontaneous micro-expression, there are three major challenges. First, previous work always uses a short video from onset frame to offset frame for micro-expression research [4]. However, in practical scenarios, it is essential to detect micro-expression from long video instead of short video with clear onset and offset frame labels. A long video is the original video sequence that may contains unwanted facial movements, which can be mistakenly detected as micro-expressions. This makes detection of micro-expression in long videos very difficult. Furthermore, the duration of micro-expression is short and the movement is subtle [3]. Therefore, it is challenging to detect when the micro-expression occurs. Finally, most of the existing micro-expression detection researches [5, 6] develop algorithms with high computational complexity, these algorithms often consume relatively long time for detection of micro-expression which cannot meet the actual needs.

To address these issues in detecting spontaneous micro-expressions, in this paper, we make the following main contributions:

(1) A new and improved optical flow algorithm was proposed to track the feature points in each frame. We calculate the sum of intensity change of all facial feature points in this frame. By combining the sum of intensity change within the whole video sequence, we can obtain a feature curve which is called the optical flow feature curve in this paper. It helps to locate when micro-expressions occur.
(2) We train a LSTM network on ten groups of feature curves based on FACS [7] to detect spontaneous micro-expressions, and only one step preprocessing is required to solve the image jitter problem in the video. The proposed detection method can achieve real-time performance.

2 Related Work

In the detection of spontaneous micro-expression, Yan et al. [8] employed Constraint Local Model (CLM) and Local Binary Pattern (LBP) as a feature extractor to locate the peak frame from micro-expression videos. Liong et al. [4] used optical flow [6] to search the apex frame from short video. Patel et al. [9] used optical flow for utilizing the motion features over local regions and integrated them into spatiotemporal regions to locate the peak frame, then computed the onset and offset frames by setting thresholds. But they all detect a peak frame in the video which already been labeled with onset and offset frames, without considering of the possibility that there may be no micro-expression or more than one micro-expression in a video.

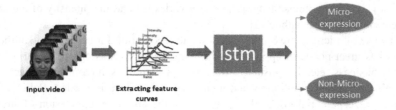

Fig. 1. Framework diagram for the proposed micro-expression detection method

Deep learning techniques are quite new in the field of micro-expression detection. Li et al. [10] proposed a micro-expression detection method based on deep multi-task learning, which utilizes histograms of oriented optical flow (HOOF) as feature descriptors. In their work, CNN was used to detect facial landmark localization and to divide the facial regions of interest. But this is just the preprocessing phase of the micro-expression data and has high computational complexity. Zhang et al. [11] presented a methodology for spotting the peak frame from video, they designed a new convolutional neural network to extract features from video clips, and a feature matrix processing was deployed to spot the apex frame from video sequences. However, before the peak frame spotted, they replace neighbor frames by the peak frame. This makes detection task easier, as in the actual circumstances the peak frame is usually unfeasible. Recently, Verburg et al. [12] used a recurrent neural network with optical flow features to detect micro-expressions. But they only roughly selected the three regions of facial landmarks to calculate HOOF, without consideration of facial action units [7].

As above-mentioned, most of the previous work on micro-expression detection only used the segmented short video with clear onset and offset frames labels for the peak frame detection, and the peak frame refers to the frame where the micro-expression reaches the climax in the video sequence. However, in real conditions, there are two problems need to be considered. First, real-world videos usually are without labels, much longer in duration, and micro-expressions may occur more than once or not occur at all. Second, we are more concerned about when micro-expression occurs rather than single apex frame. Finally, the existing micro-expression detection algorithms have high computational complexity and lower practical application performance. In our study, we use a sliding window strategy to split long videos, so that it can effectively detect whether the micro-expression occurs in each video sequence fragment, and does not rely on the labeling of the onset frame and the offset frame in the video.

3   Proposed Method

Our proposed method to detect facial micro-expressions combines the optical flow model with the LSTM network. We will further explain these in detail. The experimental method was shown in Fig. 1.

3.1 Extracting Feature Curves

In this section, we present the framework of our proposed method for feature curves extraction. An overview of our method is show in Fig. 2.

Image Jittering Elimination. During the training phase, image jittering problem is inevitable which may interfere the tracking of feature points. The jittering is usually caused by video capture environment such as stroboflash from fluorescent lamp. Histogram matching method is used to eliminate the brightness jitter of the image.

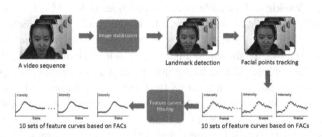

Fig. 2. Work flow diagram for the proposed feature curves extraction method

Video Sequence Segmentation. Optical flow can capture the facial motion vector between adjacent frames. However, when using optical flow method, one major challenge is feature points tracking error keep accumulate as the number of tracking frames increases. Besides, another challenge in micro-expression detection is the lack of micro-expression samples. Therefore, a sliding window strategy was developed to avoid accumulative error and expand micro-expression samples, as shown in Fig. 3.

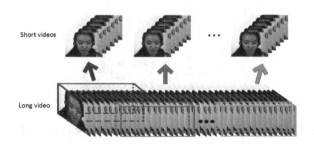

Fig. 3. Diagram of long video sequence segmentation processing

Let M = $\{m_1, m_2, \ldots m_l\}$ represent the set of all micro-expression long video samples, l is the number of micro-expression long video samples. The ith sample video is given by $m_i = \{X_{i1}, X_{i2} \cdots X_{in}\}$, where X_{ij} is the jth frame and n is the frame number of m_i.

First, the m_i was processed through a sliding window (SW). The length of the sliding window L is calculated as follows:

$$L = 0.2a + 1 \tag{1}$$

Where a is the frame rate of the input video. We use 1/5 as the coefficient of the frame rate, because the micro-expressions typically last 1/25-1/5 s [1]. Thus, when a micro-expression occurs, we can capture a complete micro-expression movement through a sliding window.

Facial Points Tracking. Ensemble of regression trees (ERT) [13] is used to detect 68 facial landmarks on the first image, then 41 facial landmarks were selected as shown in Fig. 4 and track them through the sequence using the Pyramid-Lucas-Kanade (PLK) algorithm [14], as shown in Fig. 2. The selection of 41 facial landmarks is because 17 facial contour landmarks are not stable and not helpful for represent facial expressions, so we remove them from 68 landmarks. In addition, in the field of micro-expression research, there is no clear definition of the expression represented by blinks. Taking the above reason into account, the inner corner landmark was the only one that tracked in the eye area since it is more stable [15]. As a result, 10 more facial landmarks were excluded.

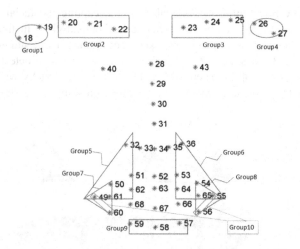

Fig. 4. Venn diagram of facial landmark groups based on FACS system

Window size is a parameter that defines the size of a small region of interest for calculating local continuous motion, which determines tracking performance of PLK algorithm. An appropriate window size can cover the exact location of the point. We set different window sizes based on different regions of the face. Details are as follows:

$$E = [0.1d + 0.5]$$
$$T = [0.73d + 0.5] \tag{2}$$
$$O = [0.7d + 0.5]$$

Where E, T, O represent the window size of the eye area, mouth area and nose area. All of these windows are squares. d is the Euclidean distance between two inner corners of eyes and plus 0.5 is for rounding. These coefficients (0.1, 0.73, 0.7) we used here was inspired by Patel et al. [9]. But different from their work, we combine the morphological proportions of the human body to calculate the value of the coefficients, and this process can reduce the impacts caused by individual facial differences. E, T and O were calculated adaptively through the distance between two inner corners of eyes.

Synthesis of Feature Curve Based on FACS. FACS is a scientific system used to measure movements of human face. It is a common standard for systematic classification of physical expression of emotions and has been shown to be useful to psychologists [16].

FACS Based Grouping. Optical flow vectors of each landmark can be grouped based on AU (action units) of FACS system [7]. The grouping method of landmarks was inspired by Patel et al. [9]. Figure 4 shows a Venn diagram illustrating the grouping principle of feature points. In normal circumstances, a person's true feelings can easily be exposed through changes in eyebrows and mouth, so we subdivide eyebrows into inner eyebrows and outer eyebrows, and subdivide mouth area by its muscle group distribution. Besides, the micro-expression may be asymmetric, so the eyebrow area is divided into 4 groups and the mouth area is divided into 6 groups.

Feature Curve Extraction. Relative motion between adjacent frames was computed as feature values, then feature curve was generated by the series of feature values in the whole sequences. The detailed calculation process is as follows:

- Calculation of the motion vector between adjacent frames of a video. The relative motion vector R is calculated as Eq. (3). When the video frame number i equals zero, the relative motion vector R_1 will be initialized to 0. When the video frame number i is greater than 0, the relative motion vector R is calculated by the location of feature point P in adjacent frame.

$$\begin{cases} R_{i+1}^{j}(x,y) = P(x_{i+1}^{j}, y_{i+1}^{j}) - P(x_i^{j}, y_i^{j}) & 1 \leq i \leq n \\ R_{i+1}^{j}(x,y) = 0 & i = 0 \end{cases} \tag{3}$$

P is a feature point tracked by optical flow algorithm. Where $i = 0, 1, 2, \cdots, n$, and n is the frame number of the video. The parameter $j = 1, 2, \cdots, 41$ denotes facial landmarks.

- A cumulative calculation of the relative motion vectors is performed to update the motion vectors of the current frame, as shown in Eq. (4).

$$F_i^j(x,y) + = R_i^j(x,y) \tag{4}$$

- Calculate the amplitude of 41 feature vectors separately in each frame, just as Eq. (5), then obtain the amplitude of each frame by Eq. (6).

$$\|F_i^j\| = \sqrt{x^2 + y^2} \tag{5}$$

$$\|F_i\| = \sum_{j=1}^{41} \|F_i^j\| \tag{6}$$

When a sequence of micro-expression video is entered, the video is presented in a series of continuous feature values, which can be fitted into a feature curve, we named it an optical flow feature curve (Fig. 2). As shown in Fig. 4, based on the FACS system, we can get 10 sets of feature curves based on 10 AU groups after video segmentation. With the increase of micro-expression duration, the magnitude of the feature points extracted by optical flow algorithm increases, resulting in an increase of the area under the optical flow feature curve.

Filtering Feature Curves. PLK algorithm is used to get motion vectors of adjacent frame. But head movements and image noises may cause errors in PLK algorithm. Following series of post-processing steps can reduce errors of PLK.

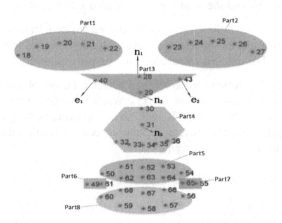

Fig. 5. A feature point partition diagram for motion error correction.

Head Movements Removal. Since inner eye corners and nasal spine point are stable and immune to facial expressions [15]. We selected them for computing the head translation and rotation. After testing plenty of micro-expression video sequences, we select nasal spine motion vector D_i as the head translation vector, and the motion vector

Rot_i of the middle point of the two eyes as the head rotation vector. The motion vector K of the middle point of the eyes is calculated as Eq. (8).

$$D_{i+1}(x,y) = P_{i+1}^{n_0}(x,y) - P_i^{n_0}(x,y) \tag{7}$$

$$K_i(x,y) = \frac{1}{2}\left(P_i^{e_1}(x,y) + P_i^{e_2}(x,y)\right) \tag{8}$$

$$Rot_{i+1}(x,y) = K_{i+1}(x,y) - K_i(x,y) \tag{9}$$

Where P_i represents the feature point of the ith frame tracked by the optical flow algorithm, n_0 represents the location of the nasal spine landmark, and e_1, e_2 represents the location of inner eye corners landmarks.

By subtracting the translation vector and rotation vector, errors caused by head translation and horizontal rotation can be reduced. This greatly improves the stability of the detection results.

Tracking Error Detection and Correction. In order to further improve the accuracy of feature points tracking and prevent tracking errors caused by image noise, we design a partition neighbor motion replacement strategy, which use motions of adjacent feature points to replace failed-tracking motions. The detail of how tracking failure is detected is explained below. The above method is used to produce more stable tracking efficiency. The partitioning method is shown in Fig. 5.

For the eye triangle region (part3 in Fig. 5), when the motion amplitude of the feature vectors is greater than 0.002d, Eq. (10) is performed. Where d refers to the Euclidean distance of the inner corner, and the parameters n_1, n_2 are two landmarks on the bridge of the nose closest to the corner of the eye, F refers to the relative motion vector of the current frame and the initial frame.

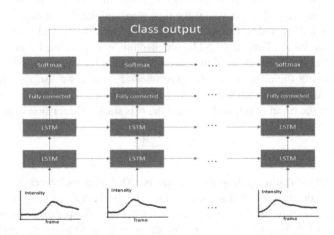

Fig. 6. The architecture of our LSTM network

$$F_i^j(x,y) = \frac{1}{2}(F_i^{n_1}(x,y) + F_i^{n_2}(x,y)), \text{ for } j \in (e_1, e_2) \tag{10}$$

For other regions of the facial, when the relative motion intensity of the feature point changes by more than $0.03d$, the movement of the point is considered to be deviated. To correct that, we use the relative motion results of the nearest neighbor point instead. The coefficient 0.002 and 0.03 is based on experimental tests. And the use of d takes individual facial differences into account.

Normalization. After above two steps, we select the distance from nasal root feature point n_1 to nasal spine feature point n_0 as the normalized distance. The normalization process is shown in Eq. (11). $Vec_i^{\,j}$ (x, y) is relative motion vector of the jth feature point in the ith frame by using post-processing, where $\|N_i\|$ is value of the modulo operation on N_i, F refers to the relative motion vector of current frame and initial frame.

$$N_i(x,y) = F_i^{n_1}(x,y) - F_i^{n_0}(x,y)$$

$$Vec_i^j(x,y) = \frac{F_i^j(x,y) - D_i(x,y) - Rot_i(x,y)}{\|N_i\|} \tag{11}$$

3.2   Feature Curves Classification

In this paper, LSTM network was used as the classifier for micro-expression detection. Figure 6 illustrate the network architecture used in subsequent sections, starting from the input data layer and ending with the class output layer. At each moment, the input of the network is a feature curve include 40 consecutive feature values. The first LSTM layer with 30 neurons to extract the characteristics of the feature curve data. Its output is a high-dimensional data eigenvalue matrix, which the first dimension is the size of input batches, the second dimension is the time step, and the third dimension represents the number of hidden nodes. Unlike the first LSTM layer, the second layer returns only the last output value. Then the LSTM architecture is completed by an output fully connected layer, followed by a softmax layer and finally the classification output layer.

To improving the accuracy of the experimental results, we use z-score standardization method to process feature curves of network input. The formula is as follows, where the μ is the mean of original data and the σ is standard deviation of original data.

$$x = \frac{x - \mu}{\sigma} \tag{12}$$

To prevent overfitting, a dropout structure is added after each layer of the LSTM. It can randomly delete some hidden layer nodes in the neural network, but retain the weight of the nodes to provides convenience for the next sample processing. The drop factor value is 0.5. Furthermore, we use gradient clipping to avoid the exploding and vanishing gradients problem. The threshold intervals are performed from -1 to 1.

4 Experimental Results

We next present experiments and discuss our results. We used two benchmark Facial Action Coding System (FACS) coded databases here: CASMEII [17] and SAMM [18].

4.1 Datasets

CASMEII [17] is a comprehensive spontaneous micro-expression database consists of 247 spontaneous facial micro-expressions from 35 subjects with Point Grey GRAS-03K2C camera. Frame resolution in CASMEII videos is 640 × 480 pixels.

SAMM [18] is a relatively new spontaneous micro-expression database containing 159 video samples from a diverse population of 32 participants. The resolution is set to 2048 × 1088, which is higher than that of CASMEII.

Both databases are recorded at frame rate of 200 fps. CASMEII provides long video clips include extra frames before onset frame and after offset frame. But SAMM only including frames from onset to offset.

4.2 Constructing the Data Set

We use spontaneous micro-expressions video sequences from the CASMEII or SAMM dataset to construct a binary classification database. The index of the onset and offset frames of each video sequence is known. Onset frame is the moment when muscles contraction and facial changes become stronger, and the offset frame is the moment where muscles are relaxing and the face expression disappears [15]. Positive samples are frame sequence from onset to offset which include micro-expressions. Negative samples are complementation of frames between onset and offset which without micro-expressions include in.

4.3 Parameters

The window length is 41, which base on the frame rate of videos in database is 200 fps.

The sliding step is set to 5. Each window includes landmarks updating and 41 times tracking by PLK algorithm. After that we get a feature curve of a video sequence consisting of 41 feature values. Then, we remove the first feature point of the obtained feature curve since there is no magnitude of the point. Thus, the input to the LSTM network was a feature curve with 40 feature values.

We train the network using Adam algorithm to minimize the cross-entropy loss. We trained 600 epochs with learning rate 0.00003. The database is divided into a training set and test set, and the sample labels are processed by one-hot to correspond the samples. The network training is done with the TensorFlow backend.

We conducted the following two sets of experiments:

- Single domain experiment involving only one micro-expression database (CASMEll).
- Cross domain experiment involving two micro-expression databases (CASMEll and SAMM), specifically, a database combines all positive and negative samples of two databases (SAMM contains only positive samples).

4.4   Results

Our method achieves an accuracy rate of 89.87% in the single database experiment and achieves 87.30% accuracy in the cross-database experiment. Table 1 provides a comparison to the state-of-the-art algorithms on CASMEll and SAMM, where Mag refers to the method of Eulerian video magnification [19]. It should be noted that Li et al. [5] focused on micro-expression classification and peak frame detection in a video sequence has been determined to have micro-expressions. Their method has achieved very good results. * are experimental results achieved by using Li et al. method [5]. To avoid evaluation error, we use five-fold stratified sampling cross-validation.

Table 1. Results of micro-expression detection of our method compare to state-of-the-art

Method		CASMEll	CASMEll + SAMM
PLK + LSTM	This paper	89.87%	87.30%
HOG3D + Mag	Li et al. [5]	85.33%*	85.89%*
LBP-TOP + Mag	Li et al. [5]	80.09%*	81.70%*

4.5   Runtime

The extraction of feature curves is implemented in Visual Studio and executed on an Intel Xeon E5-2620 CPU @ 2.10 GHz, using 64-bit Windows 10 and 64 GB RAM. The LSTM is training on a NVidia GeForce GTX 1080 GPU. It takes 1.48 s average to predict whether there was a micro-expression in a 41-frames video sequence and the frame rate is about 28 fps. Still pictures shown at 16 frames per second are seen by the human eye as continuous. In our experiment, the video frame rate reached 28 fps, which met the real-time requirements. Table 2 shows that the most of the time spent during the forecast period is used for the Pyramid-Lucas-Kanade (PLK) algorithm.

Table 2. Time required for prediction of each component

Component	Runtime
Landmark detection	250 ms
PLK algorithm	720 ms
Image stabilization	120 ms
LSTM	1.62 ms
Anything else	390 ms

5   Conclusion

In this paper, we proposed a novel method for detecting micro-expressions from long videos. This method combines landmark detection and optical flow tracking (PLK algorithm) to generate optical flow vectors, and then sliding window strategy was used to obtain feature curves based on FACS. Furthermore, the refined feature curves can be obtained by applying a series of post-processing steps referred to as the filter-feature-curves method. Finally, we used LSTM to classify feature curves. We validated the proposed method on CASMEII and SAMM databases, and the results suggest that our method are well suited for micro-expressions detection and even for applications that require real-time performance.

Future work will focus on the following three-fold. First, further improve the runtime performance of micro-expression detection. Secondly, the current micro-expression databases do not define a specific expression of blinking, however, according to psychological studies, some blinks might reveal repressed emotions. In the future, new spontaneous micro-expression databases with richer emotions will be needed to help us achieve better results. Thirdly, in future works we plan to develop real-time algorithm that can jointly detect micro-expression, macro expression, and neutral expression.

Acknowledgement. This research is supported in part by The Director Foundation Project of National Engineering Laboratory for Public Safety Risk Perception and Control by Big Data (PSRPC), in part by funding from Beijing Key Laboratory for Mental Disorders, and in part by China Postdoctoral Science Foundation (No. 2018M641437).

References

1. Ekman, P.: Micro Expression Training Tool (METT) and Subtle Expression Training Tool (SETT). Paul Ekman Company, San Francisco, CA (2003)
2. Matsumoto, D., Hwang, H.S.: Evidence for training the ability to read micro-expressions of emotion. Motiv. Emot. **35**(2), 181–191 (2011)
3. Brinke, P.L.T.: Reading between the lies: identifying concealed and falsified emotions in universal facial expressions. Psychol. Sci. **19**(5), 508–514 (2008)
4. Liong, S.T., See, J., Wong, K., Le Ngo, A.C., Oh, Y.H., Phan, R.: Automatic apex frame spotting in micro-expression database. In: 2015 3rd IAPR Asian Conference on Pattern Recognition (ACPR), pp. 665–669. IEEE (2015)
5. Li, X., et al.: Towards reading hidden emotions: a comparative study of spontaneous micro-expression spotting and recognition methods. IEEE Trans. Affect. Comput. **9**(4), 563–577 (2018)
6. Shreve, M., Godavarthy, S., Manohar, V., Goldgof, D., Sarkar, S.: Towards macro-and micro-expression spotting in video using strain patterns. In: 2009 Workshop on Applications of Computer Vision (WACV), pp. 1–6. IEEE (2009)
7. Friesen, E., Ekman, P.: Facial action coding system: a technique for the measurement of facial movement, Palo Alto, 3 (1978)
8. Yan, W.-J., Wang, S.-J., Chen, Y.-H., Zhao, G., Fu, X.: Quantifying micro-expressions with constraint local model and local binary pattern. In: Agapito, L., Bronstein, M., Rother, C.

(eds.) ECCV 2014. LNCS, vol. 8925, pp. 296–305. Springer, Cham (2015). https://doi.org/10.1007/978-3-319-16178-5_20

9. Patel, D., Zhao, G., Pietikäinen, M.: Spatiotemporal integration of optical flow vectors for micro-expression detection. In: Battiato, S., Blanc-Talon, J., Gallo, G., Philips, W., Popescu, D., Scheunders, P. (eds.) ACIVS 2015. LNCS, vol. 9386, pp. 369–380. Springer, Cham (2015). https://doi.org/10.1007/978-3-319-25903-1_32

10. Li, X., Yu, J., Zhan, S.: Spontaneous facial micro-expression detection based on deep learning. In: 2016 IEEE 13th International Conference on Signal Processing (ICSP), pp. 1130–1134. IEEE (2016)

11. Zhang, Z., Chen, T., Meng, H., Liu, G., Fu, X.: SMEConvNet: a convolutional neural network for spotting spontaneous facial micro-expression from long videos. IEEE Access 6, 71143–71151 (2018)

12. Verburg, M., Vlado M.: Micro-expression detection in long videos using optical flow and recurrent neural networks. arXiv preprint arXiv:1903.10765 (2019)

13. Kazemi, V., Sullivan, J.: One millisecond face alignment with an ensemble of regression trees. In: Proceedings of the IEEE Conference on Computer Vision and Pattern Recognition, pp. 1867–1874 (2014)

14. Bouguet, J.Y.: Pyramidal implementation of the affine Lucas Kanade feature tracker description of the algorithm. Intel Corp. 5(1–10), 4 (2001)

15. Valstar, M.F., Pantic, M.: Fully automatic recognition of the temporal phases of facial actions. IEEE Trans. Syst. Man Cybern. Part B (Cybern.) 42(1), 28–43 (2012)

16. Hamm, J., Kohler, C.G., Gur, R.C., Verma, R.: Automated facial action coding system for dynamic analysis of facial expressions in neuropsychiatric disorders. J. Neurosci. Methods 200(2), 237–256 (2011)

17. Yan, W.J., et al.: CASME II: an improved spontaneous micro-expression database and the baseline evaluation. PLoS ONE 9(1), e86041 (2014)

18. Davison, A.K., Lansley, C., Costen, N., Tan, K., Yap, M.H.: SAMM: a spontaneous micro-facial movement dataset. IEEE Trans. Affect. Comput. 9(1), 116–129 (2018)

19. Wu, H.Y., Rubinstein, M., Shih, E., Guttag, J., Durand, F., Freeman, W.: Eulerian video magnification for revealing subtle changes in the world (2012)

A Global-Matching Framework
for Multi-View Stereopsis

Wendong Mao, Minglun Gong$^{(\boxtimes)}$, Xin Huang, Hao Cai, and Zili Yi

Department of CS, Memorial University of Newfoundland, St. John's, Canada
{wm0330,gong,xhuang,hc1864,yz7241}@mun.ca

Abstract. As deep neural network demonstrated its success on various Computer Vision problems, a number of approaches have been proposed for applying it to multi-view stereopsis. Most of these approaches train networks over small cropped image patches so that the requirements on GPU's processing power and memory space are manageable. The limitation of such approaches, however, is that the networks cannot effectively learn global information and hence have trouble handling large textureless regions. In addition, when testing on different datasets, these networks often need to be retrained to achieve optimal performances. To address this incompetency, we present in this paper a robust framework that is trained on high-resolution (1280×1664) stereo images directly. It is therefore capable of learning global information and enforcing smoothness constraints across the whole image. To reduce the memory space requirement, the network is trained to output the matching scores of different pixels under each depth hypothesis at a time. A novel loss function is designed to properly handle the unbalanced distribution of matching scores. Finally, trained over binocular stereo datasets only, we show that the network can directly handle the DTU multi-view stereo dataset and generate results comparable to existing state-of-the-art approaches.

Keywords: 3D reconstruction · CNN · MVS · Point cloud

1 Introduction

Visual information captured by optical sensors are normally stored as 2D images, from which 3D models can be inferred. Reconstructing 3D models from images captured under different perspectives based on stereo correspondence is termed as Multi-View Stereopsis (MVS). Substantial efforts have been made in this research field. A well established pipeline starts from imagery collection to model refinement [8].

Given a 3D point p captured by a set of images, supporting domains from neighboring images are used to compute p's 3D location under the epipolar constraint. Although traditional matching algorithms generate promising results, many attempts on training neural networks to select potential matching pairs have been made over the past few years. Unlike many state-of-the-art methods,

© Springer Nature Switzerland AG 2019
M. Vento and G. Percannella (Eds.): CAIP 2019, LNCS 11678, pp. 635–647, 2019.
https://doi.org/10.1007/978-3-030-29888-3_52

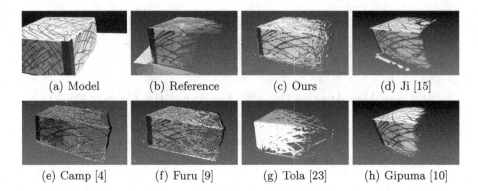

(a) Model   (b) Reference   (c) Ours   (d) Ji [15]

(e) Camp [4]   (f) Furu [9]   (g) Tola [23]   (h) Gipuma [10]

Fig. 1. Comparison with the state of the arts on 3D reconstruction for model 10 from the DTU dataset [1]. Our approach generates the most completed result.

which use local cropped image patches as input for training and enforce smoothness of depth values in post-processing stage, our framework aims at computing matching scores on entire images. This scheme allows pixels having the same depth value in the reference image to be computed at the same time and hence the global smoothness of the depth map can be learned by the neural network. To reconstruct the scene, each depth map is further integrated into a point cloud using the camera transformation matrix.

The main contributions of this paper are two-fold: (1) a novel network is presented that can learn global smoothness constraint and directly perform MVS matching based on global information; (2) the method is highly robust and can be applied to different image datasets without the needs for retraining, regardless how the resolution and depth range change. Based on the evaluation on the DTU dataset [1], the proposed approach outperforms all existing algorithms in terms of completeness and is comparable in terms of accuracy; see Fig. 1.

2   Related Work

Over the past decade, many practical approaches using traditional stereo algorithms for 3D modeling have been developed. Campbell et al. [4] utilized Normalised Cross-Correlation (NCC) to calculate patch-wise matching costs. To address false predictions in the depth maps caused by repeated texture, they enforced a spatial consistency constraint on neighboring pixels and demonstrated how to select accurate depth from multiple depth hypotheses using Markov Random Field (MRF) optimization. Furukawa and Ponce [9] proposed using photometric and visibility consistency to enhance the effectiveness of multi-view stereopsis based on epipolar geometry, and introduced two filtering steps to remove patches lying outside and inside the surface separately. For the usage of modeling applications, they further merged the collected patches into meshes through smoothness control.

The above approaches tend to assume that pixels within a supporting patch have constant depth and therefore may miscalculate depth values for slanted surfaces. Targeting this challenge, Bleyer et al. [2] introduced an effective algorithm referred to as PatchMatch, which initializes a random 3D plane for each pixel and gradually discovers the optimal plane through iterations of spatial and view propagation. As advanced optical sensors were developed to catch images with higher resolution, attempts were also made to accelerate the reconstruction process for stereopsis. Following the idea of PatchMatch, Galliani et al. [10] presented a novel diffusion-like approach which categorizes pixels into different groups as a checkerboard pattern so that high-resolution images can be addressed by an extensively parallel scheme implemented on GPU. Tola et al. [23] proposed using DAISY descriptors, which generate gradient histograms from different orientation layers, to efficiently implement similarity score computation on whole images, and directly selected matching pairs with notably larger scores than other candidates to generate depth maps. Moreover, depth prediction was performed on sparse areas first to restrict disparity searching range on neighboring pixels for fast performance. The past few years have witnessed a rapid expansion of learning-based approaches for 3D reconstruction. We here briefly group them into two categories: patch-wise and global matching.

2.1 Patch-Wise Methods

Inspired by the successful practice of patch-wise stereo matching within traditional algorithms, early learning-based approaches are devoted to using neural networks to replace window-based matching cost computation. Prosperous works [14,19,25,26] were first proposed to address binocular stereo matching and then extended to multi-view cases.

Galliani and Schindler [11] opted for the matching algorithm in [10] to generate initial 3D points and vector fields, and trained a convolutional neural network (CNN) model to perform normal prediction on raw image patches from multiple views. To obtain 3D models, depth and normal maps are merged together with Poisson reconstruction. The obtained surface normals are beneficial for reliable reconstruction of areas that have no valid MVS points. Huang et al. [13] presented a deep CNN model, which exploits the structure of U-net [21], to generate a bunch of plane-sweep volumes by performing stereo matching on 64×64 patches and further compute depth maps for MVS. Hartmann et al. [12] proposed to directly learn multi-patch similarity using n-way Siamese network architecture [3]. To enact this idea, a reference image patch together with multiple matching patches from neighboring views are assembled as an input sample for training. A similar work can be found in [24], where much wider patches and homography warping are harnessed to train an end-to-end deep learning framework. In addition, matching cost aggregation and depth map regression are integrated into the training pipeline. Ji et al. [15] proposed another end-to-end structure. They converted images to 3D voxel representations through projection and trained a CNN model, referred to as SurfaceNet, to predict each

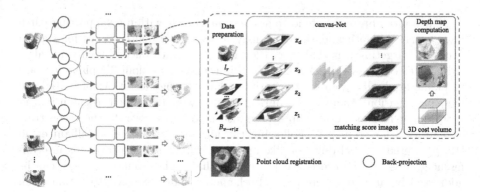

Fig. 2. MVS framework. Given a set of images with geometry parameters, fronto-parallel back-projections are first obtained to generate matching score images stored in a matching cost volume, from which depth and confidence maps are then computed and filtered for point cloud registration. In the depth maps, the warmer the color, the higher the predicted depth values are.

voxel's probability lying on the surface of models. SurfaceNet takes cropped voxel cubes as input, therefore the learning process is also based on local information.

Since patch-wise approaches generally perform prediction for each pixel individually, the computation cost tend to hinder their capability for larger datasets with high-resolution images. A solution [20] to accelerate patch-wise matching is to apply prediction only on image patches with enough vision cues at the cost of loss in completeness.

2.2 Global Methods

When it comes to objects lacking texture, patch-based approaches mostly require overall smoothness control during their post-processing steps. In contrast, this operation is automatically tackled by learning-based approaches using neural networks trained on global information. Inspiring results achieved on binocular stereo cases can be found within [5,16,18], but few attempts have been made to apply global matching on MVS. Performing global matching on multiple high-resolution images directly demands tremendous parallel computation resource, but separately applying two-view global matching on MVS presented in this paper is likely to be manageable.

3   Methodology

As discussed above, our approach is robust enough to handle different datasets without the need of retraining. It only requires that the input images have known intrinsic/extrinsic camera parameters and are lens-distortion corrected. All images from public stereo datasets, such as DTU [1], KITTI [17], and Middlebury [22], satisfy this requirement. A few notable differences among these datasets are image resolutions, experimental objects, and light conditions, which makes it challenging for a learning-based approach to process them without retraining. Note that camera calibration [27] can be additionally applied when lacking the above parameters. The overall pipeline of the proposed MVS approach is shown in Fig. 2. Given an MVS dataset, we use each image I_r as a reference image and locate its neighboring views. We then pair I_r with each of its neighboring views I_v to compute a depth map and an associated confidence map (Sect. 3.1). The former map provides us the best depth hypothesis for each pixel in I_r, whereas the latter indicates how likely this depth hypothesis is correct. The depth map computed using individual image pair can be noisy and hence we merge the depth/confidence maps computed using all I_r's neighboring views together to obtain a clean depth map under the image space of I_r (Sect. 3.2). Finally the clean depth maps computed under the image spaces of different views are registered into a 3D point cloud (Sect. 3.3).

3.1 Pair-Wise Image Matching

When matching points between a pair of images, the epipolar geometry defines that a 3D point seen in the reference image I_r only appears along the epipolar line in each neighboring view I_v. For a rectified binocular stereo image pair, the epipolar lines are parallel to scanlines. However, for general input images from multi-view stereo, the epipolar lines have arbitrary directions, making the search for matching points more difficult.

To simplify the problem, we back-project I_v to the fronto-parallel planes of I_r and maintain same resolution; see Fig. 3. Here we refer the image obtained through back-projecting I_v to the fronto-parallel planes of I_r at depth z as $B_{v \to r|z}$. Under this strategy, to find the matching pixel for a given pixel p in I_r, we only need to search among pixels at the same coordinates as p in $B_{v \to r|z}$ under different z values. In addition, 3D points having the same depth value with respect to I_r will find matches in the same back-projected image [7] and hence matching smoothness can be effectively enforced. Note that the same scheme can be also applied to binocular stereo pairs, where the back-projection only shifts the image along X axis, resulting matching pixels show at the same location on the corresponding back-projection plane.

3.2 Canvas-Net

As mentioned above, our goal is to train a neural network that can directly process high resolution stereo images from a variety of datasets. Since images from these datasets have different resolutions, we need the network to accommodate the highest resolution images. When the reference image I_r and back-projected images $B_{v \to r|z}$ have lower resolutions, we simply process them using the center portion of the network, without the need for scaling the images to match the network resolution. Here we refer to the network as canvas-Net and use $H_C \times W_C$ to denote the resolution of the network (canvas).

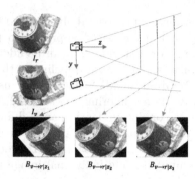

Fig. 3. Fronto-parallel back-projection. Given a reference image I_r and one of its neighboring view I_v, fronto-parallel planes at different depth z are used to back-project I_v toward the image space of I_r. The resulting images, referred to as $B_{v \rightarrow r|z}$, are used for searching matching pixels.

When training the canvas-Net, always placing I_r and $B_{v \rightarrow r|z}$ at the center of the canvas, however, will cause neurons in the area of missing data not properly trained. To address this problem, we randomly shift both I_r and $B_{v \rightarrow r|z}$ within the range of the canvas size. That is: $r_h = \text{rand}(e, H_C - h_I - e)$ and $r_w = \text{rand}(e, W_C - w_I - e)$, where the padding size $e = 5$ is set to exclude invalid convolutional operation on the edges, $h_I \times w_I$ is the resolution of I_r, r_h and r_w are random offsets used for shifting I_r and all back-projected images $B_{v \rightarrow r|z}$ in each training batch. Owing to image regularization in the previous stage, two canvases carrying grayscale information from the reference image I_r and one of its neighboring back-projected image $B_{v \rightarrow r|z}$ can be stacked together as a 3D canvas to be fed into our canvas-Net collaterally. Note that the input can be extended to accommodate RGB channels of images or one reference image with multiple back-projected images. The main goal of our model is to select all accurate matches between corresponding pixels in I_r and $B_{v \rightarrow r|z}$.

Our canvas-Net has a similar structure with U-net [21] but with a much larger receptive field; see Table 1. To accommodate high-resolution image pairs from all selected datasets in the $H_c \times W_C \times 2$ canvas, we set $H_C = 1280$ and $W_C = 1664$. This allows us to handle high-resolution images without the need for down-sampling them, a process that affects the accuracy of generated depth maps. For the reference image under each depth hypothesis, our canvas-Net outputs a matching score map to accentuate the locations of precisely matched pixels by marking them with higher confidence values.

To train the model for matching computation, stereo images with ground truth are desired. Since the input only consists of two layers, we can extract our training samples from multi-view and/or binocular imagery. Given I_r and $B_{v \rightarrow r|z=d}$, an ideal matching score image here should filter out all domains among them with same coordinates offering invalid depth estimation. In practice, a pixel (x, y) in the expected depth map is considered as mismatched *iff.* $\|D_t(x,y) - d\| > T$, where D_t denotes the ground truth and T is a threshold value. The model

Table 1. Parameters of the canvas-Net. Here "Conv", "Dconv", "Mp" and "⌢" denote convolutional, deconvolutional, max pooling and concatenation operation respectively. The final output can be compressed into a 1280×1664 canvas by excluding redundant dimensions.

Input	Operation	Kernel and channel	Stride	Output, size and channel
3D canvas	Conv	$1 \times 1 \times 2, 16$	$1 \times 1 \times 1$	O_1, $1280 \times 1664 \times 2, 16$
O_1	Conv	$5 \times 5 \times 1, 16$	$1 \times 1 \times 1$	O_2, $1280 \times 1664 \times 2, 16$
O_2	Conv	$5 \times 5 \times 2, 16$	$1 \times 1 \times 1$	O_3, $1280 \times 1664 \times 2, 16$
O_3	Conv	$5 \times 5 \times 2, 16$	$1 \times 1 \times 1$	O_4, $1280 \times 1664 \times 2, 16$
O_4	Mp	$2 \times 2 \times 2, 16$	$2 \times 2 \times 1$	O_5, $640 \times 832 \times 2, 16$
O_5	Conv	$5 \times 5 \times 2, 32$	$1 \times 1 \times 1$	O_6, $640 \times 832 \times 2, 32$
O_6	Mp	$2 \times 2 \times 2, 32$	$2 \times 2 \times 1$	O_7, $320 \times 416 \times 2, 32$
O_7	Conv	$5 \times 5 \times 2, 64$	$1 \times 1 \times 1$	O_8, $320 \times 416 \times 2, 64$
O_8	Mp	$2 \times 2 \times 2, 64$	$2 \times 2 \times 1$	O_9, $160 \times 208 \times 2, 64$
O_9	Conv	$5 \times 5 \times 2, 64$	$1 \times 1 \times 1$	O_{10}, $160 \times 208 \times 2, 64$
O_{10}	Mp	$2 \times 2 \times 2, 64$	$2 \times 2 \times 1$	O_{11}, $80 \times 104 \times 2, 64$
O_{11}	Conv	$5 \times 5 \times 2, 64$	$1 \times 1 \times 1$	O_{12}, $80 \times 104 \times 2, 64$
O_{12}	Mp	$2 \times 2 \times 2, 64$	$2 \times 2 \times 1$	O_{13}, $40 \times 52 \times 2, 64$
O_{13}	Dconv	$5 \times 5 \times 1, 64$	$2 \times 2 \times 1$	O_{14}, $80 \times 104 \times 2, 64$
$O_{14} ⌢ O_{12}$	Dconv	$5 \times 5 \times 1, 64$	$2 \times 2 \times 1$	O_{15}, $160 \times 208 \times 2, 64$
$O_{15} ⌢ O_{10}$	Dconv	$5 \times 5 \times 1, 64$	$2 \times 2 \times 1$	O_{16}, $320 \times 416 \times 2, 64$
$O_{16} ⌢ O_8$	Dconv	$5 \times 5 \times 1, 32$	$2 \times 2 \times 1$	O_{17}, $640 \times 832 \times 2, 32$
$O_{17} ⌢ O_6$	Dconv	$5 \times 5 \times 1, 32$	$2 \times 2 \times 1$	O_{18}, $1280 \times 1664 \times 2, 32$
$O_{18} ⌢ O_4$	Conv	$5 \times 5 \times 2, 6$	$1 \times 1 \times 1$	O_{19}, $1280 \times 1664 \times 2, 6$
O_{19}	Mp	$1 \times 1 \times 2, 6$	$1 \times 1 \times 2$	O_{20}, $1280 \times 1664 \times 1, 6$
O_{20}	Conv	$5 \times 5 \times 1, 1$	$1 \times 1 \times 1$	O_{21}, $1280 \times 1664 \times 1, 1$

is then trained to output "0" for each mismatched pixel and "1" the rest in the matching score image.

Unlike other attempts to improve U-net [21] by involving abundant layers and complicated substructures, the novelty of our canvas-Net lies in the well-designed scheme of loss calculation so that effective learning process can be performed without greatly increasing the computation cost. The loss function in U-net [21] cannot be directly adopted here, since it impartially addresses each pixel in the output and lacks a scheme to highlight those pixels that require more attention. To compute training loss between an estimated matching score image $S_{(e,d)}$ and its ground truth $S_{(t,d)}$, we first remove the peripheral regions generated by canvas fitting. The masks of "0" M_0 and "1" M_1 divided by T within $S_{(t,d)}$ are highly unbalanced, i.e., the output at most pixel locations should be "0" whereas only a small number of pixels should output "1". Hence, a coefficient mask M is introduced to counteract the amount variation. In addition, we select

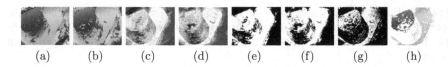

(a)   (b)   (c)   (d)   (e)   (f)   (g)   (h)

Fig. 4. Depth filtering. Two separated depth maps (a, b) and their confidence maps (c, d) are generated when the same reference is paired with different neighboring views. Their confidence masks (e, f) and depth variation mask (g) are computed by setting $G = 0.7$ and $V = 1.0$, and merged into one mask to filter out invalid values for precise estimation (h).

another threshold R in M_0 to isolate the minor mismatches forming mask M_a from the rest M_b by fulfilling $\|D_t(x, y) - d\| < R$, where R is slightly larger than T. We then compute M by:

$$M = (\frac{|M_0|M_1}{|M_1|} + w_1 \frac{|M_1+M_b|M_a}{|M_a|} + w_2 M_b)), \tag{1}$$

where $|U|$ is the size of set U. The two weight parameters w_1 and w_2 can be set additionally to achieve an optimal trade-off among all regional influences. Moreover, the training loss is computed by:

$$\text{loss} = \text{mean}(\|S_{(e,d)} - S_{(t,d)}\| \cdot M). \tag{2}$$

The canvas-Net trained above computes a set of matching score images stacked as a 3D cost volume $C_s(x, y, d)$ for each reference image. To generate the depth map $D_e(x, y)$, we here simply employ the Winner-Take-All (WTA) algorithm to select the best depth hypothesis for each pixel by $D_e(x, y) = \arg\max_d C_s(x, y, d)$.

3.3   Point Cloud Registration

For a reliable point cloud registration, we apply filtering on both $F_e(x, y)$ and $D_e(x, y)$ mentioned above to exclude the depth outliers and isolated points in the reconstruction stage.

Dramatic errors are likely to be generated when 3D points projected in I_r do not occur in other views. An effective method to partially remove them is to demand $F_e(x, y) > G$, where G is the minimum matching score required for a valid depth value. By assembling the same reference image I_r with different neighboring views, multiple depth maps together as P_e can be generated and combined for an optimal one $D_o(x, y)$, where each valid depth shares no more than a variation threshold V with all its candidates from P_e. This integration scheme further filter out more outliers; see Fig. 4.

A 3D point cloud can then be reconstructed by merging all pruned depth maps provided with the geometry parameters of camera views. For each registered point p, we utilize the k-Nearest-Neighbors (KNN) algorithm to search p's N closest neighbors and compute their mean distance. Isolated noisy points are not supported by their neighbors and hence their KNN generally spread over a large area, leading to high mean distance value. When the value is larger than a threshold K, the corresponding point will be eliminated from the point cloud.

4   Experimental Results

Our goal is to develop a robust approach that can handle different scenes without the needs for retraining the network. To validate whether we achieved this goal, the DTU [1] dataset, which consists of a large variety of scenes compared to other accessible MVS datasets, is selected for testing. In addition, we deliberately chose to use binocular stereo datasets, KITTI [17] and Middlebury [22], to train our network. This is a more challenging experimental setup than existing approaches that retrain the network before testing it on a given dataset. An added benefit of this setup is to avoid overfitting. The multi-view images from DTU are limited to objects in an experimental environment under stable lighting conditions. Combining KITTI and Middlebury, by contrast, populates the training dataset with indoors and outdoors scenes and facilitates feature extraction capability.

The algorithm is implemented with Tensorflow on a GTX 1080 Ti GPU. We generate 4,000 training samples with random offsets for each training epoch, and a stable state is achieved after 20 epochs by embedding an exponentially decreasing learning rate from 0.005 to 0.00001. Additionally, $T = 1.0$, $R = 3.0$, $w_1 = 0.5$ and $w_2 = 0.5$ are set to calculate the loss, and the entire process takes about 4 days to complete. When applying our canvas-Net on DTU, it takes around $0.3s$ to generate each matching score map.

4.1   Testing on DTU

The DTU dataset [1] contains 124 experimental scenes in total, and 49 fixed positions are set up for the most part to capture views from different perspectives. For a fair and direct comparison with existing approaches, we chose two metrics, *accuracy* and *completeness* in [1], to evaluate our approach. The former is specified by measuring the Euclidean distance from a point cloud to its ground truth and vice versa for the latter. The better performance of the algorithm, the lower the values for both metrics. All results here are built on the calibrated

Table 2. Evaluation on model 13 in [1] under different settings.

$U_z(mm)$	$K(mm)$	$|P_e|$	Accuracy	Completeness	Method	Accuracy	Completeness
	Settings				Ji [15]	0.417	3.974
1.0	3.0	2	0.526	**3.848**	Camp [4]	0.477	4.517
0.5	1.5	2	0.441	3.954	Furu [9]	0.406	4.943
0.5	3.0	2	0.460	3.879	Tola [23]	**0.313**	5.041
0.5	3.0	3	0.369	4.359	Gipuma [10]	0.340	5.630

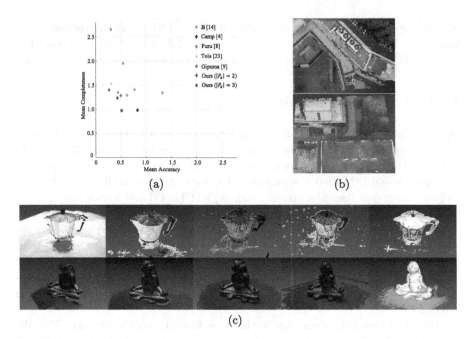

(a)   (b)

(c)

Fig. 5. Qualitative comparison using 22 models [1] on completeness v.s. accuracy plot (a) shows that our framework outperforms state-of-the-art approaches on mean completeness. Visual comparisons (c) show the ground truth (1st column), our results (2nd column), and the point clouds generated by [4,9,23], respectively. The proposed MVS framework is also used for reconstructing large scale outdoor scenes (b).

1200×1600 images with both internal and external camera parameters. To comply with the trained model above, each reference image, along with one of its neighboring views, is regulated as an input pattern for testing. With regards to DTU, we set the sampling unit $U_z = 0.5$ mm along the Z axis when generating the back-projected images. To remove invalid depth estimates precipitated by WTA, we set $G = 0.7$ and $V = 1.0$ and reconstruct the initial point clouds; see Table 2 for more parameter settings.

4.2 Quantitative Comparison

When applying patch-wise CNN models as in [6,13,20,24] on the DTU [1] dataset, it is barely manageable to generate quantitative results since a large amount of high-resolution images are captured for each scene. In addition, existing binocular global-matching algorithms [5,14,16,18] lack the flexibility to address resolution and depth range variations. Therefore, we here focus our comparison with 3 traditional algorithms [4,9,23] and 2 learning-based methods [10,15]. Note that the latter two approaches are directly trained on DTU, and therefore scenes selected for evaluation require to be isolated from their training data. For a fair comparison, we chose the same 22 scenes suggested in [15].

Mean accuracy and completeness are calculated for all selected scenes. Although direct numerical comparison based on either metric can be made, a accuracy v.s. completeness plot is used here to compare different algorithms on both aspects; see Fig. 5(a). The proposed framework makes full use of global feature correlation and therefore is more capable of performing stereo matching when lacking vision cues. Figure 5(c) visually compares the point clouds produced by different approaches.

4.3 Real-World Application

We intend to present a cross-library framework to eliminate the needs for retraining when handling different datasets. To verify this, we also directly applied the canvas-Net trained the above to the task of reconstructing large scale outdoor scenes captured by a DJI drone. Even though the input images (750 × 1000 in resolution) barely resemble our training data, our framework still successfully reconstructs dense 3D point clouds; see Fig. 5(b).

5   Conclusions

A competent learning-based MVS approach is presented in this paper. Unlike existing learning-based methods that work at patch level, the network in our approach is trained over the entire high-resolution images. As a result, the network can learn global features and implicitly enforce global smoothness constraint. Novel data preparation approach and loss function are proposed to reduce memory requirement and handle imbalanced classes. The experiments demonstrate the robustness of the proposed approach. When training on binocular datasets (KITTI and Middlebury) and tested on multi-view dataset (DTU), our approach achieved overall best performance in terms of completeness vs. accuracy among the state-of-the-art approaches. For future research, more multi-view datasets will be selected for training and evaluation.

References

1. Aanæs, H., Jensen, R.R., Vogiatzis, G., Tola, E., Dahl, A.B.: Large-scale data for multiple-view stereopsis. Int. J. Comput. Vis. **120**, 153–168 (2016)
2. Bleyer, M., Rhemann, C., Rother, C.: Patchmatch stereo-stereo matching with slanted support windows. In: BMVC, vol. 11, pp. 1–11 (2011)
3. Bromley, J., Guyon, I., LeCun, Y., Säckinger, E., Shah, R.: Signature verification using a "siamese" time delay neural network. In: Advances in Neural Information Processing Systems, pp. 737–744 (1994)
4. Campbell, N.D.F., Vogiatzis, G., Hernández, C., Cipolla, R.: Using multiple hypotheses to improve depth-maps for multi-view stereo. In: Forsyth, D., Torr, P., Zisserman, A. (eds.) ECCV 2008. LNCS, vol. 5302, pp. 766–779. Springer, Heidelberg (2008). https://doi.org/10.1007/978-3-540-88682-2_58

5. Chang, J.R., Chen, Y.S.: Pyramid stereo matching network. In: Proceedings of the IEEE Conference on Computer Vision and Pattern Recognition, pp. 5410–5418 (2018)
6. Choi, S., Kim, S., Sohn, K., et al.: Learning descriptor, confidence, and depth estimation in multi-view stereo. In: 2018 IEEE/CVF Conference on Computer Vision and Pattern Recognition Workshops (CVPRW), pp. 389–3896. IEEE (2018)
7. Collins, R.T.: A space-sweep approach to true multi-image matching. In: Proceedings CVPR IEEE Computer Society Conference on Computer Vision and Pattern Recognition, pp. 358–363. IEEE (1996)
8. Furukawa, Y., Hernández, C., et al.: Multi-view stereo: a tutorial. Found. Trends® Comput. Graph. Vis. 9(1–2), 1–148 (2015)
9. Furukawa, Y., Ponce, J.: Accurate, dense, and robust multiview stereopsis. IEEE Trans. Pattern Anal. Mach. Intell. 32(8), 1362–1376 (2010)
10. Galliani, S., Lasinger, K., Schindler, K.: Massively parallel multiview stereopsis by surface normal diffusion. In: Proceedings of the IEEE International Conference on Computer Vision, pp. 873–881 (2015)
11. Galliani, S., Schindler, K.: Just look at the image: viewpoint-specific surface normal prediction for improved multi-view reconstruction. In: Proceedings of the IEEE Conference on Computer Vision and Pattern Recognition, pp. 5479–5487 (2016)
12. Hartmann, W., Galliani, S., Havlena, M., Van Gool, L., Schindler, K.: Learned multi-patch similarity. In: 2017 IEEE International Conference on Computer Vision (ICCV), pp. 1595–1603. IEEE (2017)
13. Huang, P.H., Matzen, K., Kopf, J., Ahuja, N., Huang, J.B.: DeepMVS: learning multi-view stereopsis. In: Proceedings of the IEEE Conference on Computer Vision and Pattern Recognition, pp. 2821–2830 (2018)
14. Im, S., Jeon, H.G., Lin, S., Kweon, I.S.: DPSNet: end-to-end deep plane sweep stereo. In: International Conference on Learning Representations (2019)
15. Ji, M., Gall, J., Zheng, H., Liu, Y., Fang, L.: SurfaceNet: an end-to-end 3D neural network for multiview stereopsis. arXiv preprint arXiv:1708.01749 (2017)
16. Kendall, A., et al.: End-to-end learning of geometry and context for deep stereo regression. In: Proceedings of the International Conference on Computer Vision (ICCV) (2017)
17. Menze, M., Heipke, C., Geiger, A.: Joint 3D estimation of vehicles and scene flow. In: ISPRS Workshop on Image Sequence Analysis (ISA) (2015)
18. Pang, J., Sun, W., Ren, J.S., Yang, C., Yan, Q.: Cascade residual learning: a two-stage convolutional neural network for stereo matching. In: ICCV Workshops, vol. 7 (2017)
19. Park, H., Lee, K.M.: Look wider to match image patches with convolutional neural networks. IEEE Signal Process. Lett. 24(12), 1788–1792 (2017)
20. Poms, A., Wu, C., Yu, S.I., Sheikh, Y.: Learning patch reconstructability for accelerating multi-view stereo. In: Proceedings of the IEEE Conference on Computer Vision and Pattern Recognition, pp. 3041–3050 (2018)
21. Ronneberger, O., Fischer, P., Brox, T.: U-Net: convolutional networks for biomedical image segmentation. In: Navab, N., Hornegger, J., Wells, W.M., Frangi, A.F. (eds.) MICCAI 2015. LNCS, vol. 9351, pp. 234–241. Springer, Cham (2015). https://doi.org/10.1007/978-3-319-24574-4_28
22. Scharstein, D., et al.: High-resolution stereo datasets with subpixel-accurate ground truth. In: Jiang, X., Hornegger, J., Koch, R. (eds.) GCPR 2014. LNCS, vol. 8753, pp. 31–42. Springer, Cham (2014). https://doi.org/10.1007/978-3-319-11752-2_3
23. Tola, E., Strecha, C., Fua, P.: Efficient large-scale multi-view stereo for ultra high-resolution image sets. Mach. Vis. Appl. 23(5), 903–920 (2012)

24. Yao, Y., Luo, Z., Li, S., Fang, T., Quan, L.: MVSNet: depth inference for unstructured multi-view stereo. In: Ferrari, V., Hebert, M., Sminchisescu, C., Weiss, Y. (eds.) ECCV 2018. LNCS, vol. 11212, pp. 785–801. Springer, Cham (2018). https://doi.org/10.1007/978-3-030-01237-3_47
25. Ye, X., Li, J., Wang, H., Huang, H., Zhang, X.: Efficient stereo matching leveraging deep local and context information. IEEE Access **5**, 18745–18755 (2017)
26. Zbontar, J., LeCun, Y.: Stereo matching by training a convolutional neural network to compare image patches. J. Mach. Learn. Res. **17**(1–32), 2 (2016)
27. Zhang, Z.: A flexible new technique for camera calibration. IEEE Trans. Pattern Anal. Mach. Intell. **22**(11), 1330–1334 (2000). https://doi.org/10.1109/34.888718

Quality Analysis of Fingerprint Images Using Local Phase Quantization

Ram Prakash Sharma[✉] and Somnath Dey

Indian Institute of Technology Indore, Indore, India
{phd1501201003,somnathd}@iiti.ac.in

Abstract. The recognition performance of Automatic Fingerprint Identification System (AFIS) is immensely affected by the quality of the input fingerprint images. In a low-quality fingerprint image, various spurious minutiae points may be detected which may degrade the recognition performance of the AFIS system. Effective analysis of the low-quality fingerprint images prior to the fingerprint matching stage can aid in improving the recognition performance of the system. In this work, low quality fingerprint images are identified using a well known local textural descriptors called local phase quantization (LPQ). The local texture descriptors are gaining popularity due to their excellent performance and flexibility in analyzing the texture patterns. The experimental evaluations are carried out on low quality fingerprint images of publicly available FVC 2004 DB1 dataset. The achieved results show the high performance and robustness of the proposed method. As the proposed method outperforms the current state-of-the-art fingerprint classification methods, it can be utilized as a quality control unit during the fingerprint acquisition phase of the AFIS. The proposed method also has an advantage of computing only a single feature for fingerprint quality classification which makes it simple and fast approach.

Keywords: Biometrics · Fingerprint quality · Texture feature · Local phase quantization

1 Introduction

Fingerprint recognition is one of the most reliable and widely accepted biometric characteristics due to its high recognition performance, use of low-cost devices, non-invasiveness, distinctiveness, and permanence. Fingerprint recognition is widely adopted in various applications of personal identification, forensic investigations, e-commerce, border control, and airports, etc. However, the major problem in the fingerprint recognition is to provide accurate identification for the poor quality fingerprint images. In these poor quality fingerprint images, various spurious features (minutiae points) may be detected which can degrade the performance of the fingerprint recognition system. Therefore, it is essential to identify and process the poor quality fingerprint images before using them for

© Springer Nature Switzerland AG 2019
M. Vento and G. Percannella (Eds.): CAIP 2019, LNCS 11678, pp. 648–658, 2019.
https://doi.org/10.1007/978-3-030-29888-3_53

recognition. The fingerprint quality can be degraded due to various factors such as dryness, wetness, less or more pressure, dirt on the sensor, partial fingerprint images, and residual noise. The fingerprint sensors are sensitive to these factors. If any of these factors is/are present during the fingerprint acquisition, a low-quality fingerprint image will be acquired using the fingerprint sensor. In such scenarios, a quality improving feedback to the end-user can help to acquire a better quality fingerprint image. The obtained quality improving feedback can also be utilized for removing low-quality images, updating or replacing samples, and quality enhancement [17].

There are various on-going and past studies [1, 13, 27] for the estimation of fingerprint image quality. Most of the methods present in the literature either assign an overall quality score to the fingerprint images [21, 26] or label fingerprint images with a graded quality index i.e., high or low, good or bad [7, 18, 22, 25]. If the identification of the problem which causes the low quality of fingerprint images can be identified during the initial stage (fingerprint acquisition) of the fingerprint recognition, it can potentially help to improve the recognition performance of the system. Various recent studies of the fingerprint quality classification methods [2, 7, 10, 16, 23, 24] are present in the literature which identifies the cause of low quality of a fingerprint image. These methods utilize a classifier which is trained using ridge-based features such as ridge continuity, ridge line count, ridge fragmentation, ridge valley area uniformity, and ridge/valley ratio, etc. These existing methods require the computation of multiple quality-related features for analyzing the fingerprint texture quality. Also, there is not much research work done to detect the deficient quality of the fingerprint images. Therefore, the motive of this work is to propose a robust and high performing single feature based fingerprint texture quality classification method. The effective assessment of the fingerprint texture quality will help to acquire better quality fingerprint images during fingerprint acquisition of gallery fingerprint images. Consequently, it will improve the overall performance of the automatic fingerprint identification system (AFIS).

In this work, a powerful local texture descriptor called the local phase quantization (LPQ) [4] is utilized to analyze texture quality (dry, wet, and good) of the fingerprint images. The LPQ descriptor is invariant to blur and rotation which makes it a suitable feature for the texture classification of fingerprint images. The experimental evaluations are carried out on the publicly available FVC 2004 DB1 dataset. The fingerprint images of FVC 2004 DB1 dataset are divided into blocks of size 32×32. After that, support vector machine (SVM) classifier is trained using the LPQ features of dry, wet, and good quality fingerprint blocks marked by the human experts. Finally, the proposed block quality classification method is utilized iteratively to assign a suitable quality class to the fingerprint images of FVC 2004 DB1 dataset. The major contributions of the proposed work are highlighted in the following points:

- The proposed work identifies the low-quality fingerprint images using a well known local textural descriptors called local phase quantization (LPQ).

- The LPQ descriptor is invariant to blur and rotation. This makes it suitable for the texture quality classification of fingerprint images.
- Performance evaluations of the proposed block texture quality classification method affirm the suitability of the LPQ feature for fingerprint quality assessment.
- Experimental evaluations show that the proposed fingerprint quality classification method outperforms current state-of-the-art fingerprint quality classification methods.

The rest of the paper is organized as follows. In Sect. 2, related works of the fingerprint quality assessment are presented. Section 3 describes the proposed method for quality classification of fingerprint images. The experimental results are thoroughly discussed and compared with the current state-of-the-art in Sect. 4. Finally, the concluding remarks with future works are given in Sect. 5.

2   Related Works

The performance of fingerprint-based recognition systems is heavily influenced by the condition of the fingertip surface which varies based on the environmental conditions or other causes [1,27]. Here, an overview of some of the well-known and recent approaches of the fingerprint quality classification in terms of their quality nature i.e., dry, wet, good, etc. are presented.

Recently, Tertychnyi et al. [23] proposed a deep learning based method to classify the low-quality fingerprint images based on the various distortion such as dryness, wetness, etc. They have utilized VGG16- based deep network to recognize the low quality (dry, wet, etc.) fingerprint images. Wu et al. [24] proposed a ridge feature based dry fingerprint detection method. They have utilized ridge continuity, ridge fragmentation, and ridge/valley ratio features for the detection of dry fingerprint images. They have also utilized Random Forest (RF) and SVM classifier to test the performance of their approach. However, the performance of deep learning based model outperforms RF and SVM classifier. Wu et al. [24] proposed a dry fingerprint detection method using ridge features of fingerprint images with different resolution (500–1200 dpi). They have utilized ridge continuity, ridge fragmentation, and ridge/valley ratio features for the detection of dry fingerprint images. Finally, SVM classifier is used to classify fingerprint images into dry and normal quality classes. Sharma et al. [16] proposed a local (block-wise) fingerprint quality assessment method using various ridge based features, i.e., mean, variance, moisture, ridge valley area uniformity, and ridge line count. These features are utilized to classify the fingerprint images into good, dry, normal dry, normal wet, and wet quality classes using decision tree (DT) classifier. Awasthi et al. [2] proposed a block-based fingerprint quality impairment (dry, wet, and good) assessment method utilizing orientation and consistency based features, pixel intensity and directional contrast based features, and ridge based features. They have also given an overall quality score to fingerprint images utilizing the fraction of dry, wet, and good quality blocks in a fingerprint image. Munir et al. [10] proposed a fingerprint quality assessment method using hierarchical k-means clustering. In their approach, classification of fingerprint images into dry, wet, and normal quality classes is done using a set of statistical (mean, uniformity, smoothness, image inhomogeneity, etc.) and frequency (energy concentration) features. Another block-wise quality assessment method is proposed by Lim et al. [7]. They extracted directional strength, sinusoidal local ridge/valley pattern, ridge/valley uniformity, and core occurrences features from fingerprint blocks. Three different classifiers, namely self-organizing map (SOM), radial basis function neural network (RBFNN), and naive Bayes classifier are used to classify the fingerprint blocks into good and bad quality class. Olsen et al. [12] analyzed how fingerprint skin moisture affects the recognition performance of the system. Experimental evaluations on their in-house dataset show that a controlled level of moisture is essential to achieve good biometric performance. Labati et al. [6] proposed a method using Histogram of Oriented Gradients (HOG), mean, variance, gray-level co-occurrence matrix, and ridge orientation features to detects a set of non-ideal fingertip conditions such as dirt, grease, carrying a shoulder bag, carrying a handbag, and normal in Automated Border Control (ABC) systems. Other works analyzing the impact of fingerprint moisture on the recognition performance can be found in [19,20,28].

3   Proposed Method

Assessment of the fingerprint quality is an essential part of the AFIS to control or improve the quality of captured fingerprint images during fingerprint acquisition. The proposed work assesses the fingerprint quality using a well-known local texture descriptor called LPQ. The LPQ descriptor is invariant to blur and rotation which makes it a suitable feature for the texture classification of fingerprint images. The block diagram of the proposed fingerprint quality classification method is given in Fig. 1. The proposed method works in two phases (i) block texture quality classification and (ii) fingerprint texture quality classification. In the first stage, a block texture quality classification model is built to assess the dry, wet, and good quality nature of fingerprint blocks. In the second stage, the obtained block texture quality classification model is utilized iteratively to assign a suitable quality class to blocks of the fingerprint image. Based on the maximum membership of dry, wet, or good quality blocks, a fingerprint image is classified into dry, wet, and good class. In this work, three human experts have assigned the dry, wet, and good texture quality class to the fingerprint blocks. Sample blocks of different quality are given in the Fig. 2.

In literature, a large number of local texture image descriptors are present. In this work, we have utilized the well-known LPQ for quality classification of fingerprint images in dry, wet, and good quality classes. The description of the LPQ is given in the following section.

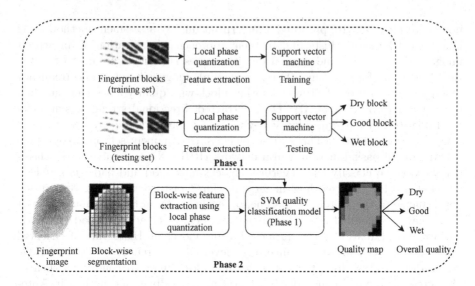

Fig. 1. Block diagram of the proposed method. Phase 1: Block texture quality assessment and Phase 2: Fingerprint texture quality assessment

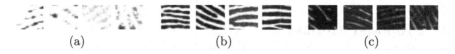

(a)   (b)   (c)

Fig. 2. Manually labeled blocks of (a) Dry (b) Good (c) Wet quality

3.1 Local Phase Quantization (LPQ)

The local phase quantization (LPQ) [11,14] was proposed for blur and rotation invariant texture classification. As per the description is given in [14], the patch surrounding the target pixel x is analyzed in the frequency domain by using short-time Fourier transform (STFT) analysis. The advantage of STFT is that the phase of the low-frequency coefficients is insensitive to centrally symmetric blur, which is found commonly in real images. In LPQ, the phase is computed in local neighborhoods N_x at each pixel position $x = [x_1, x_2]^T$ of the image $f(x)$ using Eq. 1.

$$F(u, x) = \sum f(y) w_R(y - x) e^{-j2\pi u^T \cdot y} \qquad (1)$$

Here, x, y are the spatial bi-dimensional coordinates and u represents the bi-dimensional spatial frequencies, $w_R(.)$ is a suitably compact window function defining the neighborhood N_x that enforces locality of the transform, and $F(u, x)$ is the output STFT around x. After this, the local Fourier coefficients are computed at four frequencies corresponding to the $0°$, $45°$, $90°$, and $135°$ directions, $u_0 = (a, 0)$, $u_1 = (a, a)$, $u_2 = (0, a)$, and $u_3 = (a, -a)$, where $a << 1$. The phase of $F_{(x)}$ is computed for each of these frequencies using Eq. 2.

$$F_{(x)} = [F(u_0, x), F(u_1, x), F(u_2, x), F(u_3, x)] \qquad (2)$$

The phase of the Fourier coefficients is computed by observing the signs of the real and imaginary parts of each component in $F(x)$ using a simple scalar quantization as given in Eq. 3.

$$q_j = \begin{cases} 1, & \text{if } g_j \geq 0. \\ 0, & \text{otherwise.} \end{cases} \tag{3}$$

Where g_j is the jth component of the vector $G(x) = [ReF(x), ImF(x)]$. This will result in an 8-bit feature vector $[q_1, \ldots, q_8]$ which can be converted into an integer value in the range $[0-255]$ using Eq. 4.

$$LPQ = \sum_{i=1}^{8} q_i 2^{i-1} \tag{4}$$

Finally, from all image positions, these integer values form a histogram. This histogram is used as a 256-dimensional feature vector for classification. The features of $F_{(x)}$ can also be viewed as the output phases of four Gabor filters oriented along directions $45°$ apart with proper choice of the parameters. This suggests that LPQ can effectively describe images having local wave-like behavior, like fingerprint and iris images. In [14], a rotation-invariant version of LPQ has also been proposed where the patch is preliminarily rotated along a characteristic direction $\beta(x)$ computed in advance. The average computational time required for feature extraction from a single image is 1.507 CPU time (seconds) and coding time of 0.03 CPU time (seconds) in matlab implementation [5]. Further details regarding the implementation of LPQ can be found in [11,14].

4   Experimental Results

The experimental results of the proposed fingerprint quality classification method are evaluated on the DB1 dataset of FVC 2004 database [8]. The fingerprints images of DB1 dataset of FVC 2004 are acquired by varying the conditions of fingertip surface (dry, wet, and normal). Therefore, this dataset is suitable for evaluating the performance of a fingerprint texture quality classification method. The FVC 2004 DB1 dataset contains eight samples of 100 fingers each which constitutes a dataset of 800 fingerprint images of dry, wet, and good quality.

4.1   Block Texture Quality Assessment

The performance of the block texture quality classification is evaluated on the blocks of FVC 2004 DB1 dataset. The dataset for assessment of block texture quality classification is constituted by partitioning the fingerprint images of FVC 2004 DB1 dataset into blocks of size 32×32. After the block partitioning, three human experts have marked 1000 blocks into each of the quality class (dry, wet, and good). Thereafter, a 256-dimensional feature vector is extracted using LPQ from the quality labeled blocks. Training and testing sets are constituted by using 5-fold cross-validation on each of the quality class. It results in 2400 blocks (800 of each quality class) for the training set and remaining 600 blocks (200 of each quality class) for testing the classification model. To evaluate the classification performance, SVM classifier [15] is used with radial basis function (RBF) kernel. The RBF kernel requires two parameters, namely C and γ which represent penalty and kernel parameters, respectively. The penalty parameter C controls the cost of misclassification of training examples against the simplicity of the decision surface. γ is the parameter of a Gaussian kernel to handle the non-linear classification problems. The optimal values of the parameter C and γ are obtained by grid search algorithm [3]. In our experiments, $C = 2$ and $\gamma = 0.0625$ are found as optimal resulting in the highest classification accuracy. The classification results of the block texture quality classification are presented in Table 1. Results indicate that the dry, good, and wet blocks are classified with the accuracy of 100%, 86.50%, and 99.00%, respectively. Overall classification accuracy of the proposed block texture quality classification is 95.16%. The comparative study of the proposed method is performed with Lim et al. [7] (using SOM, RBFNN, and naive Bayes classifiers) and Sharma et al. [16] methods. The Lim's et al. method [7] classifies the fingerprint blocks into good and bad quality classes. Therefore, to compare our proposed method with Lim's method, the dry and wet quality class are merged in bad quality class while good quality class remains the same. The comparative study reported in Table 2 indicates that the proposed method outperforms the other methods. The proposed approach achieves the highest 86.50% and 99.50% accuracy for the prediction of good and bad quality blocks, respectively.

Table 1. Experimental results of the block texture quality classification using LPQ features

		SVM			
		Dry	Good	Wet	Total
Subjective quality	Dry	**200**	0	0	200
	Good	3	**173**	24	200
	Wet	0	2	**198**	200
	Total	203	175	222	600
	Accuracy	100%	86.50%	99.00%	95.16%

4.2 Fingerprint Texture Quality Assessment

This section reports the experimental results of the fingerprint texture quality classification. As the fingerprint images of FVC 2004 DB1 dataset are acquired using a quality-based approach, the fingerprint images are classified into dry, good, and wet quality classes by three human experts. The block texture quality assessment method is used iteratively to assign the dry, wet or good quality

Table 2. Comparative evaluations of the block texture quality classification. Values in the brackets represents the accuracy.

Methods	Classifier	Quality		
		Good	Bad	Overall
Subjective quality	Manual	200	400	600
Proposed method	SVM	173 (86.50%)	**398 (99.50%)**	**571 (95.16%)**
Sharma et al. [16]	DT	**191 (95.50%)**	379 (94.75%)	570 (95.00%)
Lim et al. [7]	SOM	175 (87.50%)	359 (89.75%)	534 (89.00%)
Lim et al. [7]	RBFNN	186 (93%)	378 (94.50%)	564 (94.00%)
Lim et al. [7]	Naive Bayes	181 (90.50%)	375 (93.75%)	556 (92.66%)

class to foreground blocks of a fingerprint image identified using [9]. Based on the maximum membership of a particular quality class blocks, the fingerprint images are assigned to dry, wet, and good quality class. The obtained results are compared with subjective quality assigned by the human experts, Terty et al. [23] method, Awasthi et al. [2] method, and Munir et al. [10] method. The comparative results are reported in Table 3. To make all the methods comparable, the method proposed by Terty et al. [23] is used to classifies fingerprint images in dry, good, and wet quality classes. The fingerprint images belonging to normal quality in the Munir et al. [10] method are considered in the good quality class for the comparative analysis. The comparative results show that the proposed method achieves the best performance (92.87%) as compared with the other methods. These results indicate that the proposed method is more suitable for texture quality classification of fingerprint images. The quality map of some of the fingerprint images are shown in Fig. 3. Different colors are used to show the dry, good, and wet quality regions in a fingerprint image. Due to the variance based segmentation [9], some of the blocks around the boundary region of a fingerprint image are partial blocks (Fig. 3(b) and (c)), therefore, they are classified as dry. These maps can be shown to the users of AFIS system while fingerprint acquisition to provide a better quality fingerprint image by adjusting the conditions of their fingertip. The performance of AFIS can be improved by using this quality control approach.

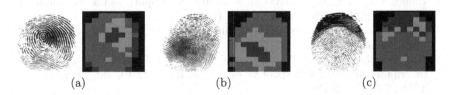

(a)	(b)	(c)

Fig. 3. Quality maps of some of the fingerprint images. Regions with red, green, and blue indicate dry, good, and wet quality, respectively. (Color figure online)

Table 3. Comparative results of the fingerprint texture quality classification for FVC 2004 DB1 dataset. Values in the brackets represents the accuracy.

	Quality class			
	Dry	Good	Wet	Overall
Subjective quality	187	441	172	800
Proposed method	**182 (97.32%)**	**393 (89.11%)**	**168 (97.67%)**	**743 (92.87%)**
Terty et al. [23]	175 (93.58%)	387 (87.75%)	163 (94.76%)	725 (90.62%)
Awasthi et al. [2]	174 (93.04%)	405 (91.83%)	159 (92.44%)	738 (92.25%)
Munir et al. [10]	169 (90.37%)	393 (89.11%)	168 (97.67%)	730 (91.25%)

5   Conclusion

In this work, a block-based fingerprint texture quality classification method is proposed using a well-known local texture descriptor called LPQ. The proposed method classifies the dry, wet, and good quality blocks with an average accuracy of 95.16% using SVM classifier. The assessment of overall fingerprint quality using the block texture quality classification method shows that it can classify the fingerprint images into appropriate quality class more accurately as compared with other recent methods. The proposed method also has an advantage of computing only a single feature for fingerprint quality classification which makes it simple and fast approach. In future work, the potential of other local texture descriptors can be evaluated for efficient texture quality assessment of the fingerprint images. Efficient assessment of fingerprint quality can work as a quality control unit during the fingerprint acquisition phase of the fingerprint recognition systems.

References

1. Alonso-Fernandez, F., et al.: A comparative study of fingerprint image-quality estimation methods. IEEE Trans. Inf. Forensics Secur. **2**(4), 734–743 (2007)
2. Awasthi, A., Venkataramani, K., Nandini, A.: Image quality quantification for fingerprints using quality-impairment assessment. In: IEEE Workshop on Applications of Computer Vision (WACV), pp. 296–302 (2013)
3. Chang, C.C., Lin, C.J.: LIBSVM: a library for support vector machines. ACM Trans. Intell. Syst. Technol. **2**(3), 1–27 (2011)
4. Chen, J., et al.: WLD: a robust local image descriptor. IEEE Trans. Pattern Anal. Mach. Intell. **32**(9), 1705–1720 (2010)
5. Gragnaniello, D., Poggi, G., Sansone, C., Verdoliva, L.: An investigation of local descriptors for biometric spoofing detection. IEEE Trans. Inf. Forensics Secur. **10**(4), 849–863 (2015)
6. Labati, R.D., Genovese, A., Ballester, E.M., Piuri, V., Scotti, F., Sforza, G.: Automatic classification of acquisition problems affecting fingerprint images in automated border controls. In: IEEE Symposium Series on Computational Intelligence, pp. 354–361 (2015)

7. Lim, E., Toh, K.A., Suganthan, P.N., Jiang, X., Yau, W.Y.: Fingerprint image quality analysis. In: International Conference on Image Processing (ICIP), vol. 2, pp. 1241–1244 (2004)
8. Maio, D., Maltoni, D., Cappelli, R., Wayman, J.L., Jain, A.K.: FVC2004: third fingerprint verification competition. In: Zhang, D., Jain, A.K. (eds.) ICBA 2004. LNCS, vol. 3072, pp. 1–7. Springer, Heidelberg (2004). https://doi.org/10.1007/978-3-540-25948-0_1
9. Mehtre, B.M.: Fingerprint image analysis for automatic identification. Mach. Vis. Appl. **6**(2), 124–139 (1993)
10. Munir, M.U., Javed, M.Y., Khan, S.A.: A hierarchical k-means clustering based fingerprint quality classification. Neurocomputing **85**, 62–67 (2012)
11. Ojansivu, V., Rahtu, E., Heikkila, J.: Rotation invariant local phase quantization for blur insensitive texture analysis. In: 2008 19th International Conference on Pattern Recognition, pp. 1–4 (2008)
12. Olsen, M.A., Dusio, M., Busch, C.: Fingerprint skin moisture impact on biometric performance. In: 3rd International Workshop on Biometrics and Forensics (IWBF 2015), pp. 1–6 (2015)
13. Olsen, M.A., Smida, V., Busch, C.: Finger image quality assessment features: definitions and evaluation. IET Biometrics **5**(2), 47–64 (2016)
14. Rahtu, E., Heikkilä, J., Ojansivu, V., Ahonen, T.: Local phase quantization for blur-insensitive image analysis. Image Vis. Comput. **30**(8), 501–512 (2012)
15. Schölkopf, B., Williamson, R., Smola, A., Shawe-Taylor, J., Platt, J.: Support vector method for novelty detection. In: Proceedings of the 12th International Conference on Neural Information Processing Systems, pp. 582–588 (1999)
16. Sharma, R.P., Dey, S.: Fingerprint image quality assessment and scoring. In: Ghosh, A., Pal, R., Prasath, R. (eds.) MIKE 2017. LNCS, vol. 10682, pp. 156–167. Springer, Cham (2017). https://doi.org/10.1007/978-3-319-71928-3_16
17. Sharma, R.P., Dey, S.: Two-stage quality adaptive fingerprint image enhancement using Fuzzy C-means clustering based fingerprint quality analysis. Image Vis. Comput. **83–84**, 1–16 (2019). https://doi.org/10.1016/j.imavis.2019.02.006
18. Shen, L.L., Kot, A., Koo, W.M.: Quality measures of fingerprint images. In: Bigun, J., Smeraldi, F. (eds.) AVBPA 2001. LNCS, vol. 2091, pp. 266–271. Springer, Heidelberg (2001). https://doi.org/10.1007/3-540-45344-X_39
19. Sickler, N.C., Elliott, S.J.: An evaluation of fingerprint image quality across an elderly population vis-a-vis an 18–25 year old population. In: Proceedings 39th Annual International Carnahan Conference on Security Technology, pp. 68–73 (2005)
20. Syam, R., Hariadi, M., Purnomo, M.H.: Determining the dry parameter of fingerprint image using clarity score and ridge-valley thickness ratio. IAENG Int. J. Comput. Sci. **38**(4), 350–357 (2011)
21. Tabassi, E.: Development of NFIQ 2.0. NIST (2015). https://www.nist.gov/services-resources/software/development-nfiq-20
22. Tabassi, E., Wilson, C.L.: A novel approach to fingerprint image quality. In: International Conference on Image Processing, vol. 2, pp. 37–40. IEEE (2005)
23. Tertychnyi, P., Ozcinar, C., Anbarjafari, G.: Low-quality fingerprint classification using deep neural network. IET Biometrics **7**(6), 550–556 (2018)
24. Wu, C., Chiu, C.: Dry fingerprint detection for multiple image resolutions using ridge features. In: IEEE International Workshop on Signal Processing Systems (SiPS), pp. 1–5, October 2017
25. Yang, X.K., Luo, Y.: A classification method of fingerprint quality based on neural network. In: International Conference on Multimedia Technology, pp. 20–23 (2011)

26. Yao, Z., Le Bars, J., Charrier, C., Rosenberger, C.: Quality assessment of fingerprints with minutiae delaunay triangulation. In: International Conference on Information Systems Security and Privacy (ICISSP), pp. 315–321 (2015)
27. Yao, Z., Le Bars, J.M., Charrier, C., Rosenberger, C.: Literature review of fingerprint quality assessment and its evaluation. IET Biometrics **5**(3), 243–251 (2016)
28. Zhao, Y., Jiang, C., Fang, X., Huang, B.: Research of fingerprint image quality estimation. In: IEEE International Conference on Dependable, Autonomic and Secure Computing, pp. 791–795 (2009)

Intrinsic Calibration of Depth Cameras for Mobile Robots Using a Radial Laser Scanner

David Zuñiga-Noël[(✉)], Jose-Raul Ruiz-Sarmiento,
and Javier Gonzalez-Jimenez

Machine Perception and Intelligent Robotics Group (MAPIR),
Department of System Engineering and Automation,
Instituto de Investigación Biomédica de Málaga (IBIMA),
University of Malaga, Malaga, Spain
{dzuniga,jotaraul,javiergonzalez}@uma.es

Abstract. Depth cameras, typically in RGB-D configurations, are common devices in mobile robotic platforms given their appealing features: high frequency and resolution, low price and power requirements, among others. These sensors may come with significant, non-linear errors in the depth measurements that jeopardize robot tasks, like free-space detection, environment reconstruction or visual robot-human interaction. This paper presents a method to calibrate such systematic errors with the help of a second, more precise range sensor, in our case a radial laser scanner. In contrast to what it may seem at first, this does not mean a serious limitation in practice since these two sensors are often mounted jointly in many mobile robotic platforms, as they complement well each other. Moreover, the laser scanner can be used just for the calibration process and get rid of it after that. The main contributions of the paper are: (i) the calibration is formulated from a probabilistic perspective through a Maximum Likelihood Estimation problem, and (ii) the proposed method can be easily executed automatically by mobile robotic platforms. To validate the proposed approach we evaluated for both, local distortion of 3D planar reconstructions and global shifts in the measurements, obtaining considerably more accurate results. A C++ open-source implementation of the presented method has been released for the benefit of the community.

Keywords: Sensor calibration · Depth cameras · Mobile robotics

1 Introduction

Nowadays, many mobile robots get awareness of their workspaces using RGB-D cameras [1,2]. These compact and affordable sensors provide per-pixel depth measurements along with colour information at high frame rates, simplifying a variety of robotic tasks that would be more involved if using a regular camera

© Springer Nature Switzerland AG 2019
M. Vento and G. Percannella (Eds.): CAIP 2019, LNCS 11678, pp. 659–671, 2019.
https://doi.org/10.1007/978-3-030-29888-3_54

only, such as 3D object detection and localization [3, 4], safe autonomous navigation [5], or map building/scene reconstruction [6–8], among others. Alternative sensors providing 3D depth information are LiDAR [9] or Time-of-Flight cameras [10], but they are not as widely spread as structured-light depth sensors, mainly due to their higher price [11].

Unfortunately, affordability of structured-light depth cameras comes at a cost: depth estimates are affected by significant distortion, not always well modeled by factory calibration parameters [12, 13]. These errors can be unacceptable for some common robotic applications, and thus require a further calibration by the user. For example, we empirically observed that an obstacle-free path through an open door can be narrowed by intrinsic depth errors up to a point where it appears to the robot as a colliding path. We also experienced the negative effect of inaccurate measurements in algorithms for plane segmentation, scene reconstruction, and human pose estimation [2, 14, 15].

With the massive deployment of robotic platforms [16], calibration methods suitable to be executed automatically by robots are desirable, seeking to prevent the manual calibration of each depth sensor prior to deployment. However, existing intrinsic calibration methods for structured-light depth cameras cannot be easily automated. For example, the method described in [17] aims to correct depth measurements via visual SLAM and, therefore, has the underlying requirement of a well illuminated, textured enough environment. Authors in [18] argue that their method could be executed automatically, however, it is applicable only for sensors mounted with a near zero pitch angle. Recently, authors in [19] proposed another calibration approach based on the observation of a known checkerboard pattern with a regular RGB camera. In order to enable automatic calibration, their approach requires manipulating the environment to include the visual pattern which, in turn, hampers the deployment process.

In this paper, we first empirically analyze the behaviour of structured-light depth cameras and then present a method to compensate for systematic errors in the measurements, which can be easily executed automatically by mobile robotic platforms. More precisely, the proposed method requires observing, at different distances, a vertical planar surface (e.g. a wall) from both the depth camera and another extrinsically calibrated sensor (e.g. a 2D laser scanner, device commonly found in robotic platforms) not suffering from those errors. In this way, the second sensor is used to obtain depth references for calibration. Note that planar surfaces are ubiquitous in human-made environments and specific visual calibration patterns are not required. Bias functions for systematic depth errors are then calibrated in a Maximum Likelihood Estimation framework. The output of the calibration method is a per-pixel quadratic approximation of the depth bias, from which systematic errors in the measurements can be corrected in an online fashion.

To demonstrate the suitability of our proposal, we collected data from two RGB-D cameras and a 2D laser scanner mounted on a mobile robot (the robotic platform Giraff [20]) when approaching a vertical, planar surface, and carried out an experimental evaluation showing both quantitative and qualitative performance results. A C++, ROS integrated open-source implementation of the presented method is available at: https://github.com/dzunigan/depth_calibration

2   Related Work

Early works in depth error calibration aimed to calibrate distortions along with the extrinsic parameters with respect to an RGB camera. For example, the authors in [21] considered the calibration of an RGB-D camera pair resorting to a linear depth distortion function, while Herrera et al. [22] tackled the calibration of two colour cameras and a depth one. In the latter case the disparity distortion was modelled as a per-pixel offset with exponential decay governed by two global parameters. Both approaches employ planar surfaces for depth compensation, tendency that still holds in recent works. An example of this is the work by Basso et al. [19], which proposed a calibration method based on the observation of a planar pattern with a regular camera, while the extrinsic calibration is more a "side effect".

All above-mentioned works require a visual pattern (typically a checkerboard) in order to compute reference depth measurements, and thus it must be included in the robot workspace to perform the calibration. A different approach is presented in [18], where the authors get rid of the visual pattern requirement and proposed a non-parametric calibration approach. However, they require another sensor in order to provide reference measurements and the depth camera has to be mounted with a zero pitch angle for the calibration.

Another way to get rid of known visual patterns is by using a visual SLAM pipeline to provide the depth references. To the best of our knowledge, depth correction via SLAM was first introduced by Teichman et al. [17]. Their method makes the strong assumption that the errors at close ranges (below 2 m) are negligible, and thus are used as reference within the SLAM pipeline. Depth correction factors are then estimated for each pixel and at a number of fixed distances. Another work based on a similar idea was presented in [23], where the authors assume known extrinsic calibration between the RGB and the depth cameras. Their method projects features from a sparse map (generated from the RGB camera) into the depth camera poses in order to estimate the correction factors. They use the thin plate spline as a tool for approximating a dense representation of the sparse correction factors. As previously stated, the main drawback of these approaches is that they have to fulfill the requirements of the SLAM pipeline in order to provide reliable estimates (e.g. high processing rates, well illuminated and textured enough environments, etc).

The calibration method presented in this work does not require any visual pattern and thus can be easily executed automatically by mobile robots. As in [18], another sensor is needed to provide reference measurements, concretely a radial laser scanner. Notice that this assumption is not very restrictive, since these sensors are commonly used in mobile robotic platforms. Moreover, we can use the laser scanner temporally just for the calibration process and get rid of it after that. In contrast to [18], we argue that the systematic depth errors can be well modeled from a more compact parametric representation. Additionally, our method does not assume a specific orientation of the depth camera to carry out the calibration.

3 Depth Error Model

In this work, as in [19], we consider both the "local distortion" and "global" errors as the main source of systematic errors. The *local distortion* has the characteristic effect of deforming the resulting point cloud, while the *global errors* shift the average observed depth. Illustrative examples of these errors are shown in Fig. 1. We argue that both sources of error can be explained by a depth bias $\beta_{u,v}$:

$$z_{u,v} = z^*_{u,v} + \beta_{u,v}, \tag{1}$$

for each pixel $(u, v) \in \Omega$ in the image domain independently, where $z^*_{u,v}$ and $z_{u,v}$ represent the true and the measured depths, respectively. We consider the bias to be normally distributed:

$$\beta_{u,v} \sim \mathcal{N}\big(\mu_{u,v}(z_{u,v}), \sigma^2(z_{u,v})\big), \tag{2}$$

where $\mu_{u,v}$ is a per-pixel mean function and σ is a global standard deviation function modeling the uncertainty in the measurements.

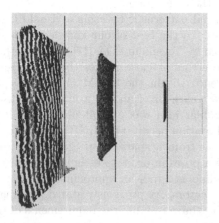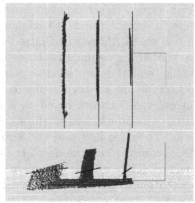

Fig. 1. Illustration of the errors and their variation with distance. Left, a depth camera observing a perpendicular wall at 1–4 m. Right, another camera with a 60 deg pitch observing the same wall, at 1–3 m. Note that the reconstructed ground is parallel to the x-y plane, while the wall has a noticeable inclination.

The bias, computed as the difference between the measured depth and the real one, are plotted in Fig. 2a as a function of the measured depth, for different pixels. The lines in that figure represent fitted quadratic models (see Sect. 4.2). It becomes clear that each pixel is affected by a different bias, but the evolution of the biases with respect to depth are well explained by quadratic functions.

Regarding the uncertainty in the measurements, previous research [24] found that it follows a quadratic evolution with respect to depth. We verified this behaviour empirically by analyzing the standard deviation of the measurements in a similar setting as for the biases. The standard deviation plotted against the measured depth are reported in Fig. 2b. Notice that, unlike the bias, the uncertainty of the measurements is similar for different pixels. This phenomenon has also been considered in our framework by modeling a single variance function for all pixels (see Sect. 4.2).

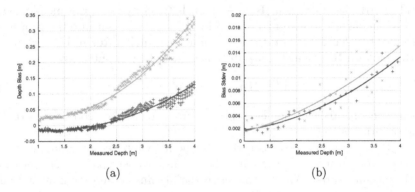

(a)   (b)

Fig. 2. The observed bias (2a) and bias noise (2b) as a function of the measured depth, along with quadratic curve fits, for two different pixels.

Finally, the systematic depth errors can be compensated by subtracting the bias mean:

$$\bar{z}_{u,v} = z_{u,v} - \mu_{u,v}(z_{u,v}) = z^*_{u,v} + \epsilon, \quad \epsilon \sim \mathcal{N}\big(0, \sigma^2(z_{u,v})\big), \tag{3}$$

yielding unbiased depth measurements.

4   Calibration Approach

In this section we describe the proposed calibration approach. First, Sect. 4.1 discusses the process of computing depth reference measurements from the observation of a planar surface by the sensors. Then, the formulation of the calibration problem in a Maximum Likelihood framework and its solution are described in Sect. 4.2.

4.1 Computation of the Depth References

The input of the calibration method are observations of a vertical, planar surface from both a depth camera and another sensor not suffering from the same errors. For the former, observations are in the form of depth images, while for the latter they are in the form of geometric parameters of the observed plane. These parameters are $(\mathbf{n}, d) \in \mathbb{R}^3 \times \mathbb{R}^+$ such that:

$$\mathbf{n} \cdot \mathbf{x} - d = 0, \tag{4}$$

for any point $\mathbf{x} \in \mathbb{R}^3$ lying on the plane. Here, $\mathbf{n}$ represents the unit normal vector (from the origin to the plane) and $d \geq 0$ the perpendicular distance to the origin (Hessian normal form).

The extrinsic calibration $(\mathbf{R}, \mathbf{t}) \in SE(3)$ between the two sensors allow us to express the plane parameters observed by the second sensor into the coordinate system of the depth camera. Clearly, the new normal vector $\mathbf{n}'$ is affected only by the rotation $\mathbf{R}$, while the new distance d' can be computed as:

$$\mathbf{n}' = \mathbf{R}\mathbf{n}, \quad d' = -\mathbf{n}' \cdot \mathbf{t} - d, \tag{5}$$

which is the distance of the new origin $-\mathbf{t}$ from the rotated coordinates (before translation).

Depth cameras allow to reconstruct 3D points via back-projection, using the associated depth measurements and the intrinsic camera parameters (provided by the manufacturer). We parameterize the 3D line representing an incoming ray with respect to depth $z \in \mathbb{R}$ as:

$$\mathbf{l}_{u,v}(z) = z \left(\frac{u - c_x}{f_x}, \frac{v - c_y}{f_y}, 1 \right)^\top, \tag{6}$$

where $(c_x, c_y) \in \mathbb{R}^2$ refers to the camera center, and $f_x, f_y \in \mathbb{R}$ to the focal lengths (in each axis). In this way, the reconstructed 3D point can be computed as $\mathbf{l}_{u,v}(z_{u,v})$. Therefore, we define the reference depth measure $z^*_{u,v}$ such that:

$$\mathbf{n}' \cdot \mathbf{l}_{u,v}(z^*_{u,v}) - d' = 0, \tag{7}$$

i.e. enforcing the plane constraint in Eq. (4) on the reconstructed 3D point. Finally, since Eq. (7) is linear with respect to $z^*_{u,v}$, the solution can be computed as:

$$z^*_{u,v} = \frac{d'}{\mathbf{n}' \cdot \mathbf{l}_{u,v}(1)}, \tag{8}$$

yielding pairs $(z_{u,v}, z^*_{u,v})$ that relate measured and reference depth values.

4.2 Maximum Likelihood Estimation of the Bias Functions

Once having computed the depth measurement-reference pairs, the estimation of the bias functions is divided into two main steps. First, we fit a quadratic function to the observed deviations, which is common for all pixels (recall Fig. 2b). Next, for each pixel independently, we solve for the actual bias parameters (recall Fig. 2a).

In first place, we want to estimate the parameters of a quadratic function that best represents the evolution of the bias noise. In a Least Squares sense, this is:

$$\arg\min_{a,b,c} \sum_{k \in \Pi} \|\sigma_k - \sigma(k)\|^2, \quad \sigma(k) = ak^2 + bk + c, \qquad (9)$$

given the discrete deviation samples σ_k over the discrete sampling interval Π. In order to compute observed standard deviations, we divide the observed bias into discrete bins for each pixel independently:

$$S_{u,v}^k = \{z - z^* \mid t > |z - k|, \forall (z, z^*) \in M_{u,v}\}, \qquad (10)$$

where $t \in \mathbb{R}$ is a discretization threshold and $M_{u,v}$ is the set of depth pairs for a pixel $(u, v) \in \Omega$. Then, for each set of observations S_k with $k \in \Pi$, we compute the deviation σ_k as:

$$\sigma_k^2 = \frac{1}{\sum_{(u,v) \in \Omega} |S_{u,v}^k|} \sum_{(u,v) \in \Omega} \left(\sum_{z \in S_{u,v}^k} (z - \bar{S}_{u,v}^k)^2 \right), \qquad (11)$$

where $|S|$ represents the set's cardinality and $\bar{S}$, the mean. Equation 11 aims to compute the variance of a range of depth measurements, where each pixel can have a different bias mean. This way, we obtain the discrete samples σ_k used to fit the function modeling the bias noise in Eq. (9).

Having an estimation of the uncertainty, we proceed to solve for the parameters of a quadratic approximation to the bias function for each pixel independently. We formulate the calibration problem in a Maximum Likelihood Estimation fashion as:[1]

$$\arg\max_{a,b,c} \prod_{i=1}^{N} p(z_i \mid z_i^*, \mu(z_i), \sigma(z_i)), \quad \mu(z) = az^2 + bz + c, \qquad (12)$$

for a likelihood function p and N independent observations. Under the assumption of normality, the likelihood function becomes:

$$p(z \mid z^*, \mu, \sigma) = \frac{1}{\sqrt{2\pi\sigma^2}} \exp\left(-\frac{(z - z^* - \mu)^2}{2\sigma^2} \right). \qquad (13)$$

Taking the negative logarithm of Eq. (12) yields an equivalent Least Squares problem:

$$\arg\min_{a,b,c} \sum_{i=1}^{N} \frac{1}{\sigma^2(z_i)} \|z_i - z_i^* - \mu(z_i)\|^2, \qquad (14)$$

which has a closed form solution since the residual expression is linear with respect to the optimization parameters. In this way, solving Eq. (14) we approximate a bias function that can be used to compensate for the measured depths in a per-pixel fashion.

---

[1] Hereafter, we drop the u, v subscript to improve readability.

5   Experimental Evaluation

The goal of the experimental evaluation is to validate our approach in a real setting. In this respect, we provide a quantitative evaluation of how well the error model presented in Sect. 3 can handle both the local distortions (Sect. 5.1) and the global errors (Sect. 5.2). We also show qualitative improvements in 3D reconstructions after calibration (Sect. 5.3).

To carry out these evaluations, we recorded two independent sequences with two RGB-D sensors (Orbbec Astra) and a 2D laser scanner (Hokuyo URG-04LX-UG01). The sensors were mounted on a Giraff [20] mobile robot and we recorded the sequences while moving it towards and away a wall. The sensor setup and a snapshot of the collection procedure are depicted in Fig. 3. Note that the upper RGB-D camera has a non-negligible pitch, while the other camera and the laser are mounted horizontally, *i.e.* with near zero pitch. The extrinsic calibration parameters between the sensors were estimated using the automatic multi-sensor method proposed in [25]. From the two recorded sequences, one was used to perform the depth calibration described in Sect. 4, while the other one was used for evaluation purposes. For the sake of reproducibility, the collected data is available at: https://doi.org/10.5281/zenodo.2636878.

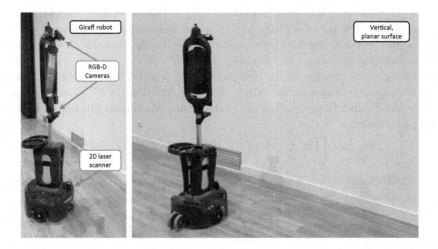

Fig. 3. Left, Giraff robot with annotations of the sensors involved in the calibration process. Right, the robot facing a planar surface during data collection.

5.1   Local Distortion Evaluation

In order to evaluate the undistortion performance, we follow a similar approach as described in [19]. Since the local distortion errors deform the reconstructed 3D structure, the evaluation method consists of fitting a plane to the point cloud acquired while observing a wall, and then computing the Root Mean Square

(RMS) perpendicular distance to the extracted plane for each point belonging to the planar surface.

This is, for a plane π, we have:

$$e_\perp(\pi) = \sqrt{\frac{1}{N} \sum_{i=1}^{N} \|\mathbf{n}_\pi \cdot \mathbf{x}_i - d_\pi\|^2}, \tag{15}$$

for each 3D point $\mathbf{x}_i \in \mathbb{R}^3$ of the planar surface.

The evaluation results for the lower and upper cameras, in terms of the RMS perpendicular error, are shown in Fig. 4a and b, respectively. We can see that calibrated depth measurements achieve better performance in both cases when compared to the original ones. For example, the calibration improves $\sim$2.5 cm the RMSE at 4 m for the lower camera, and $\sim$1 m near 3 m for the upper one. It is also noticeable the difficulties that calibrated measurements have in reaching error-free measurements, and how the error grows with respect to depth. This behaviour can be explained by the quantization error of the sensor, as argued in [19]. In the case of the upper camera, errors are even larger. This phenomenon is caused by the nonzero pitch angle of the camera, as noise in the measurements increases when observing surfaces away from the perpendicular orientation, as shown in [26].

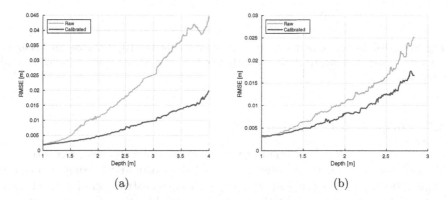

(a)   (b)

Fig. 4. Local distortion performance evaluation for the two RGB-D cameras (4a lower camera; 4b upper camera). In both cases, calibrated depth measurements show better performance.

5.2   Global Error Evaluation

In order to evaluate the global error, we follow a similar approach as before, but in this case we computed the perpendicular error with respect to a reference plane. Recall that the global error shifts the measurements away from their true value. Thus, we can evaluate the error function in Eq. (15) with respect to the plane as observed by the laser scanner.

The RMSE of the compensated and original depth measurements are reported in Fig. 5a and b for the lower and upper cameras, respectively. Here, the calibration improves up to 4 cm the RMSE for the lower camera (at 4 cm) and up to 2.5 cm for the upper one (at 1.5 m). Errors also tend to grow with depth, for the same reasons as before. Additionally, global errors after calibration are higher than the local distortion ones. This is mainly due to other external sources of errors affecting the evaluation, as *e.g.* errors in the laser measurements, extrinsic calibration errors or time delays between the laser and the cameras. Despite of this, in both cases, the use of calibrated depth measurements improves the accuracy of the measurements.

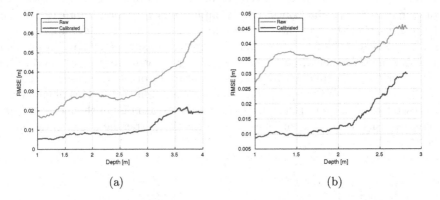

(a)   (b)

Fig. 5. Global distortion performance evaluation for the two RGB-D cameras (5a lower camera; 5b upper camera). A significantly lower error is shown when using calibrated measurements.

5.3   Qualitative Evaluation

In this section, we provide a qualitative evaluation of the obtained, reconstructed 3D point clouds when using compensated depth measurements compared to the original ones. For that purpose, we compare the reconstruction of vertical walls to ground truth measurements before and after calibration. For space reasons, only the results for the lower camera are shown.

The reconstructed point clouds using the raw, original depth measurements are shown in Fig. 6-left, while Fig. 6-right reports the corrected point clouds after calibration. At closer distances, the distortion is negligible, while small offsets are noticeable in the raw measurements. At higher distances, distortions are clearly visible. It can be observed that, after calibration, both the small offsets in the measurements as well as distortions are significantly corrected.

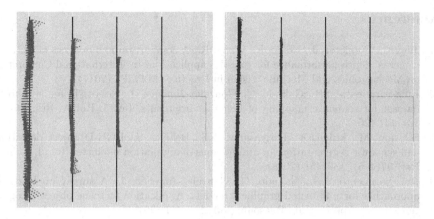

Fig. 6. Reconstructed point clouds form raw (left) and calibrated measurements (right), with reference measurements shown as black lines at 1–4 m.

6   Conclusion

In this work, we presented a method to calibrate systematic errors arising from depth cameras that can be easily executed by mobile robot platforms. First, we analyzed and characterized these errors, and then proposed a calibration method based on Maximum Likelihood Estimation. This method requires to observe a planar surface with both the depth camera and another sensor (*e.g.* a radial laser scanner), used to compute reference depth measurements. The output of the calibration are per-pixel parametric bias functions that can be used to compensate for these systematic depth errors. We evaluated the proposed method in a real robotic platform equipped with two RGB-D cameras and a 2D laser scanner, and showed that the proposed model can handle both local distortions and global errors, producing considerably more accurate measurements. We also provided a qualitative evaluation of the method performance, reporting noticeable error corrections. In the future we plan to incorporate a robust plane detection mechanism in order to enhance the method performance in cluttered environments.

Acknowledgments. This work has been supported by the research projects *WISER* (DPI2017-84827-R), funded by the Spanish Government and the European Regional Development's Funds (FEDER), *MoveCare* (ICT-26-2016b-GA-732158), funded by the European H2020 program, the European Social Found through the Youth Employment Initiative for the promotion of young researchers, and a postdoc contract from the I-PPIT program of the University of Malaga.

References

1. Jing, C., Potgieter, J., Noble, F., Wang, R.: A comparison and analysis of RGB-D cameras' depth performance for robotics application. In: International Conference on Mechatronics and Machine Vision in Practice (M2VIP) (2017)
2. Ruiz-Sarmiento, J.R., Galindo, C., Gonzalez-Jimenez, J.: Robot@Home, a robotic dataset for semantic mapping of home environments. Int. J. Robot. Res. **36**(2), 131–141 (2017)
3. Schwarz, M., Milan, A., Periyasamy, A.S., Behnke, S.: RGB-D object detection and semantic segmentation for autonomous manipulation in clutter. Int. J. Robot. Res. **37**(4–5), 437–451 (2018)
4. Ruiz-Sarmiento, J.R., Galindo, C., Gonzalez-Jimenez, J.: A survey on learning approaches for undirected graphical models. Application to scene object recognition. Int. J. Approximate Reasoning **83**, 434–451 (2017)
5. Jaimez, M., Blanco, J.L., Gonzalez-Jimenez, J.: Efficient reactive navigation with exact collision determination for 3D robot shapes. Int. J. Adv. Robot. Syst. **12**(5), 63 (2015)
6. Kähler, O., Prisacariu, V.A., Murray, D.W.: Real-time large-scale dense 3D reconstruction with loop closure. In: Leibe, B., Matas, J., Sebe, N., Welling, M. (eds.) ECCV 2016. LNCS, vol. 9912, pp. 500–516. Springer, Cham (2016). https://doi.org/10.1007/978-3-319-46484-8_30
7. Jamiruddin, R., Sari, A.O., Shabbir, J., Anwer, T.: RGB-depth SLAM review. arXiv preprint arXiv:1805.07696 (2018)
8. Ruiz-Sarmiento, J.R., Galindo, C., Gonzalez-Jimenez, J.: Building multiversal semantic maps for mobile robot operation. Knowl.-Based Syst. **119**, 257–272 (2017)
9. Zhang, J., Singh, S.: LOAM: lidar odometry and mapping in real-time. In: Robotics: Science and Systems, vol. 2 (2014)
10. Foix, S., Alenyà, G., Torras, C.: Lock-in time-of-flight (ToF) cameras: a survey. IEEE Sens. J. **11**(9), 1917–1926 (2011)
11. Rusu, R.B., Cousins, S.: 3D is here: point cloud library (PCL). In: International Conference on Robotics and Automation (2011)
12. Song, X., Zheng, J., Zhong, F., Qin, X.: Modeling deviations of RGB-D cameras for accurate depth map and color image registration. Multimed. Tools Appl. **77**(12), 14951–14977 (2018)
13. Fiedler, D., Müller, H.: Impact of thermal and environmental conditions on the kinect sensor. In: Jiang, X., Bellon, O.R.P., Goldgof, D., Oishi, T. (eds.) WDIA 2012. LNCS, vol. 7854, pp. 21–31. Springer, Heidelberg (2013). https://doi.org/10.1007/978-3-642-40303-3_3
14. Ruiz-Sarmiento, J.R., Galindo, C., Gonzalez-Jimenez, J.: Experimental study of the performance of the Kinect range camera for mobile robotics. Technial report, University of Malaga, Department of System Engineering and Automation (2013)
15. Fernandez-Moral, E., Gonzalez-Jimenez, J., Rives, P., Arevalo, V.: Extrinsic calibration of a set of range cameras in 5 seconds without pattern. In: International Conference on Intelligent Robots and Systems (2014)
16. Della Corte, B., Andreasson, H., Stoyanov, T., Grisetti, G.: Unified motion-based calibration of mobile multi-sensor platforms with time delay estimation. IEEE Robot. Autom. Lett. **4**(2), 902–909 (2019)
17. Teichman, A., Miller, S., Thrun, S.: Unsupervised intrinsic calibration of depth sensors via SLAM. In: Robotics: Science and Systems, vol. 248 (2013)

18. Di Cicco, M., Iocchi, L., Grisetti, G.: Non-parametric calibration for depth sensors. Robot. Auton. Syst. **74**, 309–317 (2015)
19. Basso, F., Menegatti, E., Pretto, A.: Robust intrinsic and extrinsic calibration of RGB-D cameras. IEEE Trans. Robot. **34**(5), 1315–1332 (2018)
20. González-Jiménez, J., Galindo, C., Ruiz-Sarmiento, J.R.: Technical improvements of the Giraff telepresence robot based on users' evaluation. In: 2012 IEEE RO-MAN: The 21st IEEE International Symposium on Robot and Human Interactive Communication (2012)
21. Zhang, C., Zhang, Z.: Calibration between depth and color sensors for commodity depth cameras. In: Shao, L., Han, J., Kohli, P., Zhang, Z. (eds.) Computer Vision and Machine Learning with RGB-D Sensors. ACVPR, pp. 47–64. Springer, Cham (2014). https://doi.org/10.1007/978-3-319-08651-4_3
22. Herrera, D., Kannala, J., Heikkilä, J.: Joint depth and color camera calibration with distortion correction. IEEE Trans. Pattern Anal. Mach. Intell. **34**(10), 2058–2064 (2012)
23. Quenzel, J., Rosu, R.A., Houben, S., Behnke, S.: Online depth calibration for RGB-D cameras using visual SLAM. In: International Conference on Intelligent Robots and Systems (2017)
24. Smisek, J., Jancosek, M., Pajdla, T.: 3D with Kinect. In: Fossati, A., Gall, J., Grabner, H., Ren, X., Konolige, K. (eds.) Consumer Depth Cameras for Computer Vision. ACVPR, pp. 3–25. Springer, London (2013). https://doi.org/10.1007/978-1-4471-4640-7_1
25. Zuñiga-Noël, D., Ruiz-Sarmiento, J.R., Gomez-Ojeda, R., Gonzalez-Jimenez, J.: Automatic multi-sensor extrinsic calibration for mobile robots. IEEE Robot. Autom. Lett. **4**(3), 2862–2869 (2019). https://doi.org/10.1109/LRA.2019.2922618
26. Nguyen, C.V., Izadi, S., Lovell, D.: Modeling Kinect sensor noise for improved 3D reconstruction and tracking. In: International Conference on 3D Imaging, Modeling, Processing, Visualization Transmission (2012)

Multilinear Subspace Method Based on Geodesic Distance for Volumetric Object Classification

Hayato Itoh[1(✉)] and Atsushi Imiya[2]

[1] Graduate School of Informatics, Nagoya University, Nagoya, Japan
hitoh@mori.m.is.nagoya-u.ac.jp
[2] Institute of Management and Information Technologies, Chiba University,
Chiba, Japan

Abstract. Organs, cells in organs and microstructures in cells are mathematically spatial textures. Tensors allow us to directly analyse, manipulate and recognise such volumetric data in medical image computing. Tensor-based data expression provides a classification method for temporal morphogenesis of spatiotemporal volumetric sequences using geodesic distances between tensor subspaces. Geodesic measures are introduced both for the Grassmann and Stiefel manifolds in multilinear space. Experimental evaluations of cardiac MRI dataset for 17 patients show the validity of the method for discrimination and classification.

1 Introduction

Analysis, manipulation and recognition of patterns in biomedical images play essential roles in applications such as computer-aided diagnosis for anatomical structure extraction, abnormality detection and image-based histological and pathological classifications. Organs, cells in organs and microstructures in cells, which are the main targets in these medical procedures, are spatial and temporal textures. From cells in ultramagnified observation to the whole human body in nonmagnified observation, medical data used in biomedical image analysis are captured as volumetric data by several modalities such as CT, micro-CT, PET, MRI and EEG scanners. Furthermore, for longitudinal analysis, these collected statistical data are represented as volumetric video sequences. For the analysis, classification, recognition and retrieval of multiway data, data analysis methodologies based on multiway structures are required [1,2].

Using tensor-based data expression, we propose a classification method for temporal morphogenesis of spatiotemporal volumetric sequences. By expressing a digital object in a volumetric video sequence as a set of third-order tensors, orthogonal tensor decomposition yields an extension of the subspace method for classification in vector spaces to that in tensor spaces [1,3]. Using tensor-based data expression, the geodesic distances between tensor subspaces [2] are

M. Vento and G. Percannella (Eds.): CAIP 2019, LNCS 11678, pp. 672–683, 2019.
https://doi.org/10.1007/978-3-030-29888-3_55

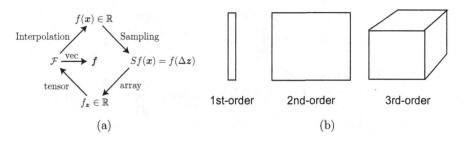

Fig. 1. Sampling and tensor representation of multidimensional objects. We can reconstruct f from $\mathcal{F}$ using an interpolation procedure. (a) Relationship among sampled data and multiway data. The sampled values of a multivariate function derive multiway array data that are dealt with as a high-order tensor to preserve the multilinear properties of the data. (b) Examples of Nth-order tensors for $N = 1, 2, 3$.

computed for our classification method for temporal morphogenesis of spatiotemporal volumetric data. Experimental evaluations of cardiac MIR dataset for 17 patients [4] show the validity of the method for discrimination and classification.

2   Preliminaries

2.1   Tensor Representation and Tensor Projection

We summarise the tensor-based multilinear expression of three-dimensional arrays [3]. A third-order tensor $\mathcal{X}$ in $\mathbb{R}^{I_1 \times I_2 \times I_2}$ is expressed as $\mathcal{X} = (x_{i_1 i_2 i_3})$ for $x_{i_1 i_2 i_3} \in \mathbb{R}$ with three indices i_1, i_2 and i_3, as shown in Fig. 1. The subscript n of i_n and I_n denotes the mode n of $\mathcal{X}$. For $\mathcal{X}$, the n-mode vectors, where $n = 1, 2, 3$, are defined as the I_n-dimensional vectors obtained from $\mathcal{X}$ by varying index i_n while fixing all other indices. The unfolding of $\mathcal{X}$ along the n-mode vectors of $\mathcal{X}$ is defined as $\mathcal{X}_{(n)} \in \mathbb{R}^{I_n \times (I_m I_l)}$, where the column vectors of $\mathcal{X}_{(n)}$ are the n-mode vectors of $\mathcal{X}$. For a tensor and its unfolding, we have the bijection $\mathcal{F}_n$ such that $\mathcal{F}_n \mathcal{X} = \mathcal{X}_{(n)}$ and $\mathcal{X} = \mathcal{F}_n^{-1} \mathcal{X}_{(n)}$. Figure 2(a) illustrates unfoldings of a third-order tensor for each mode. The n-mode product $\mathcal{G} = \mathcal{X} \times_n \mathbf{U}^\top$ of an orthogonal matrix $\mathbf{U} \in \mathbb{R}^{J_n \times I_n}$ and tensor $\mathcal{X}$ is defined by

$$\mathcal{G} = \mathcal{F}_n^{-1} \mathcal{G}_{(n)} = \mathcal{F}_n^{-1} \mathbf{U}^\top \mathcal{X}_{(n)}. \tag{1}$$

Figure 2(b) shows the linear projection form $\mathcal{G}_{(n)} = \mathbf{U}^\top \mathcal{X}_{(n)}$ of the 1-mode projection for a third-order tensor. For the m- and n-mode products with matrices $\mathbf{U}^\top$ and $\mathbf{V}^\top$, $\mathcal{X} \times_m \mathbf{U}^\top \times_n \mathbf{V}^\top = \mathcal{X} \times_n \mathbf{V}^\top \times_m \mathbf{U}^\top$ holds since n-mode projections are commutative [5].

As the tensor $\mathcal{X}$ is in the tensor space $T_{I_1 I_2 I_3} = \mathbb{R}^{I_1} \otimes \mathbb{R}^{I_2} \otimes \mathbb{R}^{I_3}$, the tensor space can be interpreted as the Kronecker product of three vector spaces $\mathbb{R}^{I_1}, \mathbb{R}^{I_2}, \mathbb{R}^{I_3}$. For two tensors, $\mathcal{X}, \mathcal{Y} \in T_{I_1 I_2 I_3}$, we define the inner product of these two tensors as $\langle \mathcal{X}, \mathcal{Y} \rangle = \sum_{i_1} \sum_{i_2} \sum_{i_3} x_{i_1 i_2 i_3} y_{i_1 i_2 i_3}$. Using this inner product,

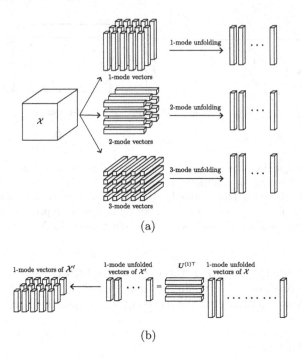

(a)

(b)

Fig. 2. (a) Unfoldings of a third-order tensor showing 1-, 2-, and 3-mode unfoldings of the third-order tensor $\mathcal{X} \in \mathbb{R}^{4 \times 5 \times 3}$. (b) 1-mode projection of $\mathcal{X} \in \mathbb{R}^{4 \times 5 \times 3}$ to a lower-dimensional tensor $\mathcal{Y} \in \mathbb{R}^{3 \times 5 \times 3}$.

we introduce the Frobenius norm of tensor $\mathcal{X}$ as $\|\mathcal{X}\|_F = \sqrt{\langle \mathcal{X}, \mathcal{X} \rangle}$. Therefore, the tensor space is a metric space. To project $\mathcal{X} \in T_{I_1 I_2 I_3}$ to another tensor $\mathcal{Y}$ in a lower-dimensional multilinear subspace $\Pi_{P_1 P_2 P_3} = \mathbb{R}^{P_1} \otimes \mathbb{R}^{P_2} \otimes \mathbb{R}^{P_3}$, where $P_n \leq I_n$ for $n = 1, 2, 3$, we need three orthogonal matrices $\{U^{(n)} \in \mathbb{R}^{I_n \times P_n}\}_{n=1}^3$. Using the three orthogonal matrices, the multilinear projection is given by

$$\mathcal{Y} = \mathcal{X} \times_1 U^{(1)\top} \times_2 U^{(2)\top} \times_3 U^{(3)\top}. \tag{2}$$

This projection is established in three steps, where each n-mode vector is projected to the P_n-dimensional space by $U^{(n)}$ at the nth step. We refer to this operation as the multilinear projection of $\mathcal{X}$ to $\mathcal{Y}$.

2.2 Multilinear Subspace of Pattern Sets

A third-order tensor, $\mathcal{X} \in \mathbb{R}^{I_1 \times I_2 \times I_3}$, which is the array $X \in \mathbb{R}^{I_1 \times I_2 \times I_3}$, is denoted as a tuple of indices (i_1, i_2, i_3). We set the identity matrices I_j, $j = 1, 2, 3$, in $\mathbb{R}^{I_j \times I_j}$. Setting $\{U^{(j)}\}_{j=1}^3$ to be orthogonal matrices of the multilinear projection $\mathcal{Y} = \mathcal{X} \times_1 U^{(1)\top} \times_2 U^{(2)\top} \times_3 U^{(3)\top}$ for third-order tensors, we have the multilinear subspace

$$\mathcal{C}(\delta) = \{\mathcal{X} \mid \|\mathcal{Y} \times_1 U^{(1)} \times_2 U^{(2)} \times_3 U^{(3)} - \mathcal{X}\|_F \ll \delta\}, \tag{3}$$

where a positive constant δ is the bound for a small perturbation to a pattern set.

For a collection of tensors $\{\mathcal{X}_i\}_{i=1}^N \in \mathbb{R}^{I_1 \times I_2 \times I_3}$, we compute

$$\mathcal{Y}_i = \mathcal{X}_i \times_1 \boldsymbol{U}^{(1)\top} \times_2 \boldsymbol{U}^{(2)\top} \times_3 \boldsymbol{U}^{(3)\top}, \tag{4}$$

where $\boldsymbol{U}^{(j)} = [\boldsymbol{u}_1^{(j)}, \dots, \boldsymbol{u}_{I_j}^{(j)}]$, which minimises the criterion

$$J = \mathrm{E}\left(\|\mathcal{X}_i - \mathcal{Y}_i \times_1 \boldsymbol{U}^{(1)} \times_2 \boldsymbol{U}^{(2)} \times_3 \boldsymbol{U}^{(3)}\|_{\mathrm{F}}^2\right) \tag{5}$$

with respect to the conditions $\boldsymbol{U}^{(j)\top}\boldsymbol{U}^{(j)} = \boldsymbol{I}_j$.

Eigendecomposition problems are derived by computing the extremes of

$$E_j = J_j + tr((\boldsymbol{I}_j - \boldsymbol{U}^{(j)\top}\boldsymbol{U}^{(j)})\boldsymbol{\Sigma}^{(j)}), \; j = 1, 2, 3, \tag{6}$$

where we set

$$J_j = \mathrm{E}\left(\|\boldsymbol{U}^{(j)\top}\mathcal{X}_{i,(j)}\mathcal{X}_{i,(j)}^{\top}\boldsymbol{U}^{(j)}\|_{\mathrm{F}}^2\right). \tag{7}$$

For matrices $\boldsymbol{M}^{(j)} = \frac{1}{N}\sum_{i=1}^N \mathcal{X}_{i,(j)}\mathcal{X}_{i,(j)}^{\top}, j = 1, 2, 3$, the optimisation of J yields the eigenvalue decomposition

$$\boldsymbol{M}^{(j)}\boldsymbol{U}^{(j)} = \boldsymbol{U}^{(j)}\boldsymbol{\Sigma}^{(j)}, \tag{8}$$

where $\boldsymbol{\Sigma}^{(j)} \in \mathbb{R}^{I_j \times I_j}$, $j = 1, 2, 3$, are diagonal matrices satisfying the relationships $\lambda_k^{(j)} = \lambda_k^{(j')}$, $k \in \{1, 2, \dots, K\}$, for

$$\boldsymbol{\Sigma}^{(j)} = \mathrm{diag}(\lambda_1^{(j)}, \lambda_2^{(j)} \cdots, \lambda_K^{(j)}, 0 \cdots, 0). \tag{9}$$

For the optimisation of $\{J_j\}_{j=1}^3$, there is no closed-form solution to this maximisation problem [5]. For practical computation, we use the iterative procedure of multilinear principal component analysis (MPCA) [1,3]. This is an extension of orthogonal decomposition from a vector representation to a tensor one (see Appendix A).

3   Distance-Based Classification to Multilinear Forms

3.1   Geodesic Distance of Grassmann Manifolds

A Grassmann manifold (Grassmannian) $\mathcal{G}(m, D)$ is the set of m-dimensional linear subspaces of $\mathbb{R}^D$ [6,7]. An element of $\mathcal{G}(m, D)$ can be represented by an orthogonal matrix $\boldsymbol{Y}$ of size $D \times m$, where $\boldsymbol{Y}$ comprises the m basis vectors for a set of patterns in $\mathbb{R}^D$. The geodesic distance between two elements on a Grassmannian has been defined in terms of principal angles [8].

Let $\boldsymbol{Y}_1$ and $\boldsymbol{Y}_2$ be orthogonal matrices of size $D \times m$. The canonical angles (principal angles) $0 \leq \theta_1 \leq \cdots \leq \theta_m \leq \frac{\pi}{2}$ between the two subspaces $\mathrm{span}(\boldsymbol{Y}_1)$ and $\mathrm{span}(\boldsymbol{Y}_2)$ are defined by

$$\cos\theta_k = \max_{\boldsymbol{u}_k \in \mathrm{span}(\boldsymbol{Y}_1)} \max_{\boldsymbol{v}_k \in \mathrm{span}(\boldsymbol{Y}_1)} \boldsymbol{u}_k^{\top}\boldsymbol{v}_k \; \text{s.t.} \; \boldsymbol{u}_k^{\top}\boldsymbol{u}_i = 0, \; \boldsymbol{v}_k^{\top}\boldsymbol{v}_i = 0, \tag{10}$$

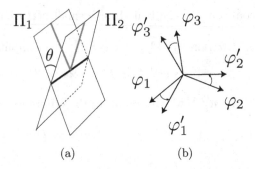

(a)   (b)

Fig. 3. Distance computation for Grassmann and Stiefel manifolds. (a) Distance between linear subspaces Π_1 and Π_2 on a Grassmann manifold computed using canonical angle θ. (b) Distance between Stiefel manifolds computed using angles between each pair of bases φ_i and φ_i'.

for $i = 1, 2, \ldots, k - 1$.

For two linear subspaces Π_1 and Π_2, we have projection matrices $P = Y_1^{\top} Y_1$ and $Q = Y_2^{\top} Y_2$, respectively. We have a set of canonical angles $\{\theta_i\}_{i=1}^m$ between these two linear subspaces with the conditions $\theta_1 \leq \theta_2 \leq \ldots . \theta_m$. We obtain the canonical angles from the solution of the eigendecomposition problem

$$PQPu = \lambda u \text{ or } QPQu = \lambda u. \tag{11}$$

For the eigenvalues λ_i for $i = 1, 2, \ldots m$ in the eigendecomposition in Eq. (11), we have the relation

$$\lambda_i = \cos^2 \theta_i. \tag{12}$$

By using the canonical angles shown in Fig. 3(a), we define the geodesic distance [7,9] on a Grassmann manifold as

$$d_G(Y_1, Y_2) = \sqrt{\sum_{i=1}^m \theta_i^2}. \tag{13}$$

We extend the Grassmann distance to measure the difference between multilinear subspaces. We define a Grassmann manifold $g(\Pi_{P_1 P_2 P_3}, T_{I_1 I_2 I_3})$ as a set of multilinear subspaces of $\mathbb{R}^{P_1} \otimes \mathbb{R}^{P_2} \otimes \mathbb{R}^{P_3}$ in a tensor space $T_{I_1 I_2 I_3}$. Let $\{P^{(j)}\}_{j=1}^3$ and $\{Q^{(j)}\}_{j=1}^3$ be the sets of projection matrices for two different multilinear subspaces Π_1 and Π_2, respectively. For each mode j, we have a set of canonical angles $\{\theta_i^{(j)}\}_{i=1}^{m_j}$ between $P^{(j)}$ and $Q^{(j)}$. Using these projection matrices of these two multilinear subspaces, we define the Grassmann distance between multilinear subspaces Π_1 and Π_2 as

$$d(\Pi_1, \Pi_2) = \sqrt{\sum_{i=1}^{m_1} (\theta_i^{(1)})^2 + \sum_{i=1}^{m_2} (\theta_i^{(2)})^2 + \sum_{i=1}^{m_3} (\theta_i^{(3)})^2}. \tag{14}$$

3.2 Geodesic Distance of Stiefel Manifolds

A Stiefel manifold $S_{m,D}$ is a set of m orthonormal vectors in $\mathbb{R}^D$, represented by a $D \times m$ matrix Y. While the Grassmannian in a vector space is defined by the dimension of the linear subspaces and the dimension of the original space, this Stiefel manifold $S_{m,D}$ is defined by a set of basis vectors. Let two Stiefel manifolds be orthogonal matrices Y_1 and Y_2. For $p = 1, 2$, the distance between the two Stiefel manifolds is defined by

$$d_S(Y_1, Y_2) = \min_{c_{ij}} \left(\sum_{i=1}^{m} \sum_{j=1}^{m} c_{ij} \theta_{ij}^p \right)^{1/p}, \tag{15}$$

where $\theta_{ij} \geq 0$ is the angle between the ith basis in $\mathrm{span}(Y_1)$ and the jth basis in $\mathrm{span}(Y_2)$ shown in Fig. 3(b), and const $c_{ij} \geq 0$ is the transportation cost between the two bases. This geodesic distance is based on angles between bases in two linear subspaces.

The geodesic distance between multilinear subspaces $\Pi_{\mathcal{G}}$ and $\Pi_{\mathcal{C}_k}$ is

$$d_{W_p}(\Pi_{\mathcal{G}}, \Pi_{\mathcal{C}_k}) = \min_{c_{ij}^{(1)}, c_{ij}^{(2)}, \ldots, c_{ij}^{(N)}} \left(\sum_{l=1}^{N_C} \sum_{i,j=1}^{I_l} (d_{ij}^{(l)})^p c_{ij}^{(l)} \right)^{1/p} \quad \text{for} \ \ p = 1, 2, \tag{16}$$

where we set three constraints, singular-value, eigenvalue, and energy constraints, as

$$\sum_j c_{ij}^{(n)} = \sqrt{\lambda_i^{(n)}} / \sum_{i=1}^{I_n} \sqrt{\lambda_i^{(n)}}, \quad \sum_i c_{ij}^{(n)} = \sqrt{\lambda_j^{(n)}} / \sum_{j=1}^{I_n} \sqrt{\lambda_j^{(n)}}, \tag{17}$$

$$\sum_j c_{ij}^{(n)} = \lambda_i^{(n)} / \sum_{i=1}^{I_n} \lambda_i^{(n)}, \quad \sum_i c_{ij}^{(n)} = \lambda_j^{(n)} / \sum_{j=1}^{I_n} \lambda_j^{(n)}, \tag{18}$$

$$\sum_j c_{ij}^{(n)} = \left(\lambda_i^{(n)} \right)^2 / \sum_{i=1}^{I_n} \left(\lambda_i^{(n)} \right)^2, \quad \sum_i c_{ij}^{(n)} = \left(\lambda_j^{(n)} \right)^2 / \sum_{j=1}^{I_n} \left(\lambda_j^{(n)} \right)^2, \tag{19}$$

respectively [2]. This is an extension of the Wasserstein distance [10]. For $p = \infty$, we define the supremum Wasserstein distance

$$d_{W_\infty}(\Pi_{\mathcal{G}}, \Pi_{\mathcal{C}_k}) = \max (d_{ij}^{(1)} c_{ij}^{(1)*}) + \max (d_{ij}^{(2)} c_{ij}^{(2)*}) + \max (d_{ij}^{(3)} c_{ij}^{(3)*}), \tag{20}$$

where $c_{ij}^{(1)*}, c_{ij}^{(2)*}, c_{ij}^{(3)*}$ are the solutions of Eq. (16).

3.3   Tensor Subspace Method and Its Extension

As the extension of the subspace method (see Appendix B) for Nth-order tensor objects, the tensor subspace method has been proposed [1]. For a third-order tensor $\mathcal{X}$, we set $\boldsymbol{U}^i, i = 1, 2, 3$, to be projection matrices in a multilinear projection from $\mathcal{X}$ to $\mathcal{Y}$. For the collection of normalised third-order tensors $\{\mathcal{X}_i\}_{i=1}^M$ such that $\|\mathcal{X}_i\|_{\mathrm{F}} = 1$ and $E(\mathcal{X}_i) = 0$, the minimisers of Eq. (5) define a multilinear subspace of a category. Using projection matrices $\{\boldsymbol{U}_k^{(j)}\}_{j=1}^3$ to the kth-category multilinear subspace, we can define the similarity of $\mathcal{G}$ to a category as

$$s = \frac{\|\mathcal{G} \times_1 \boldsymbol{U}^{(1)\top} \times_2 \boldsymbol{U}^{(2)\top} \times_3 \boldsymbol{U}^{(3)\top}\|_{\mathrm{F}}}{\|\mathcal{G}\|_{\mathrm{F}}}. \tag{21}$$

For a set $\{s_l\}_{l=1}^{N_C}$ of similarities to N_C subspaces, if an input query $\mathcal{G}$ satisfies the relation

$$l^* = \arg \max_l s_l, \tag{22}$$

the tensor subspace method concludes that $\mathcal{G}$ belongs to the pattern set $\mathcal{C}_{l^*}$.

We set $\{\boldsymbol{U}_k^{(j)}\}_{j=1}^N$ to be orthogonal matrices for multilinear projection to the kth-category multilinear subspace $\Pi_{\mathcal{C}_k}$. This set $\{\boldsymbol{U}_k^{(j)}\}_{j=1}^N$ spans the multilinear subspace defined in Eq. (3). For the collection of normalised query tensors $\{\mathcal{G}_i\}_{i=1}^L$, such that $\|\mathcal{G}_i\|_{\mathrm{F}} = 1$, the minimisers of Eq. (5) give a multilinear subspace of queries $\Pi_{\mathcal{G}}$ in the same manner as Eq. (5). For two multilinear subspaces Π_k and $\Pi_{\mathcal{G}}$, we have projection matrices for vectorised tensor objects as

$$\boldsymbol{P}_k = \boldsymbol{U}_k^\top \boldsymbol{U}_k, \quad \boldsymbol{U}_k = \boldsymbol{U}_k^{(3)} \otimes \boldsymbol{U}_k^{(3)} \otimes \boldsymbol{U}_k^{(1)}, \tag{23}$$

$$\boldsymbol{Q} = \boldsymbol{V}^\top \boldsymbol{V}, \quad \boldsymbol{V} = \boldsymbol{V}^{(3)} \otimes \boldsymbol{V}^{(2)} \otimes \boldsymbol{V}^{(1)}, \tag{24}$$

for pattern set and query multilinear subspaces, respectively. As a straightforward extension of the mutual subspace method of vector representation (see Appendix C), we have canonical angles between two subspaces as the result of eigendecomposition of $\boldsymbol{P}_k \boldsymbol{Q} \boldsymbol{P}_k$ or $\boldsymbol{Q} \boldsymbol{P}_k \boldsymbol{Q}$. However, the spatial and temporal complexity of this eigendecomposition is apt to be high because of the multidimensional structure of tensors. Furthermore, this form discards the tensor structure of multiway data.

Instead of the above straightforward extension, if input query subspace $\Pi_{\mathcal{G}}$ satisfies the condition

$$l^* = \arg \min_l d_W(\Pi_{\mathcal{G}}, \Pi_{\mathcal{C}_k}), \tag{25}$$

the tensor mutual subspace method concludes that the closest pattern set to the query subspace is pattern set $\mathcal{C}_{l^*}$.

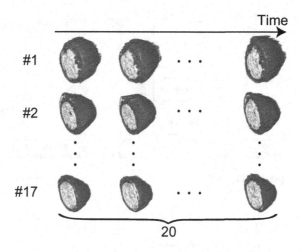

Fig. 4. Volumetric image sequences of beating left ventricles. The number of frames in each of the 17 volumetric video sequences is 20. Each sequence is a record of one cycle of the beating motion of the left ventricle.

4   Numerical Examples

We have evaluated the robustness and accuracy of classification using the qualities of the query spaces and the selection of their dimensions. We use 17 volumetric video sequences of beating left ventricles [4] as shown in Fig. 4. Each sequence is a series of 20 still volumetric images with $81 \times 81 \times 63$ voxels. Training set is constructed from even-numbered frames of each sequence. Then, odd-numbered frames of each sequence are used in the test set to compute linear subspaces of queries.

To evaluate the qualities of linear subspaces constructed from test sets, we use n randomly selected frames from each of the 17 sequences. For $n = 1$, the number of queries is 170. For $n = 2$, we randomly select 500 pairs of queries from each of the 17 sequences. For $n = 3$, we randomly select 500 triplets from each of the 17 sequences. Then from these selected frames, we compute the subspaces of $k \times k \times k$ bases for queries. For the tensor mutual subspace method, we use the Grassmann distance in Eq. (15) and the Wasserstein distances in Eqs. (16) and (20). These distances yield the geodesic between multilinear subspaces. For the computation of the Wasserstein distance, constraints based on singular values, eigenvalues, and energies with $p = 1, 2, \infty$ are used.

Figure 5 summarises the results of classifications. The results for $n = 1$ are shown in Figs. 5(a) and (b) for the tensor subspace method and tensor mutual subspace method (eigenvalue-based constraint with $p = 1$). The recognition ratios for both cases are 1.0 with $2 \times 2 \times 2$ and $3 \times 3 \times 3$ multilinear subspaces. In Fig. 5(c) to (f) show the results for $n = 2, 3$. In Fig. 5, for the Wasserstein distances except for the singular-value-based constraint and energy-based constraint for $p = \infty$, the recognition ratios are 1.0.

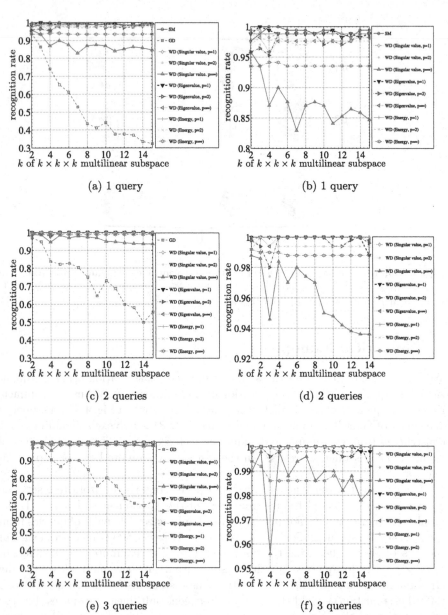

(a) 1 query

(b) 1 query

(c) 2 queries

(d) 2 queries

(e) 3 queries

(f) 3 queries

Fig. 5. Recognition rate for multilinear subspace methods. Left and right columns show whole and close-up curves of recognition rates, respectively. Top, middle and bottom rows illustrate evaluation results for $k = 1, 2, 3$, respectively. In (a)–(f), horizontal and vertical axes represent the dimensions of each mode in a selected multilinear subspace and recognition rate, respectively. For $n = 1$, we use the tensor subspace method and tensor mutual subspace method for classification. For $n = 2, 3$ we use the tensor mutual subspace method. The Grassmann distance (GD) and Wasserstein distance (WD) are evaluated. In the computation of the Wasserstein distance, the constraints based on singular value, eigenvalue and energy with $p = 1, 2, \infty$ are evaluated.

For $n = 1, 2, 3$, the Wasserstein distance of the eigenvalue constraint for $p = 1$ gives a recognition ratio of 1.0. The results in Fig. 5(a), (c) and (e) imply that the tensor mutual subspace method gives a higher and more stable classification against as n increases. For all $n = 1, 2, 3$, the classification based on the Grassmann distance has a high recognition ratio, even if low-dimensional multilinear subspaces are selected. These observations regarding on the results imply that the small number of canonical angles between multilinear subspace is discriminative, since these angles are computed form the bases corresponding to the leading major eigenvalues of multilinear spaces, which express the dominant part of each pattern set. On the other hand, the bases that corresponding to the leading minor eigenvalues of multilinear spaces express geometric perturbation in each pattern set.

The Wasserstein distance yields robust results for classification, since this distance expresses the transport among the Stiefel manifolds. We adopt the sum of singular values, sum of eigenvalues and the total energy given by MPCA as the transportation cost. Furthermore, compared with the Grassmann distance, this property between the Wasserstein distance and transportation problem indicates the advantage of the Wasserstein distance for classification.

5   Conclusions

We proposed a tensor-subspace-based method for the spatiotemporal analysis of the geometric morphogenesis of objects in volumetric video sequences. We firstly extended the subspace method in vector spaces to multilinear spaces using tensor decomposition. Secondly this decomposition yields the geodesic distance between tensor subspaces, which allows us to measure differences among pattern sets in multilinear subspaces. This geodesic distance between pattern sets in manifolds is computed by using angles between two multilinear subspaces. Numerical examples using cardiac MRI dataset show that the geodesic distance based on Stiefel manifolds in the tensor expression results in the highest recognition rates.

Appendices

A   Pattern Set as a Linear Subspace

For a set of patterns $\mathcal{C} = \{f_i\}_{i=1}^{N}$ in $\mathbb{R}^D$, using PCA, we compute the orthogonal projection P to the linear subspace spanned by vectors $\{f_i\}_{i=1}^{N}$. The linear pattern set is defined as

$$\mathcal{C}(\delta) = \{f \mid \|Pf - f\|_2 \ll \delta, \ P^\top P = I\}, \tag{26}$$

where δ is a small positive constant [11–14].

B   Subspace Method

Setting P to be the orthogonal projection matrix to subspace $\mathcal{C}(\delta)$, the similarity of input pattern g to the pattern set is given by

$$\cos \theta = \frac{\|Pg\|_2}{\|g\|_2}. \tag{27}$$

The angle $\theta = \cos^{-1} \frac{\|Pg\|_2}{\|g\|_2}$ is the geodesic distance between an input vector and the linear subspace defined by a pattern set.

For the set $\{\theta_l\}_{l=1}^{N_C}$ of angles between the query vector and the linear subspace i for $i = 1, 2, \ldots, N_c$, if

$$l^* = \arg \max_l \cos \theta_l \quad \text{and} \quad l^* = \arg \min_l \theta_l, \tag{28}$$

the results of the subspace method indicate that g belongs to pattern set $\mathcal{C}_{l^*}$ [11–13] shown in Fig. 6(b).

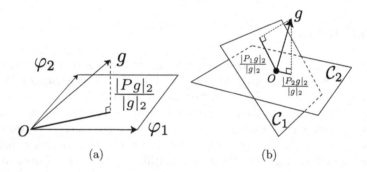

(a)   (b)

Fig. 6. Subspace method. (a) Similarity to a category subspace. φ_1 and φ_2 are set to be the basis of a linear subspace. (b) Classification of input pattern on the basis of similarities to two category subspaces.

C   Mutual Subspace Method

As an extension, the mutual subspace method assumes that queries are linear subspaces. Setting Π_G to be the linear subspace constructed from a set of queries $G = \{g_i\}_{i \in I}$ using PCA, the query subspace is defined as

$$\mathcal{C}_q = \{q \mid \|Qq - q\|_2 < \delta, \ Q^\top Q = I\}, \tag{29}$$

for the orthogonal projection Q to the subspace Π_q.

Setting P_i to be the orthogonal projection to pattern set $\mathcal{C}_i$, for $\mathcal{C}_i$ and $\mathcal{C}_q$, canonical angles are computed. The minimum canonical angle θ_l between $\mathcal{C}_l$

and $\mathcal{C}_q$ is the dissimilarity between these two subspaces. The minimum canonical angle between two subspaces is one of seven Grassmann distances [7,9]. These local geometric structures of linear subspaces derives a robust classification method with perturbations in both pattern sets and query sets.

For a set of the minimum canonical angles $\{\theta_l\}_{l=1}^{N_C}$, where θ_l is the minimum canonical angle between $\boldsymbol{P}_i$ and $\boldsymbol{Q}$, if the query subspace satisfies the condition

$$l^* = \arg\min_l \theta_l, \tag{30}$$

the results of the tensor mutual subspace method indicate that pattern set $\mathcal{C}_{l^*}$ is closest to the query subspace [14].

References

1. Itoh, H., Imiya, A., Sakai, T.: Pattern recognition in multilinear space and its applications: mathematics, computational algorithms and numerical validations. Mach. Vis. Appl. **27**(8), 1259–1273 (2016)
2. Itoh, H., Imiya, A., Sakai, T.: Analysis of multilinear subspaces based on geodesic distance. In: Felsberg, M., Heyden, A., Krüger, N. (eds.) CAIP 2017. LNCS, vol. 10424, pp. 384–396. Springer, Cham (2017). https://doi.org/10.1007/978-3-319-64689-3_31
3. Lu, H., Plataniotis, K.N., Venetsanopoulos, A.N.: MPCA: multilinear principal component analysis of tensor objects. IEEE Trans. Neural Netw. **19**(1), 18–39 (2008)
4. Andreopoulos, A., Tsotsos, J.K.: Efficient and generalizable statistical models of shape and appearance for analysis of cardiac MRI. Med. Image Anal. **12**, 335–357 (2008)
5. Cichoki, A., Zdunek, R., Phan, A.H., Amari, S.: Nonnegative Matrix and Tensor Factorizations. Wiley, Hoboken (2009)
6. Absil, P.-A., Mahony, R., Sepulchre, R.: Riemannian geometry of Grassmann manifolds with a view on algorithmic computation. Acta Applicandae Mathematicae **80**(2), 199–220 (2004)
7. Hamm, J., Lee, D.D.: Grassmann discriminant analysis: a unifying view on subspace-based learning. In Proceedings of International Conference on Machine Learning, pp. 376–383 (2008)
8. Cock, K.D., Moor, B.D.: Subspace angles between ARMA models. Syst. Control Lett. **46**, 265–270 (2002)
9. Edelman, A., Arias, T.A., Smith, S.T.: The geometry of algorithms with orthogonality constraints. SIAM J. Matrix Anal. Appl. **20**(2), 303–353 (1998)
10. Wasserstein, L.N.: Markov processes over denumerable products of spaces describing large systems of automata. Probl. Inf. Transm. **5**, 47–52 (1969)
11. Iijima, T.: Pattern Recognition. Corona Publishing, Tokyo (1973). (In Japanese)
12. Watanabe, S., Pakvasa, N.: Subspace method of pattern recognition. In: Proceedings of the 1st International Joint Conference of Pattern Recognition (1973)
13. Oja, E.: Subspace Methods of Pattern Recognition. Research Studies Press, New York (1983)
14. Maeda, K.: From the subspace methods to the mutual subspace method. In: Cipolla, R., Battiato, S., Farinella, G.M. (eds.) Computer Vision. SCI, vol. 285, pp. 135–156. Springer, Heidelberg (2010). https://doi.org/10.1007/978-3-642-12848-6_5

Author Index

Printed in the United States
by Bookmasters

Printed in the United States
By Bookmasters